THE
ULTIMATE
FILM
FESTIVAL
SURVIVAL GUIDE

THIRD EDITION

GORE

THE ULTIMATE FILM FESTIVAL SURVIVAL GUIDE, 3RD EDITION
The Essential Companion for Filmmakers and Festival-Goers

LONE EAGLE PUBLISHING COMPANY™
A division of Watson-Guptill Publications
770 Broadway
New York, NY 10003
www.watsonguptill.com

Book design by Carla Green
Edited by Lauren Rossini

Library of Congress Cataloging-in-Publication Data

Gore, Chris.
    The ultimate film festival survival guide / Chris Gore.--3rd ed.
        p. cm.
    ISBN 1-58065-057-0
    1. Film festivals--Directories. 2. Film festivals. I. Title.
PN1993.4.G67 2004
791.43'079--dc22

                                    2004048770

Books may be purchased in bulk at special discounts for promotional or educational purposes. Special editions can be created to specifications. Inquiries for sales and distribution, textbook adoption, foreign language translation, editorial, and rights and permissions inquiries should be addressed to: Lori Horak, Watson-Guptill Publications, 770 Broadway, New York, NY 10003 or send an e-mail to: lhorak@watsonguptill.com

Printed in the United States of America
  5 6 7 8 9 10 / 12 11 10 09 08

Lone Eagle Publishing Company™ is a registered trademark.

This book is dedicated to filmmakers who strive
to make breakthrough independent movies.
Be realistic about your dreams and remember—never quit.

cineswitch II

It's on the streets – the AG-DVX100A, the dramatically-improved successor to Panasonic's revolutionary, progressive-scan camera. Now with over 20 new features, including improved color reproduction, additional cine-like gamma settings, slower shutter speeds, squeeze mode for 16:9 recording, and much more. And still the only Mini-DV camera with CineSwitch™ technology for 480i/60, 480p/24fps and 480p/30fps image capture. Finally, a sequel that's better than the original. Visit **panasonic.com/dvcinema** or call **1-800-528-8601** to learn more.

AG-DVX100A is supported by your favorite
24P native non-linear editing solutions.

Panasonic ideas for life

CONTENTS

SECTION 3 – FORMING A FESTIVAL STRATEGY

SECTION 4 — FILM FESTIVAL LISTINGS

APPENDICES

TRiBUTE

A special tribute is due to filmmaker Sarah Jacobson.

The vibrant voice behind such indie movies as *I Was a Teenage Serial Killer* and Sundance fave *Mary Jane's Not a Virgin Anymore* and a friend of mine, she lost her battle with cancer in February, 2004. She died just as she was planning a benefit screening of her work to help pay her medical bills.

Sarah made underground films that I loved, and she never sold out or compromised her vision. She was the embodiment of the do-it-yourself filmmaker attitude. Lack of money or resources (the always-popular filmmaker excuses) never stopped her. Nothing did. If there was a goal in mind, she found a way there and her glowing attitude brought a lot of people along for the ride, including me. Sarah's tenacity was one of a kind and her always upbeat attitude was one that I wish more filmmakers would adopt.

I remember when *Mary Jane's Not a Virgin Anymore* premiered at Sundance — Sarah was the undisputed queen of guerilla promotion. Armed with *Not a Virgin* stickers and cheap cherry-flavored cigars, she packed the house by creating word of mouth with about twenty bucks worth of promo items. It was a joy to see her success at Park City that year. Sarah was an inspiration to me.

In the end, life really is more important than film.

DEDICATION

I'd like to dedicate this book to all the festival staffers who sacrifice financial security, months of their lives, and their collective sanity while working tirelessly to bring independent film to their local communities.

Acknowledgement is due to every member of the festival staffs and the many volunteers at every film festival who work for peanuts — or nothing at all — to support the art of film in all of its infinite variety. Your contributions are appreciated more than you may realize, and I thank you.

You inspire me.

ACKNOWLEDGEMENTS

There are so many people to thank, here is a list, in no particular order, of the people without whom this book would not have been possible: the unbelievably cool Jeff Black; my amazing editor, Lauren Rossini, who still continues to laugh at all my jokes; the outstanding Carla Green, who makes this book look so damn sexy; and my research assistants Mark Bell and Shannon Shull, who have spent several lifetimes collecting data from the Internet and on the phone. The cheerleaders who keep me going: my manager, Stephen Gates; Jason Redmond of the Independent Film Festival of Boston, Sean Lorenz of Four Yard Design, Joe Deagnon of Shem Co, Eric Campos, Mitchell Bard, Philip Zlotorynski, Barry Robison, Mike Ruggiero, Debbie Demontreux, and the whole gang at the Independent Film Channel, Patrick Hubley from Sundance, Jeremy Taylor of *Film Festival Today* magazine, the readers of FilmThreat.com, and especially my wife, Marion.

A special thanks to all of my interview subjects for their cooperation and candor. I'd also like to thank all the various members of the film festival staffs for their assistance in this project — you really make this book possible. I thank you all sincerely. There are just so many of you to thank, I wish I could list you all, but suffice to say: I owe you all a drink.

The biggest thanks goes out to all the filmmakers themselves — without their daily battles to make uncompromising films, there wouldn't be any film festivals. To those filmmakers who battle against impossible odds: remember to be realistic about your dreams and *never* quit.

Thank you.

RE-iNTRODUCTiON...

MY BiG FAT FiLM FESTiVAL EXPERiENCE

Since I am more widely known as someone who writes about film, one question I hear often is a big one: Have *you* ever made a film? Usually this question is asked of me after some festival panel discussion where I've spent a lot of time dispensing advice to filmmakers.

The answer is "yes." In fact, I've been making films since I was a kid. One of my shorts called *Red* starred Lawrence Tierney of *Reservoir Dogs* and told the story of a beleaguered booze jockey tortured by prank phone calls. The 30-minute black and white short, while a humorous crowd-pleaser, failed to get into one film festival. Not even *one*. It was too long, shot in Super 8 and finished on video, the sound was an afterthought in the process and I rushed to get the film finished to meet a deadline for a festival. My short was denied acceptance everywhere. It was disheartening, but I never gave up. And strangely *Red* went on to become a cult movie shown at bars, screening events and the occasional drunken party. I released *Red* independently on video and this little $4,000 short went onto sell thousands of copies on video. I recently put the film on DVD through my new distribution label, Film Threat DVD, where I expect it to find a whole new audience. While the film didn't enjoy any kind of festival run, I never predicted that it would find success as a cult video. I learned from that experience and later traveled the festival circuit as a journalist; the result is this series of books.

I have this desire, well, more of a mission, to pass useful information and advice along to others through my books and web site FilmThreat.com. When I was initially making *Red*, I really could have used a book like this. In some way, this is not just a resource for filmmakers and festivalgoers, but it's part of my personal crusade to dispense the cold hard truth about the world of independent film. (Trust me, I learned first hand the hard way and you can benefit from my mistakes.) I feel the need to tell filmmakers what they truly need to know, and not fill them with some BS self-help style rhetoric, which only serves to inspire and not inform. The truth about this business can be frustrating and the odds are against you from the start. That shouldn't stop you from moving forward but I believe you need about 10 percent passion and 90 percent real information to succeed.

I look for ways to dramatically improve each edition of this book and this one is no different. As I began to compile information for the third volume, the web had already emerged as a great resource for festival data and I realized that it was important to address the needs of filmmakers using this tool. I believe that print is the ultimate random access medium, and in that spirit the festival listings in the directory portion of this book contain data you will not find in any other source. Valuable new information is included in the expanded entries such as your odds of getting into a festival based on the number of submissions, what travel expenses do festivals cover and better yet, perks that are provided attendees. In addition, I've included

Gore meets Gore. Former VP and indie film fan Al Gore with the author at Sundance.

my own comments on more than 100 festivals and compiled listings of "Best" festivals that excel in specific categories to help filmmakers make informed choices about where to submit. You won't get information like this anywhere, including on the web. The improved listings aren't the only helpful addition, there are all-new filmmaker interviews including detailed conversations with Morgan Spurlock of *Super Size Me* and Jared Hess of *Napoleon Dynamite*. Morgan and Jared's films' were the biggest sales at the Sundance Film Festival and both provide revealing analysis of what got them there. Everything is updated and I've also added fresh sections on everything from creating an individualized festival strategy to web promotion to postcard design to writing a film synopsis to focus testing to putting together a festival promotion budget and even new party crashing tips. What's really odd is that I could actually use all this information myself. I guess you could say, I'm not just the author, I'm also the audience. I'm about to hit the festival circuit again as a filmmaker, this time with my first feature. And I am determined not to make the same mistakes I did with *Red.* After years of writing several feature scripts, all of which "almost" sold, I vowed that the next movie I wrote, I would produce myself. In the spirit of poking fun at the indie film world, I wrote and produced *My Big Fat Independent Movie.* As of this writing, it's just getting ready to make its way onto the festival circuit and we have not yet premiered. The film has already screened out of competition in rough cut form at a major festival in Texas; the information we gathered there helped us cut 10 minutes out of the movie so we could lock picture. Already *My Big Fat Independent Movie* has been both *invited* to premiere at several fests and *rejected* by one major fest, so I am fully prepared to endure the hardships experienced by all indie filmmakers. It's why I wrote the first edition of this book — to give filmmakers the tools they need to traverse the world of fests and to get distribution.

I'll see you at the next fest.

Your pal,
Chris Gore

A BRiEF HiSTORY OF FiLM FESTiVALS

Film, being only about 100 years old, is a young art form. The film festival, a medium for exhibiting and celebrating film, is likewise still in its youth.

While the date of the very first film festival may be lost, the oldest still in business is the Venice Film Festival, founded in the 1930s by Italian Dictator Benito Mussolini. It was originally an adjunct to a larger, pre-existing arts festival, but proved so popular that within a few years it had become a free-standing festival of its own. Unfortunately, in the days leading up to World War II, the Venice festival leaned heavily toward films from the Axis powers — Americans ultimately boycotted the gathering, which was subsequently suspended for the remainder of the war. While Il Duce did not survive the global conflict, the Venice Film Festival was revived in the late forties and remains an important international exposition today.

The Cannes Film Festival was also conceived in the 1930s and materially affected by the war. Set to debut on September 1, 1939, such Hollywood luminaries as Mae West, Gary Cooper, and Tyrone Power traveled to the French seaside community for the festivities. Establishing a Cannes tradition of excess, a replica of the Notre Dame cathedral was built on the beach to promote the release of the *Hunchback of Notre Dame.* As it happened, *Hunchback* was the only film presented at the fledgling festival because that same day Adolph Hitler invaded Poland and began his own festival of destruction: the Second World War. The first Cannes Film Festival was cancelled and Hitler went on to invade France. Ultimately the good guys won, Hitler was defeated, and the Cannes festival made its real debut in 1946.

The third of the old-line European festivals, the Berlin Film Festival, was established in 1951 as an outpost of post-war culture sanctioned by the occupying Allied forces in West Berlin. Initially slighted by the commission that tried to oversee and coordinate the

European festivals, Berlin eventually rose to its current position as one of the top-ranking European film festivals.

And so it went during the early years. Organizations like the Society for Cinephiles established festivals that were quietly run by aficionados and favored older films. Film festivals were not a rarity, but you didn't find them everywhere you turned. Ironically, rather than one of the big international festivals, it was America's own Society for Cinephiles' Cinecon, which traveled to different cities each Labor Day to screen rare silents, that was the forerunner of the festival that ushered in the modern era.

Like Cinecon, The Telluride Film Festival was created as a film buff's festival. It even involved some of the same fans, such as the late William K. Everson. But unlike the humble Cinecon, Telluride was a pricey and exclusive affair held (also during the Labor Day holiday) in the privacy of remote Telluride, Colorado. When the Sundance Film Festival was founded, it used Telluride as a model.

The Sundance Film Festival, devoted to independent films, was founded in 1978 as the United States Film Festival. The first two sessions were in Salt Lake City; in January 1981, the festival moved to its current home in Park City, Utah. Robert Redford's Sundance Institute (founded in 1983) took over festival operations in 1984. The name was formally changed to the Sundance Film Festival in 1989, the year *sex, lies and videotape* put the festival on the map as the place where an iconoclastic young director could achieve a commercial breakthrough. Bloated and weighted by success, Sundance eventually became its own kind of establishment film festival and a concurrent festival of Sundance rejects, the Slamdance festival, debuted in 1995, also in Park City. The Sundance organizers reportedly admired their pluck.

With the success of Sundance and the upstart Slamdance, the floodgates were well and truly opened. Aspiring filmmakers who couldn't make the cut at Sundance might instead opt for Ohio's Cleveland Film Festival. In the realm of tourist-bait, there was the late Sonny Bono's Palm Springs Film Festival. Over the years, significant film festivals have established themselves in Chicago, Denver, Portland (Oregon), Edinburgh, Krakow, and Hong Kong.

Today, if you are a professional or a lover of film, you can go to Santa Barbara. If you want to see naked starlets, you can go to Cannes. If you're into animation, you can go to Annecy or Ottawa.

If you like your films edgy and inexpensive, there is the New York Underground Film Festival. There are also the film buyers markets, such as those held in Milan and Los Angeles.

Film festivals have both proliferated and changed. Once upon a time, festivals were predominately creatures of the arts, and powerfully connected to politics. In 1968, the Cannes festival was shut down as a result of French student riots. Similarly, in 1970, the Berlin festival was cancelled as a result of controversy over a German film titled *O.K.*, about a rape and murder committed by US soldiers stationed in Vietnam. This kind of excitement is lacking at the more modern film festivals, which seem built around the entertainment/business model rather than the traditional art/politics combination. The current era features a different kind of excitement.

Since the year 2000, the festival circuit has exploded with new festivals being created every month. The largest area of growth has occurred in regional festivals in the United States, generally tourist hotspots (without an art house theater) seeking to bring independent films to their communities. The added benefit of these regional festivals is the opportunity to promote their cities to the entertainment business at large. Other festivals on the fast track are "genre" festivals that embrace science fiction, fantasy, and horror movies. Considered "B-movies" by cinema snobs, these films are often marginalized and ignored by the mainstream festivals. As a result, fans have sought to create festivals and events dedicated solely to the celebration of the genre picture. This exciting spurt of growth in the festival circuit has resulted in more than 400 new festivals created since the year 2000 — and this increase shows no signs of stopping even with sponsorships on the decline.

As entertainment has become the central element of our culture, film festivals have become veritable markets of celluloid, wherein dreams are bought and sold; lives are made and destroyed. On that very human level, they are exciting as hell.

10 DIRTY SECRETS OF INDEPENDENT FILM

If one is going to enter the sometimes brutal world of independent film, it helps to be armed with the knowledge of all the harsh realities. So in order to save you from having to experience them all first-hand, let me just spell all of this out for you now — even if it's painful, you need to know.

1. **Corporate independents rule. Deal with it.** Today, every major studio has an independent film division, or what might be called a "low budget studio division." Basically, these are studio-backed arty dramas in which the actors work for scale. These corporate indies have co-opted the independent spirit and turned it into a section in the video store. You can look on this as a good or a bad thing, but that's the way it is, so learn to live with it.

2. **It's a business of relationships.** Yes, it really *is* who you know. There are those who say that the film world is all "politics." Well, yeah. Get good at politics. Get to know the acquisitions executives at the major distributors that still buy movies and get those people to your screening — no matter what it takes.

3. **Casting counts.** Unfortunately. The first question any acquisitions executive — or moviegoer, for that matter — is going to ask, is, "Who's in it?" Which explains low budget, independent digital features starring Ethan Hawke (*Tape*), Sigourney Weaver (*Tadpole*), and Kevin Kline (*The Anniversary Party*). So, put together a cast that will get your film noticed. Actors are always on the lookout for good material, so get it to them any way you can. Director Rod Lurie played in a weekly poker game with actor Kevin Pollack — and Lurie ended up directing his independent feature debut by casting his card-playing pal. Cultivating relationships with recognizable talent is valuable; pursue these assets by establishing a relationship first, and not by shoving a script in an actor's face.

4. **Be original. But not *too* original.** As much as film executives say they want something original, they really don't. What they mean by "original" is simply "old wine in a new bottle." They want a familiar genre or story or tried and true formula told in a completely original way. For example: a sucessful rock and roll musical (familiar) about a man with a botched sex change operation (very original) called *Hedwig and the Angry Inch*. That works.

5. **Want to get into a film festival? Get to know the "Phantom Programmers."** Sure, everyone knows that Geoffrey Gilmore is the chief gatekeeper at the Sundance Film Festival. And there is no chance he is going to return the call of an unknown emerg-

ing indie filmmaker. That's why it is critical to get to know the "Phantom Programmers." These are the trusted friends of festival programmers — people they rely on for advice about how to fill a programming slot. So, if you can't get to guys like Gilmore, get to the people close to him — people like John Sloss, Bob Hawk, or Jeff Dowd, among others. The main programmer has The Power, but enlisting support from people who have The Influence just might make all the difference.

> **BE WARY**
>
> Beware of the leeches who feed on naïve filmmakers, like festival screening events that charge exorbitant fees. If you are paying more than $100 for an entry fee and the festival is *not* Telluride, you are being scammed. Be wary of any unsolicited phone calls from festivals seeking you out, especially if they want to charge you. An invite to a festival is one thing, but when you are "invited," you should never have to pay a fee.

6. **Get a good review from Roger Ebert.** Seven "Roger Eberts" can be found in just the Los Angeles area phone book and one of them is bound to love your movie. (You do know I'm kidding with this, right?) But really, there are more outlets covering film today than there are films released in a year. No joke. If you can't get a decent review in a recognizable media outlet, there are plenty of lesser-known media outlets on the web just salivating at the chance of being quoted on your movie poster. Just ask the major movie studios — they use this technique all the time.

7. **Awards are meaningless.** Unless, of course, you are the one receiving said award. Be sure to tout any kind of award you receive, no matter how cheesy or meaningless it might seem to you. The graphic of the two laurels and those magical words "Award Winner" in the center will make a perfect piece of marketing to use on the poster or video sleeve.

8. **Don't be an orphan.** There are thousands of "cine-orphans" out there — movies without distribution. It's important not to end up as one. After all of the large and small distributors have passed on your film, don't concern yourself with making back your money. At this point it's all about your career, so it's critical to get the film into the commercial marketplace, even if you have to self-distribute it on DVD. And DVDs make great giveaways at meetings about your next project.

9. **Get a look.** Yes, as irrelevant as it seems, fashion sense is important and a distinct look does count for something. If fame matters in moving up the indie film career ladder, then it's important to be recognizable in a crowd, or at least in the photos that the trades run. Picture the writer and director of such films as *Spanking the Monkey* and *Three Kings.* You can't. That's because Writer/Director David O. Russell — while a very talented director — is about as nondescript as they come. He's an average looking guy and there's no crime in that. Now picture the writer and director of such films as *Welcome to the Dollhouse, Happiness,* and *Storytelling.* Yes, Todd Solondz is that dork with the goofy hair and big glasses. But his unique "look" also gets him recognized at festivals, events, and parties — and *that* will get even his geeky mug into the trendy sections of magazines. Fame does help.

10. **The Truth.** The reality is that the indie film world is a freelance business in which most rarely get paid and even fewer get paid well. Success is garnering good press, winning an award at a festival, receiving rave reviews, or the simple pleasure of getting distribution and seeing your film open on the big screen. All of this perceived "success" still won't pay the bills, so it's important to take that tried and true parental advice and have a fallback plan to actually make money. Otherwise, you'll be racking up credit card debt, filing for bankruptcy, and moving back in with your folks before your first feature even hits the festival circuit. Sad, but true.

Of course, once you reach that "perceived success status," your job is to start lying to everyone about how great life is in "the industry" and continue to perpetuate the myths about the glamour of entertainment industry. No one likes reality.

SECTION 1
CONQUERING FILM FESTIVALS

"Like the lottery, you can't win if you
don't play. Sundance is the mother of
all film festivals — you MUST apply."

— Joal Ryan, filmmaker, *Former Child Star*

10 STUPiD THiNGS iNDiE FiLMMAKERS DO TO MESS UP THEiR MOViES

There are countless books that explain how to make movies. And while that is not the subject of this book, I do feel the need to chime in with some kernels of advice every once in a while.

One fact many people have a tough time accepting is that, per-centage-wise, there are far more bad independent films out there than there are bad Hollywood movies. Here are the common mistakes to avoid if you wish to make a successful independent film that rises above the pack and solidifies your career as a filmmaker. Meaning, you'll get paid to make films instead of paying to make them.

1. **Weak script.** Here is where more indie films fail than in any other area. If the running time is around seventy minutes, then the feature script was probably pretty thin to begin with. But one only has to look at Kevin Smith's *Clerks* to learn why the script is such an important element. *Clerks* is perhaps the most technically inept film ever to get a theatrical release. Almost any decent student film looks better than *Clerks*. But today's audiences are not as concerned with the technical quality of a film. Content is king for indies and this is where *Clerks* succeeds brilliantly. We don't care about the gritty look (actually that look contributes overall to the mood) — the characters engage us, the story is well-paced, and we laugh our asses off at the snappy dialogue. Kevin's amazing script rose above the limitations under which he made the movie, resulting in what is now an indie film classic. They say that paper is cheaper than film, so buy some paper. And keep buying it until you write a great screenplay (then, other people will buy it for you).

2. **Casting non-film actors.** Most first-time filmmakers think that in order to hire actors, they must go to the theater. I can spot a theater actor in an indie film on a 13" black and white TV running a fifth generation VHS screener from across the room. Theater actors are used to "projecting" their performances to

the back of the playhouse, which often leads to over-the-top performances on camera. Bring it down a notch. Or maybe ten notches. Actors' performances are magnified onscreen, so if you use non-actors or actors with little film experience, you'll often spend time asking them to tone it down. Casting is perhaps the most important decision you'll face as a filmmaker. In fact, some say half of directing is casting, so choose actors who will elevate your material, not butcher it. Talent from the Screen Actors Guild is of a higher caliber, and worth the extra money. SAG has several contracts geared toward helping independents get their films made, some even allow you to defer their pay entirely — but there are strings attached, so examine them all carefully. You can get more info at www.SAGIndie.com.

3. **Sacrificing quality to meet a deadline.** Okay, you're going to hear this one more than once in this book, but you *cannot* sacrifice the quality of your film to make the deadline for a festival. You are not only cheating yourself, you are betraying everyone on your crew (who worked so hard to do their jobs), as well as your investors (who trusted you with their money). So many filmmakers rush to meet a deadline for a major festival like Sundance and they end up with a film that is less than it could have been. And then they are surprised when the film is rejected. Take the time. It's one of the only luxuries that comes with making an independent film. Take the time to edit, to get feedback through a focus group, and be sure you have made the best film possible. Only then are you ready to submit to a festival.

4. **Wearing too many hats.** So, you're the writer/director/producer/editor and you star in your movie. Great. We all understand that making an indie film requires you to do, well, everything. But *taking credit* for doing everything makes you look naïve and inexperienced. And the opposite of humble. It might also make you look just the tiniest bit presumptuous. Consider delegating a few of those hats, along with the responsibilities that come with them, to talented people in their respective fields.

5. **Clearances.** The Number One stumbling block to getting a distribution deal has to be getting legal clearances. Have your legal house in order so that when you go to sell your movie, all your paperwork is clean. This goes for everything from actor contracts, to clearing locations, to clearing any names or items and

music. Get an attorney to look at the script for any legal stumbling blocks *before* you shoot. Do not, I repeat, *do not* accept "festival clearance" for the music in your film, hoping to get full clearance later. Yeah, I know, you love that Chemical Brothers song and it's perfect and no other song will do — but that doesn't help you because you will still have to get the song fully cleared before you can sell your movie. One very smart idea: Craig Brewer, who made the digital indie *The Poor & Hungry*, approached Icehouse Records in his hometown of Memphis, Tennessee. They provided him with a box full of CDs by local bands, and from those recordings Craig put together a soundtrack for his film, with *fully cleared* music. Do whatever it takes to clear everything, otherwise you'll be stuck having to fix it later, which can be very costly. In fact, it can cost you a distribution deal.

6. **Bad sound.** If it's a choice between sound or picture, put your cash into the sound. Nothing ruins a film experience more than being unable to follow a storyline because the dialogue is inaudible or so badly mixed that it's become incoherent. While film is a visual medium, filmmakers often forget that sound is 50 percent of the experience.

7. **No money for marketing.** There should be a line item in your budget for money to be spent on promotion and festival travel. Getting the film made is only half the battle — now you have to sell it. Without money for posters, publicity, travel, etc. — the odds of selling your movie will be stacked against you.

8. **No Festival Strategy.** If you plan to attend a festival as a filmmaker, be sure to visit that festival as a filmgoer first to learn the ins and outs. Get to know the staff and anyone who might help you get the film programmed. Have a Plan B. Just because you didn't get into Sundance, Seattle, Telluride, or Toronto is no reason to give up and no reflection on your film. There are plenty of stops on the festival circuit that can result in awards, good reviews, useful contacts, attention, and a distribution deal, so include those fests in your plan.

9. **Serious documentary = Snore. Funny documentary = Sale.** Documentaries that explore a serious topic and are tempered with humor are more commercially viable than those that

aren't. And if you've made a doc about the world of porn, swingers, or strippers — hell, anything involving nudity — that will almost guarantee a sale. It's the sad truth, but isn't that what docs are supposed to explore? Naked reality?

10. **There is no "I" in team.** Don't try to do it all yourself. If you try to do it all, you will fail. Delegate, delegate, delegate. Build a strong team to help you and your film while you're at the festival, otherwise, you'll be the only one hanging up posters. And be sure to thank all those who helped you along the way. In the independent film world, genuine thanks and appreciation often go even further than money.

D.i.C. — DO iT CHEAP

In all things related to your film — whether it be casting, production, post-production, marketing, promotion, anything — you will face one seemingly impossible barrier to getting what you want: money. Money is an obstacle filmmakers face at every level, whether producing a $100 million Hollywood extravaganza, or a $900 digital indie feature. Those filmmakers who are able to master the art of Taming the Triangle will get what they want without compromising their vision. The Triangle represents the way every filmmaker wants everything done all the time: Fast/Good/Cheap. In every aspect of your film, you almost always have the luxury of choosing any *two* of those elements to achieve your goal. As an example, let's say you need an explosion for your film. The big budget Hollywood movie producer may choose to do a giant special effects-laden explosion. Hollywood can do it fast and good, but it will certainly *not* be cheap. The no-budget digital movie producer may also choose to do an explosion, but will select the path of fast and cheap; the resulting shot will *not* be good. The no-budget-at-all film may choose good and cheap, but it will *not* be fast. That producer will encounter time as an enemy. In the making of your film, you will come up against the fast/good/cheap decision many times. For most indies, the logical choice is be good and cheap, as time is usually the one thing you have available. Many filmmakers make the mistake of rushing their film to meet a festival deadline. While this may seem wise at the time, if meeting that deadline in any way compromises the quality of your film, you're only hurting your chance of being accepted. Take a look at the choices on The Triangle and choose the path that best supports your final vision. You don't think filmmakers at all levels face the same dilemma? Even George Lucas, one of the most successful independent filmmakers of all time, waited over fifteen years to revisit the *Star Wars* universe while he waited for the quality of digital filmmaking effects and technology to improve while becoming cost-effective. Live by The Triangle, and as a filmmaker, evaluate every decision with an eye toward making the best *finished* film possible.

iN FiLM, "POLiTiCS" iS NOT A DiRTY WORD

In the film industry, politics means meeting the right people, rallying them to your cause (your film) and enlisting them in your mission to get your movie made and seen by as many people as possible.

Unfortunately, the question is not always, "Who is the best filmmaker?" More often, it comes down to the question, "Who excels at the political game that is the film industry?" You must become an astute politician if you intend to be a successful (i.e., working and solvent) filmmaker. And let me clue you in on a little secret — you already know how to do this. You may not be aware of it, and you might not have done it on purpose, but you have used politics to your advantage every moment you have been working on your film.

- You raised the money you needed for your film from somewhere.
- You secured the perfect location — for free!
- You begged the lab to go the extra mile — and they did.
- You fought to have that scene kept and shot your way.
- You convinced the rental house to give you a break on your equipment.
- You kept spirits up when disaster struck and rain ruined a day of shooting.

- You inspired the cinematographer to come up with a solution for that troublesome set-up — and it turned out beautifully.
- You talked the entire crew into working through the night.
- Your sense of humor saved your first A.D.'s life when the entire crew wanted to kill him.
- You even persuaded your actor to do that embarrassing nude scene. (Full frontal. You rock!)
- You assembled a group of people to create a film and see your vision through to completion and you smiled through it all (even though you know you could have made a better film under more ideal circumstances).

So you see, you are a political animal, you just never thought of it that way before. Now, you must take these Svengali-like abilities and translate them into selling your movie. (Pay attention and commit the next sentence to memory. It's a run-on and completely grammatically incorrect. I already know that, and I've beaten my editor over the head to keep it just the way it is; basically, it is the crux of the entire book.) All you have to do is use these very same skills to apply to festivals, lobby the festival staff, convince them your film must be seen, get into the festival, hire a publicist, a lawyer, a producer's rep, and an agent; travel to the festival — don't forget to make a killer poster, an EPK, a trailer and a website; get some press, create great buzz for your movie, pack the screening with a real audience along with press, friends, celebrities, and acquisitions executives; be humble, engaging, and funny at the post-screening Q&A session, get some good reviews, create more good buzz; get "the call," make the distribution deal, negotiate tough to get the best deal, read the trades to look for your name and the announcement, travel the world showing your film at other festivals, support the release of the film by doing interview after interview — and during this whole process get into as many parties and have as much fun as possible while exhibiting your ability to remain witty after far too many drinks. That's it. That's all you have to do.

William H. Macy and Mario Bello promote The Cooler *at Sundance.*

The rest of this book explains how all of that can be achieved. It's important to point out that no two filmmakers realize success by following the same path. Each one "makes it" differently and your experience will be completely different and totally your own.

WHAT MAKES A GREAT FiLM FESTiVAL?

I've been attending film festivals since I was a kid, so I've had my share of good and bad experiences. I rate a film festival as "great" based on a very specific set of criteria. I try not to judge a festival by a few technical mistakes, because those can plague even the largest and most respected festivals. As a festival-goer, there are three key elements that make a festival enjoyable for me: great films, solid organization, and fun parties.

10 STUPiD THiNGS PROGRAMMERS DO TO MESS UP THEiR FiLM FESTiVALS

When I was given the opportunity to program Cinema Epicuria: The Sonoma Valley Film Festival, I was determined not to make the same mistakes I had seen at other festivals. I figured, hell, if I wrote a book about film festivals, I better damn well know how to put one on. Having traveled to more than 100 festivals worldwide, I've seen the best and the worst, and I've seen the same mistakes made over and over again. While the following ten gaffes are geared toward festival staffs, it helps for filmmakers to get an inside perspective on how a festival works. As the program director for two years, I learned a lot from my experiences, so now I present to you my list of the Top Ten things to avoid when programming a festival:

1. **Screening bad movies.** The primary reason an avid filmgoer travels to a festival is to see good movies. But somehow plenty of awful films get screened — films so bad that you wouldn't watch them even if they were airing free on network television. So, why do really terrible movies constantly turn up on the festival circuit? A lot of reasons. Sometimes the director is a friend of the programmer's, or a programmer is pushing some kind of personal agenda, or another movie pulls out at the last minute and a suitable replacement has to be found quickly. Whatever

the reason, the programmer must be responsive to the needs of the local community. Personal taste will always vary, but don't screen a documentary about punk rock in the 1970s at a festival whose local demographic consists of senior citizens. You must be discriminating. Asking other programmers for help is key. Hell, ask me — I see decent indies all the time and I'm happy to hand out recommendations.

2. **Poor organization.** When the program guide contains incorrect information, when screenings are running thirty minutes late, when the screening begins with five minutes of apology from the program director about the delays, when the audience sits in the dark while a damaged print is repaired, when the post-screening question and answer session begins with nervous silence — then you've got serious organizational problems. Addressing these issues with experienced theater managers and well-trained volunteer team leaders can go a long way toward resolving these simple problems quickly. There will always be some degree of chaos behind the scenes, that's normal, but as long as the chaos remains invisible to the festival-going public, those problems never happened. Good organization is often worth paying for, because a smoothly run festival is generally a profitable one.

3. **Giving sponsors control.** Bending over backwards for sponsors can be surprisingly fruitful for both parties. The festival circuit would not exist without the generous support of sponsors committed to independent film — but that doesn't mean the program should be a slave to a corporate agenda. Be wary of how a sponsor's influence may creep into the festival itself. If you alter the name of the festival (nothing sounds more lame than "The Big Corporate Dollars' Blah-Blah Film Festival"), or if you include programming "suggested" by the sponsor, you may be bending over a little too far. And I mean bending over "forward."

4. **Bad press relations.** The press can be your best friend...or your worst enemy, if you play it wrong. Make them feel special by being generous with badges and extra tickets to events, goodie bags, and be sure to invite them to all the parties. Yes, I'm saying kiss their asses. It's totally worth it because good press can make a festival and bad press can kill it. It's never too early to

cultivate press relationships, even as far as a year before the festival. Hand-feed them stories, in the form of bold press releases sent to journalists willing to report on your festival's progress. Arrange for some of your filmmakers or celebrities to do advance interviews before they arrive at the festival so those stories can appear during the event. Get select members of the press into a screening room or get them video screeners of some of your strongest films so advance reviews can appear in the local media.

5. **No local support.** Securing local support at all levels can ensure a successful event. Contact the local government, schools, and business leaders, along with media support from newspapers, television, and radio stations. Rally their support for the festival and engage them at all levels. At Sonoma, we had each event sponsored by a different local business, which helped us gather more sponsors than ever before and gave them a special spotlight each night.

6. **Boring panels without purpose.** Panels at film festivals should be two things — informative and entertaining. So, I'm constantly miffed when esoteric film professors are given the task of moderating (what often turn out to be) yawningly dull panel discussions. With all due respect to those in academia, most people don't come to a festival for an education. They just want to see movies and be entertained. Useful, concrete information about filmmaking should absolutely be discussed during the course of a panel, but I often find film professors too academic to accompish this task without it feeling like a lecture. I try to make panels fun. I wanted to put on a panel of directors, but I also wanted to make it interesting. So, I titled the panel "How to Shoot Nude Scenes." The panel explored how directors work with actors to persuade performers to become emotionally "naked" on camera. It was no surprise that this panel discussion was packed to capacity with a standing room only crowd and the discussion was raucous and informative. Mission accomplished.

7. **Trying to be the "Sundance of —."** I hear many festivals describe themselves as the "Sundance of the West Coast" or the "Sundance of the East Coast" or the "Sundance of Lower Podunk." We already *have* a Sundance and it kicks ass. Here's a message we all should have learned in pre-school: be yourself,

not a copycat. It's better to be a festival with its own distinct identity rather than just another "Sundance wannabe." I get the feeling a lot of festivals simply lack vision. At Sonoma, which takes place in the wine country just outside of San Francisco, we realized that we could not compete with any of the international or gay and lesbian film festivals in the city. So we didn't try. Considering that the local community of Sonoma consists primarily of baby boomer families and seniors, we made a conscious decision to program "life-affirming" movies. I went after heartfelt dramas and "moving" pictures, if you will. While a lot of the movies may not have appealed to my personal taste, the local community embraced this new direction. Attendance tripled as a result and Sonoma received its best feedback ever on the programming choices.

8. **Uncomfortable Q&As.** There's nothing more uncomfortable than a silent post-screening question-and-answer session with the filmmaker in which the audience simply does not know what to ask. For Sonoma, we trained a volunteer group of people who were comfortable speaking in front of an audience, and created a cheat sheet of basic questions to ask. Each Q&A kicked off with the volunteer moderator initiating applause, thanking the filmmaker, and asking that first question. With the ice broken, the audience began to step up and ask questions of their own. Every filmmaker walked away feeling good about the experience, which I know will translate into good word of mouth to other filmmakers. This is something that is worth taking the time to do right.

9. **Celebrity factor.** Raising the profile of any festival is easy if you invite a couple of big name celebrities affiliated with some of your chosen films. However, ask yourself: is the person you're flying in (First Class), putting up (in a four star hotel), granting 24-hour use of a limo, plus a generous goodie basket, and a per diem *really* a celebrity? Are they worth it? If you find yourself saying, "You know, that guy? On that one TV show? Back in the 1990s? Remember that guy? He's starring in a movie at our festival!" Your enthusiasm for "That Guy" may not be enough to convince sponsors and audiences that you have a genuine celebrity in attendance. Limit your number of VIPs — and be sure these are genuinely "VI," because they get expensive really fast.

10. **Cash bar.** The cash bar is perhaps a partygoer's greatest fear and a guaranteed buzzkill at a festival bash. It's bound to end in weak press and leave a bad taste in the mouths of festivalgoers. Remember this old saying, "If you serve free drinks, they will come." Sonoma, being in the Wine Country, made it easy to serve top quality wines at every screening and party. Lining up a liquor sponsor is critical for official events — it may not be politically correct, but AA can have its own festival, the rest of us will be meeting up at the bar.

Film critic Rich Cline has met his worst enemy — the festival party with a cash bar.

EVERY FiLMMAKER-FRiENDLY FESTiVAL MUST AVOiD THESE...

1. **Inflated entry fees.** Keep the entry fee as low as possible, you'll get more submissions as a result.
2. **Unnecessarily long entry forms.** Keep the forms simple for entries, you can always send a follow-up form for more information when a filmmaker is accepted.
3. **Cover some travel.** Filmmakers make choices about travelling to a festival based on cost. If it's a choice between a festival covering hotel only versus a festival covering airfare, hotel, and throwing in per diem, there's no choice to make. The festival offering the better travel deal will always win.
4. **Rejection letters.** Send a rejection letter to every film that does not get in. It's tough, yes, but necessary. On the next page is the one I sent out when I was at Sonoma.
5. **Avoid technical mistakes.** Be sure to hire the right people to handle your tech and print traffic so that each film is seen in the best possible way, the way the filmmaker intended. Nothing is worse than seeing a stressed out filmmaker pacing the lobby because his or her movie is being shown in the wrong aspect ratio or the sound is garbled. Make technical excellence a top priority (and not number five like it is on this list).

Dear [Filmmaker's name]:

I really hate having to send letters like this. It is my unfortunate duty to inform you that we were unable to program your film for this year's Sonoma Valley Film Festival. The final schedule will be up on the festival website in the next week, should you wish to peruse our offerings.

Please do not take this rejection as a reflection of the film itself. I really wish we could accept more films — due to schedule and timeslot restrictions, we were limited this year, but hope to expand in the coming years. In many cases, it wasn't a matter of rejecting films that weren't worthy, more that we received so many quality films that our choices proved incredibly difficult.

I encourage you to send your future projects our way. Thanks again for considering us in your festival plans.

If you have any further questions, please contact me.

Thanks,

Chris Gore

STAYiNG ALiVE

Simple Survival Tips For the Film Festival Traveler

While a tour book about your festival destination will contain the best regional information, I've learned some tried and true tips along the way that will enhance your travel experience. Sometimes, I've learned the hard way.

- **Make reservations.** For hotel, car, plane, the works. You cannot overdo it when it comes to reservations — and that includes dinner reservations. Be sure to check the restrictions, which means cover your butt and make sure to find out if there are penalties for late cancellations. Remember, the further in advance you make the reservations for flights, the more money you will save. Flights fill up fast, so reserve your ticket early. Do not wait until the last minute. Making advance dinner reservations is key as well; you don't want to wait more than an hour for a table. Robert Redford's restaurant, Zoom, is always booked up months before Sundance. Also, sign up for every frequent flyer plan in existence. You'll be surprised how quickly those points and free trips add up. And be sure to check on restrictions for flying standby. Some airlines will tell you over the phone that you must pay $75 or more to change your return flight. If you just show up to the airport and wait on standby, you can often bypass this flight change fee altogether. It depends on the type of ticket you purchase, so be sure to check.

- **Planning.** Get the festival schedule in advance from the festival website and make a plan. Don't be afraid to modify the plan as you go; you can always palm off a few tickets to a movie you discover you want to avoid. I type up a schedule before I leave so I know what films I'm seeing when, what parties I'm going to (or crashing), and who I'm meeting with and when. I never follow my plan exactly, but it helps me to start with some kind of structure before I begin to deviate from it.

- **Address book.** On my schedule, I also print a mini-address book. Essentially, this is just a collection of local phone numbers and the cell phone numbers of pals I plan to meet. This is all printed in very tiny type and I make multiple copies so I never lose it. The info is printed small enough to fit right into my wallet. (Is it just me, or am I sounding like a compulsive geek?)

- **Backpack.** You have to have one. It's the guy's version of a purse and totally essential to navigating a festival. I'm prepared for anything with my pack in tow. Mine always contains: the all-important address book, festival schedule, lip balm, water bottle, cell phone, pens, flyers, a folder of party invitations, something to read, energy bar (emergency meal), camera, map, tape recorder, notepad, batteries, breath mints, business cards, matches, aspirin or Tylenol, eyedrops, eyeglass cleaner, Kleenex, comb, sunglasses, mini flashlight, and a hat. (The hat is used for early morning screenings. When bedhead is at its worst, a hat can be a lifesaver.)

- **Vitamins and water.** Film festivals can get exhausting very quickly. Plan on sleeping less, drinking probably more alcohol than you normally would, and know that you'll be surrounded by cigarette smoke at every party. During Sundance, I get about four hours of sleep a night. I make it a point to drink lots of water and take extra vitamins (I'm partial to vitamins in the B category). I also keep a mix of over-the-counter stuff that includes Tylenol, aspirin, Pepto-Bismol pills, sinus headache medicine, migraine headache medicine, Tums, cough drops, and plenty of other remedies all crammed into one bottle. Sometimes my friends think I'm nuts — until I whip out this mini pharmacy and cure them of what ails them.

- **Clothes.** Obviously you should be prepared to bring clothes that match the climate for the festival. For most events, you'll be wearing casual clothes, but it's also important to bring at least one dressy outfit so you're ready for a meet and greet event at which you have to impress. Also keep in mind, clothes make the filmmaker. Be unique. If you want to stand out from all the other filmmakers wearing the artist's favorite uniform — you know, black — choose something really outrageous to wear. A bright hat, a loud jacket, or a bold pair of shoes is not a bad idea. When members of the audience run into you during the festival, your unique "look" will be remembered. Clothes are about image building, so have fun with them.

- **Learn a foreign language fast.** When travelling to a foreign country, it's extremely helpful to get one of those quickie learn-a-language courses on tape. While learning the language is crucial, be sure to pay as close attention to local customs, which can be even more important than words. Reciting phrases over and over again is great for getting pronunciations correct, but you might want to try my own personal favorite way to learn another language — by watching movies. Many movie geeks like myself have the dialogue for certain films memorized from beginning to end. Purchase a DVD with foreign language tracks, a foreign language version of your favorite video, or a videotape with closed captioning, or even watch television with

FOR TRAVELERS: STUDY THE PROGRAM GUIDE
Be sure to research the films you are about to see. If you depend on the cryptic descriptions in the some official program guides (which are often confusing and sometimes have little to do with the actual film) you may end up seeing some really bad movies. Look for buzzwords -- like "earnest," which can often translate into "boring." I always try to catch features or documentaries without distribution since they may not be in theaters or on TV for years to come. And when I say "research," I mean *talk to your fellow festivalgoers.* You'd be surprised what you learn by listening to the "buzz."

the SAP channel turned on. By watching your favorite flick in another language over and over, you'll know that "Que la Fuerza te acompane," means "May the Force be with you" in Spanish. You'll be quoting popular movie lines to all your new international pals in no time! And after all, movies *are* the international language.

• **See the world.** While you're travelling, don't forget to take at least a day away from the festival to see the local sights. You may never be back to this part of the country or the world. It's also refreshing to take a break from the fest and get away from people constantly talking about movies. But only for one day!

Use basic common sense when travelling. Don't hesitate to ask a festival staffer or a local for advice or help when lost. You'll almost always find them happy to give you the information you need.

APPLY YOURSELF

Getting Into the Best Festivals for You and Your Film

So, you've worked hard, had the wrap party, you're close to finishing your film — now it's time to start sending in those festival applications and travel the world showing your masterpiece. Having finished a film you certainly have the right to be on a creative high, but don't let that sway you from reality; it's time to get serious.

Aimlessly filling out applications and writing checks is generally how most filmmakers go about submitting to festivals. That method usually results in paying a cool $40 bucks for each rejection letter — a total waste of cash. You can do better than that. You need a submission plan.

First, you need to get to know the festivals. (Which is why we included the handy festival appendix in the back of this book.) Choose a group of festivals that best fit the profile of your film. There are many factors to consider when choosing festivals that are right for you.

10 Important Factors to Consider When Applying to Festivals

As the filmmaker (writer, director, producer, or combination of the three), your job is to act as the ambassador of your film. When you travel to a festival, you represent everyone who worked on the movie and the movie itself. Make no mistake, selecting the festivals to submit your film to is an important decision. You will be throwing away vast amounts of time and money if you do not consider these ten important factors before submitting to any festival. In order of importance, they are:

1. **Prestige.** Submitting your film to a prestige festival will give your movie its best chance to be sold to a distributor, receive loads of press coverage, get your next film deal, and (cross your fingers) launch your brilliant career as a filmmaker. Also, just getting accepted into a prestige festival can make a great quote on a DVD sleeve — something as simple as "Official Selection Sundance Film Festival." I'll bet you've noticed that on more than a few films. Prestige counts for a lot. Being accepted into one of the Top Ten festivals is an honor, so keep that in mind.

2. **Distributors.** Is the fest considered a "discovery" film festival — one that distributors attend? If the ultimate goal is to sell your film, this must be of paramount concern to you. Make sure to ask the festival staff which acquisitions executives will be attending.

3. **Reviews and press coverage.** Getting exposure in newspapers like the *Los Angeles Times*, the *New York Times*, magazines like *Entertainment Weekly, Premiere, American Cinematographer, Filmmaker*, web outlets like FilmThreat.com and IndieWire, and trades like *The Hollywood Reporter* and *Variety* is another important factor to consider. Your chances of being covered and/or reviewed by these outlets increases when they actually attend the festival. But it's also your job to be sure that they see a screening of your film. Ask the festival office to provide a list of the journalists attending the festival. If the festival has only attracted local press, it may not be worth your time. Unless, of course, that local press is in one of the Top Ten markets in the US.

4. **Prizes and awards.** From sizable cash awards to film equipment to lab deals, prizes should play a role in your decision to submit. The winner of the Grand Prize for Dramatic Feature at the Heartland Film Festival gets $50,000 — that's a damn good prize! Cash awards are always a nice dividend. Be sure to research the prizes awarded and take them into consideration when submitting. Inquire about audience awards, judges

awards, and so on. Any type of award that your film receives only serves to increase its overall value. While it's an honor to receive a jury award, audience awards hold a lot of clout since they are the true gauge for whether moviegoers respond to your film. Winning an audience award will get you attention and increase the interest of other people (hopefully, well-funded people), who will now want to see your film.

5. **Location.** Could this film festival be a well-earned holiday as well as a chance to schmooze with the bigshots of the movie world? If it's a choice between the Hawaii Film Festival and a festival in Ohio, the choice is clear. Surf's up! Hawaii!

6. **Perks.** How does the festival treat you? Is the flight paid for? Are you put up for free? For example, The Florida Film Festival treats filmmakers like royalty, even offering passes to Disneyland and Universal Studios Theme Park while the film-makers are in town. Be sure to inquire about paid expenses and other perks. Travel costs can add up fast, so research what expenses festivals will cover. Almost all festivals cover lodging, fewer cover airfare, and a small few will give filmmakers per diem. Get the facts before you submit.

7. **Application fee.** Festival application fees can be really steep. Upwards of $50 for some. At that price, enter twenty fests and you've spent a $1,000 bucks. With over 1,000 festivals world-wide, those application fees can add up fast. You could end up spending enough in application fees to finance your next film!

   Be sure to ask if a festival is willing to waive the fee. It's always worth a try, and some of them will actually be willing to do it. If your film has no chance of being accepted anyway, why bother writing the check and submitting the film? Do your homework. Don't submit your talky twentysomething, ansgt-ridden, Kevin Smith-like, *Clerks* wannabe to the Asian Children's Film Festival.

8. **Research and Recommendations.** I've included lists of festivals that excel in specific categories, but you should do your own research and contact other filmmakers who have either attend-ed or had their films shown at that particular festival, if at all possible.

9. **Contacts.** It's vitally important to make useful contacts for investors in future films, distributors, acquisitions executives,

agents, lawyers, and especially other filmmakers who can help you along in your career. Or simply to make friends in the industry. You never know how these contacts can pay off later. For many, a festival can be an opportunity to meet their heroes in a social setting. I know a filmmaker who attended a small film festival for one reason only — Martin Scorsese was going to be there and he wanted to meet him. Nothing is more fun than slugging down beers and talking film until all hours of the night with a longtime film hero. You'd be shocked at what John Waters will tell you when he's feelin' loose at a party. (God, I love that guy.)

James Woods with festival directors Robin Laatz and Karl Kozak at the San Diego Film Festival.

And, if you decide to go the route of self-distribution, making contacts should be a major factor in your submission plan. You'll need to find others in the industry willing to champion your film.

10. **Fun.** Yes, fun. If it's going to be miserable, why bother? Working the festival circuit, plugging a film day in and day out, can be grueling after the fiftieth post-screening question and answer session. Select festivals in places you'd like to visit — that way, if the festival is a bore, at least you'll have the opportunity to explore a new city. Ohio may not have a beach, but there are some great bars and even better people.

Basically, you need to think of your film as an investment. The value of your film (and yourself as a filmmaker) increases as you receive good press, awards of any kind, and acceptance into prestige film festivals.

SEEKiNG ACCEPTANCE

Avoiding Mistakes on the All-important Festival Application

All you have to do is fill out the application, write a check, enclose a video, mail it off, and you're in, right? *Wrong!* Filmmakers who follow this path are only fooling themselves. There are some very simple things you can do to make the lives of the people running the festival a little easier and thereby greatly increase your chances of acceptance. Follow this advice and avoid the mistakes that turn many festival entries into recycled videotapes.

1. **Follow instructions.** The first thing that can leave a film teetering on the fence of rejection is not following the directions on the application. This only serves to upset busy festival workers. If you have any questions or extenuating circumstances regarding your film, be sure to call the festival.

2. **Label correctly.** A package sent to a festival generally includes the check, application, the film on video, the sleeve and press kit, press materials, photos, etc. Be sure to label every single one of these things and include your contact information on everything. If you send a video, the contact info should be on the video sleeve *and* the video itself.

3. **Inquire about a festival's pre-screening process.** Most festivals won't admit this, but many submissions are viewed on video, generally by subordinates, and only the first five to ten minutes are actually viewed. This is an unfortunate reality. However, when you consider that some festivals receive over 800 films, resulting in close to 1,500 hours of viewing time (that's about two straight months with no sleep in front of a VCR — hey, you try that!), you can't blame them for rushing through the screening process. If you pay the application fee, make sure someone is going to watch the entire film.

4. **Research the number of submissions accepted.** Your chances may be better at a smaller festival with fewer submissions.

5. **Save your premiere for the right festival.** It's something you'll hear more than once in this book: your premiere should be protected, as it is your film's virginity (and you can only give it up once). When submitting to a festival, full disclosure is necessary, so be honest. Lying on the application is never a good idea since the festival staff will eventually find out anyway. If the film has screened elsewhere, you *must* include this information. One way to get around "premiering" too soon is to screen at a festival as a work-in-progress out of competition and be sure you are not listed in the program guide. This means you can still officially "premiere" at a bigger festival sometime in the future.

Don't hesitate to ask a festival whether playing at another will exclude you from acceptance. Playing Toronto in September will not exclude you from playing Sundance in January, but if you play the AFI Fest in November, your chances for playing Sundance will be over.

> One way to get around "premiering" too soon is to screen at a festival as a work-in-progress out of competition and be sure you are not listed in the program guide. This means you can still officially "premiere" at a bigger festival sometime in the future.

6. *Do not* include a long apologetic letter pointing out your film's faults. "The sound is a pre-mix...this is our first rough cut...we plan to take out another twenty minutes...we're still doing some reshoots...." Dailies are for *you* to examine, not the film festival. Send as close to a finished film as possible.

   Your cover letter should include all the basic details and should be no more than one page. If the film is an answer print, certainly point that out, but don't dwell on it or go into exhausting detail.

7. **Make a personal connection.** Any kind of connection you can make in your cover letter or follow-up phone call to the festival is helpful. Attaching a voice to a name makes you human and not just another applicant. But don't be bothersome by constantly sending letters asking, "Are we in yet?" In the case of festivals, the squeaky wheel gets annoying really fast, so be understanding and respectful of festival staffers' time. There are hundreds of other filmmakers also waiting for a response.

8. *Do not* include promotional junk. T-shirts, stickers, pens, and other promotional give-aways will often make their way into the garbage. You'll need this stuff later to promote your film — *after* it's been accepted. Don't send it in with your film.

9. **Have a story.** I mean your own personal story. There is a reason you made your film, and your struggle to get it onscreen can be as compelling as the film itself. It makes a great story in a festival program and will set you apart from the pack. Is the film auto-biographical? What makes your film so important that people should be willing to pay to see it? What hardships did you endure to tell your tale? The viewers of your film will look differently at it if they know you had to sell blood to get it made.

If you really have no story, be creative. The Slamdance Film Festival program book includes information about each film-maker including a short bio. I still remember reading: "Eric Kripke is a millionaire playboy director who solves baffling crimes in his spare time." His short film, *Truly Committed*, was hilarious and went on to win the Audience Award at Slamdance.

10. **Submit on time.** Submitting late will only give the festival staff an easy excuse to reject your film. It also means that most screening slots have already been filled and that your film will most likely not be viewed in its entirety. By now, the bloodshot eyes of the screening committee in the festival are highly trained to spot films they don't like. If they are not hooked in the first five to ten minutes, your film becomes a reject.

Write a Powerful Film Synopsis

I cringe when I read poorly written descriptions of movies that appear in festival program guides. Sometimes the descriptions are so pretentious or vague, it's impossible to even tell what the movie is about. These short descriptive paragraphs are an essential piece of movie marketing and often the only thing a festivalgoer has to make choices about what film to see. Many times the film description sent in by the filmmaker is the one that is used in the program guide, so as the filmmaker, it's worth spending time writing a synopsis of your film in various word lengths.

Remember, the synopsis is made to *sell* the film. If the synopsis is poorly written, it will reflect on the film itself. Also, avoid being esoteric or pretentious like this synopsis from a rejected submission from the Atlanta Film & Video Festival:

"Put simply, this film is a romantic fable. However, as a film, it is a composition of auditory and visual components. Please keep in mind, the same person both photographed and scored this film there-by creating a structure of audio-visual counterpoint. Using an origi-nal, yet light archetypal story, the filmmaker has sought to compose a film that 'works' not only as an intensive audio-visual approach, but also as a carefree ride right into a big fat smile!"

Uh, yeah.

This handy writing primer can be used by both filmmakers and festival programmers to write eye-catching copy that will fill festival seats.

- **Getting Started:** First and foremost, a description of a movie written for a festival program guide is *not* a review — let's face it, it's advertising. You want to get audiences so excited, they'll be afraid they may miss something. You'll need to hone your writing skills by using your thesaurus. A lot. Begin by sprinkling your description with "emotional" language — like compelling, touching, moving, milestone, life-affirming, sexy, romantic, groundbreaking, or heartfelt. Adjectives like these work, so use them liberally. It's hype, there's no denying it...and it can be very successful.

- **Sound Bite:** Consider starting with a large quote underneath the title, which serves to grab the reader's attention. With only a glance, a reader can get a quick idea of what the movie is about and who it's for.

- **Synopsis:** A compelling description of the story should run about 100-500 words. The most important thing to remember is to *be specific*. Believe it or not, some of the worst festival program guide descriptions come from Sundance, where you can read 500 words about a movie and still not know what it's about. Don't go that route — tell the story, but *never* give away the ending or too much of the story. The story description should act as a *tease* and make people want to know what happens.

  And don't forget to address these questions in the copy somehow: *Why* is the film important? *Why* should audiences pay attention? *What* about this film may change the lives of audiences taking the time to see it? *Why* is this film so compelling? *Why* is this film unique? The *"why?"* is important to include since it's a chance to point out the unique nature of this film and what makes it a "must see." Every film playing at the fest is a "must see" but they each have unique attributes. Point out what your film's attributes are.

- **Review Quotes:** If you have them, include very positive quotes from prominent critics/reviewers or other sources woven into the copy. A quote needn't be a complete sentence, a phrase or even a word or two will do, as long as the credible source is quoted. If you're a filmmaker, get your movie reviewed somewhere. Anywhere. Then quote from it. Or consider getting a quote from a champion of the film, someone recognizable in the film community who gives you permission to quote him or her.

- **Extra Info:** Be sure to include additional information with the film description, such as the movie's official website, note any actors or filmmakers who may be present at the screening, as well as the premiere status of the film. (And you know, a *local premiere* is still a *premiere!*)

And don't forget to have fun with this! You're not writing a serious film "essay" — this is *marketing copy* to get audiences (you know, regular moviegoers) excited about a movie. Make it sound like a movie that *you* would want to see. Pour on the hype!

Here's an example:

Melvin Goes to Dinner

"They discuss marital infidelity, religion, schizophrenia, ghosts, stewardesses, self-pleasure..."

Starring Michael Blieden, Matt Price,
Stephanie Courtney, and Annabelle Gurwitch,
with cameos by Maura Tierney, Bob Odenkirk,
David Cross, and Jack Black

Directed by Bob Odenkirk, 80 min.

www.melvingoestodinner.com

WEST COAST PREMIERE! Have you ever gone to a dinner that changed your life? Melvin (Michael Blieden) reluctantly attends a dinner with three almost complete strangers. They discuss marital infidelity, religion, a guy in heaven wearing a Wizard's jersey, fetishes, cigarettes and schizophrenia, ghosts, stewardesses, self-pleasure, and how it's all going to get a lot worse before it gets better.

Directed by Bob Odenkirk, *Melvin Goes to Dinner* is vastly different than *Mr. Show*, his groundbreaking HBO sketch comedy series. No worries, though! Melvin has a crude sense of humor that can be linked with Odenkirk's past work and there are also laugh-out-loud cameos by David Cross and Jack Black.

GETTING A "THUMBS UP" FROM THE GATEKEEPER:
Behind the Scenes With GEOFF GILMORE,
Director of the Sundance Film Festival

The Sundance Film Festival is the leading festival in the United States, if not the world. It is where indie films are picked up for distribution, where new talent is discovered, and where people from all over the world travel to make deals. All festivals have gatekeepers, screening committees that often make group decisions about what films to accept. For Sundance there is Geoff Gilmore: the chief gatekeeper for Sundance. While the festival has a trusted group of programmers — including John Cooper, Caroline Libresco, and Trevor Groth, among others — Gilmore is the primary person responsbile for the festival program at Sundance. This makes him one of the most powerful people in the independent film industry today.

Sundance gatekeeper Geoff Gilmore
PHOTO BY
FRED HAYES

Gilmore came to Sundance in 1989, back when it was still called the United States Film Festival. He has been instrumental in the festival's emergence as the number one market for independent films in the United States. He has an unbridled passion for cinema that I have not seen in any other festival director. Gilmore truly cares about supporting independent films and has used Sundance to forward this admirable agenda.

In order to get into Sundance, you've got to get into the mind of Geoff Gilmore. He must embrace your film. In the following interview, Gilmore reveals how he selects films and his philosophies about what makes a successful independent film.

As Director of the Sundance Film Festival, what does your job entail?
Generally speaking, I am where the buck stops in terms of what gets into the Festival. I help shape the vision of Sundance — what it is and what it will become in the long term. I also manage many of the day-to-day things that we have to deal with as an institution.

Sundance sets the tone for a lot of the smaller film festivals. Many of those festival directors attend Sundance to see what's hot and then try their best to program those films at their festivals. What do you think of that?

That's partially true, although in the past few years, we've really gone out of our way to offer another thirty or forty films to those festival directors to say, "Hey, guys, this wasn't ready for us when we had to make our decision, or, we just couldn't include this one. Why don't you take a look at this?" For a number of different festivals (SXSW, Los Angeles Festival, and others), we make recommendations about work that we think they might be interested in.

This also gives the filmmaker another chance. There's a real need to support a range of different independent filmmakers. Theatrical distribution is very hard to get right now, and many independent filmmakers tend to see Sundance as an all or nothing goal. If they attain it, they've achieved victory — and if they don't, then they've lost. I very strongly want to make the point that this is not true and that good films do surface. Good films will find a way out and they'll find a way out through a number of different paths.

But playing at Sundance goes a long way toward helping a filmmaker secure distribution, doesn't it?

I am not going to argue that Sundance has a place in putting work into the marketplace or helping get work viewed, and not just for acquisition but for a lot of things. I don't think Sundance should be seen as only a market; that's too narrow. There are films at Sundance that *don't* become buzz films and therefore people don't understand that those are also very much part of the independent world. But one of the things we're really interested in trying to do is continue to expand the sense of what the aesthetic possibilities are. Ten years ago, festivals were aesthetic enterprises for critics who went and talked about the movies and talked about the nature of the film and they talked about whether it was exciting or not. Business was just not a big part of the film festival culture.

> I think probably the nicest thing you can do for young filmmakers is to get them out of debt and get their films sold.

Now you go to these festivals and the topic of conversation is acquisition deals, or whether or not new films could have been found. That's unfortunate, because it really overloads and categorizes only one aspect of a festival's function. I think there are a range of functions. That said, I never apologize for the fact that Sundance has become a market. I think probably the nicest thing you can do for young filmmakers is to get them out of debt and get their films sold.

Often I don't care whether a film was successful at the box office —
I want to know whether it was successful creatively.

It becomes a horse race; Number One is the only position that matters. They report whether or not something is the Number One grosser of the weekend; that's ridiculous because independent release distribution patterns are now similar to studio patterns. It's so much harder to keep a film in a marketplace and watch it actually find an audience.

It's amazingly difficult, the way that sets up what films the acquisitions executives are looking for — because they don't know anymore. They're finding it difficult to try to figure out what can stay out there and what can't. You can argue that it's a hit-driven marketplace. But what does that mean? So it becomes a question of what one thinks is the overall function of a festival. I am not so naïve that I think people should come there and debate Fellini; yet I would hope that at least some of the discussions would be aesthetic and ideological discussions.

The generation of filmmakers currently very much involved in producing independent films strikes me as being similar to the '90s professional athlete — very interested in what's in it for them, in making money, having their own position and their own status, but not necessarily winning championships. A lot of guys have huge contracts without ever winning a playoff game. And in some ways that seems to be what's going on with independent filmmakers. They don't really care about making films that will be memorable, films people will talk about ten years from now. They care desperately about making a film that can get them into the industry so they can recoup some of the investment they've put into the film. More than that, they want to go onto a career that's lucrative and glamorous. I meet more and more filmmakers who are extremely knowledgeable about the business side of the industry and don't really know anything about film. They have a better understanding of who's who and who is influential in the business of film than they do an appreciation for the craft.

I don't hear anyone justifying their festival by saying, "The films we showed at our festival were great." They justify themselves by saying, "We had as many films picked up as they did!" Or, "We have as many acquisitions coming out of it as they do." That should not be the justification for a festival. You have to look at your program and say, "I like this program. This is a strong program. This is what we should be showing. These are the choices we made because these are the films that have value on a number of different levels."

Hasn't Sundance become a part of this emphasis on the business side of the film industry?

One of the odd complaints of Sundance is that the agenda we've set for everyone is the business agenda, yet I don't think that's the crisis. You really have to have a degree of balance. I would hope that to some degree that balance comes from the filmmaker: that they have not chosen filmmaking as a career because they like the accoutrements that go with being a movie director, but because they actually have some passion and a kind of creative vision and a voice they need to express. I don't know if I see that as much. You can ask a lot of filmmakers questions about any of those filmmakers in their fifties, or about guys who are dead — and they don't know them; they haven't seen them. When they do, it really shows. It comes out in their work, which doesn't always make it the most commercial, but makes it interesting. And this fails to be lauded enough by critics and by journalists, who used to be part of that mechanism that helped support the aesthetic dimensions of independent film.

How does Sundance actually select the films?

When you look at about eight hundred independent fictional features and another couple of hundred documentaries and another three or four hundred films in other categories, you really just don't have time to go through them all yourself. So the primary staff is responsible for viewing that work. We have a support staff, and we make sure that no film is seen by fewer than at least a couple of people. I screen a lot of films cold, off the shelf. Recently, that percentage has dropped a bit. Instead of picking up 50 percent of those old films and taking them home, maybe the number is down to 25 percent or so. That means that there are a number of other major staff members who see material cold. And one thing I have always given my staff credit for is that they are very thoughtful. They really take a lot of time to consider work. They argue it passionately and persuasively — often fighting over different films. You are not looking for five of six people to sit there and agree. You are looking for people to support the work and you are trying to think about what they are saying. You are trying to be a professional programmer who is able to pick a film out and say, "This film should be shown. It's not necessarily my taste or a film I would buy if I were an acquisitions person, but it is a film that should be shown." You make that decision as a professional because you have reasons for this film to be shown as part of what's out there in the independent world. That's the goal for your staff and for yourself. That's what you strive for.

Unfortunately, too many people take for granted the kind of pressures that are put on you. They figure, "Well, there is a lot of political pressure coming from individuals or companies, therefore they have to respond that way." We are not about that pressure. We are certainly in a situation where some of the films we show will be distributed, but if we show six or seven films from Miramax one year, people will say, "God, Harvey [Weinstein] put in whatever he wanted this year." What people don't realize is that we looked at twenty films from Miramax and we didn't take fourteen others. The films we choose are those we think make up the best festival and represent what the independent universe is all about.

The competition is fierce, and it continues to grow.

Prints and advertising (P&A) costs have tripled in the last two years. Any film you buy has to gross theatrically at a certain level to make it profitable. You can't release a film with less than $2 million of P&A. You are going to be in that situation regardless of what the film cost to make in the first place. So, you have these acquisitions executives looking around and asking themselves, which are the films worth investing the huge amount of P&A required to make them profitable? Those are the questions that I don't think people think through clearly enough.

Are there common mistakes that you see filmmakers make over and over again?

Rushing. I keep saying don't rush. Don't create a situation where everything is dependent on a schedule only to get into X or Y festival. You know, you spend an awful lot of time putting this project together. Make it good; take the extra time to not only shoot that extra take, but to really think about quality. Try to take a step back. Have naysayers around you. Don't just let people say, "Great, great, great!" Have someone who really gives you a critical eye. You don't want a whole bunch of people arguing with you; what you really want is someone you can trust to help support your vision and not rush it.

We look for a lot of different things, but I've always said our strength is that we respond to a lot of different things. We have a very diverse and eclectic level of response that allows us to look at a work from one kind of experimental point of view to something much more casually mainstream. People really need to look at the range. You are not trying to do something as narrowly defined as "a Sundance film."

For many years, we attacked the industry for making formulaic work, and pushed the independent film as the realm in which creative vision flourished. Yet, we have now moved into an era in which the independent world has become a derivative mess. Some of the initial perspective that motivated the independent world has been lost: the capital "Q" quirky comedy that reflects only a series of quirky comedies that have come before; the generic "Tarantino-wannabe" work; the coming-of-age angst story that really isn't fresh or doesn't have the depth to make it profound, but is simply another version of the same tale.

Without being too harsh, you want to say, "Those films aren't going to make it anymore." You really need to find something or think about something that runs with freshness and originality. Filmmakers hear these words...and then go and do something straight out of a primetime network sitcom.

FOCUS TEST YOUR FILM
Paper is cheaper than film. Write. Rewrite. Get more feedback. Rewrite and repeat. Shoot some test scenes on video. Get more feedback and keep rewriting until the script is perfect. Ask yourself, "Why am I making this film?" Be willing to take helpful advice from others. When you have a copy of the film to screen, show it to a real audience. Friends and family are too polite, so recruit real moviegoers, but be prepared for brutal comments. It takes a thick skin to handle it, so be ready for a painful but ultimately worthwhile experience.

The thing that irks me is when I hear a filmmaker brag
that they wrote the film in a week.

Isn't it amazing that they do that? They say things like, "This film was done on first draft." You want to tell them — *it shows*.

If you could sit down with some of these independent filmmakers
before they started writing their screenplays and give them some advice,
what would you tell them?

Don't just go out and make a film, make a great film. It's so hard to make films and I have so much respect for people who do it. A lot of people are very often angry at us for having to make choices, for being in a position where we have to say: these are the films we have chosen and these we have decided not to take. So often, we have people filled with righteous indignation at being rejected. We have people who think, because it is so hard to make films, that just having made a film is a significant enough accomplishment in itself. It's just not enough to spend a couple of years of your life making a movie, finally finish it, think, "Oh my goodness, I've made a movie!" and pat yourself on the back. You really have to look at what you made and say, "Is this successful? Does this convey the kind of energy and inspiration and storytelling and excitement? Does it work the way I want it to work?"

They read these stories in the paper about this guy making a film or that girl making a film. They feel they have to get their film made and they go out and make it — and too often it is just not good enough. That's a phrase we use around here all the time. "It's not good enough." That doesn't mean that it's bad and it's not that it doesn't have certain elements. It means it isn't cast well or it doesn't have any visual style, or it doesn't necessarily have the kind of creativity to it that really makes it stand apart. So you have to say to yourself — if you are a filmmaker and you have to spend all these resources and all this time — why not shoot for the top? Not enough people do.

Filmmakers need to be encouraged to really take their time. Sometimes that means you won't make it this year and that you need to work on your script. People don't like hearing that their third draft wasn't good enough, that they need to go into a fourth draft. They don't want to do that; they want to say, "Let's make it!"

That sort of thinking will ultimately create something without any kind of effect and people won't care about it.

I don't believe that this generation doesn't work hard. I feel that the twenty-something generation right now is almost Protestant in its work ethic. Film students feel they should have no other life outside of their film schools. They don't even see movies because they're working so hard in school. When I was in film school, we used to say, "Are you going to go to the Nuart and watch this film?" Because it was presumed that was what you were going to do. Now, though, people are saying, "No, I've got to finish my project or I've got to work on my script or do my essay." The goal should be to go see those films. My advice is, seek that inspiration, seek that knowledge, broaden yourself, and take the time for your project to really get it right. Or else I fear we are not going to have a generation of filmmakers who will be considered memorable.

What so many of these young filmmakers forget is that you find a lot of major filmmakers doing great work in their late thirties, their forties, and their fifties rather than in their twenties. You need life experience and you just don't get it when you are twenty.

It's interesting how many of the filmmakers who have made really low-budget films have become the filmmakers of note for this generation. Maybe the creative ingenuity you need when you are working with a low budget really marks them. I wonder if there isn't something to be said for that sort of initiation. I wonder if really struggling and making those really small $100,000 budget films forces them to overcome obstacles and marks them as filmmakers with ingenuity and promise for the future.

I've heard this many times, primarily from filmmakers who have been rejected from your festival, that getting into Sundance is very "political." Some say it's "who you know." How do you respond to that kind of criticism?

That's a "I hear you've stopped beating your wife" remark. If you tell anyone what the reality of the situation is, no one believes you. I've heard a lot of people try to take credit for getting films in Sundance. They want to claim credit for getting films in based on the calls they make. I still have to smile and say, "Guys, it just isn't true." It's very hard to get inside these doors.

The ability to program comes from an ability to look at a lot of different kinds of things — even though some of them may not be your cup of tea — and say, "this one is terrific." And this is a skill that recognizes a genre film, like a *Blair Witch,* and gives it credit for what it is. *Blair Witch* knows horror. It knows documentary. It understands independent work. It understands how to mix and play with genres. It has self-reflexivity in it. It brought digital filmmaking into another world, and that hadn't been done before. For all of the lambasting the film has taken, it doesn't get credit for what it did and what made it interesting in the first place.

I've heard some say that there are too many festivals. I disagree. What do you think?

The functions of film festivals are now so numerous that you have festivals being created for regional tourist bureaus to raise the media profile of a small resort, rather than to fill any function on the national scheme of things.

But is that necessarily a bad thing? The way I see it, these festivals are providing alternative distribution outlets for indies and more people will see them on the festival circuit than after they get picked up by a distributor. It's as if the "festival tour" itself is really the thing filmmakers should focus on, rather than trying to get distribution. These films are, in a sense, already *being distributed to an audience passionate about indie film.*

Well, I agree with you. I think the film festival circuit is a little bit like the cinematheque circuit in the '60s. Except the cinematheque circuit failed because they didn't have the marketing dollars. I do think that there are audiences for this. There's very much a pay-off for filmmakers and audiences that are able to see work that is not simply what the major multiplex world and major mainstream sources would have us see. So, in some ways, it is a substitute for some kinds of theatrical distribution. In the meantime, film festivals continue to broaden the possibilities and the opportunities for filmmakers as well as audiences, for which I am grateful.

THE DUDE: A Conversation with JEFF DOWD, Indie Film's Most Notorious Producer's Rep

Producer's rep
Jeff Dowd

Jeff Dowd is The Dude. Jeff's last name, Dowd, kind of sounds like "dude," so it's not surprising that he was given this nickname in elementary school. He's been known as Dude ever since. He has enjoyed a lifelong love affair with movies, having fallen in love in the theater when he saw *Some Like it Hot* at age nine. The Dude will also tell you that he has a passion for life. This guy knows how to party. And Jeff's very often the life of the party. There is always that one guy who gets everyone fired up — the one who cranks the music, taps the keg, or starts the conga line. Jeff Dowd is that guy.

The Dude has been at the center of the indie scene at its very beginnings having helped an astonishing number of films and filmmakers including *Blood Simple, The Black Stallion, Chariots of Fire, Gandhi, Hoosiers, The Stunt Man, Desperately Seeking Susan,* and too many more to name. When the Dude talks, people listen. He knows how to get a film into the hands of the right people and form the necessary strategy to put that movie into the best possible position to get noticed and sell. It's hard to say exactly what a producer's rep like The Dude actually does, but it is a rare talent. His job involves everything from script evaluation to marketing to publicity to just plain sweet-talking. And he's damn good at all of it, especially the sweet-talking.

More recently Jeff's been involved in such films as *The Cockettes, Scratch, Neil Young's Greendale, Metallica: Some Kind of Monster,* and selling films like *Two Family House* (Sundance Audience Award Winner) to Lions Gate Films, *Dream with the Fishes* to Sony Pictures Classics, and *Eight Days a Week* to Warner Bros., *Kissing Jessica Stein* to Fox Searchlight, and *Better Luck Tomorrow* to MTV Films. The Dude also finds time to sit on the boards of the Independent Feature Project, the International Documentary Association, the Sundance Film Festival, and the Sundance Institute. Currently he is writing his autobiography.

Jeff is such a well-known and strangely unique person that film-makers Joel and Ethan Coen paid tribute to The Dude by basing a character in their film *The Big Lebowski* on him. Anyone who has spent more than five minutes with The Dude will notice that Jeff Bridges' mannerisms in that film are strikingly similar.

I met The Dude at the SXSW Film Festival where we ended up on a panel together. This resulted in a night I only half remember, bar-hopping through the streets of Austin, Texas. I don't recall everything that happened, I only know that I had an amazing time. Jeff is the cowboy I want leading the wagon train through a flurry of parties. He's also the perfect guy to have on your side when making and selling a movie.

What can a really good producer's rep do for a filmmaker?

What you do is prepare the filmmakers for what lies ahead in the marketplace. What their strategic choices are. What that means is that you help them creatively get as much feedback as they can on the movie — have screenings so they can make creative adjustments. And believe me, the best movies have made creative adjustments in post-production. Whether that means extra shooting, whether it means music addition. At the same time, it's strategic planning. How are we going to show this movie the first time? Are we going to show it at the festival? Are we going to show it to all the distributors at once? Or are we going to show it to only one distributor? What are we going to do in terms of domestic versus foreign? What's the filmmaker's agenda? There are going to be different people involved in the filmmaking team, and each one will have a slightly different agenda. Is this a stepping stone to their next movie? Do they want to get the investors' money back? Both? It's helping creative discussion so the people can focus in on the very important decisions they have to make. There are no right or wrong answers, but most of the time, people don't understand the alternatives. So, I try to get them all the information they can use to make good decisions. Also, we discuss all the things they have to do...whatever it takes to put your best foot forward. I essentially join the team in every aspect of it.

*Can a filmmaker sell a film themselves without a producer's rep
or an agent or lawyer?*

Of course you can, if you are very lucky. But even Michael Jordan tended to like to go on the court with four other guys. You're just absolutely insane if you try to do it alone. I'm all about trying to build a team. I'll work with all the agents and lawyers to put together the best possible team. Anybody who goes out into today's extremely competitive, expensive, harsh world without a good team — well, they might as well take a gun and just start shooting off the body parts of all the people who helped them make the movie. It's the most irresponsible thing to do, but it happens all the time.

The problem with independents is that they're independent. In today's world it's important to make strategic alliances. I would recommend that independents also make strategic teamwork alliances. In the worst case, it's going to get them more information.

And by the way, any smart investor really wants the best team to protect their investment. A lot of producers have underbudgeted the production and a lot of directors have underpaid themselves and so they start to think, "Why should I let someone else get involved with this and take another piece?" And that's a legitimate feeling, but they're not seeing the big picture. The big picture is getting your film into the marketplace in a proper way. It's great to have a whole team of passionate, smart players.

Before the filmmaker even begins shooting, what do they need to know?

Just because anyone *can* make a movie, doesn't mean everyone *should* make a movie. I can't believe someone thinks people would actually go see these movies on an opening Friday night as opposed to all the other choices in the world! If your movie isn't enough for people to see over every other choice, then it's never going to go theatrical. Is it so special that it's going to get on some cable show? And there's really no direct-to-video anymore, so what makes it so special?

1. Ask yourself, "Who is my intended audience?"
2. People really don't do enough dramaturgical work on their scripts. They should do readings and more readings and not just get the advice of a couple friends. Actually pay for some advice. If you're going to spend $100,000 on a film, you can use $5,000 on dramaturgical feedback. It could make the difference

between the film getting released and not getting released. That's why we started the Sundance Institute. We try to say to people, "Do not make your film yet, stop. Reassess it. Put it on its best feet. Try filming some scenes here to get some feedback."

Paper is ultimately cheaper than film.

Right! The problem is, a lot of filmmakers are filmmakers first and storytellers second. Hitchcock, Sayles, Tarantino — these filmmakers were all writers first, directors second. Audiences go to stories, not to films. Form may be equally exciting as content sometimes, but it's still about the way *the story* affects the audience emotionally and viscerally. Most of the people who end up being successful in the independent market are phenomenally well-versed in the history of cinema and they bring that to the table — Tarantino and Spielberg — these people could be working at the film library as archivists. People don't pay enough attention to stopping to get all the dramaturgical feedback that they can, studying films, and talking to people about the marketplace. I guarantee I can personally increase peoples' chances 1000 percent if they talk to me earlier rather than later in terms of whether a film will get to distribution.

So, what is a distributor looking for?

Several things: distributors are looking to see how it plays for an audience. They are assessing how it plays for critics. That's why distributors often like film festivals. They are able to get a sense of how a movie plays for audiences and how critics are likely to respond. The other thing that's important at the end of the day, is how the distributors emotionally respond to the film, how they feel about the filmmakers. They're not going to do it just for economic reasons, believe me. And, of course, there are critical and economic evaluations. So, how you assess your first showing is: maybe there's one distributor who is perfect for your film and maybe they don't like film festivals and they like to see things in their own screening room so that's the way to do it. Maybe a film festival is. But, you often want to screen a film in front of the target audience. It depends on the kind of film it is and what kind of experience you want to have. Sometimes a particular actor or director is going to be the key to selling the film. That's one thing that distributors assess. Who is going to represent this film in the media for us? They often need to see that person in action at a film festival or something. You need to come up with a way to screen the film that helps convey what it's going to do in the marketplace.

Then perhaps the distributor screening, basically a few people sitting in the room, is not the best way to go?

Maybe not, but there are certain films that have been very success-ful, and that's how they were sold. It really is case by case. It's also what you do before you screen the film. How do you position it to the distributor? How do you describe it? They are very busy people and you have to do some of the homework for them. That might mean press, artwork, trailers — coming up with a way for them to get a feel for why or how the film might interest the public. That's all part of the process. The key thing is for the studios to understand how the continuum goes all the way through to the public.

Are there other ways to get to distributors?

You can screen it at a festival, but the critical thing is what you do before, how you position it. You can do a one-two punch and screen it at a festival and then screen it right afterwards in New York and Los Angeles with audiences. Or they're going to want to screen the print so other people in their company can see it. No one is going to buy a film until the president of marketing makes a decision. That's how a big film is acquired. The other route is having distrib-utor screenings in New York and Los Angeles and there are lots of variations on those. The other alternative is to pick one or two dis-tributors and just screen it for them. The advantages of that are quite obvious. The disadvantages...well, you've only kissed one girl, so to speak, and you'll never know what everyone else might think.

What are the best ways to create buzz and build interest from distributors?

One way is to have certain people in the media doing it (e.g., *Variety, The Hollywood Reporter*). Try to position the movie for them. You can also sometimes show a film to select members of the press.

Obviously, everyone sends out postcards and faxes and things like that. A website. You can have other people, who may not be interested parties but who have some credibility with distributors, call on your behalf. You could also have a couple of screenings that

don't include distributors, but include people who have relationships with distributors.

If you're in a film festival, hiring a publicist is 100 percent recommended. If you're not in a film festival, there isn't really much for
a publicist to do, to be honest. If you have one magazine article or
something to generate some advance interest, that's okay, but you
really don't need much more than one piece. You only need one or
two examples of the buzz the film might generate. And, between the
producers, the producers' rep and the publicists, that information
will get to the distributors. Film festivals are a one-time opportunity to have people look at your film.

What are some of the important things for a filmmaker to be
aware of in any distributor negotiation?

Meet the people at the company who are going to be marketing
your film! The people who are involved acquiring your film are
going to have a lot of contact with you ahead of time, but when your
movie is coming out, they may be off in Cannes. The people who
are marketing your film, *those* are the people you're going to be
married to. The person you're going to be working with everyday is
the head of marketing. So meet those people in the company, and
have them sell you on the plan of how they are going to market your
movie. Brainstorm a little, even have some disagreements. The success of the film isn't about the price of the film, it's about how it is
handled in the marketplace.

The real test is in the extra marketing things that the distributor is going to do. How much are they really going to put into
screenings programs for word of mouth? How much are they going
to put in at a local level?

Ultimately, you're really looking for an individual in the company, an actual person, who is involved in the marketing who is
going to give you a personal commitment as to how much they're
going to do and how much they're capable of doing. You're looking
for a strategy for your film. And someone with the ability to be flexible. Can these people be focused in the season your film is coming
out? How many other films are coming out then? This is a human
business. The biggest part of the deal you're looking for is who are
the human beings you're going to be dealing with and then pray

that they're going to be there when your film comes out and that the company doesn't change hands.

What are some of the things a filmmaker needs to do to build a career?
One of the things you want most is to have some idea of what your next movie is. Either have your own script ready or go buy one. There never seems to be enough time in the day, but make time. There isn't much an agent can do for you, except maybe get you work for hire, unless you have another product they can help get made. You have to be ready for the next effort.

You want to build your team. You want to have your agents and your lawyer and your producers. I think some of the people who build a career have a team of people to work with and that team keeps them going. For example, Quentin Tarantino has Lawrence Bender.

At the end of the day, an actor will be attracted to a great script. So, doesn't it all come back to the screenplay itself?
The absolute best way is to write great parts, because actors will be your best friends. If you write a really good script, with really good parts, you can get really good actors to do it. Agents can become great allies if you have a good script. There are enough smart people who are producers, actors, agents, etc. — if you can build a good enough team, you can get your film to the critical mass. It's almost a litmus test. If your script is good, you will be able to get a name actor.

10 MYSTERiES OF THE FiLM FESTiVAL CiRCUiT REVEALED

In my travels on the film festival circuit I hear a load of gossip. I rarely pay attention, but so many disturbing rumors and pieces of pure fiction seem to get thrown around as "fact" that I thought it was time to set the record straight. Here I attempt to squash the rumors and separate the reality from the bull.

1. **Why do so many quality films never get distribution?** *My film had no stars! My film isn't commercial enough! They just don't get it!* I hear a lot of complaints from filmmakers about why their films go unsold. There are many reasons that excellent indie films get passed up for distribution, but perhaps the most common is not so obvious. Typically, movies made by novice pro-

ducers do not sell for legal reasons. Having a clean chain of title and legal clearance for all the music and copyrighted material is *critical*. In order to actually sell your film, you must have legal paper on everything. And I mean everything, not just the cast and crew, but also that box of [Kellogg's] Corn Flakes in the background. It's always best to err on the side of, well, paranoia, when shooting. So before you yell, "Action!" — before you even get on the set — have an attorney check your script for legal red flags and go about obtaining the clearances you're going to need. I can't tell you how many films I've seen that didn't sell because, in order to do so, the filmmakers would actually have to spend serious money to get those clearances. In fact, closing that coveted distribution deal can end up costing filmmakers so much money that the movie is better left unsold rather than getting deeper into debt. (Depressing thought, huh?) Get your legal papers in order *early* so that when it comes time to sell, you're covered. And don't forget to ask that attorney about E&O insurance (errors and omissions). Trust me, your lawyer will be able to explain it a lot better than I can.

2. **Why does Sundance only show big independent films with Hollywood stars?** Sundance has somehow gotten this bad rap (mainly from rejected or bitter filmmakers) that they only show celebrity-filled independent films from the big studios. The truth is that Sundance does not only show big Hollywood independents. But the media is lazy — and so are the audiences, for that matter. They tend to focus on the celebrity-driven films that screen in Park City during the festival. The reality is that close to 120 features screen at Sundance. Probably twenty-plus are films with stars — which leaves about 100 *other* films that include docs, world cinema, experimental work, and the Native Forum. For narrative features, there are about thirty or so slots open for films that are discovered via submissions. So before jumping to the cliché conclusion most often arrived at by those rejected filmmakers, do your homework, study that Sundance schedule, and take note of the other films screening. In fact, heck, take a count. I'm a documentary fan and it's a genre where I almost never see a celebrity, but I would defend any festival's efforts to bring in celebrity-driven projects. It's great for publicity, the media, and the movie-going public (who eternally

love celebs). Best of all, it can help draw much-needed attention to all those docs, experimental films, and features starring unknowns.

3. **Why do some films win jury awards while other great films go home winless?** There's one very simple reason: juries tend to award the film most in need of support (in terms of attention or securing distribution), rather than the superior work. It happens all the time. How do I know this? I've been on countless juries and the mindset is always the same — give the prize to the movie that needs the push, rather than to the best film. So, if you lose the jury prize, don't take it personally — but if you win, scream about it to everyone in the industry.

4. **Do I have to go to the major festivals like Cannes, Toronto, or Sundance?** The short answer is no. There's a small elite within the indie film community who seem to think only the big fests matter. This is simply not true anymore. Independent films are finding media attention, adoring audiences, and even distribution in the most unlikely festivals. So don't completely ignore the invite to that small, out of the way film festival — you never know what contacts you may make or what might happen.

5. **Is it absolutely necessary to have a publicist, lawyer, agent, manager, producer's rep, and image consultant?** No. I've encountered some of the worst filmmakers who had an entire team in place. It still won't guarantee a thing. It is absolutely essential first to have an outstanding film. That will attract the agent, manager, publicist, etc...and they usually come around right when you need them.

6. **Is there any way to get away with submitting late to a festival?** In reality, you can't get away with submitting past a festival deadline. But there are ways to gain yourself a few extra weeks to work on your film. One way is to be completely honest and simply call the festival to explain your situation. Their written and spoken policy will always explain that they adhere strictly to their deadlines, so it's time to beg. And sometimes this does work. Some understanding festivals will make you send in the fee, the completed entry form, and a blank tape as a placeholder so your film is in their system. Then, when they pull that videotape off the shelf, they'll call you and by that time you absolutely must be ready to turn in the final work.

Now, I didn't tell you about this last one, but you can try it. This is sneaky *and* unethical but has worked for others — not that I'm going to name any names here. All you have to do is submit on time, but send in a blank or defective videotape. By the time the festival screeners discover your defective tape (hopefully weeks later), you'll have a completed version that you can send in right away.

This is sneaky *and* unethical but has worked for others — not that I'm going to name any names here. All you have to do is submit on time, but send in a blank or defective videotape. By the time the festival screeners discover your defective tape (hopefully weeks later), you'll have a completed version that you can send in right away.

7. **Can I buy my way into a film festival?** Um, no — not a legitimate one, at least. But there is one festival that proudly allows filmmakers to buy themselves a slot in their program. So, please listen to my warning — if you are entering a festival that calls you up and informs you that their entry fee is more than $100 and it's not Telluride, you are being taken. In fact, there is a very important-sounding New York-based "film festival" that spends its time preying on naïve filmmakers by calling them to say that they have been accepted into their prestigious-sounding event. The phone call then devolves into a sales pitch involving paying more "fees" — like $300 for entering, then selling services like trailers, a website, and ads in their program guide. I know filmmakers who have been taken for more than $5,000 by these scumbags. They actually tried to sue me once for warning filmmakers about their unsavory tactics! This is a scam. Do your research and do not under any circumstance give this organization any money.

8. **The art of the sale.** Sorry to have to break this to you, but most filmmakers will not close a distribution deal in Park City during Sundance. In fact, many of the deals "announced" in the trades were closed and negotiated weeks *before* the festival even began, they are simply "announced" at Sundance because of the added media attention. The truth is that Sundance and the alternative festivals in Park City are really back-door markets for independent films. You'll find festival directors from all over the world seeking movies to program, as well as distributors (both large and small) looking for films just like yours. For most, the process of getting distribution may take a year —

after the movie has played ten or more festivals, received a few awards, and gotten great reviews from key critics.

9. **What and who are "phantom programmers"?** Okay, I have to admit something — I'm a phantom programmer. You see, I actually assist in programming many film festivals, yet I am not officially involved with festival itself. I'm not even on the advisory board! But because I see a lot of indie films before they hit the circuit through my website, FilmThreat.com, I am often asked by festival programmers looking to fill a slot, "Hey, see anything cool lately?" I always have a recommendation or two. And I'm not the only one. So consider getting your film to a festival programmer by way of a recommendation, which tends to get more attention than the usual entry form enclosed with a check.

10. **What is the one thing I must know when going to a film festival?** Be nice. I'm not kidding — being nice to people will pay off more than you ever dreamed. The indie film world is a fluid one and the assistant this year may be the festival director next year, so it's important to be cool. Just like Fonzie.

BUiLD BUZZ: EVERYTHiNG ABOUT iNDiE MOViE MARKETiNG

"The success of such films as *The Blair Witch Project*, in which millions of people knew about the film from the internet almost a year before its release, make it clear just how important the internet can be in getting the word out about your film. The pre-awareness of that project through the internet is directly responsible for the success of that film. Period."

— Linda Brown-Salmone, Publicist

INTRODUCTiON TO GUERRiLLA MARKETiNG

What do I mean by guerrilla marketing? Basically, it means "Be different." (I would also add that it means you intend to market inexpensively.) You must think beyond simply slapping the logo for your movie onto a baseball cap or a T-shirt. I know it's a cliché, but you have to think, "out of the box." And since everyone else is thinking out of the same freaking box, you have to take a sledgehammer, a bazooka, and a flamethrower to the box! Get creative when it comes to getting your film the attention it deserves from festival attendees, press — and especially distributors.

Take Morgan Spurlock, whose documentary *Super Size Me* played the 2004 Sundance Film Festival and walked away with an award and distribution. He had cheap buttons made up with the McDonald's logo on them, along with the word "Obesity." Within a few days, everyone was wearing them. One well-attended Sundance party found loads of people wearing the "Obesity" button. It was cool because it was mysterious — and because it wasn't a T-shirt.

Morgan went even further and created unique items like *Super Size Me* skull caps, french fry change purses, and even fat Ronald McDonald dolls. The *Super Size Me* posters and postcards (with screening times stickered on the back) were found everywhere. (For more on the story, see his interview later in the book.)

Morgan Spurlock's film had huge buzz with all of his screenings sold out because he was able to think "out of the box." He didn't spend a lot of money and yet he produced clever attention-getters and presented his film in a creative and unexpected way. This doesn't mean that you should be passing out buttons yourself, but it certainly means you should consider something other than T-shirts, which are very typical, and often boring and uncreative. Also, Sundance? Park City in January. It's *cold*! T-shirts either disappear under parkas or get tossed into suitcases for the trip home. (Uh, that doesn't mean you shouldn't give me a T-shirt if you see me at a festival; I always keep the cool ones.)

Following is a list of ideas that should get your creative juices flowing so you can come up with your own ideas. The ideas below are really clever and I think they're great — but they've been done, so use them to inspire your own wacky concepts.

"Out of the Box" Quick Marketing Ideas

Get your film known with these simple and cheap ideas.

- Create a flyer for your film and make it look like a parking ticket. Put it on all the cars at the festival and in the festival parking lots.
- Make a flyer that looks like a $20 bill. On the other side is info about your screening. Spread them all over town. NOTE: The Feds don't like this one, so be careful. Counterfeiting is illegal — make sure to replace Abraham Lincoln's photo on the five-dollar bill with your own, or do something else to make it really obvious that the money is fake. Many copy stores will not make copies of money, as they already know these laws.
- T-shirts are easy, but depending on the local environment, you can come up with better items of clothing like ear muffs (cold weather), sweatshirts, ski caps, boxer shorts, or G-strings. (Hey, that'll get my attention!)
- A cereal box (the single-serving, tiny kind) with the poster of your film on the front and back. Screening info is printed on the sides where the ingredients should be.
- Give Viewmaster viewers to the press with still images of your film printed on the still frames in the viewer. The frames on a Viewmaster are made from 16mm film and custom Viewmaster sleeves could be made cheaply. This one would be really cool, but likely expensive.

There are plenty of ideas to come up with on your own; the point is to do something unique so people talk will about it and ultimately attend your screening.

Find a Champion for Your Film

The single most important thing a filmmaker can do to get attention for their film on the festival circuit is to find a champion. A champion can be a film critic or reviewer, a well-known filmmaker, or someone who speaks with some kind of credibility when it comes to the content of the film. A champion provides a quote or endorsement touting the virtues of the movie that can be used to ultimately help secure a sale. For indie films with no stars, finding the "right" champion just may be the difference between getting a distribution deal or ending up as one of the thousands of cine-orphans.

One young Michigan filmmaker brought his low budget horror film to the Cannes Film Market in the early 1980s. After failing to attract attention for his gruesome movie, he happened to run into horror novelist Stephen King. The wide-eyed young filmmaker begged King to attend a screening of his little independent movie. King agreed and liked it so much that he provided a quote, which was used on the poster. The quote read:

> "*The most ferociously original horror movie of the year.*"
> – Stephen King, author of *Carrie* and *The Shining*

That famous quote was used on all the marketing and posters at the time. Just those few words from King put this little indie movie on the map. Michigan filmmaker Sam Raimi credits the quote King provided for *Evil Dead* for helping to launch his career.

The secret is to really come up with a champion who breaks convention and will get audiences (or distributors) interested in seeing the film. Securing a "thumbs up" from Roger Ebert or a positive review from Kenneth Turan of the *Los Angeles Times*, is, let's be honest, a long shot at best. Being creative about exactly who to approach is critical.

The Last Game is a new documentary about the story of a high school football coach who participates in the game of his career pitting himself in a regional playoff game with his own son. Producer's rep Jeff Dowd felt that a quote from a prominent director of sports movies would give the movie a leg up. Here's the result:

> "*I remember when I directed* Hoosiers, *the* Los Angeles Times *said, 'You don't have to be a man or a basketball fan to love this movie.' You don't have to be a man or football fan to enjoy* The Last Game. *It has a wonderful and inspirational true story with great characters and exciting real life drama that the best Hollywood screenwriters could*

only dream of inventing. And if you are a football player, coach, ath-
lete, or fan, it's a must see!"

– David Anspaugh, Director (*Hoosiers, Rudy*)

This David Anspaugh quote has been used in all the marketing for the film, including the DVD release. The film racked up positive reviews from critics and gained the attention of audiences.

My own company, Film Threat, was in need of a champion for our first DVD release. The feature-length documentary *Starwoids*, about a bunch of *Star Wars* fans waiting in line for the *Episode I* premiere, already had a great sales angle — *Star Wars*. More than a few people have heard of that film. But asking DVD consumers to watch an enter- taining documentary can be like asking a kid to eat vegetables. We had to get cre- ative. We knew we needed someone to endorse the film and give it even more credibility. Someone who could elevate an already great doc and make it a must see.

John Landis promotes his latest Slasher *at SXSW.*

We settled on independent director Kevin Smith. He perfectly represents the *Star Wars* generation to fans. Smith liked the film enough to record some voice-over narration and even provided a 10-minute interview about *Star Wars'* influence on his own films, which became an extra on the DVD. With Kevin Smith's endorse- ment, selling *Starwoids* became a lot easier (and damn if I'm not grateful to him for it). His affiliation gave us the credibility to get the film into retail chains and filmmaker Dennis Przywara will actually make a healthy profit from his indie doc.

Now, most might think that a movie reviewer might make a good champion. And they often do. But sometimes an endorsement from an unlikely source will provide a much better way to get atten- tion. Just ask my pal Silent Bob.

A POWERFUL PRESS KiT

All effective marketing begins with a press kit. It contains all the information a media person will require to do a story about your film. A large festival will be attended by hundreds, sometimes thousands, of members of the media from newspapers, magazines, television, radio, the Internet, the wire services, all types of local media, and the international media — you name it, they're here. They're all going to need a press kit in some form, whether it is contained in a folder printed on paper, on a CD-Rom or DVD or whether it's in a special press area of your website on the Internet, *everyone* will need one. Many times the press kit will act as your only communication and sales tool to convince journalists to write a story about your movie. The writing should be smart and witty, as well as completely accurate. A little humor is okay, exaggeration is fine, but outright lying will end up in the loss of all your credibility — it's always best to stick to the facts. I often find that the stories behind many indie movies are better than the movies themselves. Tell me that story and get me excited by it. An interesting story about how your film got made can prove just as helpful toward getting press as the movie itself.

> **QUICK TIP**
> If you get some really nice stickers printed, they can also be placed on anything, turning that item instantly into an inexpensive promotional piece of merchandise. A baseball bat, a candy bar, a pen, a lunchbox, a backpack, a shoe horn, a bag of microwave popcorn, a jar of olives, a lampshade — *anything* can be instantly transformed into a cool promo give-away simply by slapping on an "official" sticker.

Most festivals require that you provide them with a certain number of kits to give out to the media. Be prepared with a master press kit and enough extra materials that you can turn around several hundred kits on a moment's notice. Get your film's logo professionally printed on some slick stickers. (You can also print really nice stickers using your home computer and laser printer; it depends on how high you want the quality to be.) The stickers can be placed on the front of a folder that will hold all your materials.

The Seven Items That Must Be in Every Press Kit

1. **Cover Sheet.** The cover sheet to your press kit should include the logo for the film, the contact info for your publicist, and your own contact info. Be sure to include a local contact number for the particular festival — perhaps on business cards with your name, contact number, and description of the basic plot of your film. Having a cell phone number printed on this page is essential because you need to be available at every moment.

2. **Synopsis.** You need to have three versions of your synopsis:
   - **The One-Liner.** A sentence, but not a run-on sentence. This one-liner version is much like the logline that you use to describe the story of your film to others. Basically this sentence is how others will talk about your movie, so take the time to craft it and try it out on people. It will be used to sell your film as much as it will be to describe it. Think about this one carefully — it must be a grabber.
   - **The Short Synopsis.** About 100-250 words, this should share a page with the one-liner. This gives an overall description of the movie in a longer form and might give away some details from the first and second act of your film while offering just a hint of what might happen in the climax. If well-written, it will only encourage readers to dig into other parts of your kit.
   - **The Long Synopsis.** From 500-1000 words. This one describes the entire film and teases at what happens at the end, but it should not give away the ending. This detailed synopsis is for really lazy journalists who either skip your screening and pretend they saw your film, or who fell asleep at your screening.

   These three synopses work to the benefit of one another, offering deeper levels of information about your film depending on how far the reader wishes to delve. Most will only read the one-liner and the short synopsis, but having all three is helpful.

3. **About the production.** A behind-the-scenes story detailing the making of the film that includes brief interviews with the cast, anecdotes about the shoot, and the true tale of what inspired the filmmakers to make *this particular* movie. The best way to go about writing this is to interview the cast and crew during production and include their quotes. Journalists like numbers, so include details like how long it took to shoot, how many years you worked on the script, and so on. This document can be 500-1,000 words or more.

4. **Bios.** Include the bios of the key players in the production — the director, writer, producer, and actors — along with other key crew members, like the cinematographer. Bios can run anywhere from 100-500 words generally speaking, but there is no

rule here. If any of the crew or actors have their own bios, start there. The best way to write a bio is to tape record interviews and just say, "Tell me about yourself; how did you get into film? What is your background and experience?" Include details about schooling and other films they may have worked on. Highlight experiences with name actors or name filmmakers who journalists might recognize. If the director started as a production assistant working with someone like Quentin Tarantino, that *must* be mentioned and will be a great starting point for any journalist to ask questions. Personal details are always important. If the film is about working at a restaurant and the writer worked at one for five years, include that. As they relate to the film, personal details make the bio that much more interesting to read.

5. **Credits.** Include a list of *all* the credits that appear in your film. It's important that this is completely accurate, as anyone who writes about your film will use this document to find the correct spellings of names of the actors, characters, and anyone else associated with the picture. Also, there are reviewers who will skim those credits looking for some kind of personal connection to your film, so complete credits are always a plus.

6. **Other press clips.** Any positive press, no matter how small, should be included. If you have done your homework, you should at least have a mention of the movie in the local newspaper where shooting took place. Any mention may help. Online press counts, so include those printouts. Also, include other reviews *only* if they are positive and *especially* if they are written by name critics or for well-known outlets. You don't want someone to decide that they shouldn't write about your film because someone else has already reviewed it. Be careful about this, particularly before your debut. Critics like to think they "discovered" your movie and that by supporting it they are somehow sharing in the film's success since, hey, they saw it first. All I can say is, whatever gets them excited is fine and should be exploited. After your premiere, include as many positive reviews as will fit in the folder.

7. **Photos.** You should have at least one good photo that really represents the film. Be careful about this photo — it's likely to be the one used throughout your festival run, so choose the very

best you have. Include caption information identifying the actors, their characters, what is depicted in the photo and any other pertinent info. Captions might say something like: *Jack Jones as Dick Starkiller, a video store clerk in* Revenge of the Clerks, *an independent feature film written and directed by Keith Jones*. Don't forget to include a photo credit and copyright information. You should have three different formats for photos: black and white stills, color slides, and digital stills on a CD-ROM. Different outlets have different needs — generally newspapers want black and white stills, magazines want color (they'll also probably ask for some kind of exclusive picture, so be prepared for that), and websites will want their photos in a digital format (on a CD-ROM or DVD, or they may download them from your website — more on that later). If you're sending out press kits in advance, ask the contact what kind of photos they require rather than wasting pictures on an outlet that may not use them.

POSTER THE TOWN

Most film festival movie posters just plain suck. But don't worry, plenty of successful films have had bad posters as well. Weak tag lines are commonplace even in mainstream movies. Consider Orson Welles' *Citizen Kane,* whose "memorable" tag line was: "It's Terrific!" Wow. Or George Lucas' *Star Wars,* whose original tag line read: "It's about a boy, a girl, and a galaxy." Yikes. That sounds like *crap*!

Most posters seen at film festivals have an amateur look that, well, represents the film in a bad light. The festival is like a job interview and there you are in jeans and a grubby T-shirt. You need a poster that feels like a smooth Armani suit, not a stinky T-shirt.

The first piece of advice for any filmmaker wishing to create an eye-catching poster is to acknowledge that you are a filmmaker — not a poster designer. Filmmakers, especially on small productions, have a tendency to want to make the poster themselves. You made the film, so now back off and allow others to do their jobs. If you tell a designer exactly what you want them to do, they will do exactly as you tell them. If you allow your designer some creative freedom, you are more likely to get newer and cooler ideas. However, if your budget does not allow for a poster designer and you are forced to create your own poster, there are some basic things you should know.

Jon C. Allen designs movie posters for a living. Allen began collecting one-sheets when he was young and knew he wanted to create them for a living. He has a degree in Visual Design and has worked at various Hollywood advertising agencies. These days, Allen freelances and has designed movie posters for Sony, Castle Rock, Miramax, New Line, HBO, and many others. Allen's design credits include domestic and international posters for films like *15 Minutes, Spice World, Miss Congeniality, Gossip*, and countless home video and television projects including *American History X, The Sopranos*, and *Oz*. Now, don't blame him for some of these bad movies, the posters are all cool. However, a designer's job is also about pleasing the client and Allen is ultimately a gun for hire.

Allen suggests asking the right questions before embarking on a design. "Is the poster positioning this film in the best possible way? Can you tell what it is as you drive by it at forty miles an hour, looking at it in a bus shelter? Really, a designer has to be aware of the issues beyond the obvious aesthetics and layout. For me, a great poster is one that manages to straddle all of the fences just mentioned: sell the film, offer the slightest hint of something new, be well-balanced in layout and design — and look really cool."

This week it's marketing material, next week it's garbage.

In order for an indie to create a poster that stands out at a film festival, it's important to know your market. "There are a lot of factors — film markets, for example. Some foreign markets lean towards more action-oriented posters." says Allen. "As far as the US film market goes, I would take advantage of the fact that you aren't in the studio system and avoid some of the clichés that tend to creep into those type of projects. You don't have to do the over-used and -abused "Two-Big-Heads-Floating-in-the-Sky" look that so many studios rely on. The best piece of advice I can give you for your poster look is to *keep it simple*.

"Whenever we work on a smaller film, we always make it simple to make the movie feel *bigger*. Less really is more, in this case. So often smaller indie projects with low advertising budgets fall into the "kitchen sink design trap" — let's show everything this movie offers so they know how hard we worked on it. Granted, in some cases, a distributor wants you to show all kinds of action, explosions, sex, etc., in your poster. But sometimes, it might be better to show less. Especially if you have no stars, no photography — often in those cases, we go with a simple icon, or a concept idea that captures the viewer's attention."

Allen offers a few final thoughts: "People ask me, 'Why do the majority of movie posters suck?' Well, it's all subjective, but those same people should ask, 'Why do the majority of movies suck?' Film advertising mirrors many of the same traits, good and bad, as the rest of the film industry. Whenever you have to please a significant number of people, compromises will be made. Sometimes this will improve something, often it will not. 'Design by committee' — just like 'Filmmaking by committee' — doesn't always work. I encourage someone working on their own one-sheet to make the film poster their own vision. Please yourself first, everyone else second. Hopefully, those same rules applied when you made your movie."

Jon C. Allen can be reached via his website: www.onesheetdesign.com

~~10~~ 11 Elements of Great Movie Poster Design

Follow these simple rules and you are on your way to a memorable one-sheet.

1. **Invoke feelings.** Create some sort of emotion. This can be done through color, image, etc. A great poster sparks interest and makes people stop on the street or in a theater lobby. For example, a poster for a comedy should make you laugh, or at least smile.

2. **Well thought-out typography.** Type should compliment the image, yet not attract undue attention to itself, and it should work with the imagery as a unit.

3. **Second read.** In other words, something you don't notice the first time you look at it. For example, take a look at the FEDEX logo. Have you ever noticed the hidden arrow inside the type?

4. **Good photography.** Head strips of stars' heads on doubles' bodies sometimes work, but it's always nice to have an idea for a photo shoot, have that star shot the way you envisioned, and use the resulting photography to make your design work.

5. **Great copy.** Always important, especially for comedies. "Four Score and Seven Beers Ago..." made my *Senior Trip* poster work.

6. **Logo.** A logo that stands on its own. A great logo compliments the poster and works well in its own context, because it will often be used on its own in other mediums, such as trailers. The logo should actually compliment the poster, instead of "floating" out in front of the poster, and not acting as part of the artwork.

7. **Translatable.** Translates well to other formats. Some things may look great at 27" x 41" on a one-sheet, but how will it look on billboards, bus sides, websites, or in black and white in a newspaper?

8. **Relevant to the film's story/plot.** Sometimes a poster has nothing to do with anything that happens in a film — for example, an idea that services the marketing, but is completely removed from the film itself.

9. **Show something new.** This is always a tricky issue. Movie posters mirror the movies themselves — it's rare that something new is tried as opposed to giving them what they've seen before.

10. **Hit the target.** It should please the intended audience. Know your demographic and be sure the poster appeals to this group. Studios not only hold focus groups for movies, but for the poster ideas themselves. It's *commercial* art...it's about marketing, not just what looks good.

11. **Bad finishing skills.** Sure, you have a brilliant idea that will make you the next Saul Bass, but if it looks like crap because you aren't comfortable in Adobe PhotoShop, you're not doing yourself (or your movie) any favors.

MAKE AN IMPRESSION – PRODUCE A POSTCARD

Once you have an effective poster design, that design will translate to your actual poster (of course), your website, and eventually to a postcard, which you'll be handing out at festivals throughout your tour to advertise your screening. There are great deals on the Internet for companies that print up postcards and posters along with all the items necessary to promote your film. Be sure to leave some dead space or room on the poster to include a sticker with screening information for each particular festival. You might bring only a limited number of posters, maybe fewer than fifty, and those will have to be hung at key locations, but they're no good without the basic screening info. Same goes for the postcard. When you get them printed, leave the black and white side blank (except for maybe your website and contact info), then get some cheap stickers printed up that include basic information about your screening — like this:

"My Big Fat Independent Movie"
SXSW Film Festival 2004
Work-in-Progress Screening
TUESDAY, MARCH 16th at 2 PM
Screens once only at the
Alamo Drafthouse, 409 Colorado St

You'll be using the same postcard at every festival, so sticker a few hundred and bring them along to give away to leave on tables where they can be picked up by interested parties. Also, make a handy card holder by turning one postcard on its side and stapling it. These get attention since people can grab one and get more info. Also, if you get into town early, talk to local businesses frequented by festivalgoers and ask them if you can hang your poster in their window or leave a few postcards around. *Always ask* and ask in the nicest way possible. If you don't ask, you might as well be throwing your materials away. By getting permission (and hopefully being the first to do so), you'll make an impression with those who visit the coffee shop with your poster hanging proudly in the window. If you really target the key locations in a city, you can almost take over a festival with just a limited number of posters and a few hundred postcards.

TEASE YOUR AUDIENCE

Posters are fine; good buzz and press always help, but nothing gets an audience more hyped to see a film than a great trailer. I love movie trailers — they're just plain cool. They're my favorite part of going to the theater and I never miss them. The truth of the matter is that you really don't need a trailer to take a film to a festival. Creating a trailer can be a costly distraction when the real order of business should be to make the best film possible. Consider very seriously how setting time aside to make a trailer may impact on everything else you have to do to prepare for your festival debut. My advice is to put making a trailer at the very bottom of your "to-do" list.

However, if you have the luxury of time and some extra money to invest in a trailer, it becomes yet another helpful tool to aid in selling your movie. Trailers posted on the web get a lot of attention these days. In fact, many festival websites (like SXSW and the Los Angeles Festival) stream trailers from their programs onto their websites. This exposes a bit of your film to tens of thousands of people, whetting their appetite before your festival premiere. In addition, the trailer can be used to get distributors in seats. While I recommend that you *never* send your film on video to a distributor, an effective trailer on tape is yet another way to get a distributor or a producer's rep interested in attending a screening. It's hard to get them to sit still for ninety minutes, but two minutes of their time is not a lot to ask. In addition, a powerful teaser assists in spelling out your movie's selling points and explaining how exactly a distributor may market the film to a wider audience.

To learn about trailers, I spoke with one of the best in the business. Dave Parker is an award-winning trailer editor and has been toiling in the industry for the last fifteen years. Currently employed at Seismic Productions, he has worked on countless campaigns for everything from big Hollywood movies to independent film projects including *Saving Grace, Casino, The Mask, Philadelphia, Mortal Kombat, Tomorrow Never Dies; Me, Myself and Irene; Dungeons and Dragons,* and *The Lord of the Rings* trilogy. I met with Dave, who broke down for me exactly what makes an effective movie trailer.

10 Elements of an Explosively Effective Trailer

1. **Quick cuts.** If you've got some cool shots and a really simple-minded story, cut each shot down to about a 1/3 of a second and slap on some pumping driving music. The unfortunate reality is that often style wins over substance.

2. **Use graphics that grab you.** Decent graphics are a plus. Be creative and make an impressive title treatment that is different from your main title.

3. **Original music is important.** Be careful with the music you use. There are plenty of affordable tracks from companies that supply music specifically for trailers. Be sure to use music that is legally cleared. Of course, there *is* another way. For the purposes of the *trailer only*, if you want music that *sounds* similar to a certain movie soundtrack to capture a particular mood, have an original song or piece of music composed. The secret is this: If you want to blatantly rip off a tune, remember to *change every seventh note*. By changing the tune slightly, you can avoid being sued.

4. **Tell the story (but don't ruin it).** If you've got a great story, don't be afraid to spell it out. It doesn't hurt to do a little hand-holding. A narrator can go a long way toward dramatizing the story in broad strokes. Also, don't tell the *whole* story. Leave them wanting more.

5. **Use positive reviews.** If the film has gotten early positive reviews from notable critics or credible press outlets, use them. Big, bold quotes in a white typeface against a black background look impressive when cut quickly into the trailer. Generally, these are most effectively used near the end just before the title screen. Be sure to clear the use of these quotes from the outlets that provided them.

> **CREATE YOUR OWN MARKETING MATERIALS**
> Demonstrate to others how your film might best be sold to a paying audience in theaters. Your own early marketing materials (poster, trailer, website), along with the hype those generate in the form of publicity (articles in magazines and newspapers, on television, and the web) will show a distributor that there is a market for your movie.

6. **Great sound is critical.** Spend time on the sound mix. If you have the slightest problem understanding what your actor said, then you can bet your ass that the guy looking at your trailer doesn't have a clue. Also, don't be afraid to record dialogue for the trailer to clarify the story. In *The Negotiator* trailer, Kevin Spacey says, "They're gonna have to deal with both of us!" Spacey looped that line for the trailer only and never said anything like that in the finished feature. (Imagine that! Lying in advertising! Hard to believe, huh?)

7. **Star power.** If your film has a recognizable star, make sure to feature your star very prominently. Even if you've got only one celebrity in a brief cameo, make sure those shots are used extensively in the trailer.

8. **Keep it short.** The shorter the better, about a minute or two, but absolutely make sure it is under two and a half minutes. Why? Because that is the time limit imposed by the MPAA for all theatrical trailers. The audience watching your little masterpiece has been trained like a pack of Pavlov's dogs. Anything over two and a half minutes and they're looking at their watches.

9. **Start with a bang!** Open with an attention grabber. The opening of the trailer for David Lynch's *Lost Highway* features Robert Blake and Bill Pullman engaged in a creepy conversation. Man, that was cool. Opening with an explosive image or a memorable line of dialogue will keep them watching.

10. **End with a(nother) Bang!** Close with the best shot and/or best line. What sold *The Perfect Storm*? Was it the brooding presence of surly George Clooney? How about the clichéd dialogue mouthed by Marky Mark? C'mon — we all know it was that awesome wave!

10 Mistakes to Avoid in Making a Trailer

1. **Do *not* use a feature editor.** Don't even consider hiring your feature editor to cut the trailer. A feature editor is used to letting things play out and is not going to be as good at the short sell. A trailer is an advertisement, plain and simple. It's essentially a commercial or a music video, and is a *completely* different animal than a feature, so get a good editor with experience cutting trailers.

2. **Don't fear outtakes.** Don't be afraid to use some original scenes or outtakes that didn't make the final cut. For *My Big Fat Independent Movie*, a few key shots were done just for the trailer. These shots do not appear in the movie, but set the pefect mood for the trailer.

3. **No nudity.** Keep the trailer PG-13 or lower. Even if your film has a lot of sex, there's no reason to flaunt it. Violence, of course, is never frowned upon (thanks, MPAA!). But you never know who may see it or download it. Make sure the trailer is acceptable to air on network television.

4. **No expanded scenes.** Use sound bites only. Don't use really long expository dialogue. Make every shot concise.
5. **Boring is bad.** Get to the point. What is your movie about? Define it in the first ten seconds.
6. **Don't use uncleared music.** A distributor may assume you have the rights and you'll be shooting yourself in the foot if you use music for which you don't have the rights.
7. **Bad transfer.** Make sure not to skimp on the transfer. The picture should look as good — or better — than your feature. Footage from your dailies or rough cut is not suitable for use. Transfer clean for the trailer.
8. **Never use stolen shots.** Eventually, they'll see the finished film, so don't try to cut in expensive shots that are gratuitously lifted from another movie — like, say, a giant explosion or a train wreck.
9. **Don't give away the ending.** Never *ever* give away the ending. Yeah, I know that trailers for big studio movies do it all the time. The trailer for *Cast Away* with Tom Hanks gives away that he actually gets off the island, thus ruining a key story point at the end of the film. Look at the acquisitions people as the big fish and your trailer as the little, convulsing worm. You want them to bite, but not feel full.
10. **Too long.** The most common crime committed by an amateur trailer editor is cutting one that is too long. Shorter is better. It's better to have a 30 second trailer that leaves one wanting more than a one minute trailer that drags.

WHY AN EPK iS ESSENTiAL

An EPK or "electronic press kit" is an invaluable tool when it comes to getting press on television. While creating an EPK sounds like yet another costly distraction with all the work you already have to do to make the film, it is worth doing for several reasons.
- An EPK is incredibly helpful for television producers and makes getting press on TV much easier.
- Content from the EPK (trailer, behind-the-scenes footage, interviews) can also be used for promotion on the web and later on as extras for the DVD release.
- The material on the EPK is an asset that will have value when it comes to negotiating a distribution deal.

Television journalists are perhaps the laziest members of the media, trust me. They often need stories to be spoon-fed to them. Why not make their jobs a snap by suggesting they do a little story on your movie? In addition to your printed press kit, it's to your advantage to produce an electronic press kit that will, in a way, do a little handholding to help deadline-crazed television producers fill some airtime. The more material you provide, the chances increase that your story will go from a five second mention in a festival round-up on local television to a full blown review taking up a minute or more of time on the air. In addition, television producers will archive your EPK for use later in case the need for a follow-up story presents itself. Either they'll archive it or throw it in a pile to be turned into a blank tape, you can never tell. With this in mind, it is helpful to label the tape: *Please Return After Use.* But tapes like this are rarely returned, so you shouldn't expect it. Just be grateful to get any television press at all.

Producing the EPK Begins With the Movie

Work on the EPK should begin along with start of production. When you're shooting, you know that you should have a photographer shooting stills of key scenes such as the production at work and slick pictures of your cast. It doesn't hurt to shoot some Hi-8 or digital video footage of behind-the-scenes for use on the EPK. Members of the cast are often waiting around for the next set up. Don't waste this downtime, get those actors to sit in front of the camera for twenty minutes for an interview. Be sure that the actors are coached to speak in soundbites — no more than thirty seconds on any one question and preferably much shorter, like ten or fifteen seconds. The person off-camera will not be heard asking the question, so make sure the actor repeats the basic question within their answer so their comments are put into context. Ask the actor about their character in the film, and the actor should respond, "Well, my character, Max Power, is a blah, blah, blah." (Except, you know, make sure they say something more clever than the, "blah, blah, blah.") Prepare ten to fifteen questions, and give the actors time to formulate some clever responses. Trust me, your actors will leap at the chance to offer their own witty comments.

Here are some sample questions to ask for your EPK:
- How did you get your start in film?
- What are the differences between appearing in a big budget Hollywood film and acting in an independent film?
- How did you get involved in this project?
- What did you think when you read the script?
- What attracted you to working on this film?
- Tell me the story.
- Tell us about your character.
- Who is your favorite character, other than your own?
- Tell us about working on the film.
- What was the most challenging scene?
- What's it like to work with...?

What's on the EPK?

The EPK must include a legal disclaimer at the beginning of the tape itself. Issues such as a specific time frame that the outlet may use the material can vary, so consult your lawyer. The legal disclaimer should include the following language:

> *This film/video/digital footage is for publicity and promotional use only. Any use, re-use, or unauthorized assemblage of this film/video/digital footage is strictly prohibited without the prior written consent of [PRODUCTION COMPANY NAME]. All rights reserved. Property of [PRODUCTION COMPANY NAME], promotional use only. Sale, duplication, or transfer of this material is strictly prohibited. Use of material is granted for a six month [TIME PERIOD MAY VARY] window.*

The legal disclaimer is followed by the title card or logo. Then, a menu screen in which text scrolls that outlines the content contained on the tape. Indicate how long the tape is within the text with a TRT (total running time) in parenthesis [e.g. (31:30)] and then scroll the menu and indicate the TRT for each individual section. The sections include the following elements and should appear in the order outlined below:

1. **Two trailers.** There should be two versions of the trailer, one that includes the complete trailer and a second version of the same trailer with the sound split into two tracks — one for dialogue and effects and another track for music. In addition, if your trailer has a narrator, the second version of the trailer should either delete or isolate the narrator onto the second track. This is so television commentators can add their own commentary over clips from the film. This second version is very important. Be sure to indicate the second version has NO NARRATION and has dialogue and effects on one track and music on a separate track. Many television producers are wary of airing anything they even suspect might be uncleared music, so even if you have done your homework and cleared your music, be sure to leave them the option of omitting the music entirely when running clips.

2. **Selected scenes.** This is your opportunity to highlight the best scenes from your film. You may choose just a few or as many as ten scenes, there is no rule, but offer a variety of scenes that accentuate your film's greatest strengths. Every scene should be under a minute, in fact, the shorter the better. Spend some serious time thinking about what clips represent the best of your movie. TV time is precious and a gripping fifteen-second scene is going to deliver more of an impression than a drawn-out one-minute scene that will be cut to fit the TV show's schedule anyway. A shorter scene is more likely to be used in its entirety on television. (Especially in our soundbite driven, fast-paced modern media culture.) Be sure to introduce each clip with the title of the movie and a title, in quotes, for the scene along with a TRT for the clip. Example: *JOE INVADES PARK CITY "Joe and Bob Lose Their Car Keys" (TRT :20 sec.).*

3. **A "making of" featurette (optional).** This is totally optional and it's not likely to be used on television, but it will come in handy when talking to a distributor who will use it for promotion and for use later as an extra on the DVD. Featurettes can run anywhere from just a few minutes to up to thirty minutes. This behind-the-scenes look at your film offers another opportunity for coverage of your movie if it has already been covered in another way. It's not necessary to have behind-the-scenes footage on the EPK, but it doesn't hurt. If your featurette has a

narrator, it's also wise to put two versions on the tape with the soundtracks split so that a TV commentator can add their own spin to the footage.

4. **B-roll footage with key scenes (optional).** This is yet another optional element and often just contains raw footage of the production of certain scenes.

5. **Interviews with the cast, director, writer, producer, etc. (optional).** This should be presented in the same way that scenes are shown — with a title for the clip keeping the comments from the cast in clever soundbites under thirty seconds or less. A few comments from each crucial cast and production member are acceptable. Be sure to title each clip, for example: *JOE INVADES PARK CITY, Director Joe Jones "Joe on making a movie on a lunch-size budget." (TRT :15 sec.).*

6. **Still frame of the title.** A still frame of the title logo is crucial because this can be used as a computer graphic and appear in the background when the TV commentator mentions your film. Don't forget to include the logo or the poster, or both separately, as a still running for thirty seconds or so on the tape, so either can be turned into a graphic.

Actor Matthew Lillard and screenwriter pal James Gunn at the Sonoma Valley Film Festival.

It's not important that your EPK contain every one of the above-mentioned elements, however the two things you must have are the *trailer* and some *selected scenes*. The EPK can become a huge distraction, an animal as large to deal with as the movie itself. Do not go about producing an EPK if it will take time that is better spent on the film. Have an EPK with a trailer and scenes; that's really all you'll need.

Get Press Online with a Digital Press Kit

When most people refer to an EPK, they only think in terms of television press, but this amazing PR tool can also help toward getting press on the Internet as well. When it comes to online press, your EPK material can be digitized and used on your film's official website. In addition, you can also take the digitized content and burn it on a CD-ROM or DVD to give to major online press outlets as the digital version of your press kit. The DVD or CD-ROM version of your EPK should be readable by both Mac and PC, or any DVD player, and it must also include a decent selection of digital stills in the form of JPEGs. Stills are the most important addition to the digital press kit. It also is wise to include text from the press notes — like cast and crew bios, the synopsis, and production notes.

HYPE iT ON THE WEB

The Internet is the most important promotional tool for the independent filmmaker. The website you create for your movie has the potential to reach more people than any other mass medium — more than radio, magazines, or television. And the best part about it: You have total control over the content. In other sections I've discussed how to make various promotional materials like a press kit, a poster, a trailer, and an EPK. They are all valuable, but if you can choose only one of these marketing tools to put your time, money and energy into, I would tell you to build a website. You absolutely *must* have one. When you consider the impact that *The Blair Witch Project* website had on the success of that movie, you cannot ignore the importance of the Internet for building awareness of your own project. A website is a vital tool to build buzz in advance of your festival debut and is necessary to communicate with your greatest supporters — the moviegoing audience. In fact, promoting a movie today without a website is wasting a fantastic opportunity to increase the value of your film. Consider it this way: An effective website can help double the value of your movie. You must have a site.

> **QUICK TIP**
> Be sure that you use your "dot-com" name, your *www.thenameofyourfilm.com* on *everything*. No kidding, everything. Your website URL should be on your poster, stickers, press kit, business cards, clothes, shoes, luggage, and girlfriend. Especially your girlfriend.

Create a Supreme Website

The basic steps for creating a site don't necessarily need to be done in the order listed below; in fact, it makes sense to work on many parts simultaneously. I don't have the space for all the technical details and there are whole books on how to build a decent site, so I'm just going to give you the fundamentals here. Here's how to do it:

1. **Register the name.** It costs about $70 bucks or so to reserve a URL name for two years and takes about ten minutes — if you type *really* slowly. There are many places to register a name on the web and they even offer other services like site hosting, e-mail, etc. Start by checking out sites like www.register.com or www.dotster.com and take the time to research other places to register your name. When you have settled on a name for your film, do it as soon as possible, even if you don't plan to launch the site until much later. If the name of your film is taken, you can always do what Hollywood does and add the word "movie" to the end. I suggest registering the name of your production company as well and letting this be the home for all of your films.

2. **Create content.** Here is where the word "re-purpose" comes into play. By creating the materials for the press kit, you have already done the hard work of putting together a synopsis, bios, credits, production details, trailer, photos, and a logo for your movie. These will be elements used to launch your site. You may want to write other material exclusive to the site by keeping a production diary, but the basics from a press kit will be the early building blocks to release the initial version of the site. More elements will be added later, but starting with these key elements is essential. Don't forget the most important component — your contact info. Have this visible at the bottom of every page of the site.

3. **Flow Chart.** Here is where the site really begins to take shape. The site itself is like a collection of pages from a magazine or a book, the difference is that instead of either of those, a web surfer can bounce from page to page. The flow chart identifies all the pages of your site and shows how they connect. On paper or on a computer, build a flow chart that demonstrates how a reader will use the site and how every single page is linked. The easiest way to begin is to start with the home page and then spell out the most important aspect of the site, which is the menu bar. Make it simple, logical, and easy to navigate. The key word to keep in mind is "intuitive." Ask yourself — does it make sense that this page connects to that page? Can the reader get back to the home page or any other page on the site efficiently? The easiest way to go about this is to design a menu bar that

contains all the sections for your site. Name those sections Home, Movie Synopsis, Bios, News, About the Production, Trailer, Photos, etc. Spend considerable time poking around other sites to see what works and what doesn't. Ultimately, an intuitive site will have your readers focusing on the content instead of the flow (or the lack thereof). Visit as many other sites as you can to get a feel for what works best for you.

4. **Design the site.** When I say design, I'm talking about the way it looks. This is where you can get creative and have a blast. In a way, it's like decorating your room or apartment. Your site should, in some way, reflect the theme or mood of your film. Choose graphic elements that say something about the movie. It's like painting the outside of the house and deciding exactly how you want it to look. Almost all of the filmmakers interviewed in these pages have their own sites. Check them out and see what they've done to create a mood. The subject matter of your movie will dictate much of the design. When designing a look for the site it makes a difference to make it fun, to have it express other levels of your movie, and — for some this may be the hard part — for it to be original. Make sure it doesn't look just like every other movie site out there.

5. **Build it.** There are so many ways to build a site, it would be like me telling you exactly what kind of film you should make. Here are just some of the options you may want to consider

- **Off the shelf software.** There are plenty of programs made for building sites. They vary in levels of complexity, but for under $100 bucks, you can find numerous programs made to build a site from scratch.

- **Build it on the web.** Some websites offer space on their sites to build your own. There are thousands, like Yahoo and Homestead.com; these sites have software built into the browser that can walk you through building your own simple site, but research them all carefully before you start. The advantage here is that you won't be paying for space. The disadvantage is that you may outgrow it quickly. Be sure you have the option to move the site to another server, should that happen. All of these sites require that you click on "Terms" or "Agreement" when using their sites. Check any restrictions that apply before you put in the energy.

Explore all of these options fully and choose the best path for you.

- **Hire a web design company.** This is a smart choice *if* you have the money to do it. You'll provide them with the content, and design and they build it. Most charge upwards of $100 or more per page of the site, so if you plan on a large site that you'll want to grow, this may not be the most cost-effective option.

- **Get a friend.** Most students in high school now know HTML and web design better than they know how to spell. Get a student or a friend to do it. If you are technically inclined, you may just want to do it yourself. If not, or if you are busy making the movie, delegating this responsibility is a wise choice. The only option you don't want to exercise is putting it off. It's helpful for the site to go live during pre-production. Even if it is not perfect, you can always alter it or add to it later. And don't forget to test the site for bugs. This involves looking at every page of the site using different computers and different browsers with different types of Internet access (T1, DSL, or modems). Ask friends to look at it for you and report any problems so they can be fixed.

Ingredients for an Awesome Movie Website

Here are the do's and don'ts you must know to make a movie website that readers will not only revisit, but also tell their friends about.

1. **Don't get too flashy.** Bells and whistles like Flash animation look really cool. That intro movie to your site is great to watch — but it only works once. Web design sometimes gets too caught up in trends. (Do you remember "frames"? Does anyone use frames for their site anymore?) There is one mistake that novice web designers make time and again and that is *over*-designing a site. Just because you *can* add some cool new effect, doesn't always mean you *should*. To reach the maximum number of people with your site, avoid adding flashy extras. The design does not have to be compromised, but avoid jumping headlong into new technologies without weighing how that might limit the potential audience for your site.

2. **Interact with your audience.** Posting production diaries, interviews, exclusive video footage, and such, adds a personal touch to the site. Speak directly to your audience and have a message board so readers can offer feedback. Make it a priority to answer that feedback and keep yourself accessible.

3. **Keep it simple.** This one should be self-explanatory. An overly complex site will only turn off readers — and they'll surf elsewhere.

4. **Update the site yourself (or at least be able to).** If you design the site yourself, this should not be a problem. Make sure that you are trained to add simple updates to the site as often as you need. Don't be a slave to some web design firm that must be paid each time you add a minor update or news story. Don't be slave to the friend or student who built your site. Learn how to update the site yourself. Then, be sure to follow my next suggestion...

5. **Update often.** I can't stress this one enough. Weekly updates are preferred and even more often if that is at all possible. The latest news about your film should be right on the front page. Attach a date to each new news item so readers know when the site was last updated. If new features are added, be sure to let others know about it as well. You are taking the readers on your journey. Tell them about all the ups and downs — sometimes the personal and real-life drama you encounter making the film can make the best stories. It will also endear the audience to your cause, which is making your movie. And when you experience triumphs, like your debut festival screening, they will share in those successes.

Do-it-Yourself Internet Publicity

Now that you've spent all this time building the coolest movie site on the web — I'm sorry to have to break this to you, but I've been completely honest up to now so I have no problem telling you this — your website is worthless. Like farting in a car with the window rolled down, no one is going to notice it *unless* you promote the site. The best way to do that is to start by sending out e-mail and promoting it virally. I don't mean literally sending out a virus to all your friends; I mean a piece of e-mail that spreads virally on the 'net to everywhere it needs to go. Start with an announcement that the site is live and contains information about your movie. Send the e-mail announcement to your address book of friends and family and encourage them to tell others. Be sure to have an area on your site where readers can sign up for an e-mail newsletter about your film.

Send out updates when new things are added to the site, but not too often. There's enough junk e-mail on the 'net already, so when you send out news about your site or film be sure you really have something to say. There are no rules, but sending out an e-mail once a month or so is usually considered plenty.

One of the best places to advertise your film and website is at FilmThreat.com, which is my website. On the site, we run banner ads and classified ads in our email newsletter from new indie filmmakers who tell us they get a tremendous number of hits. (One filmmaker complained that he got 500,000 hits within two weeks and his site was nearly shut down!) Drop me an e-mail and send it to input@filmthreat.com and I'll send you information about how we can help promote your site. You'll also want to send a more formal announcement to members of the online media. Cruise those sites and build a list of general e-mail addresses to send out a mass e-mail. All entertainment and movie sites on the web have a general e-mail address for news, so gather those addresses and send out your announcement. Build your list starting from production and add everyone you meet to the list.

Kyra Sedgewick and Parker Posey enjoy the festivities at the IFC party at Cisero's.

A quick note about communicating via e-mail: Be understanding when it comes to dealing with members of the media online. I get hundreds of e-mails daily and I do my best to answer all of them. Make sure that all of your e-mail communications include the very basic details about your film so I have all the information I need. Sites like FilmThreat.com are constantly bombarded, so don't assume that members of the media will remember all the details about your film off the bat. At the end of the day, I want to do all I can to support indie filmmakers, so help me to help you.

How to Get Your Website Listed in All the Search Engines — for FREE

This is the dirty secret of the Internet industry: You don't have to pay all that money to search engine submission services. Nope, in order to get yourself listed on all those fancy search engines, first, go to www.dmoz.org. This is the search engine where *all* the other search engines get their data and it's run by people — not computers, bots, or programs. Just find the appropriate place to enter your site on dmoz.org and you will "suddenly" show up on all the other search engines — Google, Yahoo, AOL Search, etc. Look yourself up on www.dmoz.org first to see where you may already be listed, also look up sites similar to yours to see what categories they're listed in and then put yourself in similar places. To add a listing, go to www.dmoz.org/add.html. Be patient, it takes about a month to see results since this is done by humans, but it works and it will save you money.

Also, you can enter other *parts* of your site. It has really increased traffic on FilmThreat.com since we've started entering all of our reviews and interviews as individual items — it has helped make us one of the top movie sites out there. Take the time to do this once, and you will see a dramatic increase in your traffic.

Another great tool is Alexa at www.alexa.com. This is like the Nielson Ratings of the Internet and a place to see how you rank against other similar sites. Get the Alexa toolbar and mark your favorite sites. Update your listing there as well and be sure to update the thumbnail photo of your site.

HiRiNG A PUBLiCiST: WHAT YOU NEED TO KNOW

Filmmakers entering the festival game for the first time quickly learn the value of good PR. Great public relations can take an average movie and increase its value by creating hype. An average film with heat behind it is much more likely to be sold to a distributor than a great film with no heat: This is an unfortunate reality at film festivals. Really good films can and do get lost in the shuffle. However, with a great press kit, an amazing website, some well-timed articles in the trades, a few positive reviews, and some friends in the media, you'll much better positioned to achieve a sale and begin your filmmaking career.

On the Publicity Trail with
PR Pro LiNDA BROWN-SALMONE

Linda Brown-Salmone began her career at PMK Public Relations where she worked for five years on publicity campaigns with actors such as Winona Ryder, Andie MacDowell, and Gregory Hines; films such as Luc Besson's *La Femme Nikita* and Jim Sheridan's *My Left Foot*, and television shows such as Fox's *The Simpsons*. After leaving PMK in search of some kind of life, she stopped briefly at Bragman Nyman Cafarelli, then went on as Director of Motion Pictures Los Angeles for Rogers & Cowan, where she headed up campaigns and promotions for a countless number of films including *The Mask* with Jim Carrey. Currently Brown heads one of the premiere public relations firms for independent filmmakers, the Los Angeles-based Indie PR. Getting press is not just a job for Brown; she passionately believes in her clients and their films. Indie PR has been in existence since 1996 and has been successful in providing promotion, marketing campaigns, parties, festival debuts, and more for indie filmmakers. Recent films include campaigns for *Bubba Ho-Tep*, *The Big Empty*, and *Lords of Dogtown* as well as Sundance films like *D.E.B.S.*, *Below The Belt*, *Tiptoes*, *Nobody's Perfect*, *Touch of Pink*, *Harry & Max*, *Northfork*, *The Mudge Boy*, and even Slamdance movies like *Memron*.

How can a publicist help a film?

A publicist does different things at different stages of a campaign for a film. For a festival, a publicist prepares the press to receive your film in the intellectual and emotional sense. Presentation means a lot; a publicist advises you on the look of your poster, chooses the stills you use in representing your film, your clips for electronic interviews, and prepares that all-important press kit — which serves as a bible to the press when they write about your film.

Equally important, a publicist comes up with a strategy for presenting your film to the public. A filmmaker's idea of how a film should be presented may be entirely different from what is going to sell. That doesn't mean the filmmaker is wrong, it just means that it's only one opinion and it sometimes helps to go at it from other angles as well.

Why does a filmmaker need a publicist?

The smartest filmmaker takes on a publicist at the very onset of a project and keeps one throughout the entire process. That can get costly, but sometimes deals can be made.

There is so much for the press to cover during a festival, from reviewing films to covering parties to eavesdropping during breakfast for items. Unless you have someone out there vying for ink and creating a buzz about you or your movie, you run the risk of getting lost in the noise pollution. My campaigns start a month prior to the festival, which is when I start making calls to the magazines and columnists who can put a little "pre-festival buzz" on my movie. I get the press excited about your film by letting them in on it early and in a personal way. At this point, a lot of the members of the press are friends of mine, so it is very much like my calling a friend to let them in on something they just shouldn't miss.

What do filmmakers need to know when it comes to publicity?

Publicity is less effective when it is a one-shot deal. It is so much better to have continuity and a steady flow of information going out to the press throughout all of the stages of your film. That way, when it comes time to do the festival thing, it's a matter of instant recognition for both the press and distributors. It is also essential in getting all of the materials you will need to help sell the film — whether it be a press kit complete with clippings (to show a studio that your film can get press), or photos and an electronic press kit complete with interviews and behind-the-scenes footage.

What are the advantages and disadvantages of filmmakers going about their own publicity?

Filmmakers can do their own publicity as easily as publicists can make their own films...it just isn't smart. First of all, it takes up a lot of the filmmaker's time that should be spent other ways, but mostly because it's smarter to have those who do what they do best — actually *do* what they do best. The only advantage a filmmaker has in doing his/her own publicity is that it will save a few thousand dollars. That's it. Without the advice and careful planning of someone who lives this kind of work, an uninformed filmmaker could miss an opportunity to present his film with the perfect spin that

could catapult his campaign and film into the arms of a dream distributor. Think of the distributor as an audience member with a
checkbook. You still have to stand out and grab their attention.

What kind of advantages do filmmakers with publicists have?

For all of the reasons I mentioned before and because, ultimately,
the more people you have talking about your film at a festival, the
better your position. And who has bigger mouths and talks to more
press, distributors, and festival-goers than publicists? We're with the
press at breakfast, between screenings, *at* the screenings, in the bathroom, in their rooms...we never stop! We get 'em while they're
drunk and make them commit...we're relentless, and you need that
kind of energy on your side when your film is at a festival.

What sort of questions should a filmmaker ask when hiring a publicist?

When hiring a publicist, the most important question to ask is:
"How many other films are you working on at the festival?" I see it
all the time — bigger agencies pile on the clients, telling them that
they are at an advantage in being "in the company of" other big
films. This is simply not true unless you are working with a publicist who can't get Sheila Benson on the phone *without* a bunch of
big films.

There is no way you can effectively work with an exorbitant
number of films — *effectively* being the key word. I don't like to
work with more than four films per festival. Part of a campaign is
spending time with the filmmaker at the social function (it's where
most of the interviews are set up) and if you're chained to a desk in
a hotel room working on fifteen films, you just can't do that. Film
festival PR is not like publicity at time of release, where you *can*
chain yourself to a desk and pump out the calls. The press is out and
about...they're at the parties, they're at the panels. You've got to have
the freedom to pound the pavement and hunt them down.

What can a filmmaker expect to pay for a publicist?

Most agencies charge anywhere $5,000 or more for a film at a festi-
val. You should allow for expense monies as well, which should cost
you another couple of hundred depending upon the festival.

How important is it to get good online press these days?

Early on, it seemed that online activity was most effective with genre or cult films, but in the past few years, the Internet has taken over as a primary way to reach worldwide audiences with current information. The key word here being "current."

As publicists and promotions people, we used to rely on magazines or shows like *Entertainment Tonight* to get the word out. Most magazines require a three to four month leadtime, and entertainment shows give you three to four minute spots and that's that. With the Internet, it's happening right now. And the cyber-sky is the limit as to the amount of content you can have, so online press is becoming more important than any other form. The fact that studios now have entire departments of publicists and promoters who deal specifically with the online community is evidence to the fact.

How do you approach getting press on the web differently?

The web is a visual tool and its audience is more visual than, say, the *Los Angeles Times* reader, who is going to sit down and read a feature, then maybe glance at a photo. When we approach a web outlet, our job is to incorporate more interactive participation and make it more interesting for the site's audience. With print, it's a bit more cut and dry and somewhat more controlled.

Does a filmmaker need to hire a publicist to do online press?

I think that anyone can do online promotions themselves. But a publicist is able to come to the table with a more strategic campaign, which will compliment any promotions a filmmaker has already done online. Most filmmakers don't necessarily have the relationships with outlets like AOL and Yahoo, who would do the larger entertainment features on their films, and as with traditional publicity...you really need to have someone open the door for you.

What are the important things for a filmmaker to remember when working with a publicist?

A publicist is not a miracle worker. The ultimate sale of your film depends upon how good it is. But a publicist can be an essential part of your team in creating awareness and the infamous "buzz" that everyone listens for at a festival.

Know the Media Outlet You're Pitching

One should never blindly pitch a story to a media outlet. Understand the needs of that outlet before you pitch. Various media will have dramatically different areas of focus — the local newspaper will look for human interest, while a trade publication is looking for a business angle. Consider the spin you are looking for and consider the wants and needs of that outlet.

"When I worked for FilmThreat.com, I specifically looked for films that were in some way rebellious — either through the story, filmmaking style, or simply the maker's guts for doing what they did. For *American Cinematographer,* I looked for visual accomplishment, whether the picture was shot on Super 8, 16mm, 35mm, or video," says David E. Williams, currently of *CFQ* magazine.

It's important to research the outlet you're targeting *before* you make the call or send the email. Nothing will close a door faster than pitching an outlet you know nothing about and proceeding to stick your foot in your mouth. When you communicate with the outlet, be sure to compliment them, then pitch your piece to not only the publication, but a specific place. You might recommend that the story appear in their "What's Hot" or "Upcoming Movies"

> **MAKE FRIENDS WITH THE PRESS**
> Make friends with the press and, when that friendly critic bashes your movie, continue to smile and be friends. You never know when a press person will come in handy for you later.

section. Always be accommodating and accept rejection graciously, because at the end of the day your relationship with that media person or outlet is more important than whether they do that particular story. They'll remember that you were easy to deal with even in the face of rejection, and that can pay off in good press later.

Handling Q&As

After the screening of your film, you'll want to offer a few quick thank-yous, introduce members of your cast and crew in attendance, and are expected to answer some questions from the audience. It helps to be prepared. This is your opportunity to show some personality and potentially win some points. Believe it or not, it is beneficial to wear something outrageous — a bright orange jacket, a wild hat, or a loud shirt. You may even consider dying your hair a bright purple. Anything to make you stand out. When members of the audience run into you during the festival, your unique "look" will be remembered. Besides being an opportunity for a fashion statement, the Q&A is also, much like an important speech delivered by a politician, a way to win people over to your cause. The best advice is to be genuine, be honest, tell some funny stories and anecdotes, and keep your ego in check. Be gracious. Have a little humility. You may be the "filmmaker" up front doing the Q&A, but the reality is that there are at least a hundred or more people behind you that helped make the movie possible. Giving them some type of acknowledgment on stage goes a long way toward earning the respect of the audience.

As for any feelings about being nervous when speaking in front of a group, that old trick about picturing the audience naked really works, just don't let it distract you. There are some typical questions you can expect to hear at almost every Q&A, so be prepared to answer any of these:

- What was the budget?
- How long did it take to shoot?
- Is the film autobiographical?
- Where did you find that actor?
- How did you get the money?
- Where did you get the idea for your film?
- What does the title mean?
- What kind of film did you use?
- How did you shoot that one scene?
- Who are your influences?
- Where did you shoot your film?
- What's the film about?
- What's the film *really* about?
- Do you have another film in mind?

The answers to these questions should be easy; you have struggled to make your film and you know all of this. Keep the answers short, don't meander, and don't play politics — answer the question asked.

Don't fret about money questions, most audiences just don't know any better. The last thing you want to do is reveal the actual budget for your picture. Even if you do give a specific number, people will think you are either naïve or lying — so either way, they won't believe you. Just be vague and say, "Just below $10 million."

THE PARTiES

Get invited, Make an impression, Crash, Avoid Spilling Something

The single most important event at a festival other than your own screening is the party. You may be as talented as Steven Soderbergh when it comes to filmmaking, but your talent is going to be judged by how comfortable you are with idle cocktail chit-chat. Yes, yet another unfortunate entertainment industry reality.

At the parties you'll be schmoozing with agents, entertainment lawyers, acquisitions executives, distribu-tors, development executives, producers, actors, festival staff, the media, and other filmmakers — basically, the masses of the movie industry. It's important that you make a good impression.

So get social. Grab a drink, grab a table, grab some food, and scan the room. (Hey, you'll probably be too busy to grab dinner, so you'll save a little money on meals by eating party appetizers for days, keeping the cost of your trip very low.) Living on chicken fingers and wing dings for a week won't kill you. At least, not right away.)

Festival co-director Brenda Lhormer gets sandwiched by drag queens from the doc Queen of the Whole Wide World.

Now, you've got that person in your sights. The one you need to talk to. The actor for your next film. The agent you want to rep you. The festival director you want to have accept your film. The executive you want to pitch for your next film. The bartender you want to pour your next drink. (Okay, I'm getting carried away, but it can be *really* hard to get a bartender's attention some-times!) There are a few important things to remember at a party when you are there for business. Here is my version of the ever-popular list of "Do's and Don'ts."

The Party Do's

- *Do* introduce yourself to people. Most will have festival badges with their names and films and/or companies on them. At any given party you'll find at least a few people you should meet to further your personal agenda. As annoying as it sounds, remember that you are attending these parties to further your personal goals. If you think otherwise, you are only lying to yourself. Okay, *I'm* there to have fun, but everyone else has an agenda.

- *Do* try to find some common ground to begin a conversation. For example, films you each enjoy, a common city, a favorite drink, a popular actor, a sports team, a filmmaker — anything at all to establish the conversation on a positive note.

- *Do* make friends with other filmmakers and get invited to their screenings.

- *Do* tell inoffensive and clever jokes.

- *Do* talk passionately (yet unpretentiously) about your love of film and how your life was changed by the defining moment of one important film. People at film festivals get all mushy when this subject comes up.

- *Do* talk business — that's what these parties are really about anyway.

- *Do* be bold and walk up to Bob Berney of Newmarket Films and invite him to your screening.

- *Do* take every person you speak with seriously, even if they do not initially seem important to your immediate agenda. The assistant of today is the festival director, agent, or studio head of tomorrow. They'll remember that you showed them respect when no one else would. That's important.

- *Do* hand out business cards.

- *Do* make it a point to follow up and send letters to people you meet when appropriate. Again, you never know how those relationships will pay off.

The Party Don'ts

A party can be a great opportunity to make new friends, make an impression and, most importantly, to make deals. If some studio executive likes to hang out and party with you, certainly, he may also want to work with you. That's the secret of the business —

people hire other people they like. It's very simple. So keep some things in mind.

- *Do not*, as I have done, make inappropriate jokes in mixed company.
- *Do not*, as I have done, charge room service to your pals at 3 A.M.
- *Do not*, as I have done, put drinks on the tab of "the table in the corner."
- *Do not*, as I have done, drink way too much alcohol.
- *Do not*, as I have done, try to dance after drinking that alcohol.
- *Do not*, as I have done, schedule 5 A.M. wake up calls for your colleagues.
- *Do not*, as I have done, mercilessly criticize the award-winning festival film as a total piece of crap when the director is within earshot.
- *Do not*, as I have done, stand on a chair and thank everyone in the room for coming and for their support for your film, when you haven't made the film that the party is for.
- *Do not*, as I have done, avoid the festival party scene to see local bands, find the strip clubs, and visit the after-hours bars.
- *Do not*, as I have done, yell "Fire!" at a crowded party.

I really mean it. Don't do any of these things. I've made every possible mistake anyone could make at a party. Sometimes I just can't resist putting some pretentious moron in his place, or making a point through humor. Sure, I have a great time, but generally I'm attending a festival to have fun; I like to leave the business at the office. If your goal is to have fun, a few "don'ts" are fine. But more likely, you have a goal in mind — you're trying to sell a film or get another one made. Leave the hard partying for the final festival party.

Crashing Film Festival Parties

In order to get the opportunity to do some schmoozing, you have to *get into* the party. Do whatever it takes to get into the party legitimately first, but when all else fails, it's time to crash!

It's always best to get on the list before arriving at a party, but that's not always possible. Because if you're like me, you're probably not invited. But I've never let that little piece of reality stop me, and neither should you. I am the party crashing king and I'll crown you a prince or princess if you simply follow my lead.

The first piece of advice I can offer is to put on your poker face. Security is generally loose at film festival parties and it's up to you to take advantage of that. Remember: You were invited to this shindig and there must have been some mix-up. Make sure to deliver lines like an actor.

Also, never get upset. The publicists or people at the door are constantly bombarded with Hollywood egos, why add to their grief? Pretend to be understanding. Do something different — be nice. Be cool. Don't be a jackass. Knowingly shake your head as the jerk in front of you mouths off to the publicist. They'll appreciate it.

Scott Caan and Jeff Goldblum party at CineVegas.

They'll especially appreciate your patience as they frantically flip through the list, then just give up and wave you in.

You can always use someone else's business card. These days, some fancy computer work with a handy laser printer can now produce pretty convincing business cards with the click of the print button. In fact, I'm amazed how many times my own business card has been used as my golden ticket into a party.

One tried and true trick is to execute the bum's rush. Just walk in with a large group as if you know exactly what you are doing. If caught, just point way up into the crowd — too far to see — and declare, "I'm with them." Wave and act convincing. Never fails.

And heck, if all else *does* fail, there's always the back door. Yes, the back door — this is not a movie cliché, I have actually used it to gain entry. Sure, you'll be stumbling through the kitchen, but you're *in*, baby! Sometimes restrooms will have windows and those can be easily accessed from the outside. If you know of a great party that you must attend, it's best to do a little reconnaissance and check out the place first. Heck, you might even make a few new friends in the kitchen.

10 Surefire Lines to Use When Crashing a Party!

No invite? Not on the list? No problem! These lines, if delivered convincingly, will guarantee you entry into any party. However, it is getting even more difficult to crash parties now than it used to be just a few years ago. These days, the exclusive festival parties require a hard invite *and* a photo I.D. But that's never stopped me. It's not as easy to crash as it used to be, so you've got to be inventive. Try these sure-fire lines:

1. **"I RSVP'd, but I totally understand if I can't be let in. Can I just try to find my friend and tell him I'm heading back to the condo? He's in there? Somewhere?"**

2. **"Excuse me, coming through! Watch it!"** Carry a large box filled with something. Could be a case of beer, equipment, posters, flyers — the important thing is that it must be so large and heavy that people have to make way for you to get by or you may drop the damn thing and hurt yourself or somebody else. Be polite and walk right in like you know what you're doing. If stopped, say that you have to get these in there or you'll be in a heap of trouble. If you really want to go for realism, have a walkie-talkie on your belt, tons of laminated credentials around your neck, and carry a flashlight.

3. **"I think I'm going to be sick, can you tell me where the bathroom is?"** Women are much more convincing for this line. A man would never stand in the way of a sick woman. This works even better if you spit out a mouthful of corn chowder.

4. **"I'm here to drop off my roommate's keys."** Pretend to know one of the waiters, waitresses, or someone working the bar. Just in case, have an old set of keys you don't mind losing in case they decide to pass them along for you.

5. Weasel your way to the front of the line and walk in like you're supposed to be there. When stopped (and you will be), look shocked and say, **"Hey, I'm *in* the movie."** Enter party. A variation on this is to wear a baseball cap and say, **"Hey, I'm the director!"** Don't even bother to try "writer" since it won't work.

6. **"Is this the party for the *best* film at this festival?"** Now this is going to take a little pre-planning and might get you in trouble, but give it a shot. Business cards can easily be printed now from laser printers, and they look perfect. Make some phony cards from a really big press outlet. You can even go on the web and get a logo to make it ultra-realistic. When your name doesn't show up on the list, just be apologetic and pass along your card.

Once the impressive card hits the hands of the person holding the list, you'll be let in.

7. **"Hi, I was here earlier and I lost my wallet, do you have a lost and found?"** This one's called "Lost and Found." Now, here's the trick, you are *not* asking to get into the party like everyone else standing in line. No siree. Why? Because you were *already there*, why would you want to go into that awesome party? You're asking about the *lost and found*, so you have deflected the door person's attention from your true intentions. Act distraught. When your *"wallet"* (or purse, or keys, or jacket, or scarf, whatever) does not turn up in the lost and found box, ask very nicely, "May I go in and take a look around? Maybe I can find it myself." Be sure to nicely wave your wallet to the person on your way out. "Found it!" Everyone loves a happy ending, you found your missing item *and* you got in. Piece of cake.

8. **I call this one, "The Wave."** Wave like you're insane and say, *"Heeeeey!!!"* Alternatively, I call this one **"The Wave and Hug."** Wave hysterically to someone who is *way* beyond the eyesight of the people guarding the door. This could be someone you barely know — or no one at all — but wave and act like you're seeing an old friend you haven't seen in ten years. You're so caught up in seeing them after all this time that you merely "forget" to check in. Be sure to really close the deal with a convincing hug. (Ideally, you'll know the person you're hugging, if not, hopefully you've find someone really friendly.) This one only works at a really packed party.

9. This one is still effective and works even better if you learn to read upside down. Casually lean over, without letting the person see you, glance at the list and pick out a name. Try to select one that is not checked off. Then say: **"I'm the plus one with _____. I'm supposed to meet him/her here."**

10. **"Hi, I'm Billy Bale. Christian Bale's brother? I'm supposed to meet him here."** The famous always get into parties, but you're not famous. So, who's to say that Christian Bale doesn't have some less attractive brother named Billy? He might, maybe they're step-brothers, who knows. This line has actually worked for me. Celebrities are like royalty and publicists never want to offend a celebrity. Just be sure the celebrity you intend to

impersonate as a distant relative is not *actually* going to attend. If they were there, it would be bad. To say the least. You may find yourself escorted to the VIP lounge being introduced to other celebrity folk. So go ahead, pose as Kate Hudson's cousin or William H. Macy's step-brother, why not? This is also only recommended as a last ditch effort to get into a really exclusive party, since there could very well be repercussions involving the cops when using this method. Remember, I warned you about this one.

And finally, if all else fails, use "The Best Party Crashing Line Ever." If any of the above lines do not work, I have to divulge one of the best lines ever. But only to you, the readers of this book. Be sure that you do not share this with anyone — it's our secret. This one is dangerous, mainly because it's *so successful* when trying to gain entry to even the most exclusive festival parties. First, you'll need some props: bring your own pint glass and a can of juice or beer. Pour some of the liquid into the glass (not too full!) and walk casually up to the entrance so the doorman does not see you. Make sure he's distracted with the chumps waiting in line who will not be getting in. Next, pay attention to little details — if it's cold outside, take off your jacket; you don't want to look like you've just arrived. Slowly sidle up to entrance while the doorman is distracted. Once you are right next to him and just outside the door, very nonchalantly hold up your half full glass and politely ask:

"Hey, is it cool if I take this drink out here? I'm just gonna grab a smoke."

Since the party will get shut down if anyone is caught taking alcohol outside, the doorman will literally throw you into the party. He's assuming you were already in to begin with, but now you are really in!

Okay, I can't give away all my secrets. I've saved some even better entrance lines for myself, but if you ask me in person, I'll tell you a few. Now remember, I'm a master, so for me it's easy — but practice makes perfect. And you can be creative and come up with your own, you just have to be in the right mindset and remember that you are *supposed* to be there. The best advice I can give novice party crashers is this: Almost any plausible excuse, delivered with a straight face in a very polite manner, will get you in.

Putting On a Successful Party:
Create Buzz and Leave Them Talking

Nothing helps create buzz for a film better than a party. (Nothing except, well, maybe a really good film.) The most successful parties are the ones that are impossible to get into. Even as you hand your party passes to friends or associates, make sure to let them know, "This is my last pass — it's going to be really tough to get in, so show up early. I can't guarantee you'll make it in, but you can try."

Of course, this statement is repeated to every single person you hand the pass to, which will guarantee that your party becomes a "must attend" event. It's as if you are giving each person a challenge and they will rise to the occasion. The harder it is to get in, the more they will want to go.

There are certainly different opinions about what makes a great party. If you really want them to leave happy, your party must live up to the following:

1. **Make everyone RSVP.** This gives you an idea of how many will attend. The harsh reality is that 50 percent or more of those who do RSVP will *not* show up. Don't take this personally, most RSVP to everything so they have options. However, those people who choose to skip your party will be offset by the party crashers, friends, and members of the press who decide to just "show up."

2. **Hold the party at a venue that you know is too small for the number of people expected.** If you leave at least some people at the door, it's considered a party worth getting into. If it doesn't present some challenge — if it's not at least somewhat over-booked — then it's not considered a hot party.

3. **Open bar, free food.** Another unfortunate reality is that if you charge for drinks and food or use some annoying "ticket" system, you'll only piss people off. The two most feared words among journalists are "cash bar." Believe it or not, making people pay for drinks can result in bad buzz. Keep the free drinks flowing and let people know when it's last call.

4. **Avoid loud music or bands.** It's hard to have conversations with any type or distraction; music set to the max is the worst.

5. **Keep any speeches really short and funny. Better yet, how about no speeches at all.** Most "speeches" or "announcements"

given at party gatherings only serve to stop the party cold. In most cases, this is when the walk-outs begin. Start any speech about a half-hour before the scheduled end of the party and keep it to less than three minutes. Say your thank-yous, tell a joke, and then encourage people to attend your screening. That's it. Otherwise, you can kill your own party.

6. **Send 'em home with something for free.** A goodie bag is always a good idea. The bag should contain some type of useful freebie that advertises your film. A T-shirt, soundtrack CD, DVD, poster, or some useful item (like lip balm in cold climates or suntan lotion in warm climates) works wonders.

7. **Invite celebrities.** Yeah, they can be a distraction, but the fact that they showed up means something. I know, I think it's lame too, but that's reality of The Industry. A good publicist will "book" a celeb to stop by and people at the party will talk about it. I am definitely *not* a celebrity, but invite me anyway. (Please?) (See Appendix for a list of people you *must* invite to your party.)

8. **Do something different.** The party for the film *20 Dates* required that each male and female wear a badge with a number. The number corresponded with a male or female partner that partygoers were "required" to meet up with and ask a series of questions. The questions were typical of what one might ask on a date. It might sound stupid, but it was a load of fun and people talked about this party afterwards. I have always wanted to go to a film festival party with a carnival dunking booth. You know, one of those ones that people throw baseballs at so the person is "dunked" in a vat of cold water. It would be cool to see world-famous critics or movie actors in that dunk tank. Well, that's just my idea, but anything you do that is unique will get attention. Having your friend's band play will not help and is really not recommended.

"Hey, how's it going? Do I know you?" That's what Philip Seymour Hoffman said to me when we met at John Sloss' party at Sundance.

THE MOST IMPORTANT GOAL

To prepare for your film festival debut, the list of things you need to accomplish can seem insurmountable. The "to do" list in the next section is just to help you get started. You will think of many more things to add to this list, based on your individual needs. Aside from all the distractions and small tasks that come with preparing for a festival, the most important goal you have is to complete the greatest film possible with the resources at your disposal. Do not even consider compromising the integrity of your movie to make a festival deadline — making the best movie is the top priority.

HOW TO ATTEND ANY FESTIVAL FOR FREE
One of the best ways to get into a festival for free is to volunteer. All the major festivals have volunteer programs and while there's no pay, there's a ton of free swag to be had. Not to mention getting to see free movies (on your off time, of course) and most festivals even set up special "volunteer-only" screenings for their showcase films. And there's no better way to get to know the staff at a festival than to be a volunteer. So if you are thinking of entering a festival down the road, consider volunteering first to establish that personal relationship.

SECTION 3

FORMING A FESTIVAL STRATEGY

"All of a sudden, you're talking about years of work, years of dedication and you have your whole heart in this film. And suddenly that film has been turned into a monetary figure."

— Daniel Myrick, co-writer/co-director
of *The Blair Witch Project*

FORMiNG A FESTiVAL STRATEGY

Whether you have a short film, documentary, or narrative feature, in order to successfully break your film into the festival circuit, you must have a strategy. The general strategy is about the same for everyone. First, this involves getting to know your film. Consider festivals that may be more friendly to a film that fits a particular genre — whether it be gay, lesbian, documentary, digital, underground, animated, ethnic, sci-fi, fantasy, or horror — there are festivals specializing in these types and your film may best fit into one of these. It's sometimes better to be the toast of a smaller festival than be overlooked at a larger festival.

When it comes to submitting, I highly recommend that you begin by targeting the festivals on my Top Ten list. These are the "A" festivals and are also markets for indie films, heavily attended by acquisitions executives.

Next, you must plan a fallback strategy in case you do not get into any of the Top Ten. This is the category most filmmakers will fall into. There are just not enough slots, no matter how many American Spectrums or Midnight Shows Sundance schedules. Compile a list of "B" festivals — these are the ones you will submit to simultaneously. These might include strong regional festivals like the Hamptons, Austin, Atlanta, CineVegas, New Orleans, San Diego, Woodstock, or the Denver International Film Festival, among many others. (See the listings for other good "B" festivals.) These are all great festivals, don't get me wrong, but when it comes to getting a distribution deal, statistically speaking, the Top Ten have had more films walk away with distribution than all the "B" festivals combined. But these second tier fests are great for creating buzz, getting the word out, and even getting a deal. Apply to ten or even up to thirty more of these festivals and lobby just as hard for admittance as you do for the Top Ten. Plan your submission schedule around an annual calendar, mapping out the festivals you will play over the course of a year or so. If you get accepted into a "B" level festival but are still waiting to hear from a Top Ten, don't stress it. That smaller festival will keep the film in mind next year once you've made the rounds.

Then, and this is optional, take some chances; apply to some wild festivals for fun and a much deserved vacation. The weird ones and the strange sounding ones located overseas. Foreign festivals can be a blast. You may end up with a free trip to Spain for your film's European debut, all because you took a chance on a smaller festival.

All told, your plan should include applying to around twenty to forty festivals total. Sure, you could apply to hundreds, but why bother? Once your film gets circulated, it will make it to other festivals because directors of festivals talk to each other. Once your film is in the pipeline, it is in the pipeline. It's better to focus on lobbying specific film festivals first, rather than to using a scattershot strategy and applying to the more than 1,000 festivals offered in this book. Remember, lobbying festival staff (politely, correctly, in a way that gets their attention and does not annoy) is time better spent than applying randomly. Work smarter, not harder.

Once your film plays one festival, other festivals will extend invites. Some invites will be very direct and others will simply imply that *if* you send in your tape, it will most likely make it in, and oh, by the way, you don't have to send in the application fee. Anything to get around paying another forty or fifty bucks.

Strategies vary whether you are have made a short, documentary, or narrative feature. This section is broken up to individually address case studies for each kind of filmmaker and the best festivals for each type and genre of film.

No matter what kind of film you have made, your list of things to accomplish—depending on how ambitious you are—will generally be the same. The checklist on the next page is a complete rundown of the tasks you need to perform in order to take your film onto the festival circuit. Previous sections of this book have addressed how to create all the materials necessary for each task. Do not hesitate to delegate many of these tasks to others involved in the production of the film. It is important, however, that those jobs are delegated to those most qualified to see those tasks through to completion by your deadline. I suggest making a copy of this list, breaking down the responsibilities into smaller chores, then assigning deadlines to each task. It does help, however, to work on parts of this list during production, especially when it comes to gathering photos for marketing and getting video that might be used for the EPK and as extras for the DVD release. The same kind of project management that went into the monumental task of making the film should be applied here. And if you can't do it all, don't worry. Hardly any film-maker, or even team of filmmakers, has the time to generate every-thing on the list — but keep all these items on your list, anyway. It will be up to you to prioritize which items are most important.

THE ULTIMATE FiLM FESTiVAL "TO DO" LiST

1. **Submit to film festivals.** The key here is to have a focused plan of attack when submitting rather than to submit blindly.
   - Do not allow deadlines to affect the quality of your film
   - Research festivals
   - Submit to ten "A" film festivals
   - Submit to another ten to thirty "B" film festivals
   - Follow up with festivals
   - Promote movie online with website
   - Get local media to do some press
   - Set aside funds for marketing, travel and your festival debut
   - Build buzz through all of your efforts above
2. **Build the team.** Get the best team members possible with a combination of the following:
   - Publicist
   - Lawyer
   - Agent
   - Producer's Rep
   - Manager
   - Friends (for support and for assisting with tasks)
3. **Create marketing materials.** Put together a unified and clever campaign with a unique message that clearly demonstrates how the film might be sold to an audience.
   - Take production stills during shooting
   - Headshots of key cast, crew
   - Schedule photoshoot during production, for pictures that might be used on the poster, DVD sleeve, and potentially for magazine covers and press
   - Stickers with movie logo
   - Press kit (with B&W, color, and digital photos)
   - Poster

- Flyers
- Postcards
- Website (with e-mail newsletter to promote site)
- Create a "Press Only" area of your website for photos, press materials
- EPK (electronic press kit)
- CD-ROM/DVD Press Kit
- Promo item(s) (witty, clever, and original, of course)
- Trailer (post it online)
- Invitations/postcards to screening
- Plan a party

4. **Don't forget....** Be organized when it comes to the little details — your festival experience will be incalculably better for it.
   - Book travel
   - Restaurant reservations
   - Make a schedule of screenings, parties, events
   - List your goals and keep them in your wallet

5. **During the festival....** Most importantly, make valuable contacts, and, if possible, lots of new friends. (And I mean real friends, not just industry friends, there is a big difference.)
   - Invite reviewers, distributors, and VIPs
   - If necessary, make tapes available (for key critics who specifically request them)
   - Distribute postcards and posters at festival
   - Contact local media
   - Paper the town with your marketing materials
   - Give out promo items
   - Promote your screening
   - Get reviewed
   - Wear something that stands out
   - Throw a party
   - Attend parties

6. **Final thoughts....** The ultimate goal is to secure distribution and to that end, do not forget these important things:
   - Make contacts with distributors
   - Set up post-festival screenings
   - Collect all press clippings and reviews
   - Explore attending other festivals
   - Have a next project
   - Send thank you notes

SUCCESS OR FAiLURE

As you go through the process of forming your strategy, there are some key things to keep in mind. Remember that this is a marathon, not a race. Your festival tour may begin with one stop at a major festival where the film is then sold to a distributor, leading to a profitable sale, and a theatrical release. But you're more likely to win the lottery. For most, the journey is a longer one. It may last as long as two years on the festival circuit as you screen all over the world, ending with a release on home video, DVD, and cable. No two filmmakers' journeys are the same, but prepare yourself for a very long ride either way. There is no such thing as an overnight success in this business. Any "overnight" success you may have read about in the entertainment media is really just an untold story of years of preparation, planning, and hard work finally paying off. If you are disciplined and patient, success in some form will find its way to you. If you end up with only the knowledge that you failed in your intended goal, you'll have the advantage of being able to take those lessons into the next project. That knowledge, in itself, is an asset.

Luciana Pedraza and Robert Duvall in Austin, Texas to promote their film Assassination Tango *at SXSW. And they can dance the tango.*

In many ways, your *second* film is almost more important than your first. It's when you discover whether you learned from the mistakes you made the first time around. Your second film is your opportunity to apply those lessons and get another chance. You cannot control success or failure, only how you react to it. I'm going to make you read that again, because I feel this statement is so important:

You cannot control success or failure, only how you react to it.

I've observed filmmakers who had tremendous success their first time out, who then went on to do absolutely nothing. They never even made another film. I've also seen filmmakers who failed their first time out, who also, not surprisingly, never made a film again. Conversely, I've seen filmmakers fail miserably their first time — they made a bad film and never succeeded in getting into a festival and their film sits on a shelf. I've seen that very same failed filmmaker deliver a *second* movie that was absolutely brilliant. And that film went on to enjoy accolades and become a huge hit. Anything is possible. Having a strategy and a solid plan guarantees nothing, it can only help increase your chances when you have already made a fantastic film.

> "First things first, you have to really want this. No one who's on the fence about being a filmmaker ever succeeds."
> — Heidi Van Lier, writer/director of *Chi Girl*

FROM THE FRONT LiNES OF FiLMMAKiNG

I've interviewed countless filmmakers at festivals and most of the interviews turn out badly — they're just incredibly lame and boring to read. In fact, I don't think I've ever gotten a good interview at a film festival. I suspect it's because the subject is painfully aware that they are being interviewed for a magazine, newspaper, television, or whatever, so they immediately launch into "spin mode." They talk nice about the producer, nice about the director, nice about the actors, nice about the festival, *everyone* is "nice." You'd think that these interview subjects had just consumed some type of happy drug! (In some cases, they actually have.) The truth is that they are merely doing the right thing and being political. They don't want to say anything that might offend or piss someone off and hurt their chances of getting a deal, winning an award, or launching their careers.

The subjects I've gathered for this section of case studies were *not* interviewed at film festivals. They each take a truthful, and sometimes painful, look at their experiences. What you are about to read are less interviews and more like confessionals — each person offering a detailed account of their triumphs and their failures.

I carefully selected interview subjects who would avoid politics and offer useful information to filmmakers and festival-goers. These interviewees comprise the best and the brightest in independent film. Each person delivers the real deal — hard information, free of polite spin.

The filmmakers interviewed for this third edition of this book have created a strangely diverse range of films; from an earnest indie about life in the flower business, to a bittersweet romance, to a science fiction inspired by the works of Ray Bradbury, to a documentary exploring the effects of fast food, to a short film about a very personal and tragic event, to a movie that is best described as the adventures of a geek in rural America. The movies are clearly diverse and the experiences of each filmmaker are even more so. Each of these filmmakers represents one of the numerous paths a filmmaker can take when seeking success through a film festival. These myriad paths include:

- Submit to Sundance, make it into Sundance, screen at Sundance, sell film for theatrical distribution.
- Rejected from Sundance, rejected from Slamdance, enter other festivals where the movie is then discovered.
- Rejected from every Top Ten festival, only to become a hit on the international film festival circuit.
- Rejected from almost every festival, go home empty but filled with hard lessons.
- Rejected from nearly every film festival on the planet, pursue self-distribution as the final option.

There are certainly more roads than those I've mentioned, and new ones that filmmakers will invent for themselves out of necessity. And just because you are a documentary filmmaker doesn't mean you shouldn't read the sections on the short or narrative feature filmmakers. There is a lot to be learned from all types of filmmakers, so study them all. Look to these filmmakers for their inspiration, entertainment, and enlightenment, but most of all, learn from their experiences.

SHORT FiLMMAKER STRATEGiES

Personally, I love short films. Nothing is more enjoyable than discovering something that is less than ten minutes long, but makes me think about it long after the lights have come up. Too often, filmmakers are so anxious to jump into the game, placing themselves on some kind of insane personal timeline like, "I must make my feature before I turn thirty!" that they ignore the benefits to be gained by travelling the festival circuit with a short. There are just too many rewards to name, chief among them being that there are really no expectations. If you can prove that you can tell a compelling story and maintain that for the total running time, you can certainly do this in a longer format. Before you endeavor to make your feature debut, you should absolutely tour with a short. Not only will you learn about the festival circuit as a whole, you will see your film in front of an audience, and there is no better way to educate yourself about making movies than seeing your own film with a real audience. The more opportunities you have to do it, the better you will be able to see your film through the eyes of an audience — giving you much-needed insight into getting into the heads of moviegoers.

In additon to the Top Ten, short filmmakers should see the appendix in the back of the book for the complete list of festivals where the winners will be eligible for Academy Award consideration. I would like to especially point out the how important it is to play at the Palm Springs International Short Film Festival. This is a festival that *only* plays short films. The shorts screened at Palm Springs are broken down by genre, so there are various programs of children's shorts, experimental shorts, dramatic shorts, animated shorts, fantasy shorts, and so on. Also, Palm Springs attracts festival programmers from all over the world seeking shorts, so there is no better place for exposure. To make it convenient for those seeking films, the organizers at Palm Springs provide a library of videos, so if programmers miss a screening, the short may be seen on video. In addition to the above-mentioned benefits, you will be surrounded by other short filmmakers, which makes for great conversation and a lot of new friends who you will see at other fests. Your fellow short pals will impart all their knowledge of their festival journeys and filmmaking experiences. (You know, when they are not trying to beat the heat in the desert with some cool alcoholic beverages.) I cannot say enough good things about Palm Springs — for short filmmakers, this is *their* Sundance.

SHORT FILM, SHORT CREDIT SEQUENCE

Nothing is worse than watching a short film with an interminably long beginning or end credit sequence that thanks everyone on the cast, the crew, and the filmmaker's parents and pets. Do two versions of your short: one with a very brief (5-15 second maximum) end credit sequence that includes only the major people who worked on the film, and an alternate, extended version with a credit sequence that goes on as long as you'd like — send this second version to family, friends, and the crew. Include all the "thank yous" you want! Let the credits take five minutes or more to roll! Go wild!

Often short filmmakers are not treated with respect on the festival circuit, being last in line for benefits like travel or lodging or freebies. As a short filmmaker on the festival circuit, you just have to take what you can get. By focusing a good amount of your energy on the Top Ten festivals and festivals that celebrate short films only, you will find rewards in the most unlikely places.

ARI GOLD

Category:	Short Narrative Film
Film:	*Helicopter*, 21 min.
Logline:	A very personal short exploring the tragic accidental death of the filmmaker's mother.
Premiere:	SXSW Film Festival
Screenings:	More than eighty festivals worldwide, including Telluride and Sundance
Awards:	Winner of more than fifteen best short awards
Status:	Self-distributed on video, for sale on Amazon.com

Ari Gold grew up in San Francisco wishing to be a writer but later realized that directing and acting were much easier since, "you got to talk to other people." He's made eight shorts, including *Culture*, which played to huge laughs at Sundance. His most successful short to date is *Helicopter*, an autobiographical film that uses animation and a fractured narrative to tell its story. Ari's do-it-yourself approach led to an incredibly successful festival run for *Helicopter*, which went on to win a Student Oscar and screen at eighty festivals worldwide.

Ari Gold

Your first short was a one-minute joke that got a lot of attention at Sundance. How did you orchestrate that?

I ran off one afternoon and made *Culture* in one shot, and Sundance loved it. I went to Sundance armed with T-shirts and a promotional campaign totally out of proportion to the film, as a joke. It worked: By the end of the festival everyone knew about my film. I was introduced into the magical world of agents and managers who chase you out of a theater begging to work with you —

and then, when you call them in LA the next week to make it official, they tell their assistants that some annoying filmmaker is stalking them. The best result of the short was being cast in *Groove* by Gregory Harrison.

Helicopter is extremely personal, recounting the tragic true story of your mother's death. What led to wanting to make a film about such a personal subject?

Strange as this is, I just wanted to tell a story, and I thought, "Why *not* this?" Before the night I wrote it, it hadn't occurred to me as a possible movie. I'd taken notes for a novel I hoped to write about my family and the history of California, and fortunately decided to try the 170-proof version — a short film.

The hardest thing about telling a painful true story wasn't reliving the emotions, that was easy because the emotions are there anyway, the hard part was that each imperfection in the film felt like a deep failure on my part. But in the end the film finds its own truth.

Helicopter played more than 80 festivals. This is the postcard design used to promote the film during its festival run.

Did you have a strategy when you went about submitting your shorts to festivals?

Usually I tried to hit bigger festivals first. That didn't always work: Sundance rejected *Helicopter*. Later, after it won the Student Academy Award and played in Austin, they asked me to re-submit, and then they accepted it. In the end, though, I can't deny that playing Sundance opens the floodgates for all the other festival invitations. No other American festival has that kind of overblown clout, though many other festivals are fantastic affairs. Cannes has the same effect in Europe, and I'm sorry I've never played there, though I have played many other festivals in Europe.

What factors come into play when choosing what festivals to submit your short to?

Clout and travel fantasies. I mean, why wouldn't I want to be invited to Brazil to play my films? I wanted to be at least a little bit of a rock star. I didn't do much targeting. I submitted to festivals that looked cool, and there came a point, after a few prizes, that I didn't have to look for festivals; they came looking for me.

What are the advantages and/or disadvantages of being a filmmaker with a short at a festival?

The pressure is off, which is good and bad. You don't feel like this is your one and only shot at having a career, which is how it feels to friends who've had features play. On the other hand, even with the level of success I *did* have with my shorts, it didn't lead to much employment, so there you go.

I prefer the glamour of full film festivals for the industry side of things, and yet the short fests tend to be a thousand times more friendly to short filmmakers, for obvious reasons. Short fests are a good place to meet other filmmakers like you.

Do you prefer screening within a shorts program or in front of a main feature?

I prefer the excitement of being before a feature. You play first and the crowd is usually bigger. Sometimes that's uncomfortable, especially if the feature filmmakers don't want to be outshined by your little gem, but usually it's just fine. And you can only hope the programmers have a good sense of flow, which they only rarely do.

How critical is running time for a short film? Can having a longer short film actually be a burden?

The shorter the better, period. I mean, *Helicopter* was successful in spite of being twenty-one minutes, but unless you really think your short is doing something new, keep it short. Programmers, and audiences, like short shorts. Unless they're directed by Hollywood actors, in which case they can run thirty-seven minutes and suck ass.

How important are awards for short filmmakers?

They help, but only the big ones. Winning the Granite Falls Festival of Venereal Film isn't going to help you. Actually, the only ones that really help your career are the big ones. But prize money can be awesome, even if it doesn't make you a player.

Prize money can be awesome, even if it doesn't make you a player.

*It's hard enough getting critics to review a feature — how do you
get critics to pay attention to your short and write about it?*

Call them, just like I called you. You might meet a reviewer who
takes a liking to you. Or, if your short plays before a feature and it's
really, really well-received, it might happen naturally. But it's hard to
get critics to write about you, because their editors don't care about
shorts, even if the critic in question does. I've gotten more reviews
in foreign newspapers than anywhere: France, Brazil, Yugoslavia,
Japan. Here it's hard because reviewers are affected by the idea that
film is a commercial venture, and shorts aren't, so they don't merit
much coverage.

*Short filmmakers are often treated with far less respect than feature
filmmakers, so how do you get audiences to care about shorts?*

Be better than the features. Sundance is the best place to put your
short on the map; even better than the Oscars.

*When does a short filmmaker choose to put the movie online or
put it out on video themselves?*

After you've exhausted all other possibilities
of festivals and TV sales, then you can put it
online. I wouldn't recommend doing it before,
although it does increase your visibility. Though I
sold my videos on Amazon while they were still play-
ing festivals: I sell them at break-even prices, just as a way for people to see my film without having to stalk me. And having your
short on the Internet can hurt your chances of getting into a festival. Absolutely.

> Having your short on the
> Internet can hurt your
> chances of getting into
> a festival. Absolutely.

Can you really sell shorts? If so, how?

Retain as many of your rights as you can. Every deal is negotiable if
they really want your short. Having a sales agent helps a lot, unless
you want to spend a lot of time calling Japan or reading fine-print
contracts. But the sales agent takes a lot of the money. I've made
money on my shorts, but most of my friends haven't. The better
money is overseas — here, the only station that pays decently for
shorts is HBO, and they're very, very picky. The others can get you
a little money, but it's depressingly small.

Can you describe your whirlwind film festival tour?

Sundance and others — like Telluride — opened the gates. It becomes very addictive to travel with your film, especially if it's getting in to a lot of places, but it's also a real distraction from doing your next film. The best was playing in an attic filled with punk-film junkies in Yugoslavia in 2000, when I was practically the only American in the country. Being there meant a lot to them and a lot to me. The last festival I took *Helicopter* to was in Iceland. The promoters forgot to announce the festival to the national press, and nobody — I mean *nobody* — came to any of the screenings. I knew it was time to stop going to festivals. Me and the other directors got very drunk, but not as drunk as the festival organizers, who still owe me money for playing my film on TV.

Bottom line: Make a good film, promote it in a way that is eye-catching, and don't take your film too seriously. The most important thing I've learned is to never wait for anything, you have to do it yourself. And to have a million things going at once.

To learn more about Ari, visit www.arigoldfilms.com

EVAN MATHER

Category:	Short Animated Film
Films:	Various shorts, including *Icarus of Pittsburgh*, 10 min.
Logline	A digitally animated short, telling the story of a man who skydives into the midst of a pro football game.
Screenings:	*Icarus* played more than twenty festivals, including Sundance and Florida
Awards:	Winner of five Best Short awards
Status:	Streaming on the web at the Sundance Online Film Festival

Evan Mather has been making shorts since he borrowed his dad's Super-8 camera as a kid back in Baton Rouge. While he graduated from LSU with a degree in landscape architecture, he wanted to remain creative and find a way back into film. After purchasing a Power Macintosh back when QuickTime was in its infancy, he became interested in the possibilities of making movies on a computer. Evan initially took his old Super-8 films, digitized and re-edited them, and made remixes of them. At the same time, the web was new and he began posting his bizarre shorts on the Internet. Based on the attention he received, he began making original animated shorts with whatever software tools he could find.

*Evan Mather,
short film
animator*
PHOTO BY
ALICE G.
PATTERSON

What inspired you to make such unique animated shorts?

In early 1997 the *Star Wars* flicks were being reissued, and in a fit of nostalgia I asked my mother to send me all my old action figures. I promptly built a bluescreen set out of cardboard, hooked the video camera up to the Macintosh, digitized audio from the movies and started experimenting with stop-action animation. I posted the results to my website — notably *Kung Fu Kenobi* and *Quentin Tarantino's Star Wars* — and became known as, "The guy who does the homoerotic *Star Wars* action figure movies." Here I was, with a card table set up in my apartment, making short films that people around the world were watching — that was very liberating.

Did you have a strategy when you went about submitting your films to festivals?

Not really. I initially concentrated on digital film festivals like the Low Res, DFILM, and Resfest, because what I was doing seemed to be more about the technology and not so much story. What I didn't realize was — because these shorts were being distributed on the Internet, and that other people actually thought they were funny — film festival programmers started seeing my films and soliciting me to enter.

Do you prefer screening within a shorts program or in front of a main feature?

I do prefer screening in front of a main feature since the audience is concentrating on your short and then the feature. Oftentimes with shorts programs, the films are so disparate that after an hour or so, they all pretty much run together and the audience has a hard time remembering which one was yours and what they thought of it.

How critical is running time for a short film?

If your short film is more than ten minutes, you'd better have a really good reason. A good rule of thumb for me is the opening credits sequence — if the opening credits for a short are longer than about ten to fifteen seconds and are accompanied by pretentious music, then I know we're in for it. I prefer opening credits that are short and sweet and get on with it.

How important are awards for short filmmakers?

Awards inspire confidence. Unless your short gets picked up and you actually make some money off of it, an award is often the only thing left to brag about. It's a validation of all the hard work you've put into it and that can inspire you to make another film and start the process all over again. Honestly, if I hadn't won the awards I did when I was first starting, I wouldn't have continued to make so many shorts.

When should a short filmmaker put their movie online?

Personally, I use my website to instantly distribute my films and post all my current projects online. I see the Internet as just another distribution channel, like television or the festival circuit — and I figure that if people like what they see in a 3"x5" panel, they'll seek it out at a festival or on DVD. I don't feel like having a short online hurts your chances of getting into a festival — it gives the programmer a quick preview and helps spread the word about your project. Something to consider however, is that some fests, like Sundance, don't accept films that have already screened online — so these days if I make a film that has any redeeming quality, I wait until it has been rejected by these fests before I distribute it to the masses.

> I don't feel like having a short online hurts your chances of getting into a festival — it gives the programmer a quick preview and helps spread the word about your project.

How does screening at Sundance compare to other places where your short screened?

I don't like to be a festival snob — a film festival is a film festival — people go to enjoy beautiful films outside the mainstream. But at Sundance, you get a lot of free stuff. First, you get a small stipend to spend on lodging and drinks. Second, you get a load of free passes to see all the amazing features and shorts screening at the festival — when I went I saw all the movies I wanted to see for that year in one week. Third, you get excellent swag in your mailbox at festival headquarters — CDs, DVDs, magazines, T-shirts — it's an extravaganza. Finally, and most importantly, you get to ride the shuttle bus and talk trash about films with Roger Ebert. How can you beat that?

Can screening at Sundance increase your chances of other festivals screening your short?

Yes, because so many programmers attend Sundance and Slamdance. And even if they don't catch it in Park City, Sundance is a little badge of honor that makes your film stand out from the crowd.

How did you end up screening so often?

I usually contact the festival before entering and get a feel for what they are programming this year and whether my films will even fit. I also realize that film festivals pick films for a million different reasons and to not hold people personally responsible for not picking my film — there's always next year. And when you do actually attend a festival — don't be a dick. Be nice to everyone and try to relax. Programmers like to spread the word about cool filmmakers and short films.

A still from Evan Mather's animated short Fansom the Lizard.

What did you do to hype your film?

I do make postcards and send out e-mails, but I'm lucky in that my website has built up a loyal following, so I concentrate on visitors to my site to spread the word.

Were you nervous at the first screening?

I had a pretty amazing first festival experience, it was the International Film Festival Rotterdam, a very-well organized festival of great quality. They flew me out to speak on a panel about my *Star Wars* shorts and I was able to screen a few of those. Since this was my first time in front of a serious audience — as well as my first time in Europe — I was pretty nervous. But honestly, the people I met were so laid back and excited about cinema that I felt at home right away. The main thing I learned was to drop the pretension — people aren't there to write down your every word as gospel, they're there to enjoy the films and maybe pick up a few tips.

Any advice you can pass along about distribution deals for shorts?

Obviously, you have to be careful about whether the deal is exclusive or nonexclusive. In other words, will you be free to shop your film elsewhere? I have a few of my films with AtomFilms, which has exclusive rights to certain distribution elements — i.e. Internet, cable, television, etc. Be careful about the length of the contract as well. My experience has been that there is real cash money, but the deals are pretty exclusive and tie up your film for a while. So you have to decide whether this is the best deal you can get and what sort of exposure the cable channel offers.

How did you survive travelling to so many festivals?

My general rule of thumb is any festival that pays for your airfare and lodging, plus shows some cool films, makes for a great festival experience. The humble truth is that most of the time independent filmmaking pays very little, so I can't afford to go to most of the festivals my films screen in. If you want to see the world, enter foreign film festivals, which are often funded by government arts programs and have the resources to fly you out and put you up. I've been treated like royalty and had a great time at festivals in Europe and Asia that I wouldn't normally have considered going to. Unfortunately, festivals in the United States don't usually have these limitless coffers of cash.

Discover more of Evan's animated shorts at www.evanmather.com

DOCUMENTARY FiLMMAKER STRATEGiES

What I love most about documentary filmmakers is that some of the best ones never started out as filmmakers at all. They only became filmmakers when making movies became the best way to communicate their stories to an audience. Sometimes that story ends up becoming a cause, as in the case with most of Michael Moore's work, but for the most part, docs are just more entertaining than ever.

In the entertainment world as a whole, documentaries are enjoying a kind of renaissance. Technology has made it possible to make an ambitious documentary on a reasonable budget. In fact, entire home production studios often cost less than the travel and other expenses, resulting in more documentaries being produced now than at any other time in history. Now, that doesn't mean that all of them are good, but on the festival circuit, where the cream often rises to the top, documentaries are frequently the best films. In addition to submitting to the Top Ten festivals, documentary filmmakers should see the appendix in the back of this book for my list of the Best Documentary Film Festivals and specifically consider those festivals in particular.

At the very least, by visiting a "documentary only" festival, the opportunity to socialize with like-minded filmmakers talking about the business and the craft has its own obvious benefits. You can start by schmoozing with two very fascinating documentary filmmakers who came away from the festival circuit with very different results.

MORGAN SPURLOCK

Category:	Feature Length Documentary
Film:	*Super Size Me*, 90 min.
Premiere:	Sundance Film Festival 2004
Logline:	Morgan Spurlock documents his McDonald's-only diet for thirty days, with shocking results.
Awards:	Winner of Sundance's Best Director's prize in Documentary Competition
Deal:	Sold at Sundance for $1 million
Status:	Theatrical release in May, 2004, from Samuel Goldwyn Films/Roadside Attractions, fall 2004 home video and DVD release

Morgan Spurlock
PHOTO BY
AVI GERVER

West Virginia native Morgan Spurlock did not burst on the documentary scene, but looking in from the outside it just might seem that way. His documentary feature, *Super Size Me,* was *the* hit of Sundance 2004 and propelled him into the spotlight with his hilarious issue-based doc dealing with fast food's impact on obesity in America. The always-smiling Spurlock is a lot like Michael Moore, but without the chip on his shoulder. He's a filmmaker on a mission and his debut feature has secured his spot in indie film history. But what everyone wants to know is, where did he start?

So Morgan, where did you get your start?

I grew up in West Virginia. My parents rule — they were always encouraging and basically let me pursue whatever creative outlet I wanted. If it wasn't for them, I'd probably be handing out mints and towels in a bathroom somewhere.

When I graduated from high school in 1989, I went to USC to try to get into their film program. Because that's what you do, right? I was accepted into their Broadcast Journalism department and thought that once I was there it would be easy for me to get into the film school. Boy, was I wrong. I was rejected *five times*. I applied every semester...and got rejected every semester. The last time I also applied to NYU's Tisch School of the Arts and in their infinite wisdom they accepted me into the undergrad program. So, in the summer of 1991, I left LA bound for NY and the promise of a filmmaking future.

I graduated in 1993 and began working in the industry immediately. I did anything and everything. I shoveled shit on the set of *The Professional,* but I also got to shoot the last frame of film for the movie on the roof of the Essex Hotel with Director Luc Besson. I got yelled at by pedestrians while holding up traffic in Times Square on the set of *Bullets over Broadway,* but I also got to see and hear Woody Allen direct actors. I fetched coffee and fruit and danishes during the rehearsals for *Boys on the Side,* but I got take in Herb Ross breaking down a script with his entire cast in the weeks leading up to production.

While on the film *Kiss of Death* in 1994, I got a friend of mine a job working for Tracy Moore Marable (one of the coolest people on the planet) in the casting department. A few weeks later, they sent me to an audition to be the National Spokesman for Sony Electronics. I had no agent and I hadn't auditioned in years — not since my stand-up years at USC & NYU. What were they thinking? I ran downtown to drop off some film, and on my way back to the office I ran in and auditioned. Two weeks later I found out that I got the job and was off travelling the country, far away from the shlepping and the fetching.

Once on the road with Sony, I put my film degree to work by creating and shooting videos for them while also doing a lot of on-camera announcing for them and their corporate partners. Meanwhile, I kept directing and I kept writing. For Sony, Hasbro — any client that would pay me.

In 1999, my full length play, *The Phoenix*, won the Audience Favorite Award at the New York International Fringe Festival; then it won the Route 66 National Playwright Competition. However, I also had the worst music video directing experience of my life that same year — and that was the spark that lit the fuse for me to start my own production company.

In 2000, The Con was formed, and our first show, *I Bet You Will*, blew up on the web. It received more than 48 million unique visitors in 18 months and news stories were written about it worldwide. CBS optioned the idea — our worries were over! Then 9/11 happened and business in NY fell apart. I couldn't find any work, was evicted from my apartment, and had to sleep on a hammock in my office. I maxed out all of my credit cards to feed employees, pay rent, and pay other credit cards. CBS dropped the option. It was the worst of times. I was more than $300,000 in debt and the bottom seemed to be getting closer everyday.

Then MTV called after seeing us on *Sally Jessy Raphael* and bought the show. It went on to become the first program ever to go from the web to TV. In 2002, we produced fifty-three episodes for the network — when the show was cancelled in October of that year, I decided to take the small pile of money we made on the show and make our first feature. That was the foundation for *Super Size Me*. The film went on to win me the Best Director prize in Documentary Competition at the 2004 Sundance Film Festival.

What's my point in telling you all this? First, you can never dictate nor envision what ultimate path your career will take to get you to the "promised land." Also, even when I was doing the crappiest of jobs, I realized that it was merely a piece of the bigger whole and that it was only on small step of a longer journey. I've known countless talents over the years who have given up on their dreams. Be true to you, stay the path, keep working, and you *will* reap the rewards.

What made you want to make a film exposing the dangers of fast food consumption?

When I first got the idea of *Super Size Me*, I had no concept of what it would blossom into. I thought it was a funny idea that would make a great movie, be socially relevant, and tell a cohesive story. That's it. For me, it wasn't until I got deeper into the subject matter that I hoped for a film that could influence change.

How did you get into Sundance?

We had a test screening before we sent our first cut to Sundance, to ensure we were on the right track. Probably one month before the deadline. We had a second screening right after that to see what folks thought of the cut we sent. The audience loved it, so we kept moving forward. I think a lot of people send things too early — in a rush to "make Sundance." If you can get it into Sundance, great, but if not, there are plenty of other great fests out there.

Also, I was talking with a sales team early on in the process. My company was already repped by John Sloss' law firm, so it was only natural that we would also go with his sales company, Cinetic. There are plenty of reputable companies that can represent your film to buyers and having them come on early to start the ball rolling, lobbying on behalf of your film, is a huge plus.

Do your research, talk to other filmmakers, and get the lay of the land. I spoke to countless "alumni" about their experiences and asked what, in their opinions, we should do to guarantee the best Sundance experience possible. Everyone has a different answer and everyone was quite helpful in opening my eyes to the path we needed to be on at the festival. If you're applying to the festival, first you should make sure your film is a good representation of the final product. You don't need to send a finished film, we sent a rough cut, but at the time I would say the movie was about 85 percent there. Also, don't put all your eggs in the Sundance basket — there are countless fests around the world that may also be perfect for your film. We kept sending the movie out. For me, I just wanted to get the movie out there for people to see. Anywhere.

> Don't put all your eggs in the Sundance basket — there are countless fests around the world that may also be perfect for your film.

What other festivals did you apply to?

We applied to everything, probably forty festivals in all by now — all over the world. We were accepted into about half of them. It's such a bittersweet position to be in when your film is well-received, because while you want to show it everywhere, the reality is that you shouldn't. You need to be very smart about the festivals you plan to attend, outlining exactly what your goals are in attending the festival. Each festival offers a variety of pluses, so do your research and find out what would be best for your goals and your movie. (I devoured Chris' last edition of this book — Gore, you're a savior!)

How did you prepare for your first Sundance screening?

We finished our movie five days before it was to premiere at Sundance. So, needless to say, we were freaking out a little. Prior to going to Sundance, I also hired a publicist to rep the film. That will cost you anywhere from $5000-$8000 and is definitely worth every penny. I went with Dave Magdael and his team at TC:DM and Associates. Beginning in December we started putting together our marketing plan. You need to ask yourself: What do I want to get out of Sundance? For me, I wanted to (a) sell my movie, (b) create vast awareness about it and its subject matter, and (c) lay the foundation for future projects.

Having a plan in place will help you put together a cohesive strategy. You have to realize that as much as your film is art — it's also a product. The key to every successful product is developing and building the brand. It was my goal to make *Super Size Me* one of the most talked about brands at the festival. So, TC:DM and I discussed ways to get the word out. Luckily, we had hit upon a subject that most of America was passionate about. But that didn't mean our work was over. Here are the pieces of the *Super Size Me* marketing puzzle and what each meant to me and the film:

- **Branding One: The Poster.** We made posters prior to the festival that reflected the subject and were engaging. (See the "Fat Ronald" poster above.) This is a key piece of your marketing material.

- **Branding Two: The Swag.** We also made *Super Size Me* skull caps that we gave to key festival personnel: theater volunteers, parking attendants, etc. The more places you can get the name of your movie the better.
- **Branding Three: The Take Away.** We made postcards that we put in restaurants, the press office, bars — anywhere that they would let us. The Fat Ronald was a natural pick since that was our poster, but the "fry mouth" one was an afterthought. I had done a session with photographer Julie Soefer — a brilliant NYC photographer who helped out on the film — to create some publicity photos for the film. This picture came out of that session and quickly became the poster boy image for the movie. My advice to you is to have a photographer take publicity stills for your movie that reflect the film's theme. These will be staged and will deliver exactly the effect you want. It turned out to be the greatest visual tool.
- **Branding Four: The Promotional Item.** Create something else that gets the word out in an original way. We chose buttons, since it seems like everyone in Park City loves to wear them; on their jackets, hats, lanyards, you name it. We made 1,500 Obesity buttons (designed and created by NYC artist Syntax) — everywhere you went, you saw someone rocking the button. It was great branding for the film and it helped build the buzz around it.
- **Branding Five: The Gift Bag.** We wanted to take care of all the volunteers and media personnel who had taken care of us. This is such a great thing to do because these guys all bust their asses for nothing and are the biggest buzz generators when it comes to your movie. We made "Unhappy Meals": printed paper bags that were filled with goodies that related to the movie and supported the *Super Size Me* brand. We made 250 "Unhappy Meals", each contained a CD with the movie's theme song (which we burned and labeled ourselves), a postcard from the film, a skull cap, either a burger phone book or French fry coin purse, and a key chain. People *loved* these "Unhappy Meals", and being one of the filmmakers who remembers these hard working folks goes a long way.
- **Branding Six: The Street Team.** Everyone who worked on *Super Size Me* worked for free. So, as soon as we were accepted into

Sundance, I told them all that I would take them. Now I had to pay to get nineteen people to Park City! *Me and my big mouth!* Luckily, once your film gets accepted into the festival, you have something of tremendous value. I called some producer friends, Heather Winters & J.R. Morley, and hit them up for an investment. They had invested in many film projects in the past and I thought this was right up their alley. After seeing the movie, they were on board. They would get their money back first after the sale plus a percentage on top of that as well as an Executive Producer credit — in return, I would be able to take the whole team to the festival. A fair trade any day of the week in my book.

Now, why is this so important? Because when you get to the festival, you realize how overwhelming it would be to have to do everything on your own. Not only did I have my whole production team there, but now I had nineteen volunteers to help promote the movie.

I had a wardrobe supervisor friend of mine contact Ride Snowboards, who graciously donated jackets to outfit Team *Super Size Me.* You couldn't walk down Main Street without running into one of our team members. And they always had one pocket filled with postcards and another filled with buttons. Having all of them there definitely got the word out more quickly and allowed us to accomplish more in less time.

- **Branding Seven: The Super Secret Special Swag.** I wanted to make something up that only a few very special people would get at the festival. I called a friend of mine in China and had him find a manufacturer who could make the Fat Ronald Dolls.

We only made a hundred of them and they quickly became one of the hottest "must have" items at the festival. The Drawback: Since I had to have them sent overnight air from China to ensure they made it to the festival, I spent more on the shipping than I did on the dolls!

How did you go about hiring your publicist?
As soon as my sales team, Cinetic, was hired, I sat down with them and asked about publicists. They've been selling movies for years and know all the top publicists. Together we whittled the list to three — the three we all believed would have the right sensibility for

our movie. I then called each of the them. Your publicist has to be able to not only connect with you but also with your movie; you know after about two minutes whether or not you're talking to the right person.

We were all in agreement that Dave Magdael was the best choice, so we scheduled a face to face meeting immediately. Dave is great contrast to my personality; he is a very calm person. For me, especially in the heated madness of Sundance, I was ecstatic to have someone behind me who never got frazzled or bent out of shape. He and his team were so focused and they definitely maximized the exposure of both our film and me as the filmmaker.

How did that first screening go?

I was so nervous before the first screening. We had just transferred our film to an HD master five days earlier — so when the audience watched the print for the first time, it was my first time as well. Talk about nerve-wracking. For me, I just tried to relax as much as I could before I went to the theater. We rented a house with a hot tub so I spent a good hour in the tub before we had to go to the premiere. That's a big thing at Sundance — you have to take care of yourself. At that point, the movie is out of your hands. There's nothing you can do but watch, hope, and pray. I learned to let go.

Were you prepared for the questions from the audience?

I had rehearsed the answers to possible questions over and over in my head — you know, like when we all give our Academy Award acceptance speeches in the shower. So I think I was pretty prepared. Someone always throws you a curveball, but be confident and trust in yourself. No one knows your movie better than you do.

What did you do to get acquisition executives into your screenings?

Luckily, I didn't have to do anything. By hiring a topnotch sales team, I had one less thing to worry about. They made the calls and got all the biggest executives into the screening. Cinetic really made my life easy at the festival.

*What was important for you in determining which distributor
was right for the film?*

The most important thing I wanted was final cut. I wanted to make sure that whoever distributed the film would not alter it in any way. For me, this was very important in a distributor.

Second, the company had to be as passionate about the film as I was. The company we ended up going with, a tag-team release with Roadside Attractions and Samuel Goldwyn, was everything I wanted.

They were passionate, they were persistent, and they got the film completely. They were also the very first company to come forward and make an offer. Being first to the dance is something I put great value in because it shows they are thinking for themselves and not just following other companies or the press.

Did you target certain distributors before the screening, and if so, how?

Cinetic had a short list of thirty to forty distributors that they felt might be right for *Super Size Me*. Over the five days after the first screening, we narrowed that field until we were only left with a select handful. The deal was negotiated by John Sloss and myself. We got our first deals on the table at Sundance, but the negotiations for the theatrical release continued for a few weeks following the festival as we hammered it out.

Can you be specific about the deal?

The combined value of our domestic TV cable and theatrical sales was over $1,000,000. Not bad for a movie that only cost us $65,000 to get to Sundance. We also negotiated a generous backend percentage on the theatrical and video revenue. Most important to me, we held on to worldwide rights. We hired a foreign sales company just after Sundance (Fortissimo — they are fantastic!) and then, with their guidance and expertise, we sold many foreign territories separately: Spain, Portugal, France, Italy, Japan, Canada, Mexico, The Netherlands, Israel, Australia, New Zealand, the United Kingdom, Scandanavia, Russia, Poland, Switzerland, Belgium...the end result is much more money than we ever would have seen had we sold all global rights as one package.

How did you handle the vast number of press requests after Sundance?
Samuel Goldwyn's PR guru, R.J. Millard, has been juggling the requests like a champion. He hired an additional New York company to support the East Coast requests and kept on Dave Magdael to handle all the West Coast action. Once again, the less stuff you have to worry about, the more time you have to focus on the movie — which is *the most* important element of the whole equation.

How are you expected to support the release of the film?
I will travel extensively to promote the film, both in the US and abroad, to film festivals and to major media television outlets (like *Oprah* and *The Today Show*). Whatever it takes. The way I see it, I've already poured fourteen months of my life into this project — another year to really get the word out is the least I can do.

What kind of impact do you feel the film will have?
After Sundance, McDonald's announced that they were doing away with Super Size portions. Now, it doesn't take a rocket scientist to see that this is a direct preemptive step by the company to lessen the blow my film will have when it opens — even though they say that "it has nothing to do with that film whatsoever."

That is a tremendous accomplishment. Overwhelming, actually. When I heard the news I jumped and screamed and yelled and ran around the office. The little guy had won and Goliath was backpeddling.

So to all you filmmakers out there who think that what you say isn't important or who feel that what you do cannot make a difference...guess again. You work in the most influential and powerful medium in the world — your actions can move mountains and your images can inspire generations to come. Don't stop working. Persistence. Dedication. Time. And Belief. These are the foundations of success and these will help you change the world.

Get more Morgan at his official site at www.supersizeme.com

ALEX HALPERN

Category:	Feature Length Documentary
Film:	*Nine Good Teeth*, 80 min.
Logline:	A personal doc in which filmmaker Alex Halpern explores his grandmother's past through her heartfelt stories.
US Premiere:	Tribeca Film Festival, then played twenty festivals
Awards:	Grand Jury Prize for Best Documentary at the Director's View Film Festival and four other festival awards
Deal:	Sold to HBO for undisclosed sum

Alex Halpern was born in the Mongolian foothills while his parents were on an archeological expedition. As a teenager, he began to seriously consider a career in filmmaking when he met Jim Henson while on a trip to London. Jim took him to visit the creature shop for the film *Labyrinth* and it was that meeting that got Alex thinking that he could actually making a living by directing films. His short — *Zelda, Catwoman of Queens* — won him a Student Academy Award. Through his production company in New York City, he has made music videos, animation, and comedy skits for MTV.

Alex Halpern

His first feature documentary, *Nine Good Teeth*, is a very personal film. The subject is Alex's own grandmother, Mary, more affectionately known as Nana. Her unique storytelling skills (at the age of over 100) and vibrant personality made the film a tearjerker and a big hit on the festival circuit.

What made you want to make such a personal documentary film?

Every Sunday dinner, Nana would tell the most amazing stories from her own childhood — growing up at the turn of the century, when movies were still only five cents. She would recount things that had happened in her father's childhood almost 130 years ago. The stories were always so colorful and romantic that they made me want to live in that time period. Nana brought things to life in a very special way. Once she got on past ninety, I realized the only way more people could benefit from her life experiences and wisdom would be through either writing a book about her life or putting her on film.

Were you a filmmaker first, or did your subject force you to learn to be a filmmaker?

I was a filmmaker, although not a documentary filmmaker — that genre I knew nothing about. I was so misguided, I thought it would be easier and faster to make a documentary film because I wouldn't have to write a script first. I couldn't have been more wrong! It's almost twice as hard because first you accumulate the material, and then a script must be created *around* the material.

Even now I fancy myself a narrative filmmaker and storyteller, not a documentary director. In fact I don't even like the word documentary because it creates an inbred prejudice towards the work that gives critics and distributors license to dismiss its commercial potential before seeing it. It's like documentaries are supposed to be some kind of educational experience, and not entertainment — which is just bullshit.

You chose to premiere at Tribeca. Is there a whole song and dance involved with where you decide to premiere your film and what problems can this cause?

The one thing I can say with absolute certainty is there is really no way to control or influence the process from an independent's point of view. I used every means available to me to insure that my film got in front of the right screeners. I think I could have been even more aggressive, but it's a fine line. In the end you just want to make sure you've left no stone unturned in trying to get to the finish line. There are many issues, egos, and politics involved at all levels at most of the large festivals. In the end it's a shame that filmmakers have to choose because if you show at Tribeca first, then maybe Toronto or Sundance won't take the film, but every festival has it's own unique criteria and they all want to have the premiere.

I think what's often lost on first time directors is that we're in the entertainment *business* not the *art* business. We can make art, but it's a commodity that has to sell, and film festivals are a huge part of the business of selling. Festivals — just like distributors —

are controlled by business models that require the screening of a certain number of big name films — i.e. with stars on the posters and at the premieres — in order for them to meet their funding needs. If you premiere at the wrong festival, you may not get the exposure, distribution deal, or press that's needed to get the film out into theaters and onto TV.

A still from Alex Halpern's doc Nine Good Teeth

Premiering at Tribeca continues to have been an enormously special event for me and everyone involved with the film. *Nine Good Teeth* was the first film to sell out all its tickets that inaugural year. For my grandmother Nana, the 105-year-old subject of the film, it meant that she got to attend a big glitzy opening with a huge afterparty attended by family, friends, and people she loved. It was a perfect moment for which I'll always be grateful. Also, it was only about six months after 9/11 so for us it was a big deal to be part of the downtown rebirth.

What preparations did you make for your debut?

We wrote press releases, email releases, and did a huge postcard mailing. I had all these great ideas for promotional items that I wanted to have made to help juice the film — decks of playing cards, dolls, old lady whoopi cushions — but in the end I didn't have the money, so we just did the best we could by making a huge push with postcards, press kits, emails, and the phone.

Actually my film has a huge cultural draw from the Italian-American community so we did a big outreach there as well as with all the normal press outlets. We would also go to whatever festival we were in at least a few days before and paper the town with posters, postcards, and whatever it took to get people into screenings.

When did you choose to hire a publicist?

I didn't hire a publicist until the film was going to be broadcast on HBO, which I now think was a huge mistake. Some people told me if you don't get into Sundance, you don't need one. I was on a very

tight budget and afraid to spend the money, which was both practical and preposterous at the same time. I was a completely self-
financed independent and thought, "I can do this without spending
the extra money," which I didn't have to spend. *Big mistake! Hire the
publicist* even if you have to promise them something more down
the road to work for less up front. I did-
n't and while it didn't hurt the film, I think
it could have helped a lot sooner.

> A good publicist is more important
> than a good agent because
> they're actually helping you
> sell and market the film. Hire
> them as soon as you can.

Marketing a film starts the moment you
start talking about it, pitching it, and raising
money for it — well before you actually shoot anything. A good publicist is more important than a
good agent because they're actually helping you sell and market the
film. Hire them as soon as you can.

*How did you come up with your postcard, press kit, and
promo materials?*

I worked with Randy Balsmeyer, a brilliant FX and title designer
here in New York. Randy and I collaborated on the main title design
and all the still photography as well. I didn't really have the time or
money to hire a design firm that specialized in press kits and
posters, so we adapted some of the concepts used in the film for its
promotional materials.

An important point I learned really late in the game, is *don't
wait.* It sounds simple, but all this stuff should be done well before
the first frame of a film is even shot. It might seem pretentious to
have a press kit and poster for a film that's still being made, but it
helps get the word out and is how professionals work. And far too
often filmmakers assume that their work is complete when they
have a tape or print in hand, but actually that's when the hard work
begins. It's not easy to get people into the theater, so just as much
care and effort that went into making a film, must also go into marketing it.

How did you test the film before the premiere?

My first screening was a rough cut for friends and family and I was
completely nervous. My film is a meditation on life and death in a
Sicilian family as seen and told to me by my 105-year-old grandmother and it's a very personal story. Nana and I were sitting

together near the front, the lights go down, the sound starts and she's onscreen fifty feet high talking about *sex!* She turned to me and said, "That's a helluva thing to put in this picture!" For the next ninety minutes I was terrified that I'd done something to exploit her and embarrass my family, which was not my intent. At the end of the screening she turned to me and said, "Well, it's all true. Don't change a frame of it."

I must have screened the film about another forty times for various people — friends, family, strangers, whoever, just to test out the structure, the jokes, and the music. By the time I got to my first public screening I was very confident in the work and more scared of the Q&A.

Were you prepared for the questions from the audience?

The first public screening was in Munich, Germany, at DokFest about three weeks before Tribeca. It was a sold out screening, and I was floored by the audience response and questions. Keep in mind that during this screening the audience wore headsets and listened to a simultaneous translation of the film. While I thought I was prepared, it took some getting used to — being in front of two hundred people, trying to give honest responses, crack a few jokes, and keep the process moving in German, which I don't speak. Even though they loved the film it was intimidating because now I had to be witty and smart and off the cuff in front them, live.

How did the question and answer session go at Tribeca?

It was a friendly hometown audience. Nana was there, so that helped because she's very funny live and has no fear. I learned that the most successful Q&A's have three things in common:

Remember to *thank* everyone who helped you and the film get to that screening, including the festival staff.

Listen to what the audience members are asking and respond honestly without being pompous. The audience members who have the courage to stand up and ask something want to feel like they're participating in the process. I always remind myself that they've just spent two hours and ten bucks listening to what I think is important, so they deserve a few minutes.

Always have one *funny little story* to tell about the making of the film, or some bit of advice, or a weird situation that happened along the way. Audiences love to laugh at that inside story, especially when what they've just seen is emotionally dramatic.

What did you do to get acquisition executives into your screenings?

I used all available means to attract their attention and get them to the screenings. We tried to make it as easy for them as possible by providing them with free tickets and reserved seats, things like that.

I refused to send screener tapes, unless it was absolutely the *only* way they'd watch the film. Speaking of screening tapes and DVDs, I strongly advise that screeners be encoded against duplication to ensure that press, festival staff, and whomever sees the film in the best possible manner. I can't tell you how many bad dubs were made at the first couple festivals by staff to pass my film around. While it's well-intentioned on the festival's part, I didn't want the reviewer from the *New York Times* looking at a third generation VHS.

What was the most important thing in finding the right distributor?

I knew that I wanted HBO and the BBC — those brands to me signified a level of quality that I knew I could be proud of. In terms of theatrical, the field is narrow and it's important to pick a company that can help reach a wide audience. I feel it's important to feel comfortable with your distributor and be able to partner with them to ensure the greatest success for the project.

How did the deal come about?

HBO and BBC came about through personal connections. Friends put the film in front of the right people at both networks and they both wanted it. I was incredibly lucky and very tenacious. I never gave up from day one. Here's what I can say about my deal with HBO and the BBC — both had their ups and downs — neither paid a tremendous amount of money. Each network requested editorial changes in terms of running time.

Every deal is different, but I made sure that none of the deals permitted editorial changes after the film was delivered. Sometimes they'll say we need it five minutes shorter, we don't care what you cut, or they might have a specific suggestion. It's important to be firm on these points without being arrogant — arrogance is a quick exit from the business, there's just too much product and talent out there for executives to put up with it.

Also remember the "wiggly door knob." The wiggly door knob is this: when a contractor builds a house, he leaves the doorknobs loose so when the customer does a final inspection, they check the knobs and ask for them to be tightened. It gives them a feeling of being in control of the project, but the contractor isn't suffering a major headache and everyone is happy. Same idea when you're delivering a cut of the film to network — leave a couple of loose doorknobs so they don't mess with the really important stuff.

Very few documentaries get released theatrically, was your goal to go for theatrical, then see what you could get?

I wanted theatrical so badly I could taste it, but it didn't happen for me. I went about it as best I could, I had friends at some of the mini-majors and specialty places that I tried to convince, but no one understood or believed they could make money with this film. Which I still think is silly.

In terms of mini-majors, it's all dollars and cents. They need to know that if they put $500,000 dollars into a limited distribution that they're going to have a shot at making back $2.5 million, otherwise it's just not worth the risk to them.

On the other side of that, the small specialty labels have very limited resources, so they need to make sure that they've got a shot at building something up via word of mouth and festival prestige, otherwise they won't take a shot at it. A huge part of it comes down to the Sundance factor, which is this — small distributors feel that the Sundance seal of approval gives them something to sell in the marketplace; it's a way of quantifying the quality of the film. Even though *Nine Good Teeth* won many international festival prizes, it still doesn't carry the same way a Sundance or Toronto does.

Larger distributors follow the small ones into the fray and then it's a feeding frenzy. When I was at Tribeca, distributors were on their way to Cannes and they weren't really taking the festival seriously at that time. Now Tribeca is a whole different ball game.

Learn more about Alex and his film at www.ninegoodteeth.com

NARRATiVE FEATURE FiLMMAKER STRATEGiES

They are the darlings of the festival world and almost always the film-makers who open and close the festival. Narrative feature films are the most sought after, they get the lion's share of the buzz, and they generate the longest audience lines. They are also the most difficult and expensive films to pull off successfully, often resulting in a journey that takes an average of seven years from concept to completion.

In addition to applying to the Top Ten festivals, it's important to take a look at where your film may excel within a particular genre. Carefully consider submitting to festivals such as those that champion the type of movie you have made — whether it's a family film, digital picture, gay or lesbian, ethnic, animation, sports, comedy, sci-fi, fantasy, or horror among many other genres. (See those "Best" lists throughout the festival listings section.) To help you along the way and, in addition to the general Top Ten, I've separated out the Top Ten based on those best for narrative features for the US or the world. That list can be found at the end of the Top Ten festival listings (page 228).

You'll find a variety of filmmakers in this section whose advice will, more than a few times, contradict each others'. That's because there is no one correct path to follow and hearing how others have done it, no matter how different their stories, will help you in choosing your own.

JARED HESS

Category:	Narrative Feature
Film:	*Napoleon Dynamite*, 90 min.
Logline:	Following the mundane adventures and hilarious antics of a geek gone wild in rural America.
Premiere:	Sundance Film Festival 2004
Screenings:	The US Comedy Arts Festival, SXSW
Budget:	Around $250,000
Deal:	Sold at Sundance for $4.7 million
Status:	Theatrical release in May, 2004, by Fox Searchlight; Fall, 2004, home video and DVD release

At the age of only twenty-four, Jared Hess has experienced the kind of rare success few filmmakers enjoy. He not only delivered a hilariously compelling character study, but he also got into Sundance — where he sold the film and began what will surely be a long directorial career. *Napoleon Dynamite* is clearly the result of Jared's rural upbringing in places like Texas, Utah, Kansas, and Idaho. He caught

Napoleon Dynamite writer/Director Jared Hess with First Assistant Director, Tim Skousen.

the film bug when, at the age of fourteen, he worked as a camera assistant for a cinematographer in Salt Lake City, Utah. Still in his teens, he then served a volunteer two-year mission for the LDS Church in Caracas, Venezuela, and in Chicago. Upon his return, he went to film school at BYU where he met his wife and writing partner, Jerusha. Together they made the short film *Peluca*, which premiered at the Slamdance International Film Festival in 2003. He returned a year later to Park City, Utah, where his feature *Napoleon Dynamite*, which is based on his short, would premiere and become the biggest hit of Sundance 2004.

How did you prepare to enter this world of indie film?

Before making *Napoleon Dynamite* I read every book available on indie filmmaking, from breaking into the industry to how to be successful at film festivals. It all boils down to just getting out there and making the best film that you can. How people respond to what you create is totally out of your control, but most good films are able to generate a life of their own — something that is also out of anyone's control.

You first began your festival experience with a short film that contained some of the same characters and situations as your feature. Tell us about the short.

While at BYU I made the short film *Peluca*, which I had written with plans to expand it into a feature. The film was about the misadventures of an awkward Idaho teenager. Jon Heder was in a film class with me and decided it would be fun to play the main character. We gave him a perm, threw him in some moon-boots, and then headed to Idaho to make the film. *Peluca* was shot in two days on a budget of $500. I filmed it in black and white 16mm because I couldn't afford color at the time. Also, I accidentally exposed the negative wrong and the images turned out super grainy. Despite its lack of flashy production value, *Peluca* gained a very strong cult following.

Your short was a festival hit, debuting at Slamdance — what did you learn from your festival experience with the short that helped you with the feature?

Slamdance was great. Just getting accepted into the festival meant a huge deal to me. *Peluca* didn't win any awards, but the audience response was fantastic. The festival was a lot of fun, but also very nerve-wracking for me. I spent most of the week trying to convince people to go to the screenings. I'd see the fat stack of tickets that hadn't been sold yet and it would freak me out. I realized that part of the whole Slamdance experience is finding creative ways to get people to come see your film. It's exhausting, but people do turn out.

By the time the festival began, Jerusha and I had already completed our first draft of *Napoleon Dynamite*. We saw the festival as a good opportunity to screen our short for potential investors; they came and they loved it. The screenings of *Peluca* at Slamdance were instrumental in securing financing for the feature.

How did the feature version come about?

While at BYU I began collaborating with my producer, Jeremy Coon. One day I told him of the idea I had for *Napoleon Dynamite* and he assured me he could get the money. Just a few months after *Peluca*'s run at Slamdance, we had a check for $200,000. Jeremy also brought Chris Wyatt and Sean Covel on board as additional producing partners. The crew consisted of many of my good friends from film school and also people I had worked with as a camera assistant. During the month of July, 2003, we shot for twenty-two days in my hometown of Preston, Idaho. It was a very tight shooting schedule, but we tried to be as prepared as we could with a complete set of storyboards and shot lists. Our cast and crew were fantastic — there was only one motel in Preston so most of the crew slept in the basements of hospitable locals.

My wife, Jerusha, was also the costume designer for the film and was pregnant throughout production. I thought the baby was gonna pop during the shoot because she was working so hard, but luckily it didn't happen until September.

My producer, Jeremy, was also the editor of *Dynamite* and he began cutting the film in Los Angeles as soon as we wrapped. But I had to stay out in Utah to take a camera assisting job for the month — things were tight. As soon as that job finished, Jerusha, the baby, and I all drove out to California so I could work on the editing. We ended up staying out there for over a month. Those were some stressful days. I was convinced I had a piece of crap on my hands and I began to seriously consider other career options...like fishing. But Jeremy remained optimistic and sent out a rough cut to Sundance. At the time I was pretty upset, but looking back I'm glad he did.

Did you show the feature to people to get feedback in preparation for your festival debut and how did you go about that process?

Yeah. Jeremy set up a small screening for about forty people, most of whom were his friends and acquaintances. He typed up feedback sheets and everything. I was there to introduce the film, but I left to walk around outside as soon as it started. It was still a rough cut and I wasn't ready to show it. The next day I checked out what people had written, and it was mixed. I wasn't sure how accurate the responses were because of the audience's relationship to Jeremy. But later on that week I got a very genuine email from a well-known screenwriter who had attended the screening. He said that we had made a very unique and hilarious comedy. That got my spirits up a little bit.

What did you do to hype your film at Sundance?

Actually, we tried desperately *not* to hype our film at all. We didn't want to run the risk of over-hyping and fall short of audience expectations. We made the decision early on not to have a website; we wanted to remain "under the radar." But Trevor Groth, the senior programmer at Sundance, did a very clever and funny write-up for our film in the catalog. Largely because of that, many people were eager to see the film. All of our screenings sold out before the festival even began.

The postcard used to promote Napoleon Dynamite in Park City at Sundance.

What did you learn from that first screening?

I was trippin' out. I knew that the first screening would make me or break me. With comedies it's obvious whether you've succeeded or not — either people laugh or they don't. Our first screening couldn't have been better, the audience laughed through the whole thing. When the film ended we got a standing ovation. It was crazy. I got all choked up and stuff. You never realize what you have until you show it to an audience of people who have nothing to do with you.

How did the deal come about?

It all went down pretty fast. Distributors began to make us offers after our first screening, but we decided to hold off until after our third screening the next day. Our first meeting was with Fox Searchlight. Every single department head had seen the film and they were all present at the meeting — the president, the VP, head of distribution, head of marketing, head of acquisitions — everyone. I wasn't speaking to just one or two acquisitions people who could return to their studio with a film that their superiors might or might not like. I was speaking with *all* the major players who would potentially be handling the release of our film. They were all very passionate about *Dynamite* and were already coming up with ideas on how to market it. The year before I had been very impressed by how they handled films like *28 Days Later*, so I was very excited at the possibility of Fox Searchlight being our distributor.

They were determined to buy the film. They said, "We have a screening to catch at 5:00," and within the next hour we had struck a deal. The other distributors were angry that they didn't even get a chance to meet with us and make an offer. But we felt strongly that we had made the best decision for our film.

What did you look for in the deal?

Making sure they weren't going to "shelve" the film after buying it. I just wanted to make sure the film sold for what it was worth and that they were going to give it a good theatrical run. [John] Sloss made sure all that happened.

The basics of the *Napoleon* deal were the acquisition price plus 50 percent of box office net (gross receipts minus distribution fee, P&A expenses, and the acquisition price), 30 percent of home video, and a bonus of $350,000 at theatrical grosses of $20, $25, $30, and $35 million each. And we retained final cut. It's a very solid deal, especially for a film that was our first feature.

The size of the acquisition price was less important to me, because our main goal was that the film would get the attention it deserves and actually be seen in theaters. We've all heard horror stories about how such-and-such studio bought this film and then shelved it for whatever reason and then it got a lame theatrical release, dumped to video, or worse, nothing at all. That was our nightmare. After pouring two years and our hearts into making this film, it would have been devastating — both emotionally and professionally — to not even have a fair shot at reaching a wide audience.

The first thing I would recommend to a filmmaker looking for distribution is to try to get a killer producer's rep on board. We lucked out on *Napoleon* and were contacted by Cinetic Media before we had even heard anything about being accepted into Sundance. Cinetic was founded by the Godfather of reps, John Sloss, who negotiated distribution deals for many Sundance hits like *The Station Agent* and *Tadpole*. I feel that they were one of the most important reasons why the film got the attention it did and definitely the reason why our deal was so sweet. Sadly, I don't think it's just enough to make a great film because the marketplace is flooded with so many films looking for distribution and so many get lost in the shuffle. A good producer's rep can provide the validation and muscle to make sure that your film is on the distributors' radar, which allows them to negotiate a much better deal. They should also know the people working for the distributors and their personal tastes to make sure that the right person from that particular company sees the film to give it its best shot. This type of service is next to impossible to do on your own.

How important is having a good attorney?

You have to have a lawyer, and not just an entertainment lawyer, but one who has experience with distribution deals. There are so many loopholes and so much legalese that only a seasoned professional can really watch your back. The basic points to look over are a commitment to P & A (prints and advertising), backend points on theatrical and home video release, and the deliverables list.

I would also make sure that there's something in the contract about keeping you involved in the creation of any marketing materials so you are able to voice your opinion.

The biggest unknown is the deliverables list, and that can be negotiated heavily if need be. The shorter the list is, the lower your advance is likely to be, but it might be worth it sometimes. If there are a lot of things that have to be done to deliver the film, make sure that you get a percentage of the advance upon signing or that you have the money to complete it so the deal isn't jeopardized later. It can really add up, especially for music rights in our case. Every film's situation is different, but just make sure that you're comfortable with the deliverables list before you sign.

Are you, like, a gazillionaire now?

No, I'm not a gazillionaire. But I will have enough money to make a nice down payment on a house. Half of the money from the sale goes directly to our investors and the rest is divided among the above-the-line participants. So far, Fox has been great, including me in every marketing decision they make. It's been great.

MELISSA SCARAMUCCI

Category:	Narrative Feature
Film:	*Making Arrangements*, 80 min.
Logline:	This inside look at daily life in a flower shop with comedic results.
US Premiere:	Dances with Films and Big Muddy Film Festival
Screenings:	At nine festivals including Marco Island
Awards:	Winner of three Best Feature Awards
Deal:	The film remains unsold

Melissa Scaramucci is a native Oklahoman who graduated with a BA in English from the University of Oklahoma. A published writer and commercial actress, Scaramucci brings her experience as an industrial writer and director to the fictional world of feature film. Since 1999, she has directed dozens of shows for corporate and non-profit clients with PDC Multimedia Productions, where she also worked as the scriptwriter in the home office in Norman, Oklahoma. In addition, Scaramucci is the creator and director of the national keynote speaker program, Choices. Active in the local theater scene, Scaramucci worked closely with USC professor and professional screenwriter, Richard Krevolin, on his three latest scripts, either as actor, producer, or assistant director. Inspired by personal experience, *Making Arrangements* is Scaramucci's first feature length film.

Melissa Scaramucci in front of the Sooner Theater in Norman, OK, for a double bill with fellow Norman filmmaker, Bradley Beesley's Okie Noodling.

Did you have a strategy when you went about submitting the movie to festivals?

I wanted to show the film at very small festivals to start. I wanted to get an unbiased audience response to the film. Since *Making Arrangements* is a comedy, I had to know if the laughs fell where I thought they should. Since this was my first time into festival land, I wanted to start small to get my feet wet. After the first two festivals, we re-edited the film and trimmed about seven minutes, mostly at the end. Knowing when to stop when the story is over is key.

Many of the festivals we went to, we were invited to attend. That started because a few people who ran festivals liked the film and started passing our tape around. We submitted to dozens of festivals, and the film got lucky finding supporters.

Were you concerned about applying to other festivals before you got word from a large festival where you wanted to premiere?

No, and that was ignorance on my part. I didn't realize so many festivals were obsessed with the "World Premiere." I've heard many filmmakers talk about having several "World Premieres;" every time they re-cut their film, or made any change to it, the next screening was a "World Premiere." I should have been more in tune with that element of the festival circuit. My festival strategy was to start small, learn how things operate, and then finish big. Meaning, I wanted my last festivals to be nice-sized regional festivals with a lot of exposure. Hopefully this exposure would help me sell my film.

How did you prepare for your premiere screening?

I would say we had three "premiere" screenings. The first was at a small festival in Carbondale, IL, called Big Muddy. With my producing partner and two of the actresses from the film, we all road-tripped to Carbondale to attend the screening. So that's all I did to prepare for that one, hop in the car.

The second was the Oklahoma City screening, which was where we premiered the final cut of the film for cast, crew, and public. For that we had a press screening a couple of weeks before the opening, threw a party for the cast and crew, sent out notices, etc.

The real world premiere was at an LA festival called Dances with Films. We worked hard for that festival, and didn't really get much out of it. The festival directors let me know that we would be responsible for filling the seats, but they also promised many *industry* people and acquisitions folks attended screenings. This festival was really like a series of LA screenings, rather than a real festival...there wasn't a built-in festival audience. We (my producing partner and our lead actress) arrived a few days early to scope it out. The first screening we went to at that fest had four people...my actress, the filmmaker, his publicist, and myself. We realized we would have to pound the pavement — I rented a convertible, covered it in posters, and parked it on The Promenade in Santa Monica. Outfest was going on at the same time, so I made up my little cards with screening info and handed it out to folks standing in ticket lines for Outfest. I called everyone I knew who knew *anyone* in LA and bought tickets for them if they would come. I went to the pier by the theater, and to open air markets holding up posters and shouting about the screening. I also went to as many screenings at Dances with Films as possible to try to find a brotherhood of filmmakers to attend. There is so much going on in LA, it's hard to get people to commit to anything. I ended up getting about seventy-five people for a 2:45 slot on a Wednesday afternoon (including the bellman from my hotel — who gave me his headshot) so I was happy with the numbers. While I was disappointed in the festival, I learned a lot about promoting my film and the importance of learning about a festival before you submit and attend.

What did you do to hype your film?

I did the regular stuff: website, sent out emails, etc. Since my film is about a flower shop, I send out cards in envelopes to local florists with the screening info every time I screen, about two weeks before the screening. This guarantees me a built-in audience of people who will laugh and enjoy themselves. It also gives me high numbers in outside ticket sales, which festivals appreciate!

What kind of promo items did you use to get attention for your film?

I bought floral cards, "Happy Anniversary," "Happy Easter," etc., from a local floral distributor and made labels with screening info to attach to them and scattered them everywhere. As I went to more festivals, I also made small crepe paper flowers to attach to the cards to make them more noticeable. I put a flower on anyone who would hold still. Soon you would see people with *Making Arrangements* flowers hanging from lanyards all over the place.

You received a lot of local press no matter where you showed up with the film. How did you get in newspapers and on television so often — and without a publicist?

One of the first things I learned was that festivals have to publicize themselves as a whole...they don't usually have the time (or the inclination) to promote one specific film. If the festival had a publicity director, I would ask them for permission to contact the local media myself. I would always copy the publicity director on my correspondence and let them know of any interviews I set up. They were always grateful for my work — what promotes my film, promotes the festival as a whole. I also had pretty fun info packs...I painted flowers on the outside of the packages so they stood out. When I contacted a media source, I faxed them my one sheet first and followed up with a phone call the next day asking if I could send out the complete pack (including a BetaSP with clips). Once they got the pack, I tried to get myself or an actor (if I had one) on their show (whether radio or TV) or give them quotes for an article.

There is a fine line between persistence and being a bug. Bugging festivals or media people just gets you classified as a bug. Being professional in appearance and action pays off. Find something unique about your film, your tag line, whatever, and exploit it. For my film, it was all about flowers, so I focused on everything floral I could. Always keep the festival informed of your actions. It keeps them in the loop, makes you look more professional and could get you more exposure since you are staying highly visible to the festival folks.

How important was the screening time for your film?

Very important, and it's something you might not know until you get very close to the festival. I learned to start asking for *good* screening times. What that time is, depends on the festival. If it's a festival with a big audience base of people who are there to see the films — like a SXSW or Cinequest — then an afternoon screening isn't as bad as it might be at a smaller fest.

I like to be at night towards the middle or end of the fest. Being at night means you get regular people coming to your show, and towards the end of the fest, there are more festival people in attendance.

Where does the film stand now in terms of distribution?

So far, we don't have a dance partner. Lots of people have seen the film, but we haven't found the right fit. It's too grown-up for a family type film, but there aren't any boobs or blood, so the more extreme folks can't make it work either.

Sometimes I think getting a 'name' actor would help me sell it, but I love the work the actors did in the film as it stands. Sometimes I think a different storytelling style would have been more interesting, but the film makes a lot of sense, it plays well, and it looks great.

I often think that if I knew then what I know now, I never would have had the guts to make the film. People are so negative about your chances to get a film made, get it seen, etc. You can't learn anything unless you try.

What's the one thing you think filmmakers about to go on the circuit should know?

It's corny but true that you win more flies with honey than vinegar. You go to festivals and you frequently see the same filmmakers over and over. It doesn't pay to piss anyone off. At every festival I went to, there was always at least one filmmaker the festival folks were "dealing" with because they weren't happy with their accommodations, or they wanted better promotion, or whatever. Being a jerk to the festival coordinators won't win you any points. And when they need a filmmaker to run down to do the live remote for the 5 o'clock news, they're going to ask the pleasant, funny chick who's been working her ass off but staying out of everyone's way, as opposed to the guy who's sitting in the festival office whining about how no one is working for him.

GREG PAK

Category:	Narrative Feature
Film:	*Robot Stories*, 90 min.
Logline:	A sci-fi anthology film inspired by the works of Ray Bradbury exploring man's reaction to radical new technologies.
US Premiere:	Hamptons International Film Festival
Screenings:	At SXSW and fifty other festivals
Awards:	Winner of more than thirty awards
Deal:	*Robot Stories* was self-distributed theatrically and grossed a total of $120,109 at the box office over a fifteen-week run, playing in twelve different theaters.

Greg Pak grew up reading Ray Bradbury and Harlan Ellison, watching the *Twilight Zone*, and playing with robot toys. His short film, *Fighting Grandpa,* won twenty prizes, including a Student Academy Award, and played in over fifty film festivals. Greg's comic shorts — *Asian Pride Porn* and *All Amateur Ecstasy* — are among the most viewed films at AtomFilms.com.

Greg Pak
PHOTO BY
PAIGE BARR

Science fiction has always appealed to Greg, particularly Bradbury-esque science fiction, which focuses squarely on the emotional impact of human beings in fantastic situations. The ideas and characters that eventually became the subjects of his first feature, *Robot Stories*, came naturally to him over the years. He says, "As an Asian-American filmmaker, I've always been particularly interested in genre. If you're committed to telling stories that feature people of different races, I think it's a huge bonus to consider working with genre — it gives the film another way to tap into an audience, particularly an audience that might otherwise never think of going to an Asian-American film. Finally, I was very conscious of certain cliches in low-budget American independent filmmaking — the coming-of-age story, the Tarantino-esque crime movie, the romantic comedy, the six-friends-at-a-beachhouse-talking-about-sex movie, etc. I liked the idea of *Robot Stories* because I knew it would stand out from the crowd as an independent Asian-American science fiction anthology film."

Winner of over thirty awards, *Robot Stories* is "science fiction from the heart," in which human characters struggle to connect in a world of robot babies and android office workers. But even after his feature debut became a hit on the festival circuit, the film was not picked up for distribution. Taking risks is not something new to Greg and he boldly decided to self-distribute his film theatrically.

*Did your experience with your short films help prepare you
for the rigors of the festival circuit?*

I'd made about a dozen short films over nine years before I hit the festival circuit with *Robot Stories*. Doing festivals with my shorts helped me immeasurably. First, the shorts helped me establish relationships with dozens of festival programmers. Many of those programmers ended up showing *Robot Stories*. Second, attending so many festivals with my short films helped give me some notion of how these different festivals worked and how I could make the most of them. Third, a good number of press people wrote about my shorts over the years, which predisposed them later to write glowingly about *Robot Stories* in both features and reviews.

What was your approach to festivals with your first feature?

I knew the film could have a great run at the Asian-American film festivals, all of which are amazing and had supported me for years. And I knew that we had a great shot at doing very well in regional film festivals — my short films had played successfully at many great festivals like Cinequest, Florida, the Hamptons, Rhode Island, Santa Barbara, New Haven, and SXSW. But *Robot Stories* is a feature, and with an independent feature, you tend to do festivals in hopes of getting picked up by a distributor. And there are only a handful of festivals where you have a realistic chance of that happening. And those 800 pound gorilla festivals — Toronto, Sundance, Berlin, Cannes — tend to insist upon premieres. So we looked at the calendar and tried to figure out where we wanted to try to premiere. For the most part, we submitted to the big festivals first, then submitted to smaller but nonetheless outstanding festivals second.

We locked picture on the movie in the spring of 2002. In retrospect, we should have sat on the film, finished it completely, and submitted it to Sundance for 2003. But, like far too many filmmakers, I was hungry and impatient — the idea of sitting on the film for nine months drove me nuts. So we began submitting our fine cut to certain festivals, including SXSW, Cannes, Tribeca, Venice, the Los Angeles Film Festival, and Toronto. Honestly, I had no illusions that the film would get into Cannes or Venice. I get the impression that both festivals tend to go for American independents that fall into that kind of "beautiful realism" realm — films like *Raising Victor Vargas*, which is a wholly different vibe from *Robot Stories*. But I figured we had a good shot at many of the others. Alas, we didn't get into any of them, although we were a very near miss for SXSW.

I was beginning to get a little desperate. I was — rightly — angry with myself for the fact that I'd been submitting my video fine cut, without the final music, sound mix, color correction, and tape-to-film transfer, all of which meant that no one had been able to see the film the way it was meant to be seen. I also began to second-guess myself for doing a sneak preview screening at the Los Angeles Asian Pacific Film and Video Festival in May — had we foolishly popped the cherry of our film? Would other festivals consider that to be our world premiere?

Robot Stories was theatrically self-distributed.

In the end, Rajenda Roy, the programmer of the Hamptons International Film Festival, saved us. We submitted the film on a Friday, I believe. He called me on Monday to say he loved the movie and wanted to program it as one of five films in competition. I was thrilled — finally, someone got it! I struggled a bit with the choice — should we play the Hamptons or wait to hear from Sundance? Ultimately, I went for the bird in the hand. And it paid off — we won the Best Screenplay award at the Hamptons, which launched the film in a fantastic way, and eventually got into Slamdance, which gave us yet another premiere of sorts. And, amazingly enough, SXSW accepted us the next year — as did over fifty other film festivals.

Robot Stories *is a science fiction film — how did that impact what festivals you chose to submit to?*

In our big festival strategy, we knew we needed to try to play some first- and second-tier industry festivals before branching out. So it was only after we played the Hamptons and Slamdance that I focused on the science fiction or "fantastic" film festival circuit. There are a few dozen great fantastic film festivals around the world — our first was the Puchon International Fantastic Film Festival in South Korea, one of the most incredible festivals I've ever visited. We won the Best Director and Best Actress (for Wai Ching Ho) awards at Puchon. And within forty-eight hours of the awards ceremony, we'd been invited to three other fantastic film festivals in Europe. The science fiction festivals have been amazing for us — they've gotten us into countries we might not have been able to screen in otherwise, and they've helped us build awareness and credibility among science fiction fans, one of the major target audiences in our theatrical release.

Being an Asian filmmaker and Robot Stories *having a primarily Asian cast, do you think that presented any particular challenges for you?*
I know the Asian thing made it hard for some distributors to wrap their heads around the film. One distributor told my producer that the movie made him feel like he was watching a foreign movie in English. That comment still makes me mad. Some folks still don't get it, sadly enough. But I actually think the fact that we were an Asian-American film was a net advantage on the festival circuit. First, there are a host of great Asian-American festivals across the country that were huge supporters of the film (and, later, of the theatrical release). We were the opening or closing night film at most of them, which is always a tremendous experience.

Robot Stories screened on the following:
- New York - Cinema Village
- Washington, DC - AFI Silver
- Boston/Cambridge - Brattle, Coolidge
- Chicago - Facets
- Los Angeles - Laemmle Fairfax
- Pasadena - Laemmle Old Colorado
- Palm Desert - Cinema d'Or
- Worcester, MA - Bijou
- St. Louis - Landmark Tivoli

Second, I'm willing to guess that the Asian thing, like the science fiction thing, made the film stand out for programmers. If the film was junk, they wouldn't have programed it, period. But the fact that they liked it *and* that it was interestingly diverse probably made many folks even more likely to program it. In certain specific cases, my ethnicity was a huge plus. I think audiences and the press took a special liking to the film partly because I'm half-Korean and had the pride, consciousness, and gumption to make a film in America with Asian people in it.

Do you feel that ethnic-based festivals or programs marginalize ethnic filmmakers, or do they give advantages to filmmakers whose work might not otherwise be seen?

I love the Asian-American film festivals — they were the first festivals to embrace and nurture my work and they've been the first and best places for me to build the Asian-American niche audience for *Robot Stories*. Simultaneously, I've been incredibly aggressive about submitting almost all of my shorts to all kinds of festivals around the world. And those festivals and audiences have responded. We rocked the house at the Asian-American festivals. *And* we've screened around the world, selling out shows everywhere from East Lansing to Dallas to London and winning audience awards from Boston and Michigan to Spain and Sweden. So "marginalization" is a kind of fighting word with me — basically, I'm struggling to refute the industry's predisposition to equate "Asian" with "marginalized." The audiences are ready; the film's winning awards and making money. I'm trying to prove that that "Asian" can mean "niche," and that "niche" can mean dollars and a foundation for crossover success.

Was your experience at the ethnic-based festivals any different than the more broad festivals?

A good festival for filmmakers is a good festival for filmmakers, regardless of its special interest or focus. But it's worth nothing that the Asian-American festivals, for example, were founded by idealists, people who believed deeply in the importance of supporting films by and about Asian people in America. The whole point of the festivals is to nurture emerging filmmakers and connect them with audiences. Many non-ethnic festivals have essentially the same mission of supporting emerging filmmakers — as just one example, the St. Louis International Film Festival has an amazing New Filmmakers program that treats new films and their makers very nicely. But there are a few mainstream festivals out there that seem a little too enamored of their big stars and parties — small fry filmmakers sometimes get treated as an afterthought. In my experience, that's a bit less likely to happen at an ethnically based festival.

What was your secret to getting into so many festivals with
Robot Stories?

I got into the habit of including a cover letter, something I didn't bother doing with my shorts, but I think it made a big difference. If I'd had shorts at the festival before, I'd thank the programmers for showing them, mention how the festival was helpful and wonderful (being sure to thank them for any awards the festival may have given me), and then say I'm very excited to be submitting my first feature film, *Robot Stories*. And I'd give a superquick blurb about the film with our latest scintillating press quote or award. First and foremost, the letter was a way to remind folks that they'd shown my films before, because festivals tend to like showing features from their short film alums. And as I got to know my own film better, the cover letter became another place I could give a little spin about the film. Specifically, at a certain point we realized that if folks were expecting *The Matrix* when they started watching the film, then they wouldn't get it, because things don't blow up. So I started mentioning the influence of classic science fiction writers like Ray Bradbury and using the phrase "science fiction from the heart" wherever I could. I think that helped.

> When I finally learned how to make and burn DVDs on my Mac, we started submitting the film on DVD whenever possible. It just looks *so* much better on DVD, and any edge helps.

I also improved the presentation of the video itself. With my shorts, I had just sent in the tape in a cardboard sleeve with a plain typed label. With *Robot Stories*, I bought full window plastic video boxes and inserted full color sleeves I created in Photoshop and printed on high quality photo paper. In addition to spiffy graphics and the film's tagline (which eventually became *"Everything is changing...Except the human heart"*), the sleeves featured a list of our awards and a few press quotes. Sometimes programmers never see the sleeves, but sometimes they do. And it's another chance to create the right impression and mindset before they start watching the film.

Finally, we created full-on press kits, which included copies of press as well as a CD with stills and our standard materials. Lastly, when I finally learned how to make and burn DVDs on my Mac, we started submitting the film on DVD whenever possible. It just looks *so* much better on DVD, and any edge helps.

Were you concerned about applying to other festivals before you got word from a large festival that you wanted to premiere at?

Yep. This was the big strategic challenge we faced at the beginning of our run. In 2002, I held off on submitting to certain festivals with which I was very friendly because I was waiting to see what would happen with our Sundance/Slamdance applications. I knew we could submit to other festivals the next year if we had to. And that's exactly what happened — at the end of 2003, we played all the friendly festivals that I'd held off at the end of 2002. And since we'd won a ton of awards and gotten some buzz going in the meantime, we were able to get much better placement (opening and closing nights, for example) at those festivals than we would have gotten the year before.

What kind of marketing materials did you use to hype your film?

We'd had a website from the earliest days of preproduction. I'm a big believer in using the Internet to build awareness and credibility for small films. Having a decent website with a synopsis and cast and crew bios helped us get the film made — it reassured cast, crew, vendors, volunteers, location owners, product placement folks, etc., that we were legit.

And from a very early stage, we had a form on the website for people to submit their email addresses and join our mailing list. Over the months, I revamped the website several times, struggling to find the best way to present the film and our vital information, until the site became the promotional powerhouse it is today in pushing our theatrical release. But around the time of our first festival screenings, we'd heard stories about industry types giving indie films short shrift after visiting substandard websites. So until I had the chance to fully redo the site, I reduced it to a single page with our postcard image, contact info, join-the-newsletter form, choice press blurbs, and the latest screening info. At the time, we were concentrating on the targeted audiences visiting key film festivals, not on building a giant general audience through the website. So most of our outreach efforts went into sending emails and faxes to industry people to invite them to see the film, handing out postcards at the festivals, calling and emailing friends and supporters who might be in town, and talking the film up face-to-face at festival events.

Who did your publicity for you?

Laurie Blue handled our publicity for the Los Angeles sneak and the Hamptons premiere. She did a great job, although we tied her hands a bit. It's a strange thing, working publicity at festivals — you want to get enough publicity to get some attention and buzz, but you don't want to blow all of your reviews and feature stories too early — folks who run features on you during a festival run might not do it again during your theatrical, when a feature could be worth thousands in box office receipts.

Laurie got us our *Variety* review out of the Hamptons, which was very positive and perfectly timed for helping us raise the profile of the film and get consideration from other festivals.

When you didn't have a publicist, how did you do it yourself?

We did our own publicity for Slamdance and SXSW. Basically, we did what a publicist would do — compiled big lists of the press scheduled to attend the festivals and sent them emails and faxes with information about the film and a cover letter milking any personal relationship and making specific pitches based on the outlet and the content of the film. For example, I remember emailing you when we were going to screen at Slamdance. FilmThreat.com had published a five star review of my short film *Asian Pride Porn* — I mentioned that and begged you to review *Robot Stories*. Then we met on a shuttle in Park City and made a little personal connection. You guys did indeed review *Robot Stories*. And then later you hooked me up at SXSW with an interview for your Starz show. Just getting the word out and maintaining relationships — I think that's mostly what it's all about. It's also essential to get word out *on time*. I think I did the best job as my own publicist with SXSW — I got the list of press from the festival a month or so ahead of time and emailed everyone twice, I believe, over the course of two weeks. And we got tons of press, including reviews in two publications, two television interviews, and a radio show.

Any advice you'd like to pass on to other filmmakers regarding the creation of hype?

Don't waste your time with embarrassing stunts that might get you press but make you and your film look like a joke. Unless your film is a camp masterpiece for which it makes total sense to dress up like an alien and snowboard down Main Street in Park City, avoid the Troma-esque spectacle. Instead, concentrate on connecting with people at festivals in a normal way — in conversations in line or at parties — making a personal connection and encouraging them to come see the film. Even more importantly, concentrate on inviting the key industry people who you think might actually be interested in your film. Ask other filmmaker friends for advice and contact info; send people faxes and emails inviting them to come see the film. Remember their names so when you bump into them by chance you can encourage them to come see the film. Finally, remember that the only way for hype to work is when people other than you start to talk about the film in a positive way. And the only way for that to happen is for people to come see your film and like it and start talking it up on their own. So it's all about getting people into the theater. Pull favors. Get your friends and family to come, and to bring their friends. Contact groups that may have a special interest in the content of your film. Do your best to pack the house, so there's good audience reaction and the industry folks can see that this is a film with an audience.

> People *love* the buttons and typically put them on immediately upon leaving a screening. Again, it's something that gets seen right then. I'd also recommend *little* buttons. They're cooler, somehow, and more likely to be worn than big 2" or 3" buttons. They're also cheaper.

Regarding the various wingdings and geegaws that folks like to make to plug their films, I'd say avoid spending money on anything people can't use at the actual festival. For Slamdance, we made patches that we sewed onto knit caps — we wanted people to see the name of the film during the course of the festival, and in a cold place like Park City in January, a knit cap might actually get worn. For our theatrical release, we've made thousands of little 1¼" *Robot Stories* buttons with the cartoon robot from our opening credits. People *love* the buttons and typically put them on immediately upon leaving a screening. Again, it's something that gets seen right then. I'd also recommend *little* buttons. They're cooler, somehow, and more likely to be worn than big 2" or 3" buttons. They're also cheaper.

*You went about self-distributing your film, very successfully,
I might add — what led to this decision?*

We played Slamdance and SXSW and the Hamptons and a million
other highly respected festivals, getting fantastic reviews and winning dozens of awards. But we didn't play Sundance or Toronto or
Berlin or Cannes. Which, given the sad realities of the independent
film business, meant that our chances of getting a truly great distribution offer were miniscule. We did get a couple of distribution
offers from small companies. I liked the people very much, but these
were the typical no-advance offers that small companies tend to
make to small independent films without big stars. I would have
loved to have been able to make a deal and say my feature had gotten distribution. But there's no way I could go to my private
investors and say I'd given away the farm for ten to twenty years for
nothing up front.

During our festival run, I'd been pursuing a parallel strategy,
laying the groundwork for a possible self-distribution run by relentlessly collecting email addresses of fans of the film and by making
friends with art house cinema owners who might be interested in
booking the film directly through us. By the time we'd played out
the industry festivals and I realized we'd be hard pressed to find a
distributor willing to give us real money, I'd already found a half a
dozen theaters around the country which were willing to book the
film from me directly. And this wouldn't be a four-walling situation
whereby I'd be renting the theater; this would be a normal theatrical deal whereby I'd get a percentage of the door like any other distributor.

The big clinchers in making the decision came in two stages.
First, at Slamdance, Ed Arentz, who programs the Cinema Village in
New York, saw *Robot Stories*, liked it, and told me he'd book it. So I
knew we had an entirely reputable theater in Manhattan (and just a
ten minute walk from my apartment!) for our New York opening.
Then my friend Arthur Dong, an amazing documentary filmmaker,
introduced me to Sasha Berman. Sasha is an outstanding publicist
who had worked previously as the booker for a number of art house
cinemas across the country — and now she was interested in getting
into distribution. She watched the film, loved it, and we decided to
go into business together to co-distribute the movie.

What made self-distribution the best path for you?

There are a few big questions for anyone thinking about self-distribution:

1. **Do you have the time?** For a small film without a big advertising budget, a huge amount of grassroots outreach is necessary to get the word out. And successful outreach almost always depends upon the personal presence of the filmmaker. I knew I had at least a six month window in 2004 during which I wouldn't be in production or pre-production for a new movie; one big reason our self-distribution run was possible is that I committed to make myself available as much as possible during those four months to promote the theatrical release.

2. **Is there a real audience for your film — specifically, are there niche audiences you can reach for little or no money?** Of course, we all believe there's an audience for our films and that the distribution executives who have passed us by just don't get it. But for a self-distribution run to work, you have to actually *prove* it by getting folks to pony up the cash to see the movie. With *Robot Stories*, we targeted three core audiences — Asian-Americans, science fiction fans, and traditional art house theater goers. In retrospect, I'm realizing that we absolutely needed all three of those niches to make the splash we've been making. If we'd only had one of those three niches, we would have gotten a third or less of the audience, and we'd be losing money. So a film with multiple niches, while confusing to Hollywood types, can be a big win in limited or self-distribution.

3. **Can you get the money?** We're a totally bare bones operation, truly skin of our teeth. But there are certain unavoidable costs involved in distributing a feature film. I took out a loan for $50,000 to make this possible. Kind of scary. But it's already looking likely that we'll pay back that loan, and hopefully make a little money on top of that. Nonetheless, it's a big decision to take that kind of risk when you're already in the hole for however much your film cost.

How has the film performed at the box office?

We've had tremendous success — in our opening weekend in New York, we were the fourth highest grossing movie per screen in the country. Of course, we were only on one screen. But the numbers we racked up — almost $12,000 — and the reviews and features we scored were all astounding for a small, self-distributed picture. We went on to screen five weeks in Manhattan. And we've had very successful runs in Boston, DC, and Los Angeles — so far, it looks like we'll make money in every city in which we've played, which is pretty amazing. And all of this has been due to several things. First, we've had tremendous grassroots support — dedicated volunteers and friends and organizations have helped spread the word to our niche audiences. Second, we've had great press — Sasha has done an amazing job, scoring several almost unheard of coups, including getting me on NPR's *Fresh Air*. Third, my producers (Karin Chien and Kim Ima) and I have traveled as much as possible with the film, doing Q&As and special events, making friends, handing out materials, and collecting email addresses. Fourth, we have a tremendous Internet operation. We constantly collect email addresses, both in person and via our website, and send out weekly newsletters telling folks where the film is playing, what our latest press and awards are, and begging folks to get their friends out to see the movie. And I've actively encouraged bloggers to write about the film — we have our own Robot Blog on the website and frequently link to our pals' websites. All of these things together have helped us score standout numbers in most places we've played.

But we've had a handful of towns where we haven't done nearly as well as we would have liked. What I'd do differently is not necessarily accept every offer. We don't have the money to do big ads. So if a town doesn't have local press that supports independent film, and we don't have a natural constituency in the area (i.e., no college or arts community or community groups that we can contact to help us get word out to our niche audiences), it's very hard for us to do good business. Also, we've learned that there are some theaters in some towns which just don't do good business in general. We've been the top-grossing film in some theaters, but the numbers have still been totally depressing. Venue matters. Finally, when dealing with small theaters in particular, print traffic can become an issue. Print traffic arrangements need to be checked and double-checked and confirmed — otherwise you get into silly situations like we did last week when a print we thought had been shipped the week before was still sitting in someone's back room — and we ended up having to pay $200 to overnight it. Not the kind of mistake a small distribution effort like ours likes to waste money on.

Get more on Greg at www.robotstories.net and www.gregpak.com He is also is the editor of FilmHelp.com and AsianAmericanFilm.com

ADRIENNE WEHR

Category:	Narrative Feature
Film:	*The Bread, My Sweet*, 90 min.
Logline:	This romantic drama stars Scott Baio as man trapped between career, love, and family.
US Premiere:	Santa Monica International Film Festival
Screenings:	Played more than twenty festivals
Awards:	Winner of nine Festival Awards
Deal:	Distribution through Panorama Entertainment for limited theatrical grossing $1 million at the box office, DVD, and home video release through Universal Studios and Screen Media Films

Adrienne Wehr spent ten years as Associate Producer of the Emmy-award winning *Mister Rogers' Neighborhood*. Adrienne became involved with *The Bread, My Sweet* when writer and director Melissa Martin proposed the concept while the two worked on a play together at the Toronto Fringe Festival. She was immediately taken with the heartwarming script. "I loved flinging biscotti in the Strip District of Pittsburgh and I loved the screenplay. It was the type of story that is not often seen in film these days...a true mirror of humanity. It made me laugh and it made me cry."

The Bread, My Sweet Producer Adrienne Wehr and Director Melissa Martin.

Having worked mostly in television and theater, she had never produced a feature before, but agreed to help Melissa. *The Bread, My Sweet* is a charming love story starring Scott Baio in a surprisingly touching performance. As the producer, Adrienne guided the film to a successful festival run leading to a profitable limited theatrical release.

Did you have a strategy when you went about submitting to festivals?

We started with Sundance and then applied to all the other "top tier" fests. We didn't get into a single one, since we didn't fully understand the true lay-of-the-land of those particular fests. So we then set our sights on the "second tier" festivals, which were absolutely the right kind of fests for our film. We won the top award at our very first festival, the Santa Monica International Film Festival, and then swept the top two awards at our next fest, Worldfest-Houston, where we met our future distributor, Panorama Entertainment. From that meeting on, in a show of good faith since we didn't yet have a deal with them, Panorama submitted our film to multiple fests that we went on to play and where we garnered more awards. We did end up submitting to Sundance twice more over the next two years, because we still could have qualified for the American Spectrum category. But even with our screener and application being hand-delivered and well-hyped by a festival insider, we still didn't make the cut.

How did you target certain second tier festivals?

When we were submitting on our own, we sought out fests that had solid reputations, some that happened to be in industry-oriented markets. Oh, and let's not forget location, location, location. Who doesn't want to go to Sedona, AZ; Sonoma Valley, CA; or Marco Island, FL? When Panorama started submitting our film, they focused on similar target points but also submitted the film to fests that took place in markets where we hoped to open theatrically. Nothing works better to launch a theatrical run of a film — that lacks a large ad/marketing budget — than a positive word-of-mouth screening at a fest. A beautiful example of this took place in Kansas City, where we played the Halfway to Hollywood Film Festival [which has since been renamed the Kansas International Film Festival] and accomplished a major publicity tour while in town with Scott Baio, thanks to both the festival director and festival programmer. The audiences loved it, which indicated to the theater owners that they should run it theatrically. *The Bread, My Sweet* ended up playing in Kansas City theaters for months and months, and then returned yet again for a repeat theatrical run. Don't ever underestimate the power of a festival screening to launch a limited theatrical release.

How did you get into so many strong regional festivals?

We embraced the worth and value of the smaller fests and focused on them solely, especially the competitive ones. When submitting on our own, we had people who were connected to certain fests speak on our film's behalf and we wrote some "big beg" letters to certain festival programmers. When Panorama submitted our film, they were able to speak directly to the festival directors on behalf of our film. After building up a positive reputation, our film was then invited to screen at some festivals without having to go through the traditional submission process.

What did you do to hype your film?

We did a massive amount of e-mailing and phone calling. We would go on to develop a website which has proven to be an incredibly useful marketing tool. The sooner in the process you develop your website, the better.

We hired a publicist *after* our premiere to help us with future festivals, gain the attention of distributors, etc. However, keeping this publicist on retainer for three months was a total waste of money. She did little to nothing to support our film, and tried to charge us additional money to write a press release — evidently that was not included in her very steep retainer. After three months of non-work and money wasted, we released her. It's absolutely not necessary to hire a publicist for these smaller fests. Many of the festivals have their own publicists who will be willing to work with you if you just ask.

For the premiere and throughout the festival circuit, we were the queens of garnering publicity on the grassroots level. Lots of taking it to the streets — talking to people, handing out postcards and tiny bags of biscotti, partnering with local businesses; getting print, TV, and radio interviews; doing ticket giveaways; inspiring friends, family, and colleagues in every festival

The Bread, My Sweet poster used during its theatrical run. Poster design by Robert E. Bupp.

market to hype the film and spread the good word; simply doing anything and everything to get the word out.

I can honestly say that we turned into savvy publicists throughout the festival circuit and on into our theatrical run. If we weren't interested in making more films, we could start a PR firm, and I encourage all indie filmmakers to get that good at this. You'll love the results.

Any advice you'd like to pass on to other filmmakers regarding the creation of hype?

You must learn to deal with the media right off the bat. You don't need to hire a publicist to support your film at these smaller festivals, you simply have to be aggressive about targeting the key figures in print, radio, and TV who might be the right candidates to do feature coverage of your film. Be inventive on all fronts. Create a memorable give-away. Our bags of biscotti are what led our distributor to attend a screening of our film at Worldfest-Houston. Partner up with local businesses that have an obvious tie-in to your film. We did lots of partnering throughout the country with bakeries (the central action of our film takes place in a bakery) and with Italian-American organizations and districts.

Always have a second and possibly third angle to pitch to the media. For example, if the film writers or on-air film commentators were too busy hyping other product, we would turn to the food writers and or local on-air cooking show hosts to cover our film, because it's a "food film." This type of strategy is smart and it works. We also pitched the "chick filmmaking team" angle because that's who we are and that often sets us apart from the other filmmakers. Be not afraid to blow your own horn in fun, creative, and sophisticated ways.

Do you feel that having recognizable actors in your movie gave you a distinct advantage?

Yes! If you have name actors who are willing to attend the fest, then you, your film, and your actors will become the darlings of that festival. The festival publicists will be much more willing to support your film because the media always gives preference to the films with name actors in them, who may be attending the fest and be available for interviews. When Scott Baio joined us, we often ended up doing full-blown PR tours in certain festival markets, fully arranged by the festival publicist. This did not cost us a dime, yet made for incredibly valuable PR for the film. Treat your actors well and they in turn will want to extend themselves to support the film by attending festivals and making themselves available for interviews and photo ops. It's a win-win for all...the festival, the actors, your film, and you.

You ended up being distributed by Panorama Entertainment. Like a lot of smaller companies, Panorama offers no up-front advance. What are the advantages and/or disadvantages for this type of deal?

No bones about it, no advance *is* a drag, but this was the only company that was offering us a theatrical release, so it was worth it for us to do this deal. In lieu of an advance, they did agree to front the costs for the deliverables that we had not yet completed (and had no money left to complete). That helped us out at the time, and Panorama was eventually reimbursed for those expenses from box office earnings.

In the end, was this kind of theatrical release worth it?

The theatrical was a tremendous amount of hard work and extended itself over two years, but that hard work and platform-style release has paid off on many levels. Because of the success of the theatrical, the film has been released by Universal Studios and Screen Media Films on DVD/video and is selling and renting strong. Most likely these companies would not have even sneezed at our product had it not already proven its worth in theaters. Because the theatrical grossed over $1 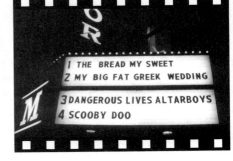 million in total box office, the film now becomes a much more valuable commodity in the foreign marketplace. We are waiting to see the ultimate results of those sales. Also, due to the release, we are now proven filmmakers, which positions us quite differently for our next project.

Any advice you can pass along about this particular type of distribution deal?

Before settling with a distributor, make certain you have investigated them thoroughly. Ask for filmmaker referrals and talk to all of those referrals, but also hunt out other filmmakers who weren't necessarily on that list. One distribution company, that courted us quite heavily, turned out to be producers and distributors of soft porn — and that's something we dug up in the eleventh hour. There's no way we were going to allow our film to exist alongside some of the other titles in their library.

You must have really good legal representation. Don't fool yourself into thinking that you can negotiate your own distribution deal. A truly sharp entertainment attorney is the only way to go here.

> You're going to encounter seemingly straight-shooters as well obvious jerks; trust no one.

If your distributor requires the option to contract out to sub-distributors, set contractual limits on the distribution fee you, as owner, are willing to pay out to both your primary distributor and sub-distributor in such arrangements. Make certain that your primary distributor holds to those terms when negotiating with sub-distributors. Even better, strive for contractual permission to review all agreements that your primary distributor makes with sub-distributors *before* they are signed. This way, you can be certain your primary distributor is honoring all terms set forth in your agreement with them, in respect to sub-distribution.

With a platform-style theatrical release, be prepared for a long wait for any return to your production company. A theatrical release is very expensive, and while it may end up paying for itself, it may not pay your production company a single dime. That's why it's extremely important to make sure that any deals made for foreign, DVD/video, and TV sales are fair and in your best interest so that you can make some of your money back in those arenas.

Do your best to stay atop the collection process. This is a tough one because there is tremendous room for creative accounting to take place at any time, starting with the box office clerk at that indie theater all the way through the many other hands along the way. You're going to encounter seemingly straight-shooters as well obvious jerks; trust no one. This is a business and the bottom line is that lots of people are out to make money by exploiting your product.

Don't simply sit back and be thrilled that your film is out there. You've got to protect your company and uphold your fiduciary responsibility to your investors in all ways possible.

Finally, if you don't want your primary distributor or any of your sub-distributors to change the title or a single frame of your film, *get that in writing in your contract.* Our film was released theatrically as *The Bread, My Sweet* but our DVD/Video releaser changed the title to *A Wedding for Bella* as a marketing strategy. It's not as if we were married to our original title because we would have gladly changed it prior to the start of our theatrical — but after branding it as *The Bread, My Sweet* for two years in the theaters (and that doesn't even count the year on the festival circuit) we were truly concerned for the loyal fan base who had been waiting patiently for the release on DVD/Video. In the end, we conceded after our releaser agreed to certain conditions which included listing *The Bread, My Sweet* on the package as a subtitle, the development of a page regarding the DVD/Video release for our website, alerting major retailers to cross-reference both titles in their computer systems, press releases that spoke to the title change, and — finally — leaving our opening credits, which include our original title, intact. The good news is that their marketing strategy has worked and we're finding a wider audience with this new title, and it appears as if *Bread* fans are catching on to the title change. When the film is released on cable and in foreign markets, it will be once again as *The Bread, My Sweet.*

Were you prepared for the kind of committment necessary to get this film out there?

This first time out, we had no real idea how long or how hard we would work all the way through post, the festival year, as well as distribution. When devising your production budget, plan ahead for a potentially long-term commitment on the part of the principals within your production company, in our case that's Melissa and me, and set salaries to be paid out over that long term. We started fundraising in 1999, produced the film in 2000, hit the gates running with a release print in January 2001, and here we are in 2004, *still* working on this project in its third year of distribution. If you asked us in 1999 if we thought we'd still be toiling diligently on this one in 2004, we would have said, "No way!" The last and only time we paid ourselves a consistent salary was during our one month of pre-production, and twenty-three days of shooting back in May and June of 2000. We will never, ever agree to compromise ourselves in that way again. There's no need to throw yourself on your sword and end up being volunteers to the cause just because you have a small budget. Remember, this is a business and you are now artist/entrepreneurs. Your time and energy are valuable. Embrace that and pay yourself your due if you plan to shepherd your project all the way thru its potentially long and drawn out journey.

Learn more about the film at www.thebreadmysweet.tv

LISA FRANCE

Category:	Narrative Feature
Film:	*Anne B. Real*, 90 min.
Logline:	A teen living in the inner city is inspired by *The Diary of Anne Frank* as she pursues her rap dreams.
US Premiere:	Pan African Film Festival
Screenings:	At Newport Beach Festival, American Black Film Festival, Zanzibar in Africa, Digifest in Berlin, Filmstock in London, and forty others
Awards:	Nominated for an IFP Independent Spirit Award and winner of several festival awards
Deal:	*Anne B. Real* is distributed by Screen Media Ventures and Universal Pictures Home Video, sold for an undisclosed sum

Lisa France

Lisa France's start came as the filmmaker behind the award-winning short *Love in Tow*, which screened at The Atlanta Film and Video Film Festival. From there it traveled across the ocean to London where it won Best Comedy at FilmStock International Film Festival. Lisa's first feature, *Anne B. Real*, is about a young African American girl whose rap songs are inspired by the *Diary of Anne Frank*. While *Anne B. Real* never played a major festival, it won top honors at the Santa

Monica International Film Festival, the Pan African, the Sedona International Film Festival, The American Black Film Festival, and Urban World among many others. Lisa's successful festival run took her to more than forty film festivals in twelve countries on four continents around the world. As co-writer and director, she received a nomination for an Independent Spirit Award for her work on *Anne* in the category of films made for under $500,000. The film went on to sell to Universal Pictures Home Video where it turned a respectable profit.

What inspired you to make Anne B. Real? *I mean, how did you come up with a story about a young black girl who aspires to be a rap artist?*

To take the life of a contemporary girl living in the ghetto and commingle it with the life of Anne Frank was quite a task to take on with respect to both worlds. To make a modern urban film with no derogatory language, no sex, and no gratuitous language was a serious challenge. The more people said we couldn't do it, of course, the more we were compelled to. The outcome was as inspiring as the actual process of making the film. In the end, I was very proud of what we had done. We made the flick for $100,000 and it looks like a hell of a lot more than that — and the message is beautiful.

Did you have a strategy when you went about submitting the movie to festivals?

We had the same strategy most filmmakers have — *get into Sundance.* We did not get into Sundance and to this day people who see our film cannot believe it. So immediately you think, "Now what?" After being rejected by Sundance, the Los Angeles Film Festival invited *Anne* to be a premiere in June. We made a rash choice and we went with the Pan African Film Festival in February instead. As wonderful a festival as PAFF is; it is not LAFF. LA holds a lot of weight in the festival world and we should have held our horses, but there was a lot of pressure from our investors and questions as to whether or not waiting was a good idea. In the end we threw the dice. We didn't loose, but we didn't win big. If I could roll back time, I would have waited for LAFF.

Anne B. Real *is an ethnic film, how did this impact what festivals you chose to submit to?*

Anne really crosses over every single demographic you can imagine. We submitted to every major festival. And after we played and won the first three festivals we were in; then we were invited to all kinds of festivals all over the world and were well received everywhere. I don't think, with our film, the "ethnic" thing really plays. Because Dean Parker composed such an amazing classical score, there is no offensive language, and because the film is narrated with Anne Frank and Otto Frank's words, the films has a wide open appeal. We had all white audiences give standing ovations and all black and Hispanic audiences do the same. Sure, we have been immediately requested by hip hop, black, and Latin film festivals, but not only them — damn, we *won* The Dubrovnik Film Festival in Croatia — tell me that isn't outside the urban box?

Did being a female director present any challenges in getting the film into festivals?

Maybe I'm an optimist, but I think the gender issues are about over. Now we, meaning women, need to persevere. I think women tend to give up more than men do. I hate generalizing, but I have noticed that men tend not to respond with weight over losses or rejection like women do. They just keep going. Women tend to take things a bit more personally and I really think that's just a matter of not being used to the repeated rejection that happens in this business. I tend to let myself hurt for about a minute and then move on. If women want to continue to be taken seriously as filmmakers, they have to keep making films no matter what.

Did you target women and/or ethnic film programs or festivals?

We really didn't have to do anything. The black, Hispanic, and hip hop festivals tracked us down.

A friend of mine, Kevin, had helped out a little on the Bermuda Film Festival and suggested we apply. I told him to see if he could get the application fee waived and put in a good word for us, then we would submit. So he did what he could and so did we. We didn't get in, but at least we didn't have to pay the fee. Those fees add up. If you are a festival darling, like *Anne* became on a small level, then you should try to get out of the submission fees. 100 submissions later you're out a good $5,000.

Also, we started getting a lot of calls for festivals. You have to be very careful about "premieres." We couldn't be in Chicago or LA because we were not going to be a premiere for them. So before you accept going to a festival, find out their rules on premiering and what other festivals in the same state or area you might want to show in because they might have rules about world, state, or regional premieres.

> If you are a festival darling, like *Anne* became on a small level, then you should try to get out of the submission fees. 100 submissions later you're out a good $5,000.

It's also important to stay on top of the schedule. The last thing you want to end up with is a 9 A.M. slot when you have a horror film. There are so many things to consider, but time slot is very important because you want people to see your film, not sleep through it.

When you realized you would not be premiering at Sundance or another big festival, how did you change your strategy?

The strategy went by the wayside. We just started playing all over the place. We really blew it by not doing Los Angeles. It's really that simple. We went to fests that we knew were right for our film and fests that would fly us in and give us a good schedule.

> There are so many things to consider, but time slot is very important because you want people to see your film, not sleep through it.

How did you prepare for your premiere screening?

We premiered at the Pan African Film Festival and didn't do much. We had postcards and a website, but nothing too exciting. We had press kits at our first distribution screening and then made them available for all the festivals, but we were so broke we didn't even have a poster made! It was bad. ATTENTION ALL FILMMAKERS: *Save money for the marketing of your film or no one will ever see it except your mom and dad!* We relied on the festival publicity folks to work hard for us. Which is a silly thing to do — if there is anything we learned, it's that a festival needs to look out for its own best interest.

I highly suggest getting a publicist early on in the venture. Have someone cover the shooting of your film if you can. Then, while you are in post-production, keep a lid on it. Once you're finished — get your publicist on it again! Eventually, for the Spirit Awards, we hired Heidi Slan at PMK.

We got lucky right away because we won our first few film festivals. *Variety* has been very kind. I've done a few little interviews here and there as a result of being at the film festivals. We also were lucky with a little company called Film Buzz — they did a wonderful bit of test marketing and graphs for *Anne*; they were so beautiful and really gave us a sense of who our audience members were and what they thought of the film.

How did the Spirit Award nomination influence interest in the film?

It has been significant to say the least. Winning would have been helpful, but being nominated doesn't suck. We love the IFP and they have been such champions of our little baby, thus it was an honor to be there and represent. I have, again, had a few little meetings for things, but nothing big.

> Winning would have been helpful, but being nominated doesn't suck.

Right now though I can't get a free bowl of soup with any one of the awards we have gotten — and I *have* tried. It's really up to you to capitalize on them. The festival did their job; they gave the award. It's now your turn to convert that award into something...I'm still waiting for my soup....

What made direct to video the best distribution path for you? Were the distribution deals you were offered simply so bad that doing it yourself became the best alternative?

There is no such thing as a "direct to video" deal being the "best" distribution path for anyone unless they make porn. "Direct to video" is what happens after you don't get a theatrical release. If you are not going to make it to the big screen, then you take a video deal. Screen Media has been great because they were still open to helping the film get to the big screen, should someone come along and want to take it there.... We were very lucky to get them to partner with us.

I'm satisfied in comparison to other filmmakers, but in general I feel we let our audiences down. People begged us not to go to video. So many people tried to support our film, but to no avail. I'm satisfied that our investors will get their money back. The actors will get paid. Those with deferred payments will likely be paid, but I don't know if I will ever see a dime. I really don't care about the money — I just want to make another film and I want the people who believed in me to get their investments back.

FROM THE ARCHiVES

JOE CARNAHAN, Writer/Director

Joe Carnahan's debut feature film, *Blood, Guts, Bullets & Octane (BGB&O)*, tells a gruesome tale of three fast-talking used car salesmen who stumble upon a car wanted by every hit man in the country. Carnahan was working at a tiny local television station, struggling at a nowhere job, shooting his film on weekends. The entire movie was shot for less than $8,000 — and he did it all while balancing the responsibilities of family life with a wife and two kids! The gutsy filmmaker just woke up

Writer/ director Joe Carnahan (left) and actor/ producer Dan Leis at the IFFM where they made a remarkable impression, which helped get them into Sundance.

and decided to do it; the result is a fast-paced debut oozing with creativity. *BGB&O* played the midnight slot at the 1998 Sundance Film Festival and later sealed a distribution deal with Lions Gate; *BGB&O* was recently released in a special edition DVD from Universal Home Video.

Joe went on to receive critical acclaim for his second feature, the harrowing crime drama *Narc*, which debuted at Sundance and went onto a successful theatrical run through Paramount Pictures. Joe earned high marks for the film's gritty look and the stellar performances from Ray Liotta and Jason Patric. Currently, he is attached to direct another crime drama for Paramount/Dreamworks and has another project in the works at Universal. With all this Hollywood success, Joe is still a straight shooter who has not forgotten his indie roots. So how does one go from an $8,000, 16mm indie movie to a $100 million studio picture in six years?

How does a filmmaker successfully apply to Sundance and gain acceptance?

Network like a sonofabitch. Anybody who believes that simply mailing in a VHS tape and a check for forty bucks will guarantee democratic privilege in the judging process is completely deluded. Don't be afraid to approach people like Geoff Gilmore or John Cooper or any of the programming staff if you see them at a festival or some other indie gathering. We have a tendency to deify these people and put them on a pedestal. Keep in mind a very basic precept — without the films to make the festivals, these people would be out of work. So strap on the same set of balls you used when you broke your ass for months on end to make your film in the first place; walk up to them and introduce yourself. If you fancy yourself the shy, inhibited, introspective type, let me tell you, that will get you about as far as the front door.

How did you find out you were in Sundance?

I was in the trenches, pulling an all night edit since we were still doing our AVID cut for the lab. My wife called in a frenzy, saying John Cooper had just phoned. I called, and Cooper confirmed that *BGB&O* was in.

Almost nine months earlier, our producer's rep — the dazzling, debonair, Patrick Lynn — had a fleeting confab with Geoff Gilmore in Toronto, and Geoff basically told Patrick that he intended to program the film. Even knowing that, we couldn't relax until we got "real" confirmation. Usually the festival programmers, particularly in Sundance, are notoriously tight-lipped about their line-up. Nothing short of the rack and razor blades around the ear can pry that priceless inside skinny from the staff.

What other festivals did you apply to?

Toronto tossed us very early on, and that was tough to swallow, but after Sundance, we were carpet-bombed with fest invites. My favorite was Berlin, hands down. It is the most structurally sound festival on the face of the planet. You could drop D-Day on that festival and it would still run as smoothly as a finely-tuned engine. Next Wave films, run by the esteemed prince of indie print, Peter Broderick, was our partner in crime since they kicked in, along with IFC/BRAVO, the necessary monies to finish the film in 35mm. They were really instrumental in landing a lot of festival attention.

Were you concerned about applying to other festivals before you got word from Sundance?

No. Primarily because I believe that it is fundamentally inane to put that much into a single film festival, even the great and almighty

Sundance. Everybody says how Sundance frowns on playing other festivals before you play theirs. While there is no arguing a preference for North American premieres and debuts in the festival, there were plenty of films that had played previously in Toronto and other big festivals prior to their Sundance dates. If your film is good enough, it's not going to be ignored.

What did you do to hype your film at Sundance?
The same way we hyped it everywhere else. We gathered en masse and marched through the streets of Park City like a parade of thugs — wearing parkas emblazoned with the film's logo, shoving it in everybody's face, creating a maelstrom of hype — getting that critical "buzz" going early and all the rest of that requisite catchphrase stuff. I openly despise and deplore ham-handed marketing techniques — the notion of jamming something down peoples' throats ad nauseum — unfortunately, the film business doesn't give you the option of subtlety. Sometimes you have to forsake your better judgment and basic common decency and just get it done...hawking your wares come hell or high water. Now, I'm not saying run up, jump on Harvey Weinstein's back, and blast your film's synopsis in his ear with a bullhorn; I *am* saying stop just short of that.

What would you have done differently in preparing for your film's debut?
I would've gotten a much earlier jump on the extensive post-production work that had to be done. This is the kind of thing you don't want to delay. Unfortunately, my lawyer and other lawyers were off doing their "lawyering" — a process requiring you to sit on your hands for weeks at a time, waiting for contractual crap to clear and a bunch of other fascinating bits of tedium that have miraculously little to do with filmmaking. I really can't say I would have changed a thing, because the PR machine we were able to put together at that point, as well as Amy Taubin's glowing review in *The Village Voice,* really put everything on track.

How can other filmmakers create the much-needed hype for their own films?
Number One, get your film into a forum where it can be shown on a screen. This means a place like the Independent Feature Film Market (IFFM), held annually in New York. This is the single best

place to develop a platform for your film. They have a marvelous staff of people who will really go the distance for you if they believe in your work. I missed the deadline for the '97 IFFM by more than a month, but because they really believed in the film, they found me a slot. This was primarily the work of two fabulous souls, Milton Tabbot and Sharon Sklar. Once you get there, adopt a style that suits your personal preference and acts in the movie's best interest. You can be obnoxious, overbearing, and pushy in a very subtle and effective way if you tailor your marketing plan to your strengths as well as your shortcomings. If you don't do well speaking to other people, or you stumble or stutter or stammer or whatever, find someone in your group who *does not do these things*. Make *that person* the point person for public relations. Understand that this is a temporary arrangement since at some point you will be required — nay, *obligated* — to speak on behalf of your work because you are the filmmaker. So beat back the bashfuls and get verbal.

Get as many press people on board as possible. If you have some outside connection or some way of getting a tape to a local critic or movie reviewer or features editor, get it to them. For me, two people were absolutely instrumental early on: Mark Ebner, formally of *Spy* Magazine and Lisa Derrick from *New Times LA*. I met them both online and they agreed to view the tape; both were jazzed about the film's prospects. They provided gutsy praise and some stellar copy for the one-sheet. I owe them both a tremendous debt since it was their initial reviews that paved the way for Amy Taubin's and others. So far, I have yet to meet Lisa in person, and it just goes to show you, you don't have to live next door to these people to get them your film.

Just don't be afraid. Don't shy away from contact and do what you need to do to make your point. There are thousands of filmmakers out there willing to do the necessary things to sell their film. Set yourself apart as much as possible, do the unusual and the extreme and ignore the whispers.

Were you nervous at the first screening?
I was more agitated than nervous because I knew the audience was not going to be seeing the film the way I intended. I sat out in the hall outside the Park City library looking at my six-month-old son and hoping the freaking roof wouldn't fall in on me and my career.

I dealt with it by staying as loose as I could and joking with my brother Matt who, like the best of the bomb squad, can always take the tension off and clip the right wires. Bob Hawk, my hero, introduced the film and that helped, too. Bob was a huge fan and his high praise for the film went miles toward calming me down and helping me focus.

What did you learn from that first screening?

That I had homicidal impulses where sound designers are concerned. That a library is just that, a library, and therefore not acoustically kind. And that what I did in two months I should have stretched over six months. And finally, that films should never start after midnight unless they have "Rocky," "Horror" or "Picture Show" in the title.

What did you do to get acquisition executives into your screenings?

That was more Patrick Lynn's doing. He, in concert with my wonderful agent Neil Friedman, drummed up early support for the film, months before the festival. We already had an idea that Lions Gate was going to come on strong — which was great since most in the business believe that Lions Gate will soon surpass October Films as the heir of the Miramax throne. Lions Gate also has a history of brilliantly handling small films like *The Daytrippers* and *The Pillow Book,* so this was a thrilling proposition for me.

Who negotiated the deal?

Neil Friedman primarily, who is truly a brilliant man. He and Patrick worked the seams to get me the best possible deal. Lions Gate put the offer on the table one week after Sundance.

What did you look for in the deal?

A company that I knew could put the film in play, which Lions Gate can so clearly do. Also, I wanted to work with guys like Mark Urman and Tom Ortenberg at a young company that is clearly going places. This was as exciting as anything else since we knew how much Mark loved the film and how doggedly he would push it. They gave us a great backend deal and a pretty substantial advance, so I was ecstatic.

The deal went for a modest six figure sum with great ancillary perks. Like $50,000 bumps as the film surpassed certain gross revenues. Remember, when a company, particularly one as upstart as Lions Gate, takes a flyer on a $7,300 film, there ain't much they can do wrong as it pertains to a relationship with their filmmakers. They even assumed the costly "Errors & Omissions" insurance and agreed to pay for the MPAA rating because they knew how little money we had. Those expenses alone more than doubled the film's original budget.

Any advice on getting the distribution deal?

Yeah — don't show the film to *anybody* who has *anything* to do with acquisitions. If distributors are going to see your film, it's best that they all see it at the same time. It's what is known as an "Acquisitions Screening" and it's done all the time in Los Angeles. Press is one thing — you need that. That's a risk you have to assume, but try to preface all conversations with potential reviewers with the request that they not show the tape around. They're going to do it anyway, but you still want to try to contain it. When you send your film in to an agency, they will almost immediately make copies of the film if they like it. They do this almost as a reflex, so at some point it's really out of your hands as to who is seeing your film. But, do your best to contain it early. In my own experience, it came to light that a rather powerful, prominent indie agent, one who reps some pretty big names, got a hold of my tape, liked it, and without my permission, passed it on to some distribution companies. He may have thought he was doing me a favor, but he wasn't and he should have known better. Guard your film. I sent mine out to only three people at the outset. One of them, Patrick Lynn, went on to rep my film. I sent my fourth out to DDA, which gave the copy to Neil Friedman, and he instantly became my agent. From that standpoint, I was fortunate.

Any advice on handling press?

Yeah, watch your ass...and keep that switchblade taped to your ankle. Understand that the people interviewing you can put whatever spin on whatever word of yours they choose. I got interviewed by this punk kid from *Variety* and thought I was coming off humble, gregarious, and generally happy to be there. What he wrote down and more importantly, put in print, made me look like a colossal ass and consequently blew my whole notion of "objective" journalism sky high. Press people want three things: funny shit, semi-scandalous shit, or shit that makes you look like you were eating Top Ramen noodles and living in a shoebox prior to making your debut film. That's it. Look at most print media about festivals and its participants and you'll find those tenets are absolutely true. You can be all bright-eyed and bushy-tailed, just so long as your answers aren't.

JOAL RYAN, Writer/Director

For each success story of filmmakers like Darren Aronofsky, Richard Linklater, and Robert Rodriguez, there are hundreds, perhaps thousands of failures. Unfortunately, while the press heaps attention on the chosen ones, the losers, the filmmakers who didn't quite make it, are left with nothing but hard lessons — learned most often in the form of a mountain of credit card debt, an unsold film and worse, an unfulfilled dream. Regrettably, these lessons are rarely passed on to those who could really use the information — first-time filmmakers ready to make their movie and enter the festival meat grinder. One such tale of woe is that of Joal Ryan.

Writer/
director
Joal Ryan

Joal Ryan is a journalist-turned-filmmaker. Her debut indie feature, *Former Child Star,* failed to get into Sundance, Slamdance, Slumdance, or Slamdunk; failed to get much good press, failed to launch her film career or get her the elusive three-picture deal; the movie itself failed to sell. Since her unheralded debut as a filmmaker, Joal has poured her considerable thoughts on the subject of TV former child stars into a book on real TV former child stars, *Former Child Stars: The Story of America's Least Wanted* (ECW Press, 2000), a groundbreaking treatise on pop culture, celebrity and, yes, Gary Coleman. Her website, *Former Child Star Central* (www.formerchildstar.net), has been featured on CNN and reviewed in *Movieline, Newsweek,* and *Entertainment Weekly.* She is self-distributing her movie *Former Child Star* through her site where a VHS copy can be purchased for only $13. Ryan is also the author of the biographical tribute *Katharine Hepburn: A Stylish Life* (St. Martin's Press, 1999), and *TV Poetry: A Collection of Television Verse* (TV Books, 2001), which is exactly what it sounds like — haiku, limericks and free verse about *Dawson's Creek, Gilligan's Island,* and the lot.

Joal is also working on a screenplay which will only be committed to film, "if somebody actually buys the stupid thing."

Showing tremendous vulnerability, Ryan documents every single mistake she made along the way. She details, with refreshing honesty and a rare flair for the truth, the trials and tribulations of making her first indie feature.

How did you begin the process of making your film?
I put an ad in *Drama-Logue,* the Los Angeles casting magazine. *Former Child Star* was, more or less, official. I was going to make a movie — a real one, with film and everything.

I was twenty-eight. A journalist. A film buff with no "official" film background. A magazine subscriber with one too many clipped-out articles about Kevin Smith. Inspired by the do-your-own-movie movement, I'd shot a 67-minute flick on Hi-8 video the year before called *How to Make a Generation X Movie*. And that project was how I came to be making a real movie.

Some quick backstory on *How to Make a Generation X Movie* — the video thing. I wrote, I directed, I cast my friends. Amateur hour? Maybe. But we approached it professionally. A month of rehearsals. I even scribbled out a couple of storyboards before I (a) got bored and (b) realized I had little talent for storyboards.

In the end, Filmmakers United, a screening series in Los Angeles, invited us to show the flick in Hollywood. A very nice gesture that turned out pretty badly. The screening was a disaster. The audience just kind of looked at it — as opposed to, you know, laughing. (It was a comedy. Or, it was supposed to be.)

And then there was the review. The bad one. The very best the old *L.A. Village View* could say was that it was "coherent." That was it. "Coherent."

How did you handle the bad press?
That word — "coherent" — became my albatross. I could do better than "coherent," couldn't I? Why, sure I could! I could make a *great* "coherent" movie. Write a better script. Extend my casting net. Get more input. Shoot on film. And, yes, spend more money. *Much* more money.

So, that was how I got to *Former Child Star.*

The story was something I'd kicked around for a while: What would happen if someone you grew up watching on TV suddenly burst into your life — became a living, breathing character in your own personal drama? Sounds kind of deep. And it probably could have been. Except when I was writing, I was studying Woody Allen's *Bananas.* I thought my video movie had been too slow, too boring. I wanted peppy, fast, funny. So, I dissected *Bananas* scene by scene and wrote a farce. Except I didn't write farcical characters. Or farcical situations. (This, I would learn later. About two years later, while squirming in my seat and watching the final product with a silent, mummified audience.)

So, fine, we had a script. The actors — a strong bunch, I still think — came mostly through *Drama-Logue* and our subsequent auditions. The locations? My apartment and a bunch of other friends' apartments. Terribly imaginative. And, as it turned out, terribly un-cinematic. The camera? Hired a camera guy who owned his own CP-16. (I thought about renting a camera and trying to shoot the thing myself, but insurance costs made that idea impossible.) The sound? Hired a sound guy who owned his own Nagra. If it sounds like I hired a lot of people, I did. Too many. There were four paid crew members, in all, I think. Ultra-cheapo, to be sure. But still too many.

Former Child Star taught me the great lesson of self-financed independent filmmaking: Don't.

Rant all you want about what a great learning experience making an ultra-indie movie is. Sooner rather than later, that deluded line leaves you with a wallet full of maxed-out credit cards. The artistic reality of moviemaking is that if your idea, script, cast, and commitment are all strong enough, you'll find funding. Maybe not as much as you want, but you'll find something. The economic reality of moviemaking is that it's an expensive hobby. And a hobby is exactly what it remains until you get someone to offer you so much as a nickel for the reels.

This was your first mistake?
Moviemaking is not novel writing. You can tap away in your attic for a year on the "Next Great Event in Fiction," produce an unreadable mass of pages and not endanger your future ability to, say, buy a can of tuna fish.

But moviemaking? The second you start rolling is the second you start losing money. The only way to stay ahead of the game is to *spend as little as possible.*

Before hindsight set in, I was seduced. I was convinced I could shoot a feature-length 16mm movie in color, with sound, for about $5,000-7,000. (I'd spent $5,000 on the video project. Also way too much but I considered it to be an "acceptable" loss.)

I probably could have pulled it off, if I'd slowed down and done my homework. Ingratiated myself to techies (I didn't know any), enrolled in a class on how to operate a camera, enrolled in a class on how to edit the old-fashioned way — by hand, with film. And, hey, genius, how about this one? Decided to shoot in *black and white.*

Where did you end up getting the money?

I talked up my movie idea to my father and — bingo! — that's where our money came from. He enthusiastically bankrolled *Former Child Star.*

Bad, *bad* idea.

Not on his part. (Hey, he's my father; he thinks he's investing in genius.) On my part.

Beg, borrow, steal, but do not — *Do Not* — let your parents subsidize your artistic whims. It'll save you the trouble of developing a taste for Pepto-Bismol and a springing a guilty head of gray hair.

Anyway, I told my father we could shoot and do a video edit for about $10,000. He ended up being in for $19,000. Not counting the $3,000-plus I spent on processing, food and assorted sundries. That's $22,000-plus on a film — without even getting to the print stage. What can I say? Shameful. Embarrassing. Stupid.

Surely an ultra low budget film will have flaws an audience will look past?

The thing you learn quick enough — even on the festival circuit — is that a $22,000 movie gets no extra credit for being a $22,000 movie. Maybe it did once, but certainly not today. You compete against the big boys and the semi-big boys. If you're not good enough, you're not good enough and your film ain't going nowhere — and you, loser, are out $22,000.

Did you apply to Sundance?

Okay, so I'm either a defeatist or a realist, but I knew *Former Child Star* wasn't getting into Sundance. Not a chance. Three reasons:

(1) In the mistaken belief that the Independent Feature Film Market (IFFM) was the place to take a brand-spanking new movie, we screened at the event in September 1996. (To give you an idea about how naïve I was — I remember nervously awaiting word on whether we'd been "accepted" to the IFFM. And then to compound naïveté with stupidity, I remember thinking that we'd "achieved" something by being "accepted." Then I got to New York and realized that quality control amounted to conferring with the bank to see if the check cleared. The IFFM is a must-*see* for an aspiring indie film-maker; it's not necessarily a must-*screen*.)

Anyway, back to our IFFM screening. People from Sundance attended. From Slamdance, too. And the Chicago Underground. And probably a half-dozen other festivals. Nobody from these out-fits contacted me after the screening. In this case, silence meant a big, fat, loud "No."

(2) I didn't do my homework. Again. Going into the IFFM, I did little to aid my cause. Sure, I hyped our screening time to as many studio and festival types as I could. But a press release and phone call are not enough. I showed up in New York with a fresh-from-the-lab print. Nobody knew me. Nobody knew my film. Nobody cared. Sure, it would have helped if the fresh-from-the-lab print fea-tured something akin to *Citizen Kane: 1996*, but it also would have helped if I'd worked the festival circuit like Sarah Jacobson, whom I met at IFFM that year.

Jacobson had made a short, *I Was a Teen-age Serial Killer,* in the early 1990s. She screened it everywhere, she pushed it relentlessly. She made people care about her passion for film. When she showed up at IFFM with her first feature, *Mary Jane's Not a Virgin Anymore,* she was ready to make people care about that project, too. And they did. A couple months later, Sarah got accepted into Sundance. That was not luck; that was hard work.

(3) My film wasn't very good. Just another waste of celluloid and money in the post-*Clerks* world of wannabe filmmakers. At least that was my review.

So why did you bother applying to Sundance?

Again, three reasons:

(1) Like I said before, filmmaking is expensive. You've got to do everything you can to protect and preserve your investment, including lying. ("It's a comedy. Really funny!") The results can be embarrassing when someone actually screens the thing and tells you, "It's a mess. Really sucky!," but consider that part of your penance.

(2) Art is subjective. Who knows? Maybe the Sundance guy will actually like the thing. It's not your job to tell him he won't like it. (See the bit about lying in the item above.)

(3) Like the lottery, you can't win if you don't play. Sundance is the mother of all film festivals — you *must* apply. Especially if your father, who paid for the movie, tells you to.

So, anyway, in the fall of 1996, I did what 800 other filmmakers did and mailed off our movie, our press kit, and a fifty dollar check. (Why Sundance needs fifty dollars to reject a film its advance team already essentially rejected at the IFFM, I don't know. "To make money," would be my first guess.)

What other festivals did you apply to?

That fall and subsequent winter I also applied to: Toronto, SXSW, Film Fest New Haven, San Francisco, New York Underground, Los Angeles Indie, Portland, Taos Talking Pictures, New York's Gen Art, Hudson Valley, Laguna Beach, and Florida. Most required entry fees — from twenty-five to forty dollars, usually. All of which I paid. Stupidly so. Not having yet learned my lesson from IFFM, I failed to realize that unless a festival scout contacts you first, the chance of your unsolicited tape working its way out of the slush pile and into the acceptance pile is minimal. That's not an indictment of festivals; that's just reality.

How do you get a festival's attention?

Think about how the screenplay business works. Do you send your hot, new script directly to Warner Bros.? Or do you send it first to an agent, who, if he likes, can get the ear of Warner Bros. on your behalf? You send it to an agent, of course. He's your "in." That's what you're looking for at film festivals.

Before you get to the check-writing, application stage, what you want to do is get your movie before the eyes of festival types. Maybe you do it at IFFM. Maybe you do it at a local fest that takes all com-ers. Maybe you do it at a private screening on your Moviola. Whatever. Just get them to watch. If they like, they'll let you know. They won't tell you you're a lock. But they'll suggest you apply. That's something; that's one person on your side. You might even get your entry fee waived.

What festivals accepted your film?

Of all the festivals I listed above, only Los Angeles Indie contacted me first. The program director called. Somebody had listed *Former Child Star* on a list of should-sees. I didn't get in, but at least I knew I had a chance. I also ended up getting invited — and accepted — to the USA Film Festival in Dallas and the Chattanooga Film Festival in, yes, Chattanooga.

Anyway, the rejection from Sundance came via the post office. Sundance was classy enough to send a "Dear Filmmaker" letter. It arrived a couple days *after* the lineup was released in the trades, but still...the other festivals I entered didn't bother to call, write or e-mail. About the best their organizations did was send a sales brochure hyping their events, i.e., the slates of movies that got picked instead of mine. Not that it's a bad idea to go to a festival where you're just an observer. In fact, it's a great idea. I need to do

JOAL RYAN'S ADVICE ON HOW TO WIN
THE FILM FESTIVAL GAME (OR AT LEAST
NOT BE REDUCED TO TEARS WHILE PLAYING):

1. Attend a film festival. Preferably the one you'd really like to get into. And, yes, that means planning a year in advance — at least. Don't sweat the lag time. Trust me. I've tried the slap-dash method; I don't recommend it.
2. Don't submit blind. Until you know at least somebody at a festival is pulling for you, it's pointless. Take the time to do the proper leg work. Unofficially show your film to as many people as you can. Solicit advice. Make contacts. If all goes well, you'll save yourself a bundle on entry fees.
3. Keep moving. Satchel Paige's baseball wisdom works for movies, too. Don't wait for word from Sundance or Slamdance. Keep working other festivals. Keep writing scripts. Keep moving.
4. If you get in, take your mother with you. I took mine to Dallas. Parents make great conversation pieces at the nightly cocktail parties.
5. Make a really, really good movie. Go figure. Quality has a way of cutting down on the number of scams you need to run to get people to notice your movie. The funny thing about *Former Child Star* is that even though I didn't enjoy, or deserve, being one of those Sundance Success Stories, the experience left me hopeful, not despairing.

it more — to see what my peers are up to, to gauge the market, and above all, to learn — maybe even steal a couple tricks.

How did you handle all the rejections?

Since Sundance never even seemed as real as a pipe dream, I wasn't exactly crushed when the rejection letter arrived. It was more like, "Next." I didn't wait for Sundance. I didn't expect Sundance. I didn't get Sundance. Fine. Next. Time to move on.

Actually, I'd begun to move on even before that. In early November 1996, I sent a video copy of *Former Child Star* to this little thing in Cleveland that promised to show *anything*. No fee, no standards, no problem. The Off-Hollywood Flick Fest. My kind of crowd.

Was I worried about blowing my Sundance virginity by hosting my world premiere in Cleveland — two months *before* Park City? No. Remember: (a) there wasn't a chance I was getting in; and, (b) if by divine act of God or mislabeling I *did* get in — what was Robert Redford going to do? Shoot me? Yell at me? *"You screened at the Off-Hollywood Flick Fest?!?! Infidel!!"* The way I figured, Sundance wouldn't boot me from its shindig. Maybe it would move me out of the competition wing, but it probably would still screen me. And that's all you want. To play Park City in January...needless to say, it was a potential problem that I spent a nanosecond worrying about.

Where did you go at this point?

After Cleveland, after the no-go with Sundance, I pursued the one solid lead I got out of the IFFM: the USA Film Fest. The program director, Alonso Duralde, saw *Former Child Star* in New York and suggested I submit. The festival didn't actually solicit features — its entry form is for short subjects — but Duralde was willing to consider *Former Child Star*. Sounded good to me. I submitted, he considered; a couple months later, he said okay. We were going to our first "real" film festival.

What did you do to build hype for your film?

It was early 1997. Pauly Shore was in a new sitcom and the reviews weren't great. But instead of cracking a joke, turning the page and looking for somebody else to make fun of (like usual), I stopped and considered the case of Pauly Shore.

The guy's never been a critical darling or a mass-audience favorite. And yet...he keeps working. The world tells him he's not funny; he says he is — and keeps working. He does what he does, figuring that someone, somewhere, will, and does, like his work.

An empowering notion.

If Pauly Shore got rejected by Sundance, I thought, would he fold and file *Bio-Dome* away on a shelf? Ha! My man Pauly would keep sellin' it. Keep sellin' himself. And why not? No one has the right to tell you you're lousy. Except yourself. So, with my new Power of Positive Pauly Shore Thinking in place, I decided to hype the one sure-fire angle of *Former Child Star* — the former child star angle.

If you grew up watching TV, you care about former child stars. You can't help but wonder what happened to Willis on *Diff'rent Strokes* or Natalie on *The Facts of Life*. These actors are our virtual peers. We wonder about their post-TV lives, like we wonder about the post-high school lives of old classmates. That was my audience. That was my cause.

This was my platform: Former Child Star-Palooza. An e-zine. An e-mail newsletter designed to shamelessly hype the movie. And designed to provide real information on real former child stars — career updates, tabloid news, first-person sightings. In February 1997, I sent out my first issue. I compiled a list of seventy-five e-mail addresses — mostly film companies, friends, and film festivals. By the second issue, readership doubled. (It's now steadied at about 2,000 a month.)

The e-zine helped you get mainstream press?

Sure. Pretty soon, I was being interviewed by the *Boston Phoenix*. Getting invites to film festivals (Wine Country, Northampton, Cinequest, and Las Vegas, none of which I ended up getting into — but, hey, at least they were waiving the entrance fees now).

By summer, the e-zine and subsequent website had been blurbed in *Newsweek, Wired,* and *Entertainment Weekly*. The e-zine took on a life of its own. It immediately found greater acclaim and acceptance than the film. In turn, it kept the film alive. It gave the film mystery. ("So, what's this *Former Child Star* we keep reading about?") It gave the film relevancy.

It *didn't* help the film get any press at our big-time film festival screening, but nothing's perfect.

How did you handle that first festival screening?

When we got into the USA Film Festival, some extra hype —
beyond the e-zine — was required. Unfortunately, all I had was me.
I know you're supposed to call in favors to get stuff like this done
right, but I was lousy at asking for freebies. Really, you should be
required to take a personality test before making an indie film.
Flunking out in the chutzpah department would have saved me
thousands of dollars.

So, anyway, I sat down, typed up a press release, attached it to
our press kit, and mailed the whole batch off to Dallas media,
newspapers, weeklies, even a couple radio and TV stations. I followed up with regular faxes and phone calls. Even got a couple people on the phone. All very nice. All very noncommittal. No one
asked for a screener. Bad sign. And, in the end, no one reviewed or
mentioned *Former Child Star.* I mean *no one.* A couple months
after the festival (we were there in April 1997), the program director sent me a round-up of clippings on the festival. Maybe twenty
to thirty articles. I went through every single one. Not one word —
bad or good — about *Former Child Star* in any of them. A complete
swing and miss.

That said, the experience in Dallas was the highlight (so far) of
the *Former Child Star* grind. The festival paid for my airline ticket
(cool!), paid for my hotel room (double cool!) and inexplicably
treated me like a real filmmaker. I got invited to a reception honoring me...and Liza Minnelli. (I showed; she didn't.) I even got asked
to sign an autograph.

Nothing like a little adulation to keep you going. And that's all
I was looking for, really. Again, I had no illusions about the USA
Fest. It's not Sundance, Slamdance, or SXSW. Agents and studio
execs don't roam the theaters with cell phones and checkbooks. It's
a local festival hosted and enjoyed by the locals. The focus in the
press is not "$20,000 movies by out-of-town nobodies," but rather
Hollywood movies *(Volcano, Traveller)* by Hollywood types. It's
Dallas' chance to rub elbows with Tommy Lee Jones, Bill Paxton,
and Molly Ringwald (a few of the names there that year).

Dallas didn't make me a media darling, but it gave me something more important: The belief that there's an audience for every
movie. Somewhere, somebody is testifying to what a fabulous character drama *Lost in Space* is. And, yes, somewhere, somebody is

attesting to what a brilliant comedy *Former Child Star* is. I don't necessarily want to meet these somebodies, but it is nice to know they exist.

Dallas was where I learned this. As much as I paced and ducked out of the theater in anticipation of the "bad" parts, the movie did okay. Aesthetically, the print never looked or sounded better. (Much better than the tin-eared closet we screened in at the IFFM.) And artistically, the film was genuinely liked. They laughed, they applauded, they stayed for the Q&A.

How did the Q&A go?

The Q&A was a breeze. In my case, again, the stakes were low. I didn't have Mike Ovitz to win over. I merely had to be nice to an auditorium of nice people who liked my movie.

I told the requisite "funny-things-that-happened-while-we-made-the-movie stories" (#1: How we caused a police incident during the filming of a robbery scene because — rim shot, please! — bystanders thought a real hold-up was in progress; #2: How I unsuccessfully sought out real former child stars to appear in cameos; #3: How I successfully recruited real former child star Rodney Allen Rippy, who starred in TV commercials for Jack in the Box in the 1970s, to do a cameo.)

I stammered when a person asked the inevitable "So, how much did it cost?" (FYI: No one is shy about pumping you for info on that one, so don't get offended.) Anyway, I mumbled an answer — afraid if anybody heard me correctly, they'd charge right back: "You spent *how much*?!?...and it looks like *that*!?!"

And then I thanked people profusely for not throwing stuff. At me or the screen. All in all, a pretty good night. To date, it's the best festival night I've had. Also, the only one.

We've had theatrical screenings in New York, Las Vegas, San Francisco, and Los Angeles (as the midnight show for a couple weekends at a local theater), but as far as festivals go, Dallas was the ballgame to date.

Sure, there were Cleveland and Chattanooga, but they didn't pay for my trip and I couldn't afford to go on my own. Also, I lacked that chutzpah thing necessary to finagle myself free airfare, á la a scene from a Jennifer Aniston film. The organizers of those two fests weren't mad about my planned absences; they said they weren't anyway. I can't say for sure now. They never took any of my follow-up phone calls.

What did you feel you've learned from the experience?
Look, I was nobody — *nobody* — and people at film festivals and studios still took the time to watch my flick, to take my calls. Did everybody like what they saw? No. But I learned the access *is* there. Film people want to see good films. They want to hear good stories. You got that; you're in.

Naïve? I don't care. That's my one plucky attitudinal vice and me and Pauly Shore are sticking to it.

HEIDI VAN LIER, First-Time Feature Filmmaker

Heidi Van Lier is a real character. Besides being a talented writer and filmmaker, she's damn funny. I would describe her as kind of a female Woody Allen with a nasal, whiny voice. In 1994 she wrote and directed a cute little short film called *Small Town Recollection*. The very next year she attended the Sundance Screenwriters Lab to develop her skills. Heidi is one of those people who is hilarious when she's doing absolutely nothing, so it's no surprise that she cast herself as the lead in her feature directing debut *Chi Girl*. In 1999, *Chi Girl* went on to win Slamdance's coveted Grand Jury Prize for Best Feature. Sold to IFC/BRAVO, *Chi Girl* will air and be in video stores at some point, fingers crossed, ending her "Cine-orphan" status.

In late 2002, Heidi gave birth to a daughter, with a little help from her husband, Joe Kraemer. In 2004, Heidi wrote and directed another feature simply titled *Monday* about one miserable loser's worst day ever, and she hopes to soon make the festival rounds. I met Heidi at the USA Film Festival in Dallas, Texas where we sat on the jury for the short film program. In addition to offering sound advice, her unique experiences making films and travelling to festivals could also provide plenty of material for a television sitcom.

Tell me about the making of Chi Girl.
I was in Los Angeles for years, attempting to be a screenwriter. Everyone kept telling me I needed something produced before I'd start getting work. So I knew at some point I was going to have to

make my own little movie, whether I liked it or not. But I had no idea how soon I was actually going to be doing that.

When I broke up with my boyfriend, I went to Chicago to get as far away from my old life as I could. In Chicago I would go see this band every Tuesday night at a little Capone speakeasy, and I met the band's manager. Out of nowhere I found myself telling him I want-

ed to use his band on the soundtrack for my movie. I wasn't even making a movie, but I didn't mention that part. I scrambled and came up with the idea for *Chi Girl* within a week. I spent two hours pitching it to the manager and at the end he said they'd do the film. Now I was screwed. I was going to have to make this movie. One thing led to another, with some good name-dropping, since my father is somewhat of a hometown hero in Chicago (having played for the Bulls in the

Filmmaker Heidi Van Lier

'70s), and now I had this band. And step by step I was putting a movie together.

One phone call to my mother and she started sending me the cash to get insurance and all the paperwork you need for pre-production. I found my only crewmember, my amazing DP, Anders Uhl. And I figured that's all I needed. Everyone I ran into told me, "Oh, no. You can't do it like that." But they were a little late, I was already about to shoot a feature, with one crew member, each scene done in only one take, on 35mm film.

Did you do research on film festivals before applying?

I'd been going to Park City and other festivals for years. The biggest mistake someone can make when applying is not knowing what they're really getting into. Sundance didn't pay much attention to my film, Slamdance did. I'd made a movie that I thought was original enough to get some attention, even though I'd ripped off all my heroes at the same time. And once I applied to Slamdance I started giving them old computers and things, not so much to bribe them (wink, wink), just so they'd remember me. It all worked. Later I found out many people try to bribe them, and with some serious cash, but most of them don't get in. After Slamdance I just started going to any festival that invited me. Most of the film festival organizers go to Park City in January to program their own festivals. They watch out for films that have "buzz" and then invite them to their festivals.

How did you find out you were in?

A friend of mine was programming, and he wasn't allowed to vote for my film as a result. He came over and first told me I had not gotten in. Then confessed he was joking. It was a big letdown to get in, for a couple reasons. First, I went through the emotional breakdown of not getting in, which was painful, and now I had to actually finish my film, and I didn't have the $30,000 to do so. Thus began six weeks of sobbing in my car on the Ventura Freeway. After that, I didn't really apply to any others, just went to festivals that invited me.

What did you do to promote your film at Slamdance and in Park City?

We talked to some publicists. But no one seemed that interested in our little $50,000 movie that I starred in myself. Fliers on the street. We were nice to everyone we met. We were willing to talk about the movie to everyone, including tourists who weren't even in Park City for the festivals. I still go to meetings now where the producer will say they met me on Main Street in Park City and I spent some time talking to them. Posters. Faxing. Calling people. We put together a street team to come up and meet the public while we were there. We made little notebooks with the *Chi Girl* logo on them. People still have those notebooks two years later. And we made Tootsie Pops with *Chi Girl* stickers on them so the audience would have a giggly sugar high in the middle of the screening. My mother spent days faxing people and we sent out thousands of postcards over the weeks before the screenings. Everyone knew our movie was at Slamdance.

How did the first screening go?

I was having some kind of strange panic attack in the lobby at the Treasure Mountain Inn. The line for our first screening was huge. My best friend was with me and watching my face go through odd contortions. The only way to get through it was to do it. I had a little silly thing I had to read before the film. I read it, people laughed, I was shaking, the lights dimmed.

I learned that it is impossible to die from nervousness. I'd seen enough Q&As to know what the deal was. I think I was a huge brat though, because I was still shaking, but for some reason people just thought I was being funny. Also, everyone tends to think I *am* the character in the film. It usually takes them a minute to realize that I'm not an obsessive stalker with a mentally ill man with a camera following me everywhere...although I did marry the guy who played the mentally ill man with the camera.

What were some of the questions you were asked at the Q&A?

"Are you seeing anyone?" When I said I was dating the other lead in the film, now my husband, the guy said, "No, I mean, like a therapist."

"Is that a prosthetic ass?" I had put on some Chicago winter weight while shooting the movie, and my ass was enormous.

"Did you ever think about cutting the film down?" I said, "Yes. I thought about cutting it down to three minutes, but that just wouldn't have been a feature film, now would it?"

Almost the entire audience stayed, and as I walked up to do the Q&A they were all leaning forward with these big smiles on their faces. I got great agents. Got a lot of distributor interest. Got a lot of press. Got a lot of buzz. It could not have been better.

When the film did not sell immediately at Slamdance, how did you continue to pursue a distribution deal?

I just made myself as available as possible. I spent two months after the festival Fed-Exing my print back and forth from New York to Los Angeles so people could decide if they wanted to buy it. That was a full time job by itself. [Now, with IFC/BRAVO,] at some point it'll see the light of day, even if it's part of some 1999 film retrospective in 2020. Other than that, my movie had a great little life. I got some jobs I love as a result. My career finally took the turn I'd been working toward, for many, many years.

Any advice on handling the press?

Be nice to everyone! And talk to as many people as humanly possible. The press will sell your film for you and get you other jobs as well. If the press like you, they'll help the distributors to pay attention to you. They can help you get an agent, and your agency can use your press as a way to get other producers to hire you.

What were some of the other festival screenings like?

The first screening at Slamdance was by far the best. But the second best had to be the Cleveland Film Festival. That is an amazing little festival! The entire population of Cleveland has a deep understanding of how film works. I was very impressed. Three screenings of 600 people were sold out, and I didn't do any promo stuff at all. The worst was a screening at the Director's Guild of America in Los Angeles, where the "large ass" was discussed again, and people seemed to be a little irritated with the shaky-cam thing. I think they'd all just seen *Blair Witch* and were already tired of the mockumentary.

Can you describe Chi Girl's *whirlwind film festival tour?*

Sex, drugs, and rock and roll in every country in the world. Very fun if you're single. I wasn't. But you have to go where you're invited, especially with your first film. It's an experience you'll never forget, and you'll get to go places you'd never go on your own.

It does get really exhausting after a while, even if you're having fun. And it can be expensive; it costs money to stay in free hotels and eat out all day, even if the festival does provide a sandwich for you on occasion. They always ask for a credit card when you check in, which I didn't have the entire year, so I'd have to leave fifty bucks there, which was generally all the money I had for food.

At the end I'd just plan on going for three days only, and on the weekend, so that I didn't have to miss any meetings in town really. And I'd spend less cash that way. Three days is the perfect amount to be at any of the smaller festivals. Bring plenty of nutrition bars, not every festival will feed you. And try not to drink, you'll end up in bed with someone who made a film you despise. I've seen it happen a thousand times.

Did the screening of the film lead to other opportunities?

Greg McKnight from William Morris was at my first Slamdance screening and he was totally enthusiastic. I moved to William Morris a week after I came back to Los Angeles, and they had me going out on so many meetings I couldn't keep track. The really weird thing is, I love my agents! How many people can say that? Sara

HEIDI VAN LIER'S 12 STEPS TO A SUCCESSFUL FILM FESTIVAL

1. Be nice to *everyone*, especially people who are bugging the hell out of you. Be nice to the other filmmakers, sometimes they'll tell people to go see your film. Better that than they're all telling the press how much they hate your arrogant ass. And always be nice to volunteers. Give the volunteers gifts; they're the ones who do all the work for you that you can't do. They'll tell everyone whether you're nice or not, and if they like you they will play a huge role in selling your film or getting you more work that year.

2. Have another project ready to go that you can pitch while you're there. If you don't, you won't get another deal or an agent and then you're a big loser. And it better be totally original or forget it.

3. Know the lay of the land by going to the big festivals before you enter.

4. Maybe make a good film, this can occasionally help. Preferably not a mockumentary. I didn't listen to this, but my film still hasn't sold. You do the math. And don't make a "you and your twenty-something friends sitting around being clever" film. Only you think your friends are clever.

5. Abstain from your drinking and drug habits while you're there. You need to be alert when Bill Bloch's people approach you. If only to make a fool out of yourself in the end anyway.

6. Promote. Let the entire planet know your screening times weeks before you go. And keep telling them until that day. Faxing. E-mailing. Posters. Postcards.

7. A billboard on Sunset with a picture of yourself naked, if you can afford it.

8. Keep your introduction short and funny. No one wants to see a bad twenty minute stand-up routine.

9. Just because you've had your first screening doesn't mean you can sleep yet. You still have the rest of the week to get press and sell your film. Sometimes people buy a film a year after it runs at one of the big festivals. This will help you start your drug habit again when the festival is over because it's even more stressful than the festival was.

10. Be careful who you bring with you on your team. Don't bring your parents or kids unless they're media savvy; they'll say the wrong thing to the press and harass celebrities while you're there and it'll only embarrass you. Don't bring friends who don't like to work hard. They'll drive you nuts when they're getting up to go skiing every day and you've been up all night stuffing press kits.

11. Don't get jealous when other filmmakers sell their movies the first day you're there. They sold their movie before they even got up there and lied about it to get into the festival. They probably didn't make any money on the deal, and it'll probably only be in theaters for five minutes. And you could still sell your movie for nothing so it can be in theaters for only five minutes.

12. Gain some weight before you go. You will lose ten pounds at every festival.

Bottfeld and Greg McKnight totally turned my career around. I started working in November on a film for MTV that I finished writing — and if all goes well, I'll be directing it soon. And there are a few other cool projects I've been working on as well, thanks to Greg and Sara and the Slamdance experience.

You've also been involved with Slamdance as a programmer, what mistakes do filmmakers make when they apply?

I have so much frustration about how people "do" festivals. Most people who apply to festivals have no idea what they're doing, and they miss out on all the opportunities when they do, and even more when they get in. First things first, you have to really want this. No one who's on the fence about being a filmmaker ever succeeds. So as a result, you should be learning everything you can about everything. Don't slack; go to these festivals and start from scratch before you think about applying. I'd say before you even think about making a film. I don't think there's much "luck" involved in a film festival. You can make the best possible scenario for yourself by doing *everything* you can to be nice, to be available, to be prepared, and to be aware of what else you could be doing. There are four things people try to get out of a festival: An award, a sale, press, other work, and/or an agent. Granted, not everyone is going to win a big festival, but it doesn't mean you can't get one of the other three. If you get even one, you've done well at your festival.

HEIDI'S NEW AND IMPROVED
INDIE FILMMAKER DO (AND DON'T) LIST:

1. DON'T get pregnant and very ill while while working on your biggest writing gig to date on your rise to indie power queen status.
2. DO get pregnant and ill while working with the very cool Maggie Malina at MTV, she'll put you on a six-month hiatus and will still talk to you like she thinks you're edgy, despite the fact that you're married, live in The Valley, drive a Hybrid, and have a kid.
3. DON'T have your best script be a comedy about the end of the world set in SoHo, despite the fact that you wrote it before September 11th. That's just not funny anymore and Saturn Films will drop it like a hot rock, and be right to do so.
4. DO go raise the money to make another groovy little film.
5. DO shoot in color this time, and of course, on film.

LiFE AFTER THE FESTiVAL DEBUT

Pursuing a career in film is an ongoing series of battles that never seem to end. One moment you're basking in the glow of the premiere, and the next, you're scrambling to get your next project produced. For some, the realities of paying the rent become all too real, and the pursuit must often be set aside in order to "get a real job." However, that so-called "real" job is generally only a minor pit stop on the path to getting back in the race. None of the filmmakers interviewed for the last edition of this book have been taking it easy. They've all been working hard on new projects, both film and non-film related. I check in with a couple of them to see what they are up to.

MARK A. ALTMAN

Mark's recent film, *House of the Dead*, earned over $15 million at the US box office. In addition to producing and co-writing *House of the Dead*, he is beginning production of *Dead Or Alive* with Constantin and Impact Films later this year as well as a sequel to *House of the Dead*, *House of the Dead 2: Dead Aim*. Also, he revisits the fertile territory of science fiction fandom with *Free Enterprise 2: My Big Geek Wedding*, a sequel to the 1999 film starring William Shatner and Eric McCormack. Mark also serves as editorial director and co-publisher of *Cinefantastique* and *Femme Fatales* magazine and is overseeing the launch of *CFQ Films*, devoted to low to medium budget genre films.

TAZ GOLDSTEIN

Taz wrote and directed the spoof short *Pearl Harbor II — Pearlmageddon*, which premiered at the 2002 Newport Beach Film Festival. It was reported that Michael Bay was seen wearing a *Pearl Harbor II — Pearlmageddon* baseball cap sent to him by Taz.

ROGER NYGARD

Roger spent a year travelling around Europe, Australia, and North and South America shooting the sequel to *Trekkies* titled *Trekkies 2*. He reports that the first *Trekkies* went into profit after its initial release — a rare occurrence for a studio film resulting in an ongoing royalty payout. The lion's share of the *Trekkies* gross came from foreign sales. In its theatrical release, *Trekkies* only grossed half of what it cost for prints and ads. But with the resulting reviews in all the major newspapers, and a "thumbs up" from Roger Ebert, the good word of mouth spread. Soon Roger negotiated with Paramount to shoot *Trekkies 2*. Get more info at www.Trekkies2.com

MARK OSBORNE

After the frustrating process of re-cutting and re-scoring all of *Dropping Out*, Mark is happy to say that a DVD and video release of the film is in the works. Although he goes on to sadly say that he has almost given up entirely on the independent film movement. Crushed by the financial failure of *Dropping Out*, he has been trying to get his foot in the door of the industry in other ways. He recently directed live-action sequences for the hugely popular *SpongeBob Squarepants* TV show as well as the feature film. Mark is currently working as a director in development at DreamWorks Feature Animation department. He has created a new website for independent stop-motion films and a brave adventure in self-distribution at www.happyproduct.com.

RICHARD SCHENKMAN

Went to Coney Island on a Mission From God, Be Back By Five had a brief theatrical run, where it garnered great reviews but little box office. It did very well at Blockbuster (over $500,000 in rentals) and they even sent a royalty check. The initial DVD release, however, was a catastrophe; the discs were all flawed, and the distributor refused to recall them. Richard also wrote and directed *A Diva's Christmas Carol* for VH1, which was a massive success for them. That film starred Vanessa Williams — Richard and Vanessa went on to become friends, and to develop a sitcom, which was sold to NBC (where it died in development).

Richard's also been keeping busy with his wife and three-year-old daughter.

SECTION 4
FiLM FESTIVAL LiSTiNGS

"...people who love independent and foreign films, going out of their way to come see movies they've never heard of, simply out of desire. They're the best audiences in the world . . . it's worth attending festivals if only for the chance to show your films to this audience."

— Richard Schenkman, filmmaker

FiND THE BEST FESTS FOR YOU

This section contains the complete list of over 1,000 film festivals world-wide. I have identified the most important festivals and included detailed information to aid you in your decision to visit a festival or enter your film. In addition to the Top Ten festivals, I have compiled more lists of festivals that excel in certain areas. In the "Even More Top Tens" section, you'll find the rosters of what I consider to be the "Best Film Festivals" in categories ranging from Documentary, Short, International, Touring, Underground, Video, Digital, Gay, Party, Vacation, and many more.

I've tried to include as many factors as possible to aid you in your selection process — such as what the entry fees are and what benefits attending filmmakers can expect. In particular, travel costs will play a huge part in your decision-making process, so the data is arranged in a way that makes it simple for you to do your own comparative analysis. I've included as much information as possible within the limits of space — I mean, I could include *everything* in this book, but then it would be 10,000+ pages, weigh a hefty twenty pounds, and you'd never be able to shove it into a backpack. You alone carry the burden of choosing which festivals to pursue, and that means you have to study.

When researching festivals to enter, let me pass along this advice — use the listings contained in this book as a launching pad for your *own* investigation. Your decisions should not be based solely on the data found within these pages; you must take your fact-finding to the Internet and thoroughly research each festival on the web. Also, use the festival listings on FilmThreat.com as well as other film festival listing sites for the most updated data. Seek out other filmmakers' opinions about their experiences at each festival and what they found to be the benefits of attending. No one festival submission plan is perfect for every filmmaker, so create your own strategy based on the data found in the listings here, supplemented by your own research.

THE TOP TEN FiLM FESTiVALS

The Top Ten film festivals have been selected based on a number of factors, one of the most important being that they qualify as "discovery" festivals — wherein new talent emerges to take center stage on the independent film scene. Each festival offers a significant amount of prestige along with better opportunities for filmmakers to gain exposure in the form of national media attention. Receiving an award from any of the Top Ten results in much-needed publicity and the attention of the industry, which can go a long way toward launching a career. The Top Ten also act as launching pads for some of Hollywood's best work — studios view these particular film festivals as a chance to premiere their most distinguished films and even their Oscar® contenders. Of paramount importance for independent filmmakers, these fests also serve as back-door film markets — movies shown at these festivals have a greater chance of getting picked up for distribution. Additionally, this select group of Top Ten film festivals also make great vacation destinations, have the best parties, and are just fantastic places to see new movies.

There's another important thing I feel compelled to point out. If your film doesn't get into one of the Top Ten festivals, your life is not over. There are hundreds of other significant festivals; rejection does not mean you that you or your film are worthless, it just may not appeal to the individual taste of the programmer for a particular festival. Move on, there is a perfect festival fit for you — and with more than 1,000 festivals listed in this book, you're going to find it.

Finally, I should add that this is *my* Top Ten list, and not anyone else's. Having spent more than twenty years traveling to festivals worldwide, I've seen the best and the worst, so trust me when I say, these *are* the best. While others may disagree with some of my choices, they probably haven't been to as many festivals as I have. I've compiled this Top Ten list as a guideline for you, so you can make intelligent choices about where to premiere your film. Debuting at any one of these will guarantee your best chance for a successful festival run, hopefully leading to distribution on a wider scale — but even more important than distribution is the launching of your film career. Collectively, the following ten festivals have seen the beginnings of some of the greats in the film business. The next one could be you.

1. Sundance Film Festival

The mother of all independent film festivals in the United States, Sundance sets the tone for the industry, which is why you will find just as many festival directors from other film fests as you will agents and acquisitions executives. Sundance is *the* place to be in January. Whether you're a film lover, filmmaker, or film student; no other festival comes close to matching the experience. There is an air of excitement and electricity about the films at Sundance. Hearing about the struggles of indie film directors at post-screening Q&A sessions only serves to motivate the next generation of filmmakers to pick up their cameras. Sundance has everything: whether you're looking for distribution, a script, an actor for your next movie, to crash some cool parties, or you just want to see some quality films. Sundance also continues to show support for shorts with the Sundance Online Film Festival, a fantastic way to showcase new work on the Internet.

Additionally, the festival's long-running commitment to supporting documentaries is demonstrated by their House of Docs program — virtually every doc that plays Sundance walks away with at least a cable or home video deal. And the unique voices of gay filmmakers' are embraced here like no other festival. In many ways, Sundance stands as the Statue of Liberty in the independent film world, collecting disenfranchised, marginalized, and challenging filmmakers — all under one recognizable brand name whose seal of approval has become an endorsement of quality filmmaking.

And while Sundance does number first on this list, the spot might be shared with the small town of Park City itself. The streets of the city turn into what I call "Park City Madness" over the ten days of the festival. The entire place is transformed into a veritable Mecca for independent film. And if your film screens at the now-established alternative film fest, Slamdance, that runs congruent to Sundance, it may well garner the same kind of frenetic attention that it would if it were running in Redford's fest. Technically speaking, it's actually *more* difficult to get into Slamdance than Sundance, because they have far fewer

Above: Sundances's Geoff Gilmore introduces a film at the spacious Eccles theater.

Below: Sundance and CineVegas programmer Trevor Groth.

screening slots — but that's not necessarily a bad thing; Sundance's enormous schedule of over two hundred films can make it possible for films to be overlooked. In fact, many speculate that the American Spectrum program was created at Sundance as a reaction to Slamdance's success.

The only negative thing one might say is that the Sundance Film Festival is a victim of its own success — there are just too many people trying to see films in too few venues. Of late, the festival has become a circus with insane media attention infringing on every event. There can be a certain amount of frustration at the festival — what with the insanely cold weather, sold-out screenings, and packed parties — but like a strained family gathering at Thanksgiving, you know you'll always come back and love every minute of it. I never miss Sundance.

sundance

c/o The Sundance Institute
8857 W. Olympic Blvd., Ste 200
Beverly Hills, CA 90211-3605
Tel.................310-360-1981; 801-328-3456 (Utah)
Fax...310-360-1969
Email ....festivalinfo@sundance.org
Web Site ....www.sundance.org

Year Festival Began: 1978 as the Utah/US Film Festival, 1991 re-named
Festival Month: Mid-January
Entry Deadline: Features: Early October
Shorts: Mid-September
Number of Submissions: 5,000
Entry Fee: $50

The hardworking volunteer staff in the Sundance press office.

Genres: Animation, Documentary, Features, Independent, International, Narrative, Online Festival, Shorts
Screening Format: 16mm - 35mm - BetaSP - DigiBeta
Number of Films Screened: 200
Odds: 1 in 25
X Factor: It's the Sundance Film Festival, if you get in, you're going.
Awards: Alfred P. Sloan Prize, Jury Awards, Other Awards
Profile: The annual Sundance Film Festival, a major program of Sundance Institute, is held each January and is considered the premier showcase for American and international independent film.
Special Events: Awards, parties, panels, special screenings, retrospectives, online festival
Filmmaker Perks: For a few days every January, the world's film industry focuses on Sundance allowing for mass amounts of press exposure, networking, and film sales.
Travel Tips: Use the festival shuttle service for theater-to-theater service, though the Park City bus system can be equally as reliable (and sometimes quicker) if you know where to go.

Geoffrey Gilmore ....Festival Director
John Cooper...........................Director of Programming

2. Toronto International Film Festival

The cosmopolitan city of Toronto in the great white north of Canada is host to one of the most respected festivals in the industry. Toronto breaks new talent and has premiered the first films of indie faves Tom DiCillo and wise-ass documentarian Michael Moore. Toronto is also the festival of choice for debuting both Hollywood's and the indie film world's best, including films like *Love Actually*, Alejandro González Iñárritu's Oscar-nominated *21 Grams*, and premieres of films from such as Jim Jarmusch's *Coffee and Cigarettes*, John Sayles' *Casa de los Babys*, and Gus Van Sants' *Elephant*.

I first attended the Toronto Film Festival in 1988. Toronto, Ontario, was just a quick train ride from Detroit, Michigan, where I lived at the time. While I had gone to smaller film festivals before (having attended my first fest at the age of twelve), nothing could have prepared me for Toronto. I was initially overwhelmed at the sheer number and variety of films. From foreign film retrospectives, to independent film premieres, to Hollywood debuts, to Canadian work — there was almost too much to choose from. Today, there is still an awesome amount to see, and it just keeps getting better. Toronto's midnight movie program proves that the festival directors are not too full of themselves. (Nothing beats a midnight showing of Japanese monster movies featuring my favorite giant turtle,

Gamera.) The atmosphere is exhilarating as the whole city seems joined in a celebration of cinema.

Toronto is one of the best-organized festivals in the world, and the amazing staff works diligently with filmmakers to help promote their films to the more than 1,000 attending members of the press. More importantly, Toronto is also a key festival for acquisitions executives looking for hot new films. The parties are a blast and the city of Toronto itself provides incredible opportunities for fun. If the bars were open later, it would be the perfect fest. As it is, it's just really, really close.

TORONTO INTERNATIONAL FILM FESTIVAL

2 Carlton St., West Mezzanine
Toronto, Ontario M5B 1J3 Canada
Tel...416-967-7371
Fax 416-967-3595; 416-967-9477
Email ....tiffg@torfilmfest.ca
Web Site ....www.tiffg.ca
Year Festival Began: 1976
Festival Month: Early September
Entry Deadline: Early June
Number of Submissions: 3,193
Entry Fee: International Features: $65
Canadian Features: $55
Canadian Shorts: $25
Genres: All, Animation, Canadian, Documentary, Features, First-Time Independent Filmmakers, Independent, International, Narrative, Shorts
Screening Format: 16mm - 35mm - DigiBeta - HDCam
Number of Films Screened: 339
Odds: 1 in 9

X Factor: It's one of the greatest film festivals in the world, and if you're Canadian, the best feature prize is worth $80,000.

Awards: AGF People's Choice Award, Citytv Award, Toronto - City Award, FIPRESCI Prize, Other Awards

Profile: The Toronto International Film Festival, one of several programming initiatives of the Toronto International Film Festival Group, is widely recognized as the most important film festival after Cannes and the largest and most successful public festival in the world. It is the discriminating and sophisticated Toronto filmgoers who make the Toronto International Film Festival a must-attend event for the public, industry, and press alike. Over the years, the filmgoing public has supported and shaped the festival into what it is today. Every September, the city opens its doors and experiences the best cinema in the world, and boasts 250,000 admissions annually.

Special Events: Panels, awards, special screenings, parties

Filmmaker Perks: The festival is an international focus, so your film will get unheard of exposure.

Travel Tips: Check with the festival for special rates on travel and accomodations.

Piers Handling ....Director & CEO
Noah Cowan ....Festival Co-Director

3. Cannes Film Festival

Cannes is home to the most prestigious film festival in the world. Held in the sprawling city on the French Riviera, this May event, known as the Festival International du Film du Cannes (Cannes Film Festival), attracts top industry players worldwide — from studio executives to moguls, to the biggest celebrities, to press and filmmakers all the way down to the struggling indies.

There are five sections of the festival: Compétition (Competitive Section), Un Certain Regard (Showcase Section), La Semaine de la Critique (Critic's Week), La Quinzaine des Réalisateurs

The Cannes Film Market can be an eye-opening experience for any filmmaker.

(Director's Fortnight) and Le Marché (the Market).

While many film festivals shy away from their obvious market appeal, Cannes embraces this business reality by offering filmmakers a chance to sell their movies to overseas buyers. Any film is welcome to be a part of the market (for a fee, of course), which makes the whole event feel more democratic. *Everyone* is welcome — both Troma and representatives from Slamdance attend every year to sell their films at the market.

Learn a little French, save up some cash (*everything* is expensive) and realize that no amount of preparation is sufficient for the largest and most prestigious film festival in the world.

Cannes does have this strange blend of festival and market. On the one hand, you have members of the overseas press praising, what we would call in the states, well, some pretty awful Hollywood movies. The international press corps views these mainstream American movies as "art." In fact, it's not just film, it's "cinema." Then there is the market. If you can't afford to buy a pass to the festival, I suggest getting a "market pass" — it's more affordable and will still give you access to many of the offbeat films playing around town. But I do have a warning about the market itself:

The view from the red carpet at Cannes.

The best way to describe it is with a cheeseburger. You see, I *love* cheeseburgers. Love 'em! That being said, I have zero desire to go to a slaughterhouse to see how they carve up the cows and grind them into beef patties. Visiting a market is a lot like visiting a slaughterhouse — seeing a necessary side of the film business that treats films like livestock ready to be sold and processed. The market-goers look on films as "product." On the market floor, buyers

representing countries all over the world are looking for films to open in their respective theaters or to stock their video store shelves. The market is, frankly, kind of creepy — with buyers milling around, large-breasted women staffing booths, salesmen in suits selling movies (many of them knock-offs of whatever the latest hot movie is), and sometimes a poster is all that exists. The enormous convention hall is lined with booths selling films; "desperation" is the prevailing smell and the market stinks of it. Any filmmaker who wishes to really learn the business should spend at least an hour there. The market is definitely an eye-opening experience.

Another important piece of advice: bring formal wear. No, seriously. An evening gown or tuxedo is actually required to attend the premieres. In fact, not only does everyone walking on the red carpet go through a security check, there is a fashion check as well. If you're wearing something a little *off,* you can be sure that your wild bow tie will be replaced with a more formal one. For men, the dress is formal and conservative, so don't forget to pack a tux or you won't get in — even if you have a ticket.

One thing that you may be surprised to learn is that the French are not the rudest people at Cannes. In fact, I have had only good experiences getting assistance when I was lost or in need of help. The Cannes Film Festival staff is outstanding and the efficiency and organization of the festival is unprecedented. Which can be a drawback because it's almost *too* organized. There are no chinks in the armor, so to speak. I can count on Sundance sometimes being in such disarray that I can — let's say "finesse" — certain rules to get what I need. That's part of the charm of Sundance. Cannes, on the other hand, is so well-organized that you have *no hope* of getting around their rules. There are ushers in blue jackets stationed at every corner and you *will* be stopped and asked to show your badge frequently. The only real trick is to smile a lot and speak at least a little French. Be polite and considerate; it's not that difficult. Most Americans receive a negative reaction because they'll just interrupt a local on the street and assume that the local can speak at least some English. If some random guy interrupted you on the street one day, blathering on in French, you'd probably assume that he was insane. Or at the very least, medicated. And yet Americans do it all the time overseas! The French are very formal and polite and you must respect that.

The rudest people I have ever encountered at Cannes are the egotistical American journalists who expect everyone to speak English. Try a few simple phrases to get around, and you'll do just fine (oh, and it's pronounced CAN, like "Yes, you CAN," not KAHN, as in *The Wrath of*).

Many exclusive parties at the Cannes Film Festival take place on yachts.

You Cannes Do It

For those traveling from outside of France, you'll find plenty of help at the Pavilions — these function like mini-embassies to help those who don't speak the French language. The American Pavilion is where you'll find your friends from the US. The staff at the American Pavilion can help with virtually everything — from Internet access, to making dinner reservations, to changing a flight, and they even serve affordable American food. You can request a mailbox there during your stay, so others may reach you while you're at Cannes — plus, it's a convenient meeting place for business. Every celebrity in town pops by and there are always parties, press events, and panels. Trust me, you will *live* at the American Pavilion while at Cannes. Get details at: www.ampav.com

3 rue Amélie
Paris 75007
France
Tel ....+33-1-53-59-61-71
Fax ....+33-1-5359-61-70
Email ....laurent.rivoire@festival-cannes.fr
Web Site ....www.festival-cannes.org
Year Festival Began: 1946
Festival Month: Late May
Entry Deadline: March
Entry Fee: VHS or DVD Feature: $30
BetaSP Feature: $115
DigiBeta Feature: $250
35mm Feature 60-105 Minutes: $350
35mm Feature Over 105 Minutes: $415
Short Films: No Fee
Genres: All, Animation, Documentary, Features,
First-Time Independent Filmmakers, Independent,
International, Markets, Narrative, Shorts
Screening Format: 35mm - VHS - BetaSP -
DigiBeta
Number of Films Screened: 70-80
X Factor: It's the Cannes Film Festival, one of the
most prestigious film festivals in history. You have to
submit.
Awards: The Palme d'Or for the best feature;
The Grand Prix - for the film that shows the most
originality; Other Awards
Profile: More widely known as the "Festival de
Cannes," the Association Française du Festival
International du Film, created in 1946, is a French
association under the auspices of the Ministry of
Culture and the Ministry of Foreign Affairs, state-
approved in 1972. The spirit of the Festival de
Cannes is one of friendship and universal cooperation. Its aim is to reveal and focus attention on
works of quality in order to contribute to the
progress of the motion picture arts and to encourage
the development of the film industry throughout the
world.
Thanks to a balance between the artistic quality of
the films and their commercial impact, the festival
has gained in fame and has become a major crossroads for the international film scene. Not only does
the presentation of a film in Cannes guarantee international publicity thanks to a high concentration of
media, but the Festival also reveals as well as
reflects the evolution and trends in world cinema
while defending the notion of "cinéma d'auteur for a
large audience."
The festival has discovered, established and hon-
oured directors who, by their presence in Cannes,

also contribute immensely to the prestige of the
event.
Special Events: Debates, tributes, retrospectives,
productions and filmed documents
Travel Tips: Check out the website for all the necessary information regarding travel and accomodations
to and around Cannes.

Giles Jacob..President
Christine Aimé ....Press Relations

4. American Film Institute (AFI) Los Angeles International Film Festival

For ten days in November, the city of Los Angeles comes together in a rare celebration of cinema. The AFI Los Angeles International Film Festival was already an established leader on the film festival circuit with a strong line-up of international films, tributes, retrospectives and American independents. The AFI Fest, as it is commonly known, is big with Hollywood and indie film celebrities, industry VIPs, and even politicians. A recent business move has shot them near the top of my list, and that is their strategic alliance with the American Film Market (AFM). With this new partnership, the festival will attract acquisitions executives from all over the world — giving filmmakers exposure not only to loving festival-goers, but also to buyers from more than eighty countries. That's a *huge* benefit for filmmakers that will surely have an impact on Sundance's "back-door market" approach.

Attending buyers with a market badge will also get access to the films screening at the festival, creating a whole new game for acquisitions execs to play.

This approach also levels the playing field in terms of filmmakers looking for exposure. Those films that do not officially get into AFI Fest now have the opportunity to screen at the market for buyers. And the market itself plays host to everything from film production companies, to financiers, to production services, to individual filmmakers seeking a sale.

I'm personally ecstatic to see this very smart approach finally being taken by a major US film festival. How many big sales come out of this AFI Fest/AFM monster over the years will be the scorecard used to determine whether this is a marriage made in heaven or a typical Hollywood coupling (you know, one that doesn't last through lunch).

This alliance certainly has the potential to turn AFI Fest into the American version of Cannes, combining a strong festival dedicated to the art of cinema, with a valuable commercial component via the market. Whatever the results, there will never be a shortage of excitement at AFI Fest.

AFI FEST
AFI LOS ANGELES INTERNATIONAL FILM FESTIVAL

American Film Institute
2021 N. Western Ave.
Los Angeles, CA 90027-1657
Tel..................................323-856-7600; 888-AFI-FEST
Fax 323-467-4578
Email ....afifest@afi.com
Web Site...www.afi.com

Year Festival Began: 1986
Festival Month: Early November
Entry Deadline: Early: June; Final: July
Number of Submissions: 2,500
Entry Fee: Early Deadline: Features - $40; Shorts - $30
Late Deadline: Features - $50; Shorts - $40
Genres: American, Animation, Digital, Documentary, Features, First-Time Independent Filmmakers, Independent, International, Narrative, Shorts
Screening Format: 16mm - 35mm - Beta SP - DigiBeta
Number of Films Screened: 135
Odds: 1 in 18
X Factor: Thanks to a new partnership with the American Film Market, filmmakers will receive an all-access AFM badge. On top of that, AFI Fest will identify festival films with all rights available and will promote them to AFM Exhibitors. Shuttles will also move festival and market participants between the Hollywood and Santa Monica headquarters.
Awards: Grand Jury Awards, Audience Awards
Profile: The AFI Los Angeles International Film Festival is the longest-running film festival in Los Angeles and one of the most influential film festivals in North America.
A program of the American Film Institute, AFI Fest spans 10 days each November, featuring international competitions of brand new films from emerging filmmakers, global showcases of the latest work from the great film masters and nightly red-carpet gala premieres.
AFI Fest offers visiting filmmakers a crucial avenue of exposure to the film community, while providing appreciative audiences with the very best of world film, right in the film capital of the world.
Special Events: Special screenings, parties, panels
Filmmaker Perks: When possible, the festival pays for travel and accomodations.
Travel Tips: Rent a car, seriously. Navigating Los Angeles without a vehicle is insane.

Christian Gaines.....................................Festival Director
Nancy Collet.............................Director of Programming

5. Berlin Film Festival

While people are recovering from Sundance and the insanity of Park City, the Berlin Film Festival is just getting started. Taking place at the beginning of February each year in Berlin, Germany, this fest is one of Europe's longest running (over fifty years) and most prestigious events. Filmmakers arriving at Berlin are given the best of treatment. Traveling overseas can be stressful for some and the incredibly helpful staff make navigating Berlin a breeze. The festival assigns a liaison to every accepted filmmaker, someone who can answer questions and attend immediately to every need — whether that is a ride to a film, help exchanging currency, taking care of problems with your flight, or where to get a cheeseburger — these liaisons are on the case. (This special attention comes in handy, especially as the theaters are spread all over town.) To say that the festival is well-organized is an understatement — Berlin is perhaps the best-organized festival in the world. For example, every person attending the festival receives a badge that is swiped for each screening. Filmmakers are given a copy of the names, as well as the audience member's designation as a filmmaker, journalist, distributor, or a viewer. In addition, there are no such things as a "wait line." The badges allow the ticketsellers to calculate precisely how many tickets are available for each screening, making attending screenings much less of a hassle. For filmmakers, there is also the European Film Market, which takes place during the festival and affords producers the opportunity to sell their films for theatrical, video, or television to European territories. Being so far from Hollywood, there is no sense of pretentiousness about the festival. This is not a Hollywood schmooze-fest, Berlin is about the appreciation of film.

Internationale Filmfestspiele Berlin
Programme Department
Potsdamer Strasse 5
Berlin D-10785
Germany
Tel ....+49-30-259-20-444
Fax ....+49-30-259-20-499
Email.......program@berlinale.de or info@berlinale.de
Web Site...www.berlinale.de

Year Festival Began: 1951

Festival Month: Early February

Entry Deadline: November

Entry Fee: Features: $150; Shorts: $60

Genres: Animation, Documentary, European, Features, Independent, International, Narrative, Shorts

Screening Format: 16mm - 35mm - BetaSP

Number of Films Screened: 23 in competition

X Factor: Beyond the competition, the European Film Market is in full effect, so if you've still got distribution rights available, you know where to find the acquisition execs.

Awards: The Golden Berlin Bear Awards, The Silver Berlin Bear Awards, Other Awards

Profile: With 15,000 accreditated attendees, including 3,500 journalists from approximately 76 countries, the Berlin International Film Festival has taken its place among the largest and most highly regarded media and industry events; it enjoys an undisputed international level of renown in artistic and film industry aspects.

Special Events: Awards, parties, panels

Travel Tips: The festival partners with local hotels to provide special rates for accredited, professional visitors (hopefully, that's you), so make sure you take advantage of the hospitality. E-mail hotel@berlinale.de for more information.

Dieter Kosslick ....Festival Director

This panel at SXSW featured festival programmers and experts.

6. SXSW: South By Southwest Film Festival

Austin is a party town and there is no better bash than SXSW. They also show some pretty cool films. I like to think that I go to Austin for the movies, but for me, Sixth Street is as much of a draw as the chance to see newest indie work. The bars, clubs, and restaurants lining Sixth Street during SXSW are not quite as wild as Mardi Gras in New Orleans (think less nudity), but they come damn close. Austin's down-to-earth folks make the non-stop partying almost as attractive as the films. SXSW screens films at a lot of venues, but the one I love the best is my favorite movie theater in America: the Alamo Drafthouse.

The informative panels, the prominent guests, and the down-home openness of the people provide a whirlwind education in filmmaking. The panels are truly the best on the fest circuit, with compelling subjects geared toward both the beginning indie filmmaker and the seasoned vet. Because of the casual atmosphere of the festival itself, the panels offer true interaction with the audience. Spend a weekend at SXSW and you'll get almost the same amount of information and inspiration you'd get from four years in film school. It really is that good. To supplement the panels, SXSW provides mini-meetings and mentoring session where filmmakers can get one-on-one support directly from industry insiders.

In addition to the panels and mini-meetings, there is a convention hall featuring booths with products and services all geared toward indies — everything from DVD replication, to locations, to the latest digital cameras, to the production of cheap promo items. The variety of exhibitors provide everything a filmmaker

SXSW programmer Matt Dentler at one of the many parties during the fest.

SXSW

PO Box 4999
Austin, TX 78765
Tel..512-467-7979
Fax...512-467-0754
Email ....film@sxsw.com
Web Site ....www.sxsw.com/film

Year Festival Began: 1994
Festival Month: Mid-March
Entry Deadline: Early December
Number of Submissions: 3,000
Entry Fee: $25-$50
Genres: Animation, Digital, Documentary, Experimental, Features, First-Time Independent Filmmakers, Independent, International, Markets, Music Videos, Narrative, Performance, Shorts, Student
Screening Format: 16mm - 35mm - BetaSP - DigiBeta
Number of Films Screened: 150
Odds: 1 in 20
X Factor: An opportunity to screen with indie and mainstream movies in a very relaxed atmosphere.
Awards: Jury Awards
Audience Awards
Profile: The South By Southwest Film Festival showcases films in both Documentary and Narrative Feature Competition, as well as a series of sidebars including: 'Round Midnight for horror/action films, Lone Star States for Texas-made features, Emerging Visions for new and innovative feature filmmakers, 24 Beats Per Second for music-related documentaries, and a Political Films Retrospective collection. SXSW also includes short films in the narrative, documentary, animated, experimental, and music video categories.
Special Events: Film conference, panels, parties, special screenings
Travel Tips: Attend the film festival and then stick around for the music festival.

Matt Dentler ....Festival Producer

could possibly need to get a project off the ground.

The fest began as an extension of the SXSW Music and Media Conference and has quickly established itself as a formidable force in the indie film world. This slightly Tex Mex-flavored independent festival has attracted the likes of Quentin Tarantino, Robert Rodriguez, Richard Linklater (Richard and Robert both live in Austin), and Kevin Smith, among others, who attend annually to sit on panels and simply enjoy the fest. Texas filmmakers are given their due with screenings, and this attention to regional artists gives out-of-towners a taste of something more than the usual indie fare. The atmosphere is incredibly laid back, which accounts for a lot of their tremendous growth. People come back to Austin year after year for this event — including me.

7. Telluride Film Festival

Telluride is one of the best vacation festivals on the planet. Sundance may be the place where the industry does business, but in Telluride you'll make lifelong friends at the movies. Set in a former mining town in the Rocky

Telluride Film Fest's Tom Luddy.

Telluride shuts down Main Street for a party and everyone is invited.

Mountains at a breathtaking (literally) 9,000 foot elevation, the September event in Telluride, Colorado, transforms the whole tiny city into a celebration of cinema. (The town itself is very small and everything is within convenient walking distance — no need to rent a car.) The charming venues will remind you of the movie theaters of yesteryear — without the modern (and sometimes annoying) sound systems of theaters today that can leave your ears ringing.

If there's one drawback, it's the cost. Attending Telluride can be prohibitively expensive. This explains the fact that most attendees are, frankly, older, white and affluent. It's definitely populated by old school film folks — which makes it a great place to learn and make valuable contacts. On another note, there are a limited number of passes. The most expensive pass is the "patron pass" and pretty much guarantees admittance. Regular passes don't guarantee admittance, but the festival repeats the best attended films later in the week, so you'll get into the popular films eventually.

There is something very special about being at Telluride. Conversation in movie lines revolves around the "art" and appreciation of movies rather than "grosses," current box office, or the latest "deal," all of which is incredibly refreshing. Leave your cell phone at home — not only will you not need it, you *will* be heckled if it starts to ring. This festival is all about an appreciation and love of film; save the deal-making for another festival. This festival is also short — a four-day event that seems to end too soon and always leaves you wanting more. There's just something in the air at Telluride that unites everyone in a cinema love-fest.

379 State St.
Portsmouth, NH 03801
Tel..603-433-9202
Fax...603-433-9206
Email.................................mail@telluridefilmfestival.org
Web Site ....www.telluridefilmfestival.org

Year Festival Began: 1974

Festival Month: Early September

Entry Deadline: Mid-July

Entry Fee: $25-$95

Genres: All, Animation, Documentary, Features, Independent, International, Narrative, Shorts, Student

Screening Format: Any Format

Number of Films Screened: 45

X Factor: The first films of Robert Rodriquez, Michael Moore, and Billy Bob Thornton debuted here.

Awards: No

Profile: A tiny one-street town nestled in the base of jaw-dropping vistas and sparkling green hills, Telluride might seem an unlikely candidate to play host to an international array of actors and writers, filmmakers, and film lovers. But it is precisely this relaxed, remote, and intimate atmosphere that makes it so ideal. The Telluride Film Festival is truly an event for people with a deep love for the art of cinema. Even while requiring that the the key filmmakers and performers attend with their works, "The Show," and its directors take great care to ensure that the films on display, and not the celebrities in attendance, are the focus. If you've filmed it, we'll watch it....

Special Events: The Guest Director, the three tributees, the Silver Medallion recipients, panels, parties

Filmmaker Perks: If you get in, the festival bends over backwards to take care of you.

Travel Tips: As flights into the Telluride area are limited, passholders are strongly urged to immediately contact Telluride Central Reservations, the Festival's travel partner, to arrange transportation.

Tom Luddy ....Festival Co-Director
Bill Pence...Festival Co-Director

8. Los Angeles Film Festival

The Los Angeles Film Festival got a huge boost when the festival management was taken over by the IFP (Independent Feature Project). The IFP is an organization that is an indispensable resource for independent filmmakers — they offer help with everything from production, to mentoring, funding, and health care. Now the same group that brings those useful resources to their members and puts on the Independent Spirit Awards has delivered a festival truly geared toward the filmmaker.

First of all, the LAFF gives out one of the largest prizes in the entire festival world — a $50,000 cash prize for Best Narrative Feature, and a $25,000 cash prize for Best Documentary (provided by their main sponsor, Target). Before the festival begins, filmmakers are pampered at a getaway retreat, which allows them to bond with other attending filmmakers and festival staff. To further assist the filmmakers in achieving their goals, indie film industry luminaries are invited to participate in a kind of "speed-dating" event. Filmmakers get to spend ten minutes each with some of the biggest in the business who consult and offer advice on taking their film and career to the next level. And if that's not enough, the

LAFF also has one of the best filmmaker goodie bags *ever*.

Sure, the extra benefits for filmmakers are numerous, but a quality line-up of movies is the key and the LAFF features perhaps the strongest line up of American independent films on the circuit. Films such as *Kissing Jessica Stein, Spellbound, Cabin Fever, Step into Liquid, The Cooler, George Washington, Lovely and Amazing, Tadpole, Biggie and Tupac,* and *24 Hour Party People*, among many others, have all made their Los Angeles debuts at LAFF. And by merely screening at the festival, a film qualifies for an Independent Spirit Award nomination.

Even more recently, the festival has been extremely supportive in seeing its alumni secure distribution. Recent acquisitions out of the festival include George Hickenlooper's *Mayor of the Sunset Strip*. It helps that the majority of acquisitions executives based in Los Angeles are willing to drive the whopping twenty minutes to the festival.

Presentation is always a concern for filmmakers, and this is where the LAFF excels. There are no screenings in converted libraries or makeshift movie houses with questionable sound. Films screen at state of the art theaters including the Directors Guild of America and the Laemmle Sunset 5, with special screenings at the John Anson Ford Amphitheatre, Laemmle Town Center 5 Encino, Wadsworth Theater, and the best movie theater in Los Angeles: the ArcLight Cinerama Dome.

The LAFF provides the best combination of hard partying fun and business. Don't miss it.

8750 Wilshire Blvd., 2nd Floor
Beverly Hills, CA 90211
Tel 323-951-7090
Email ....lafilmfest@ifp.org
Web Site ....www.lafilmfest.com

Year Festival Began: 1995

Festival Month: Mid-June

Entry Deadline: Mid-February

Number of Submissions: 2,500

Entry Fee: Features: $65; Shorts: $45; Music Videos: $30; High School Shorts: None

Genres: American, Animation, Digital, Digital Animation, Documentary, DVD, Ethnic African, Ethnic Asian, Ethnic Black, Ethnic Jewish, Ethnic Latin, Ethnic Spanish, Experimental, Features, First-Time Independent Filmmakers, Gay Lesbian, Independent, Multimedia, Narrative, Shorts, Student, Underground, Video, Weird, Women

Screening Format: 16mm - 35mm - BetaSP - DigiBeta

Number of Films Screened: 200

Odds: 1 in 12

X Factor: Held in the heart of Hollywood, the festival offers heightened industry exposure to independent filmmakers.

Awards: Jury Awards
Audience Awards

Profile: The IFP Los Angeles Film Festival, held annually for ten days in June, showcases the best of American and International independent cinema. With an attendance of over 40,000, the festival screens over 200 narrative features, documentaries, shorts, and music videos.

Special Events: Parties, panels, awards ceremony
Filmmaker Perks: Hollywood executives regularly attend screenings and despite not having an official market aspect, many films get picked up for distribution.
Travel Tips: It's LA in the summer... bring the sun tan lotion.

Richard Raddon ....Festival Director
Rachel Rosen..........................Director of Programming

9. Seattle International Film Festival

This twenty-five-day event is one of the longest festivals in the world, with a program of more than 250 films. The thirty-year-old festival mixes the best of American Independents with International debuts and secret screenings with a focus on seeking the best in cutting edge cinema — no matter where it is found. The event attracts prominent critics like David Ansen of *Newsweek* and heavy hitters from the indie film world who not only attend to see movies, but also to participate in panels. Events such as those hosted by Ray Harryhausen and the likes Quentin Tarantino (who hosted the "The Tarantino Tutorial: Q.T. Celebrates Unsung American Master William Witney") bring together students and film lovers from all over. In one of the more clever programs, called the Fly Filmmaking Challenge, filmmakers each draw one word out of a hat as the subject of their movie. They then have five days to shoot and edit a five-minute short. There are various themes to this friendly competition, but the result of one of those shorts was Dan Mirvish's feature musical comedy *Open House.*

Additionally, the festival's commitment to supporting women in film is to be applauded. Female filmmakers are embraced and included — not marginalized, as sometimes happens with other festivals. Aside from the spectacular city itself, Seattle is a town of film fanatics who crave new cinematic experiences. The adoring audiences are a filmmaker's dream, with nearly every screening nearly filled to capacity — no matter how bad the screening time slot is. Giants of the industry come to Seattle just to screen for their appreciative audiences.

Seattle International Film Festival

c/o Cinema Seattle
400 9th Ave. N
Seattle, WA 98109
Tel 206-464-5830
Fax..206-264-7919
Email ....info@seattlefilm.com
Web Site ....www.seattlefilm.com
Year Festival Began: 1975
Festival Month: Late May-June
Entry Deadline: Early March
Entry Fee: $25-$70
Genres: All, Animation, Documentary, Ethnic Asian, Features, Gay Lesbian, Independent, International, Narrative, Shorts, Women
Screening Format: 16mm - 35mm - BetaSP - DigiBeta
Number of Films Screened: 250

X Factor: The audience in Seattle is extremely appreciative of film, which is why the festival can last for almost a month.

Awards: Golden Space Needle Awards, Jury Awards, Other Awards

Profile: The Seattle International Film Festival is the largest festival in the US and has been cited by the *New York Times*, *Variety*, *Film Comment*, and *USA Today* as one of the top five festivals in North America. It is also one of only seven film festivals in North America chosen to qualify films for consideration in the Independent Spirit Awards, the Indie film world's equivalent of the Oscars®. Running a full 25 days and screening over 200 feature and short films from over 50 different countries, SIFF is considered one of the most influential festivals in the world. SIFF is produced by Cinema Seattle, a not-for-profit, membership based organization.

SIFF brings unique films from every corner of the globe to Northwest filmgoers. The festival includes gala premieres, new films from first-time and well-know directors, sneak previews, and special archival programs. Our audiences see many films months before they reach general distribution and many that will never be screened here again.

Special Events: Opening and closing parties, panels, awards

Filmmaker Perks: Networking, networking, networking. And great parties.

Travel Tips: Does it really rain all the time? No, and when it does, it's a mist so if you've got a nice windbreaker and ball cap, bring them.

Helen Loveridge ....Executive Director
Carl Spence ....Director of Programming

10. Tribeca Film Festival

No film festival in history has grown faster than Tribeca, which should be no surprise considering the face and founder of the fest is the legendary Robert DeNiro and the co-chair is Martin Scorsese. After September 11th, DeNiro and company felt that the businesses in the Tribeca area of New York needed to be revitalized and what better way to do that than a film festival?

Celebrities attend in force to be a part of the event, and

Hollywood studios, as well as important indie filmmakers, premiere their films there. In addition to the red carpet star-studded premieres and family film program, there's even a makeshift drive-in on the pier. Tribeca's primary sponsor is American Express, and the dollars appear to be well spent, as the entire city seems to transform with banners and signage everywhere. Some may claim to be the "Sundance" of their respective regions, but Tribeca is literally "The Sundance of the East Coast," having established itself very quickly as a must stop on the festival circuit. No other festival in New York gets as much national media attention, and for this reason alone, attending filmmakers will benefit greatly.

However, Tribeca's unprecedented growth has come with its share of problems. Organizational issues abound, though these are likely to be solved quickly. The primary problem is that of identity — frankly, the festival is lacking in one. Tribeca is, for lack of a better term, Frankenstein-like — as if the film programs were cobbled together from all the other New York festivals into one *monster* festival that tries to be all things to all people. This lack of identity will resolve itself over time, as long as the festival organizers are responsive to what works and what doesn't. At the moment it seems as if they are trying everything possible, throwing it against the wall to see if it sticks. Expect to see Tribeca go through some evolutionary changes over the years as it shifts direction and hones its image.

In spite of the above-mentioned (and very solvable) prob-lems, there is no doubt that the Tribeca Film Festival has earned its place on the short list of discovery festivals.

TOP TEN FILM FESTIVALS FOR AMERICAN INDEPENDENTS (U.S. only)

1. Sundance
2. SXSW
3. AFI Fest
4. IFP Los Angeles
5. Telluride
6. Seattle International
7. Tribeca
8. New York New Directors
9. Denver International
10. Cinequest San Jose

TOP TEN FILM FESTIVALS WORLDWIDE (Not including U.S.)

1. Toronto
2. Cannes
3. Berlin
4. Rotterdam
5. Oldenburg
6. Durban
7. Tokyo
8. London
9. Melbourne
10. Vancouver

TRIBECA FILM FESTIVAL

375 Greenwich St.
New York, NY 10013
Tel 212-941-2400
Fax..212-941-3939
Email ....festival@tribecafilmfestival.org
Web Site ....www.tribecafilmfestival.org

Year Festival Began: 2002
Festival Month: Early May
Entry Deadline: November
Number of Submissions: 3,300
Entry Fee: $40-$50
Genres: All, Animation, Documentary, Features, First-Time Independent Filmmakers, Independent, International, Narrative, Shorts, Student
Screening Format: 16mm - 35mm - BetaSP
Number of Films Screened: 65 in competition, 250 total
Odds: 1 in 50 for competition, 1 in 13 overall
X Factor: This festival is young, but it's on the rise to the festival elite.
Awards: Jury Awards, MTV Films Award for Student Visionary Film, The Budweiser/ TriggerStreet.com Audience Award, Other Awards
Profile: In 2002, the Tribeca Film Institute successfully launched the First Annual Tribeca Film Festival. Created by Jane Rosenthal and Robert De Niro, the mission of the Tribeca Film Festival is to enable the international film community and the general public to experience the power of film by redefining the film festival experience. The Tribeca Film Festival was founded to celebrate New York City as a major film-making center and to contribute to the long-term recovery of lower Manhattan.
Special Events: Panels, parties, special screenings, awards
Filmmaker Perks: Great networking possibilities, exposure.
Travel Tips: Venues are all over, so expect to do a bit of walking and subway riding.

Peter Scarlet ....Executive Director
Maggie Kim ....Programming Coordinator

MAJOR NORTH AMERiCAN FiLM FESTiVALS
United States and Canada

30 BELOW FiLM & ViDEO COMPETiTiON
PO Box 21084
West End Postal Outlet
Brandon R7B 3W8 Canada
Tel 204-727-9704
Fax 204-726-7649
Web Site www.filmfest.mb.ca/30below

Year Festival Began: Mid-60's

Festival Month: Mid-March

Entry Deadline: Late December

Entry Fee: $25

Genres: Canadian, Digital, Documentary, Features, First-Time Independent Filmmakers, Independent, Narrative, Shorts, Student, Video

Screening Format: 16mm - 35mm - DVD - BetaSP - DigiBeta

Profile: The 30 Below Film & Video festival is a film & video competition for emerging Canadian independent moviemakers that are the age of 30 or younger.

Special Events: Workshops, panels, parties

Travel Tips: It may be the end, but it's still Winter so bring warm clothes.

Richard Hunt ....President
Ellis Crowston.................................Vice-President

A.K.A. SHRiEKFEST, THE LOS ANGELES HORROR/SCiENCE FiCTiON FiLM FESTiVAL & SCREENPLAY COMPETiTiON
PO Box 920444
Sylmar, CA 91392-0444
Tel 818-367-9161
Fax 818-367-9861
Email ....email@shriekfest.com
Web Site ....www.shriekfest.com

Year Festival Began: 2001

Festival Month: September

Entry Deadline: Late May, Late Deadline: Late July

Entry Fee: $25-$55

Genres: Documentary, Fantasy/Science Fiction, Features, First-Time Independent Filmmakers, Horror, Independent, International, Narrative, Shorts, Student, Thriller

Screening Format: All Formats Accepted

Awards: Youngest Filmmaker & Screenplay Award; Shriekfest Award

Profile: A.K.A Shriekfest is a festival dedicated to discovering new and overlooked artists. What makes our festival unique is that we are free from any restrictions that other festivals may have...for instance, we are thrilled when your film has won in other festivals, we won't hold that against you by not allowing your film an entry possibility. The whole point of our festival is to help out the filmmakers by letting as many people see your film as possible (not by limiting when and where your film is shown). We just want to celebrate the art of filmmaking without all of the politics!

Special Events: screenplay competition

Travel Tips: Tons of parking available around the theater, but watch for meters and parking signs.

Denise Gossett ....Festival Co-Founder
Kimberlee S. Beeson......................Festival Co-Founder

AFRiCAN FiLM FESTiVAL
154 West 18th Street., Suite 3B
New York, NY 10011
Tel 212-352-1720
Fax 212-807-9752
Email ....nyaff@erols.com
Web Site ....www.africanfilmny.org

Festival Month: Early April

Entry Fee: None

Genres: Documentary, Ethnic African, Ethnic Black, Features, Independent, International, Narrative, Touring

Awards: No

Profile: The African Film Festival, a nonprofit arts organization, explores ways to introduce African film to non-African audiences, not only to develop a much needed market for this growing body of work but to open a dialogue between artists and media professionals on the two continents. Through panel discussions and post-screening events where audiences and filmmakers meet, AFF offers opportunitites for increased awareness of and interest in African culture and the development of new channels of distribution for African film throughout the US.

Special Events: Panels

Travel Tips: Forget cabs, bring comfortable shoes and use the subway.

Mahen Bonetti..................................Executive Director

AMERiCAN BLACK FiLM FESTiVAL

c/o Film Life
PO Box 688
New York, NY 10012
Tel...212-219-7267
Email..abff@thefilmlife.com
Web Site ....www.abff.com

Year Festival Began: 1997

Festival Month: Mid-July

Entry Deadline: Early April

Entry Fee: $30

Genres: American, Documentary, Ethnic Black, Features, Independent, International, Narrative, Shorts, Works in progress

Screening Format: 16mm - 35mm - BetaSP - DigiBeta - MiniDV

Awards: Blockbuster Audience Award for Best Feature Film; ABFF Filmmaker Trophy; Best Performance by an Actor Award; Best Performance by an Actress Award; HBO® Short Film Award

Profile: The American Black Film Festival (ABFF) is a five-day retreat and international film market dedicated to strengthening the independent Black filmmaking community. Formerly known as the Acapulco Black Film Festival, the festival was born out of a belief in the need to stimulate independent Black film development and promote cultural diversity within the film industry.

The ABFF is committed to nurturing filmmakers in a variety of disciplines. Through competitive film showcases and innovative annual programming initiatives (including panel discussions, workshops and seminars), the festival aims to attract and develop top-tier talent.

Filmmaker Perks: The festival takes place at the infamous South Beach in Miami, FL.

Travel Tips: Miami's climate is hot and tropical, so dress comfortably.

Jeff Friday...Founder

AMERiCAN FiLM MARKET

10850 Wilshire Blvd., 9th Fl.
Los Angeles, CA 90024 U.S.A.
Tel..310-446-1000
Fax...310-446-1600
Email ....afm@afma.com
Web Site ....www.americanfilmmarket.com

Year Festival Began: 1981

Festival Month: Early November

Entry Deadline: Mid-January

Entry Fee: $2,200 for Producer's Screening $6,030 to exhibit with an office.

Genres: 35mm, Animation, Documentary, Features, Independent, International, Markets, Narrative

Screening Format: 35mm - 70mm

Number of Films Screened: 400, 16 Producer's Screening slots

X Factor: Thanks to a new partnership with the American Film Institute (AFI) - Los Angeles International Film Festival, exhibitors will receive an all-access AFI festival pass.

Profile: The business of motion picture production and distribution - a truly collaborative process - reaches its peak every year at the American Film Market. For eight days, the AFM is the epicenter of the film industry. With over 300 motion picture companies and 7,000 film executives, the AFM assembles the largest gathering of the industry's most influential leaders. Acquisition and development execs, producers, distributors, agents, attorneys, buyers, and film financiers convene to pursue the business of film. Hundreds of films are financed, packaged, licensed, and greenlit, sealing over half a billion dollars in business for both completed films and those in preproduction.

Special Events: Seminars, premiere screenings, Producer's Screenings

Filmmaker Perks: The AFM offers discounted rates at official AFM Hotels for registered attendees.

Travel Tips: Use the shuttle to get between the AFM and the AFI Film Festival, happening concurrently.

Jonathan Wolf ....Managing Director
Robert Newman ....VP, Finance & Accounting
Robin Burt ....Director, Marketing & Corporate Alliances
Andrea Keldsen ....Manager, AFM Operations

AMERiCAN iNDiAN FiLM FESTiVAL

333 Valencia St., Suite 322
San Francisco, CA 94103
Tel..415-554-0525
Fax 415-554-0542
Email...indianfilm@aifisf.com
Web Site ....www.aifisf.com

Festival Month: Early November

Entry Deadline: Early August

Entry Fee: $50

Genres: Documentary, Ethnic Other, Features, Independent, International, Multi-Cultural, Music Videos, Narrative, Shorts

Screening Format: 16mm - 35mm - BetaSP

Awards: Jury Awards; Horizon Award

Profile: The goals of American Indian Film Festival are inherently educational: to encourage Native/non-Native filmmakers to bring to the broader media culture the Native voices, viewpoints and stories that have been historically excluded from mainstream media; to develop Indian and non-Indian audiences for this work; and to advocate tirelessly for authentic representations of Indians in the media.

Special Events: Awards

Travel Tips: November in San Francisco can be rainy, so be prepared.

Michael Smith ....Festival Founder

ANGELUS AWARDS STUDENT FiLM FESTiVAL

Family Theater Productions
7201 Sunset Blvd.
Hollywood, CA 90046
Tel..............................800-874-0999; 323-874-6633
Email...info@angelus.org
Web Site..www.angelus.org

Festival Month: Late October
Entry Deadline: Early July
Entry Fee: $25
Genres: Animation, Documentary, Independent, International, Narrative, Shorts, Student, Video
Screening Format: 16mm - 35mm - BetaSP - DigiBeta
Awards: Patrick Peyton Excellence in Filmmaking Award

Priddy Bros. Productions & Windrider Media "Triumph" Award

FujiFilm Audience Impact Award

Mole-Richardson Production Design Award

Spirit of Angelus Award

Profile: The Angelus Awards recognize and show-case student films of uncommon artistic caliber that explore the complexity of the human condition with creativity, compassion and respect. It is an international festival and seeks films with themes of redemption, equality, spirituality, triumph of the human spirit, dignity, etc.

Special Events: Award ceremony
Filmmaker Perks: All finalist films screen at the Director's Guild in Hollywood.
Travel Tips: Fly into LAX and rent a car, it's really the easiest way to do things.

Monika Moreno ....Festival Director

ANN ARBOR FiLM FESTiVAL

PO Box 8232
Ann Arbor, MI 48107
Tel...734-995-5356
Fax..734-995-5396
Email...info@aafilmfest.org
Web Site...www.aafilmfest.org

Year Festival Began: 1963
Festival Month: Mid-March
Entry Deadline: Mid-November
Number of Submissions: 1,500
Entry Fee: $35
Genres: 16mm, 35mm, Digital, Documentary, Experimental, Features, Gay Lesbian, Independent, International, Narrative, Shorts, Student, Touring
Screening Format: 35mm - 16mm - DVD - BetaSP
Number of Films Screened: 100
Odds: 1 in 15
X Factor: All screenings and events take place in the historic Michigan Theater, a restored 1920s movie house in downtown Ann Arbor. The theater has two screening spaces: the 1,700-seat main auditorium in which the entire film program is presented, and the 200-seat screening room in which additional screenings, workshops, and seminars take place.
Awards: $18,000 in cash prizes to over thirty films in a number of different categories
Profile: The Ann Arbor Film Festival is a festival of independent and experimental film and video. Established in 1963, this internationally-renowned festival is the oldest of its kind in North America. Each year the festival attracts entries from moving image artists worldwide and screens more than 100 films before audiences during six days in March.

The festival does not place emphasis on money or stars, but over the years it has fostered its fair share of luminaries. Entries have been screened by such enterprising filmmakers as Kenneth Anger, Sally Cruikshank, Brian DePalma, Barbara Hammer, Lawrence Kasdan, George Lucas, Yoko Ono, Gus Van Sant, Agnes Varda, Will Vinton, and Andy Warhol.
Special Events: The Ann Arbor Film Festival is a founder of the traveling festival tour concept. Post festival-week, the Festival Director selects a four-hour program of awarded and highlighted films for the Ann Arbor Film Festival Tour.
Filmmaker Perks: The festival doesn't pay for travel expenses, but does provide housing for programmed filmmakers.
Travel Tips: For general hotel and travel ir phone the Ann Arbor Convention & Visitor at (800) 888-9487, or visit their websit' www.annarbor.org.

Chrisstina Hamilton..............................Fr
Carrie Cecchini ....As

FiLM FESTiVAL

1401

....410-263-2388
Fax...410-263-2629
Email ....info@annapolisfilmfestival.com
Web Site ....www.annapolisfilmfestival.com

Festival Month: Early November

Entry Deadline: Mid-June, Late Deadline: Mid-July

Entry Fee: $20-$50

Genres: Animation, Documentary, Features, Independent, International, Shorts

Screening Format: 35mm - BetaSP - DVD - MiniDV

Awards: Jury Awards

Profile: The Annapolis Film Festival is an international film festival catering to all genres, bringing independent films to the scenic backyard of Washington, DC.

Special Events: Workshops, panels, awards, Masquerade Ball, parties

Travel Tips: Fly into BWI Airport and rent a car so you can enjoy the sights without trying to keep up with a bus or train schedule.

ANTiMATTER FESTiVAL OF UNDERGROUND SHORT FiLM & ViDEO

Rogue Art
F - 1322 Broad St.
Victoria, BC V8W 2A9 Canada
Tel...250-385-3327
Email...info@antimatter.ws
Web Site..www.antimatter.ws

Year Festival Began: 1998

Festival Month: Mid-September

Entry Deadline: Late May

Entry Fee: $10-$20

Genres: Animation, Canadian, Digital, Digital, Digital Animation, Digital Animation, Documentary, DVD, Experimental, Fantasy/Science Fiction, Gay Lesbian, Independent, International, Multimedia, Music Videos, Shorts, Student, Super 8/8mm, Touring, Underground, Video, Weird, Women

Screening Format: Super 8 - 16mm - DVD - MiniDV

Awards: No

Profile: Dedicated to the exhibition and nurturing of film and video as art, Antimatter has grown into the premier showcase of experimental film in the west. Encompassing screenings, installations, performances and hybrid media experiments, Antimatter provides a noncompetitive festival setting in Victoria, British Columbia, free from commercial and industry agendas.

Special Events: Video exhibitions, workshops, parties, Foreign Matter curated series

Filmmaker Perks: Lots of networking with like-minded filmmakers.

Travel Tips: Fly or take the ferry in from Vancouver, because you can't drive to an island.

Todd Eacrett..Festival Director
Deborah de Boer...Curator

ARiZONA iNTERNATiONAL FiLM FESTiVAL

PO Box 431
Tucson, AZ 85702
Tel 520-628-1737
Fax 520-628-1737
Email...reelfrontier@yahoo.com
Web Site ....www.azmac.org

Festival Month: Mid-April

Entry Deadline: Early February

Genres: Animation, Documentary, Experimental, Features, Independent, International, Narrative, Shorts

Screening Format: 16mm - 35mm - BetaSP

Awards: The Reel Frontier Film and Video Competition awards in the categories of features, documentaries, shorts, comedy, animation and experimental.

Profile: The Arizona International Film Festival is a celebration of extraordinary films not seen on ordinary screens! The festival showcases new and innovative film and video selections from artists around the world who have something to say from their very unique perspective. Every year in April, filmmakers, sponsors, volunteers, ticket buyers and the Tucson community enjoy 10 full days of events including workshops, talks, parties, special presentations, musical performances and, of course, screenings of works not shown in any mainstream exhibition venue.

Special Events: Workshops, panels, parties, special screenings

Travel Tips: Tucson is served by 14 different airlines with nonstop service to 18 cities and connections to more than 121 destinations.

Laurel Bullington....................................Festival Publicist

ARiZONA STATE UNiVERSiTY SHORT FiLM AND ViDEO FESTiVAL

ASU Art Museum
Tenth St. and Mill Ave.
Tempe, AZ 85287-2911
Tel..480-965-2787
Fax...480-965-5254
Email...spiak@asu.edu
Web Site ....asuartmuseum.asu.edu/filmfest

Year Festival Began: 1997

Festival Month: Late April

Entry Deadline: Mid-February

Number of Submissions: 320

Entry Fee: None

Genres: American, Animation, Digital Animation, Documentary, Ethnic African, Ethnic Asian, Ethnic Black, Ethnic Jewish, Ethnic Latin, Ethnic Other, Ethnic Spanish, Experimental, Fantasy/Science Fiction, First-Time Independent Filmmakers, Gay Lesbian, Independent, International, Multimedia, Shorts, Student, Super 8/8mm, Touring (Santa Ana and Santa Barbara), Underground, Video, Weird, Women

Screening Format: VHS - DVD

Number of Films Screened: 18-21

Odds: 1 in 15

Awards: LeBlanc Audience Choice Award; Juror Choice Awards; AZ Award

Profile: Arizona State University Art Museum is proud to present annually a number of short films and videos by artists from around the world. For one evening, individuals are asked to bring a lawn chair, blanket or anything else they wish to use as a seat and meet at the museum's back plaza for this free outdoor film festival event.

Special Events: Awards, outdoor screenings

Filmmaker Perks: All entrants receive a copy of the entire festival on VHS once the festival has been completed.

Travel Tips: The museum is ten minutes from Phoenix Sky Harbor airport, or a quick one-hour flight from Southern California.

John D. Spiak ....Festival Director
Bob Pece ....Festival Programmer

ASPEN SHORTSFEST

110 E Hallam, Suite 102
Aspen, CO 81611
Tel...970-925-6882
Fax..970-925 1967
Email ....shortsfest@aspenfilm.org
Web Site..www.aspenfilm.org

Festival Month: Late March-April

Entry Deadline: Mid-December

Entry Fee: $35-$45

Genres: Canadian, Commercials, Documentary, Experimental, Independent, International, Music Video, Narrative, Shorts, Student

Screening Format: 16mm - 35mm - BetaSP

Awards: Winners can qualify for Academy Award nomination.

Animated Eye Awards; The Ellen Award; The Horizon Award; Audience Favorite Award

Profile: Aspen Shortsfest is widely recognized as one of the world's premiere showcases for short film and video. The festival offers an intimate internation-

al forum for emerging artists, established film professionals, and film-loving audiences.

Aspen Shortsfest includes public screenings, tributes, retrospectives, panels, workshops, classroom visits, and other festivities, creating a unique celebration of short cinema and is attended by shorts fans, filmmakers, media journalists, buyers, bookers and other media professionals.

Special Events: Workshops, panels, parties, awards

Filmmaker Perks: Check with the festival for discounted rates at select Aspen hotels and lodges.

Travel Tips: Winter will finally be making way for spring, but make sure you've got some warm clothes just in case.

Laura Thielen......................................Executive Director

ASPIRATIONS FILM FESTIVAL

Suite 516
24-94 Bridgeport Rd. E
Waterloo ON
N2J 2J9 Canada
Tel...519-880-0894
Fax..519-885-1048
Email..info@studentfilm.ca
Web Site..www.studentfilm.ca

Festival Month: Late September

Entry Deadline: Late March

Entry Fee: $20

Genres: Animation, Canadian, Documentary, Experimental, Features, Independent, Narrative, Shorts, Student

Screening Format: Super 8 -16mm - BetaSP - VHS - HI-8 - MiniDV - DVCam

Awards: Jury Awards; People's Choice Award

Profile: Aspirations Film Festival provides a showcase for the developing talents of the next generation of film enthusiasts within Canada. AFF has become a fixture within the emerging community of student filmmaking by creating and sustaining a professional environment that supports and promotes young film artists in this country. On an annual basis, AFF assembles, organizes, promotes, and ultimately celebrates student films from across Canada. This anthology of various subjects, formats, and styles present students with the opportunity, at minimal cost, to achieve recognition, acquire experience, and gain exposure on a national level.

Special Events: Opening gala, awards

Filmmaker Perks: If you're a Canadian film student, this festival is dedicated solely to you.

Travel Tips: Bring warm clothes.

David Henderson...................................Festival Director
Eli Craig...General Manager

ATLANTA FILM FESTIVAL

75 Bennett St. NW
Suite N-1
Atlanta, GA 30309
Tel...404-352-4225
Fax..404-352-0173
Email...aff@imagefv.org
Web Site.........................www.atlantafilmfestival.com

Year Festival Began: 1977

Festival Month: Mid-June

Entry Deadline: Early February

Number of Submissions: 1,000

Entry Fee: $40

Genres: Animation, Documentary, Experimental, Features, Independent, International, Narrative, Shorts, Student

Screening Format: 35mm - BetaSP

Number of Films Screened: 150

Odds: 1 in 6

X Factor: In 2003 the festival moved from the Regal Hollywood 24 theatre to the downtown Rialto Center for the Performing Arts, which immediately boosted festival attendance, setting a record of 26,000 attendees.

Awards: Over $100,000 in cash prizes amongst a number of different categories, and all Short Film winners are eligible for Academy Award nomination

Profile: Since 1977, the Atlanta Film Festival has offered rich opportunities for the Atlanta community to experience the work of local, regional, national and international media artists. Atlanta Film Festival is widely considered one of the most respected and longest-running festivals in the United States.

Special Events: Parties, panels, and awards.

Comments: Screening films at the Image Film & Video Center, Atlanta has been a long supporter of indie shorts and features. In fact, Steven Spielberg's short *Amblin'* premiered at the festival in 1968.

Filmmaker Perks: A party is held every night, and anyone who buys a ticket to a festival film may attend.

Paul Marchant......................................Festival Director
Lorna Wilson............................Programming Associate

ATOMFILMS

Attn: Submissions
114 Sansome St., 10th Floor
San Francisco, CA 94101
Email......................submissions@atomshockwave.com
Web Site..www.atomfilms.com

Year Festival Began: 1999

Festival Month: Ongoing

Entry Deadline: None

Entry Fee: None

Genres: Animation, Digital, Multimedia, Online Festival, Web Projects
Screening Format: Flash, Quicktime, Real Media, Windows Media
Awards: No
Profile: AtomFilms provides on-demand viewing of over 1,500 world-class film and animation titles ranging from 1 to 30 minutes in length.
Filmmaker Perks: Anyone, anywhere - with Internet access - can see your film.
Travel Tips: It's online so, uh, unless you're like that guy in *Tron*, you're really not going anywhere.

Mika Salmi ....Founder and CEO

AUSTiN FiLM FESTiVAL

1604 Nueces St.
Austin, TX 78701
Tel 800-310-FEST; 512-478-4795
Fax...512-478-6205
Email ....info@austinfilmfestival.com
Web Site ....www.austinfilmfestival.com

Year Festival Began: 1994
Festival Month: Mid-October
Entry Deadline: Film Competition Deadline: Mid-July
Screenplay Competition Deadline: Early May
Number of Submissions: 1,400
Entry Fee: Films: $50
Screenplays: $40
Genres: Animation, Documentary, Features, Independent, International, Narrative, Shorts, Student
Screening Format: 16mm - 35mm - DigiBeta
Number of Films Screened: 140
Odds: 1 in 10
X Factor: Don't have a feature or short to show, how about making a trailer for the festival and competing in the Austin Film Festival Trailer Competition.
Awards: Award winning short films are eligible to be nominated for an Academy Award®; Jury Awards
Profile: Showcasing the best in independent film for the past ten years, the Austin Film Festival has become an eminent launching pad for new films and filmmakers. In addition to providing incredible networking opportunities, the Festival routinely yields immediate, practical success for participating filmmakers.
Special Events: Young Filmmakers/UT Summer Camp; Heart of Film Screenwriters' Conference
Comments: While the city of Austin, Texas, is already home to SXSW in March, the lesser-known Austin Film Festival deserves notice for simply choosing to take a different approach. AFF keeps its focus on the craft of screenwriting, making it unique among festivals where the director is always king. Their screenwriting conference takes place simulta-

neously with the festival and has attracted top screenwriters who engage in panels, seminars and workshops.
There's a kick back atmosphere and a chance to network with successful Hollywood screenwriters and indie filmmakers alike. And the best part - the city of Austin itself where Sixth Street is home to enough bars, restaurants and music venues to keep you up all night.
Filmmaker Perks: Film competition and screenplay finalists receive free airfare and accommodations courtesy of the Austin Film Festival, as well as Producer Badges to the conference.
Travel Tips: Don't stay out all night. The lobby of the Driskill Hotel, headquarters to the festival, ends up being a late night meeting place for festival guests where passionate conversations about film go on until the wee hours.

Barbara Morgan ....Executive Director/Co-Founder
Phil Scanlon ....Film Programmer (Los Angeles)
Kelly Williams ....Film Competition Director
BJ Burrow ....Screenplay Competition Director

AViGNON/NEW YORK FiLM FESTiVAL

145 Ave. of the Americas, 7th Floor
New York, NY 10013
Tel 212-343-2675
Fax..212-840-5019
Email ....jhr2001@aol.com
Web Site ....www.avignonfilmfest.com

Festival Month: Mid-April
Entry Deadline: Early March
Entry Fee: $25
Genres: American, Animation, Documentary, European, Features, First-Time Independent Filmmakers, French, Independent, International, Narrative, Shorts
Screening Format: 35mm - BetaSP
Awards: "The 21st Century Filmmaker Awards" for the best two feature films and for the best two short films as well as "Kodak Vision Award" for best cinematography. Decided by audience vote.
Profile: The Avignon/New York Film Festival celebrates French and American independent film with new films, retrospectives, round-tables on pertinent issues with industry experts, interviews with filmmakers and receptions, gourmet foods & high-caliber beverages, wines and liqueurs, and prizes for emerging filmmakers.
Special Events: Panels, retrospectives, parties, awards, screenwriting seminar
Filmmaker Perks: The festival provides a VIP pass for all screenings, panels, and parties.
Travel Tips: Try and hook up with a host family for your accomodations while in town.

Jerome Henry Rudes ....President/General Director
Sarah Knight ....Producer

BACKSEAT FiLM FESTiVAL

1730 N. 5th St. #603
Philadelphia, PA 19122
Tel 215-235-5603
Fax 425-799-9722
Email ....info@backseatconceptions.com
Web Site.........................www.backseatfilmfestival.com

Festival Month: Late January, Ongoing
Entry Deadline: Rolling Deadlines, Check Website
Entry Fee: Under 30 Minutes: $10
30-60 Minutes: $15
Over 60 Minutes: $20
Music Videos: $5
Genres: Documentary, Features, First-Time
Independent Filmmakers, Independent, International,
Music Videos, Narrative, Rock and Roll, Shorts,
Touring
Screening Format: VHS - DVD - MiniDV
X Factor: The festival tours with the Vans Warped
Tour, making sure your rock and roll movie gets to
THE rock and roll crowd.
Awards: Filmmaker Appreciation Award
Profile: The Backseat Film Festival prides itself on
showing the best rock 'n roll films from yesterday
and today. We at the festival believe that movies
have to have the right spirit, not just the right music,
to be a great rock 'n roll movie. We don't care how
much your movie cost to make, we don't care what
grades you got in film school, we don't care about the
symbolic meaning of the sunset and the circle of life,
and we don't care how funny your stupid friends
think the movie is. Your movie will be accepted into
the festival if we like it and we think people will
enjoy it when they're getting drunk at our screenings.
Special Events: After, or even during festival events,
there is a party to be found. The Backseat Film
Festival strives to provide a party enviroment at
every event. Also, there has not been one Backseat
Film Festival event that does not serve some kind of
booze, and we aim to uphold this tradition!
Filmmaker Perks: Eventually somebody will buy you
a drink, so talk to as many filmmakers as you can.
Travel Tips: Ever followed your favorite band on
tour? Get a couple of friends and a van.

Zafer Ulkucu ....Director of Programming

BEVERLY HiLLS FiLM FESTiVAL

9663 Santa Monica Blvd., Suite 777
Beverly Hills, CA 90210
Tel 310-779-1206
Email ....info@beverlyhillsfilmfestival.com
Web Site ....www.beverlyhillsfilmfestival.com

Year Festival Began: 2001
Festival Month: Early May
Entry Deadline: Early February
Entry Fee: $50-$75

Genres: Animation, Documentary, Ethnic African,
Ethnic Asian, Ethnic Black, Ethnic Jewish, Ethnic
Latin, Ethnic Spanish, Features, First-Time
Independent Filmmakers, Gay Lesbian, Independent,
International, Narrative, Shorts, Women
Screening Format: 16mm - 35mm - Other Format
Awards: Yes
Profile: Beverly Hills Film Festival is dedicated to
showcasing and promoting some of the most auspi-
cious non-studio films and screenplays to the entertainment elite. Designed to bridge the world of premier independent cinema with the renowned community of Beverly Hills, the festival is an entertainment event with world-class screenings at The
Clarity Theatre, nightly theme parties, seminars, and
a charity benefit. The festival will conclude with a
black tie awards ceremony and a special dedicated
honorary award for one of the best films of the year
acknowledged by the Academy of Motion Picture
Arts and Sciences. We welcome filmmakers and the
Beverly Hills community to share in the celebration
of art and culture in this wonderful city of international acclaim.
Special Events: Awards, parties, special screenings,
seminars, charity benefit, screenplay competition
Filmmaker Perks: Festival can arrange discounted
travel packages for filmmakers.
Travel Tips: It's okay to park on the street if you
can find it. Valet parking gets expensive.

Kathren Hanna ....Festival Director

BiG BEAR LAKE iNTERNATiONAL FiLM FESTiVAL

PO Box 1981
Big Bear Lake, CA 92315-1981
Tel 909-866-3433
Fax 909-866-3433
Email...................................BigBearFilmFest@aol.com
Web Site ....www.bigbearlakefilmfestival.com

Festival Month: Mid-September
Entry Deadline: Mid-April
Entry Fee: Features: $40
Shorts: $35
Genres: Animation, Digital, Documentary, Ethnic
Other, Family, Features, Independent, Narrative,
Shorts, Student
Screening Format: 35mm - BetaSP
Awards: Shirley Jones Family Film Award
Jury Awards
Audience Awards
Profile: The Big Bear Lake International Film
Festival is a non-profit organization dedicated to
showcasing emerging film talent and independent
films. Our goal is to create a forum by bringing
upcoming filmmakers and industry professionals
together, staged in the Big Bear Lake Community.

Special Events: Parties, awards, panels, breakfasts
Filmmaker Perks: All filmmakers get two filmmaker badges entitling them to free admittance to all screenings.
Travel Tips: It's fall, so be prepared for the temps to drop a bit at night.

Michael and Carolyn Miller ....Co-Founders

BiG FiLM SHORTS

3727 W. Magnolia Blvd., #189
Burbank, CA 91505
Tel 818-563-2633
Fax 818-955-7650
Email ....info@bigfilmshorts.com
Web Site ....www.bigfilmshorts.com
Year Festival Began: 1996
Festival Month: Ongoing
Entry Deadline: None
Entry Fee: None
Genres: All Categories - Shorts, Online Festival
Screening Format: Online
Awards: No
Profile: Big Film Shorts offers top quality, sophisticated entertainment in the form of short films, primarily via the Internet, to as wide an audience as possible.
Filmmaker Perks: Big Film Shorts is an online distribution center, working to sell and promote your short film.

David Russell ....President

BiG MUDDY FiLM FESTiVAL

Dept of Cinema and Photography
Southern Illinois University
1100 Lincoln Dr., Room 1101
Carbondale, IL 62901-6610
Tel 618-453-1482
Fax 618-453-2264
Email ....bigmuddy@siu.edu
Web Site ....www.bigmuddyfilm.com
Year Festival Began: 1979
Festival Month: Late February
Entry Deadline: Late January
Number of Submissions: 200
Entry Fee: Under 20 Minutes: $35
20-50 Minutes: $40
Over 50 Minutes: $45
Genres: Documentary, Environmental, Features, Human Rights, Independent, International, Narrative, Shorts, Student
Screening Format: 16mm - VHS - DVD - MiniDV
Number of Films Screened: 50
Odds: 1 in 4
Awards: Audience Choice; Festival Choice; John Michaels Memorial Award

Profile: The Big Muddy Film Festival showcases all independent films, and while it emphasizes the experimental and documentary filmmaker, the festival also includes narrative and feature length works. The festival provides an opportunity for filmmakers to compete and gain recognition for their work. Among the monetary awards is the newly established John Michaels Memorial Film Award, presented to the best work entered in the Big Muddy Film Festival that promotes human rights, peace and justice topics, or environmental issues.
Special Events: Awards
Travel Tips: The closest airport is in Marion, IL, about 11 miles outside of Carbondale.

Evan Smith ....Festival Director

BLACK MARiA FiLM AND ViDEO FESTiVAL

c/o New Jersey City University
2039 Kennedy Blvd. Dept. of Media Arts
Jersey City, NJ 07305
Tel 201-200-2043
Fax 201-200-3490
Email ....blackmariafest@aol.com
Web Site ....www.njcu.edu/programs/taebmff/
blackmariafest.html

Festival Month: Late January (on tour from January-June)
Entry Deadline: Mid-November
Entry Fee: Features: $45
Shorts: $35
Genres: All, Features, Independent, International, Narrative, Shorts, Touring (Alabama, Smithsonian, California, Alaska, Rhode Island, Virginia, Atlanta, Vermont, Korea, New Jersey, New York, Boston, Chicago, Ohio, Pennsylvania)
Screening Format: Super 8mm, 16mm - 35mm - VHS - DVD - DV

BEST VACATION FILM FESTIVALS

Aspen Film Festival
Bermuda International Film Festival
Cinema Epicuria Sonoma Valley Film Festival
CineVegas Film Festival
Deep Ellum Film Festival
Florida Film Festival
Hawaii International Film Festival
Marco Island Film Festival
Miami Film Festival
New Orleans Film Festival
San Diego Film Festival
Sidewalk Moving Picture Festival
Woodstock Film Festival
Waterfront Film Festival

Number of Films Screened: 50
Awards: Jury's Choice Awards
Jury's Citation Awards
Director's Choice Awards
Profile: Since 1981, the annual Black Maria Film and Video Festival, an international juried competition and award tour, has been fulfilling its mission to advocate, exhibit, and reward cutting edge works from independent film and videomakers.
Filmmaker Perks: Winning films eligible for Academy Award® consideration.

John Columbus......................................Festival Director

---

WHAT SELLS

Talk to people about the marketplace. What kind of films sell? What doesn't sell? What are the realistic expectations for my movie?

BLUE SKY INTERNATIONAL FILM FESTIVAL - LAS VEGAS

231 Horizon Ridge, Suite 225
Henderson, NV 89012
Tel 702-566-7666
Email ....info@bsiff.com
Web Site ....www.bsiff.com
Year Festival Began: 1997
Festival Month: Late September
Entry Deadline: Ongoing - Check Website or Call for Current Deadline
Entry Fee: $30; Students with Valid ID: $25
Genres: All, Animation, Documentary, Features, Independent, International, Music Videos, Narrative, Shorts, Student, World
Screening Format: 35mm - VHS - BetaSP - DVD - MiniDV - Hi8
Number of Films Screened: 30-50
X Factor: Watch a film, give a Q&A, and gamble away your life savings in Las Vegas.
Profile: Founded in 1997, BSIFF has been dedicated to the discovery and exhibition of new talent within the independent world of filmmaking.

Since that time, BSIFF has become the best source for independent and world cinema in Las Vegas. Every year BSIFF showcases a variety of films from such countries as the United States, Canada, Mexico, Brazil, Japan, Korea, Singapore, India, Australia, New Zealand, England, France, and Germany.
Travel Tips: Las Vegas has a variety of travel options, so check out www.bsiff.com/lasvegas.html for useful travel links.

Jeffrey Matthews Hill ....Festival Director/Founder

BOSTON FILM FESTIVAL

PO Box 516
Hull, MA 02045
Tel 6171421-4499
Email ....gemsad@aol.com
Web Site ....www.bostonfilmfestival.org
Festival Month: Mid-September
Entry Deadline: Early July
Number of Submissions: 50+
Entry Fee: Under 30 Minutes: $20
30-60 Minutes: $35
Over 60 Minutes: $50
Genres: 16mm, 35mm, Animation, Documentary, Features, Independent, International, Narrative, Shorts
Screening Format: 16mm - 35mm
Profile: The Boston Film Festival screens independent films from throughout the world.
Filmmaker Perks: Festival takes care of travel and accomodations when possible.
Travel Tips: Take a 2 hour trip into New Hampshire and watch the leaves change for a side experience.

BOSTON GAY & LESBIAN FILM & VIDEO FESTIVAL

c/o Museum of Fine Arts Film Program
465 Huntington Ave.
Boston, MA 02115-5597
Tel 617-369-3016
Fax 617-437-0293
Email...gaylezfest@yahoo.com
Web Site...www.mfa.org/film
Festival Month: Mid-May
Entry Deadline: Late January
Entry Fee: $20-$75
Genres: All, Animation, Documentary, Features, Gay Lesbian, Independent, International, Narrative, Shorts
Screening Format: 16mm - 35mm - BetaSP - VHS - DVD
Number of Films Screened: 15
Profile: The MFA presents Boston Gay & Lesbian Film & Video Festival celebrating gay, lesbian, bi, and trans issues and culture, which includes comedies, documentaries, and shorts.
Travel Tips: The ice of Boston has melted, and spring is in full bloom.

May Haduong...................................Festival Coordinator
James Nadeau ....Festival Coordinator

BOSTON INTERNATIONAL FESTIVAL OF WOMEN'S CINEMA

Tel 617-734-2500
Email ....connie@beaconcinema.com
Web Site ....www.beaconcinema.com/womfest

Festival Month: Early April

Entry Deadline: February

Entry Fee: None

Genres: Animation, Documentary, Features, Independent, International, Shorts, Women

Screening Format: 35mm - Other

Awards: No

Profile: Over its eleven year history, the Boston International Festival of Women's Cinema has developed as a leading showcase for commercial and independent works by and about women. Each year the festival secures "sneak preview" screenings from prominent art film distributors including Miramax Films, Fine Line Features, Sony Pictures Classics, and others. The festival also launches world and Boston-area premieres of independent works and has helped to secure theatrical film and cable television distribution for independent filmmakers.

Marianne Lampke ....Festival Director

BOSTON INTERNATIONAL FILM FESTIVAL

204 Tremont St.
Boston, MA 02116
Tel..............................781-935-0871 ; 617-426-4600
Email ....info@bifilmfestival.com
Web Site ....www.bifilmfestival.com

Festival Month: Late June

Entry Deadline: Late March

Entry Fee: $35-$70

Genres: Animation, Documentary, Features, Independent, International, Narrative, Shorts

Screening Format: 35mm - BetaSP

Awards: Indie Spirit, Soul and Spec Awards

Profile: The Boston International Film Festival was created in order to celebrate the art of filmmaking and honoring the filmmakers who make it all possible. This is a festival to reward artists for their individual talent and their expression through creativity. The festival strives to bring together local, national and international filmmakers to Boston by promoting the world's most artistic and creative independent and experimental film.

Special Events: Awards

Travel Tips: Catch a Red Sox game while you're in town at historic Fenway.

BRAINWASH MOVIE FESTIVAL

PO Box 23302
Oakland, CA 94623-0302
Tel 415 273-1545
Email ....shelby@brainwashm.com
Web Site ....www.brainwashm.com

Year Festival Began: 1994

Festival Month: Early July

Entry Deadline: Mid-May

Entry Fee: $20-$75

Genres: American, Animation, Experimental, Features, First-Time Independent Filmmakers, Independent, Markets, Microcinema, Shorts, Television, Touring, Video, Weird

Screening Format: VHS - DVD

Awards: Yes

Profile: The Brainwash Movie Festival is dedicated to presenting new, original, exciting movies at theatrical events and on television.

Special Events: Drive-In/Bike-In screenings, awards, parties

Travel Tips: Public transportation: From West Oakland BART exit left from station and cross the parking lot. Left at 5th Street to festival entrance on right.

Shelby Toland ....Festival Director

BRECKENRIDGE FESTIVAL OF FILM

PO Box 718
Breckenridge, CO 80424
Tel 970-453-6200
Email ....info@breckfilmfest.com
Web Site ....www.breckfilmfest.com

Year Festival Began: 1981

Festival Month: Early September

Entry Deadline: Early May

Entry Fee: Features: $50

Shorts: $40

Students with Valid ID: $40

Genres: Animation, Documentary, Features, First-Time Independent Filmmakers, Independent, International, Narrative, Shorts, Student

Screening Format: BetaSP - VHS - SVHS - DVD

Awards: Jury Awards; Audience Choice; Best Gay, Lesbian, or Transgender (GLBT) Film

Profile: The Breckenridge Festival of Film emphasizes a relaxed atmosphere in which filmmakers are readily accessible to film-goers. Writers, directors, producers, and actors discuss their work with audiences in informal sessions following film screenings, at receptions, and at outdoor film forums.

Special Events: Workshops, awards, parties

Filmmaker Perks: Lodging accomodations and discounts on ground transportation provided for filmmakers during the festival.

Travel Tips: Breckenridge is located approximately 80 miles west of Denver via interstate highway 70, so if you fly into Denver, you have quite a drive ahead of you.

Mitch and Vicki Kaman ....Programming Directors
Dave Downer ....Festival Contact

BRiGHTON iNTERNATiONAL FiLM FESTiVAL

6387 Brighton Rd.
Brighton, MI 48116
Email ....brightonfilmfest@hotmail.com
Web Site ....brightonfilmfest.homestead.com

Festival Month: Mid-November
Entry Deadline: Mid-October
Entry Fee: $25-$50
Genres: Animation, Documentary, Independent, International, Narrative, Shorts, Student
Screening Format: VHS - DV - CDRom
Profile: The Brighton International Film Festival purpose is to develop, encourage, sponsor, and otherwise support the appreciation, production, and growth of independent, community, and alternative media arts in southeast Michigan and the surrounding region. Special attention is placed on the encouragement of K-12 student film production. The Brighton International Film Festival also serves statewide and internationally as an advocate for greater cooperation with artists, producers, students, and other media art centers holding similar goals. Offering artists and students a chance to exchange cultural ideas through an international forum is a prime focus.
Travel Tips: Michigan winters are cold, make sure you're prepared.

BROOKLYN UNDERGROUND FiLM FESTiVAL

PO Box 050339
Brooklyn, NY 11205
Email ....info@brooklynunderground.org
Web Site ....www.brooklynunderground.org

Festival Month: October
Entry Deadline: Mid-July
Entry Fee: $30
Genres: Animation, Documentary, Experimental, Features, Independent, Narrative, Shorts, Underground
Screening Format: Super8 - 16mm - BetaSP - VHS - DV
Profile: Founded in 2002 by a small group of passionate, young filmmakers, the Brooklyn Underground Film Festival is an outlet for emerging and radical new voices from around the globe. The Brooklyn Underground's mission is to create a fresh

arena for discussion between artists, filmmakers, and audiences, with a focus on personal cinema and work driven by new processes.
Special Events: Parties
Travel Tips: Wear comfortable shoes, you'll be walking.

Josh Koury ....Co-Founder/Director of Programing

BUMBERSHOOT 1 REEL FiLM FESTiVAL

1725 Westlake Ave. N., Suite 202
Seattle, WA 98109
Tel 206-281-7788
Fax 206-281-7799
Email...filmfest@onereel.org
Web Site ....www.bumbershoot.org/film.htm

Festival Month: Early September
Entry Deadline: Mid-May
Entry Fee: $25
Genres: Animation, Documentary, Experimental, First-Time Independent Filmmakers, Independent, International, Narrative, Shorts, Student
Screening Format: 35mm - BetaSP
Awards: Best Live-Action, Best Animation and Best High School Film Awards
Profile: The 1 Reel Film Festival at Bumbershoot presents over 100 of the hottest new American-made short films - including documentaries, animation, live-action, music video, and video poems. Each film is programmed into a thematic package and the movies run non-stop each festival day.
Filmmaker Perks: The festival takes place during Bumbershoot, the West Coast's largest arts festival, lighting up over 20 stages and performance spaces with the work of more than 2,500 artists in all disciplines, including visual arts, literary arts, music, comedy, dance, theater, circus arts, and more.

CALGARY iNTERNATiONAL FiLM FESTiVAL

Suite 206
1008 17th Ave. SW
Calgary, Alberta
T2T 0A6 Canada
Tel...403-209-1490
Fax 403-283-1498
Email ....marrelli@calgaryfilm.com
Web Site...www.calgaryfilm.com

Festival Month: Late September-October
Entry Deadline: Mid-July
Entry Fee: $20
Genres: Animation, Canadian, Documentary, Features, Independent, International, Narrative, Shorts, Student
Screening Format: 16mm - 35mm - 70mm - BetaSP - DigiBeta - DVD

Awards: AGF People's Choice Award
National Film Board Award for Best Canadian Documentary
CBC Newsworld Award for Best International Documentary
Profile: The Calgary International Film Festival showcases films of all genres and formats during its ten day, competitive festival.
Special Events: Parties, Youth Film Series, awards

David Marrelli..Festival Director
Andrew Eyck ....Programming Director

CHICAGO HORROR FILM FESTIVAL

Gatlin Pictures
520 E. Bronson St.
Streator, IL 61364
Email..................................festival@gatlinsdomain.com
Web Site ....www.gatlinsdomain.com/horrorfest

Festival Month: Early April
Entry Deadline: Ongoing
Entry Fee: Features: $15
Shorts: $10
Genres: Fantasy/Science Fiction, Features, Horror, Independent, International, Narrative, Shorts, Thriller
Screening Format: 16mm - 35mm - BetaSP - MiniDV
Profile: The Chicago Horror Film Festival is dedicated to screening the best in horror, fantasy/sci-fi and thriller films.
Travel Tips: The theater is right around the corner from DePaul University and a Children's Hospital... how's that for perspective?

CHICAGO INTERNATIONAL DOCUMENTARY FESTIVAL

1112 North Milwaukee Ave.
Chicago, IL 60622
Tel 773-486-9612
Fax..773-486-9613
Email ....info@chicagodocfestival.org
Web Site ....www.chicagodocfestival.org

Festival Month: Early April
Entry Deadline: Mid-March
Entry Fee: None
Genres: Documentary, Features, Independent, International, Shorts
Screening Format: 16mm - 35mm - BetaSP - DigiBeta - DVCam - MiniDV
Awards: Chicago Doc Grand Prix
Natasha Isaacs Cinematography Award
Arie & Bozena Zweig Innovation Award
Chicago Doc Audience Award
Humanitarian Award

Profile: The Chicago International Documentary Festival is a premier US festival of documentary films. Each edition presents an array of extraordinary programs, showcasing the work of brilliant filmmakers and providing a venue for established and emerging artists of film.
Special Events: Awards
Filmmaker Perks: The Grand Prix is worth $15,000.
Travel Tips: Catch a Cubs opening game while you're in town.

CHICAGO INTERNATIONAL FILM FESTIVAL

32 West Randolph St., Suite 600
Chicago, IL 60601-9803
Tel 312-425-9400
Fax 312-425-0944
Email..................................info@chicagofilmfestival.org
Web Site............................www.chicagofilmfestival.org

Year Festival Began: 1964
Festival Month: Early October
Entry Deadline: Late July
Entry Fee: Narrative Feature: $100
Documentary Feature: $80
Short Subject (Under 30 Minutes): $50
Short Subject (30-60 Minutes): $60
Students with Valid ID: $30
Genres: All, Animation, Documentary, Ethnic Black, Ethnic Jewish, Features, Gay Lesbian, Independent, International, Narrative, Shorts, Student
Screening Format: 16mm - 35mm - 70mm - BetaSP - DigiBeta - HD
Number of Films Screened: 140
Awards: Hugo Awards; FIPRESCI Award

BEST INTERNATIONAL FESTIVALS IN THE U.S.

American Film Institute (AFI) - Los Angeles International Film Festival
Chicago International Film Festival
Cleveland International Film Festival
Denver International Film Festival
Houston International Film and Video Festival (Worldfest Houston)
Rhode Island International Film Festival
Santa Barbara International Film Festival
San Francisco International Film Festival
Seattle International Film Festival
St. Louis International Film Festival
Washington, DC International Film Festival (Filmfest DC)
West Virginia International Film Festival

Profile: The annual Chicago International Film Festival, now in its fourth decade, is the oldest competitive international film festival in the US. Many of the films shown to the public in the Film Festival participate in a number of competitions including those for feature films, short films, animation and experimental films.

At the Chicago International Film Festival, they've remained true to the spirit of discovery for over four decades. The festival annually presents the latest and greatest in world cinema with presentations of new work by veteran masters and talented newcomers.

Special Events: The festival holds a variety of panels and tributes, as well as educational programs for students, outreach programs for the deaf and hard of hearing, and special pre-release screenings.

Comments: The Chicago International Film Festival maintains an international flavor by showing amazing new work from all over the world - Argentina, England, Brazil, Mexico, Turkey, Russia, Belgium, Japan, France, Iceland, Germany, Poland, Taiwan, Australia, Spain, Thailand, and Iran among others - all while avoiding an air of pomposity.

In addition, their relentless support of issue-raising documentaries is to be commended. The programmers at Chicago are not following anyone else's lead - they're taking their own lead and running with it. With over 100 films, a truly international line-up, an impressive variety of documentaries and Hollywood galas, the Chicago International Film Festival provides a welcome alternative to the multiplexes littering the Midwest.

Filmmaker Perks: The festival pays for travel and accomodations for invited filmmakers.

Travel Tips: Late fall in Chicago - bring a warm coat.

Michael Kutza ....Artistic Director/Founder
Helen Gramates ....Director of Programming

CHICAGO UNDERGROUND FILM FESTIVAL

167 N. Racine
Chicago, IL 60607
Tel 773-327-3456
Email ....info@cuff.org
Web Site ....www.cuff.org

Festival Month: Mid-August
Entry Deadline: Early May
Entry Fee: $30
Genres: Animation, Documentary, Experimental, Features, Independent, International, Narrative, Shorts, Underground, Weird
Screening Format: Super 8- 16mm - 35mm - BetaSP - VHS - DVD - MiniDV
Number of Films Screened: 100

X Factor: The Chicago Underground Film Fund has been established to provide completion funds for films that are in keeping with the festival's defiantly independent, experimental and adventurous spirit. Recipients are awarded grants of $500- $2,000 in cash and services.
Awards: Jury Awards
Profile: The Chicago Underground Film Festival exists to showcase the defiantly independent filmmaker. Our mission is to promote films and videos that dissent radically in form, technique, or content from the "indie" mainstream and to present adventurous works that challenge and transcend commercial and audience expectations...if you suspect your film is "underground," it probably is.

When the festival was established, most film festivals catered to an older, elitist crowd. Our festival was founded to open up the film festival experience to a younger, hipper audience of film-lovers and filmmakers. We have grown into one of Chicago's major film events, a destination of choice for cutting-edge filmmakers and established the festival as an important date in Chicago's cultural scene.

Special Events: There are a number of parties and concerts associated with the festival, as well as a short film screening program at a local bar.
Comments: There is no better place to screen groundbreaking underground films than here. A sense of community also exists among the filmmakers. It's inspiring and no bullshit, all at once.
Travel Tips: Take the El or the bus to the theater, easiest mass transit around.

Bryan Wendorf ....Festival Director
Nicole Bernardi-Reis ....Marketing

CHRYSLER MILLION DOLLAR FILM FESTIVAL

c/o Hypnotic
1520 Cloverfield Blvd., Suite D
Santa Monica, CA 90404
Tel 212-809-3202
Email...steph@hypnotic.com
Web Site ....www.chryslermdff.com

Festival Month: Mid-January-September
Entry Deadline: Mid-December
Entry Fee: $30
Genres: Animation, Canadian, Documentary, Independent, International, Narrative, Shorts, Touring
Screening Format: BetaSP
Awards: Million Dollar Feature Film Deal
Profile: The Chrysler Million Dollar Film Festival begins with the submission of a short film and ends with one eligible filmmaker winning a million-dollar feature film production and distribution deal from Chrysler, Hypnotic and Universal Pictures.
Special Events: Workshops, awards

Filmmaker Perks: Universal Studios Operations Group will provide the production resources needed for the filmmakers to complete their feature film production packages.

Travel Tips: You've got to be available for all the major stops of the tour if your film advances, so be prepared to travel to Utah, New York, Toronto and Southern California.

CiNEMA EPiCURiA SONOMA VALLEY FiLM FESTiVAL

865 W. Knoll Dr.
West Hollywood, CA 90069
Tel 323-337-1006
Email ....tiffany@cinemaepicuria.org
Web Site ....www.cinemaepicuria.org

Festival Month: Early April

Entry Deadline: Mid-December

Entry Fee: Under 60 Minutes: $45-$55
Over 60 Minutes: $35-$45
Students with Valid ID: $25-$35

Genres: Animation, Documentary, Features, Independent, International, Narrative, Shorts, Student

Screening Format: 16mm - 35mm - BetaSP - DVD

Awards: The Imagery Honors, recognizing outstanding achievements in film.

Profile: Cinema Epicuria is a celebration of independent filmmaking that captures the richness of the human experience, set amidst Sonoma's epicurean pleasures of fine food, award-winning wine, soul-stirring art, and unparalleled natural beauty.

Special Events: Panels, parties, wine-tastings, lounge, awards

Filmmaker Perks: Passes to all festival events.

Travel Tips: You will have a variety of flight choices if you fly into either the San Francisco or Oakland airports. Sacramento is also an easy option. Car rentals and shuttle services are available at all airports.

Tiffany Naiman ....Program Director
Sonya Yonash ....Operations Manager

CiNEMARENO

PO Box 5372
Reno, NV 89513
Email ....cinemareno@excite.com
Web Site ....www.cinemareno.org

Festival Month: Ongoing

Entry Deadline: 1 Week Before Screening Date

Entry Fee: $20

Genres: Animation, Documentary, Features, Independent, International, Narrative, Shorts

Screening Format: 16mm - 35mm - BetaSP - VHS - DVD - MiniDV

Profile: CinemaReno is a nonprofit film society founded for the purpose of promoting the art of motion pictures in Northern Nevada. Screenings throughout the year showcase new independent films and videos, along with a selection of obscure films and classic movies. CinemaReno proudly offers an alternative to current Hollywood fare, bringing to Reno films that you are unlikely to see anywhere else.

Special Events: Varieties of screenings and events year-round

Filmmaker Perks: CinemaReno is always there, offering a venue to screen your film.

Travel Tips: Reno's like Vegas, only smaller.

CiNEMATEXAS iNTERNATiONAL SHORT FiLM & ViDEO FESTiVAL

Dept. of Radio-TV-Film
2504A Whitis Ave.
Austin, TX 78712-1091
Tel 512-471-1698
Fax 512-471-9220
Email ....cinematexas@cinematexas.org
Web Site ....www.cinematexas.org

Year Festival Began: 1995

Festival Month: Late September

Entry Deadline: Early June

Entry Fee: $30-$35

Genres: American, Animation, Digital, Digital Animation, Documentary, DVD, Ethnic African, Ethnic Asian, Ethnic Black, Ethnic Jewish, Ethnic Latin, Ethnic Spanish, Experimental, Features, First-Time Independent Filmmakers, Gay Lesbian, Independent, International, Microcinema, Multimedia, Narrative, PXL, Shorts, Student, Super 8/8mm, Underground, Video, Weird, Women

Screening Format: Super 8mm - 16mm - 35mm - BetaSP - DVD

Awards: Gecko Awards; No Budget Award; Audience Award

Profile: The Cinematexas International Short Film Festival is dedicated to screening the best and brightest short films from around the world. The only limitation is the duration of the film, any and everything else goes.

Special Events: Receptions, salons, awards, parties

Filmmaker Perks: The festival covers accomodations when possible.

Travel Tips: Summer'll be dying down. but it'll still be hot.

Ralph McKay ....Festival Director
Anne Reecer...Festival Contact

CiNEQUEST SAN JOSÉ FiLM FESTiVAL

PO Box 720040
San Jose, CA 95172-0040
Tel 408-995-5033
Fax 408-995-5713
Email ....info@cinequest.org
Web Site ....www.cinequest.org

Year Festival Began: 1990
Festival Month: Early March
Entry Deadline: May-October .
Entry Fee: $35
Genres: Animation, Documentary, Features, Independent, International, Narrative, Shorts
Screening Format: 35mm - DVD - BetaSP - DigiBeta - MiniDV
Number of Films Screened: 150
X Factor: Cinequest has gone online with the first ever full-length feature film distribution service. Users will be able to easily download or stream full-length feature films, as well as shorts, trailers and select scenes from Cinequest Online onto their computers and handheld devices, and play them back in full-screen, DVD-quality whenever they choose. Film fans and industry executives also will be able to schedule the automatic delivery of films in advance, as well as other content from Cinequest Online, including film screenings, seminar presentations or daily festival updates and other highlights delivered directly to their inboxes.
Profile: Cinequest is Northern California's premier motion picture institute that presents a soul-stirring and personable discovery festival of international films and digital media forums for movie lovers, maverick film artists and film students. Cinequest also produces and operates: Cinequest Motion Picture Studio, Youthquest, Cinequest Screenwriting Competition, and the Cinequest Membership Program.
Special Events: Maverick Spirit panels and events, Opening and Closing Night Galas, and a screenplay competition.
Comments: For more than a decade now, Cinequest has brought the best in film to San José, California. Growing at a tremendous rate, this festival screens over 100 independent films. Besides showing indie features, documentaries and several programs of shorts, Cinequest continues to champion digital filmmaking in a way unparalleled by any non-digital fest. Which is no surprise, since the festival is right in Silicon Valley's backyard. Awards are not only bestowed upon filmmakers, but also upon innovators of new filmmaking technologies. Cinequest's support of cutting edge filmmaking tools make it a must visit for the true filmmaker. Recent advances include providing DVD quality video via the internet. On the level of pure technical innovation, Cinequest is one to watch.
Filmmaker Perks: The festival covers travel and accomodations when possible.

Travel Tips: Cinequest Film Festival is proud to have American Airlines as one of its valued partners. American Airlines is offering a discount to Cinequest attendees. A 10 percent discount is available on all flights booked 30 days in advance, and a 5 percent discount is available on all flights booked within 30 days. You can take advantage of these discounts by calling 1-800-433-1790 and referring to booking code 1424BF. (Please note that these discounts are not available on Internet deals.)

Halfdan Hussey ....Executive Director/Founder
Mike Rabehl ....Director of Programming

CiNEVEGAS iNTERNATiONAL FiLM FESTiVAL

2370 Corporate Circle, Suite 300
Henderson, NV 89074
Tel 702-992-7979
Fax 702-992-7978
Email ....info-cinevegas@cinevegas.com
Web Site ....www.cinevegas.com

Year Festival Began: 1998
Festival Month: Mid-June
Entry Deadline: Early April
Number of Submissions: 700+
Entry Fee: Under 50 Minutes: $25
Over 50 Minutes: $40
Nevada Resident Films Under 50 Minutes: $15
Nevada Resident Films Over 50 Minutes: $25
Genres: Documentary, Features, Independent, International, Narrative, Shorts
Screening Format: 16mm - 35mm - Video
Number of Films Screened: 85
Odds: 1 in 8
X Factor: You'd better put on your party hats and get ready to...see some Skin! A fabulous opening gala set poolside at Skin, the sexy, outdoor nightclub venue at the Palms. Fireworks, a live band, spandex screens... the works.
Awards: Critics Awards
Profile: The CineVegas International Film Festival is one of the most successful and fastest growing festivals in the world. CineVegas' featured segments of American Independents, morning conferences with celebrated writers, nine nights of sponsor events and a one-of-a-kind poolside opening night gala make CineVegas not just a festival, but a total entertainment experience.
Special Events: Poolside opening night gala, filmmaker luncheons, and after hours parties nightly.
Comments: Combine gambling and independent film - and you've got a winning combination. CineVegas is eight days of movies, parties, panels, parties, and there are even more parties. It doesn't hurt that this festival is located in Las Vegas, which at times can be a distraction, but is that really a bad thing? After

snagging Sundance's Trevor Groth to take over film programming duties, the festival immediately brought in some of the best independent movies along with a fully stacked deck of celebrity guests. Filmmakers and guests are treated to an amazing line-up with films screened in the Palms Hotel multiplex with stadium seating and comfortable air conditioning - which is a good thing since temperatures in June can reach over 100. CineVegas is fast-becoming a must-stop on the festival circuit.

Filmmaker Perks: All filmmakers are put up in the luxurious Palms Hotel & Casino plus you'll receive tickets and coupons to a host of events around town. And, hey - you're in Vegas, baby!

Travel Tips: Don't enter any casino with more money than you're willing to lose.

Jen Jurgens ....Director of Operations
Trevor Groth ....Director of Programming

CLEVELAND INTERNATIONAL FILM FESTIVAL

2510 Market Ave.
Cleveland, OH 44113-3434
Tel 216-623-3456
Fax 216-623-0103
Email ....cfs@clevelandfilm.org
Web Site......................................www.clevelandfilm.org

Year Festival Began: 1977
Festival Month: Late March
Entry Deadline: Late November
Number of Submissions: 950
Entry Fee: $35-$75
Genres: American, Documentary, Ethnic Asian, Ethnic Black, Ethnic Latin, Ethnic Spanish, Experimental, First-Time Independent Filmmakers, Gay Lesbian, Independent, International, Short
Screening Format: 35mm - BetaSP - DVD
Number of Films Screened: 200
Odds: 1 in 5
X Factor: The three-day Midwest Independent Filmmakers Conference (MIFC) is held during the last weekend of the CIFF each year. This event features panels, workshops, equipment demonstrations, film screenings, and social events.

Awards: Yes
Profile: Founded in 1977, the Cleveland Film Society has presented the Cleveland International Film Festival every spring for nearly three decades. Ohio's premier film event features more than 200 new films from over 40 countries on six continents. Visiting directors, panel discussions, student screenings and a conference for area filmmakers are all CIFF highlights.

The Cleveland Film Society serves area film enthusiasts with film appreciation classes and year-round film exhibition. Over 1,500 people belong to its various membership and subscription groups, and tens of thousands of people enjoy its programs. The age range of participants is 8 to 80. Youngsters attend the Family Film Festival at the CIFF and senior citizens share their enjoyment of the art form in film appreciation classes.

Special Events: Cinema for Seniors, Cultural Journey, and FilmSlam screening programs in addition to FilmForums' panels.

Comments: The Cleveland Film Society's event puts together the

Salma Hayek addresses guests at a party in Park City.

most diverse film program, including foreign flicks, gay and lesbian features, documentaries, family films, Pan-African movies and American independents, resulting in perhaps the best festival in the Midwest. Those seeking international cinema will be in a state of bliss as the recent event screened over 100 features from 44 countries. It's truly a special event mixing Cleveland's richest elite patrons with film lovers from all walks of life. (Look for the moviegoers in the Browns jerseys.)

TIP: Cleveland is extremely supportive of short films showcasing more than 10 shorts programs. If you're a short filmmaker, you must submit. If you're a shorts lover, see as many as you can.

Filmmaker Perks: The festival provides travel and accomodations when possible.

Marcie Goodman ....Executive Director
William Guentzler..................Director of Programming

CMJ FILMFEST

151 W. 25th St., 12th Floor
New York, NY 10001
Tel 917-606-1908
Fax 917-606-1914
Email ....filmfest@cmj.com
Web Site ....www.cmj.com/marathon/filmfest.php

Year Festival Began: 1999
Festival Month: Late October
Entry Deadline: Late August
Entry Fee: Features and Documentaries: $30
Shorts: $20
Genres: Documentary, Features, Independent, International, Music-Related, Narrative, Rock and Roll, Shorts
Screening Format: 16mm - 35mm - BetaSP
Awards: The CMJ Signature Award is presented for Best Use Of Music In Film
Profile: CMJ FilmFest seeks the best in independent features, shorts, and documentaries that exhibit a creative and effective use of music in film.
Special Events: Awards, parties, concerts, panels

Filmmaker Perks: FilmFest goes on the same time as the CMJ Music Marathon.

Travel Tips: Use the B,D,E Subway Train to 7th Ave./53rd St. for the Hilton.

COMIC CON INTERNATIONAL INDEPENDENT FILM FESTIVAL

PO Box 128458
San Diego, CA 92112-8458
Tel 619-491-2475
Fax 619-414-1022
Email ....cci-info@comic-con.org
Web Site ....www.comic-con.org

Festival Month: Mid-July

Entry Deadline: Early May

Number of Submissions: 75

Entry Fee: None

Genres: Adventurer/Explorers, Animation, Comics, Family, Fantasy/Science Fiction, Features, Independent, International, Narrative, Shorts

Number of Films Screened: 45

Odds: 1 in 2

Awards: No

Profile: The Comic-Con International Independent Film Festival (mercifully and affectionately shortened to the CCI-IFF) screens indie short and feature films that are family-friendly genre-centric. Comic-Con will also host the *Star Wars* Fan Film Awards, in conjunction with Lucasfilm, Ltd. and AtomFilms.com.

Special Events: San Diego International Comic Con, *Star Wars* Fan Film Awards

Filmmaker Perks: It's more of a screening series than a true festival, but ICM sends agents down to seek new talent.

CROSSROADS FILM FESTIVAL

PO Box 22604
Jackson, MS 39225
Tel..601-366-3829
Email ....questions@crossroadsfilmfest.com
Web Site ....www.crossroadsfilmfest.com

Festival Month: Early April

Entry Deadline: Mid-January

Entry Fee: Features: $45

Shorts: $25

Students with Valid ID: $10

Genres: Animation, Documentary, Experimental, Features, Independent, International, Narrative, Shorts, Student

Screening Format: 16mm - 35mm - BetaSP - VHS - DV

Awards: Yes

Profile: If you think you know Mississippi...think again! Jackson, Mississippi is the cultural crossroads of the South (hence the name - Crossroads

Film Festival) and is the place where all the good stuff gets thrown together. We are also home to some real quirky and creative folks, a little Southern hospitality, fried catfish, sweet tea, and a film festival to rival the best of them.

Special Events: Receptions, workshops, parties, awards

Filmmaker Perks: Very relaxed atmosphere, unique festival in the South.

Travel Tips: Although it is Mississippi's largest city, and the state capital, Jackson feels more like a small town than a bustling city.

Monte Kraus ....Festival Director

CUCALORUS FILM FESTIVAL

PO Box 2763
Wilmington, NC 28402
Tel 910-343-5995
Fax...910-343-5227
Email ....mail@cucalorus.org
Web Site ....www.cucalorus.org

Year Festival Began: 1994

Festival Month: Late March

Entry Deadline: Early January

Number of Submissions: 400

Entry Fee: $30

Genres: American, Animation, Documentary, Experimental, First-Time Independent Filmmakers, Independent, International, Shorts, Super 8/8mm, Underground, Video, Weird

Screening Format: 35mm - BetaSP - DigiBeta

Number of Films Screened: 90

Odds: 1 in 4

X Factor: Early spring in Wilmington, NC, means fun at the beach or a round of golf.

Profile: The Cucalorus Film Festival is a five day celebration, offering a glimpse into the exciting and eclectic art of filmmaking. Each festival attracts works and audiences from all over the world, bringing people together to discuss the ever changing art. The festival is held every spring in Wilmington, North Carolina, a historic port city and growing film community on the eastern coast of the United States. Dedicated to independent filmmakers, Cucalorus strives to provide a professional showcase for challenging and exciting work from a wide range of filmmakers. The annual event is focused on providing a relaxed environment, where young and old filmmakers come together to discuss the art. Cucalorus is non-competitive, with no hefty cash prizes, offering instead a healthy dose of Southern hospitality and a few films to write home about.

Travel Tips: Call the Cape Fear Convention and Visitors Bureau at: (910) 341-4030 for all the travel info you'll need.

Dan Brawley.....................................Festival Co-Director
Craig Rogers ....Festival Co-Director

DALLAS ViDEO FESTiVAL

1405 Woodlawn Ave.
Dallas, TX 75208
Tel 214-428-8700
Fax 214-428-8702
Email ....festival@videofest.org
Web Site ....www.videofest.org

Festival Month: Early July
Entry Deadline: Mid-March
Entry Fee: $25-$40
Genres: Animation, Digital, Documentary, Experimental, Features, Independent, International, Narrative, Shorts, Video
Screening Format: BetaSP - HDCam
Awards: The Best of the Texas Show
Profile: Since 1986 The Dallas Video Festival has specialized in fiercely independent, imaginative, unusual, provocative and sometimes description-defying electronic media. In fact, we're the oldest and the largest video festival in the nation. The Dallas Video Festival has distinguished itself nationally as a veritable vortex of video, a proverbial pantheon of pixels, a place that can make your head spin, your eyeballs ache, your heart soar, and your mind expand.
Special Events: Panels, awards, parties
Travel Tips: Dress casual and cool.

Bart Weiss...Festival Director

DANCESWiTHFiLMS

The Lot
1041 N. Formosa Ave.
Formosa Bldg., Ste 217
Los Angeles, CA 90046
Tel...323-850-2929
Fax 323-850-2928
Email ....info@danceswithfilms.com
Web Site ....www.danceswithfilms.com

Year Festival Began: 1998
Festival Month: April (as of 2005)
Entry Deadline: Early January
Number of Submissions: 1,400
Entry Fee: Features: $60; Shorts: $40

Genres: American, Digital Animation, Documentary, Ethnic African, Ethnic Asian, Ethnic Black, Ethnic Jewish, Ethnic Latin, Ethnic Spanish, Experimental, Fantasy/Science Fiction, Features, First-Time Independent Filmmakers, Gay Lesbian, Independent, International, Shorts, Video, Women
Screening Format: 16mm - 35mm - BetaSP - DigiBeta - HD
Number of Films Screened: 90
Odds: 1 in 15
X Factor: No special invited films means more screens for more entries.
Profile: DancesWithFilms is the *only* film festival in the US solely geared to "unknowns" mandating that *all* competition films have no "known" actors, directors, or producers, period.

Leslee Scallon ....Co-Founder
Michael Trent..Co-Founder

DAYTONA BEACH FiLM FESTiVAL

Cinematique of Daytona
PO Box 1105
Daytona Beach, FL 32115
Tel..386-441-6504
Fax 386-323-7775
Email...sadlerds@aol.com
Web Site..www.cinematique.org

Festival Month: Mid-November
Entry Deadline: Mid-September
Entry Fee: None
Genres: Animation, Documentary, Features, Independent, International, Narrative, Shorts, Student
Screening Format: 35mm - BetaSP
Awards: Yes
Profile: American independent films, quality foreign movies, first-rate documentaries and even the occasional noteworthy animated film are all likely to turn up at the Daytona Beach Film Festival.
Special Events: Retrospectives, parties, Student Film Festival
Travel Tips: While everyone else is gearing up for winter, you'll be wondering if you've got enough time to hit the beach before your screening.

Jeff Sadler ....President

DC iNDEPENDENT FiLM FESTiVAL & SEMiNARS

2950 Van Ness St. NW, Ste 728
Washington, DC 20008
Tel..202-537-9493
Fax 202-686-7168
Email...info@dciff.org
Web Site...www.dciff.org

Festival Month: Early March

Entry Deadline: December

Genres: Animation, Documentary, Ethnic African, Features, Independent, International, Narrative, Shorts, Women

Screening Format: 35mm - BetaSP

Awards: Jury Awards; Audience Awards

Profile: The DC Independent Film Festival & Seminars (DCIFF) is a yearly event where industry professionals and the general public can see the latest most exciting independent films, whether feature, short, animation or documentary, from the United States and abroad.

Special Events: DCIFM: Film Market and Trade Show, seminars, panels, parties, awards

Filmmaker Perks: Filmmakers with a film in competition receive a "VIP Pass" giving free access to all events of the festival, seminars, tradeshow and market.

Travel Tips: Appropriate attire is required (no jeans, shorts, T-shirt, etc) for the opening and closing receptions and the DCIFF Award Ceremonies.

Carol Bidault ....Festival Contact

DEADCENTER FILM FESTIVAL

PO Box 60445
Oklahoma City, OK 73146-0445
Tel..405-808-4575
Email ....mel@deadcenterfilm.org
Web Site ....www.deadcenterfilm.org

Festival Month: Mid-June

Entry Deadline: Late March

Entry Fee: Features: $25-$35

Shorts: $15-$25

Students with Valid ID: $10-$20

Genres: Animation, Documentary, Features, Independent, International, Narrative, Shorts, Student

Screening Format: 16mm - 35mm - BetaSP - DVD

Awards: Jury Awards

Profile: The deadCENTER Film Festival was founded by Justan and Jayson Floyd in 2001. The ongoing mission of the festival is to bring quality independent films to Oklahoma City. As a result, the festival attracts filmmakers and festival attendees from around the nation who participate in an educational and dynamic forum. Designed to inspire growth in the local film industry and energize visiting film professionals, the deadCENTER Film Festival will continue to encourage the film arts through screenings, discussions, competition, special events, panels, and focused programming.

Special Events: Panels, awards, Young Filmmaker Showcase, special screenings

Comments: Bar none, the best film festival in Oklahoma. No joke, this event is put on by a group of passionate individuals in Oklahoma City dedicated to supporting independent film. Screenings take place at museums and art galleries.

Travel Tips: Bus routes shut down around 6pm, so use the trolley.

Cacky Poarch ....Festival Director

DEEP ELLUM FILM FESTIVAL

3002 B Commerce St.
Dallas, TX 75226
Tel 214-752-6759
Fax 214-752-6863
Email...info@def2.org
Web Site..www.def2.org

Year Festival Began: 1999

Festival Month: Late October

Entry Deadline: Mid-September

Entry Fee: Features: $40

Shorts: $25

Genres: American, Animation, Digital, Documentary, Ethnic Latin, Experimental, Features, First-Time Independent Filmmakers, Narrative, Online Festival, Shorts, Student, Underground, Video, Weird, Works in progress

Screening Format: 35mm - VHS - BetaSP - DigiBeta - MiniDV

Number of Films Screened: 300

X Factor: The Festival raises money for the Cancer Relief Fund, so not only will people see your film, they'll be contributing to a good cause.

Awards: Jury Awards; DEFMAN Award; Audience Awards

Profile: Deep Ellum Film Festival events take place near downtown Dallas and the Deep Ellum area. The festival opens at the historic Majestic Theater with a Film Premiere of an important independent film. In a continued effort to be one of the nation's top festivals, the Deep Ellum Film Festival is much larger than in years past. Programming includes larger, more mainstream films and filmmakers. The independent film competition highlights emerging independent film talent from all over the country. The festival also has a special showcase for films made in Dallas over the past year or made by Dallas filmmakers. Deep Ellum Film Festival screenings occur at the Angelika Film Center.

Special Events: Opening and Closing Night Galas, panels, and parties.

Comments: This 10-day event in Dallas takes place in the hip Deep Ellum district where bars, bands, booze and music thrives. The festival screens 300 works, sometimes in the most unique of circumstances. The festival supports its efforts year round with outdoor screenings and my personal favorite, the "Dive-In" - a screening that takes place outdoors where participants are encouraged to view films while relaxing in a giant pool. It must be seen to be

what are you
searching
for?

Best Discovery Film Festival
Best Truly Independent Film Festival
Best First-Time Filmmaker Festival

- Chris Gore's ULTIMATE FILM FESTIVAL SURVIVAL GUIDE 'Best Of' Lists

"the defiant fest of raw talent"

- The Hollywood Reporter

"bullish integrity has made DancesWithFilms a valuable presence on the film festival scene for six years running"

- LA Weekly

danceswithfilms

the lot • 1041 N. Formosa Ave., Formosa Bldg., 2nd Floor, West Hollywood, CA 90046
p] 323.850.2929 f] 323.850.2928 e] mail@danceswithfilms.com

w w w . d a n c e s w i t h f i l m s . c o m

believed. *Jaws* is far more entertaining to watch this way, I can guarantee you! The Deep Ellum Film Festival (often referred to as "DE/F2") is unique in its mission of promoting the art of filmmaking while supporting the ongoing battle with cancer attracting many celebrities affected by the disease. This charitable event's worthy cause is more than enough reason to attend, but the outstanding program makes it worth traveling halfway across the country to experience.

TIP: Bring a bathing suit for the Dive-In...and don't forget to wax.

Filmmaker Perks: With its diverse blend of businesses, clubs, and speciality restaurants, Deep Ellum is widely recognized as the culture and art mecca for North Texas.

Travel Tips: Check the website, www.def2.org/exper.html, for all the specifics about the area, transit, accomodations, etc.

Michael Cain..........................Artisitc Director/Founder
Melina McKinnon..............................Executive Director

STARZ DENVER
INTERNATIONAL
FILM FESTIVAL

DENVER INTERNATIONAL FILM FESTIVAL

Denver Film Society
1725 Blake St.
Denver, CO 80202
Tel..303-595-3456
Fax...303-595-0956
Email..dfs@denverfilm.org
Web Site ....www.denverfilm.org

Festival Month: Mid-October
Entry Deadline: July
Entry Fee: $20-$35
Genres: Animation, Children, Documentary, European, Experimental, Features, Independent, International, Narrative, Shorts, Student
Screening Format: 16mm - 35mm - BetaSP
Awards: John Cassavetes Award
Krzysztof Kieslowski Award For Best European Film
Starz People's Choice Award
The Stan Brakhage Vision Award
Other Awards
Profile: The Denver International Film Festival presents approximately 175 films over 10 days and plays host to more than 100 film artists. New international feature releases, independently produced fiction films and documentaries, animation, experimental works, children's programs and short subjects are included

in the festival. In addition, a number of acclaimed international film artists are honored with tributes and special "evenings with..."
Special Events: Panels, tributes, awards, seminars, parties
Comments: For more than 25 years, the Denver Film Society has brought the stars to the mile high city. Their commitment to supporting indies and maverick filmmakers is to be commended and those selected for inclusion should be honored. DIFF's John Cassavetes Award which is presented to an American director or actor for outstanding achievement in independent filmmaking is one coveted by the industry. One of the best regional fests in the US.
Filmmaker Perks: Contacts, and passes to festival events.
Travel Tips: There is a transportation center in the airport just outside baggage claim. A taxi ride costs $43-$55 to downtown from the airport.

Ron Henderson ....Festival Director

DETROIT DOCS INTERNATIONAL FILM FESTIVAL

PO Box 1235
Royal Oak, MI 48068-1235
Tel..248-214-6952
Email ....detroitdocs@msn.com
Web Site...www.detroitdocs.org

Festival Month: Mid-November
Entry Deadline: Late August
Entry Fee: $25-$30
Genres: Documentary, Features, Independent, International, Shorts, Student
Screening Format: 16mm - 35mm - BetaSP - MiniDV
Awards: No
Profile: Detroit Docs was formed by a group of devoted documentary filmmakers and film lovers. The festival is fully dedicated to bringing the world's best documentaries to Detroit area audiences.
Special Events: Seminars, parties, workshops
Filmmaker Perks: Future festivals will have a grant program.
Travel Tips: This is not a mass-transit city, so rent a car.

Chris Walny ....Executive Director

DIGITAL DAYS

2064 Alameda Padre Serra, Suite 120
Santa Barbara, CA 93103
Tel..805-730-1555
Fax 805-730-1553
Email ....digitaldaysfest@aol.com
Web Site ....www.digitaldaysfest.com

Festival Month: Early February

Entry Deadline: January

Entry Fee: Most Screenings By Invite, Check with Festival

Genres: Digital, Digital Animation, Education, Multimedia, Web Projects

Screening Format: BetaSP - DigiBeta - DVD - MiniDV

Awards: No

Profile: Highlighting state-of-the-art digital moviemaking and multimedia, Digital Days provides area youth and film enthusiasts with an up-close and hands-on experience with the latest digital software and computer technologies. Industry veterans and digital arts professionals take part in several forums and interactive discussions. Digital Days is part of the Santa Barbara International Film Festival.

Special Events: Panels, workshops, screenings

Filmmaker Perks: More of an educational showcase than a festival, seminars are sponsored by Adobe, Discreet, Canon Video, and Apple Pro-App, to name a few.

Travel Tips: Dress for warm weather, stay comfortable.

Richard Corwin ....Executive Producer
Gretchen Miller ....Producer

DiY FiLM FESTiVAL

7095 Hollywood Blvd., Suite 864
Hollywood, CA 90028-0893
Tel 323-665-8068
Fax 323-660-1776
Email ....diyconvention@aol.com
Web Site ....www.diyconvention.com

Festival Month: Early February

Entry Deadline: Late January

Entry Fee: $20-$25

Genres: Animation, Documentary, Experimental, Features, First-Time Independent Filmmakers, Independent, International, Narrative, Shorts

Screening Format: 16mm - 35mm - BetaSP - HDTV - DV

Awards: Jury Awards

Profile: The DIY Film Festival honors films from the growing field of cutting-edge, do-it-yourself storytelling. All entries must be created using commonly-available tools of independent filmmaking without financing from a major film studio or corporate backer.

Special Events: Panels, parties, awards

Filmmaker Perks: Prizes in the past have included a Panasonic digital camera package.

DOCFEST - NEW YORK iNTERNATiONAL DOCUMENTARY FESTiVAL

The New York Documentary Center
159 Maiden Lane
New York, NY 10038
Tel 212-668-1100; 212-943-6333
Fax 212-943-6396
Email ....mail@docfest.org
Web Site ....www.docfest.org

Year Festival Began: 1998

Festival Month: Spring

Entry Deadline: By Invite Only

Entry Fee: N/A

Genres: Documentary, Features, Independent, International, Shorts, Student

Screening Format: 16mm - 35mm - BetaSP - DigiBeta - MiniDV

Number of Films Screened: 20

Odds: By Invite Only

Awards: Jury Award; Audience Award

Profile: The New York International Documentary Festival is an annual event created in 1998 to present new and classic international documentaries to New York City audiences. docfest presents five days of film and video screenings and The New Technology showcase that explores up-to-the-minute developments in documentary thought, technique, and technology. docfest Dialogues with... features conversations with documentary masters. Previous guests have included Jean Rouch, Fred Wiseman, and Ricky Leacock.

The tangible intimacy of The New York Documentary Center programs is a combined result of our thoughtful and innovative programming, high standard of film selection, first class screening venues, and most importantly, the personal detailed attention that is given to both our participating filmmakers and our audience.

Special Events: Every screening and seminar presented in docfest is followed by a 45 - 60 minute panel discussion with the filmmaker, film subject(s), and often additional guests or relevant experts in the field. Additionally, after each discussion there is a meet-the-panel reception which offers the audience the opportunity to personally interact with our special guests.

Filmmaker Perks: Travel and accomodations for invited filmmakers.

Travel Tips: The subway is your friend, use it.

Cory Wynne ....Managing Director
Gary Pollard ....Founder

DRAGON CON iNDEPENDENT SHORT FiLM FESTiVAL

PO Box 16459
Atlanta, GA 30321-9998
Tel 770-909-0115
Email ....bcbc@mindspring.com
Web Site ....www.dragoncon.org

Festival Month: Late August-September
Entry Deadline: Mid-July
Entry Fee: $30
Genres: Animation, Experimental, Fantasy/Science Fiction, First-Time Independent Filmmakers, Horror, Independent, Independent, Shorts, Student, Thriller
Screening Format: VHS
Awards: Yes
Profile: The Dragon Con Independent Short Film Festival is held during Dragon Con, America's largest annual convention for fans of science fiction, fantasy and horror, comics and art, games and computers, animation, science, music, television and films.
Special Events: Panels, workshops, awards
Filmmaker Perks: Admission to Dragon Con
Travel Tips: Atlanta is one of the most accessible cities in the world by plane, train, automobile, and bus.

DURANGO FiLM FESTiVAL

PO Box 241
Durango, CO 81302
Tel 970-259-2291
Email ....info@durangofilmfestival.com
Web Site ....www.durangofilmfestival.com

Year Festival Began: 2000
Festival Month: Early March
Entry Deadline: Early December
Entry Fee: Contact Festival
Genres: Animation, Children, Documentary, Education, Features, Independent, International, Narrative, Shorts
Screening Format: 35mm - BetaSP - DVD - DVCam
Awards: Jury Awards; Audience Awards; Other Awards
Profile: The juried, 9 day Durango Film Festival presents independent narrative feature films, documentaries, animated films, shorts, children and regional films. In addition, the Festival offers educational salons, VIP panels, and filmmaker discussions, and a variety of parties and receptions.
Special Events: Parties, panels, awards
Filmmaker Perks: The Durango Film Festival has coordinated with hotel sponsors to offer special promotional rates for festival attendees.
Travel Tips: Great skiing and snowboarding in the area.

Sofia van Surksum............................Executive Director
Eric Hopper ....Programming Director

EDMONTON iNTERNATiONAL FiLM FESTiVAL

006-11523 100 Ave NW
Edmonton, AB T5K 0J8 Canada
Tel 780-423-0844
Fax 780-447-5242
Email..............................mailbox@edmontonfilm.com
Web Site ....www.edmontonfilm.com

Festival Month: Fall
Entry Deadline: Features: Mid-May
Shorts: Mid-June
Entry Fee: $20
Genres: Animation, Canadian, Documentary, Features, Independent, International, Narrative, Shorts, Student
Screening Format: 16mm - 35mm - BetaSP
Awards: No
Profile: Previously known as the Local Heroes International Film Festival, the Edmonton International Film Festival continues to cement its reputation as the "Sundance of the North" with the best independent films from around the world.
Special Events: Panels, parties, special screenings
Travel Tips: Previously a winter festival, the move to the fall season allows one to leave some of the winter gear at home.

Jan Miller ....Festival Director

EMERALD EYE SHORT FiLM FESTiVAL

303 SW Greenville Blvd.
Greenville, NC 27858
Tel 252-328-2811
Fax 252-328-1509
Email ....contact@emeraldeye.org
Web Site ....www.emeraldeye.org

Festival Month: Late September
Entry Deadline: Mid-August
Entry Fee: $25-$35
Genres: All Categories - Shorts, Independent, International
Screening Format: BetaSP - DVD - MiniDV
Awards: Grand Prize
Eastern North Carolina Filmmaker Award
Profile: The Emerald Eye Short Film Festival is a three-day competitive film, video and screenwriting festival.
Special Events: NCScreenwriters.com short-screenplay competition, awards, special screenings, parties
Filmmaker Perks: $5,000 Grand Prize.
Travel Tips: You can fly right into Pitt-Greenville Airport, so don't go to Raleigh-Durham, it's an hour from Greenville.

Jeff Lee ....Founder/Director

EURO UNDERGROUND

1658 N. Milwaukee Ave., Suite 142
Chicago, IL 60647
Tel 312-399-4531
Fax 773-292-9205
Email ....info@eurounderground.org
Web Site ....www.eurounderground.org

Year Festival Began: 1996
Festival Month: Fall
Entry Deadline: Ongoing
Entry Fee: $30

Genres: Documentary, Experimental, Features, Independent, International, Narrative, Shorts, Touring, Underground, Video, Weird

Screening Format: 16mm - 35mm - Super 8 - BetaSP - VHS

Number of Films Screened: 100 on any given country program.

Odds: 1 in 3

X Factor: Play one country or play them all: Germany, Poland, Bulgaria, Latvia, Ukraine, UK and USA.

Awards: Jury Awards

Profile: Euro Underground is a cross-cultural film organization produced by The International Film and Performance Society, a not-for-profit film organization exhibiting new and emerging work of international filmmakers. Euro Underground exhibits international work on an international level offering a built in, touring cinema network available globally for filmmakers. The types of work Euro Underground exhibits and concentrates on is independent, experimental, and underground.

Travel Tips: Depends on where your film is showing, really.

Mark Siska ....Festival Director

EYE OF THE BEHOLDER INTERNATIONAL FILM FESTIVAL

42 Highland Ave.
Asheville, NC 28801
Tel...828-225-0304
Email ....svelta@earthlink.net
Web Site.............................www.eyefilmfestival.com

Festival Month: Early December
Entry Deadline: Mid-November
Entry Fee: $10

Genres: Animation, Documentary, Features, Independent, International, Narrative, Shorts

Screening Format: Super 8mm - 16mm - 35mm - BetaSP - VHS - DV - MiniDV

Awards: Shiner Awards

Profile: Eye of the Beholder film festival is held in the mystical Appalachian mountains. Asheville, NC, is a haven for progressive socialism and artistic freaks (funny how they go hand in hand). People have moved to Asheville from all over the world to gather in a diverse and embracing community. Hungry for the power of independent thinking, the people of Asheville flock to the Eye of the Beholder Festival as a means of unconditioning their thought from the hum of modern mediocracy.

Special Events: Awards, parties, special screenings

Filmmaker Perks: Those that are accepted will receive two VIP passes to all events, an array of film promotion, and an opportunity to win cash/grant awards.

Travel Tips: Don't make fun of the local accent, because Southern hospitality still exists in Asheville.

BEST NORTH AMERICAN GENRE FESTIVALS (Sci-Fi, Fantasy, Horror)

A.K.A. Shriekfest, The Los Angeles Horror/Science Fiction Film Festival & Screenplay Competition
Another Hole in the Head San Francisco Horror Festival
Boston Fantastic Film Festival
CineMuerte International Fantastic Film Festival
Detroit International Horror Film Festival
Fantasia Film Festival
Hollywood Scarefest
Maryland Fantastique Film Fest
Screamfest Horror Film Festival
ShockerFest Film Festival
Shock-O-Rama-A-Go-Go Film Festival
Tromadance Film Festival

FANTASIA FILM FESTIVAL

460 rue St-Catherine, Suite #915
Montreal H3B IV6
Quebec Canada
Fax 514-876-1422
Email....................................info@fantasiafestival.com
Web Site .... www.fantasiafest.com

Year Festival Began: 1996
Festival Month: Early July
Entry Deadline: Early May
Entry Fee: None

Genres: American, Animation, Digital Animation, Ethnic African, Ethnic Asian, Ethnic Black, Ethnic Jewish, Ethnic Latin, Ethnic Other, Ethnic Spanish, Experimental, Fantasy/Science Fiction, Features, First-Time Independent Filmmakers, Horror, Independent, International, Multimedia, Narrative, Shorts, Women

Screening Format: 16mm - 35mm - VHS - BetaSP - DigiBeta - HD

Number of Films Screened: 200

X Factor: The audiences are enthusiastic and you don't really need to know that much French.

Awards: Jury Awards; Prix Publique Awards; Global Vision Awards

Profile: Since its inception in 1996, FanTasia has been an event hell-bent on showcasing the most exciting, innovative and individualistic examples of contemporary international genre cinema, with an emphasis on unveiling films very rarely seen in North America. It has become a hugely popular Montreal summer tradition for roughly 70,000 festi-val-goers to spend three weeks being amazed by sensational celluloid from Japan, Spain, South Korea, Italy, Hong Kong, Germany, Thailand, Denmark, France, Russia, India, New Zealand, Chile, Brazil, Australia, Holland, Scotland, Belgium, Sweden, Great Britain, the US, and of course, Quebec and Canada. As fellow film fanatics, we pride ourselves on getting the works that we love in front of an enthusiastic and knowledgeable audience. We also do everything possible to bring these films to the attention of potential distributors and the international media.

While predominantly a Fantasy/Action/Horror festi-val, FanTasia has always opened its arms to eclectic films whose sheer individuality puts them in a genre of their own. We admire films that take risks, and as programmers we feel the responsibility to match those risks by getting uniquely challenging features in front of the widest possible audiences.

Special Events: Parties, panels, and awards.

Filmmaker Perks: The festival provides travel and accomodations when possible, but regardless this is North America's biggest genre fest so it should not be missed.

Travel Tips: The friendliest city around, be prepared for cars to merge without signaling. The aren't cut-ting you off, they're just used to being let in.

FEMALE EYE FILM FESTIVAL

50 Wallace St.
Woodbridge, Ontario
L4L 2P2 Canada
Tel..905-264-6777 Ext. 1
Fax 905-964-7731
Email ....info@femaleeyefilmfestival.com
Web Site ....www.femaleeyefilmfestival.com

Festival Month: Mid-November

Entry Deadline: Late May

Entry Fee: None

Genres: Animation, Documentary, Experimental, Features, Independent, International, Music Videos, Narrative, Shorts, Women

Screening Format: 35mm - BetaSP

Awards: Jury Awards

Profile: The Female Eye Film Festival (FeFF) was established in 2001 as a nonprofit charitable organi-zation dedicated to the advancement of female direc-tors and screenplay writers who are underrepresent-ed in the film industry. The Female Eye is Ontario's one and only independent international film festival that showcases high-caliber films directed by women from around the world. The Female Eye Film Festival features films in drama, comedy, sci-fi, action, docu-mentary, experimental, animation, and cutting edge music videos all directed by debut, emerging and internationally recognized filmmakers.

Special Events: Awards, parties, screenplay compe-tition

Filmmaker Perks: Filmmakers get VIP passes to all festival screenings and events.

Travel Tips: Take a shuttle from Lester B. Pearson International Airport in Toronto.

Leslie Ann Coles ....Program Director

FILM FEST NEW HAVEN

PO Box 9644
New Haven, CT 06536
Tel 203-776-6789
Fax 203-776-4260
Email ....info@filmfest.org
Web Site...www.filmfest.org

Year Festival Began: 1995

Festival Month: Mid-September

Entry Deadline: Early June

Entry Fee: Features: $40
Shorts: $30

Genres: Animation, Documentary, Experimental, Features, First-Time Independent Filmmakers, Independent, International, Narrative, Shorts

Screening Format: 16mm - 35mm - BetaSP - VHS - DVD

Number of Films Screened: 60

Awards: Kodak Cinematography Award; Charles Schwartz Award for Exemplary Use of Sound or Music; Jury Awards; Audience Awards; Other Awards

Profile: Film Fest New Haven is a broadly focused, internationally recognized, independent festival accepting works of any type or length, on any subject matter and in any genre. A true filmmaker's festival, FFNH is known for maximizing contact between film-makers, audiences and industry professionals in a film-friendly and film-literate environment.

Special Events: Awards, parties, panels

Filmmaker Perks: The festival has deals with local hotels for discounted accomodations.

Travel Tips: Fly right into New Haven and rent a car. Visit Yale, too - not like you can escape it.

Robin Andreoli.....................................Executive Director
Nina Adams ....Artistic Director

FiLM NiTE

2029 Eastwood Rd., #131
Wilmington, NC 28403
Tel...910-395-4178
Email ....info@killingtimepictures.com
Web Site ....www.killingtimepictures.com/filmnite

Year Festival Began: 1998

Festival Month: Check Website for Next Screening

Entry Deadline: Ongoing

Genres: American, Animation, Documentary, Ethnic African, Experimental, First-Time Independent Filmmakers, Independent, International, Narrative, Shorts, Super 8/8mm, Underground, Weird

Screening Format: 8mm - Super 8mm - VHS

Awards: No

Profile: Film Nite is a year-round festival of some of the coolest short films around ... at least the ones we've been able to get our hands on. Started in June of 1998, Film Nite has shown movies made by filmmakers all over the USA and the world. Every screening has something new and different, from comedies, to dramas to documentaries, and then some don't really fit into any category. Some movies have won awards and have been screened at major festivals, while others have never been seen by an audience before.

Filmmaker Perks: The selection staff are incredibly picky, so if you get in, that's your reward.

Travel Tips: Fly into Wilmington and rent a car. Depending on when you go, there may be a hurricane warning, so watch the weather.

David Hardin ....Co-Founder
Cable Hardin..Co-Founder

FiRSTGLANCE HOLLYWOOD FiLM FESTiVAL

PO Box 571105
Tarzana, CA 91356
Tel 818-464-3544
Email...wropro1@msn.com
Web Site ....www.firstglancefilms.com

Year Festival Began: 1999

Festival Month: Early December

Entry Deadline: Mid-June

Entry Fee: Varies, starting at $20

Genres: Animation, Documentary, Experimental, Features, Independent, International, Narrative, Shorts, Student

Screening Format: BetaSP - VHS - DVD

Awards: Jury Awards

Profile: An independent, bi-coastal festival open to professionals and students from all over the world, FirstGlance has become synonymous with giving the truly independent filmmaker the time to shine in the spotlight, and the opportunity to finally breakthrough into the mainstream.

Special Events: Awards, parties

Filmmaker Perks: FirstGlance provides a complimentary entrant screening pass, discounted tickets, an All Access pass, discounts to the FirstNight reception. After parties are free admission to filmmakers and attendees. Winning projects get free entrance and exhibition to FirstGlance Philadelphia.

Travel Tips: Special hotel, car rental and airfare discounts are available by logging on to the website.

William Ostroff ....Festival Director

FiRSTGLANCE PHiLADELPHiA FiLM FESTiVAL

PO Box 571105
Tarzana, CA 91356
Tel 215-552-8566
Email...wropro1@msn.com
Web Site.................................www.firstglancefilms.com

Year Festival Began: 1996

Festival Month: Early June

Entry Deadline: Early February

Entry Fee: Varies, starting at $20

Genres: Animation, Documentary, Features, First-Time Independent Filmmakers, Independent, International, Narrative, Shorts, Student

Screening Format: BetaSP - VHS - DVD

Awards: Jury Awards

Profile: FirstGlance Philadelphia began in 1996, in response for the need for a truly indie film festival that wasn't genre specific. The festival's mission of cultivating and celebrating truly indie work by professional and student filmmakers not only makes the festival the first of its kind in Philly, but also the fastest growing. The innovative process of audience voting has brought an amazing air of competition and camaraderie to every screening program and the Philadelphia community is extremely appreciative of the participating filmmakers.

Special Events: Panels, parties, awards

Filmmaker Perks: FirstGlance provides a complimentary entrant screening pass, discounted tickets and an All Access pass. Winning projects get free entrance and exhibition to FirstGlance Hollywood.

Travel Tips: Filmmakers planning on traveling should book early, due to the large amount of travelers to the Philadelphia area in general. Philly can be hot and humid in the summer, be prepared for thunderstorms.

William Ostroff ....Festival Director

FLiCKERiNG iMAGE FESTiVAL

2240 N. Gower St.
Hollywood, CA 90068
Tel 323-960-7862
Fax 323-871-1331
Email ....shortsfest@actorsbone.com
Web Site ....www.actorsbone.com/shorts

Festival Month: Early January

Entry Deadline: Early November

Entry Fee: $25-$35

Genres: Animation, Documentary, Experimental, First-Time Independent Filmmakers, Independent, International, Narrative, Shorts

Screening Format: BetaSP - VHS - DVD - DVCam - MiniDV

Awards: Yes

Profile: The Flickering Image Festival is about moviemaking - not politics and it is definitely not "business as usual." Fair, open and forward facing - this festival will make a difference.

Special Events: Awards

Filmmaker Perks: The top ten films, selected by open-anonymous ballots (where the shorts maker will actually see how their work rated with each judge - something no other festival offers!), will be shown on the "big screen" in Hollywood and their makers will receive awards - as well as a congratulatory listing in *Variety*.

Travel Tips: The winners screen at the LA Film School, which is right in the heart of Hollywood, and within walking distance of some great restaurants, shops, and theaters.

N. Barry Carver ....Co-Director
Bonnie Gillespie...Co-Director
Paul Molinaro...Co-Director

FLORIDA
FILM FESTIVAL

FLORiDA FiLM FESTiVAL

c/o Enzian Theater
1300 South Orlando Ave.
Maitland, FL 32751
Tel ....407-629-1088 ext. 222
Fax 407-629-6870
Email ....filmfest@enzian.org
Web Site ....www.floridafilmfestival.com

Year Festival Began: 1991

Festival Month: Early March

Entry Deadline: Early December

Number of Submissions: 1,250

Entry Fee: Features: $35

Shorts: $20

Genres: Animation, Documentary, Features, Independent, International, Narrative, Shorts, Student

Screening Format: 16mm - 35mm - BetaSP - DigiBeta - HD

Number of Films Screened: 80

Odds: 1 in 15

X Factor: It seems every year this festival takes another step up the ladder to complete international prestige.

Awards: Winning live action shorts qualify for Live Action Short Film Academy Award nomination; Jury Awards; Audience Awards

Profile: The Florida Film Festival showcases the best American independent and foreign films. Produced by Enzian Theater, the Festival has become one of the most respected regional film events in the country.

The festival includes narrative and documentary features and shorts, animation, midnight movies, and a full array of educational forums, glamorous parties, and other special events. The Florida Film Festival not only prides itself in delivering the finest in independent film, but also the filmmakers who make it all possible, creating a casual interactive environment like no other.

Special Events: Educational panels, parties, and other special events.

Comments: Headquartered in Orlando, the Florida Film Festival has earned its reputation as one of the best regional film festivals, and with good reason. This festival is an intimate affair offering the opportunity for attendees and filmmakers alike to interact in an atmosphere of unpretentious revelry. Filmmakers are treated like royalty as the fest rolls out the red carpet for arriving artists. Now in its tenth year, films screen at the spectacular Enzian Theater. (The Enzian is a classic movie house that hosts other fests, such as the Central Florida Jewish Film Festival, the South Asian Film Festival and a variety of festivals of films for kids.) The festival recently moved to the cooler month of March, but the Enzian brings independent film to Orlando year round.

The festival ends with a gloriously star-studded awards ceremony attended by hundreds of filmmakers, members of the media and local luminaries. This elegant event is held on a sound stage at Universal Studios and is a gala on par with the Academy Awards®. Not to be missed for filmmakers and the lucky residents of Orlando.

Travel Tips: Travel packages and sponsor hotel and rental car discounts are available to ensure no hassle travel and accommodations for the festival.

Kat Quast..General Manager
Matthew Curtis.....................Director of Programming

FORT LAUDERDALE iNTERNATiONAL FiLM FESTiVAL

1314 E. Las Olas Blvd., Box 007
Ft. Lauderdale, FL 33301
Tel 954-760-9898
Fax 954-760-9099
Email ....brofilm@aol.com
Web Site ....www.fliff.com

Year Festival Began: 1985

Festival Month: Late October-November

Entry Deadline: Mid-August

Students: Mid-September

Number of Submissions: 1,350

Entry Fee: Features and Documentaries: $40

Shorts: $30

Students with Valid ID: $25

Genres: American, Documentary, Ethnic African, Ethnic Asian, Ethnic Black, Ethnic Jewish, Ethnic Latin, Ethnic Spanish, Experimental, Features, First-Time Independent Filmmakers, Gay Lesbian, Independent, International, Narrative, Shorts, Student, Underground, Women

Screening Format: 16mm - 35mm - VHS - BetaSP - MiniDV - DVD

Number of Films Screened: 135

Odds: 1 in 10

X Factor: With a month's worth of screenings, you know your film has a better-than-average shot at being programmed.

Awards: Jury Awards

Vespa Spirit of the Independent Award

Vespa People's Choice

Profile: Founded in 1986, the Fort Lauderdale International Film Festival is a nonprofit organization funded by grants, private memberships, corporate and private sponsorships and the City of Fort Lauderdale. The 31-day festival screens over 130 films from Boca Raton to Miami and is the longest film festival in the world, according to the *Guiness Book of World Records*.

VIRGIN PREMIERE

Protect your festival premiere status as you would your own virginity. (You know, when you *were* a virgin.) You can't "world premiere" more than once, but if you are unsure about screening at a smaller festival first, consider showing in a TBA slot as a "work in progress." You'll get valuable feedback and leave with your premiere status (and virginity) intact.

262
THE ULTIMATE FILM FESTIVAL SURVIVAL GUIDE

The festival also showcases first-time independent and student filmmakers, with a student-specific film competition outside of the festival's main competitions.

Special Events: Gala opening and closing night parties, panels.

Filmmaker Perks: The festival has numerous travel partners including hotel, rental car and airlines. Special discounts are available.

Travel Tips: While the rest of the US is getting ready for winter, you'll be hanging in the sun. Dress accordingly, leave the snow boots at home.

Gregory von Hausch..President
Bonnie Leigh Adams...............Senior Program Director

Robin Williams meets filmmakers Ray Jarrell and Adam Reist at a party in Sonoma.

FREE FILM FESTIVAL FITCHBURG (THE F4)

68 N. Washington St.
N. Atleboro, MA 02760
Tel 877-246-4300
Email ....info@f4festival.org
Web Site www.f4festival.com

Year Festival Began: 2000
Festival Month: Early April
Entry Deadline: Late February
Entry Fee: None
Genres: American, Documentary, Experimental, Features, First-Time Independent Filmmakers, Independent, Shorts, Student, Underground, Weird
Screening Format: 16mm - 35mm - BetaSP - DV - DVD
Awards: "Fitchys" Awards
Profile: F4 is a film and digital media festival born of ethics fostered by a public education in filmmaking: practical skill, creative thinking, and the knowledge that ideas can only be realized through honest effort and hard work.

Special Events: Workshops, awards
Filmmaker Perks: Past prizes have included a $10,000 digital editing system.
Travel Tips: You've got to fly into Boston and then find your way to Fitchburg, which can be extremely annoying to drive.

J.C. Bouvier ....Co-Founder
Keith Gerrard ....Co-Founder

FREEDOM FILM FESTIVAL

9911 W. Pico Boulevard, Suite 1060
Los Angeles, CA 90035
Tel 310-286-9420
Fax 310-286-7914
Email ....acinema@cinemafoundation.com
Web Site............................www.cinemafoundation.com

Year Festival Began: 1997
Festival Month: Mid-February
Entry Deadline: By Invitation Only
Genres: Animation, Documentary, Ethnic Other, European, Features, International, Narrative, Shorts
Screening Format: 16mm - 35mm
Profile: The American Cinema Foundation founded the Freedom Film Festival in 1997 to honor filmmakers from the new democracies of Europe, those former communist countries that are now on the verge of joining the European Union. These are filmmakers whom we celebrate for their creativity, visual talent, and storytelling skill, and whom we can also honor for their integrity and sense of social concern. It's our hope that this work will inspire thoughts about history and the future, in addition to providing purely cinematic enjoyment.
Filmmaker Perks: An important festival for sociopolitical cinematic relations, and possibly the only festival for the types of filmmakers to whom it caters.
Travel Tips: Events take place in LA and Berlin.

Gary McVey ....Executive Director

FRESNO REEL PRIDE INTERNATIONAL GAY & LESBIAN FILM FESTIVAL

PO Box 4647
Fresno, CA 93744
Tel 559-488-6562
Email ....info@reelpride.com
Web Site ....www.reelpride.com

Festival Month: Mid-September
Entry Deadline: August
Entry Fee: None
Genres: Animation, Documentary, Features, Gay Lesbian, Independent, International, Narrative, Shorts, Student
Screening Format: 35mm - BetaSP - VHS - DVD
Awards: Audience Awards; Director's Club Awards

Profile: Since its inception in a classroom at CSU Fresno in 1990, Fresno REEL Pride is the sixth oldest – and has grown to become one of the largest – gay and lesbian film festivals in the US.

Special Events: Parties, panels, awards

Filmmaker Perks: Filmmakers get a complimentary festival pass.

Travel Tips: The festival is held at the Tower Theatre, the dominant vertical landmark in Fresno. Yes, it's big, don't stare.

Dave Houck ....Festival Director

GEN ART

access to emerging talent

GEN ART FILM FESTIVAL

133 W. 25th St., 6th Floor E.
New York, NY 10001
Tel 212-255-7300
Fax...212-255-7400
Email ....film@genart.org
Web Site...www.genart.org

Year Festival Began: 1996

Festival Month: Mid-April

Entry Deadline: By Invite

Genres: American, Animation, Documentary, Experimental, Features, First-Time Independent Filmmakers, Gay Lesbian, Independent, Narrative, Shorts, Video, Weird, Women

Screening Format: 16mm - 35mm - BetaSP - DigiBeta - DVD - MiniDV - HD

Number of Films Screened: 14

X Factor: Filmmakers make their New York debut through this successful festival which will make his/her film the center of attention for an entire day of the festival. Forget about choosing from one of 25 films screened on one day - at Gen Art, each day is about the New York premiere of one short and one feature film - and that's it. And every filmmaker gets his/her own massive high-profile after-party - to which everyone in the audience is invited to attend!

Awards: Audience Award; Jury Award

Profile: Gen Art's Film Program began in 1996 with the launch of the Gen Art Film Festival. The festival's unique format showcases a single New York Premiere (short & feature) each night followed by a gala afterparty. The festival's celebratory environment attracts new audiences and focuses all of the attention on that evening's film.

The Gen Art Film Festival was established to showcase the work of emerging American Independent filmmakers and is curated with an emphasis on highlighting the diversity of their visions and talents.

Our goal is to create a festival where filmmakers, audiences and film industry professionals can interact together in a fun and inviting atmosphere.

Special Events: Nightly open-bar parties

Filmmaker Perks: The selected fourteen participating filmmakers will receive VIP treatment the evening of their premiere (including several guest tickets and open bar table service at the afterparty). And attending filmmakers will be guaranteed at least one meeting with a New York-based production company or agency.

Travel Tips: Bring your hippest clothing, you'll need it when you're hanging at the best clubs New York has to offer.

Jeffrey Abramson...............................Festival Director

GREAT PLAINS FILM FESTIVAL

Mary Riepma Ross Media Arts Center
313 N. 13th St., Suite 128
PO Box 880253
Lincoln, NE 68588-0253
Tel 402-472-9100
Fax 402-472-2576
Email ....dladely1@unl.edu
Web Site..www.theross.org

Festival Month: Early August

Entry Deadline: Early June

Entry Fee: Features: $30; Shorts: $20

Genres: Animation, Canadian, Documentary, Features, First-Time Independent Filmmakers, Independent, International, Narrative, Shorts, Student

Screening Format: 16mm - 35mm - BetaSP - VHS

Awards: Grand Prize; Rainbow Award; Nebraska Humanities Council Award; Jury Awards; Young Media Artists Awards

Profile: The Great Plains Film Festival is a biennial regional venue for independent film/video artists working in the US and Canadian heartland. We are committed to providing a showcase for presenting work to the public as well as to potential distributors and exhibitors from throughout the region and the nation. The festival is nurturing a better understanding and a greater awareness of the media arts being produced in this region in terms of their aesthetic, cultural, and social values. In addition, the festival encourages and promotes film/video which accentuates and enhances appreciation of our nation's extraordinary multicultural diversity and conveys the rich vibrancy of our cultural heritage.

Special Events: Tributes, parties, panels, screenplay competition

Travel Tips: Lincoln, Nebraska, may be home to some of the nicest people in the Great Plains, so be respectful.

Danny Lee Ladely ....Festival Director
Nicole Zink ....Assistant Director

H.P. LOVECRAFT FILM FESTIVAL

2626 NE 31st Ave.
Portland, OR 97212
Tel 503-282-3155
Email ....info@hplfilmfestival.com
Web Site ....www.hplfilmfestival.com

Festival Month: Early October
Entry Deadline: Mid-July
Entry Fee: None
Genres: Animation, Documentary, Experimental, Features, First-Time Independent Filmmakers, Horror, Independent, International, Narrative, Shorts, Student, Thriller
Screening Format: 16mm - 35mm - BetaSP - DVD - MiniDV
Awards: No
Profile: The purpose of the H.P. Lovecraft Film Festival is simple: to promote the works of H. P. Lovecraft through cinematic adaptations by student, amateur and professional filmmakers.

The fiction of H. P. Lovecraft, though still popular in print, has fared rather poorly when adapted to film by commercial filmmakers. Most of the problem stems from both a failure to capture the essence of Lovecraft's unique and meticulously developed atmosphere and an inability to remain faithful to the themes of his stories without adding unnecessary Hollywood devices in order to sell the film.

Special Events: Seminars, parties, special guests
Filmmaker Perks: If you made a film based on H.P. Lovecraft material, this whole festival's existence is a perk.
Travel Tips: Downtown Portland can be hell to drive through, so stay calm and don't road rage.

Andrew Migliore ....Founder

HAMPTONS INTERNATIONAL FILM FESTIVAL

3 Newtown Mews
East Hampton,, NY 11937
Tel 631-324-4600; 212-431-6292
Fax 631-324-5116
Email ....hiff@hamptonsfilmfest.org
Web Site ....www.hamptonsfilmfest.org

Festival Month: Late October
Entry Deadline: Early June
Entry Fee: Features: $35
Shorts: $25
Genres: Animation, Documentary, Features, Independent, International, Narrative, Shorts, Student
Screening Format: 16mm - 35mm - BetaSP - DVD
Number of Films Screened: 120+
X Factor: The Independents' Ball. "Everyone" who comes to the festival goes to the Independents' Ball.

Filmmakers, actors, celebrities, VIPs, sponsors, board members, and the general movie-loving public included.

Awards: Golden Starfish Prizes; Audience Awards
Profile: The Hamptons International Film Festival (HIFF) was founded to celebrate the American Independent film - long, short, fiction and documentary - and to introduce a unique and varied spectrum of international films and filmmakers to our audiences. The festival is committed to exhibiting films that express fresh voices and differing global perspectives, with the hope that these programs will enlighten audiences, provide invaluable exposure for filmmakers and present inspired entertainment for all.
Special Events: Annual Independents' Ball, panels, special screenings, and parties
Filmmaker Perks: When possible, the festival pays for travel and accomodations for invited filmmakers.
Travel Tips: Altour International is the official travel agency of the festival. Call 1-800-847-7466 or visit www.altour.com.

Denise Kasell ....Executive Director
Rajendra Roy ....Director of Programming
Stephanie Saylor ....Festival Coordinator

HAWAII INTERNATIONAL FILM FESTIVAL

1001 Bishop St, ASB Tower, Suite 745
Honolulu, HI 96813
Tel 808-528-3456
Fax 808-528-1410
Email ....info@hiff.org
Web Site ....www.hiff.org

Year Festival Began: 1981
Festival Month: Late October-November
Entry Deadline: Early June
Number of Submissions: 1,000
Entry Fee: $35
Entry fee is waived for all Hawaii-based filmmakers
Genres: Documentary, Ethnic Asian, Experimental, Features, Independent, International, Music Videos, Narrative, Pacific Rim, Shorts
Screening Format: 16mm - 35mm - BetaSP
Number of Films Screened: 150
Odds: 1 in 6
X Factor: You'll get lei'd as soon as you get off the plane.
Awards: Golden Maile Awards; Audience Awards; NETPAC Awards
Profile: Established in 1981, the Hawaii International Film Festival (HIFF) is dedicated to advance understanding and cultural exchange among the peoples of Asia, the Pacific, and North America through the medium of film. From its beginning, the Festival's constant theme has been "When Strangers Meet."

HIFF has become the premiere international film event in the Pacific and has won the praise of governments, filmmakers, scholars, educators, programmers, and film industry leaders throughout the world. As the largest "East meets West" festival in the United States, HIFF is the primary source for the discovery and exhibition of Asian and Pacific feature films, documentaries and videos in the nation. The festival is an eagerly anticipated annual event for residents of Hawaii, as well as visitors to the state.

Special Events: Opening and closing night parties, panels, awards

Filmmaker Perks: The festival takes care of travel and accomodations when possible.

Travel Tips: The nicer you are, the better you're treated!

Chuck Boller ....Festival Director
Anderson Lo ....Programmer
Chris Dacus ....Promotions Coordinator

HEARTLAND FiLM FESTiVAL

200 South Meridian St., Suite 220
Indianapolis, IN 46225-1076
Tel 317-464-9405
Fax 317-464-9409
Email..............................info@heartlandfilmfestival.org
Web Site..........................www.heartlandfilmfestival.org

Year Festival Began: 1991
Festival Month: Late October
Entry Deadline: Mid-June
Number of Submissions: 300
Entry Fee: Features: $55
Shorts: $20
Student Projects: $10
Genres: Animation, Documentary, Family, Features, Human Rights, Independent, International, Multi-Cultural, Narrative, Shorts, Student
Screening Format: 35mm - BetaSP - DVD
Number of Films Screened: 15
Odds: 1 in 20
X Factor: At Heartland, you're not a filmmaker, you're a visionary. Think on that.
Awards: Grand Prize; Crystal Heart Awards
Profile: Established in 1991, the Heartland Film Festival has developed many ways to pursue its mission: To recognize and honor filmmakers whose work explores the human journey by artistically expressing hope and respect for the positive values of life.

Over the course of ten exciting days each October, Heartland screens films from around the world, ranging from dramas to documentaries to animation, all of which take entertainment to a higher level.

The rewards of this festival are many. The audience of a Heartland film is lifted up and inspired. The recognition filmmakers receive at the Heartland Film Festival encourages them to continue to make films that move and inspire.

Special Events: Parties, seminars, and Crystal Heart Award ceremony

Filmmaker Perks: Heartland Film Festival expects the visionary selected to receive an award to attend the festival (at Heartland's expense, less incidentals) and be present at the Crystal Heart Awards Ceremony.

Travel Tips: Bring warm clothes - just in case - as the festival is on the cusp of the winter months.

Jeffrey L. Sparks...President
Jennifer A. Gardner ....Film & Research Coordinator

Hi/LO FiLM FESTiVAL

PO Box 170309
San Francisco, CA 94117
Tel 415-558-7721
Email ....marc@killingmylobster.com
Web Site ....www.hilofilmfestival.com

Festival Month: Early April
Entry Deadline: Mid-January
Entry Fee: Contact Festival
Genres: Animation, Documentary, Features, First-Time Independent Filmmakers, Independent, International, Narrative, Shorts, Touring
Screening Format: 8mm - 16mm - 35mm - DV
Awards: No
Profile: From humble beginnings at a sofa-saturated screening room in the city's North Beach District in 1997 to the posh theater at the San Francisco Art Institute, the hi/lo film festival has evolved into a major West Coast showcase for independent low-budget film makers. Each year hundreds attend the festival, which receives press coverage from numerous local and national magazines and newspapers.

Special Events: Parties

BEST GLOBAL CONSCIOUSNESS FESTIVALS

Amnesty International Film Festival
Big Muddy Film Festival
Global Peace Film Festival
Heartland Film Festival
Human Rights Nights Film Festival
Human Rights Watch International Film Festival
Kuala Lumpur World Film Festival
One World Human Rights Documentary
    Film Festival
Taos Mountain Film Festival
Wild Spaces Film Festival
World Population and Video Festival

Filmmaker Perks: The festival routinely tours Northern California with accepted films.

Travel Tips: Find a place to stay in San Francisco to save yourself money that otherwise would be spent on bridge toll.

HOLLYWOOD BLACK FILM FESTIVAL

PO Box 34858
Los Angeles, CA 90034-0858
Tel 310-712-3998
Fax 310-943-2326
Email ....Info@hbff.org
Web Site ....www.hbff.org

Year Festival Began: 1999
Festival Month: Late June
Entry Deadline: Check Website
Entry Fee: $40

Genres: American, Animation, Digital, Documentary, Ethnic Black, Features, First-Time Independent Filmmakers, Gay Lesbian, Independent, International, Narrative, Shorts, Student, Super 8/8mm, Video, Women
Screening Format: 16mm - 35mm - BetaSP - DVD
Number of Films Screened: 60

Awards: Jury Awards; HBFF Audience Choice Award
Profile: The Hollywood Black Film Festival (HBFF) is an annual film festival which showcases the work of emerging and established black filmmakers (directors and/or writers) from North America. The festival brings the work of these talented filmmakers to an environment encompassing the mainstream Hollywood community and Southern California film-going audiences. The festival's juried competition screens a selection of independently produced features and shorts, including narrative, documentary, student and animation works. In addition to the festival's competitive program, an invitational program screens out-of-competition theatrical premieres of works by black filmmakers, including studio and made-for-cable television productions.

Special Events: Awards, parties, tributes, panels, Infotainment Conference, workshops
Filmmaker Perks: In addition to the film screenings, the adjunct Infotainment Conference will feature dozens of informational seminars, panels and workshops covering a wide variety of topics which range from film production, distribution and marketing to pitching, writing for television and film, in addition to specific programs of interest to actors.

Travel Tips: Keep cool, rent a car with A/C.

Tanya Kersey-Henley...................Festival Management
Jacqueline Blaylock ....Programming

HOLLYWOOD FILM FESTIVAL

433 N. Camden Dr., Suite 600
Beverly Hills, CA 90210
Tel 310-288-3040
Fax 310-288-0060
Email.........................hollyinfo@hollywoodnetwork.com
Web Site ....www.hollywoodfilmfestival.com

Year Festival Began: 1997
Festival Month: Mid-October
Entry Deadline: Late March
Entry Fee: Features and Documentaries: $55 Shorts: $45

Genres: Animation, Documentary, Features, Independent, International, Narrative, Shorts
Screening Format: 16mm - 35mm - BetaSP - DigiBeta - HD
Number of Films Screened: 75

X Factor: Hanging with Hollywood celebrities and industry big-wigs in Beverly Hills ain't a bad way to spend a couple days.
Awards: The Hollywood Discovery Awards
The Hollywood Awards
Profile: The Hollywood Film Festival was created to bridge the gap between Hollywood and the global creative community, while at the same time honoring established Hollywood professionals. The festival includes the prestigious Hollywood Film Conference and the Hollywood Awards Gala Ceremony.

Special Events: The Hollywood Awards, Panels, Screenplay Competition, Hollywood Film Conference
Comments: No one brings out the stars like the Hollywood Film Festival. In fact, they own the name "Hollywood." Part awards event and festival screening series, the recent addition of a genre festival program shows their commitment to supporting bridging the gap between established Hollywood players with emerging filmmakers.

Filmmaker Perks: The HFF Program Catalog will feature all of the finalists, and will be mailed to over 35,000 industry executives including agents, attorneys, distributors, financiers, and producer reps. Plus, you get a VIP pass.

Travel Tips: Rent a car and give the LA Visitors Bureau a call at 323-624-7300

Carlos de Abreu ....Executive Director

HONOLULU RAINBOW FILM FESTIVAL

1877 Kalakaua Ave.
Honolulu, HI 96815
Tel 808-381-1952
Fax 808-943-1724
Email ....info@hglcf.org
Web Site ....www.hglcf.org

Festival Month: Late May
Entry Deadline: Mid-March
Entry Fee: Features: $25; Shorts: $15

Genres: Animation, Documentary, Features, Gay Lesbian, Narrative, Shorts

Screening Format: 16mm - 35mm - BetaSP - VHS

Profile: The Honolulu "Rainbow" Film Festival, sponsored by the Honolulu Gay & Lesbian Cultural Foundation, is a showcase of gay and lesbian cinema from around the world in all genres.

Special Events: Parties

Filmmaker Perks: It's held in Hawaii.

Travel Tips: When they attempt to put a lei around your neck, don't freak out. If they try to steal your wallet, run.

Jon Bryant..Festival Director

HOT DOCS CANADIAN INTERNATIONAL DOCUMENTARY FESTIVAL

517 College St., Suite 420
Toronto, Ontario
M6G 4A2 Canada
Tel..416-203-2155
Fax 416-203-0446
Email ....info@hotdocs.ca
Web Site ....www.hotdocs.ca

Festival Month: Early April

Entry Deadline: Mid-December

Entry Fee: $35

Genres: Canadian, Documentary, Features, Independent, International, Markets, Shorts

Screening Format: 16mm - 35mm - BetaSP - DigiBeta

Awards: Jury Awards; Audience Award; Outstanding Achievement Award

Profile: Hot Docs Canadian International Documentary Festival is North America's largest documentary festival. Each year, the festival presents a selection of over 100 cutting-edge documentaries from Canada and around the globe. Through its industry programmes, the festival also provides a full range of professional development, market, and networking opportunities for documentary professionals.

Special Events: Panels, parties, awards, Doc Shop market

Filmmaker Perks: All films/videos submitted to Hot Docs 2004 will automatically be included in The Doc Shop, an international documentary market running in conjunction with the festival.

Travel Tips: Whether approaching Toronto by car or by bus, the traveller will reach Toronto by one of several major routes paralleling the shore of Lake Ontario. Highways 401 and 2, and the Queen Elizabeth Way, enter Toronto from the west. Highways 401 and 2 also enter Toronto from the east. Hwy 400 runs from the north and connects with Hwy 401.

Chris McDonald ....Executive Director
Michaelle Mclean...TDF Director
Brett Hendrie ....Managing Director

Rose Belosillo...............................Director, Development
Shannon Abel ....Programme Manager &
International Programmer
Caroline Veldhuis ....Communications Manager
Rhonda Costas........................Administrative Manager
Jennifer Hobbs.........................Development Manager,
Corporate Affairs
Brett Hendrie ....Managing Director

HOT SPRINGS DOCUMENTARY FILM FESTIVAL

819 Central Ave.
P.O. Box 6450
Hot Springs National Park, AR 71902
Tel 501-321-4747
Fax..501-321-0211
Email ....hsdfi@hsdfi.org
Web Site ....www.docufilminst.org

Year Festival Began: 1992

Festival Month: Late October

Entry Deadline: Late April

Entry Fee: Domestic: $25

International: $35

Genres: Documentary, Features, Independent, International, Shorts

Screening Format: 16mm - 35mm - BetaSP - DVD - VHS

Number of Films Screened: 85

X Factor: If you're a documentary filmmaker, this festival was made specifically for you.

Awards: No

Profile: The Hot Springs Documentary Film Festival began in 1992, launched by a small group of arts activists in Hot Springs. That year, 10 Academy Award® nominated documentary films were screened to the public free of charge. Veteran actor James Whitmore lent his presence to this first event and spoke of a bright future: "[Hot Springs] could be the documentary capital of the world."

The Hot Springs Documentary Film festival is now regarded as one of the world's premier documentary film festivals. The Film Institute's mission is to promote and advance the documentary film genre and to utilize documentary film as an educational tool to facilitate the understanding of real life issues, places and events. The Film Institute is a nonprofit organization funded in part by the Hot Springs Advertising and Promotion Commission, the Arkansas Department of Economic Development, the National Endowment for the Arts, the Arkansas Arts Council, and the Academy Foundation of the Academy of Motion Picture Arts and Sciences, along with numerous other corporate and private sponsors.

Special Events: Opening gala reception, seminars

Travel Tips: Call the Hot Springs Visitors Bureau at 1-800-SPA-CITY.

Melanie Masino ....Executive Director

HOUSTON ANNUAL WORLDFEST

9494 SW Freeway, 5th Floor
Houston, TX 77074
Tel 713-965-9955
Fax 713-965-9960
Email...mail@worldfest.org
Web Site ....www.worldfest.org

Year Festival Began: 1961

Festival Month: Mid-April

Entry Deadline: Mid-February

Number of Submissions: 4,300

Entry Fee: $45-$175 Check website for applicable fee

Genres: All, Commercials, Documentary, Features, First-Time Independent Filmmakers, Independent, International, Music Videos, Narrative, PSA (Public Service Announcement), Shorts, Student, Television

Screening Format: 35mm - DVD

Number of Films Screened: 50-60

Odds: 1 in 71

X Factor: With only 60 films screened over a 10-day period, each film gets plenty of attention.

Awards: The Grand Remi Awards

Profile: WorldFest was founded August 1961 as an international film society and became a true competitive film & video festival for features, shorts and documentaries in April 1968, making it the 3rd oldest film festival in North America. The mission/vision statement of WorldFest is to recognize and honor outstanding creative excellence in film & video, to validate brilliant abilities and to promote cultural tourism for Houston, to develop film production in the region and to add to the rich cultural fabric of the city of Houston. All members of the WorldFest staff are filmmakers.

Special Events: Parties, seminars, Grand Remi award ceremony

Travel Tips: It can get hot in Houston, so be prepared.

Kathleen Haney.......................................Artistic Director
Hunter Todd...Founder

FOR TRAVELERS: MAKE A PLAN "B"

Each morning make a list of films to see and an alternate list in case those screenings are sold out. And leave time between screenings for one decent meal, which is all you'll have time for.

HUMAN RiGHTS WATCH INTERNATiONAL FiLM FESTiVAL

350 Fifth Ave., 34th floor
New York, NY 10118
Tel...212-216-1264
Fax...212-736-1300
Email...burresb@hrw.org
Web Site ....www.hrw.org/iff

Year Festival Began: 1988

Festival Month: Late February-March (San Francisco), Mid-March (London), Mid-June (New York)

Entry Deadline: Mid-January

Number of Submissions: Submissions are eligible only for the New York festival.

Entry Fee: None

Genres: Animation, Documentary, Experimental, Features, Human Rights, Independent, International, Narrative, Peace, Shorts, Touring

Number of Films Screened: 30

X Factor: The selection process is particularly strict so if you get invited, it's more than just a screening, it's validation.

Awards: Yes

Profile: In recognition of the power of film to educate and galvanize a broad constituency of concerned citizens, Human Rights Watch decided to create the Human Rights Watch International Film Festival. Human Rights Watch's International Film Festival has become a leading venue for distinguished fiction, documentary and animated films and videos with a distinctive human rights theme. Through the eyes of committed and courageous filmmakers, we showcase the heroic stories of activists and survivors from all over the world. The works we feature help to put a human face on threats to individual freedom and dignity, and celebrate the power of the human spirit and intellect to prevail. We seek to empower everyone with the knowledge that personal commitment can make a very real difference.

In selecting films for the festival, Human Rights Watch concentrates equally on artistic merit and human rights content. The festival encourages filmmakers around the world to address human rights subject matter in their work and presents films and videos from both new and established international filmmakers. Each year, the festival's programming committee screens more than 500 films and videos to create a program that represents a range of countries and issues. Once a film is nominated for a place in the program, staff of the relevant division of Human Rights Watch also view the work to confirm its accuracy in the portrayal of human rights concerns.

Special Events: Opening Night Gala, seminars, parties

Filmmaker Perks: Invited filmmakers will have travel and accomodation costs covered, budget permitting.

Travel Tips: New York in June can be extremely humid, so air conditioning - whether it be in a subway, hotel room, or taxi - is a must.

Bruni Burres ....Festival Director
John Anderson ....Associate Director
Andrea Holley ....Manager - Traveling Festival

HUMBOLDT iNTERNATiONAL SHORT FiLM FESTiVAL

Department of Theatre, Film and Dance
Humboldt State University
Arcata, CA 95521
Tel..707-826-4113
Fax 707-826-4112
Email ....filmfest@humboldt.edu
Web Site ....www.humboldt.edu/~filmfest

Year Festival Began: 1967

Festival Month: April

Entry Deadline: Late January

Entry Fee: $10-$50

Genres: Animation, Documentary, Experimental, Independent, International, Narrative, Shorts, Student

Screening Format: 16mm - DVD

Awards: Best of the Festival

The Alice Guy Blache Award for Celebration of Cinema

Jury Awards

Profile: The Humboldt International Short Film Festival has the proud distinction of being the oldest student-run film festival in the world. We are a not-for-profit organization, funded by the Associated Students of Humboldt State University, grants, community, and individual donations, fundraising events and festival entry fees. The festival is organized by a volunteer committee of students, from a wide range of academic interests, who dedicate their time and energy to the festival because of a genuine respect for the art of film.

Special Events: Awards

Filmmaker Perks: Fuji and Kodak both offer prizes in the form of film stock.

Travel Tips: Arcata's weather is typical of the Northern California coast, with an average year-round temperature of 59 degrees.

YOUR LIFE IS NOT OVER

When you pick up the trades and read that this film or that film sold for a million bucks, don't let it get you down when yours does not sell. The cold truth is that the entertainment business moves at a glacial pace. Things happen very, very slowly, so you must have patience. You may not close a distribution deal for your film, but you'll have made many new friends and useful contacts that will help you along on your eighteenth month (or more!) journey in getting your work seen in front of appreciative festival audiences.

HYPEFEST FiLM & ViDEO FESTiVAL

5225 Wilshire Blvd., Suite 403
Los Angeles, CA 90036
Tel...323-938-8363
Fax 323-938-8757
Email ....info@hypefest.com
Web Site ....www.hypefest.com

Festival Month: Late July

Entry Deadline: Early April

Entry Fee: $40

Students with Valid ID: $25

Genres: Animation, Commercials, Documentary, Experimental, Independent, International, Music Videos, Narrative, Shorts

Screening Format: BetaSP - DigiBeta

Awards: Yes

Profile: HypeFest is a high-energy film & video festival showcasing creativity in film, commercials and music videos from a diversity of filmmakers and storytellers. The weekend-long event, held in Hollywood offers film screenings and nightly parties, complete with mixing and mingling opportunities.

Special Events: Parties, screenplay competition, awards

Filmmaker Perks: HypeFest has a growing list of media partners who will be promoting HypeFest during the months leading up to the festival's premiere.

Travel Tips: Hollywood and Highland is a great place to stand with flyers to promote your film.

Leigh Godfrey ....Festival Co-Director
Jessie Nagel ....Festival Co-Director

ᴀRKET/GOTHAM AWARDS

29th Street, 12th Floor
New ᴊork, NY 10001-5310
Tel 212-465-8200
Fax 212-465-8525
Email ....info@ifp.org
Web Site ....www.ifp.org

Festival Month: October

Entry Deadline: Late May

Entry Fee: $40-$50

Genres: Animation, Documentary, Features, Independent, International, Markets, Narrative, Shorts, Television, Works in progress

Screening Format: 16mm - 35mm - BetaSP - DigiBeta - MS Windows Media Player Series 9

Awards: Emerging Narrative Awards; Short Film Award; Screenplay Award; Work-in-Progress Completion Award; Gotham Awards

Profile: The IFP Market is a week-long showcase, held each autumn in New York, for new features, works-in-progress, shorts, and scripts. For independent filmmakers, it is the only market in the US where one can present new film and television work-in-development directly to the film industry in a selective and professional atmosphere. For the film industry, it is a vital exhibition and discovery forum for new talent and a place to discover new films before they hit the festival circuit.

Special Events: Screenplay competition, awards, parties, Gotham Awards

Filmmaker Perks: Beyond the networking and possibility of selling your film, the Work-in-Progress Completion Award is worth $65,000.

Travel Tips: It's been said before but it's true, if you don't want to walk everywhere, take the subway. It's not that bad.

Michelle Byrd ....Executive Director

iMAGE+NATiON MONTREAL'S iNTERNATiONAL LESBiAN & GAY FiLM AND ViDEO FESTiVAL

4067 St. Laurent, Suite 404
Montréal, Québec
H2W 1Y7 Canada
Tel 514-285-4467
Fax..514-285-1562
Email ....info@image-nation.org
Web Site.......................................www.image-nation.org

Year Festival Began: 1987

Festival Month: Late September-October

Entry Deadline: Contact Festival for Details

Entry Fee: $10

Genres: Documentary, Experimental, Features, Gay Lesbian, Independent, International, Multimedia, Narrative, Shorts, Video

Screening Format: 16mm - 35mm - BetaSP

Awards: Jury Award; Audience Choice Award

Profile: Image+Nation is the largest and fastest growing festival of its kind in Canada. Montréal's International lesbian and gay film and video Festival brings together the best queer media works from around the globe for 11 days of exciting and moving queer images. Image+Nation also produces make the pleasure last, a series of monthly screenings of new works and old favourites. With an impressive selection of local and international titles, the festival stands as a premiere event for showcasing gay, lesbian, bisexual, and transgendered films and videos

Special Events: Awards, parties

Filmmaker Perks: Filmmakers receive a festival pass (access to all films and festival events). If invited, the festival will pay for accomodations and travel.

Travel Tips: Bring warm clothes, and enjoy the changing leaves.

Charlie Boudreau ....Festival Director

iMAGES FESTiVAL OF iNDEPENDENT FiLM AND ViDEO

401 Richmond St. W, Suite 448
Toronto ON M5V 3A8 Canada
Tel 416-971-8405
Fax 416-971-7412
Email................................images@imagesfestival.com
Web Site.................................www.imagesfestival.com

Year Festival Began: 1988

Festival Month: Mid-April

Entry Deadline: Early November

Entry Fee: Features: $45

Shorts: $15

Genres: Animation, Canadian, Digital, Documentary, Experimental, First-Time Independent Filmmakers, Independent, International, Multimedia, Narrative, Shorts, Super 8/8mm, Video

Screening Format: 8mm - Super 8mm - 16mm - 35mm - BetaSP - DV

Awards: Images Prize; National Film Board of Canada Award; Other Awards

Profile: The Images Festival is the largest festival in Canada for independent media, showcasing international excellence and innovation both on and off the screen. Many of the world's most influential and challenging artists show their work at Images. From Super-8 and hand-tinted celluloid to DV, performance and interactive media, the Images Festival goes out of its way and over the edge to present Toronto with an annual extravaganza of worldwide image making.

Special Events: Awards, panels, parties, exhibitions

Filmmaker Perks: The festival offers travel and accomodations to select filmmakers.

Travel Tips: Use the TTC system to get around. It consists of a subway system linked with bus and streetcar surface routes that service all of Toronto.

Petra Chevrier ....Executive Director
Chris Gehman ....Artistic Director

INDEPENDENT BLACK FILM FESTIVAL

PO Box 18914
Atlanta, GA 31126
Tel 404-524-0065
Fax 404-524-3760
Email ....info@indieblackfilm.com
Web Site ....www.indieblackfilm.com

Festival Month: Late January
Entry Deadline: Late October
Entry Fee: $35-$45
Genres: All, Animation, Documentary, Ethnic Black, Features, Independent, International, Markets, Narrative, Shorts
Screening Format: 16mm - 35mm - BetaSP - VHS
Awards: Final Draft Screenplay Award; Jury Awards
Profile: The Independent Black Film Festival (IBFF) is an annual event that showcases diverse and provocative independent feature films, animated films, documentaries, shorts, experimental, and new media works.

Each year, the Independent Black Film Festival will provide independent black filmmakers the opportunity to screen features, shorts, student, documentary and animation film projects, to a culturally diverse audience.
Special Events: Bootcamps, panels, parties, awards, screenplay competition, market
Filmmaker Perks: With a Vendor's Marketplace and Expo going on, you're likely to find even more industry contacts then normal.
Travel Tips: Try the new "buc" shuttle service. It's free, and it picks up at all the normal bus stops.

Asante Addae ....Festival Director

INDEPENDENT EXPOSURE

Microcinema International
531 Utah St.
San Francisco, CA 94110
Tel 415-864-0660
Email ....info@microcinema.com
Web Site ....www.microcinema.com

Year Festival Began: 1996
Festival Month: Ongoing
Entry Deadline: Ongoing
Entry Fee: $5
Genres: Animation, Digital, Digital Animation, Documentary, Experimental, First-Time Independent Filmmakers, Independent, International, Microcinema, Online Festival, PXL, Shorts, Super

8/8mm, Touring (has been played in 25 countries), Underground, Video, Weird, Women
Screening Format: 16mm - 35mm - VHS - MiniDV - DVD
Number of Films Screened: 10-12 per month
X Factor: Not only can you submit your film whenever, but it could be playing all over the world.
Awards: No
Profile: Independent Exposure is Microcinema's well known series of short film, video and digital media compilations Since 1996, Independent Exposure has screened in 41 countries plus Palestine and Antarctica and it continues to intrigue audiences at microcinemas, festivals, and special events around the world, every year. Exposure is normally "premiered" in San Francisco or Houston and then travels around the world.
Filmmaker Perks: All artists will be paid an honorarium when their work is screened in the San Francisco and Houston shows. Artists also will qualify for a non-exclusive Microcinema Distribution through Exhibition Agreement for subsequent international screenings. Microcinema pays its artists royalties for screenings, TV broadcast, VHS/DVD, and Internet sales. If we make money, the artists make money!
Travel Tips: Depends, where is your film playing?

Joel S. Bachar ....Co-Founder
Douglas Fraser...................................Staff Programmer
Patrick Kwiatkowski.....................................Co-Founder

INDEPENDENT FILM FESTIVAL OF BOSTON

44 School St., PMB 385
Boston, MA 02108
Tel 617-966-4236
Email ....info@ifsboston.org
Web Site ....www.iffboston.org

Festival Month: Late April-May
Entry Deadline: Early March
Entry Fee: $15-$45
Genres: Animation, Documentary, Features, Independent, International, Narrative, Shorts
Screening Format: 35mm - BetaSP
Awards: Grand Jury Awards; Audience Awards
Profile: The Independent Film Festival of Boston's mission is to showcase emerging filmmakers, musicians and visual artists and provide attendees direct access in interactive environments to these artists.
Special Events: Panels, awards, parties
Comments: In a few short years the IFFB has established itself as the premier festival in Boston. Bringing in key filmmakers and talent, as well as providing informative panels, it has all the elements of a successful festival. Hip audiences provide a per-

fect showcase for emerging indies. Also, a great place to party.

Filmmaker Perks: Great parties and contacts.

Travel Tips: The festival recommends using jetBlue if you're in a city that offers flights to Boston.

Anne Fazio ....Festival Director
Jason Redmond..................................Executive Director

INDIANAPOLIS INTERNATIONAL FILM FESTIVAL

c/o ME Dettner
1431 N. Delaware St.
Indianapolis, IN 46202
Tel 317-513-9379
Email ....info@indyfilmfest.org
Web Site ....indyfilmfest.org

Festival Month: Early March

Entry Deadline: Late December

Entry Fee: Contact Festival for Details

Genres: Animation, Documentary, Features, Independent, International, Narrative, Shorts

Screening Format: 35mm - BetaSP

Awards: Yes

Profile: The Indianapolis International Film Festival is a young festival that screens the best of independent cinema from around the world. Next to international premieres, the festival has a competitive section for independent shorts and features.

Special Events: Awards, parties

Travel Tips: The weather will still be a bit chilly at night, but overall it'll be mild.

INSIDE OUT LESBIAN AND GAY FILM FESTIVAL OF TORONTO

401 Richmond St. W, Suite 219
Toronto, Ontario
M5V 3A8 Canada
Tel...416-977-6847
Fax 416-977-8025
Email..............................submissions@insideout.on.ca
Web Site ....www.insideout.ca

Year Festival Began: 1991

Festival Month: Late May

Entry Deadline: Mid-January

Entry Fee: None

Genres: Canadian, Documentary, Experimental, Features, Gay Lesbian, Independent, International, Narrative, Shorts

Screening Format: 16mm - 35mm - VHS - BetaSP

Number of Films Screened: 275

X Factor: Toronto is home to one the largest and most vibrant gay and lesbian communities in the world and there's always something to do day or night.

Awards: Inside Out has the most extensive awards program of any queer film festival in Canada, honouring work in ten categories. Awards are given for both Canadian and international work.

Profile: Toronto is a major film center and home to one of the most vibrant queer communities in North America. The Toronto Lesbian and Gay Film and Video Festival is renowned for its innovative programming, enthusiastic audiences, comprehensive media coverage and hospitality. Our venues offer state-of-the-art exhibition facilities in the heart of downtown Toronto, making the festival an ideal place to launch new work.

Inside Out hosts numerous parties, receptions and special events that provide excellent opportunities to schmooze and network with industry professionals, funders, and other independent film and video makers. Our strong relationships in the film and television industry with Alliance Atlantis, Mongrel Media, the Independent Film Channel, Showcase, Pridevision TV, City TV, and CBC TV, have assisted in securing theatrical and broadcast distribution for numerous films and videos.

Special Events: Opening and closing night gala, daily parties

Filmmaker Perks: All filmmakers get an all-access pass to screenings, parties, etc.

Travel Tips: There are a limited number of travel packages through Rainbow High Vacations that include airfare, hotel, and tickets. Check out www.rainbowhighvacations.com.

Scott Ferguson.....................................Executive Director
Kathleen Mullen ....Director of Programming

INTERNATIONAL FESTIVAL OF FILMS ON ART (FIFA)

640 Saint-Paul St. W, Suite 406
Montréal, Québec
H3C 1L9 Canada
Tel...514-874-1637
Fax 514-874-9929
Email ....info@artfifa.com
Web Site ....www.artfifa.com

Festival Month: Mid-March

Entry Deadline: Late October

Entry Fee: $35

Genres: Art-Related, Avant Garde, Documentary, Features, Independent, International, Shorts

Screening Format: 16mm - 35mm - BetaSP - DVD

Awards: Pratt & Whitney Canada Grand Prize; Jury Awards; Award for Best Canadian Work; Other Awards

Profile: The International Festival of Film on Art (FIFA) encompasses all the arts, from all periods and in all styles, in the following categories: painting, sculpture, design, arts and crafts, fashion, decoration, museology, restoration, history of art, photography, cinema (profiles of directors and actors, filming, special effects), literature, dance, music, theatre. The selected films are classified in one of six sections of the Festival.

Filmmaker Perks: Grand Prize award is worth $5,000.

Travel Tips: Montreal is one of the cleanest cities in Canada, keep it that way.

Rene Rozon ....Festival Director
Andre Vailancourt ....Assistant Director

iNTERNATiONAL WiLDLiFE FiLM FESTiVAL MONTANA

718 S. Higgins Ave.
Missoula, MT 59801
Tel..406-728-9380
Fax 406-728-2881
Email ....iwff@wildlifefilms.org
Web Site ....www.wildlifefilms.org

Year Festival Began: 1978
Festival Month: Early May
Entry Deadline: Late January
Entry Fee: Television Program: $150
Television Series: $200
Children's Program: $100
Children's Series: $200
News Story: $50
Independent: $75
Point of View: $75
Music Video: $50
Conservation and Environmental: $150
Human-Wildlife Interactions: $150
Advertising/PSA: $50
Government Agency: $100
Non-Broadcast Program: $100
Amateur: $35
Newcomer: $50
Youth Group: $25
Presenter/Host: $150
Large Format: $150

Genres: All, Children, Commercials, Environmental, Episodic Television/Television Pilots, Features, Independent, International, Music Videos, Narrative, PSA (Public Service Announcement), Shorts, Student, Television, Wildlife

Screening Format: BetaSP - DigiBeta
Number of Films Screened: 50
X Factor: If you like the outdoors, this festival is for you.
Awards: Jury Awards
Profile: The International Wildlife Film Festival Montana's mission is to foster appreciation and understanding for wildlife and natural habitats through accurate and honest wildlife filmmaking. IWFF-Missoula is often called "The Filmmakers Festival," known as much for its intimacy as for the incredible setting in which the festival takes place. Once you arrive, virtually all of our festival locales are within walking distance of each other and most accomodations. For those events that are out of town, we satisfy all of your transportation needs. If you're thinking of bringing family members, there will be plenty to keep them busy and they're more than welcome to participate in many of the festival events. But some of the most exciting habitats and many of the most wonderful species in the world are right here in Montana and getting out to see them is relatively easy and affordable.
Special Events: Parades, receptions, award ceremony, field trips, workshops, parties
Travel Tips: Missoula, Big Sky Country. Bring some sturdy shoes as you'll be walking.

Janet Rose ....Executive Director
Lisa "Kersch" Kerscher ....Festival Associate

BEST GAY FiLM FESTIVALS

Atlanta Gay and Lesbian Film Festival - Out on Film
Brussels Gay and Lesbian Film Festival
Image+Nation Montreal's International Queer Film Festival
ImageOut - The Rochester Lesbian & Gay Film & Video Festival
Inside Out Lesbian and Gay Film Festival of Toronto
Melbourne Queer Film & Video Festival
Out At The Movies: San Antonio's Annual Festival of Lesbian & Gay Film
OutFar! - Annual Phoenix International Lesbian and Gay Film Festival
Out Fest: Los Angeles International Gay and Lesbian Film & Video Festival
Queersicht – Schwul-lesbisches Filmfestival Bern
Philadelphia International Gay and Lesbian Film Festival
San Francisco Lesbian and Gay Film Festival
Seattle Lesbian & Gay Film Festival

ISRAEL FILM FESTIVAL

Israfest Foundation, Inc.
6404 Wilshire Blvd., Suite 1240
Los Angeles, CA 90048
Tel 323-966-4166; 877-966-5566
Fax...323-658-6346
Email ....meir@israelfilmfestival.com
Web Site............................www.israelfilmfestival.com/

Year Festival Began: 1982
Festival Month: April-November
Entry Deadline: Mid-January
Entry Fee: None
Genres: Documentary, Episodic Television/Television
Pilots, Ethnic Jewish, Ethnic Other, Features,
Independent, International, Narrative, Shorts,
Student, Television, Touring
Screening Format: 16mm - 35mm - BetaSP
Awards: Israel Film Festival Lifetime Achievement
Award; IFF Visionary Award; IFF Cinematic Award;
IFF Humanitarian Award
Profile: The Israel Film Festival provides a greatly
expanded perception of Israel by presenting the lat-
est films and television programs and by welcoming
Israeli filmmakers to the United States, thereby
sharing with American audiences the country's rich
culture, diverse stories, and unique modern Israeli
life. Through the generosity of the Hollywood community, the Israeli government, foundations, corpora-
tions, organizations and individuals, the Israel Film
Festival continues to be the largest annual Israeli
cultural event in the United States.
Special Events: Parties, special screenings, awards
Filmmaker Perks: The festival assists with accomodations when possible.
Travel Tips: The tour lasts through the summer -
visiting Chicago, Los Angeles, New York, and Miami
- so be prepared to rack up the frequent flyer miles.

JACKSON HOLE WILDLIFE FILM FESTIVAL

PO Box 3940
Jackson, WY 83001
Tel 307-733-7016
Fax..307-733-7376
Email ....info@jhfestival.org
Web Site ....www.jhfestival.org

Year Festival Began: 1991
Festival Month: Late September (Odd Numbered
Years)
Entry Deadline: Early June
Entry Fee: $75-$80
Genres: Documentary, Environmental, Features,
Independent, International, Shorts, Wildlife
Screening Format: BetaSP - DigiBeta - DVD
Awards: Grand Teton Award; Marion Zunz
Newcomer Award; Other Awards

Profile: The Jackson Hole Wildlife Film Festival, held
in the fall of each odd-numbered year, is an unparalleled industry gathering focused on film competition;
cutting-edge equipment presentations; and an exceptional slate of seminars, panel discussions, and
screenings. The festival is attended by hundreds of
television and film professionals from more than 30
countries.
Special Events: Awards, special screenings
Filmmaker Perks: Throughout the day, delegates
will have access to the lodge's restaurant, coffee
shop, and lounge.
Travel Tips: At an elevation of 6,200 feet, Jackson
Hole is likely to be sunny and warm during the day,
with temperatures in the low 70s (Fahrenheit), but
the nights in September can dip into the 30s.
Jackets, sweaters, and similar warm clothing are
recommended.

Lisa Samford ....Executive Director

JOHNS HOPKINS FILM FESTIVAL

c/o Adam Lareau
315 E. 30th St
Baltimore, MD 21218
Tel ....(410) 235-8719
Email ....bracklives@hotmail.com
Web Site ....www.jhu.edu/~jhufilm/fest

Year Festival Began: 1998
Festival Month: Mid-April
Entry Deadline: Mid-January
Entry Fee: $25-$35
Genres: American, Animation, Documentary,
Experimental, Features, First-Time Independent
Filmmakers, Independent, International,
Microcinema, Narrative, Shorts, Student, Super
8/8mm, Underground, Weird
Screening Format: Super 8mm - 16mm - 35mm -
VHS - DVD
Awards: No
Profile: The Johns Hopkins Film Festival is a non
profit organization that seeks to promote works by
budding independent and student filmmakers.
Documentaries, features, and short films that have
been hitting the festival circuits as well as little-seen
local, national, and international films will be dis-
played.
Special Events: Special screenings, parties
Filmmaker Perks: The festival assists with travel
and accomodations when possible.
Travel Tips: Taking the Light Rail (Baltimore's
attempt at a trolley) from the airport to Penn Station
costs $1.35 and takes 35 minutes.

Adam Lareau...Festival Director

Get hip. Shoot in Montana.

Montana.
A BETTER BRAND OF LOCATIONS.

(800) 553-4563
montanafilm@visitmt.com
www.montanafilm.com

LAKE PLACID FILM FORUM

26 Main St.
PO Box 489
Lake Placid, NY 12946
Tel 518-523-3456
Fax 518-523-4746
Email ....adkfilm@adelphia.net
Web Site ....www.lakeplacidfilmforum.com

Year Festival Began: 1998
Festival Month: Early June
Entry Deadline: Early April
Entry Fee: Features and Documentaries: $45
Shorts: $25
Genres: American, Animation, Digital, Digital Animation, Documentary, DVD, Europe, Asia, South America, Canada and the U.S., Experimental, Features, First-Time Independent Filmmakers, Independent, International, Multimedia, Narrative, Shorts, Student, Video, Women
Screening Format: 35mm - BetaSP - DVD
Number of Films Screened: 60
X Factor: Very laid back atmosphere, lots of opportunity for networking.
Awards: Emerging Filmmaker Awards
Robin Pell Award
The Silver Deer Audience Award
Profile: The Lake Placid Film Festival is an intimate setting for filmmakers and film lovers to see films and discuss issues of content and the medium. The Forum screens over 60 outstanding shorts, documentaries and feature films and presents forums, roundtables, master classes and readings of screenplays, honors the lifetime achievement of a distinguished filmmaker, and provides an array of opportunities for teen filmmakers.
Special Events: Digital Filmmaking Workshop, forums, panels, parties, and book store signings
Travel Tips: Give the festival housing coordinator a call at 518-523-3456 ext. 106 to find out the latest travel and housing deals available.

Muriel Luderowski ....Managing Director
Alan Hofmanis.......................Director of Programming
Timothy Brearto............................Submissions Director
Russell Banks.............................Festival Co-Founder
Kathleen Carroll ....Festival Co-Founder

LONG ISLAND INTERNATIONAL FILM EXPO

The Malverne Cinema 4
350 Hempstead Ave.
Malverne, NY 11565
Tel..516-572-0012
Fax...516-572-0565
Email ....debfilm@aol.com
Web Site ....www.longislandfilm.com

Festival Month: Mid-July

Entry Deadline: Early May
Entry Fee: Features: $50
Shorts: $25
Genres: Animation, Documentary, Features, Independent, International, Narrative, Shorts, Student
Screening Format: 16mm - 35mm - BetaSP - VHS
Awards: Jury Awards; Audience Awards; Other Awards
Profile: The Long Island International Film Festival is devoted to the screening and support to independently produced films. Over 70 short and feature length independent films from all over the globe are screened during this weeklong film festival.
Special Events: Awards, parties, panels
Filmmaker Perks: The festival covers travel and accomodations when possible.
Travel Tips: The Malverne Train Station is half a block South of the Malverne Cinema 4.

Bob Hansen ....Chairman

LOS ANGELES INTERNATIONAL SHORT FILM FESTIVAL

2700 Cahuenga Blvd., Ste. 3206
Los Angeles, CA 90068
Tel 323-851-9100
Fax...323-851-9100
Email ....info@lashortsfest.com
Web Site ....www.lashortsfest.com

Year Festival Began: 1997
Festival Month: September
Entry Deadline: Mid-May
Number of Submissions: 1,100
Entry Fee: Under 40 Minutes: $45
40-60 Minutes: $50
Features: $60
Genres: Animation, Digital, Documentary, Features, First-Time Independent Filmmakers, Independent, International, Narrative, Shorts, Student, Touring
Screening Format: 16mm - 35mm - BetaSP - DigiBeta
Number of Films Screened: 250
Odds: 1 in 4
X Factor: Win an award and qualify for an Academy Award® nomination.
Awards: Jury Awards
Profile: LA Shorts Fest is dedicated to the celebration and cultivation of the short film. Through a variety of yearlong activities, LA Shorts Fest educates, entertains and honors those who have mastered the craft. LA Shorts Fest is the largest short film festival in the world and one of the few recognized by the Academy of Motion Pictures Arts & Sciences.
LA Shorts Fest attracts the highest caliber of short films made each year. Since its inception, sixteen

festival participants have gone on to earn Academy Award® nominations and three have won the Oscar® for their films.

The festival is now accepting feature film submissions as part of their on-going efforts to support the short filmmaker. Directors must have completed a short film sometime during their career.

Special Events: Screenplay competition, panels, parties, High School Outreach, and College Tour

Filmmaker Perks: Meet other shorts filmmakers and network in the heart of Hollywood.

Travel Tips: The weather will still be warm during the day - but the nights can get a bit chilly, so bring appropriate gear.

Robert Arentz ....Festival Director/Founder

LOS ANGELES LATiNO iNTERNATiONAL FiLM FESTiVAL

6777 Hollywood Blvd., Suite 500
Hollywood, CA 90028
Tel 323-469-9066
Fax 323-469-9067
Email ....latinofilm@yahoo.com
Web Site ....www.latinofilm.org

Year Festival Began: 1996
Festival Month: Mid-July
Entry Deadline: Mid-April
Entry Fee: Features: $20
Shorts and Documentaries: $10
Genres: Animation, Documentary, Ethnic Latin, Features, Independent, International, Narrative, Shorts
Screening Format: 16mm - 35mm - BetaSP - DigiBeta
Number of Films Screened: 110
Awards: Yes
Profile: The Los Angeles Latino International Film Festival has been recognized as the largest Latino International Film festival in the country, and is the preeminent venue for the exhibition of the highest caliber Latino films from the United States, Spain, and Latin America and creates a bridge between Hollywood and independent filmmakers from all the Spanish-speaking countries.
Special Events: Panels, workshops, awards, parties
Filmmaker Perks: The festival provides food and accomodations when possible.
Travel Tips: Films screen at the Egyptian Theater, right on the famed Hollywood Blvd. Find street parking if you can, otherwise you'll be dropping some bucks at a lot.

LOST FiLM FESTiVAL

4434 Ludlow St.
Philadelphia, PA 19104
Tel 215-662-0397
Email...info@lostfilmfest.com
Web Site ....www.lostfilmfest.com

Year Festival Began: 1998
Festival Month: Mid-April
Entry Deadline: Early March
Entry Fee: Features: $30
Shorts: $15
Genres: Animation, Digital, Digital Animation, Documentary, Ethnic African, Ethnic Asian, Ethnic Black, Ethnic Jewish, Ethnic Latin, Ethnic Spanish, Experimental, Features, First-Time Independent Filmmakers, Gay Lesbian, Independent, International, Microcinema, Narrative, Online Festival, Shorts, Student, Touring, Underground, Video, Weird, Women
Screening Format: 8mm - Super 8mm - 16mm - 35mm - VHS - DVD - BetaSP - MiniDV - CDRom
Number of Films Screened: 20+
X Factor: With a touring festival that hooks itself up with Cannes, Sundance, and SXSW, your film could really get around.
Awards: No
Profile: The Lost Film Festival is an annual festival in Philadelphia that also includes a traveling event that attaches itself to larger host festivals with name recognition to put on screenings, lecture series, and media pranks before moving on to a new host festival. The touring aspect of the festival travels worldwide.
Special Events: Panels and parties
Comments: This touring festival is about as underground, alternative and political as one will find. The Philadelphia-based festival organizers take guerilla film to the extreme and support their efforts year round with screening series and releases of shorts on DVD.
Filmmaker Perks: It's all about the meeting up with other underground, guerilla filmmakers.
Travel Tips: Philly in April can get a bit rainy, but it's typical spring weather.

Scott Beibin ....Festival Director
Elizabeth-Jane Cole ....US Booking

MADCAT WOMEN'S iNTERNATiONAL FiLM FESTiVAL

639 Steiner St.
San Francisco, CA 94117
Tel 415-436-9523
Fax 415-934-0642
Email ....info@madcatfilmfestival.org
Web Site ....www.madcatfilmfestival.org

Year Festival Began: 1996
Festival Month: Early September-October

THE ULTIMATE FILM FESTIVAL SURVIVAL GUIDE

Dustin Hoffman and the author enjoy the snow in Park City.

Entry Deadline: Late May

Number of Submissions: 880

Entry Fee: $10-$30

Genres: Animation, Avant Garde, Digital, Digital Animation, Documentary, DVD, Ethnic African, Ethnic Asian, Ethnic Black, Ethnic Jewish, Ethnic Latin, Ethnic Spanish, Experimental, Features, First-Time Independent Filmmakers, Gay Lesbian, Independent, International, Narrative, PXL, Shorts, Student, Super 8/8mm, Touring, Underground, Video, Weird, Women

Screening Format: Super8 - 16mm - 35mm - BetaSP - VHS - SVHS - MiniDV

Number of Films Screened: 60-85

Odds: 1 in 14

X Factor: Quite possibly the best film festival in the US for independent women filmmakers.

Awards: No

Profile: In 1996 the MadCat Women's International Film Festival was born and with it a new platform for women artists to screen their work. MadCat showcases some of the best avant-garde independent and experimental films and videos from around the world. At MadCat, female directors and artists are not only the centerpiece - they *are* the festival. From MadCat's beginning as a 3 day festival at one location to their current line-up of four local venues and a month long festival with over 25 touring spots around the country - MadCat is truly a festival to be reckoned with in the Bay Area and beyond.

Special Events: Free barbecue, cocktails, pool tournaments

Travel Tips: To quote SanFrancisco.com, "Fall in San Francisco is truly the best time of year for weather. Days are warm and sunny, sometimes blisteringly so, and nights are mild and clear. Rainfall is rare, the fog has cleared and the long warming process has reached its magnificent zenith, making September, October and early November the three best months to visit ."

Ariella Ben-Dov ....Festival Director/Founder

MAKING SCENES QUEER FILM & VIDEO FESTIVAL

c/o Arts Court
2 Daly Ave., Suite 250
Ottawa, ON K1N 6E2 Canada
Tel 613-566-2113
Email ....scenes@magma.ca
Web Site ....www.makingscenes.ca

Festival Month: Late October

Entry Deadline: Late July

Entry Fee: None

Genres: AIDS/HIV-related, Animation, Documentary, Features, Gay Lesbian, Independent, International, Multi-Cultural, Narrative, Shorts

Screening Format: 16mm - 35mm - BetaSP - VHS

Number of Films Screened: 75

Awards: No

Profile: The goal of the Making Scenes Queer Film & Video Festival is to provide an annual film and video festival featuring gay and lesbian works that present images of gay and lesbian lives and issues; emphasize issues of multicultural diversity, gender and HIV/AIDS; encourage local artists, critics and audiences to participate in the discussion of cultural identities and aesthetics.

Special Events: Special screenings, panels, parties

Filmmaker Perks: Free travel - not usually, but it depends

Travel Tips: Bring your jacket, the weather is going to start getting chilly.

Daniel Grummisch ....Executive Director
José Sánchez..........................Director of Programming

MALIBU INTERNATIONAL FILM FESTIVAL

PO Box 4166
Malibu, CA 90264-4166
Tel 310-452-1180
Email ....info@malibufilmfestival.org
Web Site ....www.malibufilmfestival.org

Festival Month: Mid-September

Entry Deadline: Early July

Entry Fee: $50-$100

Genres: Animation, Documentary, Features, Independent, International, Narrative, Shorts

Screening Format: 35mm - BetaSP

Awards: Yes

Profile: The Malibu Film Festival focuses on showcasing new independent films and filmmakers from around the world. After winning top honors at the Malibu Film Festival, filmmakers have gone on to be represented by the major talent agencies and have signed multi-picture deals with the movie studios.

Special Events: Parties, awards

Filmmaker Perks: Each film accepted into the festival will be granted (2) VIP screening passes.

Travel Tips: Fly into LAX and head for the Pacific Coast Highway.

David Katz ....Festival Director

MANiA FEST

PO Box 807
Venice, CA 90294
Tel 310-399-8001
Email ....festivaldirector@mania.com
Web Site ....www.maniafest.com

Festival Month: Mid-September
Entry Deadline: Mid-August
Entry Fee: Contact Festival for Details
Genres: Fantasy/Science Fiction, Features, Horror, Independent, International, Narrative, Shorts, Thriller
Screening Format: 35mm - BetaSP - VHS
Awards: Jury Awards
"Friday the 13th" Cut 'Em Up Film
Maniac Career Achievement Award
Profile: ManiaFest is a major genre film festival, celebrating the work of science fiction, fantasy, and horror screenwriters & filmmakers. This four-day event applauds the efforts and imagination of those who push the boundaries between reality and fiction, whether with nightmarish visions or views of other worlds. A portion of the proceeds will be donated to the Boys and Girls Clubs of Santa Monica.
Special Events: Awards, parties, retrospectives
Filmmaker Perks: Retrospective screenings bring horror movies, long since gone from the big screen, back.
Travel Tips: Venice is extremely laid back, even by Southern California standards.

MARCO ISLAND
FILM FESTIVAL

MARCO iSLAND FiLM FESTiVAL

601 Elkcam Circle, B6
Marco Island, FL 34145
Tel 239-642-3378
Fax 239-394-1736
Email ....info@marcoislandfilmfest.com
Web Site ....www.marcoislandfilmfest.com

Year Festival Began: 1998
Festival Month: Early November
Entry Deadline: Mid-August
Entry Fee: $25-$40

Genres: American, Animation, Children, Documentary, Features, First-Time Independent Filmmakers, First-Time Independent Filmmakers, Gay Lesbian, Independent, International, Narrative, Shorts, Student, Super 8/8mm, Video
Screening Format: 16mm - 35mm - BetaSP - DigiBeta
Number of Films Screened: 80
Awards: Audience Awards
The Marco Island Film Festival's Pelican Awards
Other Awards
Profile: The annual Marco Island Film Festival showcases and promotes film projects developed by independent film makers while creating opportunities through education and awareness for students pursuing a career in the film industry.
Special Events: Panels, parties, beach screening, awards
Comments: Marco Island is a beautiful oasis off the coast of Florida, which is reason enough to plan a trip. Films are shown at several venues, but the best is at Marco Movies which features stadium seating as well as dinner theater-style seats. Audiences viewing films at this venue can order from a full menu of food items along with beer and wine. Filmmakers are treated to a champagne cruise, elegant parties, and may also choose to participate in a host of summer activities - including jet-skiing and more. Guests and filmmakers are put up in hotels and private homes, which often end up becoming the location for all-night parties. The nightly beach screenings feature movies accented by the soft sound of the ocean. Pure heaven.
Filmmaker Perks: Opening night screening on the beach.
Travel Tips: Beach clothes, keep it casual.

Patricia Berry.......................................Executive Director

MARGARET MEAD FiLM FESTiVAL

American Museum of Natural History
Central Park West at 79th
New York, NY 10024-5192
Tel 212-769-5305
Fax...212-769-5329
Email...meadfest@amnh.org
Web Site ....www.amnh.org/programs/mead

Festival Month: Early November
Entry Deadline: Late May
Entry Fee: None
Genres: Animation, Documentary, Experimental, Features, Independent, International, Shorts, Touring
Screening Format: 16mm - 35mm - BetaSP - Other Digital
Awards: No
Profile: The Margaret Mead Film & Video Festival is the longest-running showcase for international docu-

mentaries in the United States, encompassing a broad spectrum of work, from indigenous community media to experimental nonfiction. The festival is distinguished by its outstanding selection of titles, which tackle diverse and challenging subjects, representing a range of issues and perspectives, and by the forums for discussion with filmmakers and speakers.

Special Events: Panels, special screenings, workshops

Filmmaker Perks: Select titles will be invited to participate in the Margaret Mead Traveling Film & Video Festival, featured at independent film and community centers, museums, and universities throughout the United States and abroad. An honorarium is provided.

Travel Tips: Take the B (weekdays only) or C to 81st Street. Two blocks west of the Museum, the 1 and 9 trains stop at Broadway and West 79th Street. For a subway map, visit the Metropolitan Transit Authority website (www.mta.nyc.ny.us).

MARYLAND FiLM FESTiVAL
107 East Read St.
Baltimore, MD 21202
Tel 410-752-8083
Fax 410-752-8273
Email ....info@mdfilmfest.com
Web Site ....www.mdfilmfest.com

Year Festival Began: 1999
Festival Month: Early May
Entry Deadline: Mid-February
Entry Fee: Under 5 Minutes: $10
5-20 Minutes: $20
20-50 Minutes: $30
Over 50 Minutes: $50
Entry fee waived for any production shot more than 50 percent in Maryland
Genres: Animation, Documentary, Experimental, Features, Independent, International, Narrative, Shorts
Screening Format: 16mm - 35mm - BetaSP - DVD
Awards: No
Profile: The Maryland Film Festival, funded by an unusual public/private partnership in Maryland, has two practical economic development goals: 1) to create a world class film festival centered in Baltimore, and 2) to bring filmmakers to Maryland as a way to encourage future production in the state.

We want a festival experience that is fun - celebrating the whole film culture, with no distinction between types of films. To us a great movie is a great movie. We realize this is a privilege the marketplace does not have. We strive to make Maryland Film Festival screenings distinct.

Special Events: Parties, special screenings

Travel Tips: Fly right into Baltimore and while you're in the terminal, you really owe it to yourself to visit the BWI Observation Gallery.

Jed Dietz ....Festival Director
Skizz Cyzyk ....Programming Manager

MAUi FiLM FESTiVAL
PO Box 790669
Paia, HI 96779
Tel 808-579-9996
Fax 808-579-9552
Email ....info@mauifilmfestival.com
Web Site ....www.mauifilmfestival.com

Year Festival Began: 1997
Festival Month: Mid-June
Entry Deadline: Mid-March
Entry Fee: Under 21 Minutes: $35
21-55 Minutes: $55
Over 55 Minutes: $75
Genres: All, Animation, Documentary, Experimental, Features, Independent, International, Narrative, Shorts
Screening Format: 35mm - BetaSP - DV
Awards: Stella Award; Lights!Camera!Passion! Award
Profile: The Maui Film Festival is five-day celebration of life-affirming filmmaking that features under-the-stars premieres, filmmakers panels and world-class culinary events at the Wailea Resort and Maui Arts & Cultural Center.

Special Events: Awards, panels, parties, Celestial Cinema

Filmmaker Perks: It's in Maui, that's all the perk you need!

Travel Tips: Celestial Cinema seating is on the grass; bring a blanket, mat or low backed beach chair. Beach chairs are also available for rent or purchase.

Barry and Stella Rivers ....Co-Directors
Tide Maya and Kiva Rivers ....Co-Directors

MELBOURNE iNDEPENDENT FiLMMAKERS FESTiVAL - MiFF
c/o Terry Cronin
1399 South Harbor City Blvd.
Melbourne, FL 32901
Tel...321-726-1711
Email ....terry@3boysproductions.com
Web Site.....................3boysproductions.com/miff.htm

Festival Month: Early September
Entry Deadline: Early May
Entry Fee: None
Genres: Animation, Charity, Documentary, Features, Independent, International, Narrative, Shorts
Screening Format: VHS - DVD - VCD
Awards: No

Profile: The Melbourne Independent Filmmakers Festival - MIFF is a film festival particularly aimed at promoting filmmakers and local interest in film. Filmmakers, talent agencies, and production groups will be on hand to promote their work as well as to network.

Special Events: Parties

Filmmaker Perks: Contacts.

Travel Tips: Not the best mass transit system in the world, so rent a car.

Terry Cronin ....Program Chairman

METHOD FEST INDEPENDENT FILM FESTIVAL

880 Apollo St., Suite 337
El Segundo, CA 90245
Tel 310-535-9230
Fax 310-535-9128
Email ....don@methodfest.com
Web Site..www.methodfest.com

Year Festival Began: 1999

Festival Month: Early April

Entry Deadline: Mid-January

Entry Fee: Features: $40-$50

Shorts: $30-$40

Students with Valid ID: $25

Genres: Experimental, Features, Gay Lesbian, Independent, International, Narrative, Shorts

Screening Format: 35mm - BetaSP - DigiBeta

Awards: Jury Awards

Profile: The Method Fest is the only film festival in the US that puts its focus on the actor, believing acting is the core ingredient to independent film. Dubbed as "The Actor's Festival," and named after Stanislavski's "Method" school of acting, the Method Fest showcases story-driven films featuring outstanding acting performances by emerging stars and career-defining roles by established actors.

Special Events: Method Fest Acting Competition, parties, panels, awards

Filmmaker Perks: If you're an actor, this festival is all about you.

Travel Tips: In honor of Method Fest's focus on acting, visit the "Former Child Actors'" Taco Bell across from the Warner Bros. studio lot.

Don Franken ....Festival Director

MIAMI INTERNATIONAL FILM FESTIVAL

Miami Dade College
300 NE 2nd Ave.
Miami, FL 33132-2204
Tel..305-237-3456
Fax 305-237-7344
Email ....info@miamifilmfestival.com
Web Site ....www.miamifilmfestival.com

Year Festival Began: 1984

Festival Month: Late January-February

Entry Deadline: Mid-October

Entry Fee: Features: $50

Shorts: $15

Genres: American, Animation, Digital, Documentary, Ethnic African, Ethnic Asian, Ethnic Black, Ethnic Jewish, Ethnic Latin, Ethnic Spanish, Experimental, Features, First-Time Independent Filmmakers, Independent, International, Narrative, Shorts, Women

Screening Format: 35mm - BetaSP - DVD

Number of Films Screened: 60+

X Factor: It's only natural to go south for the winter!

Awards: Jury Awards; Audience Awards

Profile: The Miami International Film Festival (MIFF) brings the best of world cinema to South Florida and plays a leading role in maintaining and further enriching its film culture.

MIFF uses the unique geographical and cultural position of Miami to be a premiere venue for the exhibition of international and US films, with a special focus on Iberoamerican cinema. Both juried and audience awards are given in Documentary and Dramatic categories.

Special Events: Panels, seminars, parties, Awards Brunch

Filmmaker Perks: The festival provides travel and accomodations for selected guests.

Travel Tips: Leave the skis and parkas at home, bring the shorts and the sunglasses.

Nicole Guillemet....................................Festival Director
T. Vincent ....Filmmaker Liaison

MICROCINEFEST

3700 Beech Ave.
Baltimore, MD 21211
Tel 410-243-5307
Email ....bfink@bcpl.net
Web Site ....www.microcinefest.org

Year Festival Began: 1997

Festival Month: October

Entry Deadline: Late July

Entry Fee: Contact Festival for Details

Genres: Animation, Independent, Microcinema, Narrative, Rock and Roll, Shorts, Touring (Atlanta, GA; Liverpool, England; Washington DC), Underground, Video, Weird

BEST FESTIVALS FOR ACTORS

Methodfest
Hollywood Film Festival
iEmmys Festival
Cannes International Film Festival
Toronto International Film Festival

Screening Format: 8mm - Super 8mm - 16mm - 35mm - VHS - DVD - DV

Awards: Low-Budget Awards

Profile: MicroCineFest screens the most ambitious, creative, daring, do-it-yourself, low-budget, offbeat, original, psychotronic, substream, underground films and videos from all over the world.

Special Events: Parties, bowling, awards

Filmmaker Perks: Any filmmaker who comes to the festival gets an all-access festival pass. We can also make arrangements for filmmakers who bring guests. Any filmmaker coming from out of town can make arrangements with us to pick him/her up at the airport/bus depot/train station and put them up with at least a floor to crash on, if not a couch or bed.

Travel Tips: Like any city, be smart after dark and don't go walking down any poorly-lit alleys.

Skizz Cyzyk ....Festival Director
J.R. Fritsch ....Assistant Director

MILL VALLEY FILM FESTIVAL

California Film Institute
38 Miller Ave., Suite 6
Mill Valley, CA 94941
Tel ....415.383.5256 ext. 119
Email ....info@cafilm.org
Web Site ....www.cafilm.org

Festival Month: Early October

Entry Deadline: Late June

Entry Fee: $25-$35

Youth: $10-$15

Genres: American, Animation, Children, Documentary, Experimental, Family, Features, Independent, International, Narrative, Shorts, Student

Screening Format: 16mm - 35mm - BetaSP

Awards: No

Profile: The Mill Valley Film Festival, California's longest-running fall festival, is known internationally as a high-profile, prestigious event celebrating the best of independent international cinema. MVFF's long-term commitment to helping launch independent films - both American and foreign - into the US market, has made it the festival of choice for filmmakers worldwide.

Special Events: Tributes, parties, New Media Lab, concerts

Filmmaker Perks: The festival covers travel and accomodations for select filmmakers. Networking with industry contacts for all.

Travel Tips: Mill Valley is north of San Francisco, but San Fran is still the closest airport. Fly in, rent a car, visit the wineries, have a friend drive you home.

Zoë Elton ....Festival Contact

MINICINE VISITING FILMMAKER SERIES

824 Texas Ave.
Shreveport, LA 71101
Email ....minicine@swampland.org
Web Site ....www.swampland.org

Year Festival Began: 1997

Festival Month: September-May

Entry Deadline: Ongoing, Check with Festival

Genres: Ethnic Other, Experimental, First-Time Independent Filmmakers, Microcinema, Multimedia, Narrative, Performance, PXL, Shorts, Super 8/8mm, Touring, Underground, Video

Screening Format: Super 8mm - 16mm - VHS

Awards: No

Profile: Minicine is a roving, pop-up suitcase, grocery cart, thrift store, hands on, volunteer run venue for experimental and independent film and video located in Shreveport, Louisiana. Screening in galleries, coffee shops, or vacant buildings, Minicine strives to create an artist/audience interactive environment and welcomes filmmakers and multimedia visual artists to present new works. Minicine is outfitted for 16mm, Super-8, VHS etc. and, in conjunction with Mother's Gallery/A Visual Sound and Movement Company, can host traveling performance art, dance, and music.

Filmmaker Perks: Festival can help find accomodations, but won't pay for them.

Travel Tips: Fly into Shreveport Airport, rent a car.

Twister ....Festival Director
Tevin ....Festival Programmer
David ....Festival Contact
Ryan ....Festival Staff
Folded Bread ....Festival Staff
Libby ....Festival Staff

MINIDV FILM FESTIVAL

Tel 877-997-2957
Fax..877-733-2987
Email ....info@minidvfestival.com
Web Site ....www.minidvfestival.com

Festival Month: Mid-December

Entry Deadline: Late October

Entry Fee: $15

Genres: Animation, Comedy, Digital, Digital Animation, Documentary, Experimental, Features, Music Videos, Narrative, Shorts

Screening Format: DVCam - MiniDV

Awards: Robert Rodriguez Award; Jury Awards

Profile: Some of the best filmmakers in the world may never get noticed because they couldn't shoot their film in a format that they could afford. The MiniDV Film Festival, a bold anarchist move to promote the world of film-making in the new digital format.

Everyone has a MiniDV camera...and everyone wants to be a star! The MDVF has been established to bring these two together by giving futurist writers, producers, and directors the opportunity to showcase their talents utilizing equipment they can financially afford, while still producing creative stories & ideas that will leave the audience in standing ovations.

Special Events: Parties, awards

Filmmaker Perks: All DV/All the time.

MINNEAPOLIS/ST PAUL INTERNATIONAL FILM FESTIVAL

2331 University Ave. SE, Suite 130-B
Minneapolis, MN 55414-3067
Tel 612-627-4431
Fax 612-627-4111
Email ....filmsoc@tc.umn.edu
Web Site www.ufilm.org/ufilm/international_fest.htm

Festival Month: Early April

Entry Deadline: Early February

Entry Fee: Features: $50

Shorts: $35

Genres: Animation, Documentary, Features, Independent, International, Narrative, Shorts

Screening Format: 16mm - 35mm - BetaSP - VHS

Awards: Jury Awards; "Minnesota Spirit" Award

Profile: Ranked among the top film festivals in the region, the Minneapolis/St. Paul International Film Festival is the largest of its kind in the Upper Midwest.

Special Events: Awards, parties

Travel Tips: The Twin Cities are home to Northwest Airlines, so you figure there've got to be travel deals to be found there.

MONTREAL INTERNATIONAL FESTIVAL OF NEW CINEMA AND NEW MEDIA

3530, St-Laurent Blvd., office 304
Montreal (Quebec) H2X 2V1 Canada
Tel 514-847-9272; 514-847-1242
Fax 514-847-0732
Email ....info@fcmm.com
Web Site ....www.fcmm.com

Year Festival Began: 1972

Festival Month: Early October

Entry Deadline: Early May

Entry Fee: $25

Genres: All, Animation, Digital, Documentary, Features, Independent, International, Narrative, Shorts

Screening Format: 16mm - 35mm - BetaSP - DigiBeta - DV - VHS

Number of Films Screened: 200

Awards: DVcolor Best Feature Award; Volkswagen Audience Award; NFB Best Documentary Award; Other Awards

Profile: The Montreal International Festival of New Cinema and New Media focuses on new approaches and technologies while working as a springboard for artists eager to explore the confines of their art.

Special Events: Awards, screenplay competition, panels

Filmmaker Perks: The Best Feature Award is worth $10,000, the other awards are worth $5,000, but the real kicker is the $80,000 SODEC Sprint for your Script Prize

Travel Tips: Beware the bicyclists - they rule the road.

Claude Chamberlan ....Festival Director

MONTREAL WORLD FILM FESTIVAL

1432 de Bleury St.
Montreal (Quebec)
H3A 2J1 Canada
Tel 514-848-3883
Fax 514-848-3886
Email ....info@ffm-montreal.org
Web Site ....www.ffm-montreal.org

Year Festival Began: 1977

Festival Month: Late August-September

Entry Deadline: Mid-June for Shorts

Mid-July for Features

Entry Fee: Features: $50

Shorts: $25

Genres: Animation, Documentary, Features, Independent, International, Narrative, Shorts, Student

Screening Format: 35mm - 70mm - BetaSP - DVD

Number of Films Screened: 400+

X Factor: With an international market and a huge screening slate, one has to wonder if your film will get lost in the masses.

Awards: Grand Prize of the Americas; Jury Awards; Other Awards

Profile: The goal of the World Film Festival (Montreal International Film Festival) is to encourage cultural diversity and understanding between nations, to foster the cinema of all continents by stimulating the development of quality films, to promote filmmakers and innovative works, to discover and encourage new talent, and to promote meetings between cinema professionals from around the world.

The festival is open to all cinema trends. The eclectic aspect of its programming makes the festival exciting for the growing number of participants from the five continents. Every year, films from more than seventy countries, including well known and first-time filmmakers alike, are selected. Many films have been discovered in Montreal

Special Events: Montreal International Film Market panels, parties, awards

Filmmaker Perks: Networking opportunities abound as the Montreal International Film Market is in full-swing and all attendees of the market have exclusive access to all festival screenings.

Travel Tips: All screening venues are within a few minutes walk of each other, so bring comfortable shoes.

Serge Losique ....President
Danièle Cauchard.....................................Vice-President
Gilles Bériault...............................Film Market Director

MOONDANCE INTERNATIONAL FILM FESTIVAL

970 Ninth St.
Boulder, CO 80302
Tel 303-545-0202; 303-818-5771
Fax 303-545-0202
Email ....info@moondancefilmfestival.com
Web Site ....www.moondancefilmfestival.com

Year Festival Began: 1999
Festival Month: Late May
Entry Deadline: Mid-March
Entry Fee: $50-$75
Genres: American, Animation, Documentary, Experimental, Features, First-Time Independent Filmmakers, Independent, International, Markets, Narrative, Shorts, Video, Women
Screening Format: BetaSP - DVD
Number of Films Screened: 50-75
X Factor: Most of the Moondance winning and finalist films have been purchased and distributed world-wide, for television and theatrical release.
Awards: Spirit of Moondance Awards; Seahorse Awards; Sandcastle Awards; Columbine Awards
Profile: The mission of the Moondance International Film Festival is to entertain, to inform, to inspire, to

BEST PARTY FESTIVALS

Chicago Underground Film Festival
CineVegas Film Festival
Deep Ellum Film Festival
Florida Film Festival
GEN ART Film Festival
Hamptons International Film Festival
Los Angeles Film Festival
New Orleans Film Festival
San Diego Film Festival
Slamdance International Film Festival
Sundance Film Festival
SXSW Film Festival
Toronto Film Festival
USA Film Festival

encourage, and to educate. We believe that films and scripts can contribute to a healthier society and that films and scripts should encourage the active involvement of audiences to connect and act collectively to address social challenges. Winning and finalist films and scripts are innovative, distinctive, compelling and engaging, relevant to varied audiences and encourage participation. We are eager to continue to be one of the most important film festivals in the world by being innovative, risk-taking, and open to new thinking, new concepts, new talent, and new ways of telling stories.

Our work on reaching out toward female filmmakers and female writers everywhere in the world is primary and ongoing. Female writers and filmmakers from all six continents, and from a wide diversity of ethnic and linguistic groups, are an integral part of our mission and goals. We seek to inspire and invigorate this creative potential of women to perceive, conceptualize, and produce their works for the benefit of the world society. We are dedicated to preserving their accumulated accomplishments and visions as expressed through the art of film and writings.

Special Events: Panels, parties, workshops, awards, screenplay competition
Filmmaker Perks: Top film studios and producers in LA, NY, and worldwide request Moondance winners' and finalists' screenplays.
Travel Tips: Fly into Denver and rent a car or taxi to Boulder.

Elizabeth English ....Founder/Executive Director
Dave Riepe........................Festival Screenings Director

MOUNTAINFILM FESTIVAL

PO Box 1088
Telluride, CO 81435
Tel 970-728-4123
Fax 970-728-6458
Email...info@mountainfilm.org
Web Site...................................www.mountainfilm.org

Year Festival Began: 1979
Festival Month: Late May
Entry Deadline: April
Entry Fee: $45
Genres: Documentary, Environmental, Features, Independent, International, Mountain Sports, Shorts, Touring
Screening Format: 16mm - 35mm - BetaSP
Number of Films Screened: 50
Awards: Yes
Profile: The Mountainfilm Festival, now entering its 26th year in Telluride, Colorado, is founded on the power of geography to shape our view of the world. Mountains are a metaphor for us, a representation of wild and different places and people – and Mountainfilm is an event that celebrates distinctive cultures and the landscapes they occupy. Each spring

we gather some of the most extraordinary films and special guests from around the world to share and celebrate their real, and metaphorical, mountains.

Special Events: Parties, panels, awards

Filmmaker Perks: There are few festivals for the mountain-related genre.

Travel Tips: Flights are available directly into Telluride or nearby Montrose, Durango, Cortez, Gunnison, and Grand Junction.

Rick Silverman ....Festival Director

NANTUCKET FiLM FESTiVAL

1633 Broadway, Suite 14-334
New York, NY 10019
Tel...212-708-1278
Fax..212-654-4784
Email ....ackfest@aol.com
Web Site ....www.nantucketfilmfestival.org

Year Festival Began: 1996

Festival Month: Late June

Entry Deadline: Mid-April

Entry Fee: Features: $40

Shorts: $25

Genres: Animation, Documentary, Features, Independent, International, Narrative, Shorts, Student

Screening Format: 16mm - 35mm - DigiBeta

Number of Films Screened: 45

X Factor: Beach screenings aren't as common as you might suspect.

Awards: Jury Awards; Audience Awards; Other Awards

Profile: The Nantucket Film Festival has established itself as a premiere US film festival that provides an intimate forum for screenwriters, producers, agents and development executives to interact with and enjoy the notable films presented on the island. The festival screens both domestic and international features, world premieres, shorts, documentaries and videos from every genre, all selected with an eye towards storytelling. Q&As with the writers and filmmakers follow each screening. Panel discussions, staged readings, beach screenings and other live events round out the festival program.

Special Events: Panels, tributes, awards, staged readings, parties, Morning Coffee and Teen View programs

Travel Tips: Don't rent or drive a moped. Most accidents in Nantucket occur on them.

Jill Goode ....Executive Director
Tom Hall ....Film Programming Director
Mystelle Brabbee ....Artistic Director

NASHViLLE FiLM FESTiVAL

PO Box 24330
Nashville, TN 37202-4330
Tel 615-742-2500
Fax..615-742-1004
Email ....info@nashvillefilmfestival.org
Web Site ....www.nashvillefilmfestival.org

Year Festival Began: 1969

Festival Month: Late April-May

Entry Deadline: Late November

Number of Submissions: 1,000

Entry Fee: $35-$60

Genres: Children, Digital Animation, Documentary, Documentary, Episodic Television/Television Pilots, Experimental, Family, Features, Independent, Markets, Music-Related, Narrative, Shorts, Student

Screening Format: 35mm - BetaSP

Number of Films Screened: 200

Odds: 1 in 5

X Factor: Winning a prize and being considered for an Academy Award® nomination isn't offered everywhere - but getting a week-long run at a Regal theater in LA can console you even if you don't get an Oscar®.

Awards: Freedom in Film Award

Dreammaker Award (Qualifies a feature for Academy Award consideration)

Best Short (Qualifies for Academy Award consideration)

Profile: The Nashville Film Festival (NFF) was founded in 1969 and is one of the longest running film festivals in the country. Because it takes place in "Music City," it is only natural that part of the focus of the NFF be on music in films. Some of the most memorable songs in films have been written and performed by Nashville's songwriters and artists. The NFF presents showcases, workshops, and other events where these songwriters and artists come together with film professionals from Hollywood and around the world to promote collaboration.

Special Events: Workshops, panels, parties, awards

Comments: Film is the thing during NFF, but for music fans, you will discover heaven for your ears.

Filmmaker Perks: Transportation is offered to get you from event to event.

Travel Tips: If you're not against meat, order the "meat and three" for lunch sometime.

Brian Gordon ....Artistic Director
Sallie Mayne...General Manager

NATiVE AMERiCAN FiLM & ViDEO FESTiVAL

Film and Video Center
National Museum of the American Indian
One Bowling Green
New York, NY 10001-1415
Tel...212-514-3732
Email...svensonm@si.edu
Web Site.............................www.nativenetworks.si.edu

Festival Month: Early December
Entry Deadline: April
Entry Fee: By Invite
Genres: American, Documentary, Ethnic Other, Features, Independent, Narrative, Shorts, Television
Screening Format: 35mm - Beta SP
Awards: No
Profile: The Native American Film and Video Festival celebrates the many remarkable recent accomplishments in the field of Native media, presenting 85 outstanding productions from Bolivia, Brazil, Canada, Chile, El Salvador, Mexico, Arctic Russia, the continental United States, and Hawaii.
Special Events: Tributes, parties, panels
Filmmaker Perks: Screenings are held throughout cultural centers in New York City

Wendy Allen...Festival Contact

NEW DiRECTORS/NEW FiLMS FESTiVAL

70 Lincoln Center Plaza
New York, NY 10023-6595
Tel...212-875-5638
Fax..212-875-5636
Email..sbensman@filmlinc.com
Web Site...www.filmlinc.com

Festival Month: Late March-April
Entry Deadline: Mid-January
Entry Fee: None
Genres: Animation, Documentary, Features, First-Time Independent Filmmakers, Independent, International, Narrative
Screening Format: 16mm - 35mm
Awards: No
Profile: The New Directors/New Films festival at the Museum of Modern Art brings New York an early look at some of the world's best films by new directors, many of which have earned acclaim at top film festivals around the world and some of which will be indie hits in the year to come.
Special Events: Parties
Filmmaker Perks: Contacts, the industry looks to the festival for new filmmaking voices.
Travel Tips: Make sure you take a look around the Museum of Modern Art instead of just screening and bolting.

Sarah Bensman......................................Festival Contact

NEW FESTiVAL: NEW YORK LESBiAN, GAY, BiSEXUAL, & TRANSGENDER FiLM FESTiVAL

139 Fulton St., Suite PH-3
New York, NY 10038
Tel...212-571-2170
Fax..212-571-2179
Email...info@newfestival.org
Web Site.......................................www.newfestival.org

Year Festival Began: 1988
Festival Month: Early June
Entry Deadline: Early March
Entry Fee: $20-$25
Genres: Animation, Documentary, Features, Gay Lesbian, Independent, International, Narrative, Shorts
Screening Format: 16mm - 35mm - BetaSP - VHS - DVD - MiniDV
Number of Films Screened: 150
X Factor: The festival has presentations with other prominent New York film festivals.
Awards: Jury Awards
The Showtime No Limits Award
The Peter S. Reed Achievement Award
The Vito Russo Award
The Audience Award
Profile: Since 1988, NewFest: the annual New York Lesbian, Gay, Bisexual, & Transgender Film Festival has been one of the most comprehensive forums of international LGBT film/video, and an important exhibition platform for independent film/video makers. NewFest provides a professional and public context for the presentation of innovative and challenging work that reflects the broad range of practice and ideas found in contemporary media.
Special Events: Awards, parties
Travel Tips: New York in June can be humid and hot, so be prepared and hang in the air-conditioning when possible.

Basil Tsiokos...Festival Director

NEW ORLEANS FiLM FESTiVAL

843 Carondelet St.
New Orleans, LA 70130
Tel...............................504-524-5271; 504-523-3818
Fax..208-975-3478
Email..............incompetition@neworleansfilmfest.com
Web Site........................www.neworleansfilmfest.com

Festival Month: Early October
Entry Deadline: Mid-June
Entry Fee: $35-$45
Genres: Animation, Documentary, Experimental, Features, Independent, International, Narrative, Shorts, Video

Screening Format: Super 8mm - 35mm - BetaSP - VHS - DVD

Number of Films Screened: 80

Awards: Jury Awards

Profile: Over the past decade, New Orleans Film Festival has grown into a prominent vehicle for exhibitions and premieres of local, regional, national and international independent

film. Each year NOFF showcases the best new American and foreign films including premieres of major feature films and short works - all with directors, actors, screenwriters, cinematographers, film critics, and fans in attendance.

Special Events: Parties, awards, special screenings

Comments: Skip Mardi Gras and get to this festival for one reason - it's New Orleans! Let me repeat: New Orleans. Need I say more?

Travel Tips: New Orleans is the birthplace of jazz but the city is deeply rooted in the history of rock music. Enjoy the history while you're partying.

Lindsay Ross ....Executive Director
John Desplas ....Artistic Director

NEW YORK EXPO OF SHORT FiLM AND ViDEO

224 Centre St., Suite 2E
New York, NY 10013
Tel 212-505-7742
Email ....nyexpo@aol.com
Web Site ....www.nyexpo.org

Festival Month: November

Entry Deadline: July

Entry Fee: $45

Genres: Animation, Documentary, Experimental, Independent, International, Narrative, Shorts

Screening Format: 16mm - 35mm - BetaSP

Number of Films Screened: 45

Awards: Jury Awards

Profile: The New York EXPOsition of Short Film and Video is the nation's longest-running annual festival of independent short film and video. The Expo celebrates the art of the short film and over its long history has sought out and presented challenging, unconventional, cutting-edge and technically innovative films and videos. The festival is one of the first to recognize the talents of Spike Lee, George Lucas, and Martha Coolidge.

Special Events: Awards, panels

Travel Tips: Weather in NYC can be extremely chilly, thanks primarily to the overabundance of concrete, so bring warm clothes.

Karen Treanor ....Director
Vera Kopylova ....Program Coordinator

NEW YORK FiLM FESTiVAL

c/o Film Society of Lincoln Center
165 W. 65th St., 4th Floor
New York, NY 10023-6595
Tel 212-875-5638
Fax...212-875-5636
Email ....festival@filmlinc.com
Web Site ....www.filmlinc.com/nyff/nyff.htm

Year Festival Began: 1963

Festival Month: Early October

Entry Deadline: Early July

Entry Fee: None

Genres: 16mm, 35mm, Avant Garde, Documentary, Features, International, Narrative

Screening Format: 16mm - 35mm

Number of Films Screened: 35

X Factor: Prestigious event, no submission fee.

Awards: Grand Marnier Film Fellowship Awards

Profile: The New York Film Festival ushers autumn in with the newest and most significant works by directors - established icons and new discoveries alike - from all over the world. An enormously popular event, the festival stirs the hearts and minds of audiences and stimulates critical debate on the season's best movie-making.

Over the years, the New York Film Festival has proudly premiered films by Martin Scorsese, Jean-Luc Godard, François Truffaut, Akira Kurosawa, Jane Campion, Louis Malle, Jonathan Demme, James Ivory, Robert Altman, Barbara Kopple, and Quentin Tarantino, among others.

The New York Film Festival prefers to screen a small number of films despite its large nature. It has previously showcased a number of popular films such as *Pulp Fiction* (1994), *Secrets & Lies* (1996) and *The People vs. Larry Flynt* (1996).

BEST UNDERGROUND FESTiVALS

20,000 Leagues Under the Industry Film Festival
Antimatter Festival of Underground Short Film
   & Video
B-Movie Film Festival
Boston Underground Film Festival
Chicago Underground Film Festival
Euro Underground
Exground - Das Filmfest
Independent Exposure
Lost Film Festival
MicroCineFest
New York Underground Film Festival
Renegade Film Festival
Seattle Underground Film Festival
Slamdance International Film Festival
TromaDance Film Festival

Co-sponsored with the Museum of Modern Art, New Directors/New Films has earned an international reputation as the foremost forum for film art that breaks or re-makes the cinematic mold. As a festival dedicated to discovering emerging and overlooked artists, newcomers on the verge of mainstream success and distinguished veterans whose work deserves wider public attention, New Directors nurtures directorial talent by creating an invaluable opportunity for that talent to win public support and acceptance.

Since its beginning in 1972, New Directors' audiences have been treated to an early preview of such diverse talents as Wim Wenders, Steven Spielberg, John Sayles, Spike Lee, Sally Potter, Pedro Almodóvar, Chen Kaige, Ken Burns, Peter Greenaway, and Whit Stillman.

Special Events: Retrospectives, awards

Travel Tips: Bring a coat for chilly NYC nights.

Richard Peña..Festival Director
Sarah Bensman.................................Festival Contact

NEW YORK LESBIAN AND GAY EXPERIMENTAL FILM AND VIDEO FESTIVAL (MIX FESTIVAL)

29 John St., #132
New York, NY 10038-4005
Tel 212-742-8880
Email ....info@mixnyc.org
Web Site ....www.mixnyc.org

Festival Month: Late November

Entry Deadline: July

Genres: Experimental, Features, Gay Lesbian, Independent, International, Shorts

Screening Format: 16mm - 35mm - BetaSP

Number of Films Screened: 100-150

Awards: No

Profile: The New York Lesbian and Gay Experimental Film/Video Festival seeks to integrate the lesbian, gay and experimental film communities by creating an innovative festival that serves as a home for both established and emerging makers while promoting and encouraging the awareness, making, and preservation of work that challenges and expands our vision of media and the world.

Special Events: Parties

Filmmaker Perks: Nightly parties in the heart of NYC.

Travel Tips: Take the F Train to the 2nd Ave stop, then walk 2 blocks north for the theater.

Larry Shea.......................................Festival Co-Director
Kara Williamson..............................Festival Co-Director
Stephen Winter ....Festival Co-Director

NEW YORK UNDERGROUND FILM FESTIVAL

195 Chrystie St., #503
New York, NY 10002
Tel 212-614-2775
Fax 212-614-2776
Email ....info@nyuff.com
Web Site ....www.nyuff.com

Festival Month: Mid-March

Entry Deadline: Mid-January

Entry Fee: $30

Genres: Animation, Documentary, Experimental, Features, Independent, International, Narrative, Shorts, Underground

Screening Format: 16mm - 35mm - BetaSP - VHS

Number of Films Screened: 75

Awards: Jury Awards

Profile: The annual New York Underground Film Festival showcases independent and unique films, focusing on innovative projects that go beyond mainstream filmmaking.

Special Events: Parties, awards, panels, retrospectives

Comments: The first underground film festival that helped support a growing movement among filmmakers, the fest screens work which might be considered by some offensive. Of course, this is the reason to actually attend and screen work that others may find "difficult."

Filmmaker Perks: Nightly parties.

Travel Tips: All screenings are at Anthology Film Archives, 32 Second Ave. at Second St. There are a number of subway options: F Train to Second Ave stop. Get out at Second Ave exit. Walk two blocks north to Second St., 6 Train to Bleecker St. stop. Walk east to Second Ave & Second St. J, M, Z to Bowery stop. Walk north on Chrystie past Houston to Second St., and the L to First Ave stop. Walk south to Second St, turn right to Second Ave.

Kendra Gaeta ....Festival Director
Ed Halter ....Executive Producer

NEWPORT BEACH FILM FESTIVAL

4540 Campus Dr.
Newport Beach, CA 92660
Tel 949-253-2880
Fax 949-253-2881
Web Site ....www.newportbeachfilmfest.com

Festival Month: Late April

Entry Deadline: Late January

Entry Fee: $75

Genres: Animation, Children, Digital, Documentary, Experimental, Independent, International, Short, Student

Screening Format: 35mm - BetaSP

Number of Films Screened: 250

Awards: Jury and Audience Awards

Profile: The Newport Beach Film Festival showcases more than 250 films from around the world, offering an ambitious and international selection of features, shorts, documentaries and animation. The festival treats its audience to World and US premieres, Academy Award® entries, Sundance Selections, a Spotlight Series, and Children's Festival, from both the independent and studio worlds, including submissions from Asia, Europe, South/Central America, and Africa.

Special Events: Parties, panels, yacht parties

Filmmaker Perks: The festival offers deals through sponsors for accomodations and food.

Travel Tips: The city boasts one of the largest movie consumer groups in the world, a rich filmmaking history as well as fine dining, shopping, and exceptional recreational activities (like yachting).

Gregg Schwenk.................................Executive Director

NEXT FRAME FiLM FESTiVAL

Dept. of Film & Media Arts
009 Annenberg Hall
2020 N. 13th St.
Temple University 011-00
Philadelphia, PA 19122
Tel 215-923-3532
Fax...215-204-8740
Email ....nextfest@temple.edu
Web Site ....www.temple.edu/nextframe

Year Festival Began: 1993

Festival Month: September-June

Entry Deadline: Late May

Number of Submissions: 300

Entry Fee: $20-$25

UFVA Student Members: $15-$20

International Students: None

Genres: Animation, Documentary, Experimental, Features, First-Time Independent Filmmakers, Independent, International, Narrative, Shorts, Student, Touring

Screening Format: 16mm - BetaSP

Number of Films Screened: 25

Odds: 1 in 12

X Factor: Unlike a traditional festival, the NextFrame award-winning films embark on a year-long international tour.

Awards: Yes

Profile: NextFrame features animation, experimental, documentary, and narrative work. The festival offers low entry fees and few restrictions - such as length and format - in order to encourage the most diverse entries possible. The goal as a festival is to connect student filmmakers and provide much-deserved screening opportunities. Visiting university campuses, museums, and media arts centers, NextFrame offers audiences a glimpse of the promising next generation of filmmaking.

Special Events: Awards, Festival Tour

Filmmaker Perks: NextFrame is not only for student filmmakers, it's run by student filmmakers.

Travel Tips: Depends on which stop on the world tour you're hooking up with.

Sunrise Tippeconnie ....Festival Co-Director
Stephanie Garoian ....Festival Co-Director

NODANCE FiLM FESTiVAL

703 Pier Ave. #675
Hermosa Beach, CA 90254
Tel 323-512-7988
Email ....info@nodance.com
Web Site ....www.nodance.com

Year Festival Began: 1998

Festival Month: January (Park City), June (Los Angeles)

Entry Deadline: Mid-December

Entry Fee: Contact Festival for Details

Genres: American, Digital, Documentary, DVD, Features, First-Time Independent Filmmakers, Gay Lesbian, Independent, International, Markets, Microcinema, Multimedia, Narrative, Online Festival, Shorts, Touring (Austin, TX; Cannes, France; Toronto, Canada; Los Angeles, CA), Underground

Screening Format: DVD

Awards: Grand Jury Awards; Audience Awards; Golden Orbs Award

Profile: The Nodance Film Festival celebrates the alternative digital film culture, with an emphasis on first-time filmmakers and digital filmmaking. Held annually in Park City, Utah, as well as screening in Los Angeles during the Summer, Nodance holds the distinction of being the world's first DVD-projected film festival.

Special Events: Awards, panels, parties

Filmmaker Perks: Once again, Nodance will present the "Out of the Box" sign-up program at the Nodance HQ. The program will provide screening space for any filmmaker with any project. "Out of the Box" provides an alternative opportunity for all filmmakers to present their films in the unique Park City environment without having to face the normal festival screening process.

Travel Tips: Accomodations can be tricky in Park City, so find out who else is playing Nodance and see if you can share lodging.

James Boyd...Festival Director

NORTH CAROLINA JEWISH FILM FESTIVAL

309 West Morgan St.
Durham, NC 27701
Tel 919-560-3040
Fax 919-560-3065
Email ....toby@carolinatheatre.org
Web Site ....carolinatheatre.org/ncjff

Year Festival Began: 1995

Festival Month: Late February

Genres: Animation, Documentary, Ethnic Jewish, Features, Independent, International, Narrative, Shorts

Screening Format: 16mm - 35mm

Number of Films Screened: 27

Profile: The North Carolina Jewish Film Festival serves to explore the diversity of Jewish life and culture and promote the discussion of relevant issues and concerns pertinent to the Jewish community. As many of the NCJFF's films are produced without the support of a major studio, and are often made for a non-mainstream audience, they bring fresh interpretations of Jewish culture and identity.

Special Events: Parties, youth art exhibit

Filmmaker Perks: Festival covers travel and accomodations when possible.

Travel Tips: Fly right into Raleigh-Durham International Airport and rent a car.

Jim Carl ....Senior Director
Toby Kennedy ....Director of Operations

NORTHWEST FILM & VIDEO FESTIVAL

The Northwest Film Center
1219 SW Park Ave.
Portland, OR 97205
Tel 503-276-4264
Fax 503-294-0874
Email ....info@nwfilm.org
Web Site ....www.nwfilm.org

Year Festival Began: 1972

Festival Month: Early November

Entry Deadline: Early August

Number of Submissions: 300+

Entry Fee: None

Genres: American, Animation, Digital, Documentary, Experimental, Features, First-Time Independent Filmmakers, Independent, Independent, Multimedia, Narrative, Performance, Shorts, Student, Super 8/8mm, Touring (Seattle, WA; Vancouver, BC; Anchorage, AK; Olympia, WA; Boise, ID; Helena, WA; Eugene OR), Video, Weird

Screening Format: 8mm - Super 8mm - 16mm - 35mm - BetaSP - VHS - DVD - MiniDV - CDRom

Number of Films Screened: 30-45

Odds: 1 in 10

X Factor: Festival and tour participants will share approximately $15,000 in lab service awards and tour honoraria.

Awards: Yes

Profile: The Northwest Film & Video Festival is the most prominent forum for independent work by artists living in the Northwest. The Festival presents features, documentaries, and short films, chosen by a prominent member of the independent film community such as Gus Van Sant, Todd Haynes, producer Christine Vachon, and *The Simpsons* creator Matt Groening.

Special Events: Awards, parties, Festival Tour

Filmmaker Perks: Following presentation in Portland the Film Center will assemble selected works for the Best of the Northwest Touring Program which will circulate throughout the region in 2004.

Travel Tips: Portland in the wintertime can have some of that famous Northwest rain, but overall it's not that bad.

Andrew Blubaugh...................................Festival Contact

NSI FILMEXCHANGE CANADIAN FILM FESTIVAL

206-70 Arthur St.
Winnipeg R3B 1G7 Canada
Tel 1-800-952-9307
Fax 204-956-5811
Email ....info@nsi-canada.ca
Web Site ....www.nsi-canada.ca/filmexchange

Year Festival Began: 1986

Festival Month: Early March

Entry Deadline: November

Entry Fee: None

Genres: Animation, Canadian, Documentary, Features, Independent, International, Narrative, Shorts

Screening Format: 35mm - BetaSP - VHS

Awards: Jury Awards

Profile: Each winter Winnipeg plays host to Canada's only 100% Canadian Film Festival. Featuring a line up of the best feature and short Canadian films of the year from the country's top filmmakers, and an amateur filmmaking competition, NSI FilmExchange is a sizzling celebration of Canadian Film and Canadian filmmaking in one very cool city.

The main objective of NSI FilmExchange is to further the development of Canadian film, television and new media by providing a forum in which emerging and established filmmakers come together to showcase their works and exchange ideas and information. NSI FilmExchange is the only major film festival to profile Canadian works exclusively.

Special Events: Workshops, awards, parties

Filmmaker Perks: Festival covers travel and acco-modations when possible.

Travel Tips: Take the bus, only $1.65. A taxi will run you about $16.

Liz Hover...Festival Contact

OHiO iNDEPENDENT FiLM FESTiVAL

1392 W. 65th St.
Cleveland, OH 44102
Tel..216-651-7315
Fax...216-651-7317
Email ....ohioindiefilmfest@juno.com
Web Site.................................www.ohiofilms.com

Year Festival Began: 1993

Festival Month: November

Entry Deadline: Early July

Entry Fee: $20-$70

Genres: American, Animation, Digital, Digital Animation, Documentary, Ethnic African, Ethnic Asian, Ethnic Black, Ethnic Jewish, Ethnic Latin, Ethnic Other, Ethnic Spanish, Experimental, Features, First-Time Independent Filmmakers, Gay Lesbian, Independent, International, Markets, Multimedia, Narrative, Online Festival, Shorts, Student, Super 8/8mm, Underground, Video, Weird, Women

Screening Format: 16mm - BetaSP - DVD

Number of Films Screened: 135

X Factor: More than a festival, a filmmaking educa-tion.

Awards: Jury Awards

Profile: The Ohio Independent Film Festival (estab-lished in 1993) is the leading organization in Ohio dedicated to freedom of expression through the art of independent media. We accomplish this mission by encouraging emerging media artists and providing a consistent, reputable venue for media work the pub-lic may not otherwise see.

The OIFF facilitates grass roots networking for inde-pendent media makers, is the accessible step between local filmmakers and the larger world of independent film, and produces educational pro-grams and workshops.

We value integrity, innovation, and the exchange of knowledge.

Special Events: Screenplay competition, awards, workshops

Travel Tips: Fly into Cleveland and rent a car. Bring warm clothes.

Bernadette Gillota ....Festival Co-Founder
Annetta Marion ....Festival Co-Founder

OTTAWA iNTERNATiONAL ANiMATiON FESTiVAL

2 Daly Ave. Suite 120
Ottawa, ON K1N 6E2
Tel..613-232-8769
Fax...613-232-6315
Email.................................info@animationfestival.ca
Web Site ....www.awn.com/ottawa

Year Festival Began: 1976

Festival Month: Late September

Entry Deadline: Early July

Entry Fee: None

Genres: Animation, Features, Independent, International, Narrative, Shorts

Screening Format: 16mm - 35mm - BetaSP

Awards: Jury Awards

Profile: The aim of the Ottawa International Animation Festival is to foster the development and growth of animation talent found within our country and region. Our animators and animation companies are among the most creative and successful in the world. The Ottawa festival helps them achieve both artistic excellence and commercial success.

We also seek to provide a means of inter-linking the regional, national, and international animation com-munities. The festival exists in part to provide an artistic and commercial forum wherein aesthetic and artistic excellence, as well as commercial expertise, can be shared and exchanged among these various communities.

Special Events: Retrospectives, panels, parties, awards

Filmmaker Perks: Invitations are given to filmmak-ers with films in competition.

Travel Tips: Everything is within walking distance, so bring comfortable shoes.

Kelly Neall...Managing Director
Chris Robinson ....Artistic Director

SCREENING TIMES MATTER

Unless your film is opening or closing night (generally taken up by studio indies anyway), the best screening slot is usually a Friday or Saturday in the evening at 7 or 9 PM. Check to be sure your screening does not conflict with any parties or major events. Usually you can count on getting at least one lousy time slot, like 11 AM on a weekday, but this should be countered by an evening screening. Be sure to ask your screening times and if there is time to make a change, ask for at least one good slot.

OUT FAR! – ANNUAL PHOENiX iNTERNATiONAL LESBiAN AND GAY FiLM FESTiVAL

Vista Events, Inc.
619 E. Vista Ave.
Phoenix, AZ 85020
Tel...602-410-1074
Fax..425-928-1074
Email..outfarfest@aol.com
Web Site ....www.outfar.org

Year Festival Began: 1997
Festival Month: Early February
Entry Deadline: Early December
Entry Fee: None
Genres: American, Animation, Documentary, First-Time Independent Filmmakers, Gay Lesbian, Independent, International, Markets, Shorts, Video
Screening Format: 35mm - BetaSP - DVD
Awards: No
Profile: OutFar! seeks to program current, compelling, entertaining and educational films or video for the LGBT community. The film festival occurs every February over the Valentine's Day weekend. Films are geared towards the alternative community at large and include a variety of subjects, themes, and messages.
Special Events: Parties, special screenings
Filmmaker Perks: The festival assists in providing or finding accomodations when possible.
Travel Tips: Make your housing arrangements early.

Amy B. Ettinger ....Festival Director

OUTFEST: LOS ANGELES GAY AND LESBiAN FiLM FESTiVAL

3470 Wilshire Blvd., Suite 1022
Los Angeles, CA 90010
Tel 213-480-7088
Fax 213-480-7099
Email..outfest@outfest.org
Web Site ....www.outfest.org

Year Festival Began: 1982
Festival Month: Early July
Entry Deadline: Mid-March
Entry Fee: Features: $35
Shorts: $25
Genres: Animation, Documentary, Experimental, Features, First-Time Independent Filmmakers, Gay Lesbian, Independent, International, Narrative, Shorts
Screening Format: 16mm - 35mm - BetaSP - VHS
Number of Films Screened: 200+
X Factor: Outfest is the only gay and lesbian film festival in the heart of the entertainment industry, and more industry executives attend Outfest than any other gay and lesbian film festival.

Awards: HBO Outstanding First Narrative Feature Award; Other Awards
Profile: Outfest is the oldest and largest continuous film festival in Southern California. Since its founding in 1982, Outfest has presented more than 3,500 films and videos for audiences of nearly half a million people.
Special Events: Awards, parties, screenplay competition, panels
Filmmaker Perks: One-on-one industry meetings with an agent/manager, production company executive, entertainment lawyer, or distribution company executive for every director in the festival.
Travel Tips: Sunglasses and a good attitude, s'all you need.

Stephen Gutwillig ....Executive Director
Kirsten Schaffer ....Director of Programming

PALM BEACH iNTERNATiONAL FiLM FESTiVAL

289 Via Naranjas
Royal Palm Plaza, Suite 48
Boca Raton, FL 33432
Tel 561-362-0003
Fax 561-362-0035
Email..info@pbifilmfest.org
Web Site ....www.pbifilmfest.org

Festival Month: Mid-April
Entry Deadline: Late January
Entry Fee: Under 30 Minutes: $30-$37
30-60 Minutes: $45-$52
Over 60 Minutes: $60-$70
Genres: All, Animation, Documentary, Features, First-Time Independent Filmmakers, Independent, International, Narrative, Shorts, Student
Screening Format: 35mm - BetaSP - DigiBeta
Awards: Audience Favorite Awards
Jury Awards
Profile: The Palm Beach International Film Festival has enjoyed a remarkable level a success to date. While competing on a national level with over 800 similar events and internationally with the same level of competition, PBIFF has created a special niche within the film industry.
Whether PBIFF is hosting acclaimed celebrities at the world renowned resorts, the Grand Gala Awards, showcasing world & US premieres in our countywide theaters or honoring the achievements of student filmmakers, the festival has certainly captured the media spotlight. Documented worldwide coverage of past festivities has been valued at over $4.7 million with an average of 57+ impressions on an annual basis.
Special Events: Awards, panels, tributes, parties, Student Showcase
Filmmaker Perks: Tons of networking possibilities.

Travel Tips: Palm Beach offers 47 miles of pristine beaches, superb parks, an average temperature of 78° F, outstanding restaurants and hotels, more than 150 golf courses, sport fishing, cruises, magnificent homes, one-of-a-kind attractions, exquisite cultural venues, and a great nightlife.

Randi Emerman ....Operations Manager
Allen Elrod..Programming

PALM SPRINGS INTERNATIONAL FESTIVAL OF SHORT FILMS

1700 East Tahquitz Canyon Way, Suite #3
Palm Springs, CA 92262
Tel 760-322-2930; 800-898-7256
Fax 760-322-4087
Email..info@psfilmfest.org
Web Site..www.psfilmfest.org

Festival Month: Early September
Entry Deadline: Early August
Entry Fee: $50
Students with Valid ID: $40
Genres: All Categories - Shorts
Profile: The Palm Springs International Festival of Short Films (PSIFSF) is the largest showcase of short films in North America.

Comments: Perhaps the best organized short festival in the world, the fest allows attendees to view shorts they've missed in a video lounge. Shorts are grouped by subject matter and festival directors come from all over to seek out shorts for their own fests. A true celebration of short films - and you'll *want* to stay indoors and watch movies most of the time as temperatures reach north of 100. Also, don't forget to visit one of the town's casinos. For short filmmakers, this is a must-stop on your festival tour.

Darryl Macdonald...............................Executive Director

PALM SPRINGS INTERNATIONAL FILM FESTIVAL

1700 E. Tahquitz Canyon Way, Suite 3
Palm Springs, CA 92262
Tel..760-322-2930
Fax 760-322-4087
Email..info@psfilmfest.org
Web Site..www.psfilmfest.org

Year Festival Began: 1990
Festival Month: Early January
Entry Deadline: November
Entry Fee: $50-$75
Genres: Documentary, Features, Independent, International
Screening Format: 16mm - 35mm - BetaSP - DVD
Number of Films Screened: 200
X Factor: Hobnob with the Oscar-contenders in a gorgeous setting.

Awards: Distinguished Achievement Award for Directing and Producing
International Filmmaker Award
Sonny Bono Visionary Award
The Rising Star Award
Other Awards
Profile: Located in the beautiful Coachella Valley desert at the base of Mt. San Jacinto in Southern California, the Palm Springs International Film Festival is one of the largest film festivals in the country, screening over 200 films from more than 60 countries to an audience of over 70,000.
Special Events: Awards, panels, parties
Filmmaker Perks: Huge networking potential.
Travel Tips: The Palm Springs International Airport is serviced by most major US airlines and several commuter airlines.

Darryl Macdonald...............................Executive Director
Carl Spence ....Director of Programming
Rhea Lewis-Woodson.......................Managing Director

PHILADELPHIA FILM FESTIVAL

c/o Philadelphia Film Society
234 Market St., Fifth Floor
Philadelphia, PA 19147
Tel ....215-733-0608, ext. 237
Fax...215-733-0637
Web Site ....www.phillyfests.com/pff/templates/
home.cfm

Festival Month: Early April
Entry Deadline: Mid-January
Entry Fee: None
Genres: Animation, Features, First-Time Independent Filmmakers, Independent, International, Narrative, Shorts, Student
Screening Format: 16mm - 35mm - BetaSP
Awards: Artistic Achievement Award
TLA Phantasmagoria Award
Profile: The Philadelphia Film Festival screens nearly 250 films from 43 countries that are sure to entertain, engage and enlighten: the latest triumphs from the masters of today and stunning debuts from the masters of tomorrow; visceral live-action and ingenious animation; guaranteed crowd-pleasers and hidden treasures waiting to be discovered.

Special Events: Panels, awards, parties, special screenings
Filmmaker Perks: The festival helps with travel and accomodations when possible.

Raymond Murray ....Festival Director

PHILADELPHIA FRINGE FESTIVAL

211 Vine St.
Philadelphia, PA 19106
Tel 215-413-9006
Fax 215-413-9007
Email ....pafringe@aol.com
Web Site ....www.pafringe.org

Festival Month: Early September
Entry Deadline: Mid-April
Entry Fee: $50-$100
Genres: Animation, Documentary, Features, Independent, International, Markets, Narrative, Shorts
Screening Format: Depends on venue you select
Awards: No
Profile: Each September, the Philadelphia Fringe takes over with a festival of new art. Since beginning in 1997, the Fringe has tripled in size and seen tremendous attention, support, and community involvement. In 2002, our sixteen-day festival drew over 42,000 people, with over 1,300 artists and company members performing for more than 700 performances. The festival presents a full spectrum of colorful work that falls within, between and sometimes beyond the standard categories of theater, dance, performance art, music, poetry, puppetry, and visual arts. National and international performers come to present new visions and thought-provoking work.
Special Events: Performances, parties, exhibitions
Filmmaker Perks: All artists who wish to participate will be listed in the guide. You may choose to have either a description or a description with a photo. You must choose one. This is as much for the audiences as it is for the artists.
Travel Tips: Run up the Philadelphia Art Museum steps, you know you want to.

Deborah Block.....................................Program Director
Barry Becker ....Fringe Coordinator

PHILADELPHIA INTERNATIONAL GAY AND LESBIAN FILM FESTIVAL

Philadelphia Film Society
234 Market St., 4th Floor
Philadelphia, PA 19106
Tel ....215-733-0608 ext. 249
Fax..215-733-0668
Email ....apreis@phillyfests.com
Web Site ....www.phillyfests.com

Year Festival Began: 1995
Festival Month: Early July
Entry Deadline: Late April
Entry Fee: None
Genres: Animation, Documentary, Features, Gay Lesbian, Independent, International, Shorts
Screening Format: 16mm - 35mm - BetaSP

Number of Films Screened: 200
X Factor: If you're a LGBT filmmaker or a filmmaker with a LGBT-themed film, this is the biggest event on the East Coast.
Awards: Jury Awards; Audience Awards
Profile: The Philadelphia International Gay & Lesbian Film Festival continues its reign as the premier presenter of GLBT film and video on the East Coast. The festival is presented by the Philadelphia Film Society and offers a full program of full-length and short films and video, documentaries and animation celebrating the imagination and determination of the world's gay, lesbian, bisexual, and transgendered communities.
Special Events: Parties, outdoor screenings, awards, workshops
Filmmaker Perks: Travel and accomodations covered for select filmmakers.
Travel Tips: Humidity is insane in Philly during the Summer months. Drink lots of water, stay cool.

Andrew R. Preis ....Festival Contact

PHOENIX FILM FESTIVAL

2345 E. Thomas Rd., Suite 100
Phoenix, AZ 85016
Tel 602-955-6444
Email ....greg@phxfilm.com
Web Site.........................www.phoenixfilmfestival.com

Year Festival Began: 2000
Festival Month: Early April
Entry Deadline: Late December
Entry Fee: Features: $25
Medium-Length: $20
Shorts: $15
Student Shorts: $5
Genres: Animation, Documentary, Features, First-Time Independent Filmmakers, Independent, International, Narrative, Shorts, Student
Screening Format: 16mm - 35mm - BetaSP - VHS
Awards: Copper Wing Awards
Profile: The Phoenix Film Festival is an international event held annually in the Spring to celebrate independent film and filmmaking. The festival celebrates the independent filmmaker by being the only festival in the world to showcase feature films made for less than $1 million and short films made for less than $50,000. It is also a gathering of film aficionados (both film lovers and creators of cinema) who come together from all over the world and from all walks of life to see and discuss and celebrate the art of independent film.
Special Events: Seminars, parties, tributes, golf tournament, awards
Filmmaker Perks: They have a golf tournament and parties nightly.

Travel Tips: Bring your golf clubs.

Chris LaMont......................................Executive Director
Greg Hall..Program Director

PORTLAND INTERNATIONAL FILM FESTIVAL

The Northwest Film Center
1219 SW Park Ave.
Portland, OR 97205
Tel...503-276-4264
Fax 503-294-0874
Email ....info@nwfilm.org
Web Site ....www.nwfilm.org

Year Festival Began: 1977

Festival Month: Mid-February

Entry Deadline: Late November

Entry Fee: $25

Genres: American, Documentary, Experimental, Features, First-Time Independent Filmmakers, Independent, International, Narrative, Shorts, Video

Screening Format: 8mm - Super 8mm - 16mm - 35mm - BetaSP - VHS - DVD - MiniDV - CDRom

Number of Films Screened: 100

X Factor: One of the premier international film events in the Northwest.

Awards: Audience Awards

Profile: Oregon's major film event, the Portland International Film Festival, is a rich snapshot of world cinema. The annual festival features nearly 100 films from over 30 countries in just over two weeks. This non-competitive festival focuses primarily on work from outside the United States but American features, documentaries, and shorts are included.

Special Events: Special screenings, parties

Travel Tips: American Airlines and Alaska Airlines are the two official airlines serving the Portland International Film Festival.

Bill Foster...Festival Director

RED BANK INTERNATIONAL FILM FESTIVAL

Freedom Film Society, Inc.
PO Box 447
Red Bank, NJ 07701
Tel 732-741-8089
Fax 732-741-8093
Email..contact@rbiff.org
Web Site ....www.rbiff.org

Festival Month: Early October

Entry Deadline: Early June

Entry Fee: Features: $45; Shorts: $25

Genres: Animation, Documentary, Experimental, Features, Independent, International, Narrative, Shorts

Profile: It is our belief that the general public is enriched through alternative forms of media and entertainment. For this reason, we at the RBIFF believe we are obligated to present the public with such alternative forms of media and entertainment and to grant artists the opportunity to showcase such work through the organization's screenings.

Special Events: Parties

Travel Tips: Watch the parking. The meter readers are vaguely tyrannical.

Matt Blackhall ....President

REEL AFFIRMATIONS FILM FESTIVAL

One In Ten
PO Box 73528
Washington, DC 20056
Tel 202-986-1119
Fax 202-939-0981
Email ....info@reelaffirmations.org
Web Site ....www.reelaffirmations.org

Festival Month: Mid-October

Entry Deadline: Late June

Entry Fee: $20

Genres: Animation, Documentary, Features, Gay Lesbian, Independent, Narrative, Shorts

Screening Format: 16mm - 35mm - BetaSP - VHS

Awards: Audience Awards

Profile: Reel Affirmations is the third most attended gay and lesbian film festival in the country and continues to build a reputation for a quality event and the ability to bring new and ground-breaking films to the Washington, DC area.

Special Events: Parties, awards

Filmmaker Perks: Screening fees for every film shown in the festival.

Travel Tips: If you're on the East Coast, you mights as well drive it. Interstate 95 in either direction.

Sarah Kellogg ....Festival Director

RENDEZVOUS WITH MADNESS FILM FESTIVAL

Workman Theatre Project
1001 Queen St. W
Toronto M6J 1H4 Canada
Tel 416-583-4339
Fax 416-583-4354
Email ....info@rendezvouswithmadness.com
Web Site ....www.rendezvouswithmadness.com

Festival Month: Early November

Entry Deadline: Late July

Genres: Documentary, Features, Independent, International, Mental Illness, Narrative, Shorts, Television

Screening Format: 35mm - BetaSP - VHS

Awards: No

Profile: Rendezvous with Madness Film Festival is an annual film festival that presents features and shorts touching upon the facts and mythology surrounding mental health and addiction. Each program focuses on a different theme. Post-screening panel discussions involve filmmakers, artists and people with professional and personal experience with mental illness and addiction.

Special Events: Panels, parties

Filmmaker Perks: A very supportive environment for films and filmmakers of the theme.

Travel Tips: The average temperature in Toronto in November is the 40s, so bundle up.

Lisa Brown ....Festival Director
Mike Twamley ....Festival Contact

RESFEST DIGITAL FILM FESTIVAL

601 West 26th St., Suite 1150
New York, NY 10001
Tel 212-320-3750
Email ....resfest2004@resfest.com
Web Site...www.resfest.com

Year Festival Began: 1997

Festival Month: September

Entry Deadline: Mid-May

Number of Submissions: 1,000+

Entry Fee: $20-$25

Genres: Animation, Digital, Digital Animation, Documentary, DVD, Experimental, Features, Independent, Music Videos, Performance, Shorts, Super 8/8mm, Touring

Screening Format: BetaSP - DigiBeta - MiniDV

Number of Films Screened: 75

Odds: 1 in 13

X Factor: More than just a touring fest, ResFest has a magazine behind it as well, so your work will get seen and publicized.

Awards: Audience Choice Awards

Profile: ResFest is a global touring festival exploring the dynamic interplay of film, art, music, and design. Each year the festival showcases the year's best shorts, features, music videos and animation in an environment that combines screenings, live music events, parties, panel discussions, and technology demonstrations.

Special Events: Seminars, studio tours, parties, concerts

Filmmaker Perks: Producers, creative directors, and production companies attend the festival, scouting for the next generation of creators, and ResFest makes every effort to promote the festival and its filmmakers to the press, through numerous releases, notes in the program guide, and profiles in our newsletter, ResAlert.

Travel Tips: Touring festival, so you could be going anywhere in the world...which is pretty exciting.

Jonathan Wells......................................Festival Director

RHODE iSLAND iNTERNATiONAL FiLM FESTiVAL

PO Box 162
Newport, RI 02840
Tel 401-861-4445
Fax 401-847-7590
Email...info@film-festival.org
Web Site......................................www.film-festival.org

Year Festival Began: 1997
Festival Month: Mid-August
Entry Deadline: Early June
Entry Fee: $40-$50
Genres: American, Animation, Digital, Digital Animation, Documentary, DVD, Ethnic African, Ethnic Asian, Ethnic Black, Ethnic Jewish, Ethnic Latin, Ethnic Spanish, Experimental, Fantasy/Science Fiction, Features, First-Time Independent Filmmakers, Gay Lesbian, Independent, International, Markets, Multimedia, Narrative, Online Festival, Shorts, Student, Underground, Video, Weird, Women
Screening Format: 16mm - 35mm - BetaSP - VHS - DVD - DV
Number of Films Screened: 186
X Factor: We offer a relaxed environment perfect for chilling with other like-minded filmmakers.
Awards: Kodak Vision Award Best Feature
Jury Awards
Viola M. Marshall Audience Choice Awards
Other Awards
Profile: The Rhode Island International Film Festival celebrates the independent spirit in film and has become a haven for independent filmmakers from throughout the world. RIIFF is dedicated to the creation of opportunities for artistic interaction and exchange among independent filmmakers, directors, producers, distributors, backers, and the film-going community. Of special note is that the Academy of Motion Picture Arts and Sciences has elected to recognize the Rhode Island International Film Festival as a qualifying festival for the Short Films category for the Annual Academy Awards.
Special Events: Screenplay competition, awards, panels, parties

Filmmaker Perks: The festival provides each attending filmmaker with an hospitality package which will include maps, passes, special offers at restaurants, entertainment complexes and local attractions.
Travel Tips: Bring your summer clothes, and prepare for cool nights.

Michael Drywa ....Festival President
Michel Coutu ....Chairman/President

RiVERRUN iNTERNATiONAL FiLM FESTiVAL

305 West Fourth St., Ste. 1-B
Winston-Salem, NC 27101
Tel 336-724-1502
Fax...336-724-1112
Email.....................................festival@riverrunfilm.com
Web Site.......................................www.riverrunfilm.com

Festival Month: Late April
Entry Deadline: Late January
Entry Fee: $25
Students with Valid ID: $15
NC Students: Free
Genres: Animation, Documentary, Experimental, Features, International, Narrative, Shorts, Student
Screening Format: 16mm - 35mm - BetaSP - VHS
Awards: Audience Award; Jury Awards;
Other Awards
Profile: The RiverRun International Film Festival places emphasis in presenting a wide variety of feature length fictional and documentary films, along with live-action, documentary, animated, experimental, and student short films.
Special Events: Awards, parties, special screenings, panels, workshops
Filmmaker Perks: All filmmakers with a film in competition will receive one "Filmmaker Pass" and one "VIP Pass" giving free access to all events and screenings (subject to availability) at the festival.
Travel Tips: Piedmont Triad International Airport is rapidly growing up from regional airport status, but it's still primarily Delta and America Airlines.

Butter Birkas...Festival Director

ROCHESTER iNTERNATiONAL FiLM FESTiVAL

Movies on a Shoestring
PO Box 17746
Rochester, NY 14617
Tel 716-288-5607
Email ....president@rochesterfilmfest.org
Web Site ....www.rochesterfilmfest.org

Year Festival Began: 1959
Festival Month: Early May
Entry Deadline: Mid-February
Entry Fee: $40

Genres: Animation, Documentary, Experimental, Independent, International, Narrative, Shorts, Student, Touring

Screening Format: 16mm - 35mm - BetaSP - VHS

Awards: No

Profile: The Rochester International Film Festival, the oldest continuously-held short film festival in the world, has been presented each year since 1959 by Movies on a Shoestring, Inc. Each festival includes a wide variety of original and imaginative works by film students, advanced amateurs, and professional filmmakers from all over the world.

Special Events: Best of Fest screenings, parties

Filmmaker Perks: If your entry is selected for showing at the festival, we might also contact you about including it in our permanent traveling collection, The Best of the Fest, which includes the most popular films from previous festivals, based on audience surveys taken at each show.

Travel Tips: If you're out and about late at night, Rochester's transit buses have a Night Deposit Program that authorizes bus operators to meet your safe-stop request after 9:00 PM. The bus driver determines the safest location nearest to your requested stop.

ROME INTERNATIONAL FILM FESTIVAL

c/o Rome Area Council for the Arts
217 East First St.
PO Box 203
Rome, GA 30162
Email..barry@diff.tv
Web Site ....www.riff.tv

Festival Month: Early September

Entry Deadline: Mid-May

Entry Fee: Under 10 minutes: $10
10 to 20 minutes: $20
21 to 45 minutes: $30
Over 45 minutes: $50

Genres: Animation, Documentary, Experimental, Features, Independent, International, Narrative, Shorts

Screening Format: 16mm - 35mm - BetaSP - DigiBeta - DVD - DV - DVCam - MiniDV

Awards: Yes

Profile: The maker of the so-called "calling card" film, with slick production values and a laundry list of high-end this or big name person doing that, but the final product looks like bad late night TV or attempts to pass itself off like a "real" movie, that follows paint-by-numbers Hollywood directions...is a true dullard and not RIFF at all (now *there's* a run-on sentence). Or are you sick of pretentious plots that are so skewed from reality that the maker insists that "Hollywood would never make *this* film, - 'Bill, a narcoleptic ice cream vendor, is accidentally mistaken for an Iraqi hit man when he wears a cer-

tain sweater while attending the circus.'" These films just make us cringe, and there's a reason that even Hollywood wouldn't touch 'em. If these things make you want to pass gas in public, then welcome to The RIFF. The RIFF doesn't see short film as the thing we make when we don't have enough funding for a feature, or as a way of killing time until we "hit it big," or at least gain entrance into a Park City Mall festival. The RIFF shows the work people want to make, not what they think "people with clout" want to see. The work we show is diverse, smart, funny - and how's this for a concept - entertaining! And we love to see the stuff people can create when they're not trying specifically to impress you.

Special Events: Parties, panels, awards

Filmmaker Perks: Festival organizers are passionate about film, and are there to help you.

Travel Tips: The mega-popular band REM is from Rome, Georgia.

Barry Norman.....................Founder/Executive Director
Jake Jacobson ....Festival Director/Programmer

SACRAMENTO INTERNATIONAL GAY AND LESBIAN FILM FESTIVAL

1008 10th St.
PO Box 379
Sacramento, CA 95814
Tel 916-319-2348
Email ....film_submissions@siglff.org
Web Site ....www.siglff.org

Year Festival Began: 1992

Festival Month: Early October

Entry Deadline: Ongoing

Genres: Animation, Documentary, Features, Gay Lesbian, Independent, International, Narrative, Shorts, Video

Screening Format: 16mm - 35mm - BetaSP - VHS

Awards: Jury Awards

Profile: The Sacramento International Gay and Lesbian Film Festival in Sacramento started in 1992, based on the student run gay and lesbian film festival at Fresno State. Organizers joined forces with the students from the California State University, Sacramento Gay and Lesbian Alliance and the brothers of the Delta Lambda Phi Fraternity and received grant funds from CSUS Associated Students Inc. to use as seed money and get the festival started.

Special Events: Awards, parties

Filmmaker Perks: The festival provides travel and accomodations for select filmmakers.

Travel Tips: You need to rent a car, otherwise you'll be walking for a long time.

Jay Kirkman ....Festival Director

SAN ANTONiO UNDERGROUND FiLM FESTiVAL

8065 Callaghan Rd #611 PMB
San Antonio, TX 78230
Tel 210-977-9004
Email ....info@safilm.com
Web Site ....www.safilm.com

Year Festival Began: 1993
Festival Month: Late June
Entry Deadline: Late April
Entry Fee: $25
Genres: Animation, Digital, Documentary, Experimental, Features, Independent, Narrative, Shorts, Underground
Screening Format: BetaSP - DVD - MiniDV
X Factor: Win the Grand Prize, get a low-rider bicycle.
Awards: Yes
Profile: The San Antonio Underground Film Festival started out in 1993 with videos that ran the gamut of styles, themes, filming techniques, and aesthetics. Though all films will be digitally projected, some have been shot directly on video and others transferred from film, unified by the DIY punk ethic of filmmaking.
Special Events: Parties, awards
Filmmaker Perks: You get a free festival t-shirt.
Travel Tips: There are plenty of motels and hotels in San Antonio, so pick your poison.

Dago Patlan ....Festival Director

SAN DiEGO FiLM FESTiVAL

7974 Mission Bonita Dr.
San Diego, CA 92120
Tel 619-582-2368
Fax 619-286-8324
Email ....info@sdff.org
Web Site ....www.sdff.org

Festival Month: Late September-October
Entry Deadline: Early July
Entry Fee: Features: $45
Shorts: $35
Genres: Animation, Documentary, Features, Independent, International, Narrative, Shorts

Screening Format: 35mm - BetaSP - DVD
Awards: Jury Awards; Audience Choice; Other Awards
Profile: The goal of the San Diego Film Festival is to bring about a greater knowledge and appreciation of cinema through creative programming which educates, enlightens and entertains.
Special Events: Awards, panels, parties, screenplay competition
Comments: San Diego is already one of America's most breathtaking cities and this spectacular weekend of indie film is like a vacation getaway come true. Screenings take place at the local stadium seating multi-plex and even an art gallery. The event has quickly become the premier festival in San Diego by focusing on delivering quality movies, informative panel series for filmmakers and a load of star-studded parties. In addition, San Diego's Gaslamp District is filled with bars, restaurants, and the best nightlife on the west coast.
Filmmaker Perks: The festival assists with travel and accomodations when possible.
Travel Tips: Bring sunglasses and sunscreen, get a tan.

Robin Laatz-Kozak ....Co-Founder/Executive Director
Karl Kozak ....Co-Founder/Programming Director

SAN FRANCiSCO iNDEPENDENT FiLM FESTiVAL

530 Divisadero St. 183
San Francisco, CA 94117
Tel 415-820-3907
Email ....info@sfindie.com
Web Site ....www.sfindie.com

Festival Month: Early February
Entry Deadline: Early November
Entry Fee: Contact Festival for Details
Genres: Animation, Documentary, Experimental, Features, First-Time Independent Filmmakers, Independent, International, Narrative, Shorts
Screening Format: 35mm - BetaSP
Awards: No

BEST KEPT SECRET FESTIVALS

Ann Arbor Film Festival
Ohio Independent Film Festival
Peachtree International Film Festival
Portland International Film Festival
Rhode Island International Film Festival
San Diego Film Festival
San Francisco Independent Film Festival
  (aka SF IndieFest)
Sedona International Film Festival and Workshop
Temecula Valley International Film Festival

Profile: IndieFest screens entertaining passionate work that provokes a response. Your reaction might be positive, or it might be negative - but you will have a reaction. We solemnly swear not to subject you to an endless series of bleak, torpid fare with doomed characters silently suffering in static frames - other festivals can play those.

Special Events: Parties, Best of Fest screenings, retrospectives, panels, special screenings

Filmmaker Perks: After-party every night, eclectic special screenings

Travel Tips: If you dig cheesesteaks, check out the Philly Cheesesteak Shop on Divisadero.

Jeff Ross...Founder/Director
Bruce Fletcher........................Director of Programming

SAN FRANCISCO INTERNATIONAL ASIAN AMERICAN FILM FESTIVAL

145 Ninth St., Suite 350
San Francisco, CA 94103
Tel 415-863-0814
Fax..415-863-7428
Email ....festival@naatanet.org
Web Site ....www.naatanet.org/festival

Year Festival Began: 1982
Festival Month: Early March
Entry Deadline: Early October
Entry Fee: $25-$35
Genres: Documentary, Ethnic Asian, Ethnic Other, Experimental, Features, First-Time Independent Filmmakers, Gay Lesbian, Independent, International, Narrative, Shorts, Touring
Screening Format: 16mm - 35mm - BetaSP
Awards: No

BEST SHORT FILM FESTIVALS IN THE U.S.

Most of these festivals are recognized by the Academy — short film winners are eligible for Oscar® consideration.

Aspen Shortsfest
Austin Film Festival
Florida Film Festival
Nashville Independent Film Festival
Palm Springs International Short Film Festival
Rhode Island International Film Festival
San Francisco International Film Festival
Santa Barbara International Film Festival
Slamdance International Film Festival
St. Louis International Film Festival
SXSW Film Festival
USA Film Festival

Profile: Presented by the National Asian American Telecommunications Association (NAATA), the San Francisco International Asian American Film Festival (SFIAAFF) is the largest annual exhibition event in North America dedicated to showcasing the best in Asian American and Asian cinema.

Special Events: Panels, parties, concerts, workshops

Filmmaker Perks: The festival tours San Francisco, Berkeley, and San Jose.

Chi-hui Yang ....Festival Director
Taro Goto..Assistant Director

SAN FRANCISCO INTERNATIONAL FILM FESTIVAL

San Francisco Film Society
39 Mesa St., Ste 110, The Presidio
San Francisco, CA 94129
Tel 415-929-5000; 415-931-3456
Fax...415-561-5099
Email ....sffs@sffs.org
Web Site ....www.sffs.org

Year Festival Began: 1957
Festival Month: Mid-April
Entry Deadline: Mid-November
Number of Submissions: 2,000+
Entry Fee: $20-$200
Genres: American, Animation, Documentary, Experimental, Features, First-Time Independent Filmmakers, Independent, International, Narrative, Shorts, Student, Video
Screening Format: 16mm - 35mm - BetaSP - DVD - MiniDV
Number of Films Screened: 175
Odds: 1 in 12
X Factor: $10,000 and $5,000, respectively, SKYY Prize for First Feature and Golden Gate Award Grand Prizes could really help a filmmaker out.
Awards: Film Society Directing Award; Golden Gate Awards; SKYY Prize; Other Awards
Profile: The San Francisco International Film Festival is presented by the San Francisco Film Society, a nonprofit arts and educational organization dedicated to celebrating international film and the moving image. The festival highlights current trends in international film and video production with an emphasis on work that has not yet secured US distribution.
Special Events: Tributes, seminars, parties, and Golden Gate Awards
Comments: Cultural diversity is the order of the day in the city by the bay. Brace yourself for adoring audiences and loads of attention.
Filmmaker Perks: Receptive audiences and massive opportunities for networking.

Travel Tips: It can get chilly and windy, so bring a nice jacket.

Roxanne Messina Captor ....Executive Director

SAN FRANCiSCO iNTERNATiONAL LESBiAN AND GAY FiLM FESTiVAL

c/o Frameline
346 9th St.
San Francisco, CA 94103
Tel 415-703-8650
Fax...415-861-1404
Email ....info@frameline.org
Web Site ....www.frameline.org/festival

Festival Month: Mid-June

Entry Deadline: Early February

Entry Fee: Contact Festival for Details

Genres: Animation, Documentary, Features, First-Time Independent Filmmakers, Gay Lesbian, Independent, International, Narrative, Shorts

Screening Format: 35mm - BetaSP

Awards: Audience Awards; Jury Awards; Frameline Award

Profile: The San Francisco International Lesbian & Gay Film Festival is the world's oldest and largest celebration of LGBT cinema. The festival delights over 80,000 attendees with nearly 80 features, including many world and US premieres, and over 150 shorts.

Special Events: Awards, parties, panels

Filmmaker Perks: The cash prizes for debut features are the highest on the LGBT festival circuit.

Travel Tips: The festival ends on Pride Day, so be prepared for a closing night party to end all parties.

SANTA BARBARA iNTERNATiONAL FiLM FESTIVAL (SBiFF)

2064 Alameda Padre Serra, Ste 120
Santa Barbara, CA 93103
Tel...805-963-0023
Fax 805-962-2524
Email ....info@sbfilmfestival.org
Web Site ....www.sbfilmfestival.org

Year Festival Began: 1986

Festival Month: Late January-February

Entry Deadline: Late November

Entry Fee: $40-$60

Genres: Animation, Digital, Documentary, Features, Independent, International, Narrative, Shorts

Screening Format: 16mm - 35mm - BetaSP - DigiBeta - DV

Number of Films Screened: 150

X Factor: Warm weather, receptive audiences, what more do you want?

Awards: Award winners receiving a first place prize are automatically eligible for consideration by the Academy of Motion Picture Arts and Sciences for an Academy Award nomination.

Jury Awards; Audience Awards; Other Awards

Profile: The Santa Barbara International Film Festival (SBIFF) is a nonprofit organization dedicated to enriching local culture and raising consciousness of film as an art form. It presents American Independent, Foreign, and Documentary cinema in the beautiful setting of downtown Santa Barbara, a premier tourist destination. SBIFF is also committed to education through its Master Class Program, Field Trip to the Movies, Kids' Fest, and educational seminars.

Special Events: Awards, parties, special screenings, panels, seminars

Filmmaker Perks: Travel and accomodations are taken care of by the festival and you get a platinum festival pass.

Travel Tips: Prepare to chill.

Roger Durling...Artistic Director
Candace Schermerhorn ....Program Director
Amanda Lee ....Festival Contact

SANTA MONiCA FiLM FESTiVAL

3000 W Olympic Blvd.
Santa Monica, CA 90404
Tel 310-264-4274
Fax 310-264-4273
Email ....info@smff.com
Web Site ....www.smff.com

Year Festival Began: 1997

Festival Month: Summer

Entry Deadline: Contact Festival for Details

Genres: Charity, Digital Animation, Documentary, Ethnic Latin, Ethnic Spanish, Experimental, Features, Independent, International, Multimedia, Narrative, Online Festival, Shorts, Touring

Screening Format: 16mm - 35mm - BetaSP

Awards: Jury Awards; Audience Awards

Profile: Over the past few years, the Deep Ellum Film Festival has worked to become a world-class event, screening the most innovative works of today's emerging filmmakers. Then they expanded the horizons of the festival to take over the reigns of the Santa Monica Film Festival and worked to create a celebration of film, music and art as DEFMAN (Deep Ellum Film, Music, Art and Noise) headed to the beach. SM/F2 maintains DEFMAN's mission by promoting the arts while raising funds to help support families affected by cancer.

Special Events: Awards, parties, panels

Filmmaker Perks: Deep Ellum has taken over the reins of the Santa Monica Film Festival, marrying two very fun, and important events. Getting into one could easily equal a two-fer.

Travel Tips: Santa Monica is a great place to hang-out, but not necessarily to park. Find a nice garage that won't take you for all you're worth.

Albert de Quay ....Executive Director

SARASOTA FILM FESTIVAL

635 S. Orange Ave., Suite 10B
Sarasota, FL 34236
Tel 941-364-9514
Fax...941-364-8411
Email..............................info@sarasotafilmfestival.com
Web Site ....www.sarasotafilmfestival.com

Year Festival Began: 1999
Festival Month: Late January-February
Entry Deadline: Early November
Entry Fee: $15-$40
Genres: Animation, Documentary, Features, Independent, International, Narrative, Shorts
Screening Format: 35mm - BetaSP - DigiBeta
Number of Films Screened: 175
X Factor: Appreciative audience, a festival by the beach.
Awards: Audience Award
Emerging Filmmaker Award
Programmer's Choice Award
Best of the Fest Films
Profile: The Sarasota Film Festival (SFF) is a non-profit arts organization with year-round activities, culminating in an annual celebration of film each January. Hosted by Regal Cinemas Hollywood 20 in beautiful downtown Sarasota, SFF offers programming and events for film enthusiasts of all economic, cultural and educational backgrounds. With the support of a passionate arts community, the Sarasota Film Festival attracts the best filmmakers, today's hottest stars, distinguished industry guests, and thousands of film enthusiasts from around the world.
Special Events: Panels, Filmmaker Breakfasts, awards, parties
Travel Tips: Fly into Sarasota-Bradenton Airport on either American, Continental, Delta, Northwest, TWA, United, or US Airways

Jody Kielbasa ....Executive Director
Jennifer Silva ....Festival Manager

SAVANNAH FILM AND VIDEO FESTIVAL

c/o Savannah College of Art and Design
PO Box 3146
Savannah, GA 31402-3146
Tel 912-525-5051
Fax 912-525-5052
Email..............................filmfest@scad.edu
Web Site ....www.scad.edu/filmfest

Year Festival Began: 1998
Festival Month: Late October

Entry Deadline: Early July
Entry Fee: $40; Students: $20
Genres: American, Animation, Documentary, Features, First-Time Independent Filmmakers, Independent, International, Narrative, Shorts, Student
Screening Format: BetaSP - VHS - DVD - DVCam
Awards: Lifetime Achievement Award
Profile: Since its inception in 1998, the Savannah Film Festival has focused on enriching and educating an expanding audience, while promoting quality independent films and filmmakers. The festival features more than 50 films, selected from more than 600 entries in the categories of feature, short, animation, documentary, and student competition, which are submitted from all over the world. The featured screenings represent a variety of independent filmmakers, while a cross section of workshops, lectures, receptions, and special events gives the festival participants an opportunity to meet colleagues active in all of areas of film production.
Special Events: Workshops, panels, awards
Filmmaker Perks: Emphasis on student filmmakers.
Travel Tips: Southern hospitality is in full-swing in Savannah, so nice manners are appreciated.

Len Cripe ....Managing Director

SCOTTSDALE INTERNATIONAL FILM FESTIVAL

619 E. Vista Ave.
Phoenix, AZ 85020
Tel..602-410-1074
Email ....scottsdaleiff@aol.com
Web Site ....www.scottsdalefilmfestival.com

Festival Month: Late October-November
Entry Deadline: Early September
Entry Fee: None
Genres: Animation, Documentary, European, Features, First-Time Independent Filmmakers, Independent, International, Narrative
Screening Format: 35mm
Awards: No
Profile: The annual Scottsdale International Film Festival (SIFF) takes place in late October through early November each year. The festival partners with the Toronto International Film Festival while also showcasing winners from such film festivals as Cannes, Sundance, and Venice.
Special Events: Special screenings, parties
Filmmaker Perks: Festival takes care of travel and accomodations for invited filmmakers.
Travel Tips: After a summer where the heat is almost unbearable (though dry), Scottsdale finally becomes comfortable in November. Bring a light jacket to wear at night.

Amy Ettinger ....Festival Director

SCREAMFEST HORROR FiLM FESTiVAL

8840 Wilshire Blvd.
Beverly Hills, CA 90211
Tel 310-358-3273; 323-656-4727
Fax..310-358-3272
Email ....screamfestla@aol.com
Web Site ....www.screamfestla.com

Festival Month: Late October
Entry Deadline: Mid-August
Entry Fee: Under 10 Minutes: $25-$35
10-40 Minutes: $30-$40
Over 40 Minutes: $40-$50
Genres: Animation, Documentary, Experimental, Fantasy/Science Fiction, Horror, Independent, Narrative, Shorts
Screening Format: 16mm - 35mm - BetaSP - DigiBeta
Awards: KOLOBOS; Jury Awards
Profile: Screamfest was formed in August 2001 by film producers Rachel Belofsky and Ross Martin in order to give filmmakers and writers in the horror/scf-fi genres a venue to have their work showcased to people in the industry.
Special Events: Screenplay competition, awards, parties
Travel Tips: The weather gets colder at night, so bring a jacket.

Rachel Belofsky...Co-Founder

SEATTLE LESBiAN & GAY FiLM FESTiVAL

c/o Three Dollar Bill Cinema
1122 E. Pike St., #1313
Seattle, WA 98122-3934
Tel 206-323-4274
Fax 206-323-4275
Email ....info@seattlequeerfilm.com
Web Site ....www.seattlequeerfilm.com

Year Festival Began: 1996
Festival Month: Mid-October
Entry Deadline: Early July
Entry Fee: $10-$15
Genres: Animation, Documentary, Experimental, Features, Gay Lesbian, Independent, International, Narrative, Shorts
Screening Format: 16mm - 35mm - BetaSP - VHS
Awards: Three Dollar Bill Cinema Awards
Audience Choice Awards
Profile: The Seattle Lesbian & Gay Film Festival is a week-long international film festival celebrating the best LGBT films from around the world.
Special Events: Parties, awards
Filmmaker Perks: The festival assists with travel and accomodations when possible.

Travel Tips: Lots of one-way streets in Seattle; plan your route before you get in the car.

Justine Barda ....Executive Director
Jason Plourde..............................Programming Director

SEATTLE UNDERGROUND FiLM FESTiVAL (THE)

The Little Theatre
608 19th Ave. E
Seattle WA 98112
Tel..206-675-2055

Year Festival Began: 1999
Festival Month: Early October
Entry Deadline: Early May
Genres: American, Digital, Documentary, Ethnic Black, Experimental, Features, First-Time Independent Filmmakers, Gay Lesbian, Independent, International, Narrative, Shorts, Super 8/8mm, Underground, Video, Weird
Screening Format: 16mm - 35mm - BetaSP
Awards: No
Profile: The Seattle Underground Film Festival (SUFF) is dedicated to bringing you the very best in avant garde, experimental, and offbeat short and feature films from around the world. The festival generally piggie-backs the Seattle International Film Festival, but is the more clandestine of the two.
Travel Tips: The Little Theater is not a clever name, it's actually a very small venue. But what it lacks in size it makes up for in programming.

Jon Behrens...Co-Founder
Steve Creson ....Co-Founder

SEDONA iNTERNATiONAL FiLM FESTiVAL AND WORKSHOP

PO Box 162
Sedona, AZ 86339
Tel 928-282-1177
Fax 928-282-1789
Email ....info@sedonafilmfestival.com
Web Site ....www.sedonafilmfestival.com

Year Festival Began: 1994
Festival Month: Early March
Entry Deadline: Late January
Number of Submissions: 500
Entry Fee: Features: $50
Shorts: $35
Genres: American, Animation, Documentary, Ethnic African, Ethnic Asian, Ethnic Black, Ethnic Jewish, Ethnic Latin, Ethnic Other, Ethnic Spanish, Features, First-Time Independent Filmmakers, Gay Lesbian, Independent, International, Narrative, Shorts, Women
Screening Format: 35mm - BetaSP - DVD - DV
Number of Films Screened: 50-60

Odds: 1 in 10

X Factor: It's held in "the most beautiful place in America".

Awards: Audience Choice Awards

Director's Choice Awards

Profile: The annual Sedona International Film Festival and Workshop is staking its claim as a signature showcase for independent filmmakers in the Southwest. Sedona is a growing southwestern US arts and culture community 90 miles north of Phoenix, Arizona, located in the place *USA Today* voted as "the most beautiful place in America."

Special Events: Southwest Classics and Emerging Filmmakers Series, children's hands-on filmmaking workshops, panels, parties

Filmmaker Perks: Passes to the festival and gala events, hotel accomodations for select filmmakers.

Travel Tips: The temp can drop below freezing and just as easily be up around the 70s, so bring a jacket you may or may not need.

Mindy Mendelsohn ....Festival Contact

SHORT SHORTS FILM FESTIVAL

1007 Montana Ave., Suite 534
Santa Monica, CA 90403
Tel 310-656-9767
Fax 310-451-4845
Email...info@shortshortsla.org
Web Site...www.shortshortsla.org

Year Festival Began: 1999

Festival Month: Summer Tour

Entry Deadline: Early November

Number of Submissions: 1,500

Entry Fee: None

Genres: Animation, Documentary, Experimental, Independent, International, Narrative, Shorts, Touring (Japan, Singapore, Los Angeles, San Diego, and Tijuana)

Screening Format: BetaSP - DigiBeta

Number of Films Screened: 50

Odds: 1 in 30

X Factor: Your film tours the world in an extremely selective program.

Awards: The Short Shorts Award

The Jury Award

The Audience Award

The Short Shorts in Los Angeles FujiFilm Award

Profile: The mission of the Short Shorts Film Festival is to celebrate short films as a fertile arena

for new cinematic talent and to raise public awareness of the format as powerful entertainment in and of itself, not merely an appetizer before the feature.

Special Events: Awards, panels

Filmmaker Perks: The festival truly cares about the short filmmaker, sponsoring travel for a select number of filmmakers to attend the Tokyo tour dates.

Travel Tips: Get a travel agent.

Douglas Williams ....Festival Director

SIDEWALK MOVING PICTURE FILM FESTIVAL

500 23rd St. S
Birmingham, AL 35233
Tel 205-324-0888
Fax 205-324-2488
Email ....festival@sidewalkfest.com
Web Site ....www.sidewalkfest.com

Festival Month: Late September

Entry Deadline: Mid-June

Entry Fee: Under 30 Minutes: $25-$30

Over 30 Minutes: $40-$55

Genres: Animation, Children, Documentary, Experimental, Family, Features, Independent, International, Music Videos, Narrative, Shorts, Student

Screening Format: 35mm - BetaSP - DigiBeta - HD - DVD

Awards: Jury Awards; Audience Awards; Homegrown Awards

Profile: The Sidewalk Moving Picture Film Festival was created to bring new films to a new audience. Since its debut in 1999, filmmakers from across the country and around the world have come to Birmingham to screen their work at Sidewalk and have been thrilled to discover fresh, enthusiastic crowds eager to devour new independent cinema. In 2002, Sidewalk attracted over 10,000 attendees during the festival weekend, some flying in from as far away as Denmark and the United Kingdom to attend the festivities.

Special Events: Awards, parties, panels, tributes

Comments: Birmingham, Alabama is probably not the first place that springs to mind when you think independent film, but once you attend this festival, you will change your mind. Festival Executive Director Alan Hunter (yes, he was one of MTV's original five VJs) has built a film production and recording studio in his old hometown of Birmingham and the facility hosts just some of the events during the festival. Films are screened at a variety of venues, the most impressive being the historic Alabama Theatre which seats 2,500. Rave parties are held at the studio along with an impressive array of panels. Not to be missed. And prepare yourself for amazing BBQ along with the friendly people.

Filmmaker Perks: Sidewalk's partner hotels offering special rates for festival attendees.

Travel Tips: Be sure you don't miss WorkPlay – the WorkPlay bar is a great place for a martini.

Erik Jambor...Festival Director

SiLVER LAKE FiLM FESTiVAL

2658 Griffith Park Blvd., #389
Los Angeles, CA 90039
Tel...323-993-7225
Email................................info@silverlakefilmfestival.org
Web Site..........................www.silverlakefilmfestival.org
Year Festival Began: 1999
Festival Month: Late September
Entry Deadline: Mid-April
Entry Fee: Features: $40-$70
Shorts: $30-$60
Students with Valid ID: $20-$30

Genres: Animation, Digital, Documentary, Ethnic Black, Ethnic Chicano, Ethnic Jewish, Experimental, Features, First-Time Independent Filmmakers, Gay Lesbian, Independent, International, Markets, Narrative, Retro Classics, Retro Science, Retro Westerns, Shorts, Student, Underground, Video, Weird
Screening Format: 16mm - 35mm - BetaSP
Awards: No
Profile: A California nonprofit, public benefit corporation, the Silver Lake Film Festival was created to celebrate through cinema the cultural diversity and avant-garde creativity that historically has characterized Silver Lake in LA. The SLFF serves as a conduit for bringing together the film community in this local area with the rest of Hollywood and hopefully the rest of the world, both filmmakers and fans alike.
Special Events: Parties, panels
Comments: One of the hippest areas of Los Angeles is home to a festival which seeks the best in cutting edge indie work. Unafraid to program challenging movies, Silver Lake prides itself on programming the best in alternative film. Prepare to have your eyes opened.
Travel Tips: Silver Lake may be hip, but parking is horrendous.

Greg Ptacek ....Co-Director
David Andrusia ....Programming Director
Roger M. Mayer ....Co-Director

SiLVERDOCS: AFi/DiSCOVERY CHANNEL DOCUMENTARY FESTiVAL

AFI Silver Theatre and Cultural Center
8633 Colesville Rd.
Silver Spring, MD 20910
Tel 301-495-6720
Fax 301-495-6798
Email...info@silverdocs.com
Web Site...www.silverdocs.com

Festival Month: Mid-June

Entry Deadline: Early March

Entry Fee: Under 50 Minutes: $25-$30
Over 50 Minutes: $30-$40

Genres: Documentary, Features, Independent, International, Shorts

Screening Format: 16mm - 35mm - 70mm - BetaSP - DigiBeta - HD

Awards: Sterling Awards; Audience Awards

Profile: SilverDocs was created by AFI in alliance with the Discovery Channel to support, honor and showcase documentaries that exhibit a personal cinematic vision and celebrate the spirit of independent filmmaking. Headquartered at the AFI Silver Theatre and Cultural Center, a newly restored 1938 art deco theatre, SilverDocs is able to provide audiences with the rare and exceptional experience of viewing world-class documentaries in a state-of-the-art theatrical setting.

Special Events: Panels, parties, awards, special screenings

Filmmaker Perks: Beyond the films and post-screening discussion, SilverDocs provides filmmakers with opportunities to engage with programming executives and other industry professionals in a program designed to foster new business relationships. Plus, the best feature doc and best short doc Sterling Awards are worth $10,000 and $5,000, respectively.

Travel Tips: From New York City or Washington, DC, take I-95.

Patricia Finneran ....Festival Director

SLAMDANCE iNTERNATiONAL FiLM FESTiVAL

5634 Melrose Ave.
Los Angeles, CA 90038
Tel 323-466-1786
Fax 323-466-1784
Email...mail@slamdance.com
Web Site...www.slamdance.com

Year Festival Began: 1995

Festival Month: Mid-January

Entry Deadline: Mid-October

Number of Submissions: 3,000

Entry Fee: Features: $55
Shorts: $35

Genres: All, Animation, Digital, Documentary, Features, Independent, International, Narrative, Shorts

Screening Format: 16mm - 35mm - BetaSP - DigiBeta - DV - MiniDV

Number of Films Screened: 75

Odds: 1 in 40

X Factor: The first, and best, alternative to Sundance. You need to play Park City.

Awards: Sparky Awards; Audience Awards; Kodak Vision Award for Best Cinematography; Other Awards

Profile: Slamdance Film Festival serves as a showcase for emerging film talent. Slamdance's mission is to support and nurture innovative artists. By Filmmakers, for Filmmakers.

Slamdance's feature competition is devoted to first-time directors who have made films that do not have domestic distribution or big budgets. The festival welcomes films in any subject matter, length, technical format, finished or not. Each year several Slamdance films are picked-up for distribution and almost all films get invited to other festivals around the world.

Special Events: Fireside chats, awards, parties, Slamdance/Sundance sledding competition, screenplay competiton, Anarchy Online festival

Comments: If your film is not accepted into Sundance, there is only one viable alternative if you desire to screen during Park City Madness. While each year brings new fests to Park City, Utah, who seek some clever variation on the name "dance," there is only one alternative festival that has gained the respect of the industry. Slamdance remains the true rebel film festival living up to their slogan "by filmmakers for filmmakers." Besides the garage band-like atmosphere, what I admire most about Slamdance is their never-ending refusal to grow up and become a real festival. The filmmaker-friendly atmosphere is everywhere as festival founder and host of the event, the Mad-Hatter Dan Mirvish, keeps a low-key cool to the screenings. Slamdance screens about a dozen features by first-time directors in an environment devoid of industry snobbery or elitism. The spirit of DIY filmmaking is present in the halls, in the lines, and at the parties in an incredibly supportive environment that at times feels more like a college dorm room than a festival. Coinciding with Sundance, screenings take place in January at the Treasure Mountain Inn at the top of Main Street. (The timing is by design and attracts acquisitions executives willing to find their way to the top of Main Street to discover new talent.)

Slamdance has continued to stay ahead of the curve by discovering new talent. In fact, their new screenwriting competition resulted in no less than four Sundance films in 2004. Several Slamdance premiere films have graduated to theatrical distribution, making acceptance to the event an achievement in

3 DAYS
23 HRS OF PARTIES
69.5 HRS OF FILM

SIDEWALK MOVING PICTURE FESTIVAL
BIRMINGHAM, AL

ONE OF 20 FILM FESTIVALS
WORTH THE ENTRY FEE
IN MOVIEMAKER

ONE OF THE TOP 10
FILM FESTIVAL GETAWAYS
IN FILM FESTIVAL TODAY

" Birmingham is probably not the first place
that springs to mind when you think independent
film, but once you attend this festival you will
change your mind... Not to be missed."
CHRIS GORE, FILM THREAT

CASH AWARDS INCLUDE
$1000 FOR BEST FEATURE,
SHORT AND DOCUMENTARY

WWW.SIDEWALKFEST.COM
CALL: 205.324.0888

PARISIAN   Hoegaarden   FILMMAKER
                                      THE MAGAZINE OF INDEPENDENT FILM

Slamdancers Peter Baxter, Margot Gerber, Paul Rachman and Dan Mirvish.

itself. And festival directors from all over the world attend to discover new films to invite to their own festivals. One word of advice, when you enter Slamdance, leave the cell phone and phony industry crap at the door. This festival kicks serious ass.

Filmmaker Perks: All filmmakers get a festival pass for all parties and screenings.

Travel Tips: Drink lots of water and go easy on the alcohol. The elevation does some damage to your tolerance.

Peter Baxter ....President
Dan Mirvish ....Co-Founder-at-Large
Paul Rachman ....Head of Slamdance/New York

SMOGDANCE FiLM FESTiVAL

dA Center for the Arts
252-D S. Main St.
Pomona, CA 91767
Tel............................909-997-0761; 909-397-9716
Email..info@smogdance.com
Web Site..www.smogdance.com

Festival Month: Mid-January

Entry Deadline: Early December

Entry Fee: None

Genres: American, Animation, Comedy, Documentary, Experimental, Fantasy/Science Fiction, First-Time Independent Filmmakers, Narrative, Shorts

Screening Format: 16mm - BetaSP - VHS

Awards: Yes

Profile: The Smogdance Film Festival is a unique festival featuring over a dozen short subjects and documentaries from emerging filmmakers across the continent.

Special Events: Awards, parties

Travel Tips: Take Amtrak right into Pomona.

Charlotte Cousins ....Festival Director
Enid Baxter Blader ....Festival Contact

SPLiT SCREEN FiLM FESTiVAL

Attn: Ethan Bennett, Director of Cinema
UK Student Activities Board
203 Student Center
Lexington, KY 40506-0030
Tel..859-257-8867
Fax 859-323-1024
Email ....cbrogers1@msn.com
Web Site ....www.splitscreenfilmfest.com

Festival Month: Late September

Entry Deadline: Mid-July

Entry Fee: $25

Genres: Animation, Documentary, Experimental, Features, First-Time Independent Filmmakers, Independent, International, Narrative, Shorts, Student

Screening Format: 8mm - Super 8mm - 16mm - 35mm - VHS - DVD - VCD

Awards: No

Profile: Splitscreen is an indie film fest made for and by students. For two days in September, up and coming filmmakers from all of the US and the world come together to celebrate their art. Live music, free screenings, filmmakers workshops and forums, a chance to meet an award-winning director/producer, and a whole lot more awaits...

Special Events: Workshops, panels, parties, concerts

Filmmaker Perks: Contacts, concerts

Travel Tips: Fly right into Blue Grass Airport, rent a car, and find a motel.

Ethan Bennett.....................................Director of Cinema

SPROCKETS TORONTO iNTERNATiONAL FiLM FESTiVAL FOR CHiLDREN

Attn: Tania Reilly
2 Carlton St., W Mezzanine
Toronto, Ontario M5B 1J3 Canada
Tel..416-967-7371
Fax 416-967-9477
Email ....sprockets@torfilmfest.ca
Web Site ....www.bell.ca/sprockets

Festival Month: Mid-April

Entry Deadline: Early January

Entry Fee: None

Genres: Animation, Canadian, Children, Documentary, Family, Features, Independent, International, Narrative, Shorts, Student

Screening Format: 16mm - 35mm - BetaSP

Awards: Pharma Plus Drugmarts Audience Choice Award; Other Awards

Profile: Sprockets is a division of the Toronto International Film Festival Group, a charitable, cultural and educational institution devoted to celebrating excellence in film and the moving image. Sprockets is always an enlightening event - as much for us as for young people and their parents and guardians.

Special Events: Awards

Travel Tips: Toronto is one of the most multicultural cities in the world, it is home to more than 80 ethnic groups and more than 100 languages. That means there's room for you.

Jane Schoettle ....Festival Director

ST. LOUiS iNTERNATiONAL FiLM FESTiVAL

394 A N. Euclid Ave.
St. Louis, MA 63108-1247
Tel ....314-454-0042 ext. 12
Fax 314-454-0540
Email ....mailroom@cinemastlouis.org
Web Site ....www.cinemastlouis.org

Festival Month: Mid-November

Entry Deadline: Mid-July

Entry Fee: Features: $45-$100

Shorts: $20-$50

Genres: Animation, Documentary, Experimental, Features, Independent, Narrative, Shorts, Student

Screening Format: 16mm - 35mm - BetaSP

Awards: Audience Choice Awards; Other Awards

Profile: The St. Louis International Film Festival is an open invitational to features, documentaries and short subjects from all over the world, with special emphasis on American independents, world cinema and prize-winning short subjects. Our festival has achieved an official designation from the Academy of Motion Picture Arts and Sciences as a sanctioned short subject qualification event.

Special Events: Parties, panels, awards

Comments: Be sure to spend some time enjoying the best Blues in the world. And if you're a sports fan, catch a Rams game during the fest.

Filmmaker Perks: Festival covers travel and accomodations when possible.

Travel Tips: Four interstate highways – I-44, I-55, I-70, and I-64/Highway 40 – go through St. Louis, so you've got options.

Chris Clark ....Artistic and Managing Director

STONY BROOK FiLM FESTiVAL

Staller Center for the Arts, Room 2030A
University at Stony Brook
Stony Brook, NY 11794
Tel 631-632-7235
Fax 631-632-7354
Email ....filmfestival@stonybrookfilmfestival.com
Web Site ....www.stonybrookfilmfestival.com

Year Festival Began: 1996

Festival Month: Late July

Entry Deadline: Early May

Entry Fee: Features: $40

Shorts: $20

Genres: 16mm, 35mm, American, Animation, Documentary, Experimental, Features, First-Time Independent Filmmakers, Independent, International, Narrative, Shorts

Screening Format: 16mm - 35mm

Awards: Jury Awards; Audience Awards; Festival Award for Excellence

Profile: The Stony Brook Film Festival showcases dozens of independent films, growing rapidly with over 14,000 moviegoers attending in 2003. The Staller Center for the Arts, which boasts a 40′ wide screen and state-of-the-art 35mm and 16mm projection equipment, is a great festival venue.

Special Events: Awards, parties, panels

Filmmaker Perks: The festival assists with travel and accomodations when possible.

Travel Tips: Long Island's Islip-MacArthur Airport is 16 miles from the campus and is serviced by direct flights by major airlines and commuter lines.

Alan Inkles...Festival Director

TELLURiDE iNDiEFEST

PO Box 860
Telluride, CO 81435
Tel 970-708-1529
Fax..970-728-8128
Email ....festival@tellurideindiefest.com
Web Site...........................www.tellurideindiefest.com

Festival Month: Late August-September

Entry Deadline: Late May

Entry Fee: Under 10 Minutes: $40

11-30 Minutes: $45

31-60 Minutes: $50

61-120 Minutes: $55

Genres: Animation, Documentary, Features, Independent, International, Narrative, Shorts

Screening Format: 35mm - BetaSP - VHS - DVD

Awards: No awards. All selected artists are considered winners - providing more opportunities to more artisans!

Profile: Telluride IndieFest showcases the best *independent* films and screenplays in the world and does not require films to "premiere" at its event.

Special Events: Screenplay competition, screenings, seminars, parties, gala reception

Comments: What Slamdance is to Sundance, IndieFest is to the Telluride Film Festival. Indiefest features screenings of independent works without distribution in Telluride. Unfortunately, most of these films have little appeal to the highbrow tastes of the mostly older, mostly white, and mostly wealthy attendees of the Telluride Film Festival. The organizers of Indiefest also screen films in other cities.

Filmmaker Perks: The festival helps with travel and accomodations when possible.

Travel Tips: The airport in Montrose isn't close, but a shuttle ride is generally a reliable way to bridge the gap.

Michael Carr ....Festival Director

TEMECULA VALLEY iNTERNATiONAL FiLM FESTiVAL

27740 Jefferson Ave. Ste 100
Temecula, CA 92590
Tel...909-699-6267
Fax 909-506-4193
Email ....jmmoulton@earthlink.net
Web Site ....www.tviff.com

Year Festival Began: 1995
Festival Month: Early September
Entry Deadline: Mid-July
Entry Fee: $25
Students with Valid ID: $10

Genres: American, Animation, Digital, Documentary, Ethnic Asian, Ethnic Black, Ethnic Jewish, Ethnic Spanish, Experimental, Features, First-Time Independent Filmmakers, Independent, International, Narrative, Shorts, Student

Screening Format: 35mm - BetaSP

Awards: Jury Awards; Audience Awards

Profile: Since 1995, the Temecula Valley International Film Festival has screened over 600 films from over 20 countries, showcasing U.S. and International full-length features, short films, student films, documentaries and animation.

Special Events: Awards, parties, music competition, workshops

Comments: Located in the lush vacation environment of Temecula Valley (also home to some rockin' Indian casinos), the entire town turns out for this amazing event. Add a complimentary music festival to the event and the combination is a worthwhile weekend of fun and film.

Filmmaker Perks: Free access to all festival events.

Travel Tips: Try getting around by bicycle. The city, in conjunction with Caltrans, has made efforts to ensure that you will be able to ride your bike safely within the community.

Jo Moulton ....Festival Director

TEXAS FiLM FESTiVAL

PO Box J-1
College Station, TX 77844
Tel 979-845-1515
Fax 979-845-5117
Email ....txfilmfest@msc.tamu.edu
Web Site ....www.txfilmfest.org

Year Festival Began: 1992
Festival Month: Mid-February
Entry Deadline: Early January
Entry Fee: $10-$30

Genres: Animation, Documentary, Features, First-Time Independent Filmmakers, Independent, Narrative, Shorts, Student

Screening Format: 8mm - Super 8mm - 16mm - 35mm - BetaSP - VHS - DVD - Hi8 - CDRom

Number of Films Screened: 50

X Factor: By students, for all indie filmmakers.

Awards: Yes

Profile: The Texas Film Festival began in 1993 on the Texas A&M University Campus. Since its inception it has grown to be the largest student-run independent film festival in the nation. For the people of the Brazos Valley, the festival is the only source of independent films.

The festival has had the privilege to showcase the talent of independent filmmakers from around the globe. Past festival guests have included Spike Lee, Oliver Stone, Tim McCanlies, Robert Rodriguez, and Sean Astin. Every year the festival is able to grow and reach an even wider audience.

Special Events: Panels, workshops, parties, awards

Filmmaker Perks: The festival covers travel and accomodations when possible.

STAND OUT

Some might advise against doing something outrageous to promote your film, but I encourage it. If you're one of the many filmmakers without distribution or Brad Pitt in your movie, you'll need some kind of extra push. Be creative.

Travel Tips: Talk to the festival for the best place to stay while in town.

Hallie Gardiner ....Festival Director
Michael Venner ....MSC Film Society Chairman

THAW VIDEO, FILM, AND DIGITAL MEDIA FESTIVAL

E. 100 Art Building
Iowa City, IA 52242
Tel 319-335-1348
Fax 319-335-2930
Email ....thaw@uiowa.edu
Web Site ....www.uiowa.edu/~thaw

Year Festival Began: 1996
Festival Month: Late October
Entry Deadline: Mid-May
Entry Fee: $20-$30
Genres: Animation, Digital, Digital Animation, Documentary, DVD, Experimental, Features, Independent, International, Microcinema, Multimedia, Narrative, Online Festival, Shorts, Student, Super 8/8mm, Underground, Video, Weird
Screening Format: Super 8mm - 16mm - 35mm
Number of Films Screened: 70+
X Factor: A very unique, hands-on festival.
Awards: Jury Awards
Profile: Thaw is an annual international festival of experimental video and film that features new work by emerging media artists. Thaw involves an exploration of the medium of film, video, performance, and digital art by providing a forum for experimental work that pushes the boundaries of the form. Thaw is open to all artists who challenge conventional standards in search of independent expression.
Special Events: Awards, parties
Filmmaker Perks: Each work exhibited will be monetarily recognized. Visiting filmmakers will also be invited to present their work and program unique screenings and events.
Travel Tips: Bring a jacket, it'll be getting colder.

Laren Leland ....Festival Contact

TIBURON INTERNATIONAL FILM FESTIVAL

1680 Tiburon Blvd.
Tiburon, CA 94920
Tel..415-381-4123
Fax..415-388-4123
Email ....info@tiburonfilmfestival.com
Web Site ....www.tiburonfilmfestival.com

Festival Month: Mid-March
Entry Deadline: December
Entry Fee: None
Genres: Animation, Documentary, Experimental, Features, Independent, International, Narrative, Shorts

Screening Format: 16mm - 35mm - BetaSP - DV
Awards: Golden Reel Awards; Audience Award; Other Awards
Profile: The Tiburon International Film Festival seeks to provide the community with top-quality films from around the world that would not be accessible without such an event. Our goal is one of cultural enrichment and heightened cultural awareness.
Special Events: Awards, special screenings
Travel Tips: Even though you could fly in Oakland, fly into San Francisco. It's slightly closer.

Saeed Shafa ....Festival Director

TIE INTERNATIONAL EXPERIMENTAL CINEMA EXPOSITION

TIE/Film Entry Committee
2 N. Cascade, Ste 1100
Colorado Springs, CO 80903
Tel 719-277-6657
Email ....entry@experimentalcinema.com
Web Site ....www.experimentalcinema.com

Festival Month: Mid-November
Entry Deadline: Early September
Entry Fee: $35
Genres: 16mm, 35mm, Avant Garde, Experimental, Features, Independent, International, Shorts, Super 8/8mm
Screening Format: 8mm - Super 8mm - 16mm - 35mm
Awards: No
Profile: The International Experimental Cinema Exposition (TIE) exists to illuminate experimental film of the highest caliber, as well as join, recognize and serve filmmakers who are dedicated to the art and experimentation of the motion picture film.
Special Events: Retrospectives, workshops, panels, parties, tributes
Filmmaker Perks: Forums for experimental filmmakers can be hard to find, this festival caters to them.
Travel Tips: Fly into the Colorado Springs Airport, which is very easy to get in and out of, has a wonderful variety of ground transportation options.

Christopher May ....Festival Founder/Director
David Torrey de Frescheville.........Festival Co-Founder

TORONTO JEWISH FILM FESTIVAL

17 Madison Ave.
Toronto, Ontario
M5R 2S2 Canada
Tel 416-324-8226
Fax 416-324-8668
Email ....tjff@tjff.ca
Web Site ....www.tjff.com

Festival Month: Early May
Entry Deadline: Early February

Entry Fee: None

Genres: Animation, Canadian, Documentary, Ethnic Jewish, Features, Independent, International, Multi-Cultural, Narrative, Shorts

Screening Format: BetaSP

Awards: No

Profile: The Toronto Jewish Film Festival is the second largest Jewish film festival in North America, and one of the largest Jewish film festivals in the world. The TJFF presents the best feature films, documentaries and shorts from around the world on themes of Jewish culture and identity. It is dedicated to using film for its contemporary, popular value and reflecting the diversity of the Jewish experience internationally.

Special Events: Parties, panels, sing-alongs, art exhibits

Filmmaker Perks: Contacts, increased international exposure.

Helen Zukerman ....Executive Director
Shlomo Schwartzberg ....Director of Programming

TRENTON FILM FESTIVAL

Trenton Film Society
PO Box 22430
Trenton, NJ 08607
Tel 609-396-6966
Fax 609-392-3634
Email ....submissions@trentonfilmfestival.org
Web Site ....www.trentonfilmfestival.org

Festival Month: May

Entry Deadline: January

Entry Fee: Contact Festival for Details

Genres: Animation, Avant Garde, Documentary, Experimental, Features, Independent, International, Narrative, Shorts

Screening Format: 16mm - 35mm - BetaSP - VHS

Awards: Yes

Profile: The Trenton Film Festival is a weekend-long event showcasing independent and foreign films. This event features a jury of critics, scholars and film professional and will award prizes in each category. The Trenton Film Festival is held in Trenton, NJ, which is centered in one of the most affluent areas of the country with over 3 million people living within 40 minutes of our venues. Trenton is also conveniently located mid-way between New York and Philadelphia on the NorthEast corridor train line.

Special Events: Awards, panels, seminars, parties

Filmmaker Perks: Possibility for a large audience turn-out.

Travel Tips: Conveniently located 30 min. north of Philadelphia and 60 min. south of NYC, Trenton is easily reachable by car, train, or bus.

Kevin Williams..Artistic Director

TRIGGERSTREET.COM ONLINE SHORT FILM FESTIVAL

9 Desbrosses St., 2nd Fl.
New York, NY 10013
Web Site.....................................www.triggerstreet.com

Festival Month: February

Entry Fee: None

Genres: All, Online, Shorts

Awards: Official Selections

Profile: Triggerstreet.com Online Short Film Festival's mission is to encourage the creative process of filmmaking and screenwriting by providing hands on, peer-to-peer, objective criticism and letting the material be judged on its own merit. We offer an engaging avenue of exploration for both first time and veteran film directors, writers, and enthusiasts - anyone at all - who is attempting to bring his or her vision to the screen.

Special Events: Awards

Filmmaker Perks: Your short becomes a part of an online network of shorts viewable at any time by a worldwide audience.

Travel Tips: Well, you might take a trip to the bathroom every once and a while.

Dana Brunetti ....President/Co-Founder
Ross Partridge ....Creative Operations Director
Kevin Spacey ....Co-Founder

TROMADANCE FILM FESTIVAL

The Troma Building
733 Ninth Ave.
New York, NY 10019
Tel...212-757-4555 ext 18
Web Site ....www.tromadance.com

Year Festival Began: 2000

Festival Month: Late January

Entry Deadline: Late December

Entry Fee: None

Genres: Animation, Digital, Digital Animation, DVD, Ethnic African, Ethnic Asian, Ethnic Black, Ethnic Jewish, Ethnic Latin, Ethnic Other, Ethnic Spanish, Experimental, Fantasy/Science Fiction, Features, First-Time Independent Filmmakers, Gay Lesbian, Horror, Independent, International, Narrative, Shorts, Student, Super 8/8mm, Touring, Underground, Video, Weird, Women

Screening Format: VHS - DVD

Awards: Kodak/TromaDance Film Festival; Independent Soul Award

Profile: TromaDance is the first film festival wholeheartedly devoted to filmmakers and fans. Unlike every other film festival, TromaDance does not charge filmmakers to submit their films. Entrance to all screenings is free and open to the public. Also, there are no VIP reservations or preferential treatment regarding films, panels, or parties of any kind given.

The organizers of TromaDance believe films are meant to be seen, especially when it comes to new filmmakers. Art...in all its forms...is for the people!

Special Events: Parties, panels, TromaDance North

Filmmaker Perks: Just being associated with Troma means publicity. Plus, you could be a part of TromaDance North, Winnipeg, Canada's TromaDance festival.

Travel Tips: It's Park City, so bring a warm coat and gloves - you'll promoting your film on Main St.

Lloyd Kaufman ....Founder
Jonathan Lees......................................Program Director

U.S. COMEDY ARTS FESTiVAL

2049 Century Park E, Ste 4300
Los Angeles, CA 90067
Tel 800-778-4633; 310-201-9200
Email ....uscafindustry@hbo.com.
Web Site ....www.hbocomedyfestival.com

Festival Month: Early March

Entry Deadline: Early December

Entry Fee: Contact Festival for Details

Genres: Animation, Comedy, Documentary, Features, Independent, International, Narrative, Performance, Shorts

Screening Format: 35mm - BetaSP

Awards: Comedy Film Honors

Film Discovery Program Awards

Jury Awards

Profile: The U.S. Comedy Arts Festival presents the best in alternative comedy, stand-up sketch, theater, and independent film from around the world, culminating in jury awards for live performance and film; Honors given to innovative artists and creators who have broken new ground and become part of our culture.

Special Events: Parties, awards

Filmmaker Perks: Great nightly parties, an environment that is all about making people feel good.

Travel Tips: The St. Regis is ideally located at the base of Aspen Mountain. The hotel is 10 minutes from Aspen Airport.

Stu Smiley ....Festival Director
Kevin Haasarud ....Film Program Director

UNiTED NATiONS ASSOCiATiON FiLM FESTiVAL

PO Box 19369
Stanford, CA 94309
Tel 650-725-0012
Fax 650-725-0011
Email ....info@unaff.org
Web Site ....www.unaff.org

Festival Month: Mid-October

Entry Deadline: Early June

Entry Fee: Under 30 Minutes: $25
Over 30 Minutes: $35

Genres: Documentary, Education, Environmental, Features, Government, Human Rights, Independent, International, Multi-Cultural, Performance, Shorts

Screening Format: 16mm - 35mm - BetaSP - VHS

Awards: No

Profile: The United Nations Association Film Festival celebrates the power of international documentary films and videos dealing with UN related issues: human rights, environmental survival, women's issues, famine, protection of refugees, homelessness, racism, disease control, education for all, war and peace.

Special Events: Traveling festival, special screenings, panels, parties

Filmmaker Perks: The festival assists with accomodations.

Travel Tips: Stanford University's visitor parking system includes one-day "Visitor" scratchers (which allow parking in Pay & Display lots and at meters) available for $12.00 each. Or, take your chances with the $1.50/hour meters.

Jasmina Bojic ....Founder/Director

UNiTED STATES SUPER 8 FiLM AND DiGiTAL ViDEO FESTiVAL

c/o Rutgers University
72 Lipman Dr., 018 Loree Hall
New Brunswick, NJ 08901-1414
Tel...732-932-8482
Fax 732-932-1935
Email ....njmac@aol.com
Web Site ....www.njfilmfest.com

Festival Month: Mid-February

Entry Deadline: Mid-January

Entry Fee: $35

Genres: Animation, Digital, Documentary, Experimental, Independent, International, Narrative, Shorts, Super 8/8mm, Video

Screening Format: 8mm - Super 8mm - Hi8/8mm - DV

BEST TOURING FILM FESTIVALS

Backseat Film Festival
Euro Underground
Gadabout Traveling Film Festival
Hip Hop Film Fest
Human Rights Watch International Film Festival
Independent Exposure
Lost Film Festival
Microcinefest
NoDance Film Festival
ResFest Digital Film Festival

Awards: Jury Awards; Audience Choice Prize

Profile: United States Super 8 Film + Digital Video Festival is the largest and longest running juried Super 8mm film and digital video festival in North America. The festival encourages any genre (animation, documentary, personal, narrative, experimental, etc.) made on Super 8mm/8mm film, Hi 8mm/8mm, or digital video. Every year our festival draws large audiences to celebrate works created with these small-gauge media formats. Many audience members come to see small-budget works created by passionate film/video makers which are often more imaginative and impressive than the big-budget works produced out of Hollywood.

Special Events: Awards

Filmmaker Perks: The festival can assist with finding discount accomodations.

Travel Tips: Fly into Newark Airport because New York City is about an hour away.

Albert Gabriel Nigrin............................Festival Director

UNiVERSiTY OF OREGON QUEER FiLM FESTiVAL

EMU, Ste 2
University of Oregon
Eugene, OR 97403-1228
Tel...541-346-0007
Fax..541-346-4400
Email.....................................qff@darkwing.uoregon.edu
Web Site...........................darkwing.uoregon.edu/~qff/

Year Festival Began: 1993

Festival Month: Late February

Entry Deadline: Early December

Genres: American, Animation, Documentary, Ethnic Other, Experimental, Features, Gay Lesbian, Independent, International, Narrative, Shorts, Student, Underground, Video, Weird

Screening Format: 16mm - 35mm - BetaSP - VHS

Awards: Audience Choice Award

Profile: The University of Oregon Queer Film Festival showcases the best in LGBT cinema from around the world. The festival has a special emphasis on shorts, offering a competition.

Special Events: Parties, awards

Filmmaker Perks: Cash prizes up to $200.

Travel Tips: Eugene is right off Interstate 5, regardless of whether you're going north or south.

Douglas Hopper ....Festival Coordinator

USA FiLM FESTiVAL/DALLAS

6116 N. Central Expressway, Ste 105
Dallas, TX 75206
Tel...214-821-6300
Fax..214-821-6364
Email..usafilmfestival@aol.com
Web Site..................................www.usafilmfestival.com

Festival Month: Mid-April

Entry Deadline: Early March

Entry Fee: None

Genres: American, Animation, Documentary, Experimental, Features, First-Time Independent Filmmakers, Independent, International, Narrative, Shorts, Video

Screening Format: 16mm - 35mm - BetaSP - DigiBeta

X Factor: This festival loves its filmmakers, and treats them royally.

Awards: Yes

Profile: One of the oldest, most prestigious film festivals in the world, the USA Film Festival was the first to celebrate the American Independent Filmmaker.

Special Events: National Short Film & Video Competition, parties, panels, tributes, retrospectives

Comments: While in Dallas, Texas, be sure to make your way to Deep Ellum - the hip part of town - for a dose of good music and great rooftop bars.

Filmmaker Perks: Festival pays for filmmakers' travel and hotel to attend to present their works and discuss them with the audience. Filmmakers are also honored at nightly receptions held in private homes of local arts patrons.

Travel Tips: Everything in Texas is big, especially the meals, so don't let your eyes get bigger then your stomach when eating out.

VAiL FiLM FESTiVAL

225 E. 24th St., 5th Fl.
New York, NY 10010
Tel..............................212-448-0111; 970-333-9689
Fax...212-683-7119
Email...info@vailfilmfestival.org
Web Site..................................www.vailfilmfestival.org

Festival Month: Early April

Entry Deadline: Early March

Entry Fee: Contact Festival for Details

Genres: Animation, Documentary, Features, Independent, International, Narrative, Shorts, Student, Television

Screening Format: 35mm - BetaSP - DVD

Awards: Yes

Profile: Founded by filmmakers, writers, directors and dedicated film enthusiasts, and, in close partnership with the town of Vail and Vail Resorts, the Vail Film Festival is a platform for independent filmmakers to screen their productions in an incredible atmosphere.

Special Events: Panels, awards, parties

Filmmaker Perks: The festival will also integrate the magnificent winter sports location by scheduling afternoon and evening-only programming and offering lift ticket packages to accommodate skiing and snowboarding enthusiasts.

Travel Tips: Vail Mountain is the largest ski resort in North America with 5,289 acres and 33 strategically placed lifts - if you board or ski you may not even make it to your screening.

Scott Cross ....Festival Co-Director
Sean Cross ....Festival Co-Director
Denis Jensen ....Festival Co-Director

VANCOUVER INTERNATIONAL FILM FESTIVAL

Suite 410
1008 Homer St.
Vancouver, BC
V6B 2X1 Canada
Tel 604-685-0260
Fax 604-688-8221
Email ....viff@viff.org
Web Site ....viff.org

Festival Month: Late September-October

Entry Deadline: International Entries: Mid-July

Canadian Entries: Mid-June

Entry Fee: $30

Genres: Animation, Documentary, Features, Independent, International, Narrative, Shorts

Screening Format: 16mm - 35mm - 70mm - BetaSP - DigiBeta - DVCam - HDCam

Number of Films Screened: 300

Awards: The Air Canada People's Choice Award; Jury Awards; Other Awards

Profile: The purpose of the Vancouver International Film Festival is to encourage understanding of other nations through the art of cinema, to foster the art of cinema, to facilitate the meeting of cinema professionals from around the world, in British Columbia, and to stimulate the motion picture industry in British Columbia and Canada.

Special Events: Panels, parties, special screenings, trade forum

Comments: VIFF is the other great film festival in Canada, next to Toronto, and frankly, this one is a lot more fun. For the uninformed, Vancouver is a great town to have a good time and the festival coincides with a film and television trade forum, making it a smart move to attend for business. And pleasure.

Travel Tips: The city is beautiful, but the winter months can get rainy, so be prepared.

Alan Franey ....Festival Director
PoChu AuYeung ....Program Manager

VERMONT INTERNATIONAL FILM FESTIVAL

One Main St.
Burlington, VT 05401
Tel 802-660-2600
Fax 802-860-9555
Email ....info@vtiff.org
Web Site ....www.vtiff.org

Year Festival Began: 1985

Festival Month: Mid-October

Entry Deadline: Mid-July

Entry Fee: Features: $45

Shorts: $25

Genres: Documentary, Features, Government, Human Rights, Independent, International, Narrative, Peace, Shorts

Awards: Best of Festival Award; George and Sonia Cullinen Heart of the Festival Award

Profile: The Vermont International Film Festival is one of the longest running venues in North America focusing on showcasing socially conscious films. For over 18 years, VIFF has provided a forum for films dealing with issues of War and Peace, Justice and Human Rights, and the Environment.

Special Events: Vermont Filmmakers Showcase, awards, parties

Filmmaker Perks: Very laid back atmosphere, detailed attention paid to each film.

Travel Tips: Fly into Manchester Airport in New Hampshire. If you fly into Boston, it'll take you two hours or longer to get to Burlington.

Kenneth Peck ....Executive Director

VICTORIA INDEPENDENT FILM AND VIDEO FESTIVAL

808 View St.
Victoria, BC V8W 1K2 Canada
Tel 250-389-0444
Fax 250-389-0406
Email ....festival@vifvf.com
Web Site ....www.vifvf.com

Year Festival Began: 1995

Festival Month: Late January-February

Entry Deadline: Mid-October

Entry Fee: $10

Genres: American, Animation, Documentary, Experimental, Features, First-Time Independent Filmmakers, Gay Lesbian, Independent, International, Narrative, Shorts, Student, Video, Women

Screening Format: 16mm - 35mm - BetaSP - VHS - DVD - MiniDV

Number of Films Screened: 160

X Factor: The locale is gorgeous, and the vibe is relaxed.

Awards: Jury Awards; Audience Favourite Award; Other Awards

Profile: The Victoria Independent Film & Video Festival presents more than 160 features, documentaries and shorts to an appreciative audience during it's ten day celebration of film. Eclectic and inspiring, the festival brings hosts an array of guests including film directors, producers, distributors, festival, and TV programmers. In recent years the festival has been sited in such media as *The Globe and Mail*, *The Seattle Times*, *Variety*, and CBC's *Big Life*.

Special Events: Parties, panels, awards, student competition

Filmmaker Perks: The director of each world premiere feature length film or documentary will be invited to attend as a guest of the festival. The festival will provide complimentary VIP Passes for two representatives of each feature-length film or long-form documentary presented and for one representative of each short work.

Travel Tips: Victoria is an additional 3 hours from Vancouver, so bring a book.

Kathy Kay ....Festival Director

VIRGINIA FILM FESTIVAL

PO Box 400869
Charlottesville, VA 22904
Tel..1-800-882-3378
Fax 434-924-3374
Email ....info@vafilm.com
Web Site ....www.vafilm.com

Festival Month: Late October

Entry Deadline: Early June

Entry Fee: By Invite

Genres: American, Independent, International

Screening Format: 16mm - 35mm - BetaSP

Awards: No

Profile: The Virginia Film Festival explores American film and the international cinema. It influences and reflects in an annual academic forum that brings together authors, critics, directors, actors, artists, and scholars from across the nation.

Special Events: Parties, workshops

Filmmaker Perks: Free access to all festival events.

Travel Tips: The festival occurs right at the peak time for the leaves to change colors for Fall. If you're a Leaf-Peeper, this fest's for you.

Richard Herskowitz ....Festival Director

BUILD A TEAM

A combination of publicist, manager, producer's rep, agent, lawyer, etc. They should all be as passionate about your film as you are.

WASHINGTON, DC INTERNATIONAL FILM FESTIVAL—FILMFEST DC

PO Box 21396
Washington, DC 20009
Tel 202-724-5613
Fax 202-724-6578
Email ....filmfestdc@filmfestdc.org
Web Site..............................www.filmfestdc.org

Year Festival Began: 1986

Festival Month: Late April-May

Entry Deadline: Mid-January

Entry Fee: Features: $25

Shorts: $15

Genres: 16mm, 35mm, American, Ethnic African, Ethnic Asian, Ethnic Black, Ethnic Jewish, Ethnic Latin, Ethnic Other, Ethnic Spanish, Features, First-Time Independent Filmmakers, Independent, International, Narrative, Shorts

Screening Format: 16mm - 35mm

Number of Films Screened: 70

Awards: DC Audience Award

Profile: Filmfest DC, presented by the Washington, DC International Film Festival, has made significant contributions to the film community in Washington, both by bringing world-wide films to theaters, but also by providing a forum for local filmmakers to showcase and market their work.

Special Events: Awards, parties, Reel Talk panels

Filmmaker Perks: The festival provides travel and accomodations when possible.

Travel Tips: Don't rent a car - DC gets confusing if you're not used to driving it.

Tony Gittens..Festival Director
Shirin Ghareeb....................Assistant Festival Director

WATERFRONT FILM FESTIVAL

PO Box 387
Saugatuck, MI 49453
Tel 269-857-8351
Fax...269-857-1072
Email...........................info@waterfrontfilm.com
Web Site.....................www.waterfrontfilm.com

Year Festival Began: 1999

Festival Month: Mid-June

Entry Deadline: Late March

Entry Fee: Features: $45

Shorts: $25

Genres: American, Animation, Documentary, Features, Independent, International, Narrative

Screening Format: 16mm - 35mm - BetaSP - DV

Awards: No

Profile: Entertainment professionals from Los Angeles, New York, and Michigan created the Waterfront Film Festival in 1999 to provide a "middle coast" venue for independent filmmakers eager to show their work to sophisticated audiences. And now, in what has quickly become a tradition, the idyllic resort village of Saugatuck, Michigan, comes alive each June with filmgoers, actors, producers, and directors sharing the excitement as outstanding independent films from all over the US are screened in casual, intimate settings.

Special Events: Seminars, parties

Comments: Waterfront is one of those intimate festival experiences you'll want to have again, screening about 50 films in the small resort town of Saugatuck, this event attracts some of the hardest partiers in festival history. Filmmakers and guests are put up in a small vacation motel, that's right, "motel," located directly on the water where parties go on until morning. The festival even brews its own beer. Filmmakers and guests are taken on a champagne cruise and are also ferried to a tiny remote island for a delightful party. Afternoon barbecues provide tasty eats for all daily and the opening night film is shown on a giant screen in the middle of charming Main Street. Appreciative audiences see films in curious alternative venues such as a Veterans Hall and a converted boat hanger, however, this just adds to the down-home feel of an unforgettable weekend of movies.

Filmmaker Perks: The festival covers travel and accomodations for select filmmakers.

Travel Tips: Whether your interests include cruising the many art galleries in the Saugatuck/Douglas area, watersports, sunbathing, golf, fishing, or dining out at premiere restaurants, all tastes can be indulged.

Hopwood DePree..............................Co-Founder
Dana DePree ....Co-Founder
Dori DePree ....Co-Founder

WEST ViRGiNiA iNTERNATiONAL FiLM FESTiVAL

PO Box 2165
Charleston, WV 25328-2165
Tel 304-342-7100
Email ....wviff@aol.com
Web Site ....www.wviff.org

Year Festival Began: 1985

Festival Month: Late October-November (Fall), Early May (Spring)

Entry Deadline: Mid-March (Student Competition)

Entry Fee: $10 (Student Competition)

Genres: Animation, Documentary, Ethnic Other, Features, Independent, International, Multi-Cultural, Narrative, Student

Screening Format: 35mm - VHS (Student Competition)

Number of Films Screened: 27 (Fall), 16 (Spring)

X Factor: If you're a young student filmmaker, the spring festival competition is for you.

Awards: 1st-3rd Place for student filmmakers in grades K-8th, High School, and College.

Profile: The WVIFF's mission is to encourage, support, and promote the film arts; to plan, organize, and present an annual fall film festival of critically acclaimed and culturally diverse domestic and foreign language feature films unlikely to be exhibited theatrically in West Virginia; to plan, organize, and present an annual spring film festival of critically acclaimed and culturally diverse domestic and foreign language feature films and documentaries, West Virginia-produced/related films, and educational programming; to conduct these activities for entertainment, educational, and audience-development purposes; to encourage local and statewide film and video production; and to carry on any business connected therewith.

Special Events: Student competition, special screenings, parties, awards

Comments: WVIFF puts on two festivals, one in the spring (May) the other in the fall (November) each featuring a healthy slate of international works.

Filmmaker Perks: The festival provides select filmmakers with travel and accomodations.

Travel Tips: Fly to Charleston, save yourself the hassle.

WHiSTLER FiLM FESTiVAL

Suite 1004, 102 - 4369 Main St.
Whistler, BC V0N 1B4 Canada
Tel...604-938-3323
Fax 604-938-3209
Email ....info@whistlerfilmfestival.com
Web Site ....www.whistlerfilmfestival.com

Year Festival Began: 2001

Festival Month: Early December

Entry Deadline: Mid-October

Entry Fee: Under 45 Minutes: $25

Over 45 Minutes: $50

Genres: Adventurer/Explorers, Animation, Digital, Digital Animation, DVD, Experimental, Features, First-Time Independent Filmmakers, Independent, International, Markets, Mountain Sports, Multimedia, Narrative, Shorts, Video

Screening Format: 16mm - 35mm - VHS

Awards: Jury Awards; People's Choice Awards; Other Awards

Profile: One of Whistler's premier cultural events and emerging as the most exciting filmmakers' festival on the circuit, the Whistler Film Festival features all the things that make a film festival fun...great films, innovative workshops, informal socializing and networking, and a fantastic setting. The Whistler Film Festival's mandate is to encourage the development of arts and culture in Whistler; to support the art of cinema and the film industry; and to provide an educational and entertaining environment for film enthusiasts and industry professionals.

Special Events: Workshops, panels, awards, parties

Filmmaker Perks: The festival assists with accomodations when possible.

Travel Tips: Whistler's enchanting alpine style, pedestrian-only village features over 20,000 beds within walking distance of the base of the mountains, more than 200 shops, 90 plus restaurants, cozy pubs, lively nightclubs, a variety of outdoor activity options, and much more!

Shauna Hardy ....Festival Director

WiLLiAMSTOWN FiLM FESTiVAL

PO Box 81
Williamstown, MA 01267
Tel 413-458-9700
Fax...413-458-2702
Email ....contactus@williamstownfilmfest.com
Web Site........................www.williamstownfilmfest.com

Year Festival Began: 1999

Festival Month: Late October-November

Entry Deadline: Late August

Entry Fee: Features: $20-$30

Shorts: $15-$25

Genres: American, Animation, Documentary, DVD, Experimental, Features, First-Time Independent Filmmakers, Independent, Narrative, Shorts, Student, Weird

Screening Format: 16mm - 35mm - BetaSP - VHS

Awards: No

Profile: The Williamstown Film Festival was founded in 1998 to fill a cultural gap in a part of Massachusetts known for its world-class museums, theater, music, and dance - the Berkshires. Because film seemed the missing link in an artistically rich region, some two dozen local residents and graduates of Williams College felt strongly that a film festival could bridge the gap. After a series of meetings, the Williamstown Film Festival was incorporated as a non-profit organization and began planning. The goal was tripartite: (a) to honor America's film past in the shape of classics, (b) celebrate the present day through panels, seminars, and Q&As between audiences and the actors, writers, directors and producers of independent film, and (c) explore the new technologies that are carrying the art of film into the 21st century.

Special Events: Parties, panels

Filmmaker Perks: The festival covers travel and accomodations when possible.

Travel Tips: Williamstown is equidistant between New York City and Boston, 3 hours away from either.

Steve Lawson ....Festival Director

WILMINGTON INDEPENDENT FILM FESTIVAL

c/o Cityfest, Inc.
800 N. French St., 9th Floor
Wilmington, DE 19801
Tel 302-576-2137
Email ....bzimmer@ciw.ilmington.de.us
Web Site..........................www.wilmingtonfilmfest.com

Festival Month: Late March

Entry Deadline: January

Entry Fee: Contact Festival for Details

Genres: Animation, Documentary, Features, Independent, International, Narrative, Shorts

Screening Format: 35mm - BetaSP - VHS

Awards: No

Profile: The Wilmington Independent Film Festival is a 3-day festival dedicated to bringing the freshest independent cinema to the greater Delaware area. It's a short program but packed with a lot of entertainment!

Special Events: Parties, special screenings

Travel Tips: Philadelphia International Airport, located 30 minutes from downtown Wilmington, provides an extensive schedule of national and international flights as well as complete freight operations.

Tina Betz ..Director/Mayor's Office of Cultural Affairs
Beverly Zimmermann ....Program Manager/Mayor's Office of Cultural Affairs

WINE COUNTRY FILM FESTIVAL

1200 Henno Rd.
PO Box 303
Glen Ellen, CA 95442
Tel 707-935-FILM; 707-996-2536
Fax 707-996-6964
Email ....wcfilmfest@aol.com
Web Site..........................www.winecountryfilmfest.com

Festival Month: July-August

Entry Deadline: Early May

Entry Fee: $40-$55

Genres: Animation, Children, Documentary, Features, Human Rights, Independent, International, Multi-Cultural, Narrative, Peace, Shorts

Screening Format: 16mm - 35mm - VHS - DVD - DVCam

Awards: Charlie Chaplin Award
Gaia Film Awards
WCFF Humanitarian Award

Wine Country Film Festival Distinguished Artist Award
Margrit and Rose Mondavi Filmmaker Prize

Profile: What sets the Wine Country Film Festival apart from the zillion other film festivals worldwide is our leisurely pace. You have plenty of time to enjoy wine country's amenities during the day. Then late afternoon and early evening arrive for an experience that will last a lifetime. Our film festival is internationally known for its spectacular open air film screenings. There are 16 celestial film nights.

Special Events: Open-air film screenings, wine-tastings, parties

Filmmaker Perks: Laid back atmosphere, free wine.

Travel Tips: Venues are about an hour north of San Francisco and the East Bay, so you're definitely driving.

WISCONSIN FILM FESTIVAL

UW-Madison Arts Institute
821 University Ave., 6th Floor
Madison, WI 53706
Tel 877-963-3456
Fax 608-262-6589
Email..info@wifilmfest.org
Web Site..www.wifilmfest.org

Year Festival Began: 1999

Festival Month: Early April

Entry Deadline: Early March

Entry Fee: $15-$30

Genres: American, Animation, Documentary, Ethnic African, Ethnic Asian, Ethnic Black, Ethnic Jewish, Ethnic Latin, Ethnic Spanish, Experimental, First-Time Independent Filmmakers, Gay Lesbian, Independent, International, Multimedia, Short, Underground, Video, Women

Screening Format: 16mm - 35mm - BetaSP - MiniDV

Awards: Jury Awards

Profile: Founded in 1999, the Wisconsin Film Festival is Wisconsin's premier independent film event and film festival. This four-day annual festival takes place each spring in campus and downtown Madison venues. The festival presents the best new independent film (feature, documentary, experimental), world cinema and new media; cultivates discovery through talks, panels, performances, and coffeehouse discussions with filmmakers; and showcases the work of Wisconsin filmmakers through juried competitions. The festival is committed to independent film culture, quality programming, community involvement, and a filmmaker-friendly environment.

Special Events: Seminars, panels, performances, coffeehouse discussions, awards

Filmmaker Perks: Festival assists with travel and accomodations when possible.

Travel Tips: Fly into Dane County Regional Airport and rent a car or, if they finally have the program going, try carsharing.

Mary Carbine ....Festival Director

WOODSTOCK FILM FESTIVAL

PO Box 1406
Woodstock, NY 12498
Tel..845-679-4265
Fax...509-479-5414
Email ....info@woodstockfilmfestival.com
Web Site ....www.woodstockfilmfestival.com

Year Festival Began: 2000

Festival Month: September

Entry Deadline: Late June

Entry Fee: $25-$50

Genres: Animation, Digital, Documentary, Features, Independent, Independent, International, Music Videos, Narrative, Shorts, Student

Screening Format: 35mm - BetaSP - HDTV - DVD

Number of Films Screened: 125

X Factor: If you're a beginning filmmaker, this may be the best place to premiere in the states.

Awards: Maverick Awards

The Elmer Bernstein Award

The Haskell Wexler Award

Profile: The Woodstock Film Festival has established itself as one of the best independent film events in the country by premiering exceptional films, hosting the most talented people in the industry, presenting A-list concerts, parties and panels, and creating innovative and stimulating programming. The festival has drawn rave reviews nationwide from filmmakers, industry members, film lovers, and the media alike.

Special Events: Parties, panels, concerts, awards, special screenings

Comments: Sure, you've heard about the historic rock shows, but film is the reason to come to Woodstock in September. The landscape alone will leave you breathless as you partake in parties, films and panels surrounded by a film-loving community unprecedented around the festival circuit. While the fest screens over 125 works and attracts A-list celebrities, you still may end up bypassing a film or two just to take in this scenic locale. In addition, it should come as no surprise that music is a major component of the fest and attendees are treated to performances at all-night music shows. If you can make the time, skip the festival for an afternoon and visit one of the relaxing day spas for some special treatment. Also, forget the hotel and make arrangements to stay at one of the many bed & breakfasts in town. B&Bs are truly romantic and a welcome break from overpriced hotels.

Filmmaker Perks: Many opportunities to network.

Travel Tips: Talk to the WFF hospitality crew first, then can turn you on to some sweet travel and accomodations deals.

Meira Blaustein ....Executive Director

WORLD COMMUNITY FILM FESTIVAL

Box 3192
Courtenay BC
V9N 5N4 Canada
Tel 250-337-5412
Email ....info@worldcommunity.ca
Web Site ....www.worldcommunity.ca/wc_film.html

Festival Month: Late January

Entry Deadline: Mid-September

Entry Fee: None

Genres: Documentary, Features, Government, Human Rights, International, Narrative, Peace, Shorts

Screening Format: 35mm - BetaSP

Awards: No

Profile: The World Community Film Festival program features 31 films, covering a wide range of social issues from around the world and closer to home.

YOUR LIFE IS NOT OVER

When you pick up the trades and read that this film or that film sold for a million bucks, don't let it get you down when yours does not sell. The cold truth is that the entertainment business moves at a glacial pace. Things happen very, very slowly, so you must have patience. You may not close a distribution deal for your film, but you'll have made many new friends and useful contacts that will help you along on your eighteenth month (or more!) journey in getting your work seen in front of appreciative festival audiences.

Special Events: Parties, discussions

Travel Tips: Via Rail operates a daily service between Victoria and Courtney (part way up Vancouver Island).

Wayne Bradley ....Festival Director

YORKTON SHORT FILM FESTIVAL

Canada's Golden Sheaf Awards
49 Smith St. E
Yorkton, Saskatchewan
S3N 0H4 Canada
Tel 306-782-7077
Fax 306-782-1550
Email....................................info@yorktonshortfilm.org
Web Site................................www.yorktonshortfilm.org

Festival Month: Late May

Entry Deadline: Mid-February

Entry Fee: None

Genres: Animation, Canadian, Documentary, Experimental, Independent, International, Narrative, Shorts, Video

Awards: Golden Sheaf Awards

Profile: The Yorkton Short Film & Video Festival is the longest running festival of its kind in Canada. Over the years, the festival has garnered an esteemed reputation as one of the country's top film and video festivals; a reputation that attracts outstanding entries and personalities from across Canada.

Established in 1947 as the Yorkton Film Council, the first festival was held in 1950, making it Canada's first Short Film & Video Festival. The very first Golden Sheaf Award was introduced in 1958 and was presented to the most outstanding film entry in the festival.

Special Events: Workshops, awards

Filmmaker Perks: Following the festival, a program of Canada's Golden Sheaf Award winning productions may be taken on tour to selected Canadian centers.

Travel Tips: If you're into rafting, Saskatchewan's got some great rivers.

Fay Kowal..Executive Director

ZOiEFiLMS FESTiVAL

505 Prentiss Point
Marietta, GA 30067
Tel 404-816-0602
Email ....info@zoiefilms.com
Web Site ....www.zoiefilms.com

Festival Month: March

Entry Deadline: February

Entry Fee: $40 for Shorts (Under 30 Minutes) $50 for Features

Genres: Animation, Children, Comedy, Commercials, Documentary, Education, Experimental, Features, Features, Music Videos, Online, PSA (Public Service Announcement), Short, Television

Screening Format: Windows Media

Awards: Jury Awards

Profile: ZoieFilms is all about independent filmmaking and encourages the work of independent filmmakers to employ the Internet as a medium for the exhibition of those films.

Kathryn Elliott ....Artistic Director

ZOMBiEDANCE UNDEAD FiLM FEST

PO Box 16650
Austin, TX 78761
Tel 512-929-0837
Email ....zombie@slowkid.com
Web Site ....www.zombiedance.org

Festival Month: Mid-March

Entry Deadline: Late February

Entry Fee: None

Genres: Fantasy/Science Fiction, Features, Horror, Independent, Narrative, Rock and Roll, Shorts, Thriller

Screening Format: Super 8mm - VHS - DV

Awards: Golden Zombie

Profile: The 3 'Do's' of the Zombiedance Undead Film Fest:

We love zombies. We love rock n' roll. We love comedy. If you can successfully combine all three, then you've got a damn good shot at getting in. Hell, you'll probably even win the Golden Zombie.

We also like robots. And beer. And hot chicks. Not necessarily in that order. We're not saying you have to have them in your film. We're just saying we like them. You do the math.

Film rules. And we'll always have a special place in our hearts for anything done on Super 8. So before you go reaching for that DV camera, remember - most everything shot on video winds up looking like the filler in some bad porno, no matter what kind of 'filter' you try and put on it. So if you can, go with film. It just looks better.

Special Events: Awards, parties

Filmmaker Perks: A true independent genre fest that passionately supports you and your film.

Travel Tips: Ride the Dillo Trolleys around town. They're free.

FILM FESTIVAL TODAY MAGAZINE

SUBSCRIBE TODAY! AND NEVER MISS AN ISSUE.

PLEASE PRINT.

NAME: _____

ADDRESS: _____

CITY: _____ STATE: _____ ZIP: _____

E-MAIL (OPTIONAL): _____

PLEASE SUBSCRIBE ME FOR:

☐ 1 YEAR / US$12.00   ☐ 1 YEAR / Outside The United States US$24.00

☐ 2 YEARS / US$20.00   ☐ 2 YEARS / Outside The United States US$40.00

☐ 3 YEARS / US$27.00   ☐ 3 YEARS / Outside The United States US$54.00

☐ This Is A Renewal   FILM FESTIVAL TODAY Publishes Quarterly.

CLIP AND SEND ✂

Please Make Your US-Dollar Denominated Check Or Money Order Out To:
FILM FESTIVAL TODAY

Complete The Above Form And Send It With Your Check Or Money Order To:
FILM FESTIVAL TODAY, ATTN: SUBSCRIPTIONS
P. O. Box 1432, New York NY 10028

FOR GREATER CONVENIENCE, SUBSCRIBE ONLINE: WWW.FILMFESTIVALTODAY.COM

ADVERTISERS! Great Web And Print Package Placements.
Call: 212.592.0151 E-Mail: sales@filmfestivaltoday.com

AD SALES REPS! Excellent Commissions, Flexible Hours.
Call: 212.592.0151 E-Mail: sales@filmfestivaltoday.com

BEST OF THE REST NORTH AMERiCAN FiLM FESTiVALS
United States and Canada

$100 FiLM FESTiVAL
www.csif.org/festival
Festival Month: Mid-March
Genres: 16mm, All Categories -
Shorts, First-Time Independent
Filmmakers, Independent, Super
8/8mm

**2 KiNGS JUDGEMENT
FiLM FESTiVAL**
www.2kingsjudgementfilmfestival.com
Festival Month: Mid-July
Genres: Features, First-Time
Independent Filmmakers, Independent,
Low Budget (Under $20,000), Shorts,
Student

**20,000 LEAGUES UNDER
THE iNDUSTRY FiLM
FESTiVAL**
www.20000leagues.org
Festival Month: September
Genres: Animation, Documentary,
Experimental, Features, Independent,
International, Narrative, Shorts,
Underground

48 HOUR FiLM FESTiVAL
www.extremefilmmaker.com
Festival Month: Late August
Genres: Shorts

48 HOUR FiLM PROJECT
www.48hourfilm.com
Festival Month: May-August
Genres: Animation, Documentary,
Independent, Narrative, Shorts,
Student

(818)/VALLEY FiLM FESTiVAL
www.valleyfilmfest.com
Festival Month: Late October
Genres: Animation, Documentary,
Features, Independent, International,
Narrative, Shorts

ABBAKUS FiLM FESTiVAL
www.abbakus.tv
Festival Month: Early September
Genres: Animation, Documentary,
Features, Independent, International,
Music-Related, Narrative, Shorts

**ACCÈS CiNÉMA AFRiCAiN
(AFRiCAN FiLM ACCESS)**
www.cinema-africain.org
Festival Month: Mid-April

**ACTiON/CUT SHORT FiLM
COMPETiTiON**
http://www.actioncut.com/
    shortfilmcompetition.html
Festival Month: September
Genres: Animation, Documentary,
Narrative, Shorts

**AFRiCAN DiASPORA
FiLM FESTiVAL**
www.nyadff.org
Festival Month: Last Friday of
November during the Thanksgiving
weekend and runs for seventeen days
Genres: Documentary, Ethnic African,
Ethnic Black, Features, Narrative,
Shorts

ALGONQUiN FiLM FESTiVAL
www.algonquinfest.org
Festival Month: Mid-May
Genres: Documentary, Features,
Narrative, Shorts, Student

**ALUCINE TORONTO LATiNO
FiLM & ViDEO FESTiVAL**
www.alucinefestival.com
Festival Month: November
Genres: Documentary, Ethnic Latin,
Experimental, Independent,
International, Narrative, Shorts

**AMERiCAN CONSERVATiON
FiLM FESTiVAL**
www.conservationfilm.org
Festival Month: November
Genres: Documentary, Education,
Environmental, Features, Independent,
Narrative, Shorts

**ANCHORAGE
iNTERNATiONAL
FiLM FESTiVAL**
www.anchoragefilmfestival.com
Festival Month: December
Genres: Animation, Documentary,
Features, Independent, International,
Shorts

ANNUAL KiDFiLM FESTiVAL
www.usafilmfestival.com
Festival Month: Early January
Genres: Children, Family, Features,
International, Shorts

**ANOTHER HOLE iN THE
HEAD SAN FRANCiSCO
HORROR FESTiVAL**
www.sfhorror.com
Festival Month: Late March
Genres: Fantasy/Science Fiction,
Features, Horror, Independent,
International, Psycho Thriller, Shorts,
Thriller

ANTARCTiC FiLM FESTiVAL
www.antarctic-filmfest.com
Festival Month: August
Genres: Documentary, Features,
Narrative

**ANTELOPE VALLEY
iNDEPENDENT FiLM FESTiVAL**
www.aviff.com
Festival Month: Mid-May
Genres: Animation, Documentary,
Experimental, Features, International,
Music Videos, Narrative, Shorts

**ARLENE GROCERY
PiCTURE SHOW**
www.arlene-grocery.com
Festival Month: Late April
Genres: Animation, Documentary,
Features, Independent, International,
Narrative, Shorts

**ARPA iNTERNATiONAL
FiLM FESTiVAL**
www.affma.org
Festival Month: Mid-October
Genres: Documentary, Features,
Independent, International, Shorts

ART iN MOTiON
www.usc.edu/aim
Festival Month: March-June
Genres: Animation, Experimental,
Independent, Shorts, Student, Web
Projects

ARTiViST FiLM FESTiVAL
www.artivistfilmfestival.org
Festival Month: Late April
Genres: Animal Rights, Documentary, Education, Environmental, Features, Human Rights, Independent, International, Narrative, Shorts

ARTWALLAH FESTiVAL
www.artwallah.org
Festival Month: June
Genres: Documentary, Ethnic Asian, Features, First-Time Independent Filmmakers, International, Multimedia, Narrative, Shorts

ASBURY SHORT FiLM SHOW OF NEW YORK
www.asburyshortsnyc.com
Festival Month: November
Genres: 16mm, 35mm, Animation, Documentary, Experimental, Independent, International, Narrative, Shorts

ASHEVILLE FiLM FESTiVAL
www.ashevillefilmfestival.com
Festival Month: Early November
Genres: Documentary, Features, Narrative, Shorts, Student

ASHLAND iNDEPENDENT FiLM FESTiVAL
www.ashlandfilm.com
Festival Month: Early April
Genres: American, Documentary, Features, First-Time Independent Filmmakers, Independent, Narrative, Shorts, Student

ASiAN AMERiCAN iNTERNATiONAL FiLM FESTiVAL
www.asiancinevision.org
Festival Month: Mid-July
Genres: American, Animation, Documentary, Ethnic Asian, Experimental, Features, International, Music Video, Narrative, Shorts

ASiAN FiLM FESTiVAL OF DALLAS
www.affd.org
Festival Month: Early June
Genres: Animation, Documentary, Experimental, Features, Narrative, Shorts

ASiAN PACiFiC AMERiCAN FiLM FESTiVAL
www.apafilm.org
Festival Month: October
Genres: American, Documentary, Ethnic Asian, Features, Narrative, Shorts

ASPEN FiLMFEST
www.aspenfilm.org
Festival Month: Late September-October
Genres: Documentary, Features, Independent, International, Narrative

ATHENS iNTERNATiONAL FiLM & ViDEO FESTiVAL
www.athensfest.org
Festival Month: Late April
Genres: Animation, Documentary, Experimental, Features, International, Narrative, Shorts

ATLANTiC CiTY FiLM FESTiVAL
www.atlanticcityfilmfestival.com
Festival Month: Mid-October
Genres: Documentary, Features, Independent, International, Narrative, Shorts

ATLANTiC FiLM FESTiVAL
www.atlanticfilm.com
Festival Month: Mid-September
Genres: Animation, Documentary, Experimental, Features, Independent, International, Narrative, Shorts

AUSTiN'S GAY AND LESBiAN FiLM FESTiVAL
www.agliff.org
Festival Month: Late August-September
Genres: Documentary, Features, Gay Lesbian, Shorts

BACK ALLEY FiLM FESTiVAL
www.backalleyfilmfestival.com
Festival Month: Mid-November
Genres: Animation, Comedy, Documentary, Independent, International, Multimedia, Shorts

BACK EAST PiCTURE SHOW
www.backeastpictureshow.org
Festival Month: April
Genres: Animation, Documentary, Features, Independent, International, Narrative, Shorts

BAHAMAS ONE WORLD FiLM FESTiVAL
www.bahamasfilmfestival.com
Festival Month: Mid-November
Genres: Documentary, Features, Independent, International, Music Videos, Shorts, Student

BANFF MOUNTAiN FiLM FESTiVAL
www.banffmountainfestivals.ca
Festival Month: Late October-November
Genres: Documentary, Environmental, Features, International, Mountain Sports, Narrative

BANGKOK FiLM MARKET (BFM)
www.bangkokfilm.org/festival/film-market.aspx
Festival Month: Late January
Genres: Documentary, Ethnic Asian, Features, Independent, International, Markets, Narrative

BARE BONES iNTERNATiONAL FiLM FESTiVAL
www.barebonesfilmfestival.com
Festival Month: Mid-April, Mid-October
Genres: Animation, Comedy, Documentary, Experimental, Fantasy/Science Fiction, Independent, International, Music Videos, Narrative, Shorts, Student, Thriller, Works in progress

BAYTOWNE FiLM FESTiVAL
www.baytownefilmfestival.com
Festival Month: Late September
Genres: Animation, Documentary, Independent, International, Narrative, Shorts

BEARDED CHiLD FiLM FESTiVAL
www.beardedchild.com
Festival Month: Early August
Genres: Avant Garde, Experimental, Independent, Multimedia, Music Videos, Performance, Underground, Weird

BERKELEY ViDEO AND FiLM FESTiVAL
www.eastbaymedia.citysearch.com
Festival Month: November
Genres: Animation, Documentary, Education, Experimental, Features, Independent, Music Videos, PSA (Public Service Announcement), Shorts, Student, Video

BERLiN AND BEYOND
www.goethe.de/sanfrancisco
Festival Month: January
Genres: Documentary, European, Features, Independent, International, Narrative, Shorts

BiCYCLE FiLM FESTiVAL
www.bicyclefilmfestival.com
Festival Month: May
Genres: BMX, Cycling, Documentary, Experimental, Features, Independent, Narrative, Shorts

BiG MiNi DV FESTiVAL
www.bigminidv.com
Festival Month: Early November
Genres: Digital, Documentary, Experimental, Features, Narrative, Shorts

BiJOUFLiX
www.bijouflix.com
Festival Month: Ongoing
Genres: All, Online Festival

**BiLLYBURG SHORT
FiLM FESTiVAL**
www.rabbitinaturtleshell.com
Festival Month: Late May
Genres: All Categories - Shorts,
Student

**BiRMiNGHAM
iNTERNATiONAL
EDUCATiONAL FiLM
FESTiVAL STUDENT ViDEO
EXPO**
www.bham.net/bieff
Festival Month: May
Genres: Education, Independent,
Shorts, Student

BLACK BEAR FiLM FESTiVAL
www.blackbearfilm.com
Festival Month: Mid-October
Genres: Animation, Documentary,
Features, Independent, International,
Narrative, Shorts

BLACK EARTH FiLM FESTiVAL
www.blackearthfilmfestival.org
Festival Month: Early October
Genres: Animation, Comedy, Digital
Animation, Documentary, Drama,
Experimental, Fantasy/Science Fiction,
Features, Horror, Independent,
International, Narrative, Shorts

BLACK POiNT FiLM FESTiVAL
www.blackpointfilmfestival.com
Festival Month: Late April
Genres: Animation, Documentary,
Experimental, Features, Independent,
International, Narrative, Shorts

BLACK SOiL FiLM FESTiVAL
www.blacksoil.com
Festival Month: Late November
Genres: Animation, Documentary,
Features, Hip-Hop Related, Narrative,
Shorts

**BLOODCHALKER
iNTERNATiONAL HORROR
FiLM FESTiVAL**
www.bloodchalker.com
Festival Month: December
Genres: Features, Horror,
Independent, Shorts

**BOSTON FANTASTiC
FiLM FESTiVAL**
www.brattlefilm.org
Festival Month: Mid-October
Genres: Fantasy/Science Fiction,
Features, Horror, Independent,
International, Narrative, Shorts,
Thriller

**BOSTON iRiSH
FiLM FESTiVAL**
www.irishfilmfestival.com
Festival Month: October
Genres: Documentary, Ethnic Other,
Features, Narrative, Shorts

**BOSTON JEWiSH
FiLM FESTiVAL**
www.bjff.org
Festival Month: Early November
Genres: Animation, Documentary,
Ethnic Jewish, Experimental, Features,
Narrative, Shorts

**BRAZiLiAN FiLM FESTiVAL
OF MiAMi**
www.brazilianfilmfestival.com
Festival Month: June
Genres: 35mm, Documentary, Ethnic
Other, Features, Narrative, Shorts

**BRONX iNDEPENDENT
FiLM FESTiVAL**
www.bronxstage.com
Festival Month: Mid-June
Genres: Animation, Documentary,
Experimental, Features, Independent,
International, Narrative, Shorts

**BROOKLYN ARTS COUNCIL
FiLM AND ViDEO FESTiVAL**
www.brooklynartscouncil.org
Festival Month: March
Genres: Documentary, Experimental,
Features, Narrative, Shorts, Student

**BROOKLYN iNTERNATiONAL
FiLM FESTiVAL**
www.brooklynfilmfestival.org
Festival Month: Early June
Genres: Documentary, Experimental,
Features, Independent, Narrative,
Shorts

**CALiFORNiA iNDEPENDENT
FiLM FESTiVAL**
www.caindiefest.com
Festival Month: Early November
Genres: Documentary, Features,
Independent, Narrative, Shorts,
Student

**CANADiAN FiLM CENTRE'S
WORLDWiDE SHORT FiLM
FESTiVAL**
www.worldwideshortfilmfest.com
Festival Month: Mid-May
Genres: Animation, Digital Animation,
Documentary, Experimental,
International, Narrative, Shorts

**CANADiAN iNTERNATiONAL
ANNUAL FiLM FESTiVAL**
www.ciaff.org
Genres: Canadian, Documentary,
Experimental, First-Time Independent
Filmmakers, Independent,
International, Music Videos, Shorts,
Student

BEST DIGITAL FILM FESTIVALS

Backup Festival New Media in Film
Big Mini DV Festival
Cinequest Film Festival
DigiFest SouthWest Filmmaking Festival
DIGit Exposition
Digital Independent Film Festival
Digital Talkies Festival
Independent Exposure
International Festival of Cinema and Technology
Machinima Film Festival
New York Midnight Movie Making Madness
ResFest Digital Film Festival
Six Minute Cinema Digital Filmmaking Festival
THAW Video, Film, and Digital Media Festival
Vancouver International Digital Festival
Westcliffe Digital Film Festival

CAPE MAY NEW JERSEY STATE FILM FESTIVAL
www.njstatefilmfestival.com
Festival Month: Mid-November
Genres: Animation, Documentary, Features, Shorts

CAROLINA FILM AND VIDEO FESTIVAL
www.carolinafilmandvideofestival.org
Festival Month: Mid-February
Genres: Independent, Student

CEDAR RAPIDS INDEPENDENT FILM FESTIVAL
www.crifilms.com/festival.html
Festival Month: April
Genres: Animation, Documentary, Experimental, Features, Independent, International, Shorts, Student

CENTRAL JERSEY STUDENT FILM FESTIVAL
www.centraljerseyfilmfestival.com
Festival Month: Mid-May
Genres: Animation, Documentary, Narrative, Shorts, Student

CENTRAL STANDARD FILM FESTIVAL
www.ifpmsp.org/
centralstandard2003.htm
Festival Month: Mid-October
Genres: American, Documentary, Features, Independent, Narrative, Shorts

CENTURY CITY FILM FESTIVAL
www.centurycityfilmfestival.com
Festival Month: Late October
Genres: Animation, Avant Garde, Digital, Documentary, Experimental, Fantasy/Science Fiction, Features, Horror, Independent, International, Narrative, Shorts, Silent, Student

CHAMIZAL INDEPENDENT FILM FESTIVAL
www.chamizalfilmfestival.org
Festival Month: Late July-August
Genres: Documentary, Ethnic Latin, Features, Independent, International, Multi-Cultural, Narrative, Shorts

CHANNEL ISLANDS INDIE FILM FESTIVAL
www.channelislandsfilmfestival.com
Festival Month: September
Genres: Documentary, Features, Independent, International, Narrative

CHARLESTON FICTION & DOCUMENTARY FILM FESTIVAL
www.mamut.com/homepages/
United_States/2/9/usafestivals/
subdet37.htm
Festival Month: September
Genres: Documentary, Features, Independent, International, Narrative

CHATTAHOOCHEE FILM AND VIDEO COMPETITION
www.columbusfilmsociety.com/
festival.htm
Festival Month: September
Genres: All Categories - Shorts

CHICAGO ASIAN AMERICAN FILM FESTIVAL
www.faaim.org
Festival Month: April
Genres: Documentary, Ethnic Asian, Experimental, Features, Narrative, Shorts

CHICAGO INTERNATIONAL CHILDREN'S FILM FESTIVAL
www.cicff.org
Festival Month: Late October
Genres: Animation, Children, Education, Features, International, Narrative, Shorts

CHICAGO LATINO FILM FESTIVAL
www.latinoculturalcenter.com
Festival Month: Late April
Genres: Animation, Digital, Digital Animation, Documentary, Ethnic Asian, Ethnic Black, Ethnic Jewish, Ethnic Latin, Ethnic Other, Ethnic Spanish, Experimental, First-Time Independent Filmmakers, Gay Lesbian, Independent, International, Multimedia, Short, Video, Weird, Women

CHICAGO LESBIAN AND GAY INTERNATIONAL FILM FESTIVAL
www.chicagofilmmakers.org/
reeling2003/index.html
Festival Month: November
Genres: Documentary, Features, Gay Lesbian, Narrative, Shorts

CHLOTRUDIS AWARDS SHORT FILM FESTIVAL
www.chlotrudis.org
Festival Month: February
Genres: Documentary, Independent, International, Narrative, Shorts

CHRISTIAN WYSIWYG FILM FESTIVAL
www.wysiwygusa.com
Festival Month: Mid-October
Genres: Animation, Children, Documentary, Family, Features, Independent, International, Narrative, Performance, Shorts

CINE ACCIÓN ¡CINE LATINO!
www.cineaccion.com
Festival Month: Mid-September
Genres: Animation, Documentary, Ethnic Latin, Experimental, Features, Shorts

CINE GOLDEN EAGLE COMPETITION
www.cine.org
Festival Month: April
Genres: Animation, Children, Comedy, Commercials, Documentary, Environmental, Features, International, Narrative, PSA (Public Service Announcement), Shorts, Student

CINE LAS AMERICAS INTERNATIONAL FILM FESTIVAL OF THE AMERICAS
www.cinelasamericas.org
Festival Month: April
Genres: Animation, Documentary, Ethnic Latin, Ethnic Other, Experimental, Features, International, Narrative, Shorts

CINEKINK NYC
www.cinekink.com
Festival Month: Early October
Genres: Alternative Sexuality, Documentary, Experimental, Features, Independent, International, Narrative, Shorts, Underground

CINEMA PARADISE FILM FESTIVAL
www.cinemaparadise.org
Festival Month: Late September
Genres: Animation, Documentary, Experimental, Features, International, Narrative, Shorts

CINEMAASIA AUSTIN ASIAN FILM FESTIVAL
www.cinemaasiaaustin.org
Festival Month: Mid-April
Genres: Documentary, Ethnic Asian, Features, Independent, International, Narrative, Shorts, Student

CINEMACABRE HORROR AND SCI-FI FILM FESTIVAL
www.cine-macabre.com
Festival Month: Early October
Genres: Fantasy/Science Fiction, Features, Horror, Independent, International, Shorts, Thriller

**CINEMANIA FRENCH
FILM FESTIVAL**
www.cinemaniafilmfestival.com
Festival Month: November
Genres: Documentary, European,
Features, French, International,
Narrative

**CINEMAYAAT ARAB
FILM FESTIVAL**
www.aff.org
Festival Month: September-October
Genres: Documentary, Ethnic Other,
Features, International, Narrative,
Shorts

**CINEME CHICAGO
INTERNATIONAL ANIMATION
FILM FESTIVAL**
www.cineme.org
Festival Month: Late September
Genres: Animation, Digital,
Experimental, Features, Independent,
Multimedia, Shorts, Student,
Television

**CINEMUERTE
INTERNATIONAL FANTASTIC
FILM FESTIVAL**
www.cinemuerte.com
Festival Month: Early July
Genres: Fantasy/Science Fiction,
Features, Horror, International,
Narrative, Shorts

**CINERAMA FILM FESTIVAL
AT THE UNIVERSITY OF
FLORIDA**
grove.ufl.edu/~fuf
Festival Month: April
Genres: Animation, Documentary,
Experimental, Features, Independent,
International, Narrative, Shorts,
Underground

**CINESOL LATINO
FILM FESTIVAL**
www.cinesol.com
Festival Month: June-July
Genres: Documentary, Ethnic Latin,
Features, Narrative, Shorts, Touring

**CITY OF LIGHTS, CITY OF
ANGELS FRENCH FILM
FESTIVAL**
www.colcoa.com
Festival Month: Late March-April
Genres: Animation, Documentary,
Features, French, Independent,
International, Narrative, Shorts

COACHELLA FILM FESTIVAL
www.coachellafilmfestival.com
Festival Month: Early May
Genres: Documentary, Independent,
International, Music Videos, Narrative,
Rock and Roll, Shorts

**COLUMBUS INTERNATIONAL
FILM AND VIDEO FESTIVAL
(CHRIS AWARDS)**
www.chrisawards.org
Festival Month: October
Genres: Animation, Documentary,
Experimental, Features, Independent,
International, Narrative, Shorts,
Student

**CONEY ISLAND
FILM FESTIVAL**
www.indiefilmpage.com
Festival Month: Early October
Genres: Animation, Digital,
Documentary, Experimental, Features,
Independent, International,
Multimedia, Narrative, Shorts

**CONNECTICUT GAY &
LESBIAN FILM FESTIVAL**
www.ctglff.org
Festival Month: Early June
Genres: Features, Gay Lesbian,
Independent, International, Shorts

**COUNCIL ON FOUNDATIONS
FILM & VIDEO FESTIVAL**
www.fundfilm.org
Festival Month: Mid-April
Genres: Animation, Documentary,
Experimental, Features, Independent,
International, Narrative, Shorts

**CRESTED BUTTE REEL FEST
SHORT FILM FESTIVAL**
www.crestedbuttereelfest.com
Festival Month: Mid-August
Genres: Comedy, Drama, Narrative,
Shorts, Student

**CU 2 VIDEO AND
FILM FESTIVAL**
www.cu2vff.org
Festival Month: May
Genres: Animation, Documentary,
Experimental, Features, Independent,
International, Narrative, PSA (Public
Service Announcement), Shorts,
Student

**CUT AND PASTE
SKATEBOARDING ART &
FILM FESTIVAL**
www.capff.org
Festival Month: May
Genres: Animation, Digital,
Documentary, Experimental, Features,
Independent, Shorts, Skateboarding

**DA VINCI FILM AND VIDEO
FESTIVAL**
www.davinci-days.org
Festival Month: July
Genres: Animation, Documentary,
Independent, International, Music
Videos, Short, Student, Video

DAM SHORT FILM FESTIVAL
www.damshortfilm.org
Festival Month: Early February
Genres: Animation, Digital,
Documentary, Independent,
International, Narrative, Shorts

DAMAH FILM FESTIVAL
www.damah.com
Festival Month: Late October
Genres: Dance, Documentary,
Experimental, Independent,
International, Shorts, Spiritual

**DANCE ON CAMERA
FESTIVAL**
www.dancefilmsassn.org
Festival Month: June on, Touring
Genres: Animation, Dance, Digital,
Documentary, Experimental, Features,
Independent, International,
Multimedia, Narrative, Performance,
Shorts, Touring

**DAWSON CITY
INTERNATIONAL SHORT
FILM FESTIVAL**
www.kiac.org
Festival Month: Mid-April
Genres: All Categories - Shorts

**DC UNDERGROUND
FILM FESTIVAL**
www.dcuff.org
Festival Month: Late May
Genres: Documentary, Experimental,
Features, Government, Human Rights,
Independent, International, Multi-
Cultural, Narrative, Shorts

REWARD THE VOLUNTEERS
Volunteers get paid nothing. So why not help them, and
yourself, by rewarding them with a t-shirt or button
or promo item? The best part is, festival volunteers
will wear your t-shirt or button or hat, which
gives you extra free promotion.

DELTA FILM FESTIVAL
www.visitmanteca.org/filmfest/
home.htm
Festival Month: November
Genres: Digital, Documentary,
Features, Independent, International,
Narrative, Shorts

DENVER JAZZ ON FILM FESTIVAL
www.jazzfilmfestival.org
Festival Month: February
Genres: Documentary, Experimental,
Features, Independent, International,
Jazz, Music Videos, Narrative,
Performance, Shorts

DENVER PAN AFRICAN FILM & ARTS FESTIVAL
www.panafricanarts.org
Festival Month: April-May
Genres: Animation, Documentary,
Ethnic Black, Features, Independent,
International, Narrative, Shorts,
Student

DETROIT INTERNATIONAL HORROR FILM FESTIVAL
www.exophagy.com/exofest/exofest4/
index.html
Festival Month: Late October-
November
Genres: Animation, Experimental,
Fantasy/Science Fiction, Features,
Horror, Independent, International,
Psycho Thriller, Shorts, Thriller

DIGIFEST SOUTHWEST FILMMAKING FESTIVAL
www.digifestsouthwest.com
Festival Month: Mid-June
Genres: Digital, Independent,
International, Shorts

DIGIT EXPOSITION
www.artsalliancesite.org
Festival Month: Late April
Genres: Animation, Digital,
Documentary, Experimental, Features,
Independent, Narrative, Shorts

DIGITAL INDEPENDENT FILM FESTIVAL
diffonline.netfirms.com
Festival Month: Early May
Genres: Animation, Digital,
Documentary, Features, Independent,
International, Narrative, Shorts

DIONYSUS FILM FESTIVAL
www.dionysusfilmfestival.com
Festival Month: Late September
Genres: All Categories - Shorts,
Music Videos, PSA (Public Service
Announcement)

DIRECTOR'S VIEW FILM FESTIVAL
www.thedirectorsview.com
Festival Month: Mid-February
Genres: Documentary, Experimental,
Features, Independent, International,
Narrative, Shorts

DIVERSITY MARKET WORLDWIDE/ONLINE FILM FESTIVAL
www.onevibe.biz
Festival Month: Early March
Genres: Documentary, Episodic
Television/Television Pilots, Features,
Independent, International, Markets,
Narrative, Online Festival, Shorts,
Works in progress

DON'T KNOCK THE ROCK MUSIC AND FILM FESTIVAL
www.dontknocktherock.com
Festival Month: Mid-September
Genres: Documentary, Features,
Music Videos, Narrative, Performance,
Shorts

DOVER FILM FESTIVAL
www.doverfilmfestival.org
Festival Month: May
Genres: Animation, Documentary,
Education, Features, Independent,
International, Narrative, Shorts

DOWNSTREAM INTERNATIONAL FILM FESTIVAL
www.downstreamfest.com
Festival Month: September
Genres: Animation, Documentary,
Experimental, Features, Independent,
International, Narrative, Shorts,
Women

DRUG WAR FILM FESTIVAL
www.911media.org
Festival Month: Mid-March
Genres: Documentary, Drug-Related,
Features, Government, Human Rights,
Independent, International

EAST LANSING CHILDREN'S FILM FESTIVAL
www.elcff.com
Festival Month: Late February
Genres: Children, Education,
International, Shorts, Student

EAST LANSING FILM FESTIVAL
www.elff.com
Festival Month: March
Genres: Documentary, Features,
Independent, International, Narrative,
Shorts, Student

EAT MY SHORTS!
hahaha.com
Festival Month: Mid-July
Genres: All Categories - Shorts

ECLIPSE FILM FESTIVAL
www.eclipsefilmfest.com
Festival Month: Mid-November
Genres: Documentary, Features,
Independent, International, Narrative,
Shorts

EMPIRE FILM FESTIVAL
www.empirefilm.com
Festival Month: Mid-November
Genres: Animation, Documentary,
Features, Narrative, Shorts

ENVIRONMENTAL FILM FESTIVAL IN THE NATION'S CAPITAL
www.dcenvironmentalfilmfest.org
Festival Month: Late March
Genres: Animation, Documentary,
Education, Environmental, Features,
International, Mountain Sports,
Narrative, Shorts

ESTROFEST
www.estrofestfilms.com
Festival Month: Late March
Genres: Animation, Documentary,
Music-Related, Narrative,
Performance, Shorts, Women

EXPLORERS CLUB DOCUMENTARY FILM FESTIVAL
www.explorers.org
Festival Month: Late January
Genres: Documentary, Environmental,
Features, Short, Shorts

FAIRYTALES INTERNATIONAL GAY & LESBIAN FILM FESTIVAL
fairytalesfilmfest.com
Festival Month: Early June
Genres: Animation, Canadian,
Features, Gay Lesbian, Independent,
International, Narrative, Shorts

FARGO FANTASTIC FILM FESTIVAL
www.valleycon.com
Festival Month: Late April, Late
October
Genres: Animation, Documentary,
Experimental, Fantasy/Science Fiction,
Features, Horror, Independent,
International, Narrative, Shorts,
Thriller

FARGO FILM FESTIVAL
www.fargofilmfestival.com
Festival Month: Early March
Genres: American, Animation,
Documentary, Ethnic Other,
Experimental, Features, Narrative,
Shorts, Student

**FEARLESS TALES
GENRE FEST**
www.fearlesstales.com
Festival Month: Mid-March
Genres: Fantasy/Science Fiction,
Features, Horror, Independent,
International, Narrative, Shorts

FESTIVAL COMEDIA
hahaha.com
Festival Month: Mid-July
Genres: Animation, Comedy, Features,
International, Narrative

**FESTIVAL FOR CINEMA OF
THE DEAF**
www.deafcinema.org
Festival Month: Late May-Winter
(Touring)
Genres: Animation, Deaf,
Documentary, Features, International,
Narrative, Shorts, Silent, Touring

**FILM EXPO TEXAS/FILM DV
AND SCREENPLAY
CONTESTS**
www.filmexpotexas.com
Festival Month: June
Genres: Animation, Documentary,
Features, Independent, International,
Narrative, Shorts

FILMCOLUMBIA
www.filmcolumbia.com
Festival Month: Late October
Genres: Canadian, Documentary,
Features, First-Time Independent
Filmmakers, Independent,
International, Narrative, Shorts,
Student

**FILMI TORONTO SOUTH
ASIAN FILM FESTIVAL**
www.filmi.org
Festival Month: Early August
Genres: Animation, Documentary,
Ethnic Asian, Features, International,
Narrative, Shorts

**FINGER LAKES
ENVIRONMENTAL FILM
FESTIVAL**
cinema.cornell.edu/fleff
Festival Month: Mid-October
Genres: Children, Documentary,
Environmental, Features, International,
Narrative, Shorts

**FIRST LOOK STUDENT
FILM FESTIVAL**
www.firstlookstudentfilmfestival.com
Festival Month: Mid-April
Genres: Animation, Documentary,
Experimental, Independent, Narrative,
Shorts, Student

**FIRST SUNDAYS SHORT
COMEDY FILM FESTIVAL**
www.firstsundays.com
Festival Month: Year-long
Genres: Animation, Comedy,
Independent, International, Shorts

FLEDGLING FILMS FESTIVAL
www.fledglingfilms.com/
ff_festival2.html
Festival Month: April
Genres: Animation, Children,
Documentary, Experimental, Features,
Narrative, PSA (Public Service
Announcement), Shorts, Student

**FLYING POPCORN!
FILM FESTIVAL**
www.kidfilmmakers.com/
flyingpopcorn.htm
Festival Month: Early August
Genres: Animation, Children,
Documentary, Features, Narrative,
Shorts, Student, Touring

**FOREST GROVE SHORT FILM
AND VIDEO FESTIVAL**
Festival Month: Early May
Genres: All Categories - Shorts

**FORT WORTH'S GAY &
LESBIAN INTERNATIONAL
FILM FESTIVAL**
www.qcinema.org
Festival Month: Mid-June
Genres: All, Gay Lesbian

FREEZE FRAME
www.freezeframeonline.org
Festival Month: Mid-March
Genres: Animation, Children,
Features, Independent, International,
Shorts, Student

FROZEN DEAD GUY DAYS
www.nederlandchamber.org
Festival Month: Late March
Genres: Documentary, Shorts, Weird

**FT. LAUDERDALE
UNDERGROUND FILM
FESTIVAL**
www.fluff2004.com
Festival Month: Late October
Genres: Animation, Documentary,
Features, Independent, International,
Narrative, Shorts, Underground

**FULL FRAME DOCUMENTARY
FILM FESTIVAL**
www.fullframefest.org
Festival Month: Early April
Genres: Documentary, Features,
International, Shorts

FUNNY FILM FESTIVAL
funnyfilmfestival.com
Festival Month: October
Genres: Animation, Comedy,
Documentary, Features, Independent,
International, Narrative, Shorts,
Student

FUSION FILM FESTIVAL
fusionfilmfestival.com
Festival Month: Early March
Genres: Documentary, Features,
Independent, International, Narrative,
Shorts, Women

BEST DOCUMENTARY FILM FESTIVALS
DocFest - New York International Documentary Festival
Doubletake Documentary Film Festival
Explorers Club Documentary Film Festival
Hot Docs Canadian International Documentary Festival
Hot Springs Documentary Film Festival
International Leipzig Festival For Documentary and
    Animated Film
Message to Man International Documentary, Short and
    Animated Films Festival
San Francisco International Film Festival
Seattle International Film Festival
Sheffield International Documentary Festival
Yamagata International Documentary Film Festival

GADABOUT TRAVELiNG FiLM FESTiVAL
www.gadaboutfilmfest.com
Festival Month: June-August
Genres: All Categories - Shorts, Animation, Documentary, Features, First-Time Independent Filmmakers, Independent, International, Student, Touring

GALVESTON iSLAND iNTERNATiONAL FiLM FESTiVAL
www.ancestralfilms.org
Festival Month: Late October-November
Genres: Animation, Children, Documentary, Experimental, Family, Features, Independent, International, Narrative, Shorts, Student

GAMMA iNDiEFEST
www.gammaindiefest.com/gammafilms/indiefest03/indiefest03.html
Festival Month: Early November
Genres: American, Animation, Documentary, Experimental, Features, Independent, International, Music Video, Narrative, Shorts, Spiritual, Student

GARDEN STATE FiLM FESTiVAL
www.gsff.org
Festival Month: Late March
Genres: Animation, Commercials, Documentary, Education, Experimental, Features, Independent, International, Music Videos, Narrative, PSA (Public Service Announcement), Shorts, Student

GEORGE LiNDSEY UNA FiLM FESTiVAL
www.lindseyfilmfest.com
Festival Month: Mid-April
Genres: Animation, Children, Documentary, Features, Music Videos, Narrative, Shorts, Student

GEORGETOWN iNDY FiLM FESTiVAL
www.georgetownfilmfest.com
Festival Month: Mid-September
Genres: Documentary, Features, Independent, International, Narrative, Shorts, Student

GLADYS CRANE MOUNTAiN PLAiNS FiLM FESTiVAL
www.uwyo.edu/th&d/film/uwfilmfestival.html
Festival Month: Mid-December
Genres: Animation, Documentary, Experimental, Features, Narrative, Shorts

GLOBAL ART FiLM FESTiVAL EXPERiENCE & REPERTORY OF SACRAMENTO
www.gaffers.org
Festival Month: Mid-June
Genres: Animation, Digital, Documentary, Features, International, Multi-Cultural, Music Videos, Narrative, Shorts, Student, World

GLOBAL PEACE FiLM FESTiVAL
www.peacefilmfest.org
Festival Month: Mid-December
Genres: Documentary, Environmental, Features, Human Rights, Independent, International, Multi-Cultural, Narrative, Peace, Shorts

GLOBAL ViSiONS FiLM FESTiVAL
www.globalvisionsfestival.com
Festival Month: Early November
Genres: Documentary, Education, Features, International, Shorts

GLORiA iNTERNATiONAL FiLM FESTiVAL
www.gloriafilmfest.org
Festival Month: October
Genres: Animation, Children, Documentary, Features, International, Narrative, Shorts, Student

GOLDEN GATE FiCTiON & DOCUMENTARY FESTiVAL
www.mamut.com/homepages/United_States/2/9/usafestivals/subdet42.htm
Festival Month: Late November
Genres: Documentary, Features, Independent, International, Narrative, Shorts, Student

GOLDEN GATE FiLM FESTiVAL
www.goldengatefilmfestival.org
Festival Month: April
Genres: Animation, Documentary, Features, Independent, International, Narrative, Shorts

GREAT LAKE SUPERiOR iNTERNATiONAL FiLM FESTiVAL
personal.myvine.com/~baje/ava/
Festival Month: Mid-July
Genres: All Categories - Shorts, First-Time Independent Filmmakers, Independent, International, Student

GREAT LAKES iNDEPENDENT FiLM FESTiVAL
www.greatlakesfilmfest.com
Festival Month: Mid-September
Genres: Animation, Digital, Documentary, Experimental, Features, First-Time Independent Filmmakers, Independent, International, Narrative, Shorts, Student

GREENWiCH FiLM FESTiVAL
www.greenwichfilmfestival.org
Festival Month: Late September
Genres: Documentary, Features, Independent, International, Narrative, Shorts

GULF COAST FiLM AND ViDEO FESTiVAL
www.gulfcoastfilmfest.com
Festival Month: Mid-September
Genres: Animation, Documentary, Experimental, Features, Independent, International, Narrative, Shorts

HARDACRE FiLM FESTiVAL
www.hardacrefilmfestival.com
Festival Month: Early August
Genres: Animation, Documentary, Experimental, Features, Independent, International, Narrative, Shorts, Student

HAVANA FiLM FESTiVAL iN NEW YORK
www.hffny.com
Festival Month: April
Genres: Dance, Documentary, Ethnic Latin, Features, International, Narrative, Shorts

---

SAVE DOLLARS FOR MARKETING EXPENSES
Have a poster along with other unique promo items ready to go. Be prepared to deliver a print in time for the film festival. And most importantly, plan to have funds available in order to pay for expenses at the festival. Budget for all of these costs and be ready when you get "the call."

HAWAii'S SURF DRiVE-iN FiLM FESTiVAL
www.surfdrive-in.com
Festival Month: November
Genres: Animation, Documentary, Experimental, Features, Independent, International, Narrative, Ocean, Shorts, Surfing

HAZEL WOLF ENViRONMENTAL FiLM FESTiVAL
www.hazelfilm.org
Festival Month: March
Genres: Documentary, Education, Environmental, Features, Independent, International, Narrative, Shorts, Student

HDFEST FiLM FESTiVAL WORLD TOUR
www.hdfest.com
Festival Month: Late May-December
Genres: Animation, Commercials, Digital, Documentary, Experimental, Features, Multimedia, Music Videos, Narrative, Shorts, Television, Touring

HEARD MUSEUM iNDiGENOUS FiLM FESTIVAL
www.heard.org/filmfest.html
Festival Month: June
Genres: American, Animation, Documentary, Experimental, Family, Features, Independent, Music Videos, Narrative, Shorts, Student

HERLAND FEMiNiST FiLM AND ViDEO FESTiVAL
www.herlandfestival.com
Festival Month: Early May
Genres: Documentary, Ethnic Jewish, Ethnic Other, Experimental, Features, Gay Lesbian, Independent, International, Narrative, Shorts, Women

Hi MOM! FiLM FESTiVAL
www.himomfilmfestival.org
Festival Month: April
Genres: All Categories - Shorts, Animation, Multimedia

HiGH FALLS FiLM FESTiVAL
www.highfallsfilmfestival.com
Festival Month: Early November
Genres: Animation, Children, Independent, International, Narrative, Shorts, Women

HiP HOP FiLM FEST
www.hiphopfilmfest.com
Festival Month: Late February, Ongoing
Genres: Documentary, Features, Hip-Hop Related, Independent, International, Music Videos, Narrative, Shorts, Touring, Underground

HOLLYWOOD SCAREFEST
www.scarefestfilms.com
Festival Month: Late October
Genres: Experimental, Fantasy/Science Fiction, Horror, Shorts

HOLLYWOOD SPiRiTUAL FiLM AND ENTERTAiNMENT FESTiVAL
www.hsff.com
Festival Month: Late March-September
Genres: Animation, Documentary, Features, Independent, International, Narrative, Shorts, Spiritual

HOMETOWN ViDEO FESTiVAL
www.alliancecm.org
Festival Month: Early July
Genres: Commercials, Documentary, Education, Episodic Television/Television Pilots, International, Narrative, PSA (Public Service Announcement), Television

HONOLULU iNTERNATiONAL FiLM FESTiVAL
www.mamut.com/homepages/United_States/2/9/usafestivals/subdet21.htm
Festival Month: March
Genres: Documentary, Ethnic Other, Features, Independent, International, Narrative

HOPE AND DREAMS FiLM FESTiVAL
www.hopeanddreams.com
Festival Month: Early October
Genres: Animation, Documentary, Education, Environmental, Features, Narrative, Shorts

HOT SHOPS FiLM FESTiVAL
www.hotshopsartcenter.com/filmfest
Festival Month: Late July-August
Genres: Animation, Documentary, Features, First-Time Independent Filmmakers, Independent, Music Videos, Narrative, Silent, Student

HOT SHOTS HiGH SCHOOL FiLM AND AD FESTiVAL
www.hsfilmfest.com
Festival Month: Late May
Genres: Commercials, Ethnic Other, Shorts, Sports, Student

HOUSTON GAY AND LESBiAN FiLM FESTiVAL
www.hglff.org
Festival Month: September
Genres: Documentary, Features, Gay Lesbian, Independent, International, Narrative, Shorts

HOUSTON iNTERNATiONAL AiDS FiLM FESTiVAL
bayloraids.org/film
Festival Month: Late March-April
Genres: AIDS/HIV-related, Charity, Documentary, Features, Independent, International, Narrative, Shorts

iCED iN BLACK
www.icedinblack.ca
Festival Month: February
Genres: Documentary, Ethnic Black, Ethnic Other, Features, Narrative, Shorts, Touring

iEMMYS FESTiVAL
www.iemmys.tv
Festival Month: Mid-November
Genres: Children, Comedy, Documentary, Drama, Episodic Television/Television Pilots, International, News, Television

iMAGE FEST
www.imagefestshorts.com
Festival Month: Early August
Genres: All Categories - Shorts, First-Time Independent Filmmakers, Student

iMAGEOUT - THE ROCHESTER LESBiAN & GAY FiLM & ViDEO FESTiVAL
www.imageout.org
Festival Month: Early October
Genres: Documentary, Features, Gay Lesbian, Independent, International, Multi-Cultural, Narrative, Shorts

iMAGES DU NOUVEAU MONDE PANAMERiCAN FiLM FESTiVAL
www.festival-inm.com
Festival Month: Late March-April
Genres: Americas (North, South, and Latin America), Documentary, Education, Ethnic Other, Features, International, Multi-Cultural, Narrative, Shorts

iMAGiNENATiVE FiLM & MEDiA ARTS FESTiVAL
www.imaginenative.org
Festival Month: Late October
Genres: Digital, Experimental, Multimedia, Web Projects

iMPERiAL BEACH iNTERNATiONAL FiLM FESTiVAL
www.ibfilmfestival.com
Festival Month: EarlyOctober
Genres: Documentary, Features, First-Time Independent Filmmakers, Independent, International, Narrative, Shorts, Student

INDIAN FILM FESTIVAL OF LOS ANGELES
www.indianfilmfestival.org
Festival Month: Mid-April
Genres: Documentary, Ethnic Other, Features, International, Narrative, Shorts

INDIANAPOLIS LGBT FILM FESTIVAL
www.indylgbtfilm.com
Festival Month: Mid-September
Genres: Animation, Documentary, Experimental, Features, Features, Gay Lesbian, Narrative, Shorts

INDIE MEMPHIS FILM FESTIVAL
www.indiememphis.com
Festival Month: Late October
Genres: American, Documentary, Features, Independent, Narrative, Shorts

INDIE MUSIC VIDEO FESTIVAL
www.imvf.com
Festival Month: Mid-September
Genres: Independent, Music Videos

INFACT THEATRICAL DOCUMENTARY SHOWCASE
www.documentary.org
Festival Month: Late August
Genres: Documentary, Features, International, Shorts

INFLATABLE DUCK FILM FEST
www.inflatableduck.org
Festival Month: May
Genres: Animation, Documentary, Experimental, Fantasy/Science Fiction, Independent, International, Music Videos, Narrative, Shorts

INTERNATIONAL BLACK PANTHER FILM FESTIVAL
www.pantherfilmfest.com
Festival Month: Late July-August
Genres: Documentary, Ethnic Black, Ethnic Latin, Features, Human Rights, International, Narrative, Shorts

INTERNATIONAL BLACK WOMEN'S FILM FESTIVAL
ibwff.filmfestivals.net
Festival Month: February-June
Genres: Documentary, Ethnic Black, Ethnic Latin, Experimental, Features, Independent, International, International, Shorts, Women

INTERNATIONAL BUDDHIST FILM FESTIVAL
www.ibff.org
Festival Month: November
Genres: Animation, Children, Documentary, Ethnic Other, Experimental, Features, International, Narrative, Shorts, Spiritual

INTERNATIONAL FAMILY FILM FESTIVAL
www.iffilmfest.org
Festival Month: Late April
Genres: Animation, Children, Education, Family, Features, First-Time Independent Filmmakers, Independent, International, Shorts, Student

INTERNATIONAL FESTIVAL OF CINEMA AND TECHNOLOGY
www.ifct.org
Festival Month: August
Genres: Animation, Digital, Digital Animation, Documentary, Experimental, Features, First-Time Independent Filmmakers, Independent, International, Narrative, Shorts, Student

INTERNATIONAL STUDENT FILM FESTIVAL HOLLYWOOD
www.isffhollywood.org
Festival Month: Early November
Genres: Documentary, Features, Independent, International, Narrative, Shorts, Student

INTERNATIONAL STUDENT ORIGINAL FILM ART FESTIVAL
www.sofanet.org
Festival Month: January
Genres: Documentary, Features, Independent, International, Narrative, Shorts, Student

INTERNATIONAL SURREALIST FILM FESTIVAL
www.oniongod.com
Festival Month: Mid-April
Genres: Animation, Avant Garde, Documentary, Experimental, Features, Independent, International, Narrative, Shorts, Weird

INTERNATIONAL TEEN MOVIE FESTIVAL
www.hiltz2.com
Festival Month: August
Genres: Animation, Commercials, Documentary, Features, First-Time Independent Filmmakers, Independent, International, Music Videos, PSA (Public Service Announcement), Shorts, Teenager

IOWA CITY INTERNATIONAL DOCUMENTARY FESTIVAL
www.icdocs.org
Festival Month: April
Genres: Documentary, Features, International, Shorts

ISMF INTERNATIONAL STUDENT MEDIA FESTIVAL
www.aect.org/ISMF
Festival Month: Late October
Genres: Animation, Children, Commercials, Digital, Documentary, Education, Features, International, Multimedia, PSA (Public Service Announcement), Shorts, Sports, Student, Web Projects

IU SOUTH BEND INDEPENDENT VIDEO & FILMMAKERS FESTIVAL
www.iusb.edu/~ivff
Festival Month: Early April
Genres: Animation, Documentary, Independent, Narrative, Shorts, Student

IVY FILM FESTIVAL
www.ivyfilmfestival.com
Festival Month: Mid-April
Genres: Documentary, Features, First-Time Independent Filmmakers, Independent, International, Narrative, Shorts, Student

JACKSON HOLE FILM FESTIVAL
www.jhff.org
Festival Month: Late September
Genres: Animation, Children, Documentary, Features, Independent, International, Narrative, Shorts, Sports, Student

JACKSONVILLE FILM FESTIVAL
www.jacksonvillefilmfestival.com
Festival Month: Mid-May
Genres: Documentary, Experimental, Features, Independent, International, Narrative, Shorts

JAMERICAN FILM AND MUSIC FESTIVAL
www.jamericanfilmfest.com
Festival Month: Mid-November
Genres: Animation, Documentary, Experimental, Features, Music Videos, Shorts

JEWISH IMAGE AWARDS IN FILM AND TELEVISION
www.jewishculture.org
Festival Month: September
Genres: Documentary, Episodic Television/Television Pilots, Ethnic Jewish, Features, Narrative, Television

KALAMAZOO ANIMATION FESTIVAL INTERNATIONAL
www.kafi.kvcc.edu
Festival Month: Mid-May
Genres: Animation, Commercials, Digital Animation, Education, Independent, International, Student, Web Projects

KANSAS CITY FILMMAKERS JUBILEE
www.kcjubilee.org
Festival Month: Mid-April
Genres: Animation, Documentary, Experimental, Independent, International, Short

KANSAS CITY GAY & LESBIAN FILM FESTIVAL
www.kcgayfilmfest.org
Festival Month: Late June-July
Genres: Animation, Digital, Documentary, Experimental, Features, Gay Lesbian, Independent, International, Narrative, Short

KANSAS INTERNATIONAL FILM FESTIVAL
www.h2hfilmfest.org
Festival Month: Mid-September
Genres: Documentary, Features, Independent, International, Narrative

KERN FILM FESTIVAL
www.kernfilmfestival.com
Festival Month: Late October
Genres: Documentary, Features, First-Time Independent Filmmakers, Independent, International, Narrative, Works in progress

KEY WEST INDIEFEST
www.keywestindiefest.com
Festival Month: Mid-April (weekend after Easter annually)
Genres: Animation, Documentary, Features, Independent, International, Narrative, Shorts

KINGSTON CANADIAN FILM FESTIVAL
www.kingcanfilmfest.com
Festival Month: Late February
Genres: Animation, Canadian, Documentary, Features, Narrative, Shorts

L'CHAIM! JEWISH FILM FESTIVAL
www.lchaimjff.org
Festival Month: Late March
Genres: Animation, Documentary, Ethnic Jewish, Experimental, Features, International, Narrative, Shorts

LAKE ARROWHEAD FILM FESTIVAL
www.lakearrowheadfilmfest.com
Festival Month: September
Genres: Animation, Documentary, Features, Independent, International, Narrative, Shorts

LATIN USA INTERNATIONAL FILM FESTIVAL
www.latinusafilmfestival.com
Festival Month: October-November
Genres: Animation, Ethnic Latin, Features, International, Music Videos, Narrative, Shorts, Student

LATINO FILM FESTIVAL SAN FRANCISCO BAY AREA
www.latinofilmfestival.org
Festival Month: Mid-November
Genres: Documentary, Ethnic Latin, Features, Gay Lesbian, Narrative, Shorts, Women

LIGHT PLAYS TRICKS SHORT FILM FESTIVAL
www.lightplaystricks.com
Festival Month: Late May
Genres: Animation, Canadian, Digital, Digital Animation, Documentary, Independent, International, Multimedia, Narrative, Shorts, Web Projects, Weird

LONDON LESBIAN FILM FESTIVAL
www.llff.lweb.net
Festival Month: Early May
Genres: Documentary, Features, Gay Lesbian, Narrative, Shorts

LONG BEACH INTERNATIONAL FILM FESTIVAL
www.longbeachfilmfestival.com
Festival Month: Mid-October
Genres: Documentary, Features, Independent, International, Narrative, Shorts

LONG ISLAND GAY & LESBIAN FILM FESTIVAL
www.liglff.org
Festival Month: Mid-November
Genres: Documentary, Features, Gay Lesbian, Independent, International, Narrative, Shorts

LOS ANGELES ITALIAN FILM AWARDS (LAIFA)
www.italfilmfest.com
Festival Month: Late April
Genres: All, Documentary, Ethnic Other, Features, Narrative, Shorts

LUCKMAN U.S. LATINO FILM/VIDEO FESTIVAL-REEL RASQUACHE
www.luckmanfineartscomplex.org
Festival Month: Mid-April
Genres: American, Animation, Digital, Documentary, Ethnic Latin, Features, First-Time Independent Filmmakers, Independent, Shorts

LUNAFEST
www.lunabar.com/lunafest
Festival Month: September
Genres: Animation, Documentary, Features, Multi-Cultural, Narrative, Shorts, Touring, Women

MACHINIMA FILM FESTIVAL
www.machinima.org
Festival Month: Late October
Genres: Animation, Digital, Digital Animation, Features, Independent, International, Multimedia, Shorts, Video Games

MADE IN MIAMI FILM & VIDEO FESTIVAL
www.madeinmiami.org
Festival Month: Mid-January
Genres: Documentary, Features, Independent, International, Music Videos, Narrative, Shorts, Student, Television

MAGNOLiA iNDEPENDENT FiLM FESTiVAL
www.magfilmfest.com
Festival Month: Early February
Genres: Animation, Documentary, Experimental, Features, Independent, Narrative, Shorts, Student

MAiNE iNTERNATiONAL FiLM FESTiVAL
www.miff.org
Festival Month: Early July
Genres: American, Documentary, Features, Independent, International, Narrative

MAiNE JEWiSH FiLM FESTiVAL
www.mjff.org
Festival Month: Mid-March
Genres: Documentary, Ethnic Jewish, Features, Independent, International, Narrative, Shorts

MANHATTAN SHORT FiLM FESTiVAL
www.msfilmfest.com
Festival Month: Mid-September
Genres: All Categories - Shorts, International

MARiN COUNTY NATiONAL FESTiVAL OF SHORT FiLM AND ViDEO
marinfair.org/ex-film.htm
Festival Month: Early July
Genres: All Categories - Shorts, Digital, First-Time Independent Filmmakers, Independent, International, Student

MARYLAND FANTASTiQUE FiLM FEST
www.chesapeakearts.org/mfffindex.html
Festival Month: October-November
Genres: Animation, Documentary, Fantasy/Science Fiction, Features, First-Time Independent Filmmakers, Horror, Mystery, Shorts, Student, Teenager, Thriller

MAZATLAN iNTERNATiONAL FiLM FESTiVAL
www.mazatlanfilmfest.com
Festival Month: Early December
Genres: Animation, Documentary, Features, Independent, International, Narrative, Shorts

MCGUFFiN FiLM FESTiVAL
www.mcguffinfestival.com
Festival Month: Late February
Genres: Documentary, First-Time Independent Filmmakers, Independent, Mystery, Narrative, Shorts, Student, Thriller

MEMPHiS BLACK WRiTERS CONFERENCE & SOUTHERN FiLM FESTiVAL
lawrence.wayne.tripod.com/vipmemphis/id19.html
Festival Month: Late April
Genres: Documentary, Ethnic Black, Ethnic Other, Features, Independent, International, Narrative, Shorts

MEMPHiS iNTERNATiONAL FiLM FESTiVAL
www.memphisfilmforum.org
Festival Month: Late March
Genres: Animation, Documentary, Experimental, Features, Independent, International, Narrative, Shorts

MiAMi GAY AND LESBiAN FiLM FESTiVAL
www.miamigaylesbianfilm.com
Festival Month: Late April-May
Genres: Documentary, Experimental, Features, Gay Lesbian, Narrative, Shorts

MiAMi iNTERNATiONAL SHORT FiLM FESTiVAL
www.mamut.com/homepages/United_States/2/9/usafestivals/subdet5.htm
Festival Month: Late October
Genres: All Categories - Shorts, Online

MiAMi LATiN FiLM FESTiVAL
www.hispanicfilm.com
Festival Month: Mid-April
Genres: Documentary, Ethnic Latin, Features, International, Narrative, Shorts

MiCHiGAN iNDEPENDENT FiLM FESTiVAL
miff.lefthandfilms.net
Festival Month: October
Genres: Animation, Documentary, Features, Independent, Narrative, Shorts

MiDCOAST FiLM AND ARTS FESTiVAL
www.midcoast.org
Festival Month: Late October
Genres: Animation, Documentary, Features, Independent, International, Narrative, Shorts

MiLWAUKEE iNTERNATiONAL FiLM FESTiVAL
www.milwaukeefilmfest.org
Festival Month: Mid-October
Genres: Documentary, Features, Independent, International, Narrative, Shorts

MiNi-CiNEMA FiLM FESTiVAL
www.minicinema.tk
Festival Month: Seasonal, Check Website
Genres: Animation, Documentary, Experimental, First-Time Independent Filmmakers, Independent, Narrative, Shorts

MONTREAL iNTERNATiONAL FiLM MARKET
www.ffm-montreal.org/en_marc_index.html
Festival Month: Late August-September
Genres: Documentary, Features, Independent, International, Markets, Narrative, Television

MONTREAL JEWiSH STUDENT FiLM FESTiVAL
www.mjsff.com
Festival Month: May
Genres: Documentary, Ethnic Jewish, Experimental, Features, Independent, International, Narrative, Student

MOTOR CiTY iNTERNATiONAL FiLM FESTiVAL
www.motorcityiff.7h.com
Festival Month: August
Genres: Animation, Documentary, Ethnic Black, Experimental, Features, Independent, International, Music Video, Narrative, Shorts, Student

BEST FESTS FOR CELEBRITY SIGHTINGS

Sundance Film Festival
Cannes International Film Festival
Toronto International Film Festival
Seattle International Film Festival
Hollywood Film Festival
Berlin International Film Festival
Tribeca Film Festival
AFI Los Angeles International Film Festival

MOUNT SHASTA INTERNATIONAL FILM FESTIVAL
www.shastafilmfest.com
Festival Month: Early October
Genres: American, Animation, Documentary, Features, Independent, International, Narrative

MUSKEGON FILM FESTIVAL
www.muskegonfilmfestival.com
Festival Month: Early February
Genres: Features, Independent, International, Narrative, Shorts, Student

MYHELAN INDIE FILM FESTIVAL
www.myhelan.org/Pages/ffhome.html
Festival Month: Early March
Genres: Animation, Documentary, Features, First-Time Independent Filmmakers, Independent, Narrative, Shorts, Student, Teenager

NATIONAL STUDENT FILM AND VIDEO FESTIVAL
www.studentfilmfestival.ca
Festival Month: Mid-May
Genres: Animation, Canadian, Documentary, Experimental, Shorts, Student

NATPE CONFERENCE AND EXHIBITION
www.natpe.org
Festival Month: Mid-January
Genres: Markets, Television

NEW AMSTERDAM FILM FESTIVAL
www.newamsterdamfilmfestival.com
Festival Month: April
Genres: Animation, Documentary, Features, First-Time Independent Filmmakers, Independent, International, Narrative, Polish, Shorts, Student

NEW ENGLAND ANIMATION BASH
www.brattlefilm.org/neab
Festival Month: June
Genres: Animation, Digital Animation, Experimental, Independent, International, Narrative, Shorts, Student

NEW HAMPSHIRE FILM EXPO NHFX
www.nhfilmexpo.com
Festival Month: Early October
Genres: Animation, Documentary, Features, Independent, International, Narrative, Shorts, Student

NEW HAVEN UNDERGROUND FILM FESTIVAL
www.nhuff.com
Festival Month: Mid-May
Genres: Animation, Digital, Documentary, Experimental, Features, Music Videos, Narrative, Shorts, Underground

NEW JERSEY INTERNATIONAL FILM FESTIVAL
www.njfilmfest.com
Festival Month: June-July
Genres: Animation, Documentary, Experimental, Features, Independent, International, Music Videos, Narrative, Shorts, Student

NEW ORLEANS LESBIAN, GAY, BISEXUAL, TRANSGENDER FILM FESTIVAL
www.reelidentities.org
Festival Month: Late February
Genres: Animation, Documentary, Experimental, Features, Gay Lesbian, Independent, International, Narrative, Shorts

NEW ORLEANS MEDIA EXPERIENCE
www.neworleansmediaexperience.com
Festival Month: Late October-November
Genres: Digital, Experimental, Features, Independent, International, Multimedia, Music Videos, Narrative, Shorts

NEW VENUE
www.newvenue.com
Festival Month: Ongoing
Genres: Avant Garde, Experimental, Independent, Online, Short

NEW YORK CITY HORROR FILM FESTIVAL
www.nychorrorfest.com
Festival Month: Late October
Genres: Features, Horror, Independent, International, Shorts

NEW YORK DUSTY FILM FESTIVAL AND AWARDS
www.schoolofvisualarts.edu/04.Studio/Undergraduate/FilmVideo/dusty/default.html
Festival Month: Early May
Genres: Documentary, Features, Independent, Narrative, Shorts, Student

NEW YORK FESTIVALS INTERNATIONAL FILM & VIDEO AWARDS
www.newyorkfestivals.com
Festival Month: January
Genres: Documentary, Education, Features, Markets, Narrative, Shorts

NEW YORK INTERNATIONAL CHILDREN'S FILM FESTIVAL
www.gkids.com
Festival Month: Early March
Genres: Animation, Children, Family, Features, International, Narrative, Shorts

NEW YORK INTERNATIONAL DIGITAL FILM FESTIVAL
nydigifest.com
Festival Month: Early November
Genres: Animation, Digital, Documentary, Features, International, Narrative, Shorts

NEW YORK INTERNATIONAL LATINO FILM FESTIVAL
www.nylatinofilm.com
Festival Month: May-June
Genres: Documentary, Ethnic Latin, Experimental, Features, Narrative, Short, Student

NEW YORK LESBIAN & GAY FILM FESTIVAL
www.newfestival.org
Festival Month: Early June
Genres: Documentary, Features, Gay Lesbian, Independent, International, Narrative, Shorts

NEW YORK MIDNIGHT MOVIE MAKING MADNESS
www.nycmidnight.com
Festival Month: October
Genres: Digital, Independent, International, Shorts

NEW YORK SHORT FILM FESTIVAL
www.mamut.com/homepages/United_States/2/9/usafestivals/subdet27.htm
Festival Month: May
Genres: Online, Shorts

**NEW YORK TURKISH
FILM FESTIVAL**
www.moonandstarsproject.org
Festival Month: Mid-October
Genres: Documentary, Ethnic Other,
Features, Narrative, Shorts

**NEWPORT INTERNATIONAL
FILM FESTIVAL**
www.newportfilmfestival.com
Festival Month: Early June
Genres: Animation, Documentary,
Features, Independent, Independent,
International, Narrative, Short

NIAGARA INDIE FILMFEST
www.niagaraindiefilmfest.org
Festival Month: Late June
Genres: Animation, Canadian,
Documentary, Independent, Narrative,
Shorts, Student

**NICKEL INDEPENDENT FILM
AND VIDEO FESTIVAL**
www.nickelfestival.com
Festival Month: Late June
Genres: Documentary, Features,
Independent, International, Narrative,
Shorts

NIHILIST FILM FESTIVAL
nihilists.net/film.html
Festival Month: Early December
Genres: Avant Garde, Documentary,
Experimental, Features, Independent,
International, Narrative, Shorts,
Underground

NOISE POP FILM FESTIVAL
www.noisepop.com
Festival Month: Late February
Genres: Animation, Documentary,
Experimental, Features, Independent,
Music Videos, Music-Related, Shorts

**NORTH CAROLINA GAY &
LESBIAN FILM FESTIVAL**
www.carolinatheatre.org/ncglff
Festival Month: Early August
Genres: Documentary, Features, Gay
Lesbian, Independent, International,
Narrative, Shorts

**NORTHAMPTON
ENVIRONMENTAL
FILM FESTIVAL**
www.frugalgreen.com/neff.html
Festival Month: Late February
Genres: Documentary, Environmental,
Independent, International, Narrative,
Shorts

**NORTHAMPTON
INDEPENDENT FILM FESTIVAL**
www.niff.org
Festival Month: November
Genres: Animation, Documentary,
Experimental, Features, Gay Lesbian,
Independent, International, Narrative,
Shorts, Student

**NORTHWEST ASIAN
AMERICAN FILM FESTIVAL**
www.nwaaff.org
Festival Month: Late September-
October
Genres: Animation, Documentary,
Ethnic Asian, Features, Independent,
International, Narrative, Shorts

**OAKLAND INTERNATIONAL
FILM FESTIVAL**
www.oaklandfilmsociety.org
Festival Month: Mid-September
Genres: Animation, Documentary,
Experimental, Features, Independent,
International, Music Videos, Narrative,
Shorts

OCEAN CITY FILM FESTIVAL
www.oceancityfilmfestival.com
Festival Month: Early June
Genres: Animation, Documentary,
Features, First-Time Independent
Filmmakers, Independent, Music
Videos, Narrative, Shorts, Student

OJAI FILM FESTIVAL
www.ojaifilmfestival.com
Festival Month: Mid-October
Genres: Documentary, Features,
Independent, International, Narrative,
Shorts

**OLA KA HONUA FILM
FESTIVAL**
www.kahea.org
Festival Month: Early December
Genres: Documentary, Education,
Environmental, Features, Human
Rights, Independent, International,
Narrative, PSA (Public Service
Announcement), Shorts

OLYMPIA FILM FESTIVAL
www.olyfilm.org
Festival Month: Early November
Genres: Documentary, Features,
Independent, International, Multi-
Cultural, Narrative, Shorts

ONE IN TEN FILM FESTIVAL
www.clubs.psu.edu/up/psupride/
oneinten
Festival Month: Early April
Genres: Animation, Documentary,
Experimental, Gay Lesbian,
Independent, International, Narrative,
Shorts

ORINDA FILM FESTIVAL
www.orindafilmfestival.org
Festival Month: Late September
Genres: Documentary, Features,
Independent, International, Narrative,
Shorts, Student

**ORLANDO GAY & LESBIAN
FILM FESTIVAL**
www.gayorlando.com/goevents/films/
benefits.html
Festival Month: Late August
Genres: Documentary, Features, Gay
Lesbian, Independent, Shorts

**ORLANDO INTERNATIONAL
FILM FESTIVAL**
www.orlandofilmfestival.com
Festival Month: Early November
Genres: Animation, Commercials,
Documentary, Experimental, Features,
Narrative, Shorts, Student

**OTHER VENICE
FILM FESTIVAL**
www.veniceofilmfest.com
Festival Month: Late March
Genres: Animation, Documentary,
Features, Independent, International,
Narrative, Shorts, Underground

**OUT ON FILM ATLANTA GAY
AND LESBIAN FILM FESTIVAL**
www.outonfilm.com
Festival Month: Mid-November
Genres: Documentary, Features, Gay
Lesbian, Independent, International,
Narrative, Shorts

**OUT TAKES DALLAS ANNUAL
LESBIAN AND GAY FILM
FESTIVAL**
www.outtakesdallas.org
Festival Month: Mid-November
Genres: Documentary, Features, Gay
Lesbian, Narrative, Shorts

**OUTFEST SAN DIEGO GAY &
LESBIAN FILM FESTIVAL**
www.outfest.org/sdfest.frame.html
Festival Month: Late September
Genres: Documentary, Features, Gay
Lesbian, Narrative, Shorts

**OUTHOUSE FILM &
VIDEO FESTIVAL**
www.lsu.edu/student_organizations/
cinema
Festival Month: April
Genres: Documentary, Features,
Independent, Narrative, Shorts,
Student

OXFORD FILM FESTIVAL
www.oxfordfilmfest.com
Festival Month: Mid-June
Genres: Animation, Documentary,
Experimental, Features, Music Videos,
Narrative, Shorts, Student, Teenager

OZARK FOOTHILLS FILMFEST
www.ozarkfoothillsfilmfest.org
Festival Month: Late March
Genres: Animation, Documentary, Features, Independent, International, Shorts

PACIFIC PALISADES FILM FEST
www.friendsoffilm.com
Festival Month: Early May
Genres: Animation, Documentary, Features, Independent, International, Narrative

PALM BEACH JEWISH FILM FESTIVAL
www.palmbeachjewishfilm.org
Festival Month: Early December
Genres: Documentary, Ethnic Jewish, Features, Independent, International, Narrative, Shorts

PAN AFRICAN FILM & ARTS FESTIVAL
www.paff.org
Festival Month: Mid-February
Genres: Documentary, Ethnic Black, Features, Independent, International, Narrative, Shorts

PARK CITY FILM MUSIC FESTIVAL
www.parkcityfilmmusicfestival.com
Festival Month: Mid-January
Genres: Documentary, Features, Independent, International, Narrative, Performance, Shorts

PEACH CITY SHORT FILM FESTIVAL
www.cmc-ent.com/pcsff
Festival Month: Mid-August
Genres: All Categories - Shorts

PENSACOLA BAY INTERNATIONAL FILM AND TELEVISION FESTIVAL
www.pensacolafilmandtv.com
Festival Month: Mid-March
Genres: Animation, Documentary, Episodic Television/Television Pilots, Features, International, Narrative, Student, Television

PERSPECTIVES INTERNATIONAL FILM FESTIVAL
www.perspectives-iff.org
Festival Month: Late July
Genres: Disabled, Documentary, Education, Features, International, Narrative

PETA'S ANIMAL RIGHTS FILM FESTIVAL
www.peta.org/feat/film
Genres: Animal Rights, International, Online, Shorts

PHILADELPHIA SHORT FILM FESTIVAL
www.mamut.com/homepages/
United_States/2/9/usafestivals/
subdet45.htm
Festival Month: November
Genres: Online, Shorts

PICTURE THIS FILM FESTIVAL
www.picturethisfestival.org
Festival Month: February
Genres: Animation, Disabled, Documentary, Features, International, Narrative, Performance, Shorts

PITTSBURGH INTERNATIONAL LESBIAN AND GAY FILM FESTIVAL
www.pilgff.org
Festival Month: Mid-October
Genres: Animation, Documentary, Features, Gay Lesbian, Independent, International, Narrative, Shorts

PIXIE FLIX FEST
www.pixiefilmfest.com
Festival Month: Early June
Genres: Animation, Documentary, Experimental, Features, Gay Lesbian, Narrative, Shorts

POCONO MOUNTAINS FILM FESTIVAL
www.poconomountainsfilmfestival.com
Festival Month: Early July
Genres: Documentary, Features, Independent, International, Music Videos, Narrative, Shorts

POLISH FILM FESTIVAL IN AMERICA
www.pffamerica.com
Festival Month: November-December
Genres: Documentary, Features, Narrative, Polish, Shorts

PORT TOWNSEND FILM FESTIVAL
www.ptfilmfest.com
Festival Month: Late September
Genres: Documentary, Features, Independent, International, Narrative, Shorts

PORTLAND INTERNATIONAL SHORT SHORT FILM FEST
www.zonkerfilms.com
Festival Month: Late September
Genres: Animation, Documentary, Experimental, Narrative, Shorts

PORTLAND LESBIAN & GAY FILM FESTIVAL
www.sensoryperceptions.org
Festival Month: Mid-October
Genres: Documentary, Features, Gay Lesbian, Independent, International, Narrative, Shorts

PORTLAND PDX FILM FESTIVAL
www.peripheralproduce.com
Festival Month: Mid-April
Genres: Documentary, Experimental, Features, Independent, International, Shorts, Underground

BEST REGIONAL FILM FESTIVALS IN THE U.S.

Ann Arbor Film Festival
Atlanta Film and Video Festival
Central Standard Film Festival
Cinema Epicuria Sonoma Valley Film Festival
Cinequest Film Festival
CineVegas Film Festival
deadCenter Film Festival
Denver International Film Festival
Florida Film Festival
Hamptons International Film Festival
Kansas International Film Festival
Mill Valley Film Festival
New Orleans Film and Video Festival
San Diego Film Festival
Sidewalk Moving Picture Film Festival
Waterfront Film Festival
Woodstock Film Festival

PROViDENCE FESTiVAL OF NEW LATiN AMERiCAN CiNEMA
www.murphyandmurphy.com/plff/
Festival Month: Late April-May
Genres: Children, Documentary, Ethnic Latin, Features, International, Narrative, Shorts

PROViNCETOWN iNTERNATiONAL FiLM FESTiVAL
www.ptownfilmfest.org
Festival Month: Mid-June
Genres: Animation, Documentary, Features, Independent, International, Narrative, Shorts

PUBLiFiLM FESTiVAL
www.publifilm.com/festival.cfm
Festival Month: Every Two Months
Genres: Animation, Documentary, Experimental, Features, Independent, International, Narrative, Shorts, Student

RAGAMUFFiN FiLM FESTiVAL
www.ragamuffinfilm.org
Festival Month: Mid-July
Genres: Documentary, Ethnic Other, Features, Narrative, Shorts

REAL TO REEL FiLM FESTiVAL
www.realtoreelfest.com
Festival Month: July
Genres: Animation, Documentary, Features, Narrative, Shorts

RED FiLM FESTVAL
www.redfilmfestival.com
Festival Month: Early April
Genres: First-Time Independent Filmmakers, Independent, International, Shorts, Student

REEL MUSiC FESTiVAL
www.nwfilm.org
Festival Month: Late January-February
Genres: Documentary, Features, Narrative, Performance, Shorts

REEL SiSTERS OF THE DiASPORA FiLM FESTiVAL
www.reelsisters.org
Festival Month: Mid-March
Genres: Animation, Documentary, Ethnic Black, Features, Independent, International, Narrative, Shorts, Women

REEL VENUS FiLM FESTiVAL
www.reelvenus.com
Festival Month: Mid-July
Genres: Independent, International, Shorts, Women

REEL WOMEN iNTERNATiONAL FiLM FESTiVAL
www.rwiff.com
Festival Month: Late August
Genres: Animation, Documentary, Features, Independent, International, Narrative, Shorts, Student, Women

REELOUT QUEER FiLM AND ViDEO FESTiVAL
www.reelout.com
Festival Month: April
Genres: Documentary, Features, Gay Lesbian, Independent, International, Narrative, Shorts

REELWORLD FiLM FESTiVAL
www.reelworld.ca
Festival Month: Late March-April
Genres: Canadian, Documentary, Features, Human Rights, Independent, Multi-Cultural, Narrative, Shorts

REHOBOTH BEACH iNDEPENDENT FiLM FESTiVAL
www.rehobothfilm.com
Festival Month: Mid-November
Genres: Animation, Documentary, Experimental, Features, Independent, International, Narrative, Shorts

RENEGADE FiLM FESTiVAL
www.renegadefilmfestival.com
Festival Month: Early April
Genres: Animation, Documentary, Experimental, First-Time Independent Filmmakers, Independent, International, Narrative, Narrative, Shorts, Student, Underground

RENO FiLM FESTiVAL
www.renofilmfestival.org
Festival Month: Mid-November
Genres: Animation, Canadian, Documentary, Features, Independent, International, Narrative, Shorts

RHODE iSLAND iNTERNATiONAL HORROR FiLM FESTiVAL
www.film-festival.org/events/horror_detail.htm
Festival Month: Late October
Genres: Animation, Documentary, Features, Horror, Independent, International, Shorts, Thriller

ROCKY MOUNTAiN WOMENS FiLM FESTiVAL
www.rmwfilmfest.org
Festival Month: November
Genres: Documentary, Features, International, Narrative, Shorts, Women

ROGER EBERT'S OVERLOOKED FiLM FESTiVAL
www.ebertfest.com
Festival Month: Late April
Genres: All

ROSEBUD FiLM AND ViDEO FESTiVAL
www.rosebudact.org
Festival Month: Late March
Genres: Documentary, Experimental, Features, Independent, Narrative, Shorts, Student, Television

ROUTE 66 FiLM FESTiVAL
www.route66filmfestival.org
Festival Month: Mid-September
Genres: Animation, Documentary, Features, Independent, International, Narrative, Shorts

ROXBURY FiLM FESTiVAL
www.roxburyfilmfestival.org
Festival Month: Mid-August
Genres: Documentary, Ethnic Black, Features, Independent, Narrative, Shorts

RURAL ROUTE FiLM FESTiVAL
www.ruralroutefilms.com
Festival Month: July
Genres: Documentary, Experimental, Features, Independent, International, Narrative, Shorts

SACRAMENTO FESTiVAL OF CiNEMA
www.sacramentofilmfestival.com
Festival Month: October
Genres: Animation, Documentary, Features, Independent, International, Narrative, Shorts

SACRAMENTO FiLM AND MUSiC FESTiVAL
www.sactofilmfest.com
Festival Month: August
Genres: Documentary, Features, Narrative, Shorts

SALEM AMATEUR HORROR FiLM FESTiVAL
www.salemfilm.com
Festival Month: Late October
Genres: First-Time Independent Filmmakers, Horror, Independent, International, Shorts, Thriller

SALENTO iNTERNATiONAL FiLM FESTiVAL
www.salentofilmfestival.com
Festival Month: Mid-June
Genres: Documentary, Features, International, Narrative, Shorts

SALT LAKE ASiAN PACiFiC FiLM FESTiVAL
www.geocities.com/slapfilmfestival
Festival Month: Early April
Genres: Animation, Documentary, Ethnic Asian, Features, First-Time Independent Filmmakers, Independent, International, Narrative, Shorts, Student

SAN ANTONiO CiNEFESTiVAL
www.guadalupeculturalarts.org/ festivals/cine2k3main.htm
Festival Month: Early March
Genres: Documentary, Ethnic Chicano, Ethnic Latin, Features, Independent, International, Narrative, Shorts

SAN DiEGO ASiAN FiLM FESTiVAL
www.sdaff.org
Festival Month: Mid-October
Genres: Animation, Documentary, Ethnic Asian, Experimental, Features, Independent, International, Music Videos, Narrative, Shorts

SAN DiEGO iNTERNATiONAL FiLM FESTiVAL
ueo.ucsd.edu
Festival Month: Mid-April
Genres: Animation, Documentary, Features, Independent, International, Narrative, Shorts

SAN DiEGO JEWiSH FiLM FESTiVAL
www.lfjcc.org/filmfestival.html
Festival Month: February
Genres: Documentary, Ethnic Jewish, Features, Independent, International, Narrative, Shorts

SAN DiEGO LATiNO FiLM FESTiVAL
www.sdlatinofilm.com
Festival Month: March
Genres: Animation, Documentary, Ethnic Latin, Experimental, Features, Narrative, Shorts, Student

SAN FRANCiSCO BLACK FiLM FESTiVAL
www.sfbff.org
Festival Month: Early June
Genres: Documentary, Ethnic African, Ethnic Black, Features, Independent, International, Narrative, Shorts

SAN FRANCiSCO JEWiSH FiLM FESTiVAL
www.sfjff.org
Festival Month: Late July-August
Genres: Documentary, Ethnic Jewish, Features, Independent, International, Narrative, Shorts

SAN FRANCiSCO OCEAN FiLM FESTiVAL
www.oceanfilmfest.org
Festival Month: Late January
Genres: Children, Documentary, Family, Features, Narrative, Ocean, Shorts

SAN FRANCiSCO SHORT FiLM FESTiVAL
www.mamut.com/homepages/ United_States/2/9/usafestivals/ subdet13.htm
Festival Month: January
Genres: Online, Shorts

SAN FRANCiSCO WORLD FiLM FESTiVAL AND MARKETPLACE
www.sfworldfilmfestival.com
Festival Month: Mid-October
Genres: Animation, Documentary, Features, Independent, International, Narrative, Shorts

SANTA CRUZ ENViRONMENTAL FiLM AND ViDEO FESTiVAL
earthvisionfest.org
Festival Month: Late October
Genres: Documentary, Environmental, Features, Narrative, Shorts

SANTA CRUZ FiLM FESTiVAL
www.santacruzfilmfestival.com
Festival Month: Mid-May
Genres: Animation, Documentary, Experimental, Features, Independent, International, Narrative, Shorts

SANTA FE FiLM FESTiVAL
www.santafefilmfestival.com
Festival Month: Early December
Genres: Documentary, Features, Independent, International, Narrative, Shorts, World

SARAH LAWRENCE COLLEGE EXPERiMENTAL FiLM & ViDEO FESTiVAL
raptor.slc.edu/~xfest/
Festival Month: Mid-April
Genres: Experimental, Features, Independent, International, Shorts, Student

SCHMOOZEDANCE FiLM FESTiVAL
www.jewishfilm.com
Festival Month: Mid-January
Genres: Documentary, Ethnic Jewish, Features, First-Time Independent Filmmakers, Independent, International, Narrative, Shorts

SEA TO SKY FiLM FESTiVAL
www.sea-to-sky.net/filmfest
Festival Month: Early September
Genres: Animation, Documentary, Experimental, Independent, International, Narrative, Shorts

BEST BLACK FiLM FESTIVALS

Acapulco Black Film Festival
African Diaspora Film Festival
American Black Film Festival
BFM International Film Festival
Denver Pan African Film & Arts Festival
Hollywood Black Film Festival
Iced In Black
International Black Panther Film Festival
International Black Women's Film Festival
Memphis Black Writers Conference & Southern Film Festival
Motor City International Film Festival
Pan African Film & Arts Festival
Reel Sisters of the Diaspora Film Festival
Roxbury Film Festival
San Francisco Black Film Festival

SEATTLE JEWiSH FiLM FESTIVAL
www.ajcseattle.org
Festival Month: Mid-March
Genres: Documentary, Ethnic Jewish, Features, Independent, International, Narrative, Shorts

SEX AND DEATH SHORT FiLM FEST
www.sex-and-death.ca
Festival Month: Late March
Genres: Animation, Documentary, Experimental, Independent, International, Narrative, Shorts

SHOCK-O-RAMA-A-GO-GO FiLM FESTiVAL
www.anxietyfilms.com
Festival Month: Late November
Genres: Alternative Sexuality, Animation, Documentary, European, Experimental, Fantasy/Science Fiction, Features, Horror, Independent, International, Performance, Rock and Roll, Underground, Weird

SHOCKERFEST FiLM FESTiVAL
www.shockerfest.com
Festival Month: Late September
Genres: Animation, Documentary, Fantasy/Science Fiction, Features, Horror, Independent, International, Narrative, Shorts

SHORTTV
www.shorttv.com
Festival Month: Ongoing
Genres: All Categories - Shorts, Online

SiLVER iMAGES FiLM FESTiVAL
www.terranova.org
Festival Month: July
Genres: Digital, Documentary, Education, Experimental, Features, Independent, International, Narrative, Senior Citizen, Shorts

SiX MiNUTE CiNEMA DiGiTAL FiLMMAKiNG FESTiVAL
www.sixmincin.com
Festival Month: Late April
Genres: Animation, Commercials, Digital, Documentary, Experimental, Independent, Music Videos, Narrative, Shorts

SOCAL iNTERNATiONAL FiLM FESTiVAL
www.socalfilmfestival.com
Festival Month: Mid-August
Genres: Documentary, Features, Independent, International, Narrative, Shorts, Student

SOMETiME iN OCTOBER FiLM FESTiVAL AND SHORT SCREENPLAY COMPETiTiON
www.cfifn.org
Festival Month: Mid-October
Genres: Documentary, Features, First-Time Independent Filmmakers, Independent, International, Narrative, Shorts

SOUTHERN COMFORT CONFERENCE FiLM FESTiVAL
www.sccatl.org
Genres: Alternative Sexuality, Animation, Documentary, Features, Gay Lesbian, Independent, International, Narrative, Shorts, Transgender

SPiNDLETOP FiLM FESTiVAL
dept.lamar.edu/advancement/spinfest
Festival Month: Late January-February
Genres: Animation, Documentary, Experimental, Features, First-Time Independent Filmmakers, Independent, Music Videos, Narrative, PSA (Public Service Announcement), Shorts, Student, Teenager

SPROUT FiLM FESTiVAL
www.gosprout.org/FilmFestival.html
Festival Month: Late May
Genres: Disabled, Documentary, Features, Independent, International, Narrative, Shorts

SPUDFEST DRiVE-iN FAMiLY FiLM & MUSiC FESTiVAL
www.spudfest.org
Festival Month: Early August
Genres: Animation, Children, Commercials, Documentary, Family, Features, First-Time Independent Filmmakers, Independent, International, Narrative, Shorts

ST. BARTH FiLM FESTiVAL / CiNEMA CARAiBE
www.stbarthff.org
Festival Month: Late April
Genres: 35mm, Ethnic Other, Features, Independent, International, Multi-Cultural, Narrative

ST. JOHN'S iNTERNATiONAL WOMEN'S FiLM & ViDEO FESTiVAL
www.womensfilmfestival.com
Festival Month: Mid-October
Genres: Canadian, Documentary, Experimental, Features, Independent, International, Narrative, Shorts, Women

STUDENTFiLMS.COM: THE ONLiNE STUDENT FiLM FESTiVAL
www.studentfilms.com
Festival Month: Ongoing
Genres: All Categories - Shorts, Online, Student

SUNNYSiDE FiLM FESTiVAL
sunnyside.centerofcultures.info/filmfest.html
Festival Month: Early September
Genres: Animation, Documentary, Experimental, Independent, Multi-Cultural, Narrative, Shorts

SUPERFEST iNTERNATiONAL MEDiA FESTiVAL ON DiSABiLiTiES
www.madknight.com/cdt/superfest
Festival Month: June
Genres: Disabled, Documentary, Features, Independent, International, Shorts

SURF FiLM FESTiVAL
www.surffilmfest.com
Festival Month: Spring
Genres: Documentary, Features, Independent, International, Narrative, Shorts, Surfing

SWiSS AMERiCAN FiLM FESTiVAL
www.swisscinema.org
Festival Month: Early November
Genres: American, Animation, Documentary, Ethnic Other, Experimental, Features, International, Narrative, Shorts

SYRACUSE iNTERNATiONAL FiLM & ViDEO FESTiVAL
www.syracusefilmandvideofest.com
Festival Month: Late April-May
Genres: Animation, Children, Documentary, Experimental, Features, Independent, International, Narrative, Shorts, Student

TALLGRASS FILM FESTIVAL
www.tallgrassfilmfest.com
Festival Month: Early October
Genres: Animation, Documentary,
Features, Independent, International,
Narrative, Shorts

TAMBAY FILM FESTIVAL
www.tambayfilmfest.com
Festival Month: Late April
Genres: Animation, Documentary,
Features, Horror, Independent,
International, Narrative, Shorts,
Student

TAMPA INDEPENDENTS' FILM FESTIVAL
www.independentsfilmfest.com
Festival Month: September
Genres: Animation, Documentary,
Features, Features, Independent,
International, Narrative, Shorts,
Student

TAMPA INTERNATIONAL GAY AND LESBIAN FILM FESTIVAL
www.pridefilmfest.com
Festival Month: Early October
Genres: Documentary, Features, Gay
Lesbian, Independent, International,
Narrative, Performance, Shorts

TAOS MOUNTAIN FILM FESTIVAL
www.mountainfilm.net
Festival Month: Early October
Genres: Adventurer/Explorers,
Documentary, Environmental,
Features, Human Rights, Independent,
International, Narrative, Shorts,
Wildlife

TAOS PICTURE SHOW
Festival Month: April
Genres: Animation, Documentary,
Features, Independent, International,
Narrative, Shorts

TAOS VISION QUEST INTERNATIONAL FILM FESTIVAL
www.taosvisionquest.com
Festival Month: Late April
Genres: Animation, Documentary,
Features, Independent, International,
Narrative, Shorts

THREE RIVERS FILM FESTIVAL
3rff.com
Festival Month: November
Genres: Animation, Documentary,
Experimental, Features, Independent,
International, Narrative, Shorts

THUNDERBIRD INTERNATIONAL FILM FESTIVAL
www.thunderbirdfilmfestival.suu.edu
Festival Month: Early June
Genres: Children, Documentary,
Family, First-Time Independent
Filmmakers, Independent,
International, Narrative, Shorts,
Student

TOASTER FILM FESTIVAL
www.state.sc.us/arts/toaster
Festival Month: Mid-August
Genres: Documentary, Experimental,
Narrative, Shorts, Student, Teenager

TORONTO HISPANO AMERICAN FILM FESTIVAL
www.hispanoamericanfilm.com
Festival Month: Late May-June
Genres: Canadian, Documentary,
Ethnic Latin, Ethnic Spanish, Features,
Independent, International, Narrative,
Shorts

TORONTO INTERNATIONAL ENVIRONMENTAL FILM & VIDEO FESTIVAL
www.planetinfocus.org
Festival Month: Late September-
October
Genres: Documentary, Environmental,
Features, Independent, International,
Narrative, Shorts

TORONTO LESBIAN AND GAY FILM AND VIDEO FESTIVAL
www.insideout.on.ca
Festival Month: Late May
Genres: Animation, Canadian,
Documentary, Experimental, Features,
Gay Lesbian, Independent,
International, Narrative, Shorts

TORONTO REEL ASIAN INTERNATIONAL FILM FESTIVAL
www.reelasian.com
Festival Month: Late November
Genres: Animation, Documentary,
Ethnic Asian, Features, International,
Narrative, Shorts

TORONTO STUDENT SHORTS NATIONAL FILM FESTIVAL
www.endless-films.com
Festival Month: Late September
Genres: Animation, Canadian,
Documentary, Experimental, Narrative,
Shorts, Student

TULSA OVERGROUND INTERNATIONAL FILM FESTIVAL
www.tulsaoverground.com
Festival Month: Early September
Genres: Animation, Documentary,
Experimental, First-Time Independent
Filmmakers, Independent,
International, Narrative, Shorts

BEST LATIN FILM FESTIVALS

AluCine Toronto Latino Film & Video Festival
Cartagena International Film Festival
Chicago Latino Film Festival
Cine Acción ¡Cine Latino!
Cine Las Americas International Film Festival of the
  Americas
CineSol Latino Film Festival
Havana Film Festival In New York
Latin USA International Film Festival
Latino Film Festival San Francisco Bay Area
Los Angeles Latino International Film Festival
Miami International Film Festival
Miami Latin Film Festival
New York International Latino Film Festival
Providence Festival Of New Latin American Cinema
San Antonio CineFestival
San Diego Latino Film Festival
Sao Paulo International Short Film Festival
Toronto Hispano American Film Festival

TWIN RIVERS MEDIA FESTIVAL
www.twinriversmediafestival.com
Festival Month: Mid-September
Genres: Animation, Commercials, Digital, Documentary, Environmental, Experimental, Features, Independent, International, Mountain Sports, Multimedia, Narrative, Shorts, Web Projects

U.N.C.L.E. FEST FILM FESTIVAL
www.unclefest.com
Festival Month: Late April-May
Genres: Documentary, Features, Independent, International, Narrative, Shorts

U.S. INTERNATIONAL FILM AND VIDEO FESTIVAL
www.filmfestawards.com
Festival Month: Early June
Genres: Documentary, Education, Episodic Television/Television Pilots, Features, International, Narrative, PSA (Public Service Announcement), Shorts, Television

UAF STUDENT FILM FESTIVAL
www.uaf.edu/filmclub
Festival Month: Early December
Genres: Animation, Digital, Documentary, First-Time Independent Filmmakers, Independent, International, Narrative, Shorts, Student

UNDERGROUNDFILM.ORG
www.undergroundfilm.org
Festival Month: Ongoing
Genres: All Categories - Shorts, Online

URBAN STUYVESANT FILM FESTIVAL (USFF)
www.3mindfilms.com
Festival Month: February
Genres: Animation, Documentary, Features, First-Time Independent Filmmakers, Independent, International, Narrative, Shorts

UTAH SHORT FILM & VIDEO FESTIVAL
www.ufvc.org
Festival Month: June
Genres: Animation, Documentary, Independent, International, Narrative, Shorts, Student

VALLEY INTERNATIONAL FILM FESTIVAL
www.viffi.org
Festival Month: Late March
Genres: Animation, Commercials, Documentary, Features, Independent, International, Music Videos, Shorts, Student

VANCOUVER ASIAN FILM FESTIVAL
www.vaff.org
Festival Month: Early November
Genres: American, Animation, Canadian, Documentary, Ethnic Asian, Features, Independent, International, Narrative, Shorts

VANCOUVER INTERNATIONAL COMEDY FESTIVAL
www.comedyfest.com
Festival Month: Late July-August
Genres: Comedy, Independent, International, Shorts, Student

VANCOUVER INTERNATIONAL DIGITAL FESTIVAL
www.vidfest.com
Festival Month: Late June
Genres: Animation, Digital, Documentary, Experimental, International, Multimedia, Music Videos, Narrative, Shorts, Student

VANCOUVER INTERNATIONAL MOUNTAIN FILM FESTIVAL
www.vimff.org
Festival Month: Late February
Genres: Adventurer/Explorers, Documentary, Features, Independent, International, Mountain Sports, Narrative, Shorts

VANCOUVER JEWISH FILM FESTIVAL
www.vjff.org
Festival Month: Early May
Genres: Documentary, Ethnic Jewish, Features, Independent, International, Narrative, Shorts

VANCOUVER OUT ON SCREEN QUEER FILM & VIDEO FESTIVAL
www.outonscreen.com
Festival Month: Early August
Genres: Documentary, Experimental, Features, Gay Lesbian, Independent, International, Multi-Cultural, Narrative, Shorts, Student

VC FILMFEST: THE VISUAL COMMUNICATIONS LOS ANGELES ASIAN PACIFIC FILM & VIDEO FESTIVAL
www.vconline.org
Festival Month: Late April-May
Genres: Animation, Documentary, Ethnic Asian, Features, Independent, International, Narrative, Shorts

VIDEOKRONIK MUSIC VIDEO FESTIVAL
www.20000leagues.org
Festival Month: Late April
Genres: Music Videos

VIDEOTHEATRE NYC
www.videotheatrenyc.com
Festival Month: New Festival Every Season
Genres: Animation, Avant Garde, Experimental, Fantasy/Science Fiction, Features, First-Time Independent Filmmakers, Horror, Independent, International, Narrative, Shorts, Student

VIEWFINDERS: INTERNATIONAL FILM FESTIVAL FOR YOUTH
www.atlanticfilm.com
Festival Month: Late April
Genres: Canadian, Children, Documentary, Family, First-Time Independent Filmmakers, Independent, International, Narrative, Shorts, Student, Teenager

VINEGAR HILL FILM FESTIVAL
vinegarhillfilmfestival.com
Festival Month: Late April
Genres: Animation, Documentary, Experimental, Independent, Narrative, Shorts, Student

VISTAS FILM FESTIVAL
www.vistasfilmfestival.org
Festival Month: Late September-October
Genres: Documentary, Ethnic Other, Ethnic Spanish, Features, Independent, International, Narrative, Shorts

WASHINGTON JEWISH FILM FESTIVAL
www.wjff.org
Festival Month: Early December
Genres: Documentary, Ethnic Jewish, Features, Independent, International, Narrative, Shorts

WATERLOO FESTIVAL FOR ANIMATED CINEMA
www.wfac.ca
Festival Month: Late June
Genres: Animation, Features, Independent, International, Narrative, Shorts

WATERTON INTERNATIONAL FRENCH FILM FESTIVAL SOCIETY
www.watertoninternationalfrench filmfest.com/comp.htm
Festival Month: June
Genres: 35mm, Documentary, Features, French, Independent, International, Narrative, Shorts

WAVES: ASIAN/ASIAN AMERICAN FILM FESTIVAL
www.uiowa.edu/~waves
Festival Month: Early April
Genres: American, Documentary, Ethnic Asian, Independent, International, Multi-Cultural, Narrative, Shorts, Student

WEST VALLEY FILM FESTIVAL
www.madridtheatre.org
Festival Month: Late April
Genres: Animation, Documentary, Features, Independent, Narrative, Shorts

WESTCHESTER COUNTY FILM FESTIVAL
www.westchestergov.com/filmoffice/
Festival Month: Mid-March
Genres: Animation, Documentary, Features, Independent, International, Narrative, Shorts, Student

WESTCLIFFE DIGITAL FILM FESTIVAL
www.westcliffedigitalfilmfestival.com
Festival Month: Late August
Genres: Animation, Digital, Documentary, Experimental, Features, Independent, Narrative, Shorts

WIDESCREEN FILM FESTIVAL
www.widescreenfilmfestival.com
Festival Month: Mid-September
Genres: Animation, Documentary, Features, Independent, International, Narrative, Shorts

WILD AND SCENIC ENVIRONMENTAL FILM FESTIVAL
www.wildandscenicfilmfestival.org
Festival Month: Early January
Genres: Adventurer/Explorers, Animation, Documentary, Environmental, Features, Independent, International, Mountain Sports, Narrative, Shorts

WILD ROSE FILM FESTIVAL
www.vaudevillemews.com/wildrose/index.shtml
Festival Month: Late September
Genres: Animation, Documentary, Features, Independent, International, Narrative, Shorts

WINFEMME FILM FESTIVAL
www.winfemme.com
Festival Month: September
Genres: Documentary, Episodic Television/Television Pilots, Features, Gay Lesbian, International, Narrative, Television, Women

WINSLOW FILM FESTIVAL
www.winslowfilmfestival.org
Festival Month: Late October
Genres: Digital, Documentary, Features, Independent, International, Narrative, Shorts, Visual Effects

WOMEN IN THE DIRECTOR'S CHAIR INTERNATIONAL FILM & VIDEO FESTIVAL
www.widc.org
Festival Month: Mid-March
Genres: Documentary, Features, First-Time Independent Filmmakers, Independent, International, Narrative, Shorts, Student, Women

WOMEN OF COLOR FILM FESTIVAL
www.bampfa.berkeley.edu/pfa_programs/women_of_color
Festival Month: March
Genres: Documentary, Ethnic Asian, Ethnic Black, Ethnic Latin, Ethnic Other, Independent, International, Narrative, Shorts, Women

WOMEN'S FILM FESTIVAL
www.womensfilmfestival.org
Festival Month: Early March
Genres: Documentary, Features, Independent, International, Narrative, Shorts, Women

WOODS HOLE FILM FESTIVAL
www.woodsholefilmfestival.org
Festival Month: Late July-August
Genres: Animation, Documentary, Experimental, Features, Independent, International, Multimedia, Narrative, Shorts

BEST ASIAN FILM FESTIVALS

Asian American International Film Festival
Asian Pacific American Film Festival
Barcelona Asian Film Festival (Muestra de Cine Asiático de Barcelona)
Busan Asian Short Film Festival
Chicago Asian American Film Festival
Cinemanila International Film Festival
Cinemaya Festival Of Asian Cinema
Earth Vision - Tokyo Global Environmental Film Festival
Far East Film Festival
Film South Asia
Filmi Toronto South Asian Film Festival
Fukuoka Asian Film Festival
Jeonju International Film Festival
Kyoto International Student Film & Video Festival
Nippon Connection - Japanese Film Festival
Northwest Asian American Film Festival
Salt Lake Asian Pacific Film Festival
San Diego Asian Film Festival
Sydney Asia-Pacific Film Festival
Toronto Reel Asian International Film Festival
Vancouver Asian Film Festival
VC Filmfest : The Visual Communications Los Angeles Asian Pacific Film & Video Festival
WAVES: Asian/Asian American Film Festival

WORLD OF COMEDY INTERNATIONAL FiLM FESTiVAL
www.worldcomedyfilmfest.com
Festival Month: Mid-February
Genres: Animation, Canadian, Comedy, Documentary, Experimental, Features, Independent, International, Narrative, Shorts

WORLD POPULATiON AND ViDEO FESTiVAL
www.wpfvf.com
Festival Month: Mid-October
Genres: Animation, Documentary, Education, Environmental, Features, Human Rights, Independent, International, Music Videos, Narrative, Shorts, Student

X-DANCE ACTiON SPORTS FiLM FESTiVAL
www.x-dance.com
Festival Month: Mid-January
Genres: Adventurer/Explorers, BMX, Cycling, Documentary, Features, Independent, International, Mountain Sports, Performance, Shorts, Skateboarding, Sports, Video Games

YOUTH MEDiA JAM
www.princemusictheater.org/film/ymj
Festival Month: Late May
Genres: Animation, Children, Documentary, First-Time Independent Filmmakers, Independent, Music Videos, Narrative, Shorts, Student, Teenager

Z FiLM FESTiVAL
www.zfilmfestival.com
Festival Month: Mid-December-January
Genres: Animation, Avant Garde, Documentary, Experimental, Independent, International, Narrative, Shorts

MAJOR iNTERNATiONAL FiLM FESTiVALS

ADELAiDE iNTERNATiONAL FiLM FESTiVAL

12 King William Rd.
Unley
South Australia 5061
Australia
Tel ....+61-8-8271-1029
Fax ....+61-8-8271-9905
Email ....info@adelaidefilmfestival.org
Web Site ....www.adelaidefilmfestival.org

Festival Month: Mid-February-March

Entry Deadline: Early December

Entry Fee: None

Genres: Animation, Documentary, Features, Independent, International, Multimedia, Music Videos, Narrative, Shorts

Screening Format: 35mm - BetaSP

Number of Films Screened: 150

Awards: All films screened are eligible for the Australian IF Awards.

Profile: The Adelaide International Film Festival explores contemporary screen culture with a unique program of screenings, special events and far reaching forum sessions, incorporating feature film, documentary, shorts, animation, music video, on line and new media screenings, computer gaming, installation and exhibitions.

Special Events: Panels, workshops, screenplay competition, best of fest screenings

Filmmaker Perks: Festival travel sponsors offer special deals for filmmakers for travel and accomodations.

Travel Tips: Adelaide is the wine capital of Australia, try not to over-indulge.

Katrina Sedgwick....................................Festival Director

ALGARVE iNTERNATiONAL FiLM FESTiVAL

PO Box 8091
1801 Lisboa Codex
Portugal
Tel ....+351-21-851-36-15
Fax ....+351-21-852-11-50
Email ....algavefilmfest@mail.telepac.pt
Web Site ....www.algarvefilmfest.com

Festival Month: Mid-May

Entry Deadline: April

Entry Fee: None

Genres: 35mm, Animation, Environmental, Independent, International, Narrative, Peace, Shorts

Screening Format: 35mm

Awards: City of Portimão Grand Prize; Public Prize

Profile: The Algarve International Film Festival, is the oldest happening in Portugal every year and directs its vocation, for quite a long time, to the promotion and divulging of short films, 35mm only, with a maximum duration of 30 minutes.

Filmmaker Perks: The festival covers lodging and food for all selected filmmakers.

Travel Tips: Portimão, headquarters for the festival, may be a vacation paradise, but it also has a history as a fishing town, so bring your poles... if you like that sort of thing.

ALPE ADRiA CiNEMA TRiESTE FiLM FESTiVAL

via San Rocco 1
Trieste I-34121
Italy
Tel..+39-040-311153
Fax ....+39-040-311993
Email ....info@alpeadriacinema.it
Web Site ....www.alpeadriacinema.it

Year Festival Began: 1989

Festival Month: Mid-January

Entry Deadline: Late October

Entry Fee: None

Genres: Documentary, Ethnic Asian, European, Experimental, Features, International, Narrative, Shorts

Screening Format: 16mm - 35mm - BetaSP

Awards: Yes

Profile: The Alpe Adria Cinema Trieste Film Festival has acquired more and more importance on the national and international level, becoming a primary point of reference in Italy for the films of central Europe, Asia, and the Mediterranean region.

Special Events: Retrospective screenings, panels, awards

Filmmaker Perks: The Best Feature award will bring in a nice $5,000 Euros which, depending on the currency conversion, might wind up being a bigger windfall then it seems.

Travel Tips: Fly right into Trieste and take your pick of luxurious hotels.

Annamaria Percavassi ....Festival Director

ANIFEST FILM FESTIVAL OF ANIMATED FILMS

CORONA s.r.o.
Jindricha Plachty 28
150 00 Prague 5
Czech Republic
Tel ....+00420-257-324-507
Fax..+00420-257-324-508
Email...info@anifest.cz
Web Site...www.anifest.cz

Festival Month: Early May

Entry Deadline: Mid-January

Entry Fee: None

Genres: Animation, Commercials, Features, Independent, International, Narrative, Shorts, Student, Television

Screening Format: 35mm - BetaSP - DVD

Awards: Grand Prix for the Best Film in the Festival; Jury Awards; Audience Awards

Profile: The AniFest Film Festival of Animated Films is a specialist international competition festival. The aim of the festival is to contribute to the high quality and development of animated film. The festival provides the opportunity to see domestic and foreign work and also has an accompanying program of events. It presents the unique and diverse nature of world-wide production to both the public and professionals.

Special Events: Panels, awards

Filmmaker Perks: The festival director will invite one filmmaker to the festival for each film chosen for competition and will provide him or her with board and accommodation.

Travel Tips: If you are coming to the festival from Prague it is quicker by train, with the bus and train stations being a 15 minute walk from the festival center.

Hana Drhovská ....Festival Director
Jirí Kubícek ....Programme Director

ANKARA INTERNATIONAL FILM FESTIVAL

Farabi Sok. No: 29/1
06690 Cankaya/Ankara
Turkey
Tel..+90-312-468-77-45
Fax ....+90-312-467-78-30
Email ....festival@filmfestankara.org.tr
Web Site ....www.filmfestankara.org.tr

Festival Month: Mid-December

Entry Deadline: September

Entry Fee: None

Genres: Animation, Documentary, Features, International, Narrative, Shorts

Screening Format: 16mm - 35mm - BetaSP

Profile: The Ankara International Film Festival supports short, animation and documentary filmmakers with their yearly festival aimed at films with less than a commercial chance at getting seen in Turkey or otherwise internationally.

Special Events: Meeting of World Cinema screenings

Filmmaker Perks: Ankara will attempt to put some money down for filmmaker accomodations but, at the very least, will find out the best deals for visiting filmmakers.

Travel Tips: It's a 2 hour bus ride from Esenboga Airport to Ankara, but it only costs $3, which is cheaper than getting a taxi.

ANNECY INTERNATIONAL ANIMATED FILM FESTIVAL

c/o Conservatoire d'art et d'histoire
18 Ave. du Tresum, BP399
74013 Annecy Cedex
France
Tel ....+33-04-50-10-09-00
Fax ....+33-04-50-10-09-70
Email ....films@annecy.org
Web Site ....www.annecy.org

Festival Month: Early June

Entry Deadline: Mid-January

Entry Fee: None

Genres: Animation, Features, Independent, International, Multimedia, Music Videos, Narrative, Shorts, Student, Television, Web Projects

Screening Format: 35mm - BetaSP - DVD

Awards: The Cristal for best feature; FIPRESCI Award; The Annecy Cristal; Other Awards

Profile: The Annecy International Animated Film Festival is the top ranking competitive international festival entirely dedicated to animation. The capacity to present and promote animation in all its different forms has made Annecy a world point of reference for animation professionals and a date not to be missed.

Special Events: Retrospective screenings, awards

Filmmaker Perks: The festival covers accomodations and meals for select film directors.

Travel Tips: Annecy is a beautiful resort town in the French Alps, so make sure you book your accomodations early.

Laurent Million ....Festival Contact

ARCIPELAGO INTERNATIONAL FESTIVAL OF SHORT FILMS & NEW IMAGES

c/o Associazione Culturale 3E-medi@
PO Box 6154
00195 Rome RM
Italy
Tel...+39-06-393-87246
Fax..+39-06-393-88262
Email............................info@arcipelagofilmfestival.org
Web Site......................www.arcipelagofilmfestival.org

Festival Month: Early June

Entry Deadline: Mid-February

Entry Fee: None

Genres: Animation, Digital, Documentary, European, Experimental, Independent, International, International, Multimedia, Music Videos, Narrative, Shorts, Web Projects

Screening Format: 35mm - BetaSP

Awards: Best International Short Film; Jury Awards

Profile: Arcipelago International Festival of Short Films and New Images is a project in progress with the aim of worldwide search and acknowledgement of the most original drives and of the most innovative film languages developing inside non-standard audiovisual formats - starting with short films and including products belonging to the new "digital domain".

Special attention is paid to European production, witnessing its quakes and registering its changes, inquiring on the creative and productive diversities, as well as drawing the most updated map of new trends and of independent, marginal and experimental activities.

Special Events: Awards

Travel Tips: Summer in Rome, bring sunscreen and shorts.

Stefano Martina ....Artistic Director
Giuliana La Volpe.............................Managing Director

ATHENS INTERNATIONAL FILM FESTIVAL

Benaki St.
152 35 Metamorphosi Halandri
Athens Greece
Tel.................+30-210-6061689; +30-210-6061363
Fax...+30-210-6014137
Email...festival@pegasus.gr
Web Site...www.aiff.gr

Festival Month: Mid-September

Entry Deadline: Mid-July

Entry Fee: None

Genres: American, Animation, Documentary, Features, Independent, International, Narrative, Shorts

Screening Format: 16mm - 35mm - BetaSP - MiniDV

Awards: The Golden Athena; City of Athens Award

Profile: Dedicated to screening the best of international, independent cinema, the Athens International Film Festival has a special emphasis on American productions.

Special Events: Awards

Travel Tips: You have to see the Acropolis. It's that simple.

Christos Mitsis ....Festival Director
Lefteris Adamidis ....Program Director

AVIGNON FRENCH FILM FESTIVAL

10, montée de la Tour
30400 Villeneuve-les-Avignon
France
Tel...+33-490-25-93-23
Fax..+33-490-25-93-24
Email...jhr2001@aol.com
Web Site...............................www.avignonfilmfest.com

Festival Month: Late-June

Entry Deadline: Early May

Entry Fee: $25

Genres: American, Animation, Documentary, European, Features, First-Time Independent Filmmakers, French, Independent, International, Narrative, Shorts

Screening Format: 35mm - BetaSP

Awards: The "Tournage Awards" are given for the best three feature films (one American, one French, one European), the "Panavision Prizes" are given to the best three short films as well as "Kodak Vision Award" for best cinematography

Profile: The Avignon French Film Festival celebrates French, European and American independent film with new films, retrospectives, round-tables on pertinent issues with industry experts, Q&As with filmmakers and receptions, prizes for emerging filmmakers, group breakfasts, lunches and receptions.

BEST ANIMATION FESTIVALS

Anima Mundi
Bristol International Animation Festival
International Leipzig Festival For Documentary and Animated Film
Melbourne International Animation Festival (MIAF)
Ottawa International Animation Festival
Zagreb World Festival of Animated Films

Special Events: Panels, awards, parties, retrospectives, wine tastings

Filmmaker Perks: All filmmakers are given VIP badges for entry into screenings, receptions, panels, and daily wine tastings.

Travel Tips: If you can afford it, rent a private home for your stay, otherwise use the festival resources to find affordable accomodations.

Jerome Henry Rudes..........President/General Director
Sylvie Tanssaout ....Producer

BANGKOK iNTERNATiONAL FiLM FESTiVAL

9107 Wilshire Blvd. Mezzanine
Beverly Hills, CA 90210
Tel..310-272-1160
Web Site ....www.bangkokfilm.org

Year Festival Began: 1998

Festival Month: Late January-February

Entry Deadline: Mid-November

Entry Fee: $40-$65

Genres: American, Documentary, Ethnic Asian, Features, First-Time Independent Filmmakers, Independent, International, Narrative, Online Festival, Shorts, Touring

Screening Format: 16mm - 35mm BetaSP

Awards: Golden Kinnaree Awards; Crystal Lens Award

Profile: The Bangkok International Film Festival is a major marketing, media and entertainment platform event in Southeast Asia. Because the major box office market in Asia begins with the Chinese New Year in January this proves to be the ideal platform for International films in Asia. January is also the best time of year for Asian films to premiere to the world as they begin their major festival and market circuit in the US and Europe.

Special Events: Awards, Bangkok Film Market, panels

Filmmaker Perks: The festival covers travel and accomodations for select filmmakers.

Travel Tips: Do not get yourself involved with drugs. Penalties for drug offences are very severe in Thailand.

Juthamas Siriwan...President
Robert Rudder ....Film Festival Management

BARCELONA ASiAN FiLM FESTiVAL

València 225, 3 - 1B
08007 Barcelona
Spain
Tel ....+34-93-511-32-52
Fax ....+34-93-511-32-54
Email ....info@baff-bcn.org
Web Site..baff-bcn.org

Year Festival Began: 1999

Festival Month: Late April-May

Entry Deadline: Early March

Entry Fee: None

Genres: 35mm, Animation, Documentary, Ethnic Asian, Features, Independent, International, Multi-Cultural, Narrative

Screening Format: 35mm

Awards: Durian de Oro; Audience Award

Profile: The main goal of the Barcelona Asian Film Festival is to celebrate and exhibit the best in Asian cinema. Through the festival, many Asian films that otherwise would not be seen in Europe are screened to an appreciative and culturally active audience.

Special Events: Parties

Filmmaker Perks: Spend time at the BAFF lounge, three straight nights of the best electronica you can stomach.

Travel Tips: Except for certain seaside resorts, the schedules for meals are different from those of the rest of Europe and the U.S. so be prepared to eat dinner much later.

Amaia Torrecilla ....Festival Co-Director
Carlos R. Ríos...................................Festival Co-Director

BELGRADE iNTERNATiONAL FiLM FESTiVAL

Majke Jevrosime 20a
11000 Belgrade
Yugoslavia
Tel ....+381-11-3346-837
Fax ....+381-11-3346-837
Email...info@fest.org.yu
Web Site...www.fest.org.yu

Festival Month: Late February-MArch

Entry Deadline: Mid-January

Entry Fee: None

Genres: 35mm, Documentary, Features, Human Rights, Independent, International, Narrative, Television

Screening Format: 35mm - 70mm

Number of Films Screened: 72

Awards: No

Profile: During its not-so-short 32 year history, every year the Belgrade International Film Festival has been the place where one could see all the best, most interesting and intriguing films in international cinema.

Special Events: Parties, special screenings

Travel Tips: Pay attention to the news, decide from there.

Miroljub Vuckovic
Dragan Marinkovic................................Artistic Director

BERMUDA INTERNATIONAL FILM FESTIVAL

PO Box HM 2963
Hamilton HM MX
Bermuda
Tel 441-293-3456
Fax 441-293-7769
Email ....bdafilm@ibl.bm
Web Site ....www.bermudafilmfest.com

Year Festival Began: 1997

Festival Month: Late March

Entry Deadline: Early November

Entry Fee: None

Genres: American, Animation, Documentary, Ethnic African, Ethnic Asian, Ethnic Black, Ethnic Jewish, Ethnic Latin, Ethnic Spanish, First-Time Independent Filmmakers, Gay Lesbian, Independent, International, Narrative, Shorts, Women

Screening Format: 35mm - BetaSP

Number of Films Screened: 90

X Factor: The festival is held in BERMUDA!!!

Awards: Yes

Profile: The Bermuda International Film Festival is a registered charity established in 1997. Our mission is to advance the love of independent film from around the world, and create a community welcoming to filmmakers and filmgoers.

Special Events: Parties, panels, and awards.

Travel Tips: You can book your entire trip to BIFF through Liberty Travel, which can arrange your hotel, air travel and even your film and party tickets. Contact them at 1-800-764-1000.

Aideen Ratteray Pryse ....Festival Director
Duncan Hall ....Deputy Festival Director

BRUSSELS INTERNATIONAL FESTIVAL OF FANTASY FILMS

Peymey Diffusion asbl.
Rue de la Comtesse de Flandre 8 at B-1020
Brussels
Belgium
Tel...+32-2-201-17-13
Fax...+32-2-201-14-69
Email ....peymay@bifff.org
Web Site ....www.bifff.org

Festival Month: Mid-March

Entry Deadline: Late December

Entry Fee: None

Genres: Fantasy/Science Fiction, Features, Horror, Independent, International, Narrative, Shorts

Screening Format: 16mm - 35mm - BetaSP - DVD

Awards: "The Raven" Grand Jury Prize

Pegasus Audience Prize

"Melies D'Argent" for the Best European Fantasy Feature Film of Brussels

Profile: The Brussels International Festival of Fantasy Films has as its purpose to reveal and to valorise the cinematographic works of fantasy, science-fiction or thriller and to promote the worldwide development of the film industry towards the professionals and towards the public.

Special Events: Retrospectives, body painting, exhibitions, panels, awards, parties, fashion show

Travel Tips: Bring your paint brush, you might be doing some body painting.

CABOURG FESTIVAL OF ROMANTIC FILMS

106 bis Avenue de Villiers
75017 Paris
France
Tel ....+33-1-4267-2626
Web Site..............................www.cabourg.net/site_uk/
evenements/festivals.html#

Festival Month: Mid-June

Entry Deadline: Curated

Genres: Animation, Features, Independent, International, Narrative, Romantic, Shorts

Screening Format: 16mm - 35mm

Awards: Swan d'Or

Profile: Every year in June, during the film festival, Romanticism officially takes up residence in Cabourg. Thanks to this event, which starts off the summer season, the town lives up to its reputation as the favourite resort of lovers.

Special Events: Panels, debates, parties

Travel Tips: Take that special someone with you.

F. Mahout ....Festival Contact

CAIRO INTERNATIONAL FILM FESTIVAL

17 Kasr El Nil St.
Cairo
Egypt
Tel..202-392-3562
Fax 202-393-8979
Email ....info@cairofilmfest.com
Web Site ....www.cairofilmfest.com

Festival Month: Early October

Entry Deadline: Early August

Entry Fee: None

Genres: Animation, Documentary, Features, Independent, International, Markets, Narrative, Shorts

Screening Format: 35mm - 70mm - BetaSP - DigiBeta - VHS

Awards: Golden Pyramid Awards; Silver Pyramid Awards; Other Awards

Profile: Egypt has had a strong cinematic tradition since the early '30s. With its ancient history, and vast motion picture industry, Egypt became the cultural capital of the Arab world. Egypt's cinema's influence on the Arabs is as profound as that of the American cinema on the rest of the world. That why Cairo, and the Cairo International Film Festival, is known to be "Hollywood" of the Middle East.

Special Events: Market, tributes, retrospectives, parties

Travel Tips: While in Egypt drink the filtered bottle water or the mineral water.

Cherif El-Shoubasy............................President

CAMBRiDGE iNTERNATiONAL FiLM FESTiVAL

Cambridge Arts Picturehouse
38-39 St Andrews St.
Cambridge
CB2 3AR
UK
Tel......................................+44-0122-350-0082
Fax ....+44-0122-346-2555
Email ....cff@picturehouses.co.uk
Web Site ....www.cambridgefilmfestival.org.uk

Year Festival Began: 1977

Festival Month: Mid-July

Entry Deadline: Early May

Entry Fee: None

Genres: Children, Documentary, European, Family, Features, Independent, International, Narrative, Shorts

Screening Format: 16mm - 35mm - BetaSP

Number of Films Screened: 300

X Factor: This is an important regional film festival, close to London, receiving good media coverage not only in the regional press but also in the national newspapers. Many of the regional cinema chains attend the festival to view new films.

Awards: Audience Award for Best Short

Profile: The Cambridge Film Festival is one of the UK's most popular and influential British film festivals. It previously ran for 20 years from 1977 to 1996 before its successful re-launch in 2001 after a

5 year hiatus. The Festival was originally conceived with a two-fold purpose: as a means of screening the very best of current international cinema; and to rediscover important but neglected film-makers and their films, which were either out of distribution or unseen for many years.

Special Events: Awards

Travel Tips: Flight to Stansted. Then rail or bus to Cambridge (50 minutes)

Tony Jones...............................Festival Director

CANNES DiRECTORS' FORTNiGHT

Quinzaine des Réalisateurs
14 rue Alexandre Parodi
75010 Paris
France
Tel.......................................+01-44-89-99-99
Fax ....+01-44-89-99-60
Email......................infos@quinzaine-realisateurs.com
Web Site ....www.quinzaine-realisateurs.com/uk

Festival Month: Mid-May

Entry Deadline: Mid-April

Entry Fee: $120

Genres: 35mm, Documentary, Features, Independent, International, Narrative, Shorts

Screening Format: 16mm - 35mm - 70mm

Awards: Caméra d'Or

Profile: The members of the SRF, and, among them, its president, Robert Enrico, and vice-president, Jacques Doniol-Valcroze, heatedly debate the very idea of the Fortnight: is it appropriate to present films as part of the Cannes Film Festival, even if it is in a sidebar program for films of diverse origins? The partisans of the festival prevail, endorsing the idea of a non-competitive Fortnight refusing all forms of censorship and diplomatic considerations, serving as a showcase for all international film industries.

All films are born free and equal: we must help them to remain so.

Filmmaker Perks: Festival coincides with the Cannes International Film Festival, so you'll be near the action.

Olivier Père...............................Artistic Director

BEST INTERNATIONAL FESTiVALS

Berlin Film Festival
Cannes Film Festival
Durban International Film Festival
The Times BFI London Film Festival
Melbourne International Film Festival
Oldenburg International Film Festival
Rotterdam International Film Festival
Tokyo International Film Festival
Toronto International Film Festival
Venice International Film Festival

CAPE TOWN WORLD CiNEMA FESTiVAL

Tel..+27-021-430-8160
Fax ....+27-021-430-8186
Email....................................info@sithengi.co.za
Web Site www.sithengi.co.za/2003/festival

Festival Month: Late November

Entry Deadline: August

Genres: Documentary, Ethnic African, Ethnic Asian, Ethnic Black, Ethnic Latin, Features, Independent, International, Narrative

Screening Format: 16mm - 35mm - DigiBeta

Awards: Yes

Profile: The Cape Town World Cinema Festival aims to showcase African and more specifically South African films in the context of other "World Cinema" films. World cinema here encompasses films from South America, Asia and Africa as well as films from the Black diaspora and a special focus on films from indigenous peoples i.e. Aborigine, Maori, Native American, Inuit etc.

Special Events: Parties, awards

Travel Tips: Use the mini-buses. They'll stop whenever you need to get off, real cheap too.

Joy Lekgau...Festival Contact

CARDiFF SCREEN FESTiVAL

10 Mount Stuart Square
Cardiff CF10 5EE
Wales
Tel ....+44-02920-333323
Fax..+44-02920-333320
Email ....james@sgrin.co.uk
Web Site ....www.cardiffscreenfestival.co.uk

Year Festival Began: 1989

Festival Month: Mid-November

Entry Deadline: August

Entry Fee: None

Genres: Animation, Documentary, Features, Independent, International, Narrative, Shorts, Television

Screening Format: 35mm - BetaSP

Number of Films Screened: 170

Awards: DM Davies Award

Profile: The Cardiff Screen Festival is a high quality platform for work from around the world, as well as the main focus for new Welsh audiovisual and cinematographic works both in the English and Welsh languages. European production and talent has always received high priority in the programming of the Festival, with particular focus on new talent and productions which are yet to receive distribution deals, especially in the UK.

Special Events: Debates, special screenings, awards, parties

Filmmaker Perks: The festival offers to cover accomodations and travel when possible.

Sarah Howells ....Festival Manager

CARTAGENA iNTERNATiONAL FiLM FESTiVAL

Centro, Calle San Juan de Dios
Baluarte de San Francisco Javier
Cartagena Colombia
Tel...575-664-2345
Fax..575-660-1701
Email ....info@festicinecartagena.com
Web Site ....www.festicinecartagena.com

Year Festival Began: 1960

Festival Month: Late February-March

Entry Deadline: Mid-January

Entry Fee: None

Genres: Children, Documentary, Ethnic Latin, Features, First-Time Independent Filmmakers, Independent, International, Narrative, Shorts, Television

Screening Format: 35mm - VHS - BetaSP

Number of Films Screened: 60-70

X Factor: Catagena is a living "set" of history, architecture, beauty and romantic nights, drawing visitors through the twisting streets aboard candlelight horse drawn coaches.

Awards: Yes

Profile: The longest-running film festival in Latin America, the Cartagena International Film Festival has a reputation as being progressive and innovative, presenting the best films produced in Latin America, Spain, and Portugal. The event also features shorts, videos and documentaries. As well as awarding prizes for international films, actors and directors, it also pays homage to its national stars both in film and television.

Special Events: Retrospectives, tributes, awards

Travel Tips: Check www.cartagenainfo.com for answers to all your travel questions.

Don Victor Nieto Nunez ....Festival Director
Gerardo Nieto ....Festival Coordinator

NEXT!

Have your next movie, a "go-to" project, ready. Either a script or idea you're working on, another piece of material you'd like to adapt, or a script you want to option, it doesn't matter, *just have something*. Don't have five projects, have one that you really feel passionate about. Passion is the key. Someone may find fault with your film, but if you exude passion for it, others will want to be a part of it. Act as if your life depended on getting this next film made. (A lot of times, it does.)

CERGY-PONTOISE SHORT FILM FESTIVAL

Tant qu'il Y aura des Ohms - ENSEA
6, Ave. du Ponceau
95014 Cergy CEDEX
France
95027 Cergy, France
Tel ....+33-1-30-73-62-24
Fax ....+33-1-30-73-62-24
Email ....tyo@ensea.fr
Web Site ....assoc.tyo.free.fr/shortfilm

Festival Month: Early April

Entry Deadline: Mid-January

Entry Fee: None

Genres: Animation, Documentary, Independent, International, Narrative, Shorts, Student

Screening Format: 35mm - BetaSP

Awards: Prix du SAN; Prix du Conseil Général; Prix du Public

Profile: The Cergy-Pontoise International Short-Film Festival is opened to films made by students enrolled in any institution of higher education, no matter what their field of study or nationality are.

Special Events: Awards

Filmmaker Perks: Best film wins $2,300 Euros which, depending on the currency rate, could be bigger than it seems. Two persons who have taken part in the selected film will be invited to the Festival.

CHERBOURG-OCTEVILLE FESTIVAL OF IRISH & BRITISH FILM

15, passage Digard
50100 Cherbourg
France
Tel ....+33-02-33-93-38-94
Fax...+33-02-33-93-38-24
Email ....travelling.cherbourg@wanadoo.fr
Web Site ....www.festivalcherbourg.com

Festival Month: Early October

Entry Deadline: July

Entry Fee: None

Genres: Animation, Documentary, European, Features, First-Time Independent Filmmakers, Independent, International, Narrative, Shorts, Student, Touring

Screening Format: 35mm

Awards: Audience award for the best feature

Profile: The Cherbourg Film Festival with its tributes and retrospectives dedicated to various members of the British and Irish film industries has become a must for those interested in the discovery and promotion of films from Ireland and Great Britain.

The Cherbourg Film Festival presents new full-length feature films not yet distributed in France and organises a competition endowed with a prize discerned by a jury. Many young directors present their first or second film and some have subsequently won public recognition and approval.

Special Events: Tributes, parties

Filmmaker Perks: An entire festival dedicated to British and Irish filmmakers, young and old. If you fit that description, this festival is perfect for you.

Stephanie LeGrand.................................Festival Contact

CINÉMA DU RÉEL INTERNATIONAL FESTIVAL OF VISUAL ANTHROPOLOGY AND SOCIAL DOCUMENTARY FILMS

Centre Georges Pompidou
25 Rue du Renard
75197 Paris Cedex 04
France
Tel...........................+33-1-4478-4421; 44-78-44-21
Fax ....+33-1-4478-1224
Email..cinereel@bpi.fr
Web Site..betelgeuse.bpi.fr

Year Festival Began: 1979

Festival Month: Early March

Entry Deadline: November

Entry Fee: None

Genres: Documentary, Features, Human Rights, Independent, International, Shorts

Screening Format: 16mm - 35mm - BetaSP

Awards: Grand Prix; Pierre and Yolande Perrault scholarship; Other Awards

Profile: The Cinéma du Réel International Festival of Visual Anthropology and Social Documentary Films showcases documentaries of any length dealing with social concerns.

Filmmaker Perks: The Grand Prix is worth $8,000 Euros.

Travel Tips: It's in Paris, but try to focus on the fact that you're there for your film.

Suzette Glénadel ....Festival Contact

CLERMONT-FERRAND SHORT FILM FESTIVAL

La Jetée - 6 place Michel-de-L'Hospital
63058 Clermont-Ferrand Cedex 1
France
Tel ....+33-4-73-14-73-21
Fax ....+33-4-73-92-11-93
Email ....info@clermont-filmfest.com
Web Site ....www.clermont-filmfest.com

Festival Month: Late January-February

Entry Deadline: October

Entry Fee: None

Genres: Animation, Digital, Documentary, French, Independent, International, Narrative, Shorts

Screening Format: 16mm - 35mm - BetaSP - DigiBeta

Awards: Grand Prix; Public Prize; Digital Competition
Profile: The Clermont-Ferrand International Festival is a unique opportunity in France to savour a highly colourful planet of shorts films.
Special Events: Workshops, parties, awards
Filmmaker Perks: The festival is one of the biggest short fests in France.
Travel Tips: Fly into Kyriad Airport, get a hotel.

Christian Guinot ....Festival Contact

COPENHAGEN INTERNATIONAL FILM FESTIVAL

Kronprinsensgade 6, 1.
1114 Copenhagen K
Denmark
Tel ....+45-33-45-47-49
Fax ....+45-33-45-47-45
Email ....entry@copenhagenfilmfestival.com
Web Site ....www.copenhagenfilmfestival.com

Festival Month: Mid-August
Entry Deadline: June
Entry Fee: None
Genres: Documentary, European, Features, International, Narrative
Screening Format: VHS - 35mm
Awards: The Golden Swan
Profile: The Copenhagen International Film Festival (CIFF) has a strong European as well as an international profile featuring a main competition of European feature films and an international jury.
Special Events: Workshops, panels, parties, awards

Janne Giese............................Festival Director
Lone Korslund.............................Head of Programming

CORK INTERNATIONAL FILM FESTIVAL

10 Washington St.
Cork
Ireland
Tel ....+353-21-4271711
Fax ....+353-21-4275945
Email ....info@corkfilmfest.org
Web Site ....www.corkfilmfest.org

Year Festival Began: 1956
Festival Month: Early October
Entry Deadline: Early July
Entry Fee: None
Genres: American, Animation, Digital Animation, Documentary, Ethnic African, Ethnic Asian, Ethnic Black, Ethnic Jewish, Ethnic Latin, Ethnic Other, Ethnic Spanish, Experimental, Features, First-Time Independent Filmmakers, Gay Lesbian, Independent, International, Shorts, Video, Women
Screening Format: 16mm - 35mm - BetaSP - DVD - CDRom

Awards: Jameson Short Film Award
Claire Lynch Award for Best First Short by an Irish Director
Audience Awards
Award of the Festival
Other Awards
Profile: Cork Film Festival is Ireland's oldest and largest film event. The festival was established in 1956 to bring to Irish audiences the best of international cinema and to showcase new Irish cinema. Cork is competitive for shorts only.
Special Events: Panels, workshops, parties, awards
Filmmaker Perks: The festival offers accomodations to overseas filmmakers when possible.
Travel Tips: Cork International Airport, is off the Kinsale Road and less then 10 minutes from Cork City centre.

Mick Hannigan ....Festival Director

CRACOW FILM FESTIVAL

Al. Krasinskiego 34
30-101 Krakow
Poland
Tel ....+48-12-422-36-77
Fax ....+48-12-422-50-15
Email ....festiwal@apollofilm.pl
Web Site ....www.cracowfilmfestival.pl

Festival Month: Late May-June
Entry Deadline: Mid-February
Entry Fee: None
Genres: Animation, Documentary, Independent, International, Narrative, Shorts
Screening Format: 16mm - 35mm - BetaSP
Awards: The Golden Dragon; The Silver Dragon; Prix UIP Cracow; Diplomas of Honour; Golden Hobby-Horse of Cracow; FIPRESCI Award;

BEST JEWISH FILM FESTIVALS

Boston Jewish Film Festival
Docaviv Tel-Aviv International Documentary Film Festival
Girona Film Festival
Hong Kong Jewish Film Festival
Jerusalem International Film Festival
Jewish Image Awards in Film and Television
L'Chaim! Jewish Film Festival
Maine Jewish Film Festival
Palm Beach Jewish Film Festival
San Diego Jewish Film Festival
San Francisco Jewish Film Festival
Seattle Jewish Film Festival
UK Jewish Film Festival

Planete Channel Special Prize; "Golden Scissors"; Other Awards

Profile: The Cracow Film Festival is one of Europe's oldest events dedicated to documentary, animation and other short film forms. It has been organised year after year since 1961.

Special Events: Awards, panels, parties, tributes

Travel Tips: Cracow has a well developed nightlife scene, so get out there and boogie!

Krzysztof Gierat ....Festival Director

DOCPOiNT HELSiNKi DOCUMENTARY FiLM FESTiVAL

Perämiehenkatu 11 C
00150 Helsinki
Finland
Tel ....+358-9-672-472
Fax ....+358-9-673-998
Email ....info@docpoint.info
Web Site ....www.docpoint.info

Festival Month: Mid-February

Entry Deadline: June

Genres: Children, Documentary, Ethnic Other, European, Features, International, Shorts

Screening Format: 16mm - 35mm - BetaSP

Awards: The Aho & Soldan Award

Profile: DocPoint is the biggest documentary film festival in the Nordic countries. The festival program consists of Finnish, International and classic documentary films as well as a selection especially targeted for children.

Special Events: Awards, panels, special screenings, retrospectives

Filmmaker Perks: DocPoint routinely teams up with other European doc festivals, so you may wind up working the circuit.

Travel Tips: Helsinki can be downright frozen, bring many, many layers.

Kai Huotari ....Executive Director
Arto Halonen ....Artistic Director

DONOSTiA - SAN SEBASTiAN iNTERNATiONAL FiLM FESTiVAL

Usandizaga, 4-6
20.002 Donostia - San Sebastian
Spain
Tel ....+34-943-48-12-12
Fax ....+34-943-48-12-18
Email ....ssiff@sansebastianfestival.com
Web Site ....www.sansebastianfestival.ya.com

Year Festival Began: 1953

Festival Month: Mid-September

Entry Deadline: Late July

Entry Fee: None

Genres: 35mm, Documentary, Ethnic Latin, Ethnic Spanish, Features, Independent, International, Narrative

Screening Format: 35mm

Number of Films Screened: 18 in main competition, 50-75 total

X Factor: Beautiful location, excellent cinematic company.

Awards: Concha de Oro
Concha de Plata
The Altadis-New Directors Award
Pearl of the Audience Award

Profile: The Donostia - San Sebastian International Film Festival's primordial role is to serve as a showcase for each year's most disquieting and innovative films.

Special Events: Films in Progress section, parties, awards, seminars, Zabaltegi section

Travel Tips: Go for walk along the city streets and delightful beaches, enjoy the excellent cuisine, and above all, take in some good cinema.

Mikel Olaciregui ....President
Mikel Etxagibel ....Manager

DUBROVNiK iNTERNATiONAL FiLM FESTiVAL

PO Box 480280
Los Angeles, CA 90048
Tel 310-903-0483
Fax 310-903-0483
Email ....info@dubrovnikiff.org
Web Site ....www.dubrovnikiff.org

Festival Month: Late May

Entry Deadline: Late March

Entry Fee: $20-$50

Genres: Animation, Documentary, Features, Independent, International, Narrative, Shorts

Screening Format: 35mm - BetaSP - DigiBeta - DVD

Awards: Libertas Award; Argosy Award; DIFF Awards

Profile: Set in the picturesque Adriatic coastal city of Dubrovnik, Croatia, with its perfect combination of sun and medieval architecture, Dubrovnik International Film Festival celebrates creativity, extraordinary filmmakers and artistic diversity that both enlighten and entertain audiences.

Special Events: Tributes, awards, special screenings

Travel Tips: Many international airlines offer regular flights to Zagreb, Croatia's capital. Once you arrive in Zagreb, it's just a short domestic flight with the country's major international and domestic carrier, Croatia Airlines, to the southern city of Dubrovnik.

Ziggy Mrkich ....Festival Director

DURBAN INTERNATIONAL FILM FESTIVAL

Centre for Creative Arts
University of Natal
4041 Durban
South Africa
Tel ....+27-31-260-2506
Fax ....+27-31-260-3074
Email ....diff@nu.ac.za
Web Site ....www.und.ac.za/und/carts/ffestpage.html

Year Festival Began: 1978
Festival Month: Mid-June
Entry Deadline: Mid-April
Entry Fee: None
Genres: Documentary, Features, First-Time Independent Filmmakers, Independent, International, Narrative, Shorts, Student
Screening Format: 16mm - 35mm - VHS - BetaSP
Number of Films Screened: 100+
X Factor: The program includes screenings in township areas where cinemas are non-existent so your movie may be the only film some people see all year.
Awards: The eThekwini Film Awards
Profile: This longest-running South African international film festival screens over 100 films from around the world, most of them premiere showings in Durban. The festival also promotes local films and offers workshops featuring visiting directors, screenwriters, actors etc to stimulate developing filmmakers. The programme includes screenings in areas where cinemas are non-existent.
Special Events: The festival offers seminars and workshops featuring local and international filmmakers.
Filmmaker Perks: When budget permits, the festival helps with travel and accomodations.
Travel Tips: South Africa is *hot*! Bring short-sleeved shirts.

Peter Rorvik...Festival Director
Nashen Moodley ....Festival Manager

EDINBURGH INTERNATIONAL FILM FESTIVAL

88 Lothian Rd.
Edinburgh EH3 9BZ
Scotland
UK
Tel ....+44-131-228-4051
Fax...+44-131-229-5501
Email...info@edfilmfest.org.uk
Web Site ....www.edfilmfest.org.uk

Festival Month: Mid-August
Entry Deadline: Mid-April
Entry Fee: Shorts: $45
Features: $175

Genres: Animation, Documentary, European, Features, Independent, International, Narrative, Shorts
Screening Format: 16mm - 35mm - 70mm - BetaSP - DigiBeta
Awards: Standard Life Audience Award
Michael Powell Award for Best New British Feature Film
Guardian New Directors Award
Kodak Dazzle Award for Best British Short Film
The McLaren Award for New British Animation
European Short Film Award / Prix UIP
Saltire Society Grierson Award for Short Documentary
Profile: The longest continually running film festival in the world, the Edinburgh International Film Festival, has come a long way from its beginnings as a documentary festival in 1947 when its spirit was established as bold and international. It has become established as the true home of innovative and exciting cinema.
Special Events: Panels, tributes, parties awards
Travel Tips: Taxis are expensive, and most venues are within walking distance anyway.

Shane Danielsen ....Artistic Director
Nicola Pierson ....Deputy Artistic Director

ENTREVUES BELFORT INTERNATIONAL FILM FESTIVAL

Cinemas d'Aujourd'hui
Hotel de Ville
Place d'Armes
90020 Belfort Cedex
France
Tel ....+33-03-84-22-94-44
Fax..+33-03-84-22-94-40
Email ....info@festival-entrevues.com
Web Site ....www.festival-entrevues.com

Festival Month: Late November
Entry Deadline: September
Entry Fee: None
Genres: Animation, Documentary, Experimental, Features, First-Time Independent Filmmakers, French, Independent, International, Narrative, Shorts
Screening Format: 16mm - 35mm - BetaSP
Awards: Jury Awards; Gérard Frot-Courtaz Award; Audience Awards; Other Awards
Profile: Entrevues, the Belfort International Film Festival, pursues its mission and takes the necessary risks which involve noting, finding, and discovering yet - or almost - unknown cinematic works and artists.
Special Events: Awards, parties, retrospective screenings

Filmmaker Perks: There are nightly parties and invited directors have their food and accomodations covered.

Bernard Benoliel.....................................Festival Director
Richard Gorrieri.....................................Festival Contact

ESPOO CiNÉ iNTERNATiONAL FiLM FESTiVAL

PO Box 95
Espoo 02101
Finland
Tel ....+358-9-466-599
Fax..+358-466-358
Email ....office@espoocine.org
Web Site...www.espoocine.org

Year Festival Began: 1990
Festival Month: Late August
Entry Deadline: May
Genres: Children, European, Fantasy/Science Fiction, Features, Horror, Independent, International, Narrative, Shorts
Screening Format: 16mm - 35mm
Number of Films Screened: 60-70
Odds: 1 in 4
Awards: Méliès d'Argent for European fantastic films in association with the European Fantastic Film Festivals Federation Méliès d'Or.
Profile: Espoo Ciné International Film Festival is the biggest annual showcase of contemporary European cinema in Finland. The festival is currently a member of the European Fantastic Film Festivals Federation Méliès d'Or, making it an official European showcase for the best in genre movies from around the world.
Special Events: Special programming for children, various retrospectives, parties.
Filmmaker Perks: Filmmakers generally get accomodations covered, but outside of special invited guests, travel costs can only be covered on a case-by-case basis.
Travel Tips: Check in with Åbergin Linja, official transportation company for the festival.

Timo Kuismin ....Festival Director
Sato Elo...Festival Contact

EXGROUND - DAS FiLMFEST

Ernst-Goebel-Str. 27
65207 Wiesbaden
Germany
Tel...+49-611-174-8227
Fax ....+49-611-174-8228
Email ....info@exground.com
Web Site...www.exground.com

Year Festival Began: 1990
Festival Month: Mid-November
Entry Deadline: Early August

Number of Submissions: 1,500
Entry Fee: None
Genres: American, Animation, Digital Animation, Documentary, Ethnic Asian, Experimental, Features, First-Time Independent Filmmakers, Independent, International, Narrative, Shorts, Underground, Weird
Screening Format: 16mm - 35mm - Super 8 - BetaSP - DVD
Number of Films Screened: 300
Odds: 1 in 5
X Factor: You could do worse than a trip to Germany to premiere your film.
Awards: German Short Film, International ON VIDEO competition awards
Profile: Among the approximately 40 feature films and almost 20 short film programs (including the contests with over 240 entries), the exground filmfest offers more world premieres as well as European and German premieres than ever. This is as much proof for the increased international reputation of the Wiesbaden film festival as the record number of submissions - more than 1,500, mainly from foreign countries.
Special Events: exground filmfest's main program covers the sections American Independents, News from Asia, International, Documentaries, Focus Austria, Short Films, as well as Extras.

Andrea Wink ....Festival Director
Marion Klomfass...................................Festival Contact

FANTASY FiLMFEST - iNTERNATiONAL FiLM FESTiVAL FOR SCiENCE FiCTiON, FiCTiON, HORROR AND THRiLLER

Rosebud Entertainment
Veranstaltungs und Medien GmbH
Fregestr. 36
D-12161 Berlin
Germany
Tel ....+49-30-861-45-32
Fax ....+49-30-861-45-39
Email ....info@rosebud-entertainment.de
Web Site..............................www.fantasyfilmfest.com

Festival Month: Late July-August
Entry Deadline: Late May
Entry Fee: None
Genres: 35mm, Fantasy/Science Fiction, Features, Horror, Independent, International, Markets, Narrative, Shorts, Thriller, Touring
Screening Format: 35mm
Awards: No
Profile: The Fantasy Filmfest is one of the biggest genre events worldwide, touring seven German cities. The festival is well-respected among distributors for being a link between them as well as producers and sales companies. German buyers and

distribution companies consider the festival an extraordinary market and a promotional opportunity, often frequenting each festival city to get an up close impression of the audience's reaction.

Special Events: Panels, parties, market, special screenings

Filmmaker Perks: About 80 percent of the films that play the festival, sell.

Travel Tips: Get a rail pass and tour Germany with your film.

FESTiVAL OF DEAUViLLE FOR AMERiCAN CiNEMA (LE FESTiVAL DU CiNEMA AMERiCAiN iN DEAUViLLE)

Le Public Systeme Cinema
40 rue Anatole
Levallois-Perret Cedet
Cedex 04 F-92594
France
Tel ....+33-1-41-34-20-33
Fax ....+33-1-41-34-20-77
Email..............................jlasserre@le-public-systeme.fr
Web Site ....www.festival-deauville.com

Festival Month: Early September

Entry Deadline: Early July

Entry Fee: None

Genres: American, Documentary, Features, Independent, International, Narrative, Shorts

Screening Format: 35mm

Number of Films Screened: 70

X Factor: Harrison Ford makes this fest an annual stop, and was named an Honorary Citizen of Deauville. If it's good enough for Han Solo...

Awards: Great Prize

Jury Prize

international Critics Award

Journal du Dimanche Audience Award

Other Awards

Profile: The Festival of Deauville for American Cinema aims to increase the European audience for American cinema through an extensive presentation of new American films. The schedule includes many American films that may be deemed "mainstream", but the festival more than makes up for it with their many feature and short independent film competitions.

Special Events: Panels and parties.

Filmmaker Perks: The big-time studios and celebrities are in force, so networking is a huge plus at Deauville.

Travel Tips: Check www.deauville.org/en/ for all the Deauville transportation and tourist info you could ever want.

Bruno Barde ....Festival Director
Jérôme Lasserre ....Director of Programming

FESTiVAL OF EUROPEAN FiLMS

Abay Kunanbay Cad. Bilir Sok. No:20/13 06700
Kavaklidere Ankara
Turkey
Tel ....+00-90-312-466-34-84
Fax ....+00-90-312-466-43-31
Email ....info@europeanfilmfestival.com
Web Site ....www.europeanfilmfestival.com

Festival Month: Early October

Entry Deadline: Early August

Entry Fee: None

Genres: 16mm, 35mm, Animation, European, Features, Features, Independent, International, Narrative, Touring

Screening Format: 16mm - 35mm

Awards: Short Film Audience Award

Profile: The Festival of European Films was first organised in 1995 to present remarkable Turkish and European films to the film lovers in various cities. Being a member of the European Coordination of Film Festivals, the festival visits different cities to present its program during four weeks. Within the last few years, the festival has visited Ankara, Bursa, Çanakkale, Diyarbakir, Drama(Greece), Eskisehir, Gaziantep, Istanbul, Izmir and Mersin.

BEST ETHNIC FILM FESTIVALS

African, Asian and Latin American Film Festival
Beirut Documentary Film Festival - DocuDays
Bellaria Independent Cinema Festival
Boston Irish Film Festival
Brazilian Film Festival of Miami
Celtic Film and Television Festival
Cinemayaat Arab Film Festival
Cork International Film Festival
Eksjö Animation Festival
Fajr International Film Festival
Festival Of The 3 Continents
Haifa International Film Festival
Indian Film Festival of Los Angeles
International Buddhist Film Festival
Iranian International Market
Israel Film Festival
Jihlava International Documentary Film Festival
Los Angeles Italian Film Awards (LAIFA)
Nordic Film Days Lübeck
Norwegian Short Film Festival
Puchon International Fantastic Film Festival (PiFan)
Rome Independent Film Festival
Swiss American Film Festival
UpOverDownUnder Film Festival
Women of Color Film Festival

Traditionally, every year, the Turkish and foreign guests of the festival are hosted in Bursa, the old capital of the Ottoman Empire, near Istanbul.

Special Events: Retrospectives, awards, parties

Filmmaker Perks: The cost of transportation of the prints will be covered by the Festival.

Travel Tips: It's a whirlwind tour of Turkey and Europe in a little under a month, so take advantage of the free meals.

Basak Emre ....Festival Director

FESTIVAL OF FANTASTIC FILMS

"Penrose"
21 Winton Rd.
Bowdon, Cheshire WA14 2PE
England
UK
Tel ....+44-0161-929-1423
Fax..+44-0161-929-1067
Email.....................gil@manchesterfantasticfilms.co.uk
Web Site ....fantastic-films.com/festival

Festival Month: Mid-August

Entry Deadline: Mid-July

Entry Fee: $55-$185

Genres: Animation, Documentary, Fantasy/Science Fiction, Features, First-Time Independent Filmmakers, Horror, Independent, International, Narrative, Shorts, Student, Thriller

Screening Format: Super 8mm - 16mm - 35mm - VHS

Awards: Jury Awards

Profile: In addition to the retrospective film program that is the backbone of the event, the Festival of Fantastic Films has, within the past few years, become the premiere UK venue for new genre movies. Films that you are unlikely to see anywhere else are screened alongside the new movies from major studios right through the weekend. Each year sees an increase in the number of young and highly creative filmmakers, submitting their work into the International Competition and giving members of the festival a unique opportunity to see a great range of movies.

Special Events: Guest interviews, discussions, panels, auctions, Artshow and poster exhibition, dealer room, themed dinner, parties, awards

Filmmaker Perks: Free one day Festival pass (worth $55)

Travel Tips: Manchester Airport is only 20 minutes via direct rail to City Centre and convention hotel.

Gil Lane-Young ....Chairman

FESTIVAL OF NATIONS

Gaumbergstraße 82
A- 4060 Linz
Austria
Tel ....+0043-732-673-693
Fax ....+0043-732-666-2-666
Email ....eva-video@netway.at
Web Site www.8ung.at/filmfestival

Festival Month: Mid-June

Entry Deadline: Early April

Genres: Animation, Documentary, Experimental, Independent, International, Narrative, Shorts

Screening Format: Super 8mm - 16mm - VHS - DVD - DVCam - DV - MiniDV

Awards: Ebenseer Bear Awards; UNICA - Medaille

Profile: The Festival of Nations is the most important film festival in Austria with more than 500 entries from 40 countries every year.

Special Events: Awards, parties

Filmmaker Perks: Certificates for every participant.

Erich Riess ....Festival Contact

FILMFEST MUNCHEN

Internationale Münchner Filmwochen GmbH
Programmkoordination
Sonnenstr. 21
D-80331 München
Germany
Tel ....+49-89-38-19-04-27
Fax..+49-89-38-19-04-27
Email ....program@filmfest-muenchen.de
Web Site ....www.filmfest-muenchen.de

Festival Month: Late June-July

Entry Deadline: Late March-April

Entry Fee: None

Genres: American, Animation, Documentary, Documentary, European, Experimental, Independent, International, Narrative, Shorts, Student, Television

Screening Format: 16mm - 35mm - BetaSP - DigiBeta - VHS - DVD - MiniDV

Awards: The CineMerit Award

Young German Cinema Award

High Hopes Award

VFF TV Movie Award

Bild-Kunst Award for Experimental Film

Bernhard Wicki-Film Prize- The Bridge

Profile: Filmfest Munchen is the second largest film festival in Germany, taking place in Munich. Film fans, movie professionals, journalists well-known celebrities and young talents gather to watch new movies from all over the world. The festival programs new productions from the major Hollywood studios, fascinating projects from other parts of the world and movies from young German directors.

Special Events: Retrospectives, tributes, parties, awards

Filmmaker Perks: The Young German Cinema Award is worth $80,000 Euros. The other awards? $25,000 Euros.

Travel Tips: Try not to go souvenir crazy, there's a 16 percent sales tax on everything.

Andreas Ströhl ....Managing Director

GIJON INTERNATIONAL FILM FESTIVAL FOR YOUNG PEOPLE

Paseo de Begoña, 24, entlo.
PO Box 76
33201 Gijón
Spain
Tel ....+34-985-182-940
Fax...+34-985-182-944
Email ....festivalgijon@telecable.es
Web Site ....www.gijonfilmfestival.com/

Year Festival Began: 1963
Festival Month: Late November
Entry Deadline: Mid-September
Entry Fee: None
Genres: American, Animation, Children, Documentary, Ethnic Spanish, European, Features, First-Time Independent Filmmakers, Independent, International, Shorts, Student, Underground
Screening Format: 16mm - 35mm
Awards: Jury Awards
Profile: Gijon International Film Festival For Young People is one of the oldest films festivals in Spain. Focused primarily on cinema for young people, the festival programs innovative and independent films made by and for young people, with retrospectives, cycles, exhibitions, musical events and the different film sections with a choice for all tastes, from the fresh Official Section to the vindication of directors which have opened new ways in filmmaking.
Special Events: Retrospectives, awards, parties, panels
Filmmaker Perks: The Festival covers travel, accomodation, and meals.
Travel Tips: The weather is a mix of warm and wet, so forget the shorts, but don't bring the parka.

Jose Luís Cienfuegos ....Festival Director
Fran Gayo ....Festival Staff

GÖTEBORG FILM FESTIVAL

Olof Palmes plats
SE 413 04 Göteborg
Sweden
Tel ....+46-31-339-3000
Fax ....+46-31-41-0063
Email ....goteborg@filmfestival.org
Web Site ....www.goteborg.filmfestival.org

Year Festival Began: 1979
Festival Month: Late January-February

Entry Deadline: November
Entry Fee: None
Genres: Animation, Documentary, Ethnic Other, European, Features, Independent, International, Narrative, Shorts
Screening Format: 16mm - 35mm - BetaSP
Number of Films Screened: 300+
Awards: No
Profile: The Göteborg Film Festival festival, which is arranged annually, is a must for all who are interested in film. Every year the festival becomes more and more popular becoming a natural meeting place for filmmakers from all the Nordic countries.
Special Events: Parties, panels, special screenings
Travel Tips: Rent a bicycle to get around, just like the locals.

Jannike Åhlund ....Festival Director

HELSINKI FILM FESTIVAL - LOVE AND ANARCHY

PO Box 889
Mannerheimintie 22-24
00100 Helsinki
Finland
Tel ....+358-9-684-35-230
Fax ....+358-9-684-35-232
Email ....office@hiff.fi
Web Site ....www.hiff.fi

Year Festival Began: 1987
Festival Month: Mid-September
Entry Deadline: Late June
Entry Fee: None
Genres: American, Animation, Documentary, Ethnic Asian, European, Experimental, Features, First-Time Independent Filmmakers, Independent, International, Narrative, Shorts
Screening Format: 16mm - 35mm - BetaSP
Awards: No
Profile: The Helsinki International Film Festival - Love & Anarchy is a non-competitive film festival held since 1987 annually in September. The festival promotes the artistry of filmmaking, the inventive, visually stunning and controversial new films, revealing the promising talents of tomorrow.
Special Events: Parties, special screenings
Filmmaker Perks: Festival assists with travel and accomodations when possible.
Travel Tips: A recent survey of eight European cities (Stockholm, Oslo, Copenhagen, Vienna, Barcelona, Munich and Turin) placed Helsinki near the top of the charts for the smooth running of its public transport and the standard of its service.

HONG KONG INTERNATIONAL FILM FESTIVAL (HKIFF)

22nd Floor
181 Queen's Road Central
Hong Kong
China
Tel ....+852-2970-3300
Fax ....+852-2970-3011
Email...hkiff@hkadc.org.hk
Web Site ....www.hkiff.org.hk

Festival Month: Early April

Entry Deadline: Mid-December

Entry Fee: None

Genres: Animation, Documentary, Ethnic Asian, Features, Independent, International, Multi-Cultural, Narrative, Shorts

Screening Format: Super 8mm - 16mm - 35mm - BetaSP - DV

Awards: Firebird Awards for Young Cinema

Asian DV Competition

Humanitarian Awards for Documentaries

FIPRESCI

SIGNIS Award Co-organized with SIGNIS Hong Kong

Profile: The Hong Kong International Film Festival (HKIFF) was launched in 1977 by the Urban Council. This spectacular cinematic event of the Asia Pacific region takes place every Easter, offering film buffs a 16-day feast of films from around the globe, as well as a showcase for the historical development of Hong Kong cinema.

Special Events: Workshops, parties, retrospectives, DV competition, panels

Filmmaker Perks: There is a wealth of education and experiences to be had during the festival expansive program.

Travel Tips: Hong Kong is the major air-traffic center for the region, so there are sufficient flights in and out of the country.

Angela Tong ....Festival Contact

HUESCA INTERNATIONAL SHORT FILM FESTIVAL

Avda.Parque, 1 2
22002 Huesca
Spain
Tel ....+34-974212582
Fax...+34-974210065
Email ....info@huesca-filmfestival.com
Web Site ....www.huesca-filmfestival.com

Year Festival Began: 1973

Festival Month: Early June

Entry Deadline: April

Entry Fee: None

Genres: Animation, Documentary, Ethnic Latin, Ethnic Other, Ethnic Spanish, Independent, International, Narrative, Shorts, Student

Screening Format: 16mm - 35mm

Awards: Awards in Iberoamerican and International Short Film Sections

Profile: International Short-Film Contest, and Sample of European and Latinamerican Cinema (Feature Films).

Special Events: Tributes, awards, retrospectives, panels, parties

Filmmaker Perks: Festival pays for accomodations when possible.

Travel Tips: Fly into the Zaragoza airport, it's the closest.

Jose Maria Escriche ....Festival Director

INTERNATIONAL DOCUMENTARY FILM FESTIVAL AMSTERDAM (IDFA)

Kleine-Gartmanplantsoen 10
1017 RR Amsterdam
Netherlands
Tel ....+31-20-627-33-29
Fax ....+31-20-638-53-88
Email ....info@idfa.nl
Web Site ....www.idfa.nl

Festival Month: Mid-November

Entry Deadline: Early September

Entry Fee: None

Genres: Documentary, Features, Independent, International, Shorts

Screening Format: 16mm - 35mm - BetaSP

Awards: VPRO Joris Ivens Award

Silver Wolf Award

International Critics Awards

Audience Award

Amnesty International-DOEN Award

Profile: The International Documentary Film Festival Amsterdam (IDFA) has become one of the world's leading documentary film festivals with more than 200 documentaries and an audience of over 90,000. IDFA offers a diverse platform for screening and debating films, as well as discovering new documentary trends. IDFA is more than just a screening location for creative documentaries. Amsterdam is also the place for meeting your filmmaking colleagues, independent producers, the buyers of your film and the financiers you are looking for. IDFA is the best way of meeting the most fascinating documentary film people.

Special Events: Awards, retrospectives, panels

Filmmaker Perks: The Audience Award is worth $4,500 Euros.

Travel Tips: You're in Amsterdam for your film, not the hash bars. Well, maybe both.

Ally Derks ....General Director

INTERNATIONAL FILM FESTIVAL OF INDIA

Directorate of Film Festivals
Ministry of Information and Broadcasting
Government of India
Sirifort Auditorium
Asian Games Complex
August Kranti Marg, New Delhi 110 049
India
Tel ....+91-11-649-7214
Fax ....+91-11-649-9371
Email ....dffiffi@bol.net.in
Web Site ....www.mib.nic.in/dff

Festival Month: Early October

Entry Deadline: Early August

Entry Fee: None

Genres: Animation, Documentary, Ethnic Other, Features, Independent, International, Multi-Cultural, Narrative, Shorts

Screening Format: 16mm - 35mm - 70mm

Profile: As a vehicle of cultural exchange, International Film Festival of India promotes international friendship, provides access to new trends in world cinema, generates healthy competition and, in the process, helps to improve the standards of Indian films.

Special Events: Tributes, retrospectives, panels

Travel Tips: You can fly right to New Delhi, so don't get sidetracked in Mumbai or Calcutta.

Malti Sahai ....Festival Director

INTERNATIONAL LEIPZIG FESTIVAL FOR DOCUMENTARY AND ANIMATED FILM

Grosse Fleischergasse 11
04109 Leipzig
Germany
Tel...+49-341-9-80-39-21
Fax ....+49-341-9-80-61-41
Email ....info@dokfestival-leipzig.de
Web Site ....www.dokfestival-leipzig.de

Year Festival Began: 1955

Festival Month: Late October

Entry Deadline: Early August

Entry Fee: None

Genres: Animation, Documentary, Experimental, Features, Independent, International, Shorts

Screening Format: 16mm - 35mm - BetaSP (PAL)

Number of Films Screened: 300

X Factor: Animated films and documentaries only is a pretty unique festival format.

Awards: Gold and Silver Doves Jury Prizes

Profile: The Leipzig DOK Festival is an annual festival for documentary and animated films. The Festival is promoted and supported by Leipzig City Council, which has commissioned the limited company

Leipziger DOK-Filmwochen GmbH with the organisation, preparation and execution of the Festival. Under the motto "Films of the world for human dignity", the Festival serves the promotion and increased circulation of international documentary and animated films, and provides film-makers, producers, distributors, journalists and media specialists with an opportunity to meet and exchange views with each other and the Leipzig cinema public.

Special Events: Symposiums, parties, and local young filmmaker short competition

Travel Tips: You can reach Leipzig by plane, train, or automobile.

Claas Danielsen ....Festival Director

INTERNATIONAL LESBIAN FILM FESTIVAL IMMAGINARIA

Via L. Calori 13
40122 Bologna
Italy
Tel ....+39-051-6424276
Fax ....+39-051-6424276
Email ....info@immaginaria.org
Web Site ......http://www.immaginaria.org/Indexe.htm

Year Festival Began: 1993

Festival Month: Late November-December

Entry Deadline: October

Entry Fee: None

Genres: Animation, Documentary, Experimental, Features, Gay Lesbian, Independent, International, Narrative, Shorts

Screening Format: 16mm - 35mm - BetaSP

Awards: Audience Awards

Special Immaginaria Award

BEST CHILDREN'S/FAMILY FILM FESTIVALS

Asian Children's Film Festival
Cambridge International Film Festival
Carolina Film and Video Festival
Chicago International Children's Film Festival
Cinekid Film Festival
Dove Family Film Festival
Fledgling Films Festival
Flying Popcorn! Film Festival
Heartland Film Festival
High Falls Film Festival
KidFlix - Florida International Children's Film
  Festival
New York International Children's Film Festival
Spudfest Drive-In Family Film & Music Festival
ViewFinders: International Film Festival for Youth
Youth Media Jam

Profile: The International Lesbian Film Festival Immaginaria promotes lesbian independent cinema of the whole world realized and produced by lesbian directors. Every year lesbian production becomes more remarkable and rich in its contents: it offers both a self-representation -how lesbians see other lesbians- and a lesbian point of view on the world. The Festival rejects the clichés continuously spread by heterosexual cinema about the lesbian subject in films .

Special Events: Awards, parties, panels

Filmmaker Perks: The festival covers travel and accomodations when possible.

Travel Tips: The G. Marconi Airport handles international flights. Once in Bologna, the bus system will be your best friend.

Marina Genovese..................................Festival Director

INTERNATIONAL SCIENTIFIC FILM FESTIVAL

Tisza Mozi Kft., 5000 Szolnok
Templom utca 4.
Hungary
Tel ....+36-56-511-270
Fax ....+36-56-420-038
Email ....tiszamozi@tiszamozi.hu
Web Site ....www.tiszamozi.hu

Festival Month: Late September-October

Entry Deadline: March

Entry Fee: None

Genres: Animation, Documentary, European, Independent, International, Markets, Narrative, Scientific and Popular Science

Screening Format: 35mm

Awards: No

Profile: The history of the International Scientific Film Festival initiated in Szolnok dates back to 30 years ago. During this time it became an important event for Hungarian filmmakers, fine and applied artists as well as the connoisseur public. The festival now showcases international and European cinema on science.

Special Events: Panels, discussions

Filmmaker Perks: The festival's very existence is a perk, considering how specialized its theme.

Demeter István..................................Managing Director

INTERNATIONAL SHORT FILM FESTIVAL OBERHAUSEN

Grillostraße 34
D-46045 Oberhausen
Germany
Tel ....+49-208-825-2652
Fax ....+49-208-825-5413
Email ....info@kurzfilmtage.de
Web Site ....www.kurzfilmtage.de

Year Festival Began: 1954

Festival Month: Late April-May

Entry Deadline: Late January

Number of Submissions: 4,800

Entry Fee: None

Genres: Animation, Children, Documentary, Family, Independent, International, Markets, Music Videos, Narrative, Shorts, Video

Screening Format: Super8 - 16mm - 35mm - MiniDV - DVCam - BetaSP

Number of Films Screened: 450 total, 150 in compatiton

Odds: 1 in 32 of screening in competition

X Factor: All works submitted to the festival (more than 4,800 from over 80 countries in 2003) can be viewed at the film market. So you could sell your film and not actually screen at the festival.

Awards: Jury Awards; Other Awards

Profile: The International Short Film Festival Oberhausen, one of the oldest and most renowned film festivals in the world, has always been flexible in dealing with political and aesthetic change, choosing its own standard of quality against which the "short idea on celluloid" is to be measured. A film isn't selected in Oberhausen simply for being well produced. A work must always be judged against its own claim of being something new - regardless of genre, production quality and budget. The decisive factor is a film's position vis-à-vis social reality, cultural differences and aesthetic innovation.

The Short Film Festival presents far more than a mere medley of current short productions. One of the most outstanding features of the Festival is the meticulousness with which its program is compiled. Individual works are thus brought into relation to one another, ideas and trends are elaborated and interaction rendered possible, leading to a refreshingly new short film experience. Today, every imaginable format of moving picture is presented in Oberhausen, covering the entire spectrum of the short form. The short film has long since shed its entertainment or educational function as an opener to the main feature. Instead, it now leads a very lively existence - extending far beyond the confines of the cinema.

Special Events: Youth and Children's Competition, MuVi Award for the best German music video, parties, panels, retrospectives, award ceremony, Film Market

Filmmaker Perks: The International Short Film Festival Oberhausen purchases certain festival entries each year, with due consideration of the prize-winning entries, for the purpose of non-commercial distribution and for the Festival archive, in order to afford these films, many of whom have no other distributors, exposure to the greater public.

Travel Tips: Amidst all the nice German hotels and youth hostels is the Best Western Parkhotel Oberhausen, proving some franchises can not be stopped.

Lars Henrik Gass ....Festival Directot
Ulrike Erbslöh...................................Managing Director

INTERNATIONAL TRICKFILM FESTIVAL STUTTGART

Film-und Medienfestival GmbH
Stuttgart International Festival of Animated Film
Breitscheidstraße 4
70174 Stuttgart
Germany
Tel ....+49-711-92546-115
Fax ....+49-711-92546-150
Email ....bauer@festival-gmbh.de
Web Site..www.itfs.de

Festival Month: Early April
Entry Deadline: Early December
Entry Fee: None
Genres: Animation, Children, Digital Animation, Family, Features, International, Student
Screening Format: 35mm - BetaSP
Awards: State of Baden-Württemberg Award
City of Stuttgart Award
SWR Audience Awards

Profile: The Stuttgart International Festival of Animated Film is the second largest festival for animated film in the world and the largest event of its kind in Germany. Artistic animated film is the focal point of this Festival.

On six festival days and nights several hundred animated films from all continents will be screened in the presence of the directors and producers. In addition to four competition sections, the Festival offers an extensive supporting programme with special presentations and retrospectives, workshops and exhibitions.

Special Events: Workshops, awards, parties, retrospectives
Filmmaker Perks: The Sponsorship Prize is worth $12,500 Euros
Travel Tips: Stuttgart International Airport is served by all major airlines. After that, use the "S-Bahn" subway or "U-Bahn" tramway transit systems to get around.

Gabriele Röthemeyer ....Managing Director

INTERNATIONALES FILMFESTIVAL MANNHEIM-HEIDELBERG

Collini-Center, Galerie
D-68161 Mannheim
Germany
Tel................+49-621-1560154; +49-621-15 23 16
Fax ....+49-621-291564
Email.......................ifmh@mannheim-filmfestival.com
Web Site ....www.mannheim-filmfestival.com

Festival Month: Mid-November
Entry Deadline: Early August
Entry Fee: None
Genres: Animation, Documentary, Features, First-Time Independent Filmmakers, Independent, International, Markets, Narrative, Shorts, Student
Screening Format: 16mm - 35mm - Other Formats
Awards: The Main Award of Mannheim-Heidelberg
FIPRESCI Prize
Ecumenic Film Prize
Other Awards

Profile: No other festival in the world is specialized so consequently in the discovery of new talent, presenting only newcomer films that are to a large extent unknown to the international film industry.

Special Events: Awards, parties, special screenings, meetings, market
Comments:
Filmmaker Perks: The festival offers travel and board for select filmmakers.
Travel Tips: Get a German Rail 'n Drive Pass, allowing you to use the trains for long distances and a car for the local sights.

Daniela Koetz.....................................Program Manager

JERUSALEM INTERNATIONAL FILM FESTIVAL

11 Hebron Rd.
Wolfson Gardens
Jerusalem 91083
Israel
Jerusalem, 91083 Israel
Tel...+ 972-2-565-4333
Fax ....+ 972-2-565-4334
Email ....festival@jer-cin.org.il
Web Site ....www.jff.org.il

Year Festival Began: 1983
Festival Month: Mid-July
Entry Deadline: Mid-April
Entry Fee: None
Genres: All, Animation, Avant Garde, Documentary, Ethnic Jewish, Features, Human Rights, Independent, International, Multi-Cultural, Narrative, Shorts, Student, Television
Screening Format: 16mm - 35mm - BetaSP
Number of Films Screened: 200

Awards: The Wolfgin Awards

In the Spirit of Freedom Award

Television Drama Award

Other Awards

Profile: For two weeks each summer, the city of Jerusalem is transported into a magical movie cinema. The Jerusalem International Film Festival is a magnet for people from around the city, the country and the world. The Festival showcases more than 200 films from 40 countries. It is one of the most important cultural events of the State of Israel and one of the most distinguished international celebrations of cinema.

The Festival serves as a center stage for quality Israeli film productions. Israeli filmmakers have historically faced extraordinary economic hardship; the Festival provides them with much-needed international exposure, and affords them intellectual exchange with the world's greatest filmmakers.

Special Events: Panels, opening and closing galas, award ceremony, nightly Happy Hours

Travel Tips: The only reasonable way to get to Israel, unless you happen to be living in Jordan, is by plane. Security is tight, so don't try anything funny.

Lia van Leer ....Festival Director/Founder

KARLOVY VARY iNTERNATiONAL FiLM FESTiVAL

Film Servis Festival Karlovy Vary

Panská 1

110 00 Prague 1

Czech Republic

Tel ....+420-221-411-011 ; + 420-22-141-1026

Fax ....+420-221-411-033

Email ....festival@kviff.com

Web Site ....www.kviff.com

Festival Month: Early July

Entry Deadline: Mid-April

Entry Fee: None

Genres: 16mm, 35mm, Animation, Documentary, Features, Independent, International, Narrative, Shorts

Screening Format: 16mm - 35mm - 70mm

Awards: Grand Prix - A Crystal Globe; Jury Awards

Profile: The Karlovy Vary IFF is one of the oldest film festivals of all time (the first year took place in 1946). The festival is a non-specialised competitive festival recognised by FIAPF. Its aim is to contribute to the development and promotion of artistic cinema and film industry.

Special Events: Awards, panels, parties

Filmmaker Perks: For each film accepted into the competition, the President of the Karlovy Vary Film Festival and the Artistic Director invite a two-member delegation for a period of four days, covering all accomodations. The Grand Prix is worth $20,000.

Travel Tips: You may want to buy a tourist pass that will enable you to use any type of mass transit as many times as you want within the time period for which your pass is valid.

Jirí Bartoſka..President

Eva Zaoralová ....Artistic Director

KASSELER DOKUMENTARFiLM - UND ViDEOFEST

Goethestraße 31

34119 Kassel

Germany

Tel ....+49-0561-70764-0

Fax ....+49-561-70764-41

Email..dokfest@filmladen.de

Web Site ....www.filmladen.de/dokfest

Year Festival Began: 1982

Festival Month: Early November

Entry Deadline: August

Entry Fee: None

Genres: Documentary, DVD, Experimental, Features, Independent, International, Shorts, Video

Screening Format: 16mm - 35mm - BetaSP

Awards: No

Profile: In times of extreme political, economical, and cultural changes, documentary films and videos can play a large part in raising highly controversial topics and in examining background information. Next to other documentary film festivals like Duisburg, Munich, and Leipzig, the Kassel festival is one of the few that devotes itself completely to documentaries and its variations. In Germany Europe, this genre is still far away from public awareness since it can't be shown very often.

Special Events: Retrospectives, panels, parties

Filmmaker Perks: The festival assists with travel and accomodations when possible.

Travel Tips: Bring a jacket, temps drop close to freezing.

Wieland Höhne ....Festival Contact

Gerhard Wissner ....Festival Staff

KiNOFiLM MANCHESTER iNTERNATiONAL SHORT FiLM FESTiVAL

42 Edge St.

Manchester M4 1HN

England, UK

Tel ....+ 44-161-288-2494

Fax...+ 44-161-281-1374

Email ....kino.info@good.co.uk

Web Site ....www.kinofilm.org.uk

Year Festival Began: 1995

Festival Month: Late October

Entry Deadline: Mid-June

Number of Submissions: 1,300

Entry Fee: $10

Genres: Digital, Documentary, Ethnic Asian, Ethnic Black, Ethnic Chicano, European, Experimental, Independent, International, Narrative, Shorts

Screening Format: 8mm - Super8 - 16mm - 35mm - VHS - BetaSP (PAL) - DVD

Number of Films Screened: 250

Odds: 1 in 5

X Factor: Manchester's a great place to eat out, whether you want Chinese, Indian, Italian, Japanese, Malaysian, the latest in French nouvelle cuisine, or just a good greasy spoon cafe.

Awards: Jury Awards; Audience Award

Profile: In October 1995, Kinofilm the Manchester International Short Film Festival was born following a series of successful one-of events showcasing new short films. The festival has grown from strength to strength ever since and Kinofilm is now the largest shorts festival in the UK, with over thirty programmes and 250 shorts selected from over 1300 entries submitted from around the world. British New Wave is back by popular demand showcasing a round up of surreal, poignant, and just plain fantastic shorts from the UK and Ireland. The International Panorama is a truly mixed bag from around the globe, we have hand picked the best outstanding award winning films from festivals worldwide for your viewing pleasure, many of which are making their UK premiere.

Special Events: Panels, parties, awards ceremony, seminars

Filmmaker Perks: Free passes to screenings.

Travel Tips: Rent a car if you must, but the trains are sweet.

John Wojowski..........................Festival Director

KYiV iNTERNATiONAL FiLM FESTiVAL MOLODiST

DOM KINO, Suite 115
Saksagansky St. 6
Kyiv 01033 U
kraine
Tel ....+38-044-227-45-57
Fax ....+38-044-461-98-03
Email ....info@molodist.com
Web Site ....www.molodist.com

Year Festival Began: 1970

Festival Month: Late October-November

Entry Deadline: Early July

Entry Fee: None

Genres: Animation, Documentary, Features, Independent, International, Narrative, Shorts, Student

Screening Format: 16mm - 35mm

Awards: Grand Prix; Jury Awards; FIPRESCI Award

Profile: The main goal of the Kyiv International Film Festival Molodist is to give educational and information support for young International and Ukrainian filmmakers, to create opportunities for exchanging experiences for participants with each other and with outstanding contemporary filmmakers.

Special Events: Parties, awards, workshops, panels, special screenings

Filmmaker Perks: The Grand Prix is worth $10,000. Directors whose films have been selected for competition are invited as participants for the festival's duration. Room and board in a hotel will be provided by the festival.

Travel Tips: Boryspil Airport is about 40 km southeast of the city center on a rare stretch of four-lane road and it recently got a baggage carousel.

Andrei Khalpakhchi..........................General Director
Olena Yershova ....Executive Director

LEEDS CHiLDREN AND YOUNG PEOPLE'S FiLM FESTiVAL

PO Box 596
Leeds LS2 8YQ
UK
Tel................................+44-0113-247-952
Email ....filmfestival@leeds.gov.uk
Web Site................................www.leedsfilm.com

Festival Month: Early April

Entry Deadline: Mid-January

Entry Fee: None

Genres: Animation, Children, Documentary, Family, Features, Independent, International, Narrative, Shorts

Screening Format: 35mm - BetaSP - DigiBeta - MiniDV

BEST FESTIVALS FOR WOMEN IN FILM

Feminale Women's Film Festival
International Black Women's Film Festival
International Women Film Festival of Créteil
International Women's Film Festival of Barcelona
Lunafest
Madcat Women's International Film Festival
Moondance International Film Festival
Reel Sisters of the Diaspora Film Festival
Rocky Mountain Womens Film Festival
Seattle International Film Festival
St. John's International Women's Film & Video Festival
WinFemme Film Festival
Women in the Director's Chair International Film & Video Festival
Women Make Waves Film Festival

Awards: National Young Filmmakers Award

Profile: The Leeds Children and Young People's Film Festival is the UK's annual children's festival, complete with a Young Filmmakers Award for children filmmakers.

Filmmaker Perks: Festival assists with travel and accomodations when possible.

Travel Tips: If you're in contention for the Young Filmmakers Award, make sure you have your parent or guardian with you.

Debbie Maturi ....Festival Director
Adam Graham ....Production Manager

LEEDS INTERNATIONAL FILM FESTIVAL

PO Box 596
Leeds LS2 8YQ
UK
Tel ....+44-0113-247-8389
Email ....filmfestival@leeds.gov.uk
Web Site...www.leedsfilm.com

Year Festival Began: 1987

Festival Month: October

Entry Deadline: Mid-July

Entry Fee: None

Genres: Animation, Documentary, Features, Independent, International, Narrative, Shorts

Screening Format: 16mm - 35mm - BetaSP - DigiBeta - DVD - MiniDV

Number of Films Screened: 200+

Awards: Louis le Prince International Short Film Awards

Yorkshire Film Award

British Independent Short Film Award

Profile: The North of England's leading film event, Leeds International Film Festival has presented vast programmes of new and unseen cinema from around the world. The Festival seeks to promote the moving image as a major contributor to the cultural life of the city, the region, and the nation as a whole.

Special Events: Awards, panels, parties

Filmmaker Perks: Festival assists with travel and accomodations when possible.

Travel Tips: Bring warm clothes, the weather can be chilly. And help the festival out if you can by offering to buy the odd round of drinks - you will be rewarded with their undying admiration.

Chris Fell ....Festival Director
Debbie Maturi ....Festival Deputy Director

LOCARNO INTERNATIONAL FILM FESTIVAL

Via Ciseri 23
6600 Locarno
Switzerland
Tel ....+41-91-756-2121
Fax ....+41-91-756-2149
Email ....info@pardo.ch; programming@pardo.ch
Web Site ....www.pardo.ch

Festival Month: Early August

Entry Deadline: Early June

Entry Fee: None

Genres: 16mm, 35mm, Animation, Documentary, Features, First-Time Independent Filmmakers, Independent, International, Shorts, Student

Screening Format: 16mm - 35mm

Awards: Leopard of Honour

Raimondo Rezzonico Award

Profile: The Locarno International Film Festival is keeping alive the tradition of experimentation, discovery, eclecticism and passion for auteur cinema, at the same time maintaining the magical atmosphere of an artistic event that knows how to be friendly and convivial - never more so than when seven or eight thousand (sometimes even more) moviegoers of all ages, nationalities and backgrounds gather under the stars in Piazza Grande to watch a movie on one of the world's biggest screens.

Special Events: Awards, parties, panels, tributes, retrospectives

Filmmaker Perks: The Festival undertakes to provide accommodations for filmmakers for a maximum of 3 nights for those coming from European countries and for a maximum of 5 nights for those coming from countries outside Europe.

Travel Tips: Ticino can be reached by every means of transportation - by car or train - from all over Switzerland as well as from Italy and nearby European countries, and by air from the rest of the world.

Irene Bignardi ....Festival Director

MARSEILLES INTERNATIONAL DOCUMENTARY FILM FESTIVAL

Vue sur les Docs
3 Square Stalingrad
13001 Marseilles
France
Tel ....+33-04-95-04-44-90
Fax..+33-04-95-04-44-91
Email ....welcome@fidmarseille.org
Web Site ....www.fidmarseille.org

Festival Month: Early July

Entry Deadline: Mid-March

Entry Fee: None

Genres: Documentary, Features, Independent, International, Shorts

Screening Format: 16mm - 35mm - BetaSP - DigiBeta - VHS

Awards: The Grand Prix

The Prix de la Competition Francaise

The Prix Premiers

Profile: The Marseilles International Documentary Film Festival is an annual festival showcasing the best in international short and longform documentaries.

Special Events: Awards, panels, parties

Travel Tips: Fly into Airport Marseille-Provence and then take advantage of their expansive bus system.

Jean-Pierre Rehm..................................Artistic Director

MELBOURNE INTERNATIONAL FILM FESTIVAL

PO Box 2206

Fitzroy Mail Centre

Victoria 3065

Australia

Tel..+ 61-3-9417-2011

Fax ....+ 61-3-9417-3804

Email ....miff@melbournefilmfestival.com.au

Web Site ....www.melbournefilmfestival.com.au

Year Festival Began: 1952

Festival Month: Late July-August

Entry Deadline: Mid-March

Entry Fee: $30

Genres: Animation, Documentary, Features, Human Rights, Independent, International, Narrative, Shorts, Touring

Screening Format: 16mm - 35mm - BetaSP (Shorts) - VHS (Shorts)

Number of Films Screened: 400+

X Factor: Over 67,000 attendees attend the festival

Awards: City of Melbourne Grand Prix; Jury Awards; Other Awards

Profile: Established in 1952, the Melbourne International Film Festival is one of the country's oldest running arts events and the oldest and largest established film festival in the Southern Hemisphere. It is a major event on the Australian arts calendar every July/August

The Melbourne International Film Festival is a showcase for the latest developments in Australian and International filmmaking, offering audiences a wide range of features and shorts, documentaries, animation and experimental films.

Special Events: Forums, awards, parties

Filmmaker Perks: Travel and accommodations are only offered to guests invited to the festival.

Travel Tips: July-August in Melbourne is winter time, so expect some rain and cold weather.

James Hewison..................................Executive Director

Nick Feik..Project Coordinator

MELBOURNE QUEER FILM & VIDEO FESTIVAL

6 Claremont St.

South Yarra, VIC

3141

Australia

Tel...+ 61-3-9827-2022

Fax ....+ 61-3-9827-1622

Email........................info@melbournequeerfilm.com.au

Web Site..................www.melbournequeerfilm.com.au

Year Festival Began: 1990

Festival Month: Mid-March

Entry Deadline: Mid-December

Entry Fee: None

Genres: American, Animation, Documentary, Ethnic African, Ethnic Asian, Ethnic Black, Ethnic Jewish, Ethnic Latin, Ethnic Spanish, Experimental, Features, First-Time Independent Filmmakers, Gay Lesbian, Independent, International, Narrative, Online Festival, Shorts, Student, Super 8/8mm, Underground, Video, Weird, Women

Screening Format: 8mm - Super8 - 16mm - 35mm - VHS - DVD - BetaSP - MiniDV - Hi8

Number of Films Screened: 100

X Factor: It's the 2nd biggest queer film festival in Australia, that has to mean something.

Awards: The City of Melbourne Emerging Filmmaker Award

Profile: The Melbourne Queer Film Festival is the 2nd largest queer film festival in Australia and exhibits up to 100 features, docos, shorts, and experimental works from Australia and around the world over 10 days. It is the highlight of queer Melbourne's cultural calendar.

Special Events: Opening and closing night party

Filmmaker Perks: Festival pays for accomodations when possible.

Travel Tips: The weather turns mild in March as Autumn takes over. Bring some long sleeves and jackets just to be safe.

Lisa Daniel..Festival Director

Heidi Wharton ....Festival Assistant

MESSAGE TO MAN INTERNATIONAL DOCUMENTARY, SHORT AND ANIMATED FILMS FESTIVAL

Karavannaya 12

191011 Saint-Petersburg

Russia

Tel................+7-812-235-2660 ; +7-812-230-2200

Fax ....+7-812-235-3995

Email.................................info@message-to-man.spb.ru

Web Site.........................www.message-to-man.spb.ru

Year Festival Began: 1989

Festival Month: Mid-June

Entry Deadline: April

Number of Submissions: 1200

Entry Fee: None

Genres: 16mm, 35mm, Animation, Documentary, Features, First-Time Independent Filmmakers, Independent, International, Shorts, Student

Screening Format: 16mm - 35mm

Awards: Grand Prix "Golden Centaur"; Jury Awards

Profile: The idea of Message to Man is to emphasize the importance of non-feature films for the global culture and to let the native documentary filmmakers become the full members of the cinematographic world. Now, as the festival deals with short-feature, animation films, as well as with the documentaries, its purposes have become even more complicated.

The program of the Festival presents the new forms and styles in the world and native filmmaking to the specialists, and introduce the viewers to genres of cinema unfamiliar to them. Message to Man - is both the name and the slogan of the festival. It refers to the Bible and reflects the main issues of our meeting: Faith, Hope, Love, Mercy, and Compassion, which we are eager to find in our real life and cinematography today.

Special Events: Special screenings, retrospectives

Filmmaker Perks: Directors whose films have been selected will be invited to attend the festival and provided with hotel accommodation. Expenses for only one person per film can be paid. The invitation can be transferred to the producer in case if the director is not able to attend.

Travel Tips: If you don't speak Russian, find someone who translates and stick with them like glue.

Mikhail Litviakov.....................General Director
Alexandra Leybovitch ....Chief Coordinator
Boris Peyrik ....Executive Director

BEST FIRST-TIME FILMMAKER FESTIVALS

$100 Film Festival
Bergamo International Week of Auteur Film
Castellinaria International Young Cinema Festival
DancesWithFilms
Deep Ellum Film Festival
Gen Art Film Festival
Home Brewed International Short Film Festival
Hot Shops Film Festival
IAC British International Amateur Film & Video Competition
Imperial Beach Student Film Festival
International Teen Movie Festival
Spindletop Film Festival
up-and-coming Film Festival Hannover
ViewFinders: International Film Festival for Youth

MiDNiGHT SUN FiLM FESTiVAL

Lapintie 16 as 2
FIN-99600 Sodankylä
Finland
Tel...+358-16-614-525
Fax ....+358-16-618-646
Email ....office@msfilmfestival.fi
Web Site........................www.msfilmfestival.fi

Festival Month: Mid-June

Entry Deadline: March

Entry Fee: None

Genres: Documentary, European, Experimental, Features, Independent, International, Narrative, Shorts, Silent

Screening Format: 16mm - 35mm

Awards: No

Profile: Thousands of film enthusiasts make the journey across the Arctic Circle in June to participate in the Midnight Sun Film Festival for five days and nights. The festival showcases the works of the greatest masters of cinema over the decades, the best new films and a brilliant exposition of silent films accompanied by live music.

Special Events: Morning discussions, special screenings, retrospectives

Filmmaker Perks: Midnight Sun Film Festival gives contact informations of local realtors, who are willing to rent out discounted apartments for the festival duration.

Travel Tips: Sodankylä is pretty small town, but it can still accomodate about 20,000 visitors so find accomodations early on.

Peter von Bagh.......................Festival Director
Ari Lehtola.............................Project Manager

MiFED

Palazzina FMI
Largo Domodossola 1
20145 Milano
Italy
Tel...+ 39-02-485501
Fax ....+ 39-02-48550420
Email ....mifed@fmi.it
firstinitiallastname@fmi.it
Web Site..................................www.mifed.com

Festival Month: Mid-October

Entry Fee: $175-$900 Depending on Duration and Tech Specs for Screening Room

Genres: All, Animation, Documentary, Features, International, Markets, Multimedia, Narrative, Television

Screening Format: 16mm - 35mm - BetaSP - DigiBeta

Profile: Mifed, the International film and multimedia market, is one of the world's leading audio-visual events where supply meets demand in the field of films, television and home video rights.

Special Events: Panels, exhibitions, parties

Filmmaker Perks: Folks are there to buy and sell, you've got as good a shot as anyone else renting a screening room.

Travel Tips: During trade shows, Fiera Milano provides a shuttle bus to the venue from Linate Airport.

Carlo Bassi ....General Manager

MIX BRASIL FESTIVAL OF SEXUAL DIVERSITY

Rua Joao Moura
2432, CEP 105413.004
Sao Paulo, SP
Brazil
Tel....................................+ 55-11-3819-7390
Fax ....+ 55-11-3819-5360
Web Site ....mixbrasil.uol.com.br

Festival Month: Mid-November

Entry Deadline: Mid-July

Genres: Alternative Sexuality, Animation, Documentary, Ethnic Latin, Ethnic Other, Experimental, Features, Gay Lesbian, Independent, International, Multi-Cultural, Narrative, Performance, Shorts, Touring

Screening Format: 35mm - BetaSP

Number of Films Screened: 130 - 170

Awards: Yes

Profile: The Mix Brasil Festival of Sexual Diversity is a touring festival dedicated to showcasing new independent and international works about cultural and sexual diversity.

Special Events: Parties, retrospectives

Filmmaker Perks: One month spent touring Brazil with a lively program of films and filmmakers.

Travel Tips: Stay cool, drink lots of water... bottled water.

Suzy Capó ....Festival Director
João Federici

MUMBAI INTERNATIONAL FILM FESTIVAL

Ministry of Information & Broadcasting
Government of India
Soochana Bhavan
C.G.O. Complex, Lodhi R.d
New Delhi - 110 003 India
Tel ....+91-22-2381-0176
Fax ....+91-22-2380-0308
Email...miff@miffindia.com
Web Site.....................www.miffindia.com/home.htm

Festival Month: Early February

Entry Deadline: Mid-November

Entry Fee: $50

Genres: Animation, Documentary, First-Time Independent Filmmakers, Independent, International, Markets, Shorts, Student

Screening Format: 16mm - 35mm - BetaSP - DigiBeta

Awards: Gold and Silver Conch Awards; Other Awards

Profile: The Mumbai International Film Festival is dedicated to bringing the best and brightest short, animation, and documentary films to India. With a special emphasis is placed on first-time directors, the festival cultivates and nurtures the future of cinema in India.

Special Events: Parties, awards, retrospectives, market

Filmmaker Perks: The festival has a market component to assist with film sales.

Travel Tips: Avoid travelling at peak rush hours: 7-10 am and 5-8 pm. The buses are full of people, the streets are covered in pushcarts and merchants, and everyone with a car is trying to get home.

Dr. Gopalrao Deshmukh Marg ....Festival Director

NAPOLI FILM FESTIVAL

via A. Depretis 130
80133 Napoli
Italy
Tel...................................+39-081-1956-3340
Fax ....+39-081-1956-3345
Email................................press@napolifilmfestival.com
Web Site ....www.napolifilmfestival.com

Festival Month: Mid-June

Entry Deadline: April

Entry Fee: None

Genres: Animation, Documentary, European, Features, Independent, International, Narrative, Shorts

Screening Format: 35mm - BetaSP

Awards: Vesuvio Award

Profile: Napoli Film Festival continues with the development project it began years ago to become a Euro-Mediterranean festival, highlighting a region which is not just a center of conflict but is also a crossroads of diverse cultures and traditions. It is from this perspective that one gets a better sense of the identity of the host city, Naples, which itself is a product of frequent and controversial miscegenation.

Special Events: Awards, parties

Filmmaker Perks: Festival's dedication to Euro-Mediterranean filmmakers.

Travel Tips: When in Naples, catch a soccer game. It's a whole other world of sports.

Adriana Messina...................................Festival Contact

NEW ZEALAND FiLM FESTiVAL

PO Box 9544
Marion Square
Wellington 6001
New Zealand
Tel ....+64-4-385-0162
Fax ....+64-4-801-7304
Email ....festival@nzff.co.nz
Web Site..www.enzedff.co.nz

Festival Month: Mid-July-August

Entry Deadline: Mid-April

Entry Fee: None

Genres: Animation, Documentary, Ethnic Other, European, Experimental, Features, Independent, Independent, Narrative, Shorts

Screening Format: 16mm - 35mm - 70mm - BetaSP - DVD

Awards: No

Profile: The New Zealand Film Festival was inaugurated with seven films in 1972 to supplement the meager options of Wellington filmgoers. In 2001 those options were not at all meagre, but the Festival continued to grow, showing over 120 programmes to audiences in excess of 62,000. The Festival has a long tradition of supporting New Zealand filmmakers. The main venue is the magnificent Embassy Theatre and the Festival has played a major role in the theatre's rehabilitation and continuing refurbishment.

Special Events: Travelling Festival Circuit, parties, special screenings

Filmmaker Perks: Accepted films are eligible to travel to other New Zealand film festivals in the Travelling Festival Circuit.

Travel Tips: Bring sunscreen.

Bill Gosden ....Festival Director

NO BUDGET iNTERNATiONAL iNDEPENDENT FiLM & ViDEO FESTiVAL

Akademie f. Bildende Künste d.
Johannes Gutenberg universität
Am Taubertsberg 6
55099 Mainz
Germany
Tel..+43-01-535-28-03
Fax ....+43-01-535-28-03
Email ....agbeckmann@web.de
Web Site..www.ohnekohle.at.tf

Festival Month: July

Entry Deadline: Mid-April

Entry Fee: None

Genres: Animation, Digital, Documentary, Experimental, Features, Independent, International, Narrative, Shorts, Sports, Underground

Screening Format: BetaSP - DVD - DVCam - MiniDV

Awards: Yes

Profile: The No Budget International Independent Film & Video Festival provides a basis for "no-budget" films and their emerging makers, which is hard to find due to the economical reasons in the film-, and art-market in general. The festival offers artists the opportunity to gain exposure for their work, and so get the credit they deserve.

Special Events: Shorts competition

Filmmaker Perks: Focus on the all-digital audience, added exposure.

NORRKÖPiNG FiLM FESTiVAL FLiMMER

G:a Rådstugugatan 30
602 20 Norrköping 011 - 15 26 50
Sweden
Tel ....+46-011-152650
Email ....info@flimmer.nu
Web Site ....www.flimmer.nu

Year Festival Began: 1998

Festival Month: Late September

Entry Deadline: Late August

Entry Fee: Contact Festival

Genres: American, Animation, Digital, Documentary, Features, Gay Lesbian, Independent, International, Microcinema, Narrative, Shorts, Student, Video

Screening Format: 35mm - BetaSP - DV

Profile: The Norrköping Film Festival is southeast Sweden`s biggest film festival. The festival is aimed at filmlovers, of all ages irrespective of taste. Experiences beyond the ordinary repetoire are offered, but also reruns of earlier premiéres. A total film celebration for all the family.

Special Events: Retrospectives, parties, workshops, special screenings

Filmmaker Perks: Festival assists with accomodations when it can.

Travel Tips: Fly into Kungsangen Airport in Norrkoping and take a taxi.

Johan Karlsson....................................Festival Director

NORWEGiAN iNTERNATiONAL FiLM FESTiVAL

PO Box 145
5501 Haugesund
Norway
Tel ....+47-52-74-33-70
Fax..+47-52-74-33-71
Email ....info@filmfestivalen.no
Web Site ....www.filmfestivalen.no

Festival Month: Late August

Entry Deadline: By Invite Only

Genres: Animation, Documentary, European, Features, International, Narrative

Awards: No

Profile: The Norwegian International Film Festival program is devoted to finding feature films a theatrical release. Titles are selected on artistic merit. The Festival co-operates closely with Norwegian distributors in selecting films for screening at the Festival and Nordic bodies for screening at New Nordic Films. The Norwegian Int'l Film Festival is a non-competitive festival and the films screened are by invitation only.

Special Events: New Nordic Films market, seminars, special screenings

Filmmaker Perks: The New Nordic Films is an annual market offering a special possibility to meet other Nordic filmmakers, producers, agents, buyers and distributors during the festival.

Travel Tips: Fly into Haugesund Airport Karmøy.

Gunnar Johan Løvvik ....Festival Director
Hakon Skogrand ....Program Director

OLDENBURG INTERNATIONAL FILM FESTIVAL

Bahnhofstr. 15
26122 Oldenburg
Germany
Tel ....+ 49-441-925-0855
Fax..+ 49-441-925-0856
Email....................................info@filmfest-oldenburg.de
Web Site..............................www.filmfest-oldenburg.de

Year Festival Began: 1994
Festival Month: Early September
Entry Deadline: June
Number of Submissions: 500
Entry Fee: None
Genres: Animation, Documentary, Features, Independent, International, Narrative, Shorts, Women
Screening Format: 16mm - 35mm - 70mm
Number of Films Screened: 45 - 55

X Factor: According to Slamdance co-founder Dan Mirvish, "Oldenburg is one of the few German fests (Munich another) that really focuses on US indies. And their volunteers, though perhaps not as young and nubile as those at Avignon, are definitely the "friendliest" of any Euro-fest. Fest adds new meaning to the term "German hospitality." You're sure to have a good time!"

Awards: The German Independence Audience Award

Profile: Being a "non-competitive film festival" the Oldenburg International Film Festival has a tradition of covering the international movie scene in all of its aspects. This open minded approach leads to an interesting and inspiring mix of great premieres, surprising discoveries and original independent productions. An eclectic and attractive programme has been the result for the past years.

Special Events: Retrospectives, tributes, parties

Filmmaker Perks: Travel and accomodations offered to select filmmakers.

Travel Tips: Rent a car in Bremen and drive the world famous Autobahn into Oldenburg.

Torsten Neumann............................Festival Co-Director
Thorsten Ritter ....Festival Co-Director

ONE TAKE FILM FESTIVAL

Trg rtava faizma 14
10 000 Zagreb
Croatia
Tel ....+385-01-4612548
Fax ....+385-01-4612548
Email ....onetake@kkz.hr
Web Site ....onetake.kkz.hr

Festival Month: Mid-November
Entry Deadline: Mid-September
Entry Fee: None
Genres: Commercials, Documentary, Experimental, Features, Independent, International, Music Videos, Narrative, Shorts
Screening Format: 8mm - Super 8mm - 16mm - Super 16mm - 35mm - BetaSP - VHS - DVCam - MiniDV
Awards: Grand prix

Profile: The One Take Film Festival is an international festival of films shot in one take, that is films shot without interruption, from the moment of turning the camera on to the moment of turning the camera off. The One Take Film Festival eliminates a seemingly indispensable part of a film - namely, editing - and thus prohibits cut, dissolve, fade in/out and all other types of transitions. In that way, the One Take Film Festival makes room for a more stimulating concept of film and more exciting filmmaking.

Special Events: Concerts, parties, awards

Filmmaker Perks: This is a festival specifically geared to one type of filmmaker, there are no other festivals like it.

Travel Tips: The temperatures will be dropping so bring a jacket.

Vedran Samanovic ....Festival Director

ONEDOTZERO DIGITAL CREATIVITY FESTIVAL

Unit 212c Curtain House
134-146 Curtain Rd.
London EC2A 3AR
, England
Tel ....+44-207-729-0072
Fax...+44-207-729-0057
Email ....info@onedotzero.com
Web Site ....www.onedotzero.com

Year Festival Began: 1997
Festival Month: Early May

Entry Deadline: Ongoing, but decisions are made in March

Entry Fee: None

Genres: Animation, Digital, Digital Animation, Documentary, Features, Independent, International, Multimedia, Narrative, Shorts, Video Games, Visual Effects, Web Projects

Screening Format: BetaSP

Number of Films Screened: 70

Awards: No

Profile: Since onedotzero's inception it has collated and commissioned almost a hundred hours of original programming for the eponymous annual digital creativity festival and other innovative projects. It has been the largest dedicated digital film festival in the world since 1999 and elements of the London event are presented around the globe.

Special Events: Panels, exhibitions

Filmmaker Perks: Great networking opportunities.

Travel Tips: London Underground is the oldest and one of the largest subway systems in the world, use it.

Shane Walter ....Festival Director

OUT TAKES

PO Box 27 070
Wellington
New Zealand
Wellington, New Zealand
Tel ....+64-4-972-6775
Fax ....+64-4-801-9906
Email ....info@outtakes.org.nz
Web Site ....www.outtakes.org.nz

Festival Month: Mid-May-June

Entry Deadline: Mid-March

Entry Fee: None

Genres: Features, Gay Lesbian, Independent, International, Narrative, Shorts, Touring

Screening Format: 16mm - 35mm - BetaSP - VHS - DVD

Awards: No

Profile: Reel Queer Inc is a group of gay men and lesbians based mainly in Wellington and Auckland that organises New Zealand's annual gay and lesbian film festival, Out Takes.

Special Events: Parties

Filmmaker Perks: Festival will help with travel and accomodations when possible.

Travel Tips: The festival tours Auckland, Wellington, Christchurch, and Dunedin so be prepared to spend a month in New Zealand.

Simon Fulton...Programmer

PALESTINE FILM FESTIVAL DREAMS OF A NATION

2 Ibn Jubair St.
PO Box 54874
Jerusalem
Tel ....+972-02-626-1045
Fax ....+972-02-626-1372
Email ....info@dreamsofanation.org
Web Site ....www.dreamsofanation.org

Festival Month: Mid-January

Entry Deadline: Early November

Entry Fee: None

Genres: Documentary, Ethnic Other, Features, Human Rights, International, Multi-Cultural, Narrative, Shorts

Screening Format: 16mm - 35mm - BetaSP - DVD

Awards: No

Profile: Dreams of a Nation is a Columbia University-based project to provide resources for research into Palestinian film- and video-making. This project is strictly limited to work by Palestinians, and does not include the wide range of materials that have been produced by non-Palestinians about Palestine or related issues.

Special Events: Palestinian film archive

Filmmaker Perks: For a Palestinian filmmaker, this festival is the opportunity to exhibit your work.

Hamid Dabashi ....Festival Contact

PRIX JEUNESSE INTERNATIONAL

Bayerischer Rundfunk
Rundfunkplatz 1
D - 80300 Munich
Germany
Tel...+49-89-5900-2058
Fax ....+49-89-5900-3053
Email..info@prixjeunesse.de,
uvz@prixjeunese.de
Web Site ....www.prixjeunesse.de

Year Festival Began: 1964

Festival Month: Mid-June

Entry Deadline: Late January

Entry Fee: None

Genres: Children, Episodic Television/Television Pilots, International, Television, Web Projects

Screening Format: BetaSP - DigiBeta

Number of Films Screened: 84

Awards: Yes

Profile: Participating in Prix Jeunesse is children's television's most engaging and rewarding professional training exercise. The bi-annual competition is distinctive because prizes are not awarded by a small, select jury. All participants may help select the winners. Prizes are awarded for overall excellence and for special achievements based on specific criteria.

Special Events: Discussions, parties, awards

Filmmaker Perks: Contacts with the best in international children's programming.

Travel Tips: People in Munich have their own dialect of German, called Bavarian. If you understand German but are having trouble, that's probably why.

Ursula von Zallinger...........................Secretary General
Kirsten Schneid ....Organizational Manager

QUEERSiCHT - SCHWUL-LESBiSCHES FiLMFESTiVAL BERN

Postfach 367
3000 Bern 11
Switzerland
Tel...+41-31-311-41-48
Email ....queersicht.filme@bluewin.ch
Web Site ....www.queersicht.ch

Year Festival Began: 1997

Festival Month: 2nd weekend of November

Entry Deadline: Late June

Entry Fee: None

Genres: Animation, Documentary, Experimental, Features, Gay Lesbian, Independent, International, Narrative, Shorts

Screening Format: 16mm - 35mm - BetaSP - VHS

Awards: The Rosa Brille Award

Profile: Queersicht is the oldest gay-lesbian filmfestival in Switzerland. It's a small but beautiful festival: About 30 short films, documentaries and features are shown in five cinemas in the centre of Berne, Switzerland, every second weekend in November.

Special Events: Awards, parties

Filmmaker Perks: Very appreciative audience.

Travel Tips: If you feel up to it, most big-name Swiss towns are less than 2 hours from Bern - you could go exploring.

Maddalena Tognola ....Festival Director

RAiNDANCE FiLM FESTiVAL

81 Berwick St.
London W1F 8TW UK
UK
Tel ....+44-0207-287-3833
Fax ....+44-0207-439-2243
Email...festival@raindance.co.uk
Web Site ....www.raindance.co.uk

Festival Month: Early October

Entry Deadline: Mid-July

Entry Fee: $30-$90

Genres: Animation, Documentary, Features, Independent, International, Narrative, Shorts

Screening Format: 35mm - BetaSP - VHS - DVD

Awards: Yes

Profile: Welcome to Raindance. Dedicated to fostering and promoting independent film in the UK and around the world, Raindance spans the full spectrum of the art, craft and business of independent movies - from guerilla style low or no budget production through to big budget indie blockbusters.

Special Events: Awards, panels, parties, workshops

Filmmaker Perks: Raindance supports indie filmmakers passionately.

Travel Tips: London offers many options for travelers to get around, such as Red Buses, Black Cabs, and the Tube.

Ronni Raygun..Raindance NYC

RiO DE JANEiRO iNTERNATiONAL FiLM FESTiVAL

Rua Arnaldo Quintela, 62 - Botafogo
Rio de Janeiro, RJ - 22280-070
Brazil
Tel ....+55-21-2579-0352
Fax ....+55-21-2539-3580
Email ....films@festivaldorio.com.br
Web Site ....www.festivaldorio.com.br

Festival Month: Late September-October

Entry Deadline: Late July

Entry Fee: Primarily By Invite, Contact Festival for Details

Genres: Animation, Documentary, Ethnic Latin, Features, Independent, International, Narrative, Shorts

Screening Format: 35mm - BetaSP

Awards: Audience Awards; FIPRESCI Prize

Profile: Over 15 days, Rio de Janeiro lights up with over 300 films from around the world, presented by top celebrities and filmmakers. Screenings take place at 35 locations throughout the city, including galas at Cinema Odeon BR, a restored 1920s movie palace, and open-air presentations on Copacabana Beach.

BEST "DIFFERENT" FILM FESTIVALS

48 Hour Film Festival
Bearded Child Film Festival
Century City Film Festival
CineKink NYC
Faces Of Love International Film Festival
Frozen Dead Guy Days
Inflatable Duck Film Fest
Machinima Film Festival
Nihilist Film Festival
Rural Route Film Festival
Sex And Death Short Film Fest
Wreck-Beach Film Festival

Special Events: Cinema on the Beach, seminars, panels, parties, awards, workshops
Filmmaker Perks: Massive exposure throughout Rio de Janeiro.
Travel Tips: Sunscreen, shorts, sunglasses, smile... pack them all.

Ilda Santiago ....Co-Director
Walkiria Barbosa...Co-Director

RIVER TO RIVER FLORENCE INDIAN FILM FESTIVAL

bdjMEDIA/Belle de Jour
Via del Purgatorio, 2
50123 Florence
Italy
Tel..+39-055-2654257
Fax...+39-055-268012
Email ....info@rivertoriver.it
Web Site ....www.rivertoriver.it

Festival Month: Early December
Entry Deadline: Mid-October
Entry Fee: None
Genres: Animation, Documentary, Ethnic Other, Features, Independent, International, Narrative, Shorts
Screening Format: 35mm - BetaSP - DV
Awards: Audience Awards
Profile: River to River Florence Indian Film Festival, the only festival in Europe entirely devoted to films from or about India.

To give our audience a greater vision of India, the festival is also open to films coming from Bangladesh, Nepal, Pakistan and Sri Lanka.

Special Events: Awards, parties
Filmmaker Perks: The film chosen by the festival audience will win the River to River DigiMovies Audience Award: up to 15 minutes of it will be on streaming for one year on www.digimovies.net.
Travel Tips: The Winter days in Florence are short and cold, averaging in the 40s.

Luca Marziali ....Festival Co-Director
Selvaggia Velo ....Festival Co-Director

ROTTERDAM INTERNATIONAL FILM FESTIVAL

PO Box 21696
3001 AR Rotterdam
The Netherlands
Tel ....+31-10-8909090
Fax..+31-10-8909091
Email ....tiger@filmfestivalrotterdam.com
Web Site ....www.filmfestivalrotterdam.com

Year Festival Began: 1972
Festival Month: Late January-February
Entry Deadline: November
Entry Fee: None
Genres: Animation, Documentary, Ethnic Asian, European, Features, First-Time Independent Filmmakers, Independent, International, Markets, Narrative, Shorts
Screening Format: 16mm - 35mm - BetaSP
Number of Films Screened: 210 45 in Cinemart Market
X Factor: If you're a first-time filmmaker, Rotterdam offers one of the best prizes around, the VPRO Tiger Award worth $10,000 Euros.
Awards: VPRO Tiger Award; FIPRESCI Award; Audience Awards; Other Awards
Profile: Having started out in 1972 as Film International, the International Film Festival Rotterdam has developed into one of the biggest cultural events of the Netherlands. The original principle still applies: focusing on independent and innovative cinema. Through the years, the festival has been expanded with thematic sidebars which, for instance, explore the links with the visual arts and multimedia. Important parts of the festival are the VPRO Tiger Awards Competition for first and second features, the Hubert Bals Fund which supports filmmakers in developing countries and the co-production market CineMart.
Special Events: Cinemart Market, panels, awards, parties
Filmmaker Perks: With the Cinemart Market happening at the same time, you could wind up selling your film just as easily as you screen it.

BE A PRODUCER

If being surrounded by film biz types starts to get on your nerves, hey, just become one of them. Anyone can be a producer. Trust me, it doesn't take much. Some of the least intelligent people I have ever met at festivals have been producers. In fact, I can prove that you're a "producer" right now! Just look in the mirror and say, "I'm a producer." See, that was easy. The hard part is getting something actually produced, which is another article entirely. But "wanna-be" producers already surround you, so join in the fun and completely BS your way to a career in film. Believe me, you won't be the only one.

Travel Tips: The public transportation in Rotterdam is superb.

Simon Field ....Festival Co-Director
Sandra den Hamer ....Festival Co-Director
René van der Giessen ....Head of Programming

SÃO PAULO INTERNATIONAL FILM FESTIVAL

Abmic Mostra Internacional de Cinema
Rua Antonio Carlos, 2
88 01309-010 Cerqueira Cesar - São Paulo - SP
Brazil
Tel ....+55-11-3141-2548; + 55 11 3064-5819
Fax...+55-11-3266-7066
Email ....info@mostra.org
Web Site ....www.mostra.org

Year Festival Began: 1976
Festival Month: Late October-November
Entry Deadline: Early August
Entry Fee: None
Genres: 16mm, 35mm, Animation, Documentary, Features, First-Time Independent Filmmakers, Independent, International, Narrative, Shorts
Screening Format: 16mm - 35mm
Number of Films Screened: 300
X Factor: Summer in Brazil, how often do you do that?
Awards: Jury Awards
Profile: The Festival is a cultural, non-profit event, held by the 'Associação Brasileira Mostra Internacional de Cinema'and recognized by the International Federation of the Association of Film Producers. The Festival includes two sessions: 'International Perspective' and 'New Filmmakers Competition.'
Special Events: Panels, awards, parties, New Filmmakers Competition, International Perspective section
Travel Tips: October-November is Summer in Brazil and you can expect temperatures in the 90's day and night.

Leon Cakoff ....Festival Director

SHANGHAI INTERNATIONAL FILM FESTIVAL

11/F STV Mansions
298 Wei Hai Road
Shanghai 200041
China
Tel...+86-21-62597115
Fax ....+86-21-62552000
Email ....siff@public4.sta.net.cn
Web Site ....www.siff.com

Festival Month: Early June
Entry Deadline: Mid-April

Entry Fee: None
Genres: 35mm, Animation, Documentary, Ethnic Asian, Features, Independent, International, Markets, Narrative, Television
Screening Format: 35mm
Awards: Jin Jue Award; Asian New Talent Award
Profile: The Shanghai International Film Festival is co-directed by the State Administration of Radio, Film & TV and the Shanghai Municipal Government. According to the FIAPF International Regulations, this annual Festival comprises four major activities, including "Jin Jue" Award International Film Competition, International Film Panorama, International Film & TV Market and "Jin Jue" International Film Forum.
Special Events: Awards, market, parties, panels
Filmmaker Perks: Admissions to International Film and TV Market.
Travel Tips: Shanghai now possesses two international airports, i.e. Hongqiao International Airport in the west and Pudong International Airport on the seashore of East China Sea, so take your pick.

Fan Jie ....Executive for Asia, America and Oceania
Mao Liyun ....European Executive

SHEFFIELD INTERNATIONAL DOCUMENTARY FESTIVAL

The Workstation, 15 Paternoster Row
Sheffield, S1 2BX
England
Tel..+44-0114-276-5141
Fax...+44-0114-272-1849
Email ....info@sidf.co.uk
Web Site ....www.sidf.co.uk

Year Festival Began: 1994
Festival Month: Early November
Entry Deadline: Early June
Entry Fee: None
Genres: Documentary, Features, First-Time Independent Filmmakers, Independent, International, Markets, Shorts, Student
Screening Format: 16mm - 35mm - BetaSP
Number of Films Screened: 70
X Factor: A major gathering for documentary filmmakers and distributors in the UK.
Awards: No
Profile: The Sheffield International Documentary Festival is both a public film festival and an industry gathering dedicated to documentary film and TV. It's the only time in the UK when all of those working in documentary - independent producers, commissioners, TV company executives, academics, students and up-and-coming filmmakers can get together. In 2003 the admissions totalled over 8650 and over 650 people registered as delegates.

Filmmaker Perks: The festival is attended by established directors, independent producers, commissioners, TV company executives, academics and up-and-coming film makers from both the UK and abroad.

Travel Tips: Your best bet is to fly into Sheffield City Airport and then rent a car.

Sirkka Moeller ....Festival Programmer
Jo Wingate ....Deputy Director

SINGAPORE INTERNATIONAL FILM FESTIVAL

45A Keong Saik Road
Singapore 089149
Republic of Singapore
Tel ....+65-6225-7417
Fax ....+65-6738-7578
Email...filmfest@pacific.net.sg
Web Site ....www.filmfest.org.sg

Festival Month: Mid-April

Entry Deadline: December

Entry Fee: None

Genres: Animation, Documentary, Ethnic Asian, Features, International, Narrative, Shorts, Underground

Screening Format: 16mm - 35mm - VHS

Awards: Silver Screen Award

Profile: The Singapore International Film Festival screens 300 films consisting of features, shorts, animations in their main, fringe and special programs.

Special Events: Tributes, retrospectives, parties, special screenings, free fringe screenings

Travel Tips: Changi Airport in Singapore is 10 miles from the city center, so don't try to walk it.

Teo Swee Leng ....Festival Co-Director
Phillip Cheah....................................Festival Co-Director

SITGES INTERNATIONAL FILM FESTIVAL OF CATALONIA

Av. Josep Tarradellas, 135, esc. A, 3r. 2a.
08029 Barcelona
Spain
Tel...+34-93-419-3635
Fax..+34-93-439-7380
Email ....info@cinema.sitges.com
Web Site ....www.sitges.com/cinema

Year Festival Began: 1968

Festival Month: November

Entry Deadline: July

Entry Fee: None

Genres: Animation, Documentary, Fantasy/Science Fiction, Features, Independent, International, Narrative, Shorts

Screening Format: 35mm - BetaSP

Number of Films Screened: 180

Awards: Yes

Profile: Inaugurated in 1968 as the International Fantasy and Horror Film Week, the Sitges Festival has transformed itself over the past thirty-odd years into a fortnight-long celebration of world cinema, as well as a center for Spain's cinema producers and distributors to meet and display their latest works to a large audience.

Special Events: Awards, parties, retrospectives, panels

Filmmaker Perks: Festival covers travel and accomodations for select filmmakers.

Travel Tips: There is a regular train service from Barcelona Airport to Sitges: the Airport Railway Station is opposite to Terminal 'A'.

Angel Sala ....Festival Director

SOUR GRAPES FILM FESTIVAL

PO Box 1132
Maroubra Junction
NSW 2035
Australia
Tel...+61-2-9294-0301
Email ....info@sourgrapes.com.au
Web Site ....www.sourgrapes.com.au

Festival Month: Early July

Entry Deadline: Late May

Entry Fee: $30

Genres: Animation, Documentary, Experimental, Independent, International, Music Videos, Narrative, Shorts

Screening Format: 16mm - 35mm - BetaSP - VHS

Awards: Jury Awards; The Golden Grape; Other Awards

Profile: Sour Grapes hosts an annual screening event open to anyone that hasn't made the finals of a major short film festival! In essence...anyone that has experienced Sour Grapes! And most importantly, we screen all entrant over the week long festival at Fox Studios. We aim to overcome your Sour Grapes experience, and also we ensure you'll have a blast.

Special Events: Awards, parties, panels

Filmmaker Perks: Appreciative audience sees your film, contacts.

Travel Tips: Sydney is a big city. However, many of its key attractions are packed into a reasonably small area, making much of Sydney explorable on foot.

STOCKHOLM iNTERNATiONAL FiLM FESTiVAL

Box 3136
103 62 Stockholm
Sweden
Tel...+46-8-677-5000
Fax ....+46-8-200-590
Email ....info@filmfestivalen.se
Web Site ....www.filmfestivalen.se

Year Festival Began: 1989
Festival Month: Mid-November
Entry Deadline: September
Entry Fee: None
Genres: 35mm, American, Ethnic Asian, European, First-Time Independent Filmmakers, Independent, International, Shorts, Student
Screening Format: 35mm - 70mm
Number of Films Screened: 150
X Factor: It's the biggest and best in Sweden.

Awards: Bronze Horse
Aluminum Horse

Profile: The Stockholm International Film Festival is the leading competitive film festival in northern Europe and continues to manifest itself as a ground-breaking event. The Film Festival film sections give proof of a great width presenting films from a vast geographic spectra: from upcoming American independent stories to the visions of the Nordic and Baltics countries and the images of Asia.

Special Events: Awards, panels, retrospectives, parties

Filmmaker Perks: The festival covers accomodations and food when possible.

Travel Tips: Stockholm has the highest density of restaurants per capita in Europe, so you will not go hungry.

Git Scheynius.....................................Festival Organizer
Jakob Abrahamsson ....Festival Contact

SYDNEY FiLM FESTiVAL

PO Box 96
Strawberry Hills NSW 2012
Australia
Tel...+61-2-9280-0511
Fax ....+61-2-9280-1520
Email ....info@sydneyfilmfestival.org
Web Site ....www.sydneyfilmfestival.org

Year Festival Began: 1954
Festival Month: Mid-June
Entry Deadline: Mid-February
Number of Submissions: 2,000
Entry Fee: $15-$40
Genres: Animation, Documentary, Features, Independent, International, Narrative, Shorts, Touring

Screening Format: 16mm - 35mm - BetaSP - DigiBeta
Number of Films Screened: 200
Odds: 1 in 10
Awards: FIPRESCI Award; Audience Awards; Dendy Awards for Australian Short Films
Profile: The Sydney Film Festival, dedicated to exploring the art of film, is Australia's leading international film festival. The festival has a special emphasis on documentaries and Australian shorts, but welcomes films from throughout the world.

Special Events: Panels, awards, travelling festival
Filmmaker Perks: As a general rule, the Festival will provide hotel accommodation for director of a film screening in the festival, for a period of not more than three days.

Lynden Barber..Festival Director
Jenny Neighbour ....Manager SFF Programs

TAMPERE FiLM FESTiVAL

PO Box 305
FIN-33101 Tampere
Finland
Tel..+358-3-3146-6149
Fax ....+358-3-223-0121
Email...........................filmdept@tamperefilmfestival.fi
Web Site..............................www.tamperefilmfestival.fi

Festival Month: Early March
Entry Deadline: Early December
Entry Fee: None
Genres: Documentary, European, Experimental, International, Markets, Narrative, Shorts
Screening Format: 16mm - 35mm - BetaSP - DigiBeta - DVD
Awards: Grand Prix; "Kiss" Award
Profile: The Tampere Film Festival has established its position not only as a significant cultural event in Finland but also as the oldest and largest short film festival in Northern Europe.

BEST EUROPEAN GENRE FESTIVALS (Sci-Fi, Fantasy, Horror)

Cinenygma Luxembourg International Film Festival
Courmayeur Noir Film Festival
Dead by Dawn Horror Film Festival
Espoo Ciné International Film Festival
Fantasporto / Oporto International Film Festival
International Odense Film Festival
London Science Fiction and Fantasy Film Festival
Neuchâtel International Fantastic Film Festival
Sitges International Film Festival of Catalonia
Transilvania International Film Festival

Special Events: Awards, panels,Short Film Market, concerts, seminars, parties

Filmmaker Perks: $5,000 Euros for the top prize-winner.

Travel Tips: Take a taxi or an Airport Taxi from the Tampere-Pirkkala Airport to your hotel in the Tampere City Centre, which should run you about $20 Euros.

Jukka-Pekka Laakso ....Festival Director

TEHRAN iNTERNATiONAL ANiMATiON FESTiVAL

Cultural and Art Creative Center
Hajab St., Dr. Fatemi Ave.
Tehran 14156
Iran
Tel ....+009621-8958776
Fax ....+009621-8958778
Email ....info@tehran-animafest.com
Web Site ....www.tehran-animafest.com

Festival Month: February

Entry Deadline: November

Entry Fee: None

Genres: Animation, Children, Digital Animation, Documentary, Ethnic Other, Experimental, Features, Independent, International, Shorts

Screening Format: 16mm - 35mm - BetaSP - DigiBeta - VHS

Awards: Gold and Silver Awards

Special Awards

Crystal Prize

Profile: The Tehran International Animation Festival is the largest international animation festival in Iran, showcasing works from around the world.

Special Events: Awards, panels, workshops, special screenings

Filmmaker Perks: Numerous opportunities to expand animation appreciation and education

Travel Tips: Use a taxi, the bus system can be quite random at times.

Mohamma Reza Karimi Saremi ....Festival Director
Seyed Hossein Vaziri...........................Festival President

THE TiMES BFi LONDON FiLM FESTiVAL

National Film Theatre
South Bank
Waterloo
London SE1 8XT
UK
Tel..........+44-020-7815-1322; +44-020-7815-1323
Fax ....+44-020-7633-0786
Email ....sarah.lutton@bfi.org.uk,
carol.coombes@bfi.org.uk
Web Site ....www.rlff.com

Year Festival Began: 1957

Festival Month: Mid-October

Entry Deadline: Mid-July

Entry Fee: None

Genres: Documentary, European, Experimental, Features, International, Narrative, Shorts

Screening Format: 8mm - 16mm - 35mm - 70mm - BetaSP - DigiBeta

Number of Films Screened: 350

X Factor: You could do worse than premiering at a festival this established and this selective.

Awards: No

Profile: The Times bfi London Film Festival is an established non-competitive international film festival without a market or competition. There is no application fee for filmmakers or delegates wishing either to submit work or go to the festival. Over 115,000 attend this 16 day festival.

Special Events: Gala and special screenings

Travel Tips: London Heathrow airport is about 15 miles west of the city. The quickest way of travelling to Central London is by the Piccadily Line Undergound. If you have a lot of luggage, it would be better to take the Airbus A1/A2 to Central London. Airbus runs every 20 minutes and the journey takes about 60-70 minutes. Just follow the signs at the airport to get to the Underground station, Bus stop or the taxi point.

Sandra Hebron...Artistic Director
Sarah Lutton ....Program and Guest Coordinator

THESSALONiKi iNTERNATiONAL FiLM FESTiVAL

40 Paparigopoulou St.
11473 Athens
Greece
Tel..+30-210-87-06-000
Fax ....+30-210-64-48-143
Email ....program@filmfestival.gr
Web Site..www.filmfestival.gr

Festival Month: Mid-November

Entry Deadline: Early October

Entry Fee: None

Genres: Animation, Documentary, European, Features, Independent, International, Narrative, Shorts

Screening Format: 16mm - 35mm

Awards: Golden Alexander Jury Awards

Profile: The International Thessaloniki Film Festival has become the Balkans' primary showcase for the work of new and emerging filmmakers, as well as the leading film festival in the region. The event features the International Section, the panorama of Greek films, the New Horizons program, the Balkan Survey, and numerous retrospectives and tributes to leading figures in the world of film.

Special Events: Tributes, retrospectives, awards, parties

Filmmaker Perks: Golden Alexander and Silver Alexander awards are worth $37,000 and $22,000 Euros, respectively.

Travel Tips: The Guest Service can arrange transportation for the guests who will inform us on their arrival hour in advance. Alternatively, please check in directly to your hotel.

Michel Demopoulos ....Festival Director
Adonis Kioukas ....Deputy Director

TOKYO INTERNATIONAL FILM FESTIVAL

c/o Nippon Cine Arts Co., Ltd.
2-5 Honmura-Cho, Ichigaya, Shinjuku-ku
Tokyo 162-0845
Japan
Fax..+81-3-3268-5235
Email...info@tiff-jp.net
Web Site.....................................www.tiff-jp.net

Year Festival Began: 1985
Festival Month: Early November
Entry Deadline: Mid-July
Number of Submissions: 500+

Entry Fee: None

Genres: 35mm, Animation, Documentary, Ethnic Asian, Ethnic Other, Features, Independent, International, Narrative

Screening Format: 35mm
Number of Films Screened: 14 in competition
Odds: 1 in 35

X Factor: Festivals in Asia don't come any bigger.

Awards: Tokyo Grand Prix / The Governor of Tokyo Award; Jury Awards; Other Awards

Profile: The Tokyo International Film Festival (TIFF), approved by the International Federation of Film Producers Associations (FIAPH), has been held since 1985 as one of the 12 major film festivals of the world. The TIFF, which includes a feature-length film competition at its core, is also the biggest film festival in Asia and attaches importance to actively supporting Asian films and to discovering and cultivating new film directors from all over the world. The festival was held biannually until 1991 and then changed to an annual festival

Special Events: Special screenings, Winds of Asia section, retrospectives, awards, parties

Travel Tips: Fly into Haneda Airport otherwise it's going to take you 90 minutes to get to the venue.

Michiyasu Kawauchi...........................Festival Director

TORINO FILM FESTIVAL

Via Monte di Pietà 1
10121 Torino
Italy
Tel ....+39-011-5623309
Fax..+39-011-5629796
Email.................................info@torinofilmfest.org
Web Site.................................www.torinofilmfest.org

Year Festival Began: 1982
Festival Month: Mid-November
Entry Deadline: Late September
Entry Fee: None

Genres: Animation, Ethnic Other, European, Features, First-Time Independent Filmmakers, International, Narrative, Shorts

Screening Format: 35mm - BetaSP
Awards: Jury Awards; FIPRESCI Award; Other Awards

Profile: The Torino Film Festival's purpose is to constitute a meeting point for contemporary International cinema and to provide the opportunity for a discussion on all its perspectives and artistic trends. The Festival will pay particular attention to emerging cinemas and filmmakers. In its competitive sections it will promote awarness of new films and new directors whose work is carachterized by strong formal and stylistic research.

Special Events: Awards, parties, tributes, retrospectives

Filmmaker Perks: The top award is worth $20,500 Euros.

Travel Tips: Fly into Turin International Airport and then take the bus, a bit pricey at 5 Euros, but it beats cab fare.

Giulia D'Agnolo Vallan ....Festival Director
Roberto Turigliatto ....Festival Director

TROMSØ INTERNATIONAL FILM FESTIVAL

PO Box 285
N-9253 Tromsø
Norway
Tel....................+47-77-75-30-90; +47 77 75 30 92
Fax...+47-77-75-30-99
Email ....filmfestival@tiff.no
Web Site ....www.tiff.no

Year Festival Began: 1991
Festival Month: Mid-January
Entry Deadline: October
Entry Fee: By Invite

Genres: Documentary, European, Features, First-Time Independent Filmmakers, Independent, International, Narrative, Peace, Shorts

Screening Format: 16mm - 35mm - BetaSP

Awards: Audience Award
Aurora Award
FIPRESCI award
Don Quijote award
The Norwegian Peace Film Award

Profile: The Tromsø International Film Festival is Norway's largest film festival for regular cinema-goers. It is the world's northernmost film festival, presenting an international cutting-edge program of feature films plus the latest regional productions. Complete with a program of critic's favorites, visiting filmmakers and two international juries, the festival's main emphasis is on quality films that reflect the cultural, visual and narrative diversity of international independent filmmaking, and that would not otherwise be seen in Norwegian cinemas. The festival takes place just after the sun has returned to the horizon after a two-month absence, but while it is still possible to experience the Northern Lights in Tromsø.

Special Events: Panels, parties, awards, special screenings, retrospectives

Filmmaker Perks: The festival can help with industry contacts.

Travel Tips: You've got your choice between SAS and Braathens, the only airlines that serve Tromsø.

Martha Otte..Festival Producer

TURIN INTERNATIONAL GAY & LESBIAN FILM FESTIVAL "FROM SODOM TO HOLLYWOOD"

piazza S. Carlo 161
10123 Torino
Italy
Tel ....+39-011-534-888
Fax ....+39-011-535-796
Email ....info@turinglfilmfestival.com,
glfilmfest@assioma.com
Web Site...........................www.turinglfilmfestival.com

Year Festival Began: 1986
Festival Month: Late April
Entry Deadline: Late January
Entry Fee: None

BEST FESTIVALS FOR SCREENWRITERS

Austin Film Festival
Cinequest San Jose Film Festival
DIY Film Festival
iEmmys Festival
Memphis Black Writers Conference & Southern Film Festival
Moondance International Film Festival
Nantucket Film Festival
Slamdance International Film Festival

Genres: American, Documentary, Experimental, Features, Gay Lesbian, Independent, International, Narrative, Shorts, Video

Screening Format: 16mm - 35mm - BetaSP - VHS - DV

Awards: Jury Awards

Profile: The Turin International Gay & Lesbian Film Festival "from Sodom To Hollywood" is a festival that carries on the important task of searching new authors and characters that the public can discover, and building an informal, rich and stimulating dialogue that allows a useful and involving exchange of experiences between different cultures.

Special Events: Parties, panels, awards, retrospectives, tributes

Filmmaker Perks: The festival offers travel and accomodations to select filmmakers.

Travel Tips: For about $4 you can use the bus service between downtown Turin and Turin Airport.

Giovanni Minerba ....Festival Director

UPPSALA INTERNATIONAL SHORT FILM FESTIVAL

Box 1746
SE-751 47 Uppsala
Sweden
Tel ....+46-018-12-00-25
Fax...+46-018-12-13-50
Email ....info@shortfilmfestival.com
Web Site ....www.shortfilmfestival.com

Year Festival Began: 1982
Festival Month: Mid-October
Entry Deadline: Mid-June
Entry Fee: None

Genres: Animation, Children, Documentary, Ethnic Other, European, Experimental, International, Narrative, Shorts

Screening Format: 16mm - 35mm
Number of Films Screened: 200+
Awards: Uppsala Grand Prix; Audience Award

Profile: Founded in 1982, the Uppsala International Short Film Festival has since become Sweden's premier arena for short film, having attained both national recognition of the Swedish Film Institute and genuine international renown.

Special Events: Children's festival, awards, parties, seminars, workshops

Filmmaker Perks: The festival will try to arrange for private accommodations and reasonably priced lodgings if possible.

Travel Tips: During peak hours the airport shuttle bus, no 801 leaves 2-4 times per hour to and from the centre of Uppsala-Arlanda.

Sofia Lindskog ....Festival Director
Christoffer Olofsson ....Program Director

VENICE INTERNATIONAL FILM FESTIVAL

c/o La Biennale di Venezia Settore Cinema
60. Mostra Internazionale D'arte Cinematografica
Ca' Giustinian - San Marco 30124 Venezia
Italy
Tel............+39-041-27-26-501; + 39-041-5218-878
Fax...+39-041-27-26-520
Email ....cinema@labiennale.org
Web Site ....www.labiennale.org

Year Festival Began: 1932

Festival Month: Late August

Entry Deadline: Mid-June

Entry Fee: None

Genres: Animation, Documentary, Experimental, Features, First-Time Independent Filmmakers, Independent, International, Shorts

Screening Format: 16mm - 35mm - 70mm

Number of Films Screened: 80

X Factor: The "Luigi De Laurentiis" Award for a First Feature is worth $100,000 Euros AND 20,000 meters of Kodak film.

Awards: Golden Lion; Jury Awards; Other Awards

Profile: The Venice International Film Festival aims to encourage, in an atmosphere of freedom and tolerance, the awareness and the promotion of all aspects of world cinema as an art, as entertainment and as an industry. In addition, the Festival program will include tributes to outstanding personalities as well as retrospectives, as a contribution to a better understanding of the history of cinema.

Special Events: Awards, panels, retrospectives, parties

Travel Tips: After arrival at the railway station of Venezia S.Lucia, catch a vaporetto boat for the Lido (ACTV public transport routes 51/52). Alight at Lido/S. Maria Elisabetta.

Marco Muller ....Festival Director

VERZAUBERT - INTERNATIONAL QUEER FILM FESTIVAL

Rosebud Entertainment
Veranstaltungs Und Medien Gmbh
Fregestr. 36
Berlin, D12161 Germany
Tel..+ 49-30-861-4532
Fax..+ 49-30-861-4539
Email ....info@rosebud-entertainment.de
Web Site ....www.verzaubertfilmfest.com

Festival Month: Mid-November-December

Entry Deadline: September

Entry Fee: None

Genres: All, Animation, Experimental, Features, Gay Lesbian, Independent, International, Narrative, Shorts

Screening Format: 35mm - BetaSP - DigiBeta

Awards: Jury Awards

Profile: The Verzaubert - International Queer Film Festival has progressively become one of the biggest gay and lesbian film festivals in Europe. The festival selects about 75 films- features, shorts, and documentaries, primarily in 35mm but also in Video formats.

Special Events: Awards, parties

Filmmaker Perks: Festival assists with travel and accomodations when possible.

Travel Tips: The transit system is tops, but take a walk every once in a while.

Schorsch Müller ....Festival Contact

VIENNALE - VIENNA INTERNATIONAL FILM FESTIVAL

Siebensterngasse 2
A-1070 Wien
Austria
Tel...................+43-1-526-59-47; + 43 1 523 41 72
Fax ....+43-1-523-41-72
Email ....film@viennale.at
Web Site ....www.viennale.at

Year Festival Began: 1960

Festival Month: Mid-October

Entry Deadline: Mid-August

Entry Fee: By Invitation

Genres: Documentary, European, Features, International, Narrative, Shorts

Screening Format: 16mm - 35mm - BetaSP

Awards: FIPRESCI Prize; Vienna Film Prize; Audience Award

Profile: The Viennale is Austria's most important international film event, as well as being one of the oldest and best-known festivals in the German-speaking world. It takes place every October in beautiful cinemas in Vienna's historic centre, providing a festival with an international orientation and a distinctive urban flair. A high percentage of the approximately 70,000 visitors to the festival from Austria and abroad is made up of a decidedly young audience.

Special Events: Awards, tributes, retrospectives, special screenings, parties, panels

Filmmaker Perks: If invited the festival covers travel and accomodations.

Travel Tips: Vienna has an excellent public transportation system with buses, train and a subway. You can use one validated ticket to use all the different forms of transportation within an hour.

Hans Hurch ....Festival Director
Eva Rotter ....Managing Director

VISIONS DU RÉEL INTERNATIONAL DOCUMENTARY FILM FESTIVAL

18, rue Juste-Olivier
C.P. 593
1260 Nyon
Switzerland
Tel ....+41-22-3-65-44-55
Fax ....+41-22-3-65-44-50
Email ....docnyon@visionsdureel.ch
Web Site ....www.visionsdureel.ch

Year Festival Began: 1969
Festival Month: Late April
Entry Deadline: Mid-January
Genres: Documentary, Features, Independent, International, Markets, Shorts
Screening Format: 16mm - 35mm - BetaSP
Awards: Visions du Réel Grand Prize
Audience Prize City of Nyon
Kodak Prize
Other Awards
Profile: The objective of Visions du Réel is to show the world as it is perceived, to break away from the mainstream. All the players of the brand Visions du Réel are mobilised to ensure a very high level of quality in their work and to contribute to the common good. The Festival offers a diversity of committed and inspired points of view whilst making it possible to correlate experiences, reflections and aspirations.
Special Events: Workshops, parties, panels, awards, Doc Outlook-International Market
Filmmaker Perks: Film makers whose films have been selected to take part in the Festival program are invited to Nyon for three to five days. Their hotel expenses are paid by the Festival.
Travel Tips: Fly Swissair. Really, it's why they're around.

Jean Perret ....President

WARSAW INTERNATIONAL FILM FESTIVAL

PO Box 816
PL-00-950 Warsaw 1
Poland
Tel 48-2-635-7591
Email ....kontakty@wff.org.pl
Web Site ....www.wff.pl

Festival Month: Early October
Entry Deadline: Late June
Entry Fee: None
Genres: 35mm, Animation, Documentary, European, Features, Independent, International, Narrative
Screening Format: 35mm
Awards: Grand Prix NESCAFÉ
Audience Award

Profile: The Warsaw International Film Festival screens the best European and international films from around the world, with special emphasis on presenting the latest and most attractive films from Russia, the Czech Republic, Germany, Hungary and other nearby countries.
Special Events: Awards, parties
Filmmaker Perks: The Grand Prix is worth $5,000 Euros.
Travel Tips: The main cinemas - Relax, Bajka, Luna, Silver Screen are all right off the subway line.

Stefan Laudyn..Festival Director
Ewa Wieckowska-Mietkiewicz ....President

WELLINGTON FILM FESTIVAL

PO Box 9544
Marion Square
Wellington 6001
New Zealand
Tel ....+64-4-385-0162
Fax ....+64-4-801-7304
Email ....festival@nzff.co.nz
Web Site...www.enzedff.co.nz

Festival Month: Mid-July
Entry Deadline: Mid-April
Entry Fee: None
Genres: Animation, Documentary, Ethnic Other, European, Features, Independent, International, Narrative, Shorts
Screening Format: 16mm - 35mm - 70mm - BetaSP - DVD
Awards: No
Profile: The Wellington Film Festival is part of the New Zealand International Film Festival's Travelling Festival Circuit program.
Special Events: Parties
Filmmaker Perks: Accepted films are eligible to travel to other New Zealand film festivals in the Travelling Festival Circuit.
Travel Tips: Warm weather with a few windy days, so bring your shorts and a wind-breaker to be safe.

Bill Gosden ....Festival Director

YAMAGATA INTERNATIONAL DOCUMENTARY FILM FESTIVAL

2-3-25 Hatago-machi
Yamagata-shi, Yamagata-ken 990-8540
Japan
Tel ....+81-23-624-8368
Fax ....+81-23-624-9618
Email ....yidff.info@city.yamagata.yamagata.jp
Web Site.................www.city.yamagata.yamagata.jp/
yidff/home-e.html

Year Festival Began: 1989
Festival Month: October

Entry Deadline: March
Number of Submissions: 1,454
Entry Fee: None
Genres: Documentary, Ethnic Asian, Features, Independent, International, Video
Screening Format: 16mm - 35mm - VHS
Number of Films Screened: 177
Odds: 1 in 8
X Factor: The best doc fest in Asia, perfect for international networking.
Awards: The Robert and Frances Flaherty Prize
The Mayor's Prize
FIPRESCI Prize
Other Awards
Profile: The inaugural Yamagata International Documentary Film Festival was held in October, 1989 as one of the events commemorating the centennial of Yamagata City. Held biennially, it has become a place for the filmmakers of the world to present both old and new works and to network together. The numbers of film entries and participants from Japan and abroad have increased with each festival-and the opportunities to meet and interact at local venues at a range of enjoyable events is firmly established.
Special Events: Panels, parties, awards
Filmmaker Perks: The festival covers all travel and accomodations for the official guests.
Travel Tips: Bring a jacket as the nights can get chilly.

Saito Aiko ....Festival Contact

ZAGREB WORLD FESTIVAL OF ANIMATED FILMS
Kneza Mislava 18
10000 Zagreb
Croatia
Tel ....+385-1450-1190
Fax..+385-1461-1808
Email ....animafest@kdz.hr
Web Site...www.animafest.hr
Year Festival Began: 1972
Festival Month: Mid-June
Entry Deadline: Mid-March
Entry Fee: None
Genres: Animation, Children, Experimental, Features, First-Time Independent Filmmakers, Independent, International, Shorts, Student
Screening Format: 16mm - 35mm - BetaSP
Awards: Grand Prix
The City of Zagreb Award
Other Awards
Profile: The organizers of Zagreb Festival have always done their best to achieve what they have considered to be the aim of the festival: to make it a

BEST TRULY INDEPENDENT FILM FESTIVALS
Fests that shy away from big studio indies and screen real indie films

20,000 Leagues Under the Industry Film Festival
Arizona State University Short Film and Video Festival
Backseat Film Festival
Bare Bones International Film Festival
Brainwash Movie Festival
Central Standard Film Festival
Cucalorus Film Festival
DancesWithFilms
Gadabout Traveling Film Festival
GAMMA IndieFest
Images Festival of Independent Film and Video (the)
Independent Exposure
NoDance Film Festival
Renegade Film Festival
ResFest Digital Film Festival
Slamdance International Film Festival
UpOverDownUnder Film Festival
USA Film Festival/Dallas
VideoTheatre NYC
Westcliffe Digital Film Festival

gathering-place for authors and fans of the animated film from all over the world, at which the recent world production is judged, the past is recalled by shoving relevant national, personal, or thematic retrospectives, and meetings, exhibitions, lectures and similar events are organised - all in order to promote and advance the art of film animation and animated film production in general.
Special Events: Tributes, retrospectives, awards, parties, workshops
Filmmaker Perks: The festival will cover the cost of accommodation and meal allowance for directors whose films are chosen for official competition. The festival will pay a cash amount covering maximum 40 percent of the travel expenses to the directors of short fiction films, who, in case of being selected for official competition, confirm their arrival to Zagreb in the appropriate column of the entry form.
Travel Tips: The festival is putting you up, so focus on the right gear...June is Zagreb is pretty warm.

Margit Antauer ....Managing Director

End.

Don't let your script end here.

Get *The Independent* and become a member of AIVF, the Association of Independent Video and Filmmakers. By joining AIVF you can enjoy benefits like **trade discounts** on supplies and services; discounts on **workshops** and **resource guides**; access to affordable **health coverage**. AIVF offers a searchable **directory** of domestic and international films festivals, plus a whole lot more.....

the Independent
FILM & VIDEO MONTHLY

How to Market Your Film

AIVF
association of independent
video and filmmakers

visit us at **www.aivf.org**

BEST OF THE REST iNTERNATiONAL FiLM FESTiVALS

3 CONTiNENTS iNTERNATiONAL DOCUMENTARY FiLM FESTiVAL
www.3continentsfestival.co.za
Festival Month: September
Genres: Africa, Asia, and Latin America, Documentary, Features, International, Narrative, Shorts

ACADEMiA FiLM OLOMOUC FiLM FESTiVAL
www.afo.cz
Festival Month: Early October
Genres: Documentary, Education, Multimedia, Scientific and Popular Science, Television

AFRiCAN, ASiAN AND LATiN AMERiCAN FiLM FESTiVAL
www.festivalcinemaafricano.org
Festival Month: March
Genres: Africa, Asia, and Latin America, Documentary, Ethnic African, Ethnic Asian, Ethnic Latin, Features, Multi-Cultural, Narrative, Shorts

AGROFiLM FESTiVAL
www.agrofilm.sk
Festival Month: September
Genres: Agriculture

ALEXANDRiA iNTERNATiONAL FiLM FESTiVAL
alexfilmfest.tripod.com
Festival Month: Early September
Genres: Features, International

ALPiNALE FiLM FESTiVAL
www.alpinale.net
Festival Month: Mid-August
Genres: Animation, Documentary, European, Experimental, Features, International, Narrative, Shorts, Student

ALTERNATiVE FiLM FESTiVAL
www.digitmovies.biz/alternative
Festival Month: Mid-October
Genres: Documentary, Features, Narrative, Shorts, Student

AMiENS iNTERNATiONAL FiLM FESTiVAL
www.filmfestamiens.org
Festival Month: Early November
Genres: Animation, Children, Documentary, Education, European, Family, Features, International, Narrative, Student

AMNESTY iNTERNATiONAL FiLM FESTiVAL
www.amnesty.nl/filmfestival
Festival Month: March-April
Genres: Documentary, European, Features, Human Rights, International, Narrative

ANiMA MUNDi
www.animamundi.com.br
Festival Month: Early July
Genres: Animation, Children, Features, Shorts, Works in progress

ANiMAC iNTERNATiONAL ANiMATiON FiLM FESTiVAL
www.animac.info
Festival Month: Late February
Genres: Animation, Features, Shorts

ANiMATED EXETER
www.animatedexeter.co.uk
Festival Month: Early February
Genres: Animation, Features, Independent, Shorts, Student

APOLLO FiLM FESTiVAL
www.apollotheatre.co.za
Festival Month: September
Genres: Documentary, Features, Independent, International, Shorts

ARSENAL FiLM FORUM
www.arsenals.lv
Festival Month: Mid-September
Genres: Documentary, European, Features, Independent, International, Narrative, Shorts

ART FiLM FESTiVAL TRENCiANSKE TEPLiCE
www.artfilm.sk
Festival Month: Mid-June

Genres: Documentary, Experimental, Features, Narrative, Shorts, Student

ASOLO ART FiLM FESTiVAL
www.asolofilmfestival.it
Festival Month: Mid-September
Genres: Animation, Documentary, Features, International, Music Video, Shorts, Student, Television

ASTRA FiLM FESTiVAL
www.astrafilm.ro
Festival Month: Late October
Genres: Documentary, Features, International, Shorts

AUBURN iNTERNATiONAL FiLM AND ViDEO FESTiVAL FOR CHiLDREN AND YOUNG ADULTS
www.hotkey.net.au/~acdn/
   festival.html
Festival Month: Mid-September
Genres: Animation, Children, Education, Family, Features, Shorts, Student

AUCKLAND iNTERNATiONAL FiLM FESTiVAL
www.enzedff.co.nz
Festival Month: Mid-July
Genres: Documentary, Features, International, Narrative, Shorts

AUDiTiON iNTERNATiONAL FiLM FESTiVAL
www.auditionfilmfestival.com
Festival Month: Early November
Genres: Fantasy/Science Fiction, Features, Horror, Independent, International, Narrative, Shorts, Thriller

AUSTRALiAN iNTERNATiONAL DOCUMENTARY CONFERENCE
www.aidc.com.au
Festival Month: Late February
Genres: Documentary, International, Markets

AUSTRALIAN NATIONAL STUDENT FILM & VIDEO FESTIVAL
www.yap.com.au/filmfest
Festival Month: Early August
Genres: Animation, Documentary, Experimental, Narrative, Shorts, Shorts

BACKUP FESTIVAL NEW MEDIA IN FILM
www.backup-festival.com
Festival Month: October-November
Genres: Digital, Features, International, Multimedia, Shorts

BANGKOK FILM FESTIVAL
www.movieseer.com/bangkokfilmfestival
Festival Month: Late April-May
Genres: 35mm, Documentary, Features, Independent, International, Narrative, Underground

BEIRUT DOCUMENTARY FILM FESTIVAL – DOCUDAYS
www.docudays.com
Festival Month: November
Genres: Documentary, Ethnic Other, Features, International, Shorts

BELFAST FILM FESTIVAL
www.belfastfilmfestival.org
Festival Month: March-April
Genres: Features, International, Shorts, World

BELIZE INTERNATIONAL FILM FESTIVAL
www.belizefilmfestival.com
Festival Month: Between June and November
Genres: Ethnic Other, Features, International, Multi-Cultural, Shorts

BELLARIA INDEPENDENT CINEMA FESTIVAL
www.bellariafilmfestival.org
Festival Month: June
Genres: Animation, Documentary, Ethnic Other, European, Features, Independent, International, Narrative, Shorts

BELO HORIZONTE INTERNATIONAL SHORT FILM FESTIVAL
www.festivaldecurtasbh.com.br
Festival Month: September-October
Genres: Animation, Documentary, Experimental, International, Narrative, Shorts

BERGAMO INTERNATIONAL WEEK OF AUTEUR FILM
www.alasca.it/bfm/index.html
Festival Month: March
Genres: Avant Garde, Documentary, Features, First-Time Independent Filmmakers, Independent, International, Narrative, Shorts

BERGEN INTERNATIONAL FILM FESTIVAL (BiFF)
www.biff.no
Festival Month: Mid-October
Genres: Documentary, Features, International, Narrative, Shorts

BFM INTERNATIONAL FILM FESTIVAL
www.bfmfilmfestival.com
Festival Month: Mid-September
Genres: Animation, Documentary, Ethnic Black, Experimental, Features, International, Narrative, Shorts

BILAN DU FILM ETHNOGRAPHIQUE
www.comite-film-ethno.net
Festival Month: October
Genres: Documentary, Features, Human Rights, International, Multi-Cultural, Shorts

BIRMINGHAM SCREEN FESTIVAL
www.film-tv-festival.org.uk
Festival Month: March
Genres: Documentary, Features, International, Shorts

BITE THE MANGO FILM FESTIVAL
www.bitethemango.org.uk
Festival Month: Late September
Genres: Documentary, Features, International, Narrative, Shorts

BLACK INTERNATIONAL CINEMA BERLIN
www.black-international-cinema.com
Festival Month: May
Genres: Children, Documentary, Education, Ethnic African, Features, International, Multi-Cultural, Narrative, Shorts

BLINK FILM FESTIVAL COVENTRY
www.blinkfilmfestival.org.uk
Festival Month: Student Film Competition: Late May
Genres: Animation, Documentary, Features, First-Time Independent Filmmakers, Independent, International, Narrative, Shorts, Student

BOGOTA FILM FESTIVAL
www.bogocine.com
Festival Month: Early October
Genres: Documentary, Ethnic Other, Features, First-Time Independent Filmmakers, Independent, International, Narrative, Shorts

BEST "FILM ONLY" FESTIVALS

Algarve International Film Festival
Flickerfest Australian International Outdoor Short Film Festival
Bangkok Film Festival
Barcelona Asian Film Festival
Brazilian Film Festival of Miami
Cannes Directors' Fortnight
Donostia-San Sebastian International Film Festival
Flickerfest Australian International Outdoor Short Film Festival
Message to Man International Documentary, Short and Animated Films Festival
New York Film Festival
Oldenburg International Film Festival
São Paulo International Film Festival
Stockholm International Film Festival
Tokyo International Film Festival
Valladolid International Film Festival
Venice International Film Festival
Washington, DC International Film Festival—Filmfest DC

BRADFORD ANiMATiON FESTiVAL
www.baf.org.uk
Festival Month: Early November
Genres: Animation, Children, Digital Animation, Experimental, Features, International, Shorts

BRADFORD FiLM FESTiVAL
www.bradfordfilmfestival.org.uk
Festival Month: March
Genres: Documentary, European, Features, Independent, International, Narrative, Shorts

BRAUNSCHWEiG iNTERNATiONAL FiLM FESTiVAL
www.filmfest-braunschweig.de
Festival Month: Early November
Genres: Documentary, European, Features, International, Narrative, Shorts

BRiGHTON FESTiVAL
www.brighton-festival.org.uk
Festival Month: May
Genres: Multimedia

BRiSBANE iNTERNATiONAL FiLM FESTiVAL
www.biff.com.au
Festival Month: August
Genres: Animation, Documentary, Ethnic Asian, Features, Independent, International, Narrative, Shorts

BRiSTOL iNTERNATiONAL ANiMATiON FESTiVAL
www.animated-encounters.org.uk
Festival Month: Late April
Genres: Animation, Digital Animation, Features, Shorts

BRiSTOL iNTERNATiONAL SHORT FiLM FESTiVAL
www.brief-encounters.org.uk
Festival Month: November
Genres: Animation, Documentary, International, Narrative, Shorts

BRiTiSH FiLM FESTiVAL
www.festivaldufilm-dinard.com
Festival Month: Early October
Genres: Documentary, European, Features, International, Narrative, Shorts

BRiTSPOTTiNG iNDEPENDENT FiLM FESTiVAL
www.britspotting.de
Festival Month: May
Genres: European, Features, Independent, Shorts

BRUSSELS GAY AND LESBiAN FiLM FESTiVAL
www.fglb.org
Festival Month: January
Genres: Documentary, Features, Gay Lesbian, Independent, International, Narrative, Shorts

BUSAN ASiAN SHORT FiLM FESTiVAL
www.basff.org
Festival Month: Early May
Genres: All Categories - Shorts, Ethnic Asian

BUSTER COPENHAGEN iNTERNATiONAL CHiLDREN'S FiLM FESTiVAL
www.busterfilm.dk
Festival Month: Mid-September
Genres: Animation, Children, Documentary, European, Features, International, Narrative, Shorts

CASTELLiNARiA iNTERNATiONAL YOUNG CiNEMA FESTiVAL
www.castellinaria.ch
Festival Month: Mid-November
Genres: Documentary, European, Features, First-Time Independent Filmmakers, International, Student

CELTiC FiLM AND TELEViSiON FESTiVAL
www.celticfilm.co.uk
Festival Month: Late March- Early April
Genres: Animation, Children, Commercials, Documentary, Education, Episodic Television/Television Pilots, Ethnic Other, European, Experimental, Features, Independent, International, Narrative, Shorts

CERTAMEN DE CiNE AMATEUR
www.urriazinema.com
Festival Month: November
Genres: Documentary, Features, First-Time Independent Filmmakers, Independent, International, Narrative, Shorts

CHiCHESTER FiLM FESTiVAL
www.chichestercinema.org
Festival Month: Late August-September
Genres: Animation, Documentary, Features, First-Time Independent Filmmakers, International, Narrative, Shorts, Student

CiNANiMA iNTERNATiONAL ANiMATED FiLM FESTiVAL
www.cinanima.pt
Festival Month: November
Genres: Animation, Digital Animation, Features, International, Shorts

CiNEFEST SUDBURY iNTERNATiONAL FiLM FESTiVAL
www.cinefest.com
Festival Month: Late September
Genres: Documentary, Education, Features, International, Narrative, Shorts

CiNEKiD FiLM FESTiVAL
www.cinekid.nl
Festival Month: Mid-October
Genres: Animation, Children, Documentary, Features, International, Narrative, Shorts, Television

CiNEMA AU FEMiNiN
www.cinemafeminin.com
Festival Month: Late September-October
Genres: Documentary, Features, International, Narrative, Shorts, Women

CiNEMA JOVE iNTERNATiONAL FiLM FESTiVAL
www.gva.es/cinemajove
Festival Month: Mid-June
Genres: 16mm, 35mm, Children, Documentary, Features, First-Time Independent Filmmakers, International, Narrative, Shorts, Student

CiNEMA NOVO FESTiVAL
www.cinemanovo.be
Festival Month: Mid-March
Genres: Africa, Asia, and Latin America, Documentary, Features, Narrative

CiNÉMA TOUT ECRAN
www.cinema-tout-ecran.ch
Festival Month: Late October-November
Genres: Animation, Documentary, Episodic Television/Television Pilots, Features, International, Narrative, Shorts

CiNEMAGiC WORLD SCREEN FESTiVAL FOR YOUNG PEOPLE
www.cinemagic.org.uk
Festival Month: December
Genres: Animation, Children, Documentary, Family, Features, International, Narrative, Shorts

CiNEMAMBiENTE
www.cinemambiente.it
Festival Month: Late October
Genres: Animation, Documentary, Environmental, Experimental, Features, International, Narrative, Shorts

CINEMANILA INTERNATIONAL FILM FESTIVAL

www.cinemanila.com.ph

Festival Month: Mid-August
Genres: Children, Digital, Documentary, Ethnic Asian, Features, International, Narrative, Shorts

CINEMAYA FESTIVAL OF ASIAN CINEMA

www.cinemaya.net/cinefan/index.asp

Festival Month: July
Genres: Documentary, Ethnic Asian, Features, International, Narrative, Shorts

CINENYGMA LUXEMBOURG INTERNATIONAL FILM FESTIVAL

www.cinenygma.lu

Festival Month: March-April
Genres: Experimental, Fantasy/Science Fiction, Features, Horror, International, Mystery, Shorts, Thriller

CO-OPERATIVE YOUNG FILM-MAKERS FESTIVAL

www.film-makers.co-op.co.uk

Festival Month: Mid-October
Genres: Animation, Digital, Documentary, Experimental, Independent, International, Narrative, Shorts

COGNAC INTERNATIONAL FILM FESTIVAL OF THE THRILLER

www.festival.cognac.fr

Festival Month: April
Genres: Features, International, Psycho Thriller, Short, Thriller

COLOGNE INTERNATIONAL SHORT FILM FESTIVAL

www.short-cuts-cologne.de

Festival Month: Mid-September
Genres: Animation, Avant Garde, Documentary, Experimental, International, Narrative, Shorts

COLOGNE INTERNATIONAL TV & FILM CONFERENCE

www.cologne-conference.de

Festival Month: June
Genres: Documentary, Episodic Television/Television Pilots, Features, International, Narrative, Shorts, Television

COMMONWEALTH FILM FESTIVAL

www.commonwealthfilm.com

Festival Month: April-May
Genres: Documentary, Experimental, Features, Independent, International, Narrative, Shorts

CONSTELLATION CHANGE SCREEN DANCE FESTIVAL

www.constellation-change.co.uk

Festival Month: Early March
Genres: Dance, Documentary, Features, International, Narrative, Performance, Shorts

CORTO IMOLA FESTIVAL - INTERNATIONAL SHORT FILM FESTIVAL

www.cortoimolafestival.it

Festival Month: Early December
Genres: All Categories - Shorts, Animation, Documentary, Experimental, Shorts

CORTOITALIACINEMA INTERNATIONAL SHORT FILM FESTIVAL

www.cortoitaliacinema.com

Festival Month: November
Genres: All Categories - Shorts, European

COTSWOLD INTERNATIONAL FILM FESTIVAL

www.cotswoldfilmvideofest.co.uk

Festival Month: Early September
Genres: Animation, Documentary, Experimental, Features, First-Time Independent Filmmakers, Independent, International, Narrative, Shorts, Student

COURMAYEUR NOIR FILM FESTIVAL

www.noirfest.com

Festival Month: Early December
Genres: Fantasy/Science Fiction, Horror, International, Mystery, Shorts, Thriller

COURTISANE FESTIVAL FOR SHORT FILM VIDEO AND NEW MEDIA

www.courtisane.be

Festival Month: Mid-May
Genres: Animation, Documentary, European, Experimental, International, Multimedia, Shorts

DEAD BY DAWN HORROR FILM FESTIVAL

www.deadbydawn.co.uk

Festival Month: Late-April
Genres: Animation, Experimental, Fantasy/Science Fiction, Features, Horror, Independent, International, Psycho Thriller, Shorts, Thriller

DEAF FILM & TV FESTIVAL

www.britishdeafassociation.org.uk/film

Festival Month: November
Genres: Animation, Deaf, Documentary, Features, Narrative, Shorts

DEAF FOCUS FILM FESTIVAL

www.deaf-focus.org.uk

Festival Month: Late Winter-Early Spring
Genres: Animation, Deaf, Experimental, International, Narrative, Shorts

DIAGONALE FILM FESTIVAL

www.diagonale.at

Festival Month: Early March
Genres: Animation, Avant Garde, Documentary, European, Experimental, Features, Narrative, Shorts

DIGITAL TALKIES FESTIVAL

www.digitaltalkies.com

Festival Month: Late February-March
Genres: Animation, Digital, Documentary, Ethnic Other, Features, Independent, International, Narrative, Shorts

DISABILITY FILM FESTIVAL

www.disabilityfilmfestival.net

Festival Month: Early December
Genres: Animation, Disabled, Documentary, Experimental, Features, Independent, International, Narrative, Shorts

BEST DEAF/DISABLED FILM FESTIVALS

Festival For Cinema Of The Deaf

Deaf Film & TV Festival

Deaf Focus Film Festival

Disability Film Festival

Perspectives International Film Festival

Picture This Film Festival

Sprout Film Festival

Superfest International Media Festival on Disabilities

DOCAViV TEL-AViV INTERNATiONAL DOCUMENTARY FiLM FESTiVAL
www.docaviv.co.il
Festival Month: Late March-April
Genres: Documentary, Ethnic Jewish, Ethnic Other, Features, Shorts

DOKUFEST DOCUMENTARY & SHORT FiLM FESTiVAL
www.dokufest.com
Festival Month: Late August
Genres: All Categories - Shorts, Documentary

DORTMUND iNTERNATiONAL FiLM FESTiVAL
www.femmetotale.de
Festival Month: April
Genres: Animation, Documentary, Experimental, Features, International, Narrative, Shorts, Women

DRiFTiNG CLOUDS iNTERNATiONAL SHORT FiLM FESTiVAL
www.driftingcloudsfilmfest.com
Festival Month: February
Genres: All Categories - Shorts

DUBLiN LESBiAN AND GAY FiLM FESTiVAL
www.gcn.ie/dlgff
Festival Month: Late July-August
Genres: Animation, Documentary, Experimental, Features, Gay Lesbian, International, Narrative, Shorts

DUNDEE MOUNTAiN FiLM FESTiVAL
www.dundee.mountainfilm.btinternet.co.uk
Festival Month: Late November
Genres: Adventurer/Explorers, Documentary, Features, Independent, International, Mountain Sports, Narrative, Shorts

EARTH ViSiON - TOKYO GLOBAL ENViRONMENTAL FiLM FESTiVAL
www.earth-vision.jp
Festival Month: February
Genres: Documentary, Environmental, Ethnic Asian, Features, International, Shorts

ECOCiNEMA
www.ecocinema.gr
Festival Month: Early June
Genres: Documentary, Environmental, Features, Narrative, Shorts

EiLAT iNTERNATiONAL FiLM FESTiVAL
www.eilatfilmfest.com
Festival Month: Mid-March
Genres: Animation, Children, Documentary, Features, Gay Lesbian, International, Narrative, Scuba Diving & Marine

EKSJÖ ANiMATiON FESTiVAL
www.eksjofestival.com
Festival Month: September
Genres: Animation, Digital Animation, Ethnic Other, Features, International, Narrative, Shorts, Student

EKSPERiM[E]NTO FiLM & ViDEO FESTiVAL
www.geocities.com/eksperimento
Festival Month: Mid-March
Genres: Animation, Avant Garde, Documentary, Ethnic Asian, Experimental, Features, Independent, Narrative, Shorts, Touring, Underground, Weird

EMDEN iNTERNATiONAL FiLM FESTiVAL
www.filmfestemden.de
Festival Month: Early June
Genres: Animation, Documentary, European, Features, First-Time Independent Filmmakers, Independent, Narrative, Shorts

ENCOUNTERS SOUTH AFRiCAN iNTERNATiONAL DOCUMENTARY FESTiVAL
www.encounters.co.za
Festival Month: Cape Town: Mid-July Johannesburg: Early August
Genres: Documentary, Ethnic African, Features, International, Shorts

ERA NEW HORiZONS FiLM FESTiVAL
www.eranowehoryzonty.pl
Festival Month: Late July-August
Genres: Animation, Avant Garde, Dance, Documentary, European, Experimental, Features, Independent, International, Narrative, Shorts

EUROPACiNEMA FESTiVAL
www.europacinema.it
Festival Month: Late September-October
Genres: Documentary, European, Features, International, Narrative, Shorts

EUROPEAN CiNEMA FiLM FESTiVAL
www.europecinefestival.org
Festival Month: April
Genres: Documentary, European, Features, International, Multi-Cultural, Narrative

EUROPEAN MEDiA ART FESTiVAL
www.emaf.de
Festival Month: Late April
Genres: Animation, Avant Garde, Documentary, Experimental, Features, International, Narrative, Shorts

FACES OF LOVE iNTERNATiONAL FiLM FESTiVAL
www.kinotavr.com/fol.html
Festival Month: Mid-January
Genres: Animation, Features, International, Romantic, Shorts

FAJR iNTERNATiONAL FiLM FESTiVAL
www.fajrfilmfest.com
Festival Month: Mid-January
Genres: Documentary, Ethnic Other, Features, International, Narrative, Shorts

FANO iNTERNATiONAL FiLM FESTiVAL
www.fanofilmfestival.it
Festival Month: Mid-October
Genres: All Categories - Shorts, First-Time Independent Filmmakers, Independent, International, Student

FANTASPORTO / OPORTO iNTERNATiONAL FiLM FESTiVAL
www.fantasporto.online.pt
Festival Month: February-March
Genres: Animation, Avant Garde, Experimental, Fantasy/Science Fiction, Features, Horror, Independent, International, Shorts, Thriller

FANTASTiSK FiLM FESTiVAL SWEDEN
www.fff.se
Festival Month: Mid-September
Genres: Animation, Avant Garde, Experimental, Fantasy/Science Fiction, Features, Horror, Narrative, Shorts, Thriller

FANTOCHE iNTERNATiONAL ANiMATiON FiLM FESTiVAL
www.fantoche.ch
Festival Month: Mid-September
Genres: Animation, Features, Shorts

FAR EAST FiLM FESTiVAL
www.fareastfilm.com
Festival Month: Late April-May
Genres: Animation, Ethnic Asian, Features, International, Shorts

FEMiNALE WOMEN'S FiLM FESTiVAL
www.feminale.de
Festival Month: Early October
Genres: Animation, Documentary, Experimental, Features, International, Narrative, Shorts, Women

FESTiVAL DEi POPOLi, iNTERNATiONAL FiLM FESTiVAL OF SOCiAL DOCUMENTARiES
www.festivaldeipopoli.org
Festival Month: Late November-December
Genres: Documentary, Features, International, Multi-Cultural, Shorts

FESTiVAL DU FiLM D'ANiMATiON POUR LA JEUNESSE
perso.wanadoo.fr/festival.bourg
Festival Month: Late October
Genres: Animation, Children, Family, Family, Features, International, Narrative, Shorts, Student

FESTiVAL GARAGE
www.garage-g.de
Festival Month: August
Genres: All Categories - Shorts

FESTiVAL iNTERNACiONAL DE CiNE FANTASTiCO
www.fantastico.uma.es
Festival Month: Early March
Genres: Animation, Experimental, Fantasy/Science Fiction, Features, Horror, Independent, Shorts, Thriller

FESTiVAL iNTERNACiONAL DE CiNE REALiZADO POR MUJERES
wzar.unizar.es/siem/muestra.html
Festival Month: March
Genres: Documentary, Features, International, Narrative, Shorts, Women

FESTiVAL iNTERNATiONAL DU FiLM AMATEUR DE KELiBiA
Festival Month: July-August
Genres: Animation, Documentary, Features, First-Time Independent Filmmakers, International, Shorts, Student

FESTiVAL OF FANTASTiC FiLMS
www.fantastic-films.com/festival
Festival Month: Mid-August
Genres: Animation, Experimental, Fantasy/Science Fiction, Features, Horror, Independent, International, Shorts, Thriller

FESTiVAL OF THE 3 CONTiNENTS
www.3continents.com
Festival Month: Late November
Genres: Africa, Asia, and Latin America, American, Documentary, Ethnic Black, Features

FESTiVAL OF THE DHOW COUNTRiES
www.zanzibar.org/ziff
Festival Month: Late June-July
Genres: Animation, Documentary, Environmental, Ethnic African, Features, Narrative, Shorts

FiFA iNTERNATiONAL WiLDLiFE FiLM FESTiVAL
www.fifa.com.fr
Festival Month: Late March
Genres: Documentary, Environmental, Features, Fishing, Hunting, International, Shorts, Wildlife

FiKE ÉVORA iNTERNATiONAL SHORT FiLM FESTiVAL
www.fikeonline.net
Festival Month: Late November
Genres: Animation, Documentary, International, Narrative, Shorts

FiLM BY THE SEA
www.filmbythesea.nl
Festival Month: Mid-September
Genres: European, Features, International, Narrative

FiLM FESTiVAL COTTBUS
www.filmfestivalcottbus.de
Festival Month: Early November
Genres: Animation, Children, Documentary, European, Features, International, Narrative, Shorts

FiLM SOUTH ASiA
www.himalassociation.org/fsa
Festival Month: Late November
Genres: Documentary, Ethnic Asian, Features, Independent, Shorts, Touring

FiLMFEST HAMBURG
www.filmfesthamburg.de
Festival Month: Mid-September
Genres: Animation, Children, Documentary, Features, International, Narrative, Shorts

FiLMFESTiVAL MAX OPHÜLS PREiS
www.max-ophuels-preis.de
Festival Month: Mid-January
Genres: Documentary, European, Experimental, Features, Independent, International, Narrative, Shorts

FiLMFESTiVAL OF THE FiLM ACADEMY ViENNA
www.filmfestivalvienna.com
Festival Month: Early May
Genres: Animation, Documentary, European, Features, Independent, International, Narrative, Shorts, Student

FiLMS FROM THE SOUTH FESTiVAL
www.filmfrasor.no
Festival Month: Early October
Genres: 16mm, 35mm, Africa, Asia, and Latin America, Documentary, Experimental, Features, International

FiLMSTOCK iNTERNATiONAL FiLM FESTiVAL
www.filmstock.co.uk
Festival Month: Early June
Genres: Experimental, Features, Independent, International, Narrative, Shorts

FLANDERS iNTERNATiONAL FiLM FESTiVAL GHENT
www.filmfestival.be
Festival Month: Early October
Genres: Animation, Avant Garde, Documentary, Experimental, Features, Independent, International, Multimedia, Narrative, Performance, Shorts

BEST MUSiC-RELATED FESTiVALS

Backseat Film Festival
Black Soil Film Festival
Coachella Film Festival
Denver Jazz on Film Festival
Don't Knock The Rock Music And Film Festival
Hip Hop Film Fest
Indie Music Video Festival
Nashville Independent Film Festival
Noise Pop Film Festival
Spudfest Drive-In Family Film & Music Festival
SXSW Film Festival
Videokronik Music Video Festival

FLICKERFEST AUSTRALIAN INTERNATIONAL OUTDOOR SHORT FILM FESTIVAL
www.flickerfest.com.au
Festival Month: January
Genres: 16mm, 35mm, International, Shorts

FRENCH FILM FESTIVAL UK
www.frenchfilmfestival.org.uk
Festival Month: November-December
Genres: Animation, Documentary, Features, French, Independent, International, Narrative, Shorts

FRIBOURG INTERNATIONAL FILM FESTIVAL
www.fiff.ch
Festival Month: March
Genres: Africa, Asia, and Latin America, Animation, Documentary, Ethnic African, Ethnic Asian, Ethnic Latin, Features, International, Narrative, Shorts

FUKUOKA ASIAN FILM FESTIVAL
www2.gol.com/users/faff/english.html
Festival Month: Early July
Genres: Animation, Commercials, Documentary, Ethnic Asian, Experimental, Features, Independent, International, Music Videos, Narrative, Shorts, Student

FUTURE FILM FESTIVAL
www.futurefilmfestival.org
Festival Month: Mid-January
Genres: Animation, Digital Animation, Episodic Television/Television Pilots, Experimental, Features, International, Shorts

GALWAY FILM FLEADH
www.galwayfilmfleadh.com
Festival Month: Early July
Genres: Documentary, Ethnic Other, European, Features, International, Narrative, Shorts

GIFFONI FILM FESTIVAL
www.giffoniff.it
Festival Month: Mid-July
Genres: 35mm, Animation, Children, Features, International, Narrative, Shorts, Student

GIRONA FILM FESTIVAL
www.gironafilmfestival.com
Festival Month: Mid-September
Genres: Animation, Documentary, Ethnic Jewish, International, Narrative, Shorts

GOEAST - FESTIVAL OF CENTRAL AND EASTERN EUROPEAN FILM
www.filmfestival-goEast.de
Festival Month: Late April
Genres: Documentary, Features, International, Narrative

GOLDEN KNIGHT INTERNATIONAL FILM FESTIVAL
www.global.net.mt/macc
Festival Month: Late November
Genres: All Categories - Shorts, First-Time Independent Filmmakers, Independent, International, Student

GREEK INTERNATIONAL SHORT FILM FESTIVAL IN DRAMA
www.dramafilmfestival.gr
Festival Month: Mid-September
Genres: Animation, Documentary, International, Narrative, Shorts

HAIFA INTERNATIONAL FILM FESTIVAL
www.haifaff.co.il
Festival Month: October
Genres: Documentary, Ethnic Other, Features, Independent, International, Multi-Cultural, Narrative, Shorts, Student

HAMBURG INTERNATIONAL SHORT FILM FESTIVAL
www.shortfilm.com
Festival Month: Mid-June
Genres: All Categories - Shorts, Digital, Digital Animation, International, Short, Super 8/8mm

HERTFORDSHIRE INTERNATIONAL FILM FESTIVAL
www.hiff.co.uk
Festival Month: Early October
Genres: Animation, Documentary, Experimental, Features, Independent, International, Music Videos, Narrative, Shorts

HIROSHIMA INTERNATIONAL ANIMATION FESTIVAL
www.urban.ne.jp/home/hiroanim
Festival Month: August
Genres: Animation, Digital, Features, International, Narrative, Shorts

HOF INTERNATIONAL FILM FESTIVAL
www.hofer-filmtage.de
Festival Month: Late October
Genres: Animation, Avant Garde, Documentary, Ethnic Other, European, Experimental, Features, Independent, International, Narrative, Shorts

HOLLAND ANIMATION FILM FESTIVAL
www.awn.com/haff
Festival Month: Early November
Genres: Animation, Avant Garde, Digital Animation, Experimental, Features, International, Shorts

HOME BREWED INTERNATIONAL SHORT FILM FESTIVAL
www.homebrewedfilm.com
Festival Month: Late October
Genres: Documentary, Experimental, First-Time Independent Filmmakers, Independent, International, Narrative, Shorts, Student

HONG KONG INTERNATIONAL FILM & TV MARKET (FILMART)
www.hkfilmart.com
Festival Month: Late June
Genres: Animation, Documentary, Ethnic Asian, Features, Independent, International, Markets, Narrative, Shorts, Television

HONG KONG JEWISH FILM FESTIVAL
www.hkjewishfilmfest.org
Festival Month: November
Genres: Animation, Documentary, Ethnic Jewish, Features, International, Narrative, Shorts

HULL INTERNATIONAL SHORT FILM FESTIVAL
www.hullfilm.co.uk
Festival Month: Mid-October
Genres: Animation, Children, Documentary, Experimental, International, Narrative, Shorts

HUMAN RIGHTS NIGHTS FILM FESTIVAL
www.humanrightsnights.org
Festival Month: Late March
Genres: Documentary, Features, Human Rights, International, Narrative, Shorts

I CASTELLI ANIMATI INTERNATIONAL ANIMATED FILM FESTIVAL
www.castellianimati.it
Festival Month: Early December
Genres: Animation, Commercials, Digital Animation, Experimental, Features, International, Shorts, Television

**IAC BRITISH
INTERNATIONAL AMATEUR
FILM & VIDEO COMPETITION**
www.theiac.org.uk
Festival Month: Late April
Genres: Children, Documentary,
Features, First-Time Independent
Filmmakers, Independent,
International, Narrative, Shorts,
Student, Video

**INCURT SHORT FILM
FESTIVAL**
www.incurt.org
Festival Month: Early June
Genres: Ethnic Spanish, European,
International, Shorts

INFINITY FESTIVAL
www.infinityfestival.it
Festival Month: Late March-April
Genres: Documentary, Environmental,
Experimental, Features, Independent,
International, Narrative, Scientific and
Popular Science, Spiritual

**INTERFEST MOSCOW
INTERNATIONAL FILM
FESTIVAL**
www.miff.ru/25/eng/interfest
Festival Month: Late June
Genres: Animation, Documentary,
Ethnic Other, Experimental, Features,
Independent, International, Narrative,
Shorts

**INTERFILM – INTERNATIONAL
SHORT FILM FESTIVAL
BERLIN**
www.interfilm.de
Festival Month: Early November
Genres: Animation, Children,
Documentary, International, Narrative,
Shorts

**INTERNATIONAL ADVENTURE
AND DISCOVERY FILM
FESTIVAL**
www.valdisere.com/gb/activite/
    festival.php
Festival Month: Mid-April
Genres: Adventurer/Explorers,
Documentary, Education,
Environmental, Features, International,
Mountain Sports, Shorts

**INTERNATIONAL ANIMATED
FILM AND CARTOON
FESTIVAL**
www.awn.com/folioscope
Festival Month: Late February
Genres: Animation, Digital Animation,
Features, Narrative, Shorts

**INTERNATIONAL
DOCUMENTARY FESTIVAL OF
BARCELONA**
www.docupolis.org
Festival Month: Late October
Genres: Documentary, Features,
International, Shorts

**INTERNATIONAL
ENVIRONMENTAL FILM
FESTIVAL**
www.ficma.com
Festival Month: Early June
Genres: Documentary, Education,
Environmental, Features, International,
Shorts, Student, Television

**INTERNATIONAL FESTIVAL
OF DOCUMENTARY AND
SHORT FILM OF BILBAO**
www.zinebi.com
Festival Month: November
Genres: Documentary, Shorts

**INTERNATIONAL FESTIVAL
OF NEW FILM SPLIT**
www.splitfilmfestival.hr
Festival Month: Late June-July
Genres: Animation, Avant Garde,
Digital, Documentary, Experimental,
Features, First-Time Independent
Filmmakers, Independent,
International, Narrative, Shorts

**INTERNATIONAL FILM
FESTIVAL INNSBRUCK**
www.iffi.at
Festival Month: Early June
Genres: 16mm, 35mm, Africa, Asia,
and Latin America, Animation,
Documentary, Features, Independent,
International, Shorts

**INTERNATIONAL FILM
FESTIVAL MUMBAI**
www.iffmumbai.com
Festival Month: Late November
Genres: Documentary, Ethnic Other,
Features, Independent, International,
Narrative

**INTERNATIONAL FILM
FESTIVAL OF FESTIVALS**
www.filmfest.ru
Festival Month: Mid-June
Genres: Documentary, Ethnic Other,
Features, International, Narrative,
Shorts

**INTERNATIONAL FILM
FESTIVAL OF KERALA**
www.keralafilm.com
Festival Month: Mid-December
Genres: Africa, Asia, and Latin
America, Documentary, Ethnic Other,
Features, First-Time Independent
Filmmakers, Independent,
International, Narrative, Shorts

**INTERNATIONAL FILM
FESTIVAL OF MILAN**
www.miffmilanofestival.com
Festival Month: Late October-
November
Genres: Animation, Avant Garde,
Documentary, Ethnic Other, European,
Features, Independent, International,
Narrative, Shorts

**INTERNATIONAL FILM
FESTIVAL OF URUGUAY**
www.cinemateca.org.uy
Festival Month: July
Genres: Animation, Children,
Documentary, Ethnic Latin,
Experimental, Features, Independent,
International, Narrative, Shorts

**INTERNATIONAL HUMAN
RIGHTS FILM FESTIVAL**
www.humanrightsfilmfestival.org
Festival Month: September
Genres: Documentary, Education,
Features, Human Rights, International,
Multi-Cultural, Narrative, Shorts

**INTERNATIONAL ODENSE
FILM FESTIVAL**
www.filmfestival.dk
Festival Month: Mid-August
Genres: Documentary, European,
Experimental, Fantasy/Science Fiction,
Features, First-Time Independent
Filmmakers, Independent,
International, Student

**INTERNATIONAL PANORAMA
OF INDEPENDENT FILMAKERS**
www.independent.gr
Festival Month: Early October
Genres: Animation, Documentary,
Ethnic Other, Experimental, Features,
Independent, International, Narrative,
Shorts

**INTERNATIONAL SHORT FILM
FESTIVAL OF AMSTERDAM**
www.shorts-filmfestival.com
Festival Month: Mid-March
Genres: All Categories - Shorts

**INTERNATIONAL SHORT FILM
FESTIVAL WINTERTHUR**
www.kurzfilmtage.ch
Festival Month: Mid-November
Genres: All Categories - Shorts

**INTERNATIONAL SKOPJE
FILM FESTIVAL**
www.kinoeye.org/02/09/
    trajkov09.html
Festival Month: Mid-March
Genres: Documentary, Features,
International, Narrative, Shorts

INTERNATIONAL TOURIST FILM FESTIVAL
www.actl.it/festival
Festival Month: April
Genres: Adventurer/Explorers, Commercials, Documentary, Environmental, Ethnic Other, Features, International, Multi-Cultural, Narrative, Sports, Television

INTERNATIONAL WOMEN FILM FESTIVAL OF CRÉTEIL
www.filmsdefemmes.com
Festival Month: Mid-March
Genres: Documentary, Features, International, Narrative, Shorts, Women

INTERNATIONAL WOMEN'S FILM FESTIVAL OF BARCELONA
mostra.dracmagic.com
Festival Month: Early June
Genres: Animation, Documentary, Experimental, Features, Independent, International, Narrative, Women

INTERNATIONAL YOUNG FILMMAKERS FESTIVAL OF GRANADA
www.filmfest-granada.com
Festival Month: Mid-April
Genres: 16mm, 35mm, Animation, Children, Experimental, Narrative, Shorts, Student

IRANIAN INTERNATIONAL MARKET
www.fcf-ir.com
Festival Month: Early February
Genres: Documentary, Ethnic Other, Family, Features, Human Rights, International, Markets, Narrative

ISTANBUL INTERNATIONAL FILM FESTIVAL
www.istfest.org
Festival Month: Mid-April
Genres: Animation, Documentary, Ethnic Other, Features, International, Narrative, Shorts

ISTANBUL INTERNATIONAL SHORT FILM FESTIVAL
www.kisafilm.com
Festival Month: Early April
Genres: 16mm, 35mm, Animation, Experimental, International, Narrative, Shorts

ITALIAN FILM FESTIVAL UK
www.italianfilmfestival.org.uk
Festival Month: March-April
Genres: Animation, Avant Garde, Documentary, Ethnic Other, Experimental, Features, International, Narrative, Shorts, Touring

ITS ALL TRUE INTERNATIONAL DOCUMENTARY FESTIVAL
www.itsalltrue.com.br
Festival Month: Late March-April
Genres: Documentary, Features, International, Shorts

JAFFAS DOWN THE AISLE
www.jaffasdowntheaisle.com.au
Festival Month: Early July
Genres: Comedy, Features, Independent, Independent, Narrative, Performance, Shorts

JAMESON DUBLIN INTERNATIONAL FILM FESTIVAL
www.dubliniff.com
Festival Month: March
Genres: Animation, Documentary, Experimental, Features, International, Narrative, Shorts

JAPAN WILDLIFE FESTIVAL
www.naturechannel.jp
Festival Month: Late August
Genres: Animation, Children, Documentary, Education, Environmental, Features, International, Narrative, Shorts, Wildlife

JEONJU INTERNATIONAL FILM FESTIVAL
www.jiff.or.kr
Festival Month: Late April-May
Genres: Animation, Digital, Ethnic Asian, Experimental, Features, Independent, International, Narrative, Shorts

JIHLAVA INTERNATIONAL DOCUMENTARY FILM FESTIVAL
www.dokument-festival.cz
Festival Month: Late October
Genres: Documentary, Ethnic Other, European, Features, International, Shorts

JVC TOKYO VIDEO FESTIVAL
www.jvc-victor.co.jp/tvf/index.html
Festival Month: January
Genres: Digital, Independent, International, Shorts, Video

KARAFILM FESTIVAL
www.karafilmfest.com
Festival Month: Mid-December
Genres: Documentary, Ethnic Other, Experimental, Features, International, Narrative, Shorts

KINDER FILM FESTIVAL JAPAN
www.kinder.co.jp
Festival Month: Mid-August
Genres: Animation, Children, Family, Features, International, Shorts

KOLKATA FILM FESTIVAL
www.calfilmfestival.org
Festival Month: Mid-November
Genres: Documentary, Ethnic Other, Features, Human Rights, International, Narrative, Shorts

KUALA LUMPUR WORLD FILM FESTIVAL
www.klwff.com
Festival Month: Mid-February
Genres: 16mm, 35mm, Features, Human Rights, International, Multi-Cultural, Narrative, Peace

KYOTO INTERNATIONAL STUDENT FILM & VIDEO FESTIVAL
www.consortium.or.jp/~kisfvf2003
Festival Month: Late November
Genres: Ethnic Asian, Features, International, Shorts, Student

L'ISOLA DEL CINEMA INTERNATIONAL FILM FESTIVAL
www.isoladelcinema.com
Festival Month: July-August
Genres: Documentary, Ethnic Other, Features, International, Narrative, Shorts

LA ROCHELLE INTERNATIONAL FILM FESTIVAL
www.festival-larochelle.org
Festival Month: Late June-July
Genres: 16mm, 35mm, Features, International, Narrative

BEST COMEDY FILM FESTIVALS

Aspen Shortsfest
DIY Film Festival
Festival Comedia
First Sundays Short Comedy Film Festival
Jaffas Down the Aisle
U.S. Comedy Arts Festival
Vancouver International Comedy Festival
World of Comedy International Film Festival

**LAUSANNE UNDERGROUND
FILM & MUSIC FESTIVAL**
www.luff.ch
Festival Month: Mid-October
Genres: Animation, Documentary,
Experimental, Features, Independent,
International, Narrative, Shorts,
Underground

**LESBIAN & GAY FILM
FESTIVAL HAMBURG**
www.lsf-hamburg.de
Festival Month: Mid-October
Genres: Documentary, European,
Features, Gay Lesbian, International,
Narrative, Shorts

**LEUVEN KORT SHORT FILM
FESTIVAL**
www.shortfilmfestival.org
Festival Month: Late November-
December
Genres: Documentary, European,
Narrative, Shorts

**LISBON GAY & LESBIAN FILM
FESTIVAL**
www.lisbonfilmfest.org
Festival Month: September
Genres: Documentary, Features, Gay
Lesbian, International, Narrative,
Shorts

**LISBON INTERNATIONAL
VIDEO FESTIVAL**
www.videolisboa.com
Festival Month: Late November
Genres: Animation, Digital,
Documentary, DVD, Education,
International, Multimedia, Narrative,
Shorts, Student, Video, Web Projects

**LJUBLJANA INTERNATIONAL
FILM FESTIVAL**
www.cd-cc.si/liffe
Festival Month: Mid-November
Genres: Documentary, First-Time
Independent Filmmakers, Independent,
International, Narrative, Shorts

**LONDON LESBIAN & GAY
FILM FESTIVAL**
www.outuk.com/llgff
Festival Month: Late March-April
Genres: Documentary, Features, Gay
Lesbian, International, Narrative,
Shorts

**LONDON SCIENCE FICTION
AND FANTASY FILM
FESTIVAL**
www.sci-fi-london.com
Festival Month: Late January-
February
Genres: Animation, Documentary,
European, Fantasy/Science Fiction,
Features, Horror, Independent,
International, Narrative, Shorts

**MAGICAL AGE
INTERNATIONAL VIDEO
FESTIVAL**
Festival Month: Mid-May
Genres: Animation, Documentary,
Environmental, Experimental,
Fantasy/Science Fiction, Features,
International, Shorts, Spiritual

**MALESCO INTERNATIONAL
SHORT FILM FESTIVAL**
www.malescorto.it
Festival Month: Early August
Genres: Documentary, International,
Narrative, Shorts

MARDI GRAS FILM FESTIVAL
www.queerscreen.com.au
Festival Month: Mid-February
Genres: Documentary, Features, Gay
Lesbian, Independent, International,
Narrative, Shorts, Student

**MARRAKECH
INTERNATIONAL FILM
FESTIVAL**
www.festivalmarrakech.com
Festival Month: Early October
Genres: Documentary, Features,
International, Narrative, Shorts

MATITA FILM FESTIVAL
www.matitafilmfestival.org
Festival Month: Late September
Genres: Animation, Digital Animation,
First-Time Independent Filmmakers,
Independent, International, Shorts,
Student

MEDFILM FESTIVAL
www.mediatecaroma.org/medfilm
Festival Month: Mid-November
Genres: Documentary, Ethnic Other,
European, Features, International,
Narrative, Shorts, Television

MEDIAWAVE FESTIVAL
www.mediawavefestival.com
Festival Month: Late April-May
Genres: Animation, Dance,
Documentary, European, Features,
First-Time Independent Filmmakers,
Independent, International, Narrative,
Shorts, Student

**MELBOURNE FRINGE
FESTIVAL**
www.melbournefringe.org.au
Festival Month: September 22-
October 10, 2004
Genres: Animation, Animation, Avant
Garde, Documentary, Experimental,
Features, First-Time Independent
Filmmakers, Independent,
International, Markets, Narrative,
Performance, Shorts

**MELBOURNE INTERNATIONAL
ANIMATION FESTIVAL (MIAF)**
www.miaf.net
Festival Month: Late June
Genres: Animation, Digital Animation,
Features, First-Time Independent
Filmmakers, Independent,
International, Shorts, Student

**MELBOURNE UNDERGROUND
FILM FESTIVAL**
www.muff.com.au
Festival Month: July
Genres: Animation, Documentary,
Features, Independent, International,
Narrative, Shorts, Underground

MENISCUS FILM FESTIVAL
www.meniscusfilms.com
Festival Month: Late October-
November
Genres: Animation, Documentary,
Features, Independent, International,
Narrative, Shorts

**MINIMALEN SHORT FILM
FESTIVAL**
www.minimalen.com
Festival Month: Mid-March
Genres: Ethnic Other, European,
Independent, International, Shorts

MIPCOM JUNIOR
www.mipcom.com
Festival Month: Early October
Genres: International, Markets,
Television

MIPTV
www.mipdoc.com, www.miptv.com
Festival Month: Late March
Genres: Documentary, Markets,
Television

**MONTECATINI
INTERNATIONAL SHORT FILM
FESTIVAL**
www.filmvideomontecatini.com
Festival Month: Early July
Genres: Animation, Dance,
Documentary, Experimental, Narrative,
Shorts

MONTPELLIER FESTIVAL
www.cinemed.tm.fr
Festival Month: Late October
Genres: Documentary, Experimental,
Features, International, Narrative,
Shorts

**MOOMBA INTERNATIONAL
AMATEUR FILM FESTIVAL**
Festival Month: March
Genres: Documentary, Family,
Features, First-Time Independent
Filmmakers, Independent,
International, Narrative, Shorts,
Student

MORBEGNO FILM FESTIVAL
www.zert.it
Festival Month: Late September
Genres: Animation, Documentary, First-Time Independent Filmmakers, Independent, International, Narrative, Shorts, Silent

MORELIA INTERNATIONAL FILM FESTIVAL
www.moreliafilmfest.com/
Festival Month: Early October
Genres: Animation, Documentary, Ethnic Other, Features, First-Time Independent Filmmakers, Independent, International, Narrative, Shorts

MOSCOW INTERNATIONAL CHILDREN'S FILM FESTIVAL
www.children-animation.ru
Festival Month: Late March-April
Genres: Animation, Children, Features, First-Time Independent Filmmakers, Independent, International, Shorts, Student

MOTOVUN FILM FESTIVAL
www.motovunfilmfestival.com
Festival Month: Late July
Genres: Documentary, Features, Independent, International, Narrative, Shorts

NAPOLIDANZA
www.napolidanza.com
Festival Month: Mid-May
Genres: Dance, Digital, Documentary, Features, International, Multimedia, Narrative, Performance, Shorts

NATFILM FESTIVAL
www.natfilm.dk
Festival Month: Late March-April
Genres: Documentary, Features, International, Narrative

NEDERLANDS FILM FESTIVAL
www.filmfestival.nl
Festival Month: Late September-October
Genres: Animation, Commercials, Documentary, European, Features, International, Narrative, Shorts, Student, Television

NEUCHÂTEL INTERNATIONAL FANTASTIC FILM FESTIVAL
www.nifff.ch
Festival Month: Late June-July
Genres: Animation, European, Fantasy/Science Fiction, Horror, International, Mystery, Shorts, Thriller

BEST VIDEO FILM FESTIVALS

Antimatter Festival of Underground Short Film & Video
Arizona State University Short Film and Video Festival
Atlanta Film and Video Festival
Berkeley Video and Film Festival
Cinematexas International Short Film & Video Festival
CU 2 Video and Film Festival
Da Vinci Film and Video Festival
eKsperim[E]nto Film & Video Festival
Firstglance: Philadelphia Independent Film and Video Festival
Hometown Video Festival
JVC Tokyo Video Festival
Magical Age International Video Festival
Northwest Film & Video Festival
VideoTheatre NYC
Viper International Film Video and Multimedia Festival

NEXTFRAME JAPAN
www.tuj.ac.jp/nextframe
Festival Month: Late July-August
Genres: Documentary, Documentary, Features, First-Time Independent Filmmakers, Independent, International, Narrative, Student, Touring

NIPPON CONNECTION – JAPANESE FILM FESTIVAL
www.nipponconnection.de
Festival Month: April
Genres: Animation, Digital, Documentary, Ethnic Asian, Features, Independent, International, Shorts

NORDIC FILM DAYS LÜBECK
www.luebeck.de/filmtage/03/index.html
Festival Month: Late October-November
Genres: Documentary, Ethnic Other, European, Features, Independent, International, Narrative, Shorts

NORDIC FILM FESTIVAL
www.festival-cinema-nordique.asso.fr
Festival Month: March
Genres: Documentary, European, Features, Independent, International, Narrative, Shorts

NORTHERN LIGHTS FILM FESTIVAL
www.nlff.co.uk
Festival Month: Early September
Genres: Documentary, European, Features, International, Narrative, Shorts

NORWEGIAN SHORT FILM FESTIVAL
www.kortfilmfestivalen.no/engframeset-1.html
Festival Month: Mid-June
Genres: Documentary, Ethnic Other, European, Independent, International, Narrative, Shorts, Student

NORWICH INTERNATIONAL ANIMATION FESTIVAL
www.filmartsnorwich.co.uk
Festival Month: October
Genres: Animation, Experimental, Features, Independent, International, Shorts

ÖKOMEDIA INTERNATIONAL ENVIRONMENTAL FILM FESTIVAL
www.oekomedia-institut.de
Festival Month: October
Genres: Documentary, Environmental, Features, International, Narrative, Shorts

ONE WORLD HUMAN RIGHTS DOCUMENTARY FILM FESTIVAL
www.oneworld.cz
Festival Month: Mid-April
Genres: Documentary, Features, Human Rights, International, Shorts

OPEN AIR FILMFEST WEITERSTADT
www.filmfest-weiterstadt.de
Festival Month: Mid-August
Genres: Documentary, Features, Independent, International, Narrative, Performance, Shorts, Student

OSLO INTERNATIONAL FILM FESTIVAL
www.oslofilmfestival.com
Festival Month: Late November
Genres: Documentary, European, Features, International, Narrative, Shorts

OULU INTERNATIONAL CHILDREN'S FILM FESTIVAL
www.ouka.fi/lef
Festival Month: Mid-November
Genres: Animation, Children, Family, International, Shorts

OUT IN AFRICA SOUTH AFRICAN GAY & LESBIAN FILM FESTIVAL
www.oia.co.za
Festival Month: Mid-March-April
Genres: Documentary, Features, Gay Lesbian, Independent, International, Narrative, Shorts

OVER THE FENCE COMEDY FILM FESTIVAL
www.overthefence.com.au
Festival Month: February-May
Genres: Comedy, Ethnic Other, Independent, Shorts

PANAFRICAN FILM AND TELEVISION FESTIVAL OF OUAGADOUGOU
www.fespaco.bf
Festival Month: Late February-March
Genres: Documentary, Ethnic African, Features, International, Narrative, Shorts, Television

PARIS/BERLIN INTERNATIONAL MEETINGS
www.art-action.org
Festival Month: November
Genres: Animation, Documentary, Experimental, Features, International, Multimedia, Narrative, Shorts, Web Projects

PÄRNU INTERNATIONAL DOCUMENTARY AND ANTHROPOLOGY FILM FESTIVAL
www.chaplin.ee
Festival Month: Early July
Genres: Children, Documentary, Environmental, European, Features, International, Shorts

PINK APPLE – SCHWULLESBISCHES FILMFESTIVAL
www.pinkapple.ch
Festival Month: Early May
Genres: Documentary, Features, Gay Lesbian, Independent, International, Narrative, Shorts, Touring (Zurich, Frauenfeld, Lucerne, Basel)

PITIGLIANO FILM FESTIVAL
www.pitifest.it
Festival Month: August
Genres: Documentary, Ethnic Jewish, Features, Independent, International, Multi-Cultural, Narrative, Shorts

PLATFORMA VIDEO FESTIVAL
www.platforma.gr
Festival Month: Early October
Genres: Dance, Digital, Documentary, Features, Independent, International, Multimedia, Performance, Shorts, Video

POLITICALLY INCORRECT FILM FESTIVAL
Festival Month: Early May
Genres: Documentary, Features, Human Rights, International, Multi-Cultural, Narrative

PORDENONE SILENT FILM FESTIVAL
cinetecadelfriuli.org/gcm
Festival Month: Early October
Genres: Animation, Avant Garde, Features, Independent, International, Shorts, Silent

PORTOBELLO FILM FESTIVAL
www.portobellofilmfestival.com
Festival Month: Early August
Genres: All

PREMIERS PLANS FESTIVAL
www.premiersplans.org
Festival Month: Mid-January
Genres: Documentary, European, Experimental, Features, First-Time Independent Filmmakers, French, Independent, International, Narrative, Shorts, Underground

PRIDE INTERNATIONAL FILM FESTIVAL
piff.filmfestivals.net
Festival Month: Spring-Summer
Genres: Animation, Documentary, Education, Features, Gay Lesbian, Independent, International, Narrative, Shorts

PUCHON INTERNATIONAL FANTASTIC FILM FESTIVAL (PiFAN)
www.pifan.com
Festival Month: Mid-July
Genres: Animation, Ethnic Other, Experimental, Fantasy/Science Fiction, Features, Horror, International, Narrative, Shorts, Thriller

PUSAN INTERNATIONAL FILM FESTIVAL
info.piff.org
Festival Month: Early October
Genres: 16mm, 35mm, Animation, Documentary, Ethnic Asian, Experimental, Features, International, Narrative, Shorts

REEL MADNESS FILM FESTIVAL
www.reelmadness.co.uk
Festival Month: Mid-June
Genres: Documentary, Experimental, Experimental, Features, Independent, International, Narrative, Shorts

REELIFE SHORT FILM FESTIVAL
www.vibewire.net/reelife
Festival Month: Late September
Genres: Ethnic Other, First-Time Independent Filmmakers, Independent, International, Shorts, Student, Teenager

REVELATION PERTH INTERNATIONAL FILM FESTIVAL
www.revelationfilmfest.org
Festival Month: Early July
Genres: Animation, Documentary, Experimental, Features, Independent, International, Narrative, Shorts, Student

BEST SPORTS FILM FESTIVALS

Banff Mountain Film Festival
Hot Shots High School Film and Ad Festival
International Adventure and Discovery Film Festival
Sports Movie & TV International Festival
Trento International Film Festival
Twin Rivers Media Festival
Vancouver International Mountain Film Festival
Wild and Scenic Environmental Film Festival
Cut and Paste Skateboarding Art & Film Festival
Surf Film Festival
XDance
Bicycle Film Festival

RiO DE JANEiRO INTERNATiONAL SHORT FiLM FESTiVAL
www.curtacinema.com.br
Festival Month: Early December
Genres: All Categories - Shorts, International

RiVER CiTY FiLM FESTiVAL
www.film.wanganui.info
Festival Month: October
Genres: Ethnic Other, International, Shorts, Student, Teenager, Television

ROME iNDEPENDENT FiLM FESTiVAL
www.riff.it
Festival Month: Late February
Genres: Animation, Digital, Digital Animation, Documentary, Ethnic Other, European, Features, Independent, International, Narrative, Shorts, Student

RUSHES SOHO SHORTS FiLM FESTiVAL
www.sohoshorts.com
Festival Month: Late July-August
Genres: Animation, Documentary, First-Time Independent Filmmakers, Independent, International, Music Videos, Narrative, Shorts, Student

SABiNA iNTERNATiONAL SHORT FiLM FESTiVAL
www.festivaldelcorto.org/index-i.htm
Festival Month: Mid-July
Genres: Animation, Children, Documentary, Experimental, Independent, International, Narrative, Shorts, Student

SAO PAULO iNTERNATiONAL SHORT FiLM FESTiVAL
www.kinoforum.org
Festival Month: Late August-September
Genres: 16mm, 35mm, Documentary, Ethnic Latin, International, Narrative, Shorts

SARAJEVO FiLM FESTiVAL
www.sff.ba
Festival Month: Late August
Genres: Documentary, Ethnic Other, European, Features, Independent, International, Narrative, Shorts

SCHWULE FiLMWOCHE FREiBURG
www.schwule-filmwoche.de
Festival Month: Mid-May
Genres: Documentary, Features, Gay Lesbian, Independent, International, Narrative, Shorts

SEHSÜCHTE iNTERNATiONAL STUDENT FiLM FESTIVAL
www.sehsuechte.de
Festival Month: Late April-May
Genres: Animation, Documentary, Experimental, Features, Independent, International, Shorts, Student

SEOUL NET AND FiLM FESTiVAL
www.senef.net
Festival Month: Mid-September
Online: March-September
Genres: Digital, Documentary, Features, International, Multimedia, Online Festival, Web Projects

SHADOW FiLM FESTiVAL
www.shadowfestival.nl
Festival Month: Mid-November
Genres: Documentary, Features, Independent, International, Shorts

SHADOWLiNE SALERNO FiLM FESTiVAL
www.shadowline.it
Festival Month: Late April-May
Genres: 35mm, Digital, Features, First-Time Independent Filmmakers, Independent, International, Narrative, Shorts, Student, Teenager

SHORT CRAP FiLM FESTiVAL
www.fullyflared.com
Festival Month: TBA
Genres: Animation, Documentary, Experimental, Independent, International, Narrative, Shorts, Touring

SKiP CiTY iNTERNATiONAL D-CiNEMA FESTiVAL
www.skipcity-dcf.jp
Festival Month: Late March
Genres: Animation, Digital, Documentary, Features, Independent, International, Narrative, Shorts

SLEEPWALKERS STUDENT FiLM FESTiVAL
www.hot.ee/sleepwalkers
Festival Month: Late November
Genres: Animation, Documentary, Experimental, Features, Independent, International, Narrative, Shorts, Student

SNiFF SHORT iNTERNATiONAL FiLM FESTiVAL
www.sniff-festival.com
Festival Month: Late June
Genres: Animation, Documentary, European, Experimental, Independent, International, Narrative, Shorts, Student

SOCHi iNTERNATiONAL FiLM FESTiVAL
www.kinotavr.com/siff.html
Festival Month: June
Genres: Documentary, European, Features, Independent, International, Narrative, Shorts

SOFiA iNTERNATiONAL FiLM FESTiVAL
www.cinema.bg/sff
Festival Month: Mid-March
Genres: Documentary, European, Features, International, Narrative, Shorts

SOLOTHURN FiLM FESTiVAL
www.solothurnerfilmtage.ch
Festival Month: Late January
Genres: Animation, Documentary, Ethnic Other, European, Features, Independent, International, Narrative, Shorts, Student

SOPOT FiLM FESTiVAL
www.sopotfilm.com
Festival Month: Late June
Genres: Animation, Documentary, Experimental, Independent, International, Music Videos, Narrative, Polish, Shorts

SPORTS MOViE & TV iNTERNATiONAL FESTiVAL
www.ficts.com
Festival Month: Late October-November
Genres: Documentary, Features, International, Narrative, Shorts, Sports, Television

ST. KiLDA FiLM FESTiVAL
www.portphillip.vic.gov.au/st_kilda_filmfestival_2003.html
Festival Month: Late May
Genres: Animation, Documentary, Independent, International, Music Videos, Narrative, Shorts

STUTTGART FiLMWiNTER
www.filmwinter.de
Festival Month: Mid-January
Genres: Digital, Documentary, Features, Independent, International, Multimedia, Narrative, Online, Shorts, Web Projects

SULZBACH-ROSENBERG iNTERNATiONAL SHORT FiLM FESTiVAL
www.filmfest-abgedreht.com
Festival Month: Mid-May
Genres: International, Shorts

SYDNEY ASIA-PACIFIC FILM FESTIVAL
www.sapff.com.au
Festival Month: December
Genres: Animation, Documentary, Ethnic Asian, Features, International, Narrative, Shorts, Television

TABOR FILM FESTIVAL
www.taborfilmfestival.com
Festival Month: Mid-June
Genres: Animation, Digital, Documentary, Experimental, Independent, International, Narrative, Shorts

TAIWAN INTERNATIONAL CHILDREN'S TV & FILM FESTIVAL
www.tictff.org.tw/index_e.htm
Festival Month: Early January
Genres: Animation, Children, Documentary, Education, Episodic Television/Television Pilots, Family, Features, International, Narrative, Shorts, Television

TAIWAN INTERNATIONAL ETHNOGRAPHIC FILM FESTIVAL
www.tieff.sinica.edu.tw
Festival Month: Early October
Genres: Documentary, Ethnic Other, Features, Human Rights, International, Multi-Cultural, Shorts

TALLINN BLACK NIGHTS FILM FESTIVAL
www.poff.ee
Festival Month: Late November-December
Genres: Documentary, European, Features, International, Narrative, Shorts

TAORMINA BNL FILMFEST
www.taorminafilmfest.it
Festival Month: Mid-June
Genres: Documentary, Ethnic Other, Features, International, Narrative, Shorts

TEHRAN SHORT FILM FESTIVAL
www.shortfilmfest-ir.com
Festival Month: Late October
Genres: Animation, Documentary, Experimental, International, Narrative, Shorts

TINKLAI INTERNATIONAL SHORT FILM FESTIVAL
www.tinklai.net
Festival Month: Mid-September
Genres: Animation, Documentary, European, Experimental, International, Narrative, Shorts

TIRANA INTERNATIONAL FILM FESTIVAL
www.tiranafilmfest.com
Festival Month: Early December
Genres: Documentary, Ethnic Other, European, International, Narrative, Shorts

TOKYO INTERNATIONAL LESBIAN & GAY FILM FESTIVAL
www.tokyo-lgff.org
Festival Month: June
Genres: Animation, Documentary, Experimental, Features, Gay Lesbian, Independent, International, Narrative, Shorts

TOUGH EYE INTERNATIONAL TURKU ANIMATED FILM FESTIVAL
www.tough-eye.com
Festival Month: May
Genres: Animation, Experimental, Features, Independent, International, Shorts

TOURFILM FESTIVAL
www.tourfilm.cz/cz/index.htm
Festival Month: Early October
Genres: Commercials, Documentary, Features, International, Shorts, Tourism

TRANSILVANIA INTERNATIONAL FILM FESTIVAL
www.tiff.ro
Festival Month: Late May-June
Genres: Documentary, Experimental, Fantasy/Science Fiction, Features, Horror, Independent, International, Narrative, Shorts

TRANSPARENCY INTERNATIONAL FILM FESTIVAL
www.transparency.org/film
Festival Month: Late May
Genres: Documentary, Features, Government, International, Narrative, Shorts

TRENTO INTERNATIONAL FILM FESTIVAL
www.mountainfilmfestival.trento.it
Festival Month: Early May
Genres: Adventurer/Explorers, Documentary, Environmental, Features, International, Mountain Sports, Narrative, Shorts, Sports, Television

UK JEWISH FILM FESTIVAL
www.ukjewishfilmfestival.org.uk
Festival Month: October-November
Genres: Documentary, Ethnic Jewish, Features, Narrative, Shorts

UMEÅ INTERNATIONAL FILM FESTIVAL
www.ff.umea.com
Festival Month: Late September
Genres: Documentary, Features, Independent, International, Narrative, Shorts

UP-AND-COMING FILM FESTIVAL HANNOVER
www.up-and-coming.de
Festival Month: Early November
Genres: Animation, Avant Garde, Digital, Experimental, Features, First-Time Independent Filmmakers, Independent, International, Narrative, Shorts, Shorts

UPOVERDOWNUNDER FILM FESTIVAL
www.upoverdownunder.co.uk
Festival Month: Late September-October
Genres: Digital, Documentary, Ethnic Other, European, Features, Independent, International, Narrative, Shorts

BEST DISCOVERY FILM FESTIVALS

$100 Film Festival
Bergamo International Week of Auteur Film
Bermuda International Film Festival
Cleveland International Film Festival
DancesWithFilms
Deep Ellum Film Festival
Entrevues Film Festival
Firstglance Hollywood/Philadelphia Film Festivals
Lost Film Festival
New Venue
Northwest Film & Video Festival
up-and-coming Film Festival Hannover

URBANCHiLLERS
www.urbanchillers.com
Genres: Horror, Independent,
International, Online, Shorts

**VALDiViA iNTERNATiONAL
FiLM FESTiVAL**
www.festivalcinevaldivia.com
Festival Month: Early September
Genres: Documentary, Ethnic Other,
Ethnic Spanish, Features,
Independent, International, Shorts,
Student

**VALLADOLiD
iNTERNATiONAL FiLM
FESTiVAL**
www.seminci.com
Festival Month: Late October
Genres: 16mm, 35mm, Documentary,
Features, International, Narrative,
Shorts

VERONA FiLM FESTiVAL
www.schermidamore.it
Festival Month: Mid-April
Genres: European, Features,
Independent, International, Narrative,
Romantic, Shorts

**ViLA DO CONDE
iNTERNATiONAL SHORT FiLM
FESTiVAL**
www.curtasmetragens.pt/festival
Festival Month: Early July
Genres: Animation, Documentary,
European, Experimental, Independent,
International, Narrative, Shorts

**ViLNiUS SPRiNG
iNTERNATiONAL FiLM
FESTiVAL**
www.kino.lt
Festival Month: March
Genres: Documentary, European,
Features, International, Narrative,
Shorts

ViNOKiNO FiLM FESTiVAL
www.tuseta.fi/vinokino
Festival Month: Mid-November
Genres: Animation, Documentary,
Experimental, Features, Gay Lesbian,
Independent, International, Narrative,
Shorts

**ViPER iNTERNATiONAL FiLM
ViDEO AND MULTiMEDiA
FESTiVAL**
www.viper.ch
Festival Month: Mid-November
Genres: Animation, Avant Garde,
Digital, Experimental, Features,
International, Multi-Cultural,
Narrative, Shorts, Web Projects

BEST BEACH FiLM FESTiVALS

American Black Film Festival
Bermuda International Film Festival
Daytona Beach Film Festival
Donostia - San Sebastian International Film Festival
Hawaii International Film Festival
Imperial Beach International Film Festival
Long Beach International Film Festival
Marco Island Film Festival
Miami Film Festival
Newport Beach Film Festival
Palm Beach International Film Festival
Rehoboth Beach Independent Film Festival
San Diego Film Festival
Wreck-Beach Film Festival

**VOLADERO iNTERNATiONAL
FiLM AND ViDEO FESTiVAL**
www.voladero.com
Festival Month: Late August
Genres: Animation, Documentary,
Independent, International, Multi-
Cultural, Narrative, Shorts

**WELLiNGTON FRiNGE SHORT
FiLM FESTiVAL**
www.fringefilmfest.co.nz
Festival Month: Early July
Genres: Animation, Documentary,
Ethnic Other, Independent,
International, Narrative, Shorts

WiLD SPACES FiLM FESTiVAL
www.wildspaces.foe.org.au
Festival Month: September
Genres: Documentary, Environmental,
Features, First-Time Independent
Filmmakers, Human Rights,
Independent, International, Narrative,
Shorts, Touring

WiLDSCREEN FESTiVAL
www.wildscreenfestival.org
Festival Month: Mid-October
Genres: Documentary, Environmental,
Features, Independent, International,
Scientific and Popular Science, Shorts,
Student, Wildlife

**WOMEN MAKE WAVES FiLM
FESTiVAL**
www.wmw.com.tw
Festival Month: Mid-September
Genres: Documentary, Features,
Independent, International, Narrative,
Shorts, Women

**WOMEN'S FiLM FESTiVAL iN
SEOUL**
www.wffis.or.kr
Festival Month: Early April
Genres: Documentary, Features,
International, Narrative, Shorts,
Women

**WORLD FESTiVAL OF
UNDERWATER PiCTURES**
www.underwater-festival.com
Festival Month: Late October-
November
Genres: Documentary, Environmental,
Features, Independent, International,
Ocean, Scuba Diving & Marine,
Shorts, Wildlife

WORLD MEDiA FESTiVAL
www.worldmediafestival.org
Festival Month: Mid-May
Genres: Documentary, Features,
Independent, International, Markets,
Narrative, Shorts

**WORLD WiDE ViDEO
FESTiVAL**
www.wwvf.nl
Festival Month: Early June
Genres: Animation, Avant Garde,
Documentary, Experimental, Features,
Independent, International, Narrative,
Shorts

**WRECK-BEACH FiLM
FESTiVAL**
www.wreck-beach.org/filmfestival/
index.php
Festival Month: Mid-June
Genres: Animation, Documentary,
Experimental, Independent,
International, Narrative, Shorts

WÜRZBURG INTERNATIONAL FILM WEEKEND
www.filmwochenende-wuerzburg.de
Festival Month: Late January
Genres: Animation, Children, Documentary, Features, International, Narrative, Shorts

YORK INTERNATIONAL FILM FESTIVAL
www.yiff.co.uk
Festival Month: Mid-March
Genres: Animation, Documentary, European, Features, First-Time Independent Filmmakers, Independent, International, Narrative, Shorts

ZAGREB FILM FESTIVAL
www.zagrebfilmfestival.com
Festival Month: Mid-October
Genres: Documentary, European, Features, First-Time Independent Filmmakers, Independent, International, Narrative, Shorts, Student

ZLIN INTERNATIONAL FILM FESTIVAL FOR CHILDREN AND YOUTH
www.zlinfest.cz
Festival Month: Late May-June

BEST FILM FESTIVAL PRIZES AWARDED

$100,000 in services Southeastern Media Award (Atlanta Film Festival)

$100,000 Euros and 20,000 meters of Kodak film The "Luigi De Laurentiis" Award for a First Feature (Venice International Film Festival)

$80,000, $20,000 Tokyo Grand Prix / The Governor of Tokyo Award and Special Jury Prize respectively (Tokyo International Film Festival)

$50,000 Grand Prize for Dramatic Feature (Heartland Film Festival)

$30,000 Euros Pearl of the Audience Award (Donostia - San Sebastian International Film Festival)

$30,000 Toronto – City Award for Best Canadian Feature Film (Toronto International Film Festival)

$25,000 Best Feature Film (International Film Festival Of Kerala)

$20,000 Alfred P. Sloan Prize (Sundance Film Festival)

$20,000 Blockbuster Audience Award for Best Feature Film (American Black Film Festival)

$15,000 Eclipse Flash Best Feature (Gen Art Film Festival)

$15,000 Best Narrative Feature (Tribeca Film Festival)

$10,000 Euros VPRO Tiger Award for Best First or Second Feature (Rotterdam International Film Festival)

$10,000 Euro VPRO Tiger Awards (Rotterdam International Film Festival)

$10,000 and $5,000, respectively, SKYY Prize for First Feature and Golden Gate Award Grand Prizes (San Francisco International Film Festival)

$10,000 Grand Prize (Angelus Awards Student Film Festival)

$6,000 Euros Durian de Oro (Barcelona Asian Film Festival)

$5,000 Kodak Vision Award for Best Cinematography (Slamdance International Film Festival)

$5,000 Ken Burns Best of the Festival Award (Ann Arbor Film Festival)

$5,000 Euros Best Feature Award (Alpe Adria Cinema Trieste Film Festival)

$5,000 Euros The Golden Athena Award (Athens International Film Festival)

16mm Bolex Camera Grand Prize (International Surrealist Film Festival)

Week-Long Regal Theater Run in Los Angeles, Academy Award consideration Dreammaker Award (Nashville Film Festival)

APPENDiCES

- ⊙ index of Film Festivals by Name
- ⊙ index of Film Festivals by Month
- ⊙ index of Film Festivals by Genre
- ⊙ Hollywood Creative Directory
  Power invitation List for Distribution,
  Festival Screenings, and Parties
- ⊙ Filmmaker Resources

iNDEX OF FiLM FESTiVALS BY NAME

iNDEX OF FiLM FESTiVALS BY MONTH

JANUARY
Alpe Adria Cinema Trieste Film Festival
Annual Kidfilm Festival
Backseat Film Festival
Bangkok Film Market (BFM)
Berlin and Beyond
Black Maria Film and Video Festival
Brussels Gay and Lesbian Film Festival
Explorers Club Documentary Film Festival
Faces Of Love International Film Festival
Fajr International Film Festival
Filmfestival Max Ophüls Preis
Flickerfest Australian International Outdoor
  Short Film Festival
Flickering Image Festival
Future Film Festival
Independent Black Film Festival
International Student Original Film Art
  Festival
JVC Tokyo Video Festival
Made In Miami Film & Video Festival
NATPE Conference and Exhibition
New York Festivals International Film &
  Video Awards
Palestine Film Festival Dreams Of A Nation
Palm Springs International Film Festival
Park City Film Music Festival
Premiers Plans Festival
San Francisco Ocean Film Festival
San Francisco Short Film Festival
Schmoozedance Film Festival
Slamdance International Film Festival
Smogdance Film Festival
Solothurn Film Festival
Stuttgart Filmwinter
Sundance Film Festival
Taiwan International Children's TV & Film
  Festival
Tromadance Film Festival
Tromsø International Film Festival
Wild and Scenic Environmental Film Festival
World Community Film Festival
Würzburg International Film Weekend
X-Dance Action Sports Film Festival

JANUARY-FEBRUARY
Bangkok International Film Festival
Clermont-Ferrand Short Film Festival
Göteborg Film Festival
London Science Fiction and Fantasy Film
  Festival
Miami International Film Festival
Reel Music Festival
Rotterdam International Film Festival
Santa Barbara International Film Festival
  (SBIFF)
Sarasota Film Festival
Spindletop Film Festival
Victoria Independent Film and Video Festival

JANUARY, JUNE
NoDance Film Festival

JANUARY-SEPTEMBER
Chrysler Million Dollar Film Festival

FEBRUARY
Animac International Animation Film
  Festival
Animated Exeter
Australian International Documentary
  Conference
Berlin International Film Festival
Big Muddy Film Festival
Carolina Film and Video Festival
Chlotrudis Awards Short Film Festival
Dam Short Film Festival
Denver Jazz on Film Festival
Digital Days
Director's View Film Festival
DIY Film Festival
DocPoint Helsinki Documentary Film
  Festival
Drifting Clouds International Short Film
  Festival
Earth Vision - Tokyo Global Environmental
  Film Festival
East Lansing Children's Film Festival
Freedom Film Festival

Jameson Dublin International Film Festival
L'Chaim! Jewish Film Festival
Maine Jewish Film Festival
Melbourne Queer Film & Video Festival
Memphis International Film Festival
Minimalen Short Film Festival
Mipdoc
Miptv
Moomba International Amateur Film Festival
Myhelan Indie Film Festival
New York International Children's Film
    Festival
New York Underground Film Festival
Nordic Film Festival
NSI FilmExchange Canadian Film Festival
Other Venice Film Festival
Ozark Foothills FilmFest
Pensacola Bay International Film and
    Television Festival
Reel Sisters of the Diaspora Film Festival
Rosebud Film And Video Fesitval
San Antonio CineFestival
San Diego Latino Film Festival
San Francisco International Asian American
    Film Festival
Seattle Jewish Film Festival
Sedona International Film Festival and
    Workshop
Sex And Death Short Film Fest
Skip City International D-Cinema Festival
Sofia International Film Festival
SXSW: South By Southwest Film Festival
Tampere Film Festival
Tiburon International Film Festival
U.S. Comedy Arts Festival
Valley International Film Festival
Vilnius Spring International Film Festival
Westchester County Film Festival
Wilmington Independent Film Festival
Women in the Director's Chair International
    Film & Video Festival
Women of Color Film Festival
Women's Film Festival
York International Film Festival
ZoieFilms Festival
Zombiedance Undead Film Fest

MARCH–APRiL

Amnesty International Film Festival
Aspen Shortsfest
Belfast Film Festival
Celtic Film and Television Festival
Cinenygma Luxembourg International Film
    Festival
City of Lights, City of Angels French Film
    Festival

Docaviv Tel-Aviv International Documentary
    Film Festival
Houston International AIDS Film Festival
Images du Nouveau Monde Panamerican
    Film Festival
Infinity Festival
Italian Film Festival UK
Its All True International Documentary
    Festival
London Lesbian & Gay Film Festival
Moscow International Children's Film Festival
NatFilm Festival
New Directors/New Films Festival
Out In Africa South African Gay & Lesbian
    Film Festival
ReelWorld Film Festival

MARCH–JUNE

Art In Motion

MARCH–SEPTEMBER

Hollywood Spiritual Film and Entertainment
    Festival

APRiL

Accès Cinéma Africain (African Film Access)
African Film Festival
Arizona International Film Festival
Arizona State University Short Film and
    Video Festival
Arlene Grocery Picture Show
Artivist Film Festival
Ashland Independent Film Festival
Athens International Film & Video Festival
Avignon/New York Film Festival
Back East Picture Show
Black Point Film Festival
Boston International Festival Of Women's
    Cinema
Bristol International Animation Festival
Cedar Rapids Independent Film Festival
Cergy-Pontoise Short Film Festival
Chicago Asian American Film Festival
Chicago Horror Film Festival
Chicago International Documentary Festival
Chicago Latino Film Festival
CINE Golden Eagle Competition
Cine Las Americas International Film Festival
    of the Americas
Cinema Epicuria Sonoma Valley Film Festival
CinemaAsia Austin Asian Film Festival
Cinerama Film Festival at the University of
    Florida
Cognac International Film Festival of The
    Thriller
Council On Foundations Film & Video
    Festival

Jeonju International Film Festival
Mediawave Festival
Miami Gay and Lesbian Film Festival
Nashville Film Festival
Providence Festival Of New Latin American
    Cinema
Sehsüchte International Student Film Festival
Shadowline Salerno Film Festival
Syracuse International Film & Video Festival
U.N.C.L.E. Fest Film Festival
VC Filmfest : The Visual Communications
    Los Angeles Asian Pacific Film & Video
    Festival
Washington, DC International Film Festival—
    Filmfest DC

APRIL, OCTOBER
Bare Bones International Film Festival
Fargo Fantastic Film Festival

APRIL-NOVEMBER
Israel Film Festival

MAY
Algarve International Film Festival
Algonquin Film Festival
AniFest Film Festival of Animated Films
Antelope Valley Independent Film Festival
Beverly Hills Film Festival
Bicycle Film Festival
Billyburg Short Film Festival
Birmingham International Educational Film
    Festival Student Video Expo
Black International Cinema Berlin
Blink Film Festival Coventry
Boston Gay & Lesbian Film & Video Festival
Brighton Festival
Britspotting Independent Film Festival
Busan Asian Short Film Festival
Canadian Film Centre's Worldwide Short
    Film Festival
Cannes Directors' Fortnight
Cannes International Film Festival
Central Jersey Student Film Festival
Coachella Film Festival
COURTisane Festival For Short Film Video
    And New Media
CU 2 Video and Film Festival
Cut and Paste Skateboarding Art & Film
    Festival
DC Underground Film festival
Digital Independent Film Festival
Dover Film Festival
Dubrovnik International Film Festival
Festival For Cinema Of The Deaf
Filmfestival Of The Film Academy Vienna
Forest Grove Short Film and Video Festival

Herland Feminist Film And Video Festival
Honolulu Rainbow Film Festival
Hot Shots High School Film and Ad Festival
Inflatable Duck Film Fest
Inside Out Lesbian and Gay Film Festival of
    Toronto
International Wildlife Film Festival Montana
Jacksonville Film Festival
Kalamazoo Animation Festival International
Light Plays Tricks Short Film Festival
London Lesbian Film Festival
Magical Age International Video Festival
Maryland Film Festival
Montreal Jewish Student Film Festival
Moondance International Film Festival
Mountainfilm Festival
Napolidanza
National Student Film and Video Festival
New Haven Underground Film Festival
New York Dusty Film Festival And Awards
New York Short Film Festival
Onedotzero Digital Creativity Festival
Pacific Palisades Film Fest
Pink Apple - Schwullesbisches Filmfestival
Politically Incorrect Film Festival
Rochester International Film Festival
Santa Cruz Film Festival
Schwule Filmwoche Freiburg
Sprout Film Festival
St. Kilda Film Festival
Sulzbach-Rosenberg International Short Film
    Festival
Toronto Jewish Film Festival
Toronto Lesbian And Gay Film And Video
    Festival
Tough Eye International Turku Animated
    Film Festival
Transparency International Film Festival
Trento International Film Festival
Trenton Film Festival
Tribeca Film Festival
Vancouver Jewish Film Festival
World Media Festival
Yorkton Short Film Festival
Youth Media Jam

MAY-JUNE
Cracow Film Festival
New York International Latino Film Festival
Out Takes
Seattle International Film Festival
Toronto Hispano American Film Festival
Transilvania International Film Festival
Zlin International Film Festival For Children
    And Youth

MAY-AUGUST
48 Hour Film Project

MAY-DECEMBER
HDFEST Film Festival World Tour

JUNE
Annecy International Animated Film Festival
Arcipelago International Festival of Short
  Films & New Images
Art Film Festival Trencianske Teplice
Artwallah Festival
Asian Film Festival Of Dallas
Atlanta Film Festival
Avignon French Film Festival
Bellaria Independent Cinema Festival
Boston International Film Festival
Brazilian Film Festival of Miami
Bronx Independent Film Festival
Brooklyn International Film Festival
Cabourg Festival of Romantic Films
Cinema Jove International Film Festival
CineVegas International Film Festival
Cologne International TV & Film Conference
Connecticut Gay & Lesbian Film Festival
Dance On Camera Festival
deadCenter Film Festival
DigiFest SouthWest Filmmaking Festival
Durban International Film Festival
EcoCinema
Emden International Film Festival
Fairytales International Gay & Lesbian Film
  Festival
Festival Of Nations
Film Expo Texas/Film DV and Screenplay
  Contests
Filmstock International Film Festival
FirstGlance Philadelphia Film Festival
Fort Worth's Gay & Lesbian International
  Film Festival
Global Art Film Festival Experience &
  Repertory of Sacramento
Hamburg International Short Film Festival
Heard Museum Indigenous Film Festival
Hollywood Black Film Festival
Hong Kong International Film & TV Market
  (FILMART)
Huesca International Short Film Festival
IFP Los Angeles Film Festival
InCurt Short Film Festival
Interfest Moscow International Film Festival
International Environmental Film Festival
International Film Festival Innsbruck
International Film Festival of Festivals
International Women's Film Festival of
  Barcelona
Lake Placid Film Forum

Maui Film Festival
Melbourne International Animation Festival
  (MIAF)
Message to Man International Documentary,
  Short and Animated Films Festival
Midnight Sun Film Festival
Nantucket Film Festival
Napoli Film Festival
New England Animation Bash
New Festival: New York Lesbian, Gay,
  Bisexual, & Transgender Film Festival
New York Lesbian & Gay Film Festival
Newport International Film Festival
Niagara Indie FilmFest
Nickel Independent Film and Video Festival
Norwegian Short Film Festival
Ocean City Film Festival
Oxford Film Festival
Pixie Flix Fest
Prix Jeunesse International
Provincetown International Film Festival
Reel Madness Film Festival
Salento International Film Festival
San Antonio Underground Film Festival
San Francisco Black Film Festival
San Francisco International Lesbian and Gay
  Film Festival
Shanghai International Film Festival
SILVERDOCS: AFI/Discovery Channel
  Documentary Festival
SNIFF Short International Film Festival
Sochi International Film Festival
Sopot Film Festival
Superfest International Media Festival on
  Disabilities
Sydney Film Festival
Tabor Film Festival
Taormina BNL FilmFest
Thunderbird International Film Festival
Tokyo International Lesbian & Gay Film
  Festival
U.S. International Film and Video Festival
Utah Short Film & Video Festival
Vancouver International Digital Festival
Waterfront Film Festival
Waterloo Festival for Animated Cinema
Waterton International French Film Festival
  Society
World Wide Video Festival
Wreck-Beach Film Festival
Zagreb World Festival of Animated Films

JUNE-JULY
CineSol Latino Film Festival
Festival Of The Dhow Countries
Filmfest Munchen
International Festival of New Film Split

Kansas City Gay & Lesbian Film Festival
La Rochelle International Film Festival
Neuchâtel International Fantastic Film
Festival
New Jersey International Film Festival

JUNE-AUGUST
Gadabout Traveling Film Festival

JUNE-NOVEMBER
Belize International Film Festival

JULY
2 Kings Judgement Film Festival
American Black Film Festival
Anima Mundi
Asian American International Film Festival
Auckland International Film Festival
Brainwash Movie Festival
Cambridge International Film Festival
Cinemaya Festival Of Asian Cinema
CineMuerte International Fantastic Film
Festival
Comic Con International Independent Film
Festival
Da Vinci Film and Video Festival
Dallas Video Festival
Eat My Shorts!
Fantasia Film Festival
Festival Comedia
Fukuoka Asian Film Festival
Galway Film Fleadh
Giffoni Film Festival
Great Lake Superior International Film
Festival
Hometown Video Festival
HypeFest Film & Video Festival
International Film Festival of Uruguay
Jaffas Down the Aisle
Jerusalem International Film Festival
Karlovy Vary International Film Festival
Long Island International Film Expo
Los Angeles Latino International Film Festival
Maine International Film Festival
Marin County National Festival of Short Film
and Video
Marseilles International Documentary Film
Festival
Melbourne Underground Film Festival
Montecatini International Short Film Festival
Motovun Film Festival
NO BUDGET International Independent
Film & Video Festival
OUTFEST: Los Angeles Gay and Lesbian Film
Festival
Pärnu International Documentary and
Anthropology Film Festival

Perspectives International Film Festival
Philadelphia International Gay and Lesbian
Film Festival
Pocono Mountains Film Festival
Puchon International Fantastic Film Festival
(PiFan)
Ragamuffin Film Festival
Real to Reel Film Festival
Reel Venus Film Festival
Revelation Perth International Film Festival
Rural Route Film Festival
Sabina International Short Film Festival
Silver Images Film Festival
Sour Grapes Film Festival
Stony Brook Film Festival
Vila do Conde International Short Film
Festival
Wellington Film Festival
Wellington Fringe Short Film Festival

JULY-AUGUST
Chamizal Independent Film Festival
Dublin Lesbian and Gay Film Festival
Encounters South African International
Documentary Festival
Era New Horizons Film Festival
Fantasy Filmfest - International Film Festival
for Science Fiction, Fiction, Horror and
Thriller
Festival International Du Film Amateur De
Kelibia
Hot Shops Film Festival
International Black Panther Film Festival
L'Isola del Cinema International Film Festival
Melbourne International Film Festival
New Zealand Film Festival
NextFrame Japan
Rushes Soho Shorts Film Festival
San Francisco Jewish Film Festival
Vancouver International Comedy Festival
Wine Country Film Festival
Woods Hole Film Festival

AUGUST
48 Hour Film Festival
Alpinale Film Festival
Antarctic Film Festival
Australian National Student Film & Video
Festival
Bearded Child Film Festival
Brisbane International Film Festival
Chicago Underground Film Festival
Cinemanila International Film Festival
Copenhagen International Film Festival
Crested Butte Reel Fest Short Film Festival
dokuFEST Documentary & Short Film
Festival

Edinburgh International Film Festival
Espoo Ciné International Film Festival
Festival Garage
Festival of Fantastic Films
Festival of Fantastic Films
Filmi Toronto South Asian Film Festival
Flying Popcorn! Film Festival
Great Plains Film Festival
Hardacre Film Festival
Hiroshima International Animation Festival
Image Fest
InFACT Theatrical Documentary Showcase
International Festival of Cinema and
    Technology
International Odense Film Festival
International Teen Movie Festival
Japan Wildlife Festival
Kinder Film Festival Japan
Locarno International Film Festival
Malesco International Short Film Festival
Motor City International Film Festival
North Carolina Gay & Lesbian Film Festival
Norwegian International Film Festival
Open Air FilmFest Weiterstadt
Orlando Gay & Lesbian Film Festival
Peach City Short Film Festival
Pitigliano Film Festival
Portobello Film Festival
Reel Women International Film Festival
Rhode Island International Film Festival
Roxbury Film Festival
Sacramento Film and Music Festival
Sarajevo Film Festival
SoCal International Film Festival
Spudfest Drive-In Family Film & Music
    Festival
Toaster Film Festival
Vancouver Out On Screen Queer Film &
    Video Festival
Venice International Film Festival
Voladero International Film and Video
    Festival
Westcliffe Digital Film Festival

AUGUST–SEPTEMBER

Austin's Gay and Lesbian Film Festival
Chichester Film Festival
Dragon Con Independent Short Film Festival
Montreal International Film Market
Montreal World Film Festival
Sao Paulo International Short Film Festival
Telluride IndieFest

SEPTEMBER

20,000 Leagues Under the Industry Film
    Festival
3 Continents International Documentary
    Film Festival
A.K.A. Shriekfest, The Los Angeles
    Horror/Science Fiction Film Festival &
    ScreenPlay Competition
ABBAKUS Film Festival
Action/Cut Short Film Competition
Agrofilm Festival
Alexandria International Film Festival
Antimatter Festival of Underground Short
    Film & Video
Apollo Film Festival
Arsenal Film Forum
Asolo Art Film Festival
Aspirations Film Festival
Athens International Film Festival
Atlantic Film Festival
Auburn International Film and Video Festival
    for Children and Young Adults
Baytowne Film Festival
BFM International Film Festival
Big Bear Lake International Film Festival
Bite the Mango Film Festival
Blue Sky International Film Festival - Las
    Vegas
Boston Film Festival
Breckenridge Festival of Film
Bumbershoot 1 Reel Film Festival
Buster Copenhagen International Children's
    Film Festival
Channel Islands Indie Film Festival
Charleston Fiction & Documentary Film
    Festival
Chattahoochee Film and Video Competition
Cine Acción ¡Cine Latino!
Cinefest Sudbury International Film Festival
Cinema Paradise Film Festival
Cinematexas International Short Film &
    Video Festival
CINEME Chicago International Animation
    Film Festival
Cologne International Short Film Festival
Cotswold International Film Festival
Dionysus Film Festival
Don't Knock The Rock Music And Film
    Festival
Donostia - San Sebastian International Film
    Festival
Downstream International Film Festival
Eksjö Animation Festival
Emerald Eye Short Film Festival
Fantastisk Film Festival Sweden
Fantoche International Animation Film
    Festival

Festival of Deauville for American Cinema
(Le Festival du Cinema Americain in
Deauville)
Film By The Sea
Film Fest New Haven
Film South Asia
Filmfest Hamburg
Fresno REEL Pride International Gay &
Lesbian Film Festival
Georgetown Indy Film Festival
Girona Film Festival
Great Lakes Independent Film Festival
Greek International Short Film Festival In
Drama
Greenwich Film Festival
Gulf Coast Film And Video Festival
Helsinki Film Festival - Love and Anarchy
Houston Gay and Lesbian Film Festival
Indianapolis LGBT Film Festival
Indie Music Video Festival
International Human Rights Film Festival
Jackson Hole Film Festival
Jackson Hole Wildlife Film Festival
Jewish Image Awards in Film and Television
Kansas International Film Festival
Lake Arrowhead Film Festival
Lisbon Gay & Lesbian Film Festival
Los Angeles International Short Film Festival
Lunafest
Malibu International Film Festival
Manhattan Short Film Festival
Mania Fest
Matita Film Festival
Melbourne Fringe Festival
Melbourne Independent Filmmakers Festival
- MIFF
Morbegno Film Festival
Norrköping Film Festival Flimmer
Northern Lights Film Festival
Oakland International Film Festival
Oldenburg International Film Festival
Orinda Film Festival
Ottawa International Animation Festival
Outfest San Diego Gay & Lesbian Film
Festival
Palm Springs International Festival Of Short
Films
Philadelphia Fringe Festival
Port Townsend Film Festival
Portland International Short Short Film Fest
Reelife Short Film Festival
ResFest Digital Film Festival
Rome International Film Festival
Route 66 Film Festival
Sea to Sky Film Festival
Seoul Net and Film Festival
ShockerFest Film Festival

Sidewalk Moving Picture Film Festival
Silver Lake Film Festival
Split Screen Film Festival
Sunnyside Film Festival
Tampa Independents' Film Festival
Telluride Film Festival
Temecula Valley International Film Festival
Tinklai International Short Film Festival
Toronto International Film Festival
Toronto Student Shorts National Film Festival
Tulsa Overground International Film Festival
Twin Rivers Media Festival
Umeå International Film Festival
Valdivia International Film Festival
Widescreen Film Festival
Wild Rose Film Festival
Wild Spaces Film Festival
WinFemme Film Festival
Women Make Waves Film Festival
Woodstock Film Festival

SEPTEMBER-OCTOBER
Aspen Filmfest
Belo Horizonte International Short Film
Festival
Calgary International Film Festival
Cinema Au Feminin
Cinemayaat Arab Film Festival
EuropaCinema Festival
Image+Nation Montreal's International
Lesbian & Gay Film and Video Festival
International Scientific Film Festival
Madcat Women's International Film Festival
Nederlands Film Festival
Northwest Asian American Film Festival
Rio de Janeiro International Film Festival
San Diego Film Festival
Toronto International Environmental Film &
Video Festival
UpOverDownUnder Film Festival
Vancouver International Film Festival
Vistas Film Festival

SEPTEMBER-MAY
Minicine Visiting Filmmaker Series

SEPTEMBER-JUNE
Next Frame Film Festival

OCTOBER
(818)/Valley Film Festival
Academia Film Olomouc Film Festival
Alternative Film Festival
Angelus Awards Student Film Festival
Arpa International Film Festival
Asian Pacific American Film Festival
Astra Film Festival

Atlantic City Film Festival
Austin Film Festival
Bergen International Film Festival (BIFF)
Bilan Du Film Ethnographique
Black Bear Film Festival
Black Earth Film Festival
Bogota Film Festival
Boston Fantastic Film Festival
Boston Irish Film Festival
British Film Festival
Brooklyn Underground Film Festival
Cairo International Film Festival
Central Standard Film Festival
Century City Film Festival
Cherbourg-Octeville Festival of Irish &
    British Film
Chicago International Children's Film Festival
Chicago International Film Festival
Christian WYSIWYG Film Festival
Cinekid Film Festival
CineKink NYC
CineMacabre Horror and Sci-Fi Film Festival
Cinemambiente
CMJ Filmfest
Co-operative Young Film-Makers Festival
Columbus International Film and Video
    Festival (Chris Awards)
Coney Island Film Festival
Cork International Film Festival
Damah Film Festival
Deep Ellum Film Festival
Denver International Film Festival
Fano International Film Festival
Feminale Women's Film Festival
Festival Du Film D'animation Pour La
    Jeunesse
Festival of European Films
FilmColumbia
Films From The South Festival
Finger Lakes Environmental Film Festival
Flanders International Film Festival Ghent
Ft. Lauderdale Underground Film Festival
Funny Film Festival
Gloria International Film Festival
H.P. Lovecraft Film Festival
Haifa International Film Festival
Hamptons International Film Festival
Heartland Film Festival
Hertfordshire International Film Festival
Hof International Film Festival
Hollywood Film Festival
Hollywood Scarefest
Home Brewed International Short Film
    Festival
Hope And Dreams Film Festival
Hot Springs Documentary Film Festival
Hull International Short Film Festival

IFP Market/Gotham Awards
ImageOut - The Rochester Lesbian & Gay
    Film & Video Festival
imagineNATIVE Film & Media Arts Festival
Imperial Beach International Film Festival
Indie Memphis Film Festival
International Documentary Festival of
    Barcelona
International Film Festival of India
International Leipzig Festival For
    Documentary and Animated Film
International Panorama of Independent
    Filmakers
ISMF International Student Media Festival
Jihlava International Documentary Film
    Festival
Kern Film Festival
Kinofilm Manchester International Short
    Film Festival
Lausanne Underground Film & Music
    Festival
Leeds International Film Festival
Lesbian & Gay Film Festival Hamburg
Long Beach International Film Festival
Machinima Film Festival
Making Scenes Queer Film & Video Festival
Marrakech International Film Festival
Miami International Short Film Festival
Michigan Independent Film Festival
Microcinefest
MidCoast Film and Arts Festival
Mifed
Mill Valley Film Festival
Milwaukee International Film Festival
Mipcom
Mipcom Junior
Montpellier Festival
Montreal International Festival of New
    Cinema and New Media
Morelia International Film Festival
Mount Shasta International Film Festival
New Hampshire Film Expo NHFX
New Orleans Film Festival
New York City Horror Film Festival
New York Film Festival
New York Midnight Movie Making Madness
New York Turkish Film Festival
Norwich International Animation Festival
Ojai Film Festival
Ökomedia International Environmental Film
    Festival
Pittsburgh International Lesbian and Gay
    Film Festival
PLATFORMA Video Festival
Pordenone Silent Film Festival
Portland Lesbian & Gay Film Festival
Pusan International Film Festival

Raindance Film Festival
Red Bank International Film Festival
Reel Affirmations Film Festival
Rhode Island International Horror Film
Festival
River City Film Festival
Sacramento Festival of Cinema
Sacramento International Gay and Lesbian
Film Festival
Salem Amateur Horror Film Festival
San Diego Asian Film Festival
San Francisco World Film Festival and
Marketplace
Santa Cruz Environmental Film and Video
Festival
Savannah Film and Video Festival
Screamfest Horror Film Festival
Seattle Lesbian & Gay Film Festival
Seattle Underground Film Festival (The)
Sometime in October Film Festival and Short
Screenplay Competition
St. John's International Women's Film &
Video Festival
Taiwan International Ethnographic Film
Festival
Tallgrass Film Festival
Tampa International Gay and Lesbian Film
Festival
Taos Mountain Film Festival
Tehran Short Film Festival
Thaw Video, Film, and Digital Media Festival
The Times bfi London Film Festival
Tourfilm Festival
United Nations Association Film Festival
Uppsala International Short Film Festival
Valladolid International Film Festival
Vermont International Film Festival
Viennale - Vienna International Film Festival
Virginia Film Festival
Warsaw International Film Festival
Wildscreen Festival
Winslow Film Festival
World Population and Video Festival
Yamagata International Documentary Film
Festival
Zagreb Film Festival

OCTOBER–NOVEMBER

Backup Festival New Media in Film
Banff Mountain Film Festival
Cinéma Tout Ecran
Detroit International Horror Film Festival
Fort Lauderdale International Film Festival
Galveston Island International Film Festival
Hawaii International Film Festival
International Film Festival Of Milan
Kyiv International Film Festival Molodist

Latin USA International Film Festival
Maryland Fantastique Film Fest
Meniscus Film Festival
New Orleans Media Experience
Nordic Film Days Lübeck
São Paulo International Film Festival
Scottsdale International Film Festival
Sports Movie & TV International Festival
UK Jewish Film Festival
Williamstown Film Festival
World Festival Of Underwater Pictures

OCTOBER–NOVEMBER, MAY

West Virginia International Film Festival

NOVEMBER

African Diaspora Film Festival
AluCine Toronto Latino Film & Video
Festival
American Conservation Film Festival
American Film Institute (AFI) - Los Angeles
International Film Festival
American Film Market
American Indian Film Festival
Amiens International Film Festival
Annapolis Film Festival
Asbury Short Film Show of New York
Asheville Film Festival
Audition International Film Festival
Back Alley Film Festival
Bahamas One World Film Festival
Beirut Documentary Film Festival -
DocuDays
Berkeley Video and Film Festival
Big Mini DV Festival
Black Soil Film Festival
Boston Jewish Film Festival
Bradford Animation Festival
Braunschweig International Film Festival
Brighton International Film Festival
Bristol International Short Film Festival
California Independent Film Festival
Cape May New Jersey State Film Festival
Cape Town World Cinema Festival
Cardiff Screen Festival
Castellinaria International Young Cinema
Festival
Certamen De Cine Amateur
Chicago Lesbian and Gay International Film
Festival
Cinanima International Animated Film
Festival
Cinemania French Film Festival
Cortoitaliacinema International Short Film
Festival
Daytona Beach Film Festival
Deaf Film & TV Festival

NOVEMBER–DECEMBER

DECEMBER

Courmayeur Noir Film Festival
Disability Film Festival
Eye of the Beholder International Film
    Festival
FirstGlance Hollywood Film Festival
Gladys Crane Mountain Plains Film Festival
Global Peace Film Festival
I Castelli Animati International Animated
    Film Festival
International Film Festival Of Kerala
KaraFilm Festival
Mazatlan International Film Festival
MiniDV Film Festival
Native American Film & Video Festival
Nihilist Film Festival
Ola Ka Honua Film Festival
Palm Beach Jewish Film Festival
Rio De Janeiro International Short Film
    Festival
River to River Florence Indian Film Festival
Santa Fe Film Festival
Sydney Asia-Pacific Film Festival
Tirana International Film Festival
UAF Student Film Festival
Washington Jewish Film Festival
Whistler Film Festival

DECEMBER-JANUARY

Z Film Festival

ONGOING

AtomFilms
Big Film Shorts
BijouFlix
CinemaReno
Film Nite
First Sundays Short Comedy Film Festival
Independent Exposure
New Venue
PubliFilm Festival
ShortTV
Studentfilms.com: The Online Student Film
    Festival
Undergroundfilm.org

SEASONAL-CHECK WEBSITE

Mini-Cinema Film Festival
VideoTheatre NYC

SPRING

Docfest - New York International
    Documentary Festival
Surf Film Festival

SPRING-SUMMER

Pride International Film Festival

SUMMER

Santa Monica Film Festival
Short Shorts Film Festival

FALL

Edmonton International Film Festival
Euro Underground

WINTER-SPRING

Deaf Focus Film Festival

INDEX OF FILM FESTIVALS BY GENRE
for Major North American and International Festivals

16MM
Ann Arbor Film Festival
Boston Film Festival
Festival of European Films
Karlovy Vary International Film Festival
Locarno International Film Festival
Message to Man International Documentary, Short and Animated Films Festival
New York Film Festival
São Paulo International Film Festival
Stony Brook Film Festival
TIE International Experimental Cinema Exposition
Washington, DC International Film Festival— Filmfest DC

35MM
Algarve International Film Festival
American Film Market
Ann Arbor Film Festival
Barcelona Asian Film Festival
Belgrade International Film Festival
Boston Film Festival
Cannes Directors' Fortnight
Donostia - San Sebastian International Film Festival
Fantasy Filmfest - International Film Festival for Science Fiction, Fiction, Horror and Thriller
Festival of European Films
Karlovy Vary International Film Festival
Locarno International Film Festival
Message to Man International Documentary, Short and Animated Films Festival
New York Film Festival
São Paulo International Film Festival
Shanghai International Film Festival
Stockholm International Film Festival
Stony Brook Film Festival
TIE International Experimental Cinema Exposition
Tokyo International Film Festival
Warsaw International Film Festival
Washington, DC International Film Festival— Filmfest DC

ADVENTURER/EXPLORERS
Comic Con International Independent Film Festival
Whistler Film Festival

AIDS/HIV-RELATED
Making Scenes Queer Film & Video Festival

ALL
Black Maria Film and Video Festival
Blue Sky International Film Festival - Las Vegas
Boston Gay & Lesbian Film & Video Festival
Cannes International Film Festival
Chicago International Film Festival
Houston Annual Worldfest
Independent Black Film Festival
International Wildlife Film Festival Montana
Jerusalem International Film Festival
Maui Film Festival
Mifed
Montreal International Festival of New Cinema and New Media
Palm Beach International Film Festival
Seattle International Film Festival
Slamdance International Film Festival
Telluride Film Festival
Toronto International Film Festival
Tribeca Film Festival
Triggerstreet.com Online Short Film Festival
Verzaubert - International Queer Film Festival

ALL CATEGORIES - SHORTS
Big Film Shorts
Emerald Eye Short Film Festival
Palm Springs International Festival of Short Films

ALTERNATIVE SEXUALITY
Mix Brasil Festival of Sexual Diversity

AMERiCAN

American Black Film Festival
American Film Institute (AFI) - Los Angeles
International Film Festival
Arizona State University Short Film and
Video Festival
Athens International Film Festival
Avignon French Film Festival
Avignon/New York Film Festival
Bangkok International Film Festival
Bermuda International Film Festival
Brainwash Movie Festival
Cinematexas International Short Film &
Video Festival
Cleveland International Film Festival
Cork International Film Festival
Cucalorus Film Festival
DancesWithFilms
Deep Ellum Film Festival
Exground - Das Filmfest
Fantasia Film Festival
Festival of Deauville for American Cinema
(Le Festival du Cinema Americain in
Deauville)
Film Nite
Filmfest Munchen
Fort Lauderdale International Film Festival
Free Film Festival Fitchburg (The F4)
Gen Art Film Festival
Gijon International Film Festival For Young
People
Helsinki Film Festival - Love and Anarchy
Hollywood Black Film Festival
IFP Los Angeles Film Festival
Johns Hopkins Film Festival
Lake Placid Film Forum
Marco Island Film Festival
Melbourne Queer Film & Video Festival
Miami International Film Festival
Mill Valley Film Festival
Moondance International Film Festival
Native American Film & Video Festival
NoDance Film Festival
Norrköping Film Festival Flimmer
Northwest Film & Video Festival
Ohio Independent Film Festival
Out Far! - Annual Phoenix International
Lesbian and Gay Film Festival
Portland International Film Festival
Rhode Island International Film Festival
San Francisco International Film Festival
Savannah Film and Video Festival
Seattle Underground Film Festival (The)
Sedona International Film Festival and
Workshop
Smogdance Film Festival
Stockholm International Film Festival

Stony Brook Film Festival
Temecula Valley International Film Festival
Turin International Gay & Lesbian Film
Festival "from Sodom to Hollywood"
University of Oregon Queer Film Festival
USA Film Festival/Dallas
Victoria Independent Film and Video Festival
Virginia Film Festival
Washington, DC International Film Festival—
Filmfest DC
Waterfront Film Festival
Williamstown Film Festival
Wisconsin Film Festival

ANiMATiON

Adelaide International Film Festival
Algarve International Film Festival
American Film Institute (AFI) - Los Angeles
International Film Festival
American Film Market
Angelus Awards Student Film Festival
AniFest Film Festival of Animated Films
Ankara International Film Festival
Annapolis Film Festival
Annecy International Animated Film Festival
Antimatter Festival of Underground Short
Film & Video
Arcipelago International Festival of Short
Films & New Images
Arizona International Film Festival
Arizona State University Short Film and
Video Festival
Aspirations Film Festival
Athens International Film Festival
Atlanta Film Festival
AtomFilms
Austin Film Festival
Avignon French Film Festival
Avignon/New York Film Festival
Barcelona Asian Film Festival
Berlin International Film Festival
Bermuda International Film Festival
Beverly Hills Film Festival
Big Bear Lake International Film Festival
Blue Sky International Film Festival - Las
Vegas
Boston Film Festival
Boston Gay & Lesbian Film & Video Festival
Boston International Festival Of Women's
Cinema
Boston International Film Festival
Brainwash Movie Festival
Breckenridge Festival of Film
Brighton International Film Festival
Brooklyn Underground Film Festival
Bumbershoot 1 Reel Film Festival
Cabourg Festival of Romantic Films

Melbourne Queer Film & Video Festival
Message to Man International Documentary,
Short and Animated Films Festival
Miami International Film Festival
Microcinefest
Mifed
Mill Valley Film Festival
MiniDV Film Festival
Minneapolis/St Paul International Film
Festival
Mix Brasil Festival of Sexual Diversity
Montreal International Festival of New
Cinema and New Media
Montreal World Film Festival
Moondance International Film Festival
Mumbai International Film Festival
Nantucket Film Festival
Napoli Film Festival
New Directors/New Films Festival
New Festival: New York Lesbian, Gay,
Bisexual, & Transgender Film Festival
New Orleans Film Festival
New York Expo of Short Film and Video
New York Underground Film Festival
New Zealand Film Festival
Newport Beach Film Festival
Next Frame Film Festival
NO BUDGET International Independent
Film & Video Festival
Norrköping Film Festival Flimmer
North Carolina Jewish Film Festival
Northwest Film & Video Festival
Norwegian International Film Festival
NSI FilmExchange Canadian Film Festival
Ohio Independent Film Festival
Oldenburg International Film Festival
Onedotzero Digital Creativity Festival
Ottawa International Animation Festival
Out Far! - Annual Phoenix International
Lesbian and Gay Film Festival
OUTFEST: Los Angeles Gay and Lesbian Film
Festival
Palm Beach International Film Festival
Philadelphia Film Festival
Philadelphia Fringe Festival
Philadelphia International Gay and Lesbian
Film Festival
Phoenix Film Festival
Queersicht - Schwul-lesbisches Filmfestival
Bern
Raindance Film Festival
Red Bank International Film Festival
Reel Affirmations Film Festival
ResFest Digital Film Festival
Rhode Island International Film Festival
Rio de Janeiro International Film Festival
River to River Florence Indian Film Festival

RiverRun International Film Festival
Rochester International Film Festival
Rome International Film Festival
Rotterdam International Film Festival
Sacramento International Gay and Lesbian
Film Festival
San Antonio Underground Film Festival
San Diego Film Festival
San Francisco Independent Film Festival
San Francisco International Film Festival
San Francisco International Lesbian and Gay
Film Festival
Santa Barbara International Film Festival
(SBIFF)
São Paulo International Film Festival
Sarasota Film Festival
Savannah Film and Video Festival
Scottsdale International Film Festival
Screamfest Horror Film Festival
Seattle International Film Festival
Seattle Lesbian & Gay Film Festival
Sedona International Film Festival and
Workshop
Shanghai International Film Festival
Short Shorts Film Festival
Sidewalk Moving Picture Film Festival
Silver Lake Film Festival
Singapore International Film Festival
Sitges International Film Festival of Catalonia
Slamdance International Film Festival
Smogdance Film Festival
Sour Grapes Film Festival
Split Screen Film Festival
Sprockets Toronto International Film Festival
for Children
St. Louis International Film Festival
Stony Brook Film Festival
Sundance Film Festival
SXSW: South By Southwest Film Festival
Sydney Film Festival
Tehran International Animation Festival
Telluride Film Festival
Telluride IndieFest
Temecula Valley International Film Festival
Texas Film Festival
Thaw Video, Film, and Digital Media Festival
Thessaloniki International Film Festival
Tiburon International Film Festival
Tokyo International Film Festival
Torino Film Festival
Toronto International Film Festival
Toronto Jewish Film Festival
Trenton Film Festival
Tribeca Film Festival
Tromadance Film Festival
U.S. Comedy Arts Festival
United States Super 8 Film and Digital Video
Festival

University of Oregon Queer Film Festival
Uppsala International Short Film Festival
USA Film Festival/Dallas
Vail Film Festival
Vancouver International Film Festival
Venice International Film Festival
Verzaubert - International Queer Film
    Festival
Victoria Independent Film and Video Festival
Warsaw International Film Festival
Waterfront Film Festival
Wellington Film Festival
West Virginia International Film Festival
Whistler Film Festival
Williamstown Film Festival
Wilmington Independent Film Festival
Wine Country Film Festival
Wisconsin Film Festival
Woodstock Film Festival
Yorkton Short Film Festival
Zagreb World Festival of Animated Films
ZoieFilms Festival

ART-RELATED
International Festival of Films On Art (FIFA)

AVANT GARDE
International Festival of Films On Art (FIFA)
Jerusalem International Film Festival
Madcat Women's International Film Festival
New York Film Festival
TIE International Experimental Cinema
    Exposition
Trenton Film Festival

CANADIAN
30 Below Film & Video Competition
Antimatter Festival of Underground Short
    Film & Video
Aspen Shortsfest
Aspirations Film Festival
Calgary International Film Festival
Chrysler Million Dollar Film Festival
Edmonton International Film Festival
Great Plains Film Festival
Hot Docs Canadian International
    Documentary Festival
Images Festival of Independent Film and
    Video
Inside Out Lesbian and Gay Film Festival of
    Toronto
NSI FilmExchange Canadian Film Festival
Sprockets Toronto International Film Festival
    for Children
Toronto International Film Festival
Toronto Jewish Film Festival
Yorkton Short Film Festival

CHARITY
Melbourne Independent Filmmakers Festival
    - MIFF
Santa Monica Film Festival

CHILDREN
Cambridge International Film Festival
Cartagena International Film Festival
Denver International Film Festival
DocPoint Helsinki Documentary Film
    Festival
Durango Film Festival
Espoo Ciné International Film Festival
Gijon International Film Festival For Young
    People
International Short Film Festival Oberhausen
International TrickFilm Festival Stuttgart
International Wildlife Film Festival Montana
Leeds Children and Young People's Film
    Festival
Marco Island Film Festival
Mill Valley Film Festival
Nashville Film Festival
Newport Beach Film Festival
Prix Jeunesse International
Sidewalk Moving Picture Film Festival
Sprockets Toronto International Film Festival
    for Children
Tehran International Animation Festival
Uppsala International Short Film Festival
Wine Country Film Festival
Zagreb World Festival of Animated Films
ZoieFilms Festival

COMEDY
MiniDV Film Festival
Smogdance Film Festival
U.S. Comedy Arts Festival
ZoieFilms Festival

COMICS
Comic Con International Independent Film
    Festival

COMMERCIALS
AniFest Film Festival of Animated Films
Aspen Shortsfest
Houston Annual Worldfest
HypeFest Film & Video Festival
International Wildlife Film Festival Montana
One Take Film Festival
ZoieFilms Festival

DiGiTAL

30 Below Film & Video Competition
American Film Institute (AFI) - Los Angeles
  International Film Festival
Ann Arbor Film Festival
Antimatter Festival of Underground Short
  Film & Video
Antimatter Festival of Underground Short
  Film & Video
Arcipelago International Festival of Short
  Films & New Images
AtomFilms
Big Bear Lake International Film Festival
Cinematexas International Short Film &
  Video Festival
Clermont-Ferrand Short Film Festival
Dallas Video Festival
Deep Ellum Film Festival
Digital Days
Hollywood Black Film Festival
IFP Los Angeles Film Festival
Images Festival of Independent Film and
  Video
Independent Exposure
Kinofilm Manchester International Short
  Film Festival
Lake Placid Film Forum
Los Angeles International Short Film Festival
Lost Film Festival
Madcat Women's International Film Festival
Miami International Film Festival
MiniDV Film Festival
Montreal International Festival of New
  Cinema and New Media
Newport Beach Film Festival
NO BUDGET International Independent
  Film & Video Festival
NoDance Film Festival
Norrköping Film Festival Flimmer
Northwest Film & Video Festival
Ohio Independent Film Festival
Onedotzero Digital Creativity Festival
ResFest Digital Film Festival
Rhode Island International Film Festival
San Antonio Underground Film Festival
Santa Barbara International Film Festival
  (SBIFF)
Seattle Underground Film Festival (The)
Silver Lake Film Festival
Slamdance International Film Festival
SXSW: South By Southwest Film Festival
Temecula Valley International Film Festival
Thaw Video, Film, and Digital Media Festival
Tromadance Film Festival
United States Super 8 Film and Digital Video
  Festival
Whistler Film Festival
Woodstock Film Festival

DiGiTAL ANiMATiON

Antimatter Festival of Underground Short
  Film & Video
Antimatter Festival of Underground Short
  Film & Video
Arizona State University Short Film and
  Video Festival
Cinematexas International Short Film &
  Video Festival
Cork International Film Festival
DancesWithFilms
Digital Days
Exground - Das Filmfest
Fantasia Film Festival
IFP Los Angeles Film Festival
Independent Exposure
International TrickFilm Festival Stuttgart
Lake Placid Film Forum
Lost Film Festival
Madcat Women's International Film Festival
MiniDV Film Festival
Nashville Film Festival
Ohio Independent Film Festival
Onedotzero Digital Creativity Festival
ResFest Digital Film Festival
Rhode Island International Film Festival
Santa Monica Film Festival
Tehran International Animation Festival
Thaw Video, Film, and Digital Media Festival
Tromadance Film Festival
Whistler Film Festival

DOCUMENTARY

30 Below Film & Video Competition
A.K.A. Shriekfest, The Los Angeles
  Horror/Science Fiction Film Festival &
  ScreenPlay Competition
Adelaide International Film Festival
African Film Festival
Alpe Adria Cinema Trieste Film Festival
American Black Film Festival
American Film Institute (AFI) - Los Angeles
  International Film Festival
American Film Market
American Indian Film Festival
Angelus Awards Student Film Festival
Ankara International Film Festival
Ann Arbor Film Festival
Annapolis Film Festival
Antimatter Festival of Underground Short
  Film & Video
Arcipelago International Festival of Short
  Films & New Images
Arizona International Film Festival
Arizona State University Short Film and
  Video Festival
Aspen Shortsfest

Hollywood Film Festival
Hong Kong International Film Festival
  (HKIFF)
Honolulu Rainbow Film Festival
Hot Docs Canadian International
  Documentary Festival
Hot Springs Documentary Film Festival
Houston Annual Worldfest
Huesca International Short Film Festival
Human Rights Watch International Film
  Festival
Humboldt International Short Film Festival
HypeFest Film & Video Festival
IFP Los Angeles Film Festival
IFP Market/Gotham Awards
Image+Nation Montreal's International
  Lesbian & Gay Film and Video Festival
Images Festival of Independent Film and
  Video
Independent Black Film Festival
Independent Exposure
Independent Film Festival of Boston
Indianapolis International Film Festival
Inside Out Lesbian and Gay Film Festival of
  Toronto
International Documentary Film Festival
  Amsterdam (IDFA)
International Festival of Films On Art (FIFA)
International Film Festival of India
International Leipzig Festival For
  Documentary and Animated Film
International Lesbian Film Festival
  Immaginaria
International Scientific Film Festival
International Short Film Festival Oberhausen
Internationales Filmfestival Mannheim-
  Heidelberg
Israel Film Festival
Jackson Hole Wildlife Film Festival
Jerusalem International Film Festival
Johns Hopkins Film Festival
Karlovy Vary International Film Festival
Kasseler Dokumentarfilm - Und Videofest
Kinofilm Manchester International Short
  Film Festival
Kyiv International Film Festival Molodist
Lake Placid Film Forum
Leeds Children and Young People's Film
  Festival
Leeds International Film Festival
Locarno International Film Festival
Long Island International Film Expo
Los Angeles International Short Film Festival
Los Angeles Latino International Film Festival
Lost Film Festival
Madcat Women's International Film Festival
Making Scenes Queer Film & Video Festival

Malibu International Film Festival
Marco Island Film Festival
Margaret Mead Film Festival
Marseilles International Documentary Film
  Festival
Maryland Film Festival
Maui Film Festival
Melbourne Independent Filmmakers Festival
  - MIFF
Melbourne International Film Festival
Melbourne Queer Film & Video Festival
Message to Man International Documentary,
  Short and Animated Films Festival
Miami International Film Festival
Midnight Sun Film Festival
Mifed
Mill Valley Film Festival
MiniDV Film Festival
Minneapolis/St Paul International Film
  Festival
Mix Brasil Festival of Sexual Diversity
Montreal International Festival of New
  Cinema and New Media
Montreal World Film Festival
Moondance International Film Festival
Mountainfilm Festival
Mumbai International Film Festival
Nantucket Film Festival
Napoli Film Festival
Nashville Film Festival
Nashville Film Festival
Native American Film & Video Festival
New Directors/New Films Festival
New Festival: New York Lesbian, Gay,
  Bisexual, & Transgender Film Festival
New Orleans Film Festival
New York Expo of Short Film and Video
New York Film Festival
New York Underground Film Festival
New Zealand Film Festival
Newport Beach Film Festival
Next Frame Film Festival
NO BUDGET International Independent
  Film & Video Festival
NoDance Film Festival
Norrköping Film Festival Flimmer
North Carolina Jewish Film Festival
Northwest Film & Video Festival
Norwegian International Film Festival
NSI FilmExchange Canadian Film Festival
Ohio Independent Film Festival
Oldenburg International Film Festival
One Take Film Festival
Onedotzero Digital Creativity Festival
Out Far! - Annual Phoenix International
  Lesbian and Gay Film Festival

DVD
Antimatter Festival of Underground Short
    Film & Video
Cinematexas International Short Film &
    Video Festival
IFP Los Angeles Film Festival
Kasseler Dokumentarfilm - Und Videofest
Lake Placid Film Forum
Madcat Women's International Film Festival
NoDance Film Festival
ResFest Digital Film Festival
Rhode Island International Film Festival
Thaw Video, Film, and Digital Media Festival
Tromadance Film Festival
Whistler Film Festival
Williamstown Film Festival

EDUCATION
Digital Days
Durango Film Festival
United Nations Association Film Festival
ZoieFilms Festival

ENVIRONMENTAL
Algarve International Film Festival
Big Muddy Film Festival
International Wildlife Film Festival Montana
Jackson Hole Wildlife Film Festival
Mountainfilm Festival
United Nations Association Film Festival

EPISODIC TELEVISION/TELEVISION PILOTS
International Wildlife Film Festival Montana
Israel Film Festival
Nashville Film Festival
Prix Jeunesse International

ETHNIC AFRICAN
African Film Festival
Arizona State University Short Film and
    Video Festival
Bermuda International Film Festival
Beverly Hills Film Festival
Cape Town World Cinema Festival
Cinematexas International Short Film &
    Video Festival
Cork International Film Festival
DancesWithFilms
DC Independent Film Festival & Seminars
Fantasia Film Festival
Film Nite
Fort Lauderdale International Film Festival
IFP Los Angeles Film Festival
Lost Film Festival
Madcat Women's International Film Festival
Melbourne Queer Film & Video Festival

Miami International Film Festival
Ohio Independent Film Festival
Rhode Island International Film Festival
Sedona International Film Festival and
    Workshop
Tromadance Film Festival
Washington, DC International Film Festival—
    Filmfest DC
Wisconsin Film Festival

ETHNIC ASIAN
Alpe Adria Cinema Trieste Film Festival
Arizona State University Short Film and
    Video Festival
Bangkok International Film Festival
Barcelona Asian Film Festival
Bermuda International Film Festival
Beverly Hills Film Festival
Cape Town World Cinema Festival
Cinematexas International Short Film &
    Video Festival
Cleveland International Film Festival
Cork International Film Festival
DancesWithFilms
Exground - Das Filmfest
Fantasia Film Festival
Fort Lauderdale International Film Festival
Hawaii International Film Festival
Helsinki Film Festival - Love and Anarchy
Hong Kong International Film Festival
    (HKIFF)
IFP Los Angeles Film Festival
Kinofilm Manchester International Short
    Film Festival
Lost Film Festival
Madcat Women's International Film Festival
Melbourne Queer Film & Video Festival
Miami International Film Festival
Ohio Independent Film Festival
Rhode Island International Film Festival
Rotterdam International Film Festival
San Francisco International Asian American
    Film Festival
Seattle International Film Festival
Sedona International Film Festival and
    Workshop
Shanghai International Film Festival
Singapore International Film Festival
Stockholm International Film Festival
Temecula Valley International Film Festival
Tokyo International Film Festival
Tromadance Film Festival
Washington, DC International Film Festival—
    Filmfest DC
Wisconsin Film Festival
Yamagata International Documentary Film
    Festival

ETHNiC BLACK

African Film Festival
American Black Film Festival
Arizona State University Short Film and
Video Festival
Bermuda International Film Festival
Beverly Hills Film Festival
Cape Town World Cinema Festival
Chicago International Film Festival
Cinematexas International Short Film &
Video Festival
Cleveland International Film Festival
Cork International Film Festival
DancesWithFilms
Fantasia Film Festival
Fort Lauderdale International Film Festival
Hollywood Black Film Festival
IFP Los Angeles Film Festival
Independent Black Film Festival
Kinofilm Manchester International Short
Film Festival
Lost Film Festival
Madcat Women's International Film Festival
Melbourne Queer Film & Video Festival
Miami International Film Festival
Ohio Independent Film Festival
Rhode Island International Film Festival
Seattle Underground Film Festival (The)
Sedona International Film Festival and
Workshop
Silver Lake Film Festival
Temecula Valley International Film Festival
Tromadance Film Festival
Washington, DC International Film Festival—
Filmfest DC
Wisconsin Film Festival

ETHNiC CHiCANO

Kinofilm Manchester International Short
Film Festival
Silver Lake Film Festival

ETHNiC JEWiSH

Arizona State University Short Film and
Video Festival
Bermuda International Film Festival
Beverly Hills Film Festival
Chicago International Film Festival
Cinematexas International Short Film &
Video Festival
Cork International Film Festival
DancesWithFilms
Fantasia Film Festival
Fort Lauderdale International Film Festival
IFP Los Angeles Film Festival
Israel Film Festival
Jerusalem International Film Festival

Lost Film Festival
Madcat Women's International Film Festival
Melbourne Queer Film & Video Festival
Miami International Film Festival
North Carolina Jewish Film Festival
Ohio Independent Film Festival
Rhode Island International Film Festival
Sedona International Film Festival and
Workshop
Silver Lake Film Festival
Temecula Valley International Film Festival
Toronto Jewish Film Festival
Tromadance Film Festival
Washington, DC International Film Festival—
Filmfest DC
Wisconsin Film Festival

ETHNiC LATiN

Arizona State University Short Film and
Video Festival
Bermuda International Film Festival
Beverly Hills Film Festival
Cape Town World Cinema Festival
Cartagena International Film Festival
Cinematexas International Short Film &
Video Festival
Cleveland International Film Festival
Cork International Film Festival
DancesWithFilms
Deep Ellum Film Festival
Donostia - San Sebastian International Film
Festival
Fantasia Film Festival
Fort Lauderdale International Film Festival
Huesca International Short Film Festival
IFP Los Angeles Film Festival
Los Angeles Latino International Film Festival
Lost Film Festival
Madcat Women's International Film Festival
Melbourne Queer Film & Video Festival
Miami International Film Festival
Mix Brasil Festival of Sexual Diversity
Ohio Independent Film Festival
Rhode Island International Film Festival
Rio de Janeiro International Film Festival
Santa Monica Film Festival
Sedona International Film Festival and
Workshop
Tromadance Film Festival
Washington, DC International Film Festival—
Filmfest DC
Wisconsin Film Festival

ETHNIC OTHER
American Indian Film Festival
Arizona State University Short Film and
Video Festival
Big Bear Lake International Film Festival
Cork International Film Festival
DocPoint Helsinki Documentary Film
Festival
Fantasia Film Festival
Freedom Film Festival
Göteborg Film Festival
Huesca International Short Film Festival
International Film Festival of India
Israel Film Festival
Minicine Visiting Filmmaker Series
Mix Brasil Festival of Sexual Diversity
Native American Film & Video Festival
New Zealand Film Festival
Ohio Independent Film Festival
Palestine Film Festival Dreams Of A Nation
River to River Florence Indian Film Festival
San Francisco International Asian American
Film Festival
Sedona International Film Festival and
Workshop
Tehran International Animation Festival
Tokyo International Film Festival
Torino Film Festival
Tromadance Film Festival
University of Oregon Queer Film Festival
Uppsala International Short Film Festival
Washington, DC International Film Festival—
Filmfest DC
Wellington Film Festival
West Virginia International Film Festival

ETHNIC SPANISH
Arizona State University Short Film and
Video Festival
Bermuda International Film Festival
Beverly Hills Film Festival
Cinematexas International Short Film &
Video Festival
Cleveland International Film Festival
Cork International Film Festival
DancesWithFilms
Donostia - San Sebastian International Film
Festival
Fantasia Film Festival
Fort Lauderdale International Film Festival
Gijon International Film Festival For Young
People
Huesca International Short Film Festival
IFP Los Angeles Film Festival
Lost Film Festival
Madcat Women's International Film Festival
Melbourne Queer Film & Video Festival

Miami International Film Festival
Ohio Independent Film Festival
Rhode Island International Film Festival
Santa Monica Film Festival
Sedona International Film Festival and
Workshop
Temecula Valley International Film Festival
Tromadance Film Festival
Washington, DC International Film Festival—
Filmfest DC
Wisconsin Film Festival

EUROPE, ASIA, SOUTH AMERICA, CANADA AND THE U.S.
Lake Placid Film Forum

EUROPEAN
Alpe Adria Cinema Trieste Film Festival
Arcipelago International Festival of Short
Films & New Images
Avignon French Film Festival
Avignon/New York Film Festival
Berlin International Film Festival
Cambridge International Film Festival
Cherbourg-Octeville Festival of Irish &
British Film
Copenhagen International Film Festival
Denver International Film Festival
DocPoint Helsinki Documentary Film
Festival
Edinburgh International Film Festival
Espoo Ciné International Film Festival
Festival of European Films
Filmfest Munchen
Freedom Film Festival
Gijon International Film Festival For Young
People
Göteborg Film Festival
Helsinki Film Festival - Love and Anarchy
International Scientific Film Festival
Kinofilm Manchester International Short
Film Festival
Midnight Sun Film Festival
Napoli Film Festival
New Zealand Film Festival
Norwegian International Film Festival
Rotterdam International Film Festival
Scottsdale International Film Festival
Stockholm International Film Festival
Tampere Film Festival
The Times bfi London Film Festival
Thessaloniki International Film Festival
Torino Film Festival
Tromsø International Film Festival
Uppsala International Short Film Festival
Viennale - Vienna International Film Festival
Warsaw International Film Festival
Wellington Film Festival

EXPERIMENTAL

Alpe Adria Cinema Trieste Film Festival
Ann Arbor Film Festival
Antimatter Festival of Underground Short
  Film & Video
Arcipelago International Festival of Short
  Films & New Images
Arizona International Film Festival
Arizona State University Short Film and
  Video Festival
Aspen Shortsfest
Aspirations Film Festival
Atlanta Film Festival
Brainwash Movie Festival
Brooklyn Underground Film Festival
Bumbershoot 1 Reel Film Festival
Chicago Underground Film Festival
Cinematexas International Short Film &
  Video Festival
Cleveland International Film Festival
Cork International Film Festival
Crossroads Film Festival
Cucalorus Film Festival
Dallas Video Festival
DancesWithFilms
Deep Ellum Film Festival
Denver International Film Festival
DIY Film Festival
Dragon Con Independent Short Film Festival
Entrevues Belfort International Film Festival
Euro Underground
Exground - Das Filmfest
Fantasia Film Festival
Female Eye Film Festival
Festival Of Nations
Film Fest New Haven
Film Nite
Filmfest Munchen
FirstGlance Hollywood Film Festival
Flickering Image Festival
Fort Lauderdale International Film Festival
Free Film Festival Fitchburg (The F4)
Gen Art Film Festival
H.P. Lovecraft Film Festival
Hawaii International Film Festival
Helsinki Film Festival - Love and Anarchy
Human Rights Watch International Film
  Festival
Humboldt International Short Film Festival
HypeFest Film & Video Festival
IFP Los Angeles Film Festival
Image+Nation Montreal's International
  Lesbian & Gay Film and Video Festival
Images Festival of Independent Film and
  Video
Independent Exposure
Inside Out Lesbian and Gay Film Festival of
  Toronto

International Leipzig Festival For
  Documentary and Animated Film
International Lesbian Film Festival
  Immaginaria
Johns Hopkins Film Festival
Kasseler Dokumentarfilm - Und Videofest
Kinofilm Manchester International Short
  Film Festival
Lake Placid Film Forum
Lost Film Festival
Madcat Women's International Film Festival
Margaret Mead Film Festival
Maryland Film Festival
Maui Film Festival
Melbourne Queer Film & Video Festival
Method Fest Independent Film Festival
Miami International Film Festival
Midnight Sun Film Festival
Mill Valley Film Festival
Minicine Visiting Filmmaker Series
MiniDV Film Festival
Mix Brasil Festival of Sexual Diversity
Moondance International Film Festival
Nashville Film Festival
New Orleans Film Festival
New York Expo of Short Film and Video
New York Lesbian and Gay Experimental Film
  and Video Festival (Mix Festival)
New York Underground Film Festival
New Zealand Film Festival
Newport Beach Film Festival
Next Frame Film Festival
NO BUDGET International Independent
  Film & Video Festival
Northwest Film & Video Festival
Ohio Independent Film Festival
One Take Film Festival
OUTFEST: Los Angeles Gay and Lesbian Film
  Festival
Portland International Film Festival
Queersicht - Schwul-lesbisches Filmfestival
  Bern
Red Bank International Film Festival
ResFest Digital Film Festival
Rhode Island International Film Festival
RiverRun International Film Festival
Rochester International Film Festival
Rome International Film Festival
San Antonio Underground Film Festival
San Francisco Independent Film Festival
San Francisco International Asian American
  Film Festival
San Francisco International Film Festival
Santa Monica Film Festival
Screamfest Horror Film Festival
Seattle Lesbian & Gay Film Festival
Seattle Underground Film Festival (The)

Short Shorts Film Festival
Sidewalk Moving Picture Film Festival
Silver Lake Film Festival
Smogdance Film Festival
Sour Grapes Film Festival
Split Screen Film Festival
St. Louis International Film Festival
Stony Brook Film Festival
SXSW: South By Southwest Film Festival
Tampere Film Festival
Tehran International Animation Festival
Temecula Valley International Film Festival
Thaw Video, Film, and Digital Media Festival
The Times bfi London Film Festival
Tiburon International Film Festival
TIE International Experimental Cinema
   Exposition
Trenton Film Festival
Tromadance Film Festival
Turin International Gay & Lesbian Film
   Festival "from Sodom to Hollywood"
United States Super 8 Film and Digital Video
   Festival
University of Oregon Queer Film Festival
Uppsala International Short Film Festival
USA Film Festival/Dallas
Venice International Film Festival
Verzaubert - International Queer Film
   Festival
Victoria Independent Film and Video Festival
Whistler Film Festival
Williamstown Film Festival
Wisconsin Film Festival
Yorkton Short Film Festival
Zagreb World Festival of Animated Films
ZoieFilms Festival

FAMILY

Big Bear Lake International Film Festival
Cambridge International Film Festival
Comic Con International Independent Film
   Festival
Heartland Film Festival
International Short Film Festival Oberhausen
International TrickFilm Festival Stuttgart
Leeds Children and Young People's Film
   Festival
Mill Valley Film Festival
Nashville Film Festival
Sidewalk Moving Picture Film Festival
Sprockets Toronto International Film Festival
   for Children

FANTASY/SCiENCE FiCTiON

A.K.A. Shriekfest, The Los Angeles
   Horror/Science Fiction Film Festival &
   ScreenPlay Competition
Antimatter Festival of Underground Short
   Film & Video
Arizona State University Short Film and
   Video Festival
Brussels International Festival of Fantasy
   Films
Chicago Horror Film Festival
Comic Con International Independent Film
   Festival
DancesWithFilms
Dragon Con Independent Short Film Festival
Espoo Ciné International Film Festival
Fantasia Film Festival
Fantasy Filmfest - International Film Festival
   for Science Fiction, Fiction, Horror and
   Thriller
Festival of Fantastic Films
Mania Fest
Rhode Island International Film Festival
Screamfest Horror Film Festival
Sitges International Film Festival of Catalonia
Smogdance Film Festival
Tromadance Film Festival
Zombiedance Undead Film Fest

FEATURES

30 Below Film & Video Competition
A.K.A. Shriekfest, The Los Angeles
   Horror/Science Fiction Film Festival &
   ScreenPlay Competition
Adelaide International Film Festival
African Film Festival
Alpe Adria Cinema Trieste Film Festival
American Black Film Festival
American Film Institute (AFI) - Los Angeles
   International Film Festival
American Film Market
American Indian Film Festival
AniFest Film Festival of Animated Films
Ankara International Film Festival
Ann Arbor Film Festival
Annapolis Film Festival
Annecy International Animated Film Festival
Arizona International Film Festival
Aspirations Film Festival
Athens International Film Festival
Atlanta Film Festival
Austin Film Festival
Avignon French Film Festival
Avignon/New York Film Festival
Backseat Film Festival
Bangkok International Film Festival
Barcelona Asian Film Festival

Human Rights Watch International Film
  Festival
IFP Los Angeles Film Festival
IFP Market/Gotham Awards
Image+Nation Montreal's International
  Lesbian & Gay Film and Video Festival
Independent Black Film Festival
Independent Film Festival of Boston
Indianapolis International Film Festival
Inside Out Lesbian and Gay Film Festival of
  Toronto
International Documentary Film Festival
  Amsterdam (IDFA)
International Festival of Films On Art (FIFA)
International Film Festival of India
International Leipzig Festival For
  Documentary and Animated Film
International Lesbian Film Festival
  Immaginaria
International TrickFilm Festival Stuttgart
International Wildlife Film Festival Montana
Internationales Filmfestival Mannheim-
  Heidelberg
Israel Film Festival
Jackson Hole Wildlife Film Festival
Jerusalem International Film Festival
Johns Hopkins Film Festival
Karlovy Vary International Film Festival
Kasseler Dokumentarfilm - Und Videofest
Kyiv International Film Festival Molodist
Lake Placid Film Forum
Leeds Children and Young People's Film
  Festival
Leeds International Film Festival
Locarno International Film Festival
Long Island International Film Expo
Los Angeles International Short Film Festival
Los Angeles Latino International Film Festival
Lost Film Festival
Madcat Women's International Film Festival
Making Scenes Queer Film & Video Festival
Malibu International Film Festival
Mania Fest
Marco Island Film Festival
Margaret Mead Film Festival
Marseilles International Documentary Film
  Festival
Maryland Film Festival
Maui Film Festival
Melbourne Independent Filmmakers Festival
  - MIFF
Melbourne International Film Festival
Melbourne Queer Film & Video Festival
Message to Man International Documentary,
  Short and Animated Films Festival
Method Fest Independent Film Festival
Miami International Film Festival

Midnight Sun Film Festival
Mifed
Mill Valley Film Festival
MiniDV Film Festival
Minneapolis/St Paul International Film
  Festival
Mix Brasil Festival of Sexual Diversity
Montreal International Festival of New
  Cinema and New Media
Montreal World Film Festival
Moondance International Film Festival
Mountainfilm Festival
Nantucket Film Festival
Napoli Film Festival
Nashville Film Festival
Native American Film & Video Festival
New Directors/New Films Festival
New Festival: New York Lesbian, Gay,
  Bisexual, & Transgender Film Festival
New Orleans Film Festival
New York Film Festival
New York Lesbian and Gay Experimental Film
  and Video Festival (Mix Festival)
New York Underground Film Festival
New Zealand Film Festival
Next Frame Film Festival
NO BUDGET International Independent
  Film & Video Festival
NoDance Film Festival
Norrköping Film Festival Flimmer
North Carolina Jewish Film Festival
Northwest Film & Video Festival
Norwegian International Film Festival
NSI FilmExchange Canadian Film Festival
Ohio Independent Film Festival
Oldenburg International Film Festival
One Take Film Festival
Onedotzero Digital Creativity Festival
Ottawa International Animation Festival
Out Takes
OUTFEST: Los Angeles Gay and Lesbian Film
  Festival
Palestine Film Festival Dreams Of A Nation
Palm Beach International Film Festival
Palm Springs International Film Festival
Philadelphia Film Festival
Philadelphia Fringe Festival
Philadelphia International Gay and Lesbian
  Film Festival
Phoenix Film Festival
Portland International Film Festival
Queersicht - Schwul-lesbisches Filmfestival
  Bern
Raindance Film Festival
Red Bank International Film Festival
Reel Affirmations Film Festival
Rendezvous with Madness Film Festival

ResFest Digital Film Festival
Rhode Island International Film Festival
Rio de Janeiro International Film Festival
River to River Florence Indian Film Festival
RiverRun International Film Festival
Rome International Film Festival
Rotterdam International Film Festival
Sacramento International Gay and Lesbian
  Film Festival
San Antonio Underground Film Festival
San Diego Film Festival
San Francisco Independent Film Festival
San Francisco International Asian American
  Film Festival
San Francisco International Film Festival
San Francisco International Lesbian and Gay
  Film Festival
Santa Barbara International Film Festival
  (SBIFF)
Santa Monica Film Festival
São Paulo International Film Festival
Sarasota Film Festival
Savannah Film and Video Festival
Scottsdale International Film Festival
Seattle International Film Festival
Seattle Lesbian & Gay Film Festival
Seattle Underground Film Festival (The)
Sedona International Film Festival and
  Workshop
Shanghai International Film Festival
Sheffield International Documentary Festival
Sidewalk Moving Picture Film Festival
Silver Lake Film Festival
SILVERDOCS: AFI/Discovery Channel
  Documentary Festival
Singapore International Film Festival
Sitges International Film Festival of Catalonia
Slamdance International Film Festival
Split Screen Film Festival
Sprockets Toronto International Film Festival
  for Children
St. Louis International Film Festival
Stony Brook Film Festival
Sundance Film Festival
SXSW: South By Southwest Film Festival
Sydney Film Festival
Tehran International Animation Festival
Telluride Film Festival
Telluride IndieFest
Temecula Valley International Film Festival
Texas Film Festival
Thaw Video, Film, and Digital Media Festival
The Times bfi London Film Festival
Thessaloniki International Film Festival
Tiburon International Film Festival
TIE International Experimental Cinema
  Exposition

Tokyo International Film Festival
Torino Film Festival
Toronto International Film Festival
Toronto Jewish Film Festival
Trenton Film Festival
Tribeca Film Festival
Tromadance Film Festival
Tromsø International Film Festival
Turin International Gay & Lesbian Film
  Festival "from Sodom to Hollywood"
U.S. Comedy Arts Festival
United Nations Association Film Festival
University of Oregon Queer Film Festival
USA Film Festival/Dallas
Vail Film Festival
Vancouver International Film Festival
Venice International Film Festival
Vermont International Film Festival
Verzaubert - International Queer Film
  Festival
Victoria Independent Film and Video Festival
Viennale - Vienna International Film Festival
Visions du Réel International Documentary
  Film Festival
Warsaw International Film Festival
Washington, DC International Film Festival—
  Filmfest DC
Waterfront Film Festival
Wellington Film Festival
West Virginia International Film Festival
Whistler Film Festival
Williamstown Film Festival
Wilmington Independent Film Festival
Wine Country Film Festival
Woodstock Film Festival
World Community Film Festival
Yamagata International Documentary Film
  Festival
Zagreb World Festival of Animated Films
ZoieFilms Festival
ZoieFilms Festival
Zombiedance Undead Film Fest

FiRST-TiME iNDEPENDENT FiLMMAKERS

30 Below Film & Video Competition
A.K.A. Shriekfest, The Los Angeles
  Horror/Science Fiction Film Festival &
  ScreenPlay Competition
American Film Institute (AFI) - Los Angeles
  International Film Festival
Arizona State University Short Film and
  Video Festival
Avignon French Film Festival
Avignon/New York Film Festival
Backseat Film Festival
Bangkok International Film Festival

Bermuda International Film Festival
Beverly Hills Film Festival
Brainwash Movie Festival
Breckenridge Festival of Film
Bumbershoot 1 Reel Film Festival
Cannes International Film Festival
Cartagena International Film Festival
Cherbourg-Octeville Festival of Irish & British Film
Cinematexas International Short Film & Video Festival
Cleveland International Film Festival
Cork International Film Festival
Cucalorus Film Festival
DancesWithFilms
Deep Ellum Film Festival
DIY Film Festival
Dragon Con Independent Short Film Festival
Durban International Film Festival
Entrevues Belfort International Film Festival
Exground - Das Filmfest
Fantasia Film Festival
Festival of Fantastic Films
Film Fest New Haven
Film Nite
FirstGlance Philadelphia Film Festival
Flickering Image Festival
Fort Lauderdale International Film Festival
Free Film Festival Fitchburg (The F4)
Gen Art Film Festival
Gijon International Film Festival For Young People
Great Plains Film Festival
H.P. Lovecraft Film Festival
Helsinki Film Festival - Love and Anarchy
Hi/Lo Film Festival
Hollywood Black Film Festival
Houston Annual Worldfest
IFP Los Angeles Film Festival
Images Festival of Independent Film and Video
Independent Exposure
Internationales Filmfestival Mannheim-Heidelberg
Johns Hopkins Film Festival
Lake Placid Film Forum
Locarno International Film Festival
Los Angeles International Short Film Festival
Lost Film Festival
Madcat Women's International Film Festival
Marco Island Film Festival
Marco Island Film Festival
Melbourne Queer Film & Video Festival
Message to Man International Documentary, Short and Animated Films Festival
Miami International Film Festival
Minicine Visiting Filmmaker Series

Moondance International Film Festival
Mumbai International Film Festival
New Directors/New Films Festival
Next Frame Film Festival
NoDance Film Festival
Northwest Film & Video Festival
Ohio Independent Film Festival
Out Far! - Annual Phoenix International Lesbian and Gay Film Festival
OUTFEST: Los Angeles Gay and Lesbian Film Festival
Palm Beach International Film Festival
Philadelphia Film Festival
Phoenix Film Festival
Portland International Film Festival
Rhode Island International Film Festival
Rotterdam International Film Festival
San Francisco Independent Film Festival
San Francisco International Asian American Film Festival
San Francisco International Film Festival
San Francisco International Lesbian and Gay Film Festival
São Paulo International Film Festival
Savannah Film and Video Festival
Scottsdale International Film Festival
Seattle Underground Film Festival (The)
Sedona International Film Festival and Workshop
Sheffield International Documentary Festival
Silver Lake Film Festival
Smogdance Film Festival
Split Screen Film Festival
Stockholm International Film Festival
Stony Brook Film Festival
SXSW: South By Southwest Film Festival
Temecula Valley International Film Festival
Texas Film Festival
Torino Film Festival
Toronto International Film Festival
Tribeca Film Festival
Tromadance Film Festival
Tromsø International Film Festival
USA Film Festival/Dallas
Venice International Film Festival
Victoria Independent Film and Video Festival
Washington, DC International Film Festival—Filmfest DC
Whistler Film Festival
Williamstown Film Festival
Wisconsin Film Festival
Zagreb World Festival of Animated Films

FRENCH

Avignon French Film Festival
Avignon/New York Film Festival
Clermont-Ferrand Short Film Festival
Entrevues Belfort International Film Festival

GAY/LESBiAN

Ann Arbor Film Festival
Antimatter Festival of Underground Short
    Film & Video
Arizona State University Short Film and
    Video Festival
Bermuda International Film Festival
Beverly Hills Film Festival
Boston Gay & Lesbian Film & Video Festival
Chicago International Film Festival
Cinematexas International Short Film &
    Video Festival
Cleveland International Film Festival
Cork International Film Festival
DancesWithFilms
Fort Lauderdale International Film Festival
Fresno REEL Pride International Gay &
    Lesbian Film Festival
Gen Art Film Festival
Hollywood Black Film Festival
Honolulu Rainbow Film Festival
IFP Los Angeles Film Festival
Image+Nation Montreal's International
    Lesbian & Gay Film and Video Festival
Inside Out Lesbian and Gay Film Festival of
    Toronto
International Lesbian Film Festival
    Immaginaria
Lost Film Festival
Madcat Women's International Film Festival
Making Scenes Queer Film & Video Festival
Marco Island Film Festival
Melbourne Queer Film & Video Festival
Method Fest Independent Film Festival
Mix Brasil Festival of Sexual Diversity
New Festival: New York Lesbian, Gay,
    Bisexual, & Transgender Film Festival
New York Lesbian and Gay Experimental Film
    and Video Festival (Mix Festival)
NoDance Film Festival
Norrköping Film Festival Flimmer
Ohio Independent Film Festival
Out Far! - Annual Phoenix International
    Lesbian and Gay Film Festival
Out Takes
OUTFEST: Los Angeles Gay and Lesbian Film
    Festival
Philadelphia International Gay and Lesbian
    Film Festival
Queersicht - Schwul-lesbisches Filmfestival
    Bern

Reel Affirmations Film Festival
Rhode Island International Film Festival
Sacramento International Gay and Lesbian
    Film Festival
San Francisco International Asian American
    Film Festival
San Francisco International Lesbian and Gay
    Film Festival
Seattle International Film Festival
Seattle Lesbian & Gay Film Festival
Seattle Underground Film Festival (The)
Sedona International Film Festival and
    Workshop
Silver Lake Film Festival
Tromadance Film Festival
Turin International Gay & Lesbian Film
    Festival "from Sodom to Hollywood"
University of Oregon Queer Film Festival
Verzaubert - International Queer Film
    Festival
Victoria Independent Film and Video Festival
Wisconsin Film Festival

GOVERNMENT

United Nations Association Film Festival
Vermont International Film Festival
World Community Film Festival

HORROR

A.K.A. Shriekfest, The Los Angeles
    Horror/Science Fiction Film Festival &
    ScreenPlay Competition
Brussels International Festival of Fantasy Films
Chicago Horror Film Festival
Dragon Con Independent Short Film Festival
Espoo Ciné International Film Festival
Fantasia Film Festival
Fantasy Filmfest - International Film Festival
    for Science Fiction, Fiction, Horror and
    Thriller
Festival of Fantastic Films
H.P. Lovecraft Film Festival
Mania Fest
Screamfest Horror Film Festival
Tromadance Film Festival
Zombiedance Undead Film Fest

HUMAN RiGHTS

Belgrade International Film Festival
Big Muddy Film Festival
Cinéma du Réel International Festival of
    Visual Anthropology and Social
    Documentary Films
Heartland Film Festival
Human Rights Watch International Film
    Festival
Jerusalem International Film Festival

Melbourne International Film Festival
Palestine Film Festival Dreams Of A Nation
United Nations Association Film Festival
Vermont International Film Festival
Wine Country Film Festival
World Community Film Festival

INDEPENDENT

30 Below Film & Video Competition
A.K.A. Shriekfest, The Los Angeles
    Horror/Science Fiction Film Festival &
    ScreenPlay Competition
Adelaide International Film Festival
African Film Festival
Algarve International Film Festival
American Black Film Festival
American Film Institute (AFI) - Los Angeles
    International Film Festival
American Film Market
American Indian Film Festival
Angelus Awards Student Film Festival
AniFest Film Festival of Animated Films
Ann Arbor Film Festival
Annapolis Film Festival
Annecy International Animated Film Festival
Antimatter Festival of Underground Short
    Film & Video
Arcipelago International Festival of Short
    Films & New Images
Arizona International Film Festival
Arizona State University Short Film and
    Video Festival
Aspen Shortsfest
Aspirations Film Festival
Athens International Film Festival
Atlanta Film Festival
Austin Film Festival
Avignon French Film Festival
Avignon/New York Film Festival
Backseat Film Festival
Bangkok International Film Festival
Barcelona Asian Film Festival
Belgrade International Film Festival
Berlin International Film Festival
Bermuda International Film Festival
Beverly Hills Film Festival
Big Bear Lake International Film Festival
Big Muddy Film Festival
Black Maria Film and Video Festival
Blue Sky International Film Festival - Las
    Vegas
Boston Film Festival
Boston Gay & Lesbian Film & Video Festival
Boston International Festival Of Women's
    Cinema
Boston International Film Festival
Brainwash Movie Festival

Breckenridge Festival of Film
Brighton International Film Festival
Brooklyn Underground Film Festival
Brussels International Festival of Fantasy
    Films
Bumbershoot 1 Reel Film Festival
Cabourg Festival of Romantic Films
Cairo International Film Festival
Calgary International Film Festival
Cambridge International Film Festival
Cannes Directors' Fortnight
Cannes International Film Festival
Cape Town World Cinema Festival
Cardiff Screen Festival
Cartagena International Film Festival
Cergy-Pontoise Short Film Festival
Cherbourg-Octeville Festival of Irish &
    British Film
Chicago Horror Film Festival
Chicago International Documentary Festival
Chicago International Film Festival
Chicago Underground Film Festival
Chrysler Million Dollar Film Festival
Cinéma du Réel International Festival of
    Visual Anthropology and Social
    Documentary Films
Cinema Epicuria Sonoma Valley Film Festival
CinemaReno
Cinematexas International Short Film &
    Video Festival
Cinequest San José Film Festival
CineVegas International Film Festival
Clermont-Ferrand Short Film Festival
Cleveland International Film Festival
CMJ Filmfest
Comic Con International Independent Film
    Festival
Cork International Film Festival
Cracow Film Festival
Crossroads Film Festival
Cucalorus Film Festival
Dallas Video Festival
DancesWithFilms
Daytona Beach Film Festival
DC Independent Film Festival & Seminars
deadCenter Film Festival
Denver International Film Festival
Detroit Docs International Film Festival
DIY Film Festival
Docfest - New York International
    Documentary Festival
Donostia - San Sebastian International Film
    Festival
Dragon Con Independent Short Film Festival
Dragon Con Independent Short Film Festival
Dubrovnik International Film Festival
Durango Film Festival

Message to Man International Documentary, Short and Animated Films Festival
Method Fest Independent Film Festival
Miami International Film Festival
Microcinefest
Midnight Sun Film Festival
Mill Valley Film Festival
Minneapolis/St Paul International Film Festival
Mix Brasil Festival of Sexual Diversity
Montreal International Festival of New Cinema and New Media
Montreal World Film Festival
Moondance International Film Festival
Mountainfilm Festival
Mumbai International Film Festival
Nantucket Film Festival
Napoli Film Festival
Nashville Film Festival
Native American Film & Video Festival
New Directors/New Films Festival
New Festival: New York Lesbian, Gay, Bisexual, & Transgender Film Festival
New Orleans Film Festival
New York Expo of Short Film and Video
New York Lesbian and Gay Experimental Film and Video Festival (Mix Festival)
New York Underground Film Festival
New Zealand Film Festival
New Zealand Film Festival
Newport Beach Film Festival
Next Frame Film Festival
NO BUDGET International Independent Film & Video Festival
NoDance Film Festival
Norrköping Film Festival Flimmer
North Carolina Jewish Film Festival
Northwest Film & Video Festival
Northwest Film & Video Festival
NSI FilmExchange Canadian Film Festival
Ohio Independent Film Festival
Oldenburg International Film Festival
One Take Film Festival
Onedotzero Digital Creativity Festival
Ottawa International Animation Festival
Out Far! - Annual Phoenix International Lesbian and Gay Film Festival
Out Takes
OUTFEST: Los Angeles Gay and Lesbian Film Festival
Palm Beach International Film Festival
Palm Springs International Film Festival
Philadelphia Film Festival
Philadelphia Fringe Festival
Philadelphia International Gay and Lesbian Film Festival
Phoenix Film Festival

Portland International Film Festival
Queersicht - Schwul-lesbisches Filmfestival Bern
Raindance Film Festival
Red Bank International Film Festival
Reel Affirmations Film Festival
Rendezvous with Madness Film Festival
ResFest Digital Film Festival
Rhode Island International Film Festival
Rio de Janeiro International Film Festival
River to River Florence Indian Film Festival
Rochester International Film Festival
Rome International Film Festival
Rotterdam International Film Festival
Sacramento International Gay and Lesbian Film Festival
San Antonio Underground Film Festival
San Diego Film Festival
San Francisco Independent Film Festival
San Francisco International Asian American Film Festival
San Francisco International Film Festival
San Francisco International Lesbian and Gay Film Festival
Santa Barbara International Film Festival (SBIFF)
Santa Monica Film Festival
São Paulo International Film Festival
Sarasota Film Festival
Savannah Film and Video Festival
Scottsdale International Film Festival
Screamfest Horror Film Festival
Seattle International Film Festival
Seattle Lesbian & Gay Film Festival
Seattle Underground Film Festival (The)
Sedona International Film Festival and Workshop
Shanghai International Film Festival
Sheffield International Documentary Festival
Short Shorts Film Festival
Sidewalk Moving Picture Film Festival
Silver Lake Film Festival
SILVERDOCS: AFI/Discovery Channel Documentary Festival
Sitges International Film Festival of Catalonia
Slamdance International Film Festival
Sour Grapes Film Festival
Split Screen Film Festival
Sprockets Toronto International Film Festival for Children
St. Louis International Film Festival
Stockholm International Film Festival
Stony Brook Film Festival
Sundance Film Festival
SXSW: South By Southwest Film Festival
Sydney Film Festival
Tehran International Animation Festival

Telluride Film Festival
Telluride IndieFest
Temecula Valley International Film Festival
Texas Film Festival
Thaw Video, Film, and Digital Media Festival
Thessaloniki International Film Festival
Tiburon International Film Festival
TIE International Experimental Cinema
  Exposition
Tokyo International Film Festival
Toronto International Film Festival
Toronto Jewish Film Festival
Trenton Film Festival
Tribeca Film Festival
Tromadance Film Festival
Tromsø International Film Festival
Turin International Gay & Lesbian Film
  Festival "from Sodom to Hollywood"
U.S. Comedy Arts Festival
United Nations Association Film Festival
United States Super 8 Film and Digital Video
  Festival
University of Oregon Queer Film Festival
USA Film Festival/Dallas
Vail Film Festival
Vancouver International Film Festival
Venice International Film Festival
Vermont International Film Festival
Verzaubert - International Queer Film
  Festival
Victoria Independent Film and Video Festival
Virginia Film Festival
Visions du Réel International Documentary
  Film Festival
Warsaw International Film Festival
Washington, DC International Film Festival—
  Filmfest DC
Waterfront Film Festival
Wellington Film Festival
West Virginia International Film Festival
Whistler Film Festival
Williamstown Film Festival
Wilmington Independent Film Festival
Wine Country Film Festival
Wisconsin Film Festival
Woodstock Film Festival
Woodstock Film Festival
Yamagata International Documentary Film
  Festival
Yorkton Short Film Festival
Zagreb World Festival of Animated Films
Zombiedance Undead Film Fest

INTERNATIONAL
A.K.A. Shriekfest, The Los Angeles
  Horror/Science Fiction Film Festival &
  ScreenPlay Competition
Adelaide International Film Festival
African Film Festival
Algarve International Film Festival
Alpe Adria Cinema Trieste Film Festival
American Black Film Festival
American Film Institute (AFI) - Los Angeles
  International Film Festival
American Film Market
American Indian Film Festival
Angelus Awards Student Film Festival
AniFest Film Festival of Animated Films
Ankara International Film Festival
Ann Arbor Film Festival
Annapolis Film Festival
Annecy International Animated Film Festival
Antimatter Festival of Underground Short
  Film & Video
Arcipelago International Festival of Short
  Films & New Images
Arcipelago International Festival of Short
  Films & New Images
Arizona International Film Festival
Arizona State University Short Film and
  Video Festival
Aspen Shortsfest
Athens International Film Festival
Atlanta Film Festival
Austin Film Festival
Avignon French Film Festival
Avignon/New York Film Festival
Backseat Film Festival
Bangkok International Film Festival
Barcelona Asian Film Festival
Belgrade International Film Festival
Berlin International Film Festival
Bermuda International Film Festival
Beverly Hills Film Festival
Big Muddy Film Festival
Black Maria Film and Video Festival
Blue Sky International Film Festival - Las
  Vegas
Boston Film Festival
Boston Gay & Lesbian Film & Video Festival
Boston International Festival Of Women's
  Cinema
Boston International Film Festival
Breckenridge Festival of Film
Brighton International Film Festival
Brussels International Festival of Fantasy
  Films
Bumbershoot 1 Reel Film Festival
Cabourg Festival of Romantic Films
Cairo International Film Festival

Calgary International Film Festival
Cambridge International Film Festival
Cannes Directors' Fortnight
Cannes International Film Festival
Cape Town World Cinema Festival
Cardiff Screen Festival
Cartagena International Film Festival
Cergy-Pontoise Short Film Festival
Cherbourg-Octeville Festival of Irish &
    British Film
Chicago Horror Film Festival
Chicago International Documentary Festival
Chicago International Film Festival
Chicago Underground Film Festival
Chrysler Million Dollar Film Festival
Cinéma du Réel International Festival of
    Visual Anthropology and Social
    Documentary Films
Cinema Epicuria Sonoma Valley Film Festival
CinemaReno
Cinematexas International Short Film &
    Video Festival
Cinequest San José Film Festival
CineVegas International Film Festival
Clermont-Ferrand Short Film Festival
Cleveland International Film Festival
CMJ Filmfest
Comic Con International Independent Film
    Festival
Copenhagen International Film Festival
Cork International Film Festival
Cracow Film Festival
Crossroads Film Festival
Cucalorus Film Festival
Dallas Video Festival
DancesWithFilms
Daytona Beach Film Festival
DC Independent Film Festival & Seminars
deadCenter Film Festival
Denver International Film Festival
Detroit Docs International Film Festival
DIY Film Festival
Docfest - New York International
    Documentary Festival
DocPoint Helsinki Documentary Film
    Festival
Donostia - San Sebastian International Film
    Festival
Dubrovnik International Film Festival
Durango Film Festival
Durban International Film Festival
Edinburgh International Film Festival
Edmonton International Film Festival
Emerald Eye Short Film Festival
Entrevues Belfort International Film Festival
Espoo Ciné International Film Festival
Euro Underground

Exground - Das Filmfest
Eye of the Beholder International Film
    Festival
Fantasia Film Festival
Fantasy Filmfest - International Film Festival
    for Science Fiction, Fiction, Horror and
    Thriller
Female Eye Film Festival
Festival of Deauville for American Cinema
    (Le Festival du Cinema Americain in
    Deauville)
Festival of European Films
Festival of Fantastic Films
Festival Of Nations
Film Fest New Haven
Film Nite
Filmfest Munchen
FirstGlance Hollywood Film Festival
FirstGlance Philadelphia Film Festival
Flickering Image Festival
Florida Film Festival
Fort Lauderdale International Film Festival
Freedom Film Festival
Fresno REEL Pride International Gay &
    Lesbian Film Festival
Gijon International Film Festival For Young
    People
Göteborg Film Festival
Great Plains Film Festival
H.P. Lovecraft Film Festival
Hamptons International Film Festival
Hawaii International Film Festival
Heartland Film Festival
Helsinki Film Festival - Love and Anarchy
Hi/Lo Film Festival
Hollywood Black Film Festival
Hollywood Film Festival
Hong Kong International Film Festival
    (HKIFF)
Hot Docs Canadian International
    Documentary Festival
Hot Springs Documentary Film Festival
Houston Annual Worldfest
Huesca International Short Film Festival
Human Rights Watch International Film
    Festival
Humboldt International Short Film Festival
HypeFest Film & Video Festival
IFP Market/Gotham Awards
Image+Nation Montreal's International
    Lesbian & Gay Film and Video Festival
Images Festival of Independent Film and
    Video
Independent Black Film Festival
Independent Exposure
Independent Film Festival of Boston
Indianapolis International Film Festival

Inside Out Lesbian and Gay Film Festival of
  Toronto
International Documentary Film Festival
  Amsterdam (IDFA)
International Festival of Films On Art (FIFA)
International Film Festival of India
International Leipzig Festival For
  Documentary and Animated Film
International Lesbian Film Festival
  Immaginaria
International Scientific Film Festival
International Short Film Festival Oberhausen
International TrickFilm Festival Stuttgart
International Wildlife Film Festival Montana
Internationales Filmfestival Mannheim-
  Heidelberg
Israel Film Festival
Jackson Hole Wildlife Film Festival
Jerusalem International Film Festival
Johns Hopkins Film Festival
Karlovy Vary International Film Festival
Kasseler Dokumentarfilm - Und Videofest
Kinofilm Manchester International Short
  Film Festival
Kyiv International Film Festival Molodist
Lake Placid Film Forum
Leeds Children and Young People's Film
  Festival
Leeds International Film Festival
Locarno International Film Festival
Long Island International Film Expo
Los Angeles International Short Film Festival
Los Angeles Latino International Film Festival
Lost Film Festival
Madcat Women's International Film Festival
Making Scenes Queer Film & Video Festival
Malibu International Film Festival
Mania Fest
Marco Island Film Festival
Margaret Mead Film Festival
Marseilles International Documentary Film
  Festival
Maryland Film Festival
Maui Film Festival
Melbourne Independent Filmmakers Festival
  - MIFF
Melbourne International Film Festival
Melbourne Queer Film & Video Festival
Message to Man International Documentary,
  Short and Animated Films Festival
Method Fest Independent Film Festival
Miami International Film Festival
Midnight Sun Film Festival
Mifed
Mill Valley Film Festival
Minneapolis/St Paul International Film
  Festival

Mix Brasil Festival of Sexual Diversity
Montreal International Festival of New
  Cinema and New Media
Montreal World Film Festival
Moondance International Film Festival
Mountainfilm Festival
Mumbai International Film Festival
Nantucket Film Festival
Napoli Film Festival
New Directors/New Films Festival
New Festival: New York Lesbian, Gay,
  Bisexual, & Transgender Film Festival
New Orleans Film Festival
New York Expo of Short Film and Video
New York Film Festival
New York Lesbian and Gay Experimental Film
  and Video Festival (Mix Festival)
New York Underground Film Festival
Newport Beach Film Festival
Next Frame Film Festival
NO BUDGET International Independent
  Film & Video Festival
NoDance Film Festival
Norrköping Film Festival Flimmer
North Carolina Jewish Film Festival
Norwegian International Film Festival
NSI FilmExchange Canadian Film Festival
Ohio Independent Film Festival
Oldenburg International Film Festival
One Take Film Festival
Onedotzero Digital Creativity Festival
Ottawa International Animation Festival
Out Far! - Annual Phoenix International
  Lesbian and Gay Film Festival
Out Takes
OUTFEST: Los Angeles Gay and Lesbian Film
  Festival
Palestine Film Festival Dreams Of A Nation
Palm Beach International Film Festival
Palm Springs International Film Festival
Philadelphia Film Festival
Philadelphia Fringe Festival
Philadelphia International Gay and Lesbian
  Film Festival
Phoenix Film Festival
Portland International Film Festival
Prix Jeunesse International
Queersicht - Schwul-lesbisches Filmfestival
  Bern
Raindance Film Festival
Red Bank International Film Festival
Rendezvous with Madness Film Festival
Rhode Island International Film Festival
Rio de Janeiro International Film Festival
River to River Florence Indian Film Festival
RiverRun International Film Festival
Rochester International Film Festival

Rome International Film Festival
Rotterdam International Film Festival
Sacramento International Gay and Lesbian
  Film Festival
San Diego Film Festival
San Francisco Independent Film Festival
San Francisco International Asian American
  Film Festival
San Francisco International Film Festival
San Francisco International Lesbian and Gay
  Film Festival
Santa Barbara International Film Festival
  (SBIFF)
Santa Monica Film Festival
São Paulo International Film Festival
Sarasota Film Festival
Savannah Film and Video Festival
Scottsdale International Film Festival
Seattle International Film Festival
Seattle Lesbian & Gay Film Festival
Seattle Underground Film Festival (The)
Sedona International Film Festival and
  Workshop
Shanghai International Film Festival
Sheffield International Documentary Festival
Short Shorts Film Festival
Sidewalk Moving Picture Film Festival
Silver Lake Film Festival
SILVERDOCS: AFI/Discovery Channel
  Documentary Festival
Singapore International Film Festival
Sitges International Film Festival of Catalonia
Slamdance International Film Festival
Sour Grapes Film Festival
Split Screen Film Festival
Sprockets Toronto International Film Festival
  for Children
Stockholm International Film Festival
Stony Brook Film Festival
Sundance Film Festival
SXSW: South By Southwest Film Festival
Sydney Film Festival
Tampere Film Festival
Tehran International Animation Festival
Telluride Film Festival
Telluride IndieFest
Temecula Valley International Film Festival
Thaw Video, Film, and Digital Media Festival
The Times bfi London Film Festival
Thessaloniki International Film Festival
Tiburon International Film Festival
TIE International Experimental Cinema
  Exposition
Tokyo International Film Festival
Torino Film Festival
Toronto International Film Festival
Toronto Jewish Film Festival

Trenton Film Festival
Tribeca Film Festival
Tromadance Film Festival
Tromsø International Film Festival
Turin International Gay & Lesbian Film
  Festival "from Sodom to Hollywood"
U.S. Comedy Arts Festival
United Nations Association Film Festival
United States Super 8 Film and Digital Video
  Festival
University of Oregon Queer Film Festival
Uppsala International Short Film Festival
USA Film Festival/Dallas
Vail Film Festival
Vancouver International Film Festival
Venice International Film Festival
Vermont International Film Festival
Verzaubert - International Queer Film
  Festival
Victoria Independent Film and Video Festival
Viennale - Vienna International Film Festival
Virginia Film Festival
Visions du Réel International Documentary
  Film Festival
Warsaw International Film Festival
Washington, DC International Film Festival—
  Filmfest DC
Waterfront Film Festival
Wellington Film Festival
West Virginia International Film Festival
Whistler Film Festival
Wilmington Independent Film Festival
Wine Country Film Festival
Wisconsin Film Festival
Woodstock Film Festival
World Community Film Festival
Yamagata International Documentary Film
  Festival
Yorkton Short Film Festival
Zagreb World Festival of Animated Films

MARKETS
American Film Market
Brainwash Movie Festival
Cairo International Film Festival
Cannes International Film Festival
Fantasy Filmfest - International Film Festival
  for Science Fiction, Fiction, Horror and
  Thriller
Hot Docs Canadian International
  Documentary Festival
IFP Market/Gotham Awards
Independent Black Film Festival
International Scientific Film Festival
International Short Film Festival Oberhausen
Internationales Filmfestival Mannheim-
  Heidelberg

Mifed
Moondance International Film Festival
Mumbai International Film Festival
Nashville Film Festival
NoDance Film Festival
Ohio Independent Film Festival
Out Far! - Annual Phoenix International
    Lesbian and Gay Film Festival
Philadelphia Fringe Festival
Rhode Island International Film Festival
Rotterdam International Film Festival
Shanghai International Film Festival
Sheffield International Documentary Festival
Silver Lake Film Festival
SXSW: South By Southwest Film Festival
Tampere Film Festival
Visions du Réel International Documentary
    Film Festival
Whistler Film Festival

MENTAL ILLNESS
Rendezvous with Madness Film Festival

MICROCINEMA
Brainwash Movie Festival
Cinematexas International Short Film &
    Video Festival
Independent Exposure
Johns Hopkins Film Festival
Lost Film Festival
Microcinefest
Minicine Visiting Filmmaker Series
NoDance Film Festival
Norrköping Film Festival Flimmer
Thaw Video, Film, and Digital Media Festival

MOUNTAIN SPORTS
Mountainfilm Festival
Whistler Film Festival

MULTI-CULTURAL
American Indian Film Festival
Barcelona Asian Film Festival
Heartland Film Festival
Hong Kong International Film Festival
    (HKIFF)
International Film Festival of India
Jerusalem International Film Festival
Making Scenes Queer Film & Video Festival
Mix Brasil Festival of Sexual Diversity
Palestine Film Festival Dreams Of A Nation
Toronto Jewish Film Festival
United Nations Association Film Festival
West Virginia International Film Festival
Wine Country Film Festival

MULTIMEDIA
Adelaide International Film Festival
Annecy International Animated Film Festival
Antimatter Festival of Underground Short
    Film & Video
Arcipelago International Festival of Short
    Films & New Images
Arizona State University Short Film and
    Video Festival
AtomFilms
Cinematexas International Short Film &
    Video Festival
Digital Days
Fantasia Film Festival
IFP Los Angeles Film Festival
Image+Nation Montreal's International
    Lesbian & Gay Film and Video Festival
Images Festival of Independent Film and
    Video
Lake Placid Film Forum
Mifed
Minicine Visiting Filmmaker Series
NoDance Film Festival
Northwest Film & Video Festival
Ohio Independent Film Festival
Onedotzero Digital Creativity Festival
Rhode Island International Film Festival
Santa Monica Film Festival
Thaw Video, Film, and Digital Media Festival
Whistler Film Festival
Wisconsin Film Festival

MUSIC VIDEO
Aspen Shortsfest

MUSIC VIDEOS
Adelaide International Film Festival
American Indian Film Festival
Annecy International Animated Film Festival
Antimatter Festival of Underground Short
    Film & Video
Arcipelago International Festival of Short
    Films & New Images
Backseat Film Festival
Blue Sky International Film Festival - Las
    Vegas
Female Eye Film Festival
Hawaii International Film Festival
Houston Annual Worldfest
HypeFest Film & Video Festival
International Short Film Festival Oberhausen
International Wildlife Film Festival Montana
MiniDV Film Festival
One Take Film Festival
ResFest Digital Film Festival
Sidewalk Moving Picture Film Festival

Sour Grapes Film Festival
SXSW: South By Southwest Film Festival
Woodstock Film Festival
ZoieFilms Festival

MUSIC-RELATED

CMJ Filmfest
Nashville Film Festival

NARRATIVE

30 Below Film & Video Competition
A.K.A. Shriekfest, The Los Angeles
    Horror/Science Fiction Film Festival &
    ScreenPlay Competition
Adelaide International Film Festival
African Film Festival
Algarve International Film Festival
Alpe Adria Cinema Trieste Film Festival
American Black Film Festival
American Film Institute (AFI) - Los Angeles
    International Film Festival
American Film Market
American Indian Film Festival
Angelus Awards Student Film Festival
AniFest Film Festival of Animated Films
Ankara International Film Festival
Ann Arbor Film Festival
Annecy International Animated Film Festival
Arcipelago International Festival of Short
    Films & New Images
Arizona International Film Festival
Aspen Shortsfest
Aspirations Film Festival
Athens International Film Festival
Atlanta Film Festival
Austin Film Festival
Avignon French Film Festival
Avignon/New York Film Festival
Backseat Film Festival
Bangkok International Film Festival
Barcelona Asian Film Festival
Belgrade International Film Festival
Berlin International Film Festival
Bermuda International Film Festival
Beverly Hills Film Festival
Big Bear Lake International Film Festival
Big Muddy Film Festival
Black Maria Film and Video Festival
Blue Sky International Film Festival - Las
    Vegas
Boston Film Festival
Boston Gay & Lesbian Film & Video Festival
Boston International Film Festival
Breckenridge Festival of Film
Brighton International Film Festival
Brooklyn Underground Film Festival
Brussels International Festival of Fantasy
    Films

Bumbershoot 1 Reel Film Festival
Cabourg Festival of Romantic Films
Cairo International Film Festival
Calgary International Film Festival
Cambridge International Film Festival
Cannes Directors' Fortnight
Cannes International Film Festival
Cape Town World Cinema Festival
Cardiff Screen Festival
Cartagena International Film Festival
Cergy-Pontoise Short Film Festival
Cherbourg-Octeville Festival of Irish &
    British Film
Chicago Horror Film Festival
Chicago International Film Festival
Chicago Underground Film Festival
Chrysler Million Dollar Film Festival
Cinema Epicuria Sonoma Valley Film Festival
CinemaReno
Cinematexas International Short Film &
    Video Festival
Cinequest San José Film Festival
CineVegas International Film Festival
Clermont-Ferrand Short Film Festival
CMJ Filmfest
Comic Con International Independent Film
    Festival
Copenhagen International Film Festival
Cracow Film Festival
Crossroads Film Festival
Dallas Video Festival
Daytona Beach Film Festival
DC Independent Film Festival & Seminars
deadCenter Film Festival
Deep Ellum Film Festival
Denver International Film Festival
DIY Film Festival
Donostia - San Sebastian International Film
    Festival
Dubrovnik International Film Festival
Durango Film Festival
Durban International Film Festival
Edinburgh International Film Festival
Edmonton International Film Festival
Entrevues Belfort International Film Festival
Espoo Ciné International Film Festival
Euro Underground
Exground - Das Filmfest
Eye of the Beholder International Film
    Festival
Fantasia Film Festival
Fantasy Filmfest - International Film Festival
    for Science Fiction, Fiction, Horror and
    Thriller
Female Eye Film Festival
Festival of Deauville for American Cinema
    (Le Festival du Cinema Americain in
    Deauville)

NSI FilmExchange Canadian Film Festival
Ohio Independent Film Festival
Oldenburg International Film Festival
One Take Film Festival
Onedotzero Digital Creativity Festival
Ottawa International Animation Festival
Out Takes
OUTFEST: Los Angeles Gay and Lesbian Film
    Festival
Palestine Film Festival Dreams Of A Nation
Palm Beach International Film Festival
Philadelphia Film Festival
Philadelphia Fringe Festival
Phoenix Film Festival
Portland International Film Festival
Queersicht - Schwul-lesbisches Filmfestival
    Bern
Raindance Film Festival
Red Bank International Film Festival
Reel Affirmations Film Festival
Rendezvous with Madness Film Festival
Rhode Island International Film Festival
Rio de Janeiro International Film Festival
River to River Florence Indian Film Festival
RiverRun International Film Festival
Rochester International Film Festival
Rome International Film Festival
Rotterdam International Film Festival
Sacramento International Gay and Lesbian
    Film Festival
San Antonio Underground Film Festival
San Diego Film Festival
San Francisco Independent Film Festival
San Francisco International Asian American
    Film Festival
San Francisco International Film Festival
San Francisco International Lesbian and Gay
    Film Festival
Santa Barbara International Film Festival
    (SBIFF)
Santa Monica Film Festival
São Paulo International Film Festival
Sarasota Film Festival
Savannah Film and Video Festival
Scottsdale International Film Festival
Screamfest Horror Film Festival
Seattle International Film Festival
Seattle Lesbian & Gay Film Festival
Seattle Underground Film Festival (The)
Sedona International Film Festival and
    Workshop
Shanghai International Film Festival
Short Shorts Film Festival
Sidewalk Moving Picture Film Festival
Silver Lake Film Festival
Singapore International Film Festival
Sitges International Film Festival of Catalonia

Slamdance International Film Festival
Smogdance Film Festival
Sour Grapes Film Festival
Split Screen Film Festival
Sprockets Toronto International Film Festival
    for Children
St. Louis International Film Festival
Stony Brook Film Festival
Sundance Film Festival
SXSW: South By Southwest Film Festival
Sydney Film Festival
Tampere Film Festival
Telluride Film Festival
Telluride IndieFest
Temecula Valley International Film Festival
Texas Film Festival
Thaw Video, Film, and Digital Media Festival
The Times bfi London Film Festival
Thessaloniki International Film Festival
Tiburon International Film Festival
Tokyo International Film Festival
Torino Film Festival
Toronto International Film Festival
Toronto Jewish Film Festival
Trenton Film Festival
Tribeca Film Festival
Tromadance Film Festival
Tromsø International Film Festival
Turin International Gay & Lesbian Film
    Festival "from Sodom to Hollywood"
U.S. Comedy Arts Festival
United States Super 8 Film and Digital Video
    Festival
University of Oregon Queer Film Festival
Uppsala International Short Film Festival
USA Film Festival/Dallas
Vail Film Festival
Vancouver International Film Festival
Vermont International Film Festival
Verzaubert - International Queer Film
    Festival
Victoria Independent Film and Video Festival
Viennale - Vienna International Film Festival
Warsaw International Film Festival
Washington, DC International Film Festival—
    Filmfest DC
Waterfront Film Festival
Wellington Film Festival
West Virginia International Film Festival
Whistler Film Festival
Williamstown Film Festival
Wilmington Independent Film Festival
Wine Country Film Festival
Woodstock Film Festival
World Community Film Festival
Yorkton Short Film Festival
Zombiedance Undead Film Fest

ONLiNE

AtomFilms
Bangkok International Film Festival
Big Film Shorts
Deep Ellum Film Festival
Independent Exposure
Lost Film Festival
Melbourne Queer Film & Video Festival
NoDance Film Festival
Ohio Independent Film Festival
Rhode Island International Film Festival
Santa Monica Film Festival
Sundance Film Festival
Thaw Video, Film, and Digital Media Festival
Triggerstreet.com Online Short Film Festival
ZoieFilms Festival

PACiFiC RiM

Hawaii International Film Festival

PEACE

Algarve International Film Festival
Human Rights Watch International Film
     Festival
Tromsø International Film Festival
Vermont International Film Festival
Wine Country Film Festival
World Community Film Festival

PERFORMANCE

Minicine Visiting Filmmaker Series
Mix Brasil Festival of Sexual Diversity
Northwest Film & Video Festival
ResFest Digital Film Festival
SXSW: South By Southwest Film Festival
U.S. Comedy Arts Festival
United Nations Association Film Festival

PSA (PUBLiC SERViCE ANNOUNCEMENT)

Houston Annual Worldfest
International Wildlife Film Festival Montana
ZoieFilms Festival

PXL

Cinematexas International Short Film &
     Video Festival
Independent Exposure
Madcat Women's International Film Festival
Minicine Visiting Filmmaker Series

RETRO CLASSiCS

Silver Lake Film Festival

RETRO SCiENCE

Silver Lake Film Festival

RETRO WESTERNS

Silver Lake Film Festival

ROCK AND ROLL

Backseat Film Festival
CMJ Filmfest
Microcinefest
Zombiedance Undead Film Fest

ROMANTiC

Cabourg Festival of Romantic Films

SCiENTiFiC

International Scientific Film Festival

SHORTS

30 Below Film & Video Competition
A.K.A. Shriekfest, The Los Angeles
     Horror/Science Fiction Film Festival &
     ScreenPlay Competition
Adelaide International Film Festival
Algarve International Film Festival
Alpe Adria Cinema Trieste Film Festival
American Black Film Festival
American Film Institute (AFI) - Los Angeles
     International Film Festival
American Indian Film Festival
Angelus Awards Student Film Festival
AniFest Film Festival of Animated Films
Ankara International Film Festival
Ann Arbor Film Festival
Annapolis Film Festival
Annecy International Animated Film Festival
Antimatter Festival of Underground Short
     Film & Video
Arcipelago International Festival of Short
     Films & New Images
Arizona International Film Festival
Arizona State University Short Film and
     Video Festival
Aspen Shortsfest
Aspirations Film Festival
Athens International Film Festival
Atlanta Film Festival
Austin Film Festival
Avignon French Film Festival
Avignon/New York Film Festival
Backseat Film Festival
Bangkok International Film Festival
Berlin International Film Festival
Bermuda International Film Festival
Beverly Hills Film Festival
Big Bear Lake International Film Festival

Big Muddy Film Festival
Black Maria Film and Video Festival
Blue Sky International Film Festival - Las
  Vegas
Boston Film Festival
Boston Gay & Lesbian Film & Video Festival
Boston International Festival Of Women's
  Cinema
Boston International Film Festival
Brainwash Movie Festival
Breckenridge Festival of Film
Brighton International Film Festival
Brooklyn Underground Film Festival
Brussels International Festival of Fantasy
  Films
Bumbershoot 1 Reel Film Festival
Cabourg Festival of Romantic Films
Cairo International Film Festival
Calgary International Film Festival
Cambridge International Film Festival
Cannes Directors' Fortnight
Cannes International Film Festival
Cardiff Screen Festival
Cartagena International Film Festival
Cergy-Pontoise Short Film Festival
Cherbourg-Octeville Festival of Irish &
  British Film
Chicago Horror Film Festival
Chicago International Documentary Festival
Chicago International Film Festival
Chicago Underground Film Festival
Chrysler Million Dollar Film Festival
Cinéma du Réel International Festival of
  Visual Anthropology and Social
  Documentary Films
Cinema Epicuria Sonoma Valley Film Festival
CinemaReno
Cinematexas International Short Film &
  Video Festival
Cinequest San José Film Festival
CineVegas International Film Festival
Clermont-Ferrand Short Film Festival
Cleveland International Film Festival
CMJ Filmfest
Comic Con International Independent Film
  Festival
Cork International Film Festival
Cracow Film Festival
Crossroads Film Festival
Cucalorus Film Festival
Dallas Video Festival
DancesWithFilms
Daytona Beach Film Festival
DC Independent Film Festival & Seminars
deadCenter Film Festival
Deep Ellum Film Festival
Denver International Film Festival

Detroit Docs International Film Festival
DIY Film Festival
Docfest - New York International
  Documentary Festival
DocPoint Helsinki Documentary Film
  Festival
Dragon Con Independent Short Film Festival
Dubrovnik International Film Festival
Durango Film Festival
Durban International Film Festival
Edinburgh International Film Festival
Edmonton International Film Festival
Entrevues Belfort International Film Festival
Espoo Ciné International Film Festival
Euro Underground
Exground - Das Filmfest
Eye of the Beholder International Film
  Festival
Fantasia Film Festival
Fantasy Filmfest - International Film Festival
  for Science Fiction, Fiction, Horror and
  Thriller
Female Eye Film Festival
Festival of Deauville for American Cinema
  (Le Festival du Cinema Americain in
  Deauville)
Festival of Fantastic Films
Festival Of Nations
Film Fest New Haven
Film Nite
Filmfest Munchen
FirstGlance Hollywood Film Festival
FirstGlance Philadelphia Film Festival
Flickering Image Festival
Florida Film Festival
Fort Lauderdale International Film Festival
Free Film Festival Fitchburg (The F4)
Freedom Film Festival
Fresno REEL Pride International Gay &
  Lesbian Film Festival
Gen Art Film Festival
Gijon International Film Festival For Young
  People
Göteborg Film Festival
Great Plains Film Festival
H.P. Lovecraft Film Festival
Hamptons International Film Festival
Hawaii International Film Festival
Heartland Film Festival
Helsinki Film Festival - Love and Anarchy
Hi/Lo Film Festival
Hollywood Black Film Festival
Hollywood Film Festival
Hong Kong International Film Festival
  (HKIFF)
Honolulu Rainbow Film Festival
Hot Docs Canadian International
  Documentary Festival

Philadelphia Fringe Festival
Philadelphia International Gay and Lesbian
Film Festival
Phoenix Film Festival
Portland International Film Festival
Queersicht - Schwul-lesbisches Filmfestival
Bern
Raindance Film Festival
Red Bank International Film Festival
Reel Affirmations Film Festival
Rendezvous with Madness Film Festival
ResFest Digital Film Festival
Rhode Island International Film Festival
Rio de Janeiro International Film Festival
River to River Florence Indian Film Festival
RiverRun International Film Festival
Rochester International Film Festival
Rome International Film Festival
Rotterdam International Film Festival
Sacramento International Gay and Lesbian
Film Festival
San Antonio Underground Film Festival
San Diego Film Festival
San Francisco Independent Film Festival
San Francisco International Asian American
Film Festival
San Francisco International Film Festival
San Francisco International Lesbian and Gay
Film Festival
Santa Barbara International Film Festival
(SBIFF)
Santa Monica Film Festival
São Paulo International Film Festival
Sarasota Film Festival
Savannah Film and Video Festival
Screamfest Horror Film Festival
Seattle International Film Festival
Seattle Lesbian & Gay Film Festival
Seattle Underground Film Festival (The)
Sedona International Film Festival and
Workshop
Sheffield International Documentary Festival
Short Shorts Film Festival
Sidewalk Moving Picture Film Festival
Silver Lake Film Festival
SILVERDOCS: AFI/Discovery Channel
Documentary Festival
Singapore International Film Festival
Sitges International Film Festival of Catalonia
Slamdance International Film Festival
Smogdance Film Festival
Sour Grapes Film Festival
Split Screen Film Festival
Sprockets Toronto International Film Festival
for Children
St. Louis International Film Festival
Stockholm International Film Festival

Stony Brook Film Festival
Sundance Film Festival
SXSW: South By Southwest Film Festival
Sydney Film Festival
Tampere Film Festival
Tehran International Animation Festival
Telluride Film Festival
Telluride IndieFest
Temecula Valley International Film Festival
Texas Film Festival
Thaw Video, Film, and Digital Media Festival
The Times bfi London Film Festival
Thessaloniki International Film Festival
Tiburon International Film Festival
TIE International Experimental Cinema
Exposition
Torino Film Festival
Toronto International Film Festival
Toronto Jewish Film Festival
Trenton Film Festival
Tribeca Film Festival
Triggerstreet.com Online Short Film Festival
Tromadance Film Festival
Tromsø International Film Festival
Turin International Gay & Lesbian Film
Festival "from Sodom to Hollywood"
U.S. Comedy Arts Festival
United Nations Association Film Festival
United States Super 8 Film and Digital Video
Festival
University of Oregon Queer Film Festival
Uppsala International Short Film Festival
USA Film Festival/Dallas
Vail Film Festival
Vancouver International Film Festival
Venice International Film Festival
Vermont International Film Festival
Verzaubert - International Queer Film
Festival
Victoria Independent Film and Video Festival
Viennale - Vienna International Film Festival
Visions du Réel International Documentary
Film Festival
Washington, DC International Film Festival—
Filmfest DC
Wellington Film Festival
Whistler Film Festival
Williamstown Film Festival
Wilmington Independent Film Festival
Wine Country Film Festival
Wisconsin Film Festival
Woodstock Film Festival
World Community Film Festival
Yorkton Short Film Festival
Zagreb World Festival of Animated Films
ZoieFilms Festival
Zombiedance Undead Film Fest

SiLENT
Midnight Sun Film Festival

SPORTS
NO BUDGET International Independent Film & Video Festival

STUDENT
30 Below Film & Video Competition
A.K.A. Shriekfest, The Los Angeles Horror/Science Fiction Film Festival & ScreenPlay Competition
Angelus Awards Student Film Festival
AniFest Film Festival of Animated Films
Ann Arbor Film Festival
Annecy International Animated Film Festival
Antimatter Festival of Underground Short Film & Video
Arizona State University Short Film and Video Festival
Aspen Shortsfest
Aspirations Film Festival
Atlanta Film Festival
Austin Film Festival
Big Bear Lake International Film Festival
Big Muddy Film Festival
Blue Sky International Film Festival - Las Vegas
Breckenridge Festival of Film
Brighton International Film Festival
Bumbershoot 1 Reel Film Festival
Calgary International Film Festival
Cergy-Pontoise Short Film Festival
Cherbourg-Octeville Festival of Irish & British Film
Chicago International Film Festival
Cinema Epicuria Sonoma Valley Film Festival
Cinematexas International Short Film & Video Festival
Crossroads Film Festival
Daytona Beach Film Festival
deadCenter Film Festival
Deep Ellum Film Festival
Denver International Film Festival
Detroit Docs International Film Festival
Docfest - New York International Documentary Festival
Dragon Con Independent Short Film Festival
Durban International Film Festival
Edmonton International Film Festival
Festival of Fantastic Films
Filmfest Munchen
FirstGlance Hollywood Film Festival
FirstGlance Philadelphia Film Festival
Florida Film Festival
Fort Lauderdale International Film Festival
Free Film Festival Fitchburg (The F4)

Fresno REEL Pride International Gay & Lesbian Film Festival
Gijon International Film Festival For Young People
Great Plains Film Festival
H.P. Lovecraft Film Festival
Hamptons International Film Festival
Heartland Film Festival
Hollywood Black Film Festival
Houston Annual Worldfest
Huesca International Short Film Festival
Humboldt International Short Film Festival
IFP Los Angeles Film Festival
International TrickFilm Festival Stuttgart
International Wildlife Film Festival Montana
Internationales Filmfestival Mannheim-Heidelberg
Israel Film Festival
Jerusalem International Film Festival
Johns Hopkins Film Festival
Kyiv International Film Festival Molodist
Lake Placid Film Forum
Locarno International Film Festival
Long Island International Film Expo
Los Angeles International Short Film Festival
Lost Film Festival
Madcat Women's International Film Festival
Marco Island Film Festival
Melbourne Queer Film & Video Festival
Message to Man International Documentary, Short and Animated Films Festival
Mill Valley Film Festival
Montreal World Film Festival
Mumbai International Film Festival
Nantucket Film Festival
Nashville Film Festival
Newport Beach Film Festival
Next Frame Film Festival
Norrköping Film Festival Flimmer
Northwest Film & Video Festival
Ohio Independent Film Festival
Palm Beach International Film Festival
Philadelphia Film Festival
Phoenix Film Festival
Rhode Island International Film Festival
RiverRun International Film Festival
Rochester International Film Festival
San Francisco International Film Festival
Savannah Film and Video Festival
Sheffield International Documentary Festival
Sidewalk Moving Picture Film Festival
Silver Lake Film Festival
Split Screen Film Festival
Sprockets Toronto International Film Festival for Children
St. Louis International Film Festival
Stockholm International Film Festival

SXSW: South By Southwest Film Festival
Telluride Film Festival
Temecula Valley International Film Festival
Texas Film Festival
Thaw Video, Film, and Digital Media Festival
Tribeca Film Festival
Tromadance Film Festival
University of Oregon Queer Film Festival
Vail Film Festival
Victoria Independent Film and Video Festival
West Virginia International Film Festival
Williamstown Film Festival
Woodstock Film Festival
Zagreb World Festival of Animated Films

SUPER 8/8MM

Antimatter Festival of Underground Short
 Film & Video
Arizona State University Short Film and
 Video Festival
Cinematexas International Short Film &
 Video Festival
Cucalorus Film Festival
Film Nite
Hollywood Black Film Festival
Images Festival of Independent Film and
 Video
Independent Exposure
Johns Hopkins Film Festival
Madcat Women's International Film Festival
Marco Island Film Festival
Melbourne Queer Film & Video Festival
Minicine Visiting Filmmaker Series
Northwest Film & Video Festival
Ohio Independent Film Festival
ResFest Digital Film Festival
Seattle Underground Film Festival (The)
Thaw Video, Film, and Digital Media Festival
TIE International Experimental Cinema
 Exposition
Tromadance Film Festival
United States Super 8 Film and Digital Video
 Festival

TELEVISION

AniFest Film Festival of Animated Films
Annecy International Animated Film Festival
Belgrade International Film Festival
Brainwash Movie Festival
Cardiff Screen Festival
Cartagena International Film Festival
Filmfest Munchen
Houston Annual Worldfest
IFP Market/Gotham Awards
International Wildlife Film Festival Montana
Israel Film Festival
Jerusalem International Film Festival

Mifed
Native American Film & Video Festival
Prix Jeunesse International
Rendezvous with Madness Film Festival
Shanghai International Film Festival
Vail Film Festival
ZoieFilms Festival

THRILLER

A.K.A. Shriekfest, The Los Angeles
 Horror/Science Fiction Film Festival &
 ScreenPlay Competition
Chicago Horror Film Festival
Dragon Con Independent Short Film Festival
Fantasy Filmfest - International Film Festival
 for Science Fiction, Fiction, Horror and
 Thriller
Festival of Fantastic Films
H.P. Lovecraft Film Festival
Mania Fest
Zombiedance Undead Film Fest

TOURING

African Film Festival
Ann Arbor Film Festival
Antimatter Festival of Underground Short
 Film & Video
Arizona State University Short Film and
 Video Festival
Backseat Film Festival
Bangkok International Film Festival
Black Maria Film and Video Festival
Brainwash Movie Festival
Cherbourg-Octeville Festival of Irish &
 British Film
Chrysler Million Dollar Film Festival
Euro Underground
Fantasy Filmfest - International Film Festival
 for Science Fiction, Fiction, Horror and
 Thriller
Festival of European Films
Hi/Lo Film Festival
Human Rights Watch International Film
 Festival
Independent Exposure
Israel Film Festival
Los Angeles International Short Film Festival
Lost Film Festival
Madcat Women's International Film Festival
Margaret Mead Film Festival
Melbourne International Film Festival
Microcinefest
Minicine Visiting Filmmaker Series
Mix Brasil Festival of Sexual Diversity
Mountainfilm Festival
Next Frame Film Festival
NoDance Film Festival

Northwest Film & Video Festival
Out Takes
ResFest Digital Film Festival
Rochester International Film Festival
San Francisco International Asian American
    Film Festival
Santa Monica Film Festival
Short Shorts Film Festival
Sydney Film Festival
Tromadance Film Festival

UNDERGROUND
Antimatter Festival of Underground Short
    Film & Video
Arizona State University Short Film and
    Video Festival
Brooklyn Underground Film Festival
Chicago Underground Film Festival
Cinematexas International Short Film &
    Video Festival
Cucalorus Film Festival
Deep Ellum Film Festival
Euro Underground
Exground - Das Filmfest
Film Nite
Fort Lauderdale International Film Festival
Free Film Festival Fitchburg (The F4)
Gijon International Film Festival For Young
    People
IFP Los Angeles Film Festival
Independent Exposure
Johns Hopkins Film Festival
Lost Film Festival
Madcat Women's International Film Festival
Melbourne Queer Film & Video Festival
Microcinefest
Minicine Visiting Filmmaker Series
New York Underground Film Festival
NO BUDGET International Independent
    Film & Video Festival
NoDance Film Festival
Ohio Independent Film Festival
Rhode Island International Film Festival
San Antonio Underground Film Festival
Seattle Underground Film Festival (The)
Silver Lake Film Festival
Singapore International Film Festival
Thaw Video, Film, and Digital Media Festival
Tromadance Film Festival
University of Oregon Queer Film Festival
Wisconsin Film Festival

VIDEO
30 Below Film & Video Competition
Angelus Awards Student Film Festival
Antimatter Festival of Underground Short
    Film & Video

Arizona State University Short Film and
    Video Festival
Brainwash Movie Festival
Cinematexas International Short Film &
    Video Festival
Cork International Film Festival
Cucalorus Film Festival
Dallas Video Festival
DancesWithFilms
Deep Ellum Film Festival
Euro Underground
Gen Art Film Festival
Hollywood Black Film Festival
IFP Los Angeles Film Festival
Image+Nation Montreal's International
    Lesbian & Gay Film and Video Festival
Images Festival of Independent Film and
    Video
Independent Exposure
International Short Film Festival Oberhausen
Kasseler Dokumentarfilm - Und Videofest
Lake Placid Film Forum
Lost Film Festival
Madcat Women's International Film Festival
Marco Island Film Festival
Melbourne Queer Film & Video Festival
Microcinefest
Minicine Visiting Filmmaker Series
Moondance International Film Festival
New Orleans Film Festival
Norrköping Film Festival Flimmer
Northwest Film & Video Festival
Ohio Independent Film Festival
Out Far! - Annual Phoenix International
    Lesbian and Gay Film Festival
Portland International Film Festival
Rhode Island International Film Festival
Sacramento International Gay and Lesbian
    Film Festival
San Francisco International Film Festival
Seattle Underground Film Festival (The)
Silver Lake Film Festival
Thaw Video, Film, and Digital Media Festival
Tromadance Film Festival
Turin International Gay & Lesbian Film
    Festival "from Sodom to Hollywood"
United States Super 8 Film and Digital Video
    Festival
University of Oregon Queer Film Festival
USA Film Festival/Dallas
Victoria Independent Film and Video Festival
Whistler Film Festival
Wisconsin Film Festival
Yamagata International Documentary Film
    Festival
Yorkton Short Film Festival

ViDEO GAMES
Onedotzero Digital Creativity Festival

ViSUAL EFFECTS
Onedotzero Digital Creativity Festival

WEB PROJECTS
Annecy International Animated Film Festival
Arcipelago International Festival of Short
    Films & New Images
AtomFilms
Digital Days
Onedotzero Digital Creativity Festival
Prix Jeunesse International

WEiRD
Antimatter Festival of Underground Short
    Film & Video
Arizona State University Short Film and
    Video Festival
Brainwash Movie Festival
Chicago Underground Film Festival
Cinematexas International Short Film &
    Video Festival
Cucalorus Film Festival
Deep Ellum Film Festival
Euro Underground
Exground - Das Filmfest
Film Nite
Free Film Festival Fitchburg (The F4)
Gen Art Film Festival
IFP Los Angeles Film Festival
Independent Exposure
Johns Hopkins Film Festival
Lost Film Festival
Madcat Women's International Film Festival
Melbourne Queer Film & Video Festival
Microcinefest
Northwest Film & Video Festival
Ohio Independent Film Festival
Rhode Island International Film Festival
Seattle Underground Film Festival (The)
Silver Lake Film Festival
Thaw Video, Film, and Digital Media Festival
Tromadance Film Festival
University of Oregon Queer Film Festival
Williamstown Film Festival

WiLDLiFE
International Wildlife Film Festival Montana
Jackson Hole Wildlife Film Festival

WOMEN
Antimatter Festival of Underground Short
    Film & Video
Arizona State University Short Film and
    Video Festival
Bermuda International Film Festival
Beverly Hills Film Festival
Boston International Festival Of Women's
    Cinema
Cinematexas International Short Film &
    Video Festival
Cork International Film Festival
DancesWithFilms
DC Independent Film Festival & Seminars
Fantasia Film Festival
Female Eye Film Festival
Fort Lauderdale International Film Festival
Gen Art Film Festival
Hollywood Black Film Festival
IFP Los Angeles Film Festival
Independent Exposure
Lake Placid Film Forum
Lost Film Festival
Madcat Women's International Film Festival
Melbourne Queer Film & Video Festival
Miami International Film Festival
Moondance International Film Festival
Ohio Independent Film Festival
Oldenburg International Film Festival
Rhode Island International Film Festival
Seattle International Film Festival
Sedona International Film Festival and
    Workshop
Tromadance Film Festival
Victoria Independent Film and Video Festival
Wisconsin Film Festival

WORKS iN PROGRESS
American Black Film Festival
Deep Ellum Film Festival
IFP Market/Gotham Awards

WORLD
Blue Sky International Film Festival - Las
    Vegas

HOLLYWOOD CREATiVE DiRECTORY
POWER iNViTATiON LiST FOR DiSTRiBUTiON,
FESTiVAL SCREENiNGS, AND PARTiES

Alliance Atlantis
121 Bloor Street East
Toronto, ON M4W 3M5 Canada
416-967-1174
Patrick Roy

Attitude Films
300 Mercer Street, #26L
New York, NY 10003
212-995-9008
Andrew Chang

Castle Hill Productions
36 W. 25th Street, 2nd Floor
New York, NY 10010
212-242-1500
Mel Maron

Dimension Films
375 Greenwich St.
New York, NY 10013
212-941-3800
Bob Weinstein, Andrew Rona

Fine Line Features
116 N. Robertson Blvd., #200
Los Angeles, CA 90048
310-854-5811
Mark Ordesky, Ileen Maisel

First Look Pictures
8000 Sunset Blvd. East Penthouse
Los Angeles, CA 90046
323-337-1000
Bill Bromley, Liz Mackiewicz

First Run Features
153 Waverly Place
New York, NY 10014
212-243-0600
Seymour Wishman

Focus Features
65 Bleecker Street, 2nd Fl.
New York, NY 10012
212-539-4000
David Linde, James Schamus

Fox Searchlight
10201 Pico Blvd.
Los Angeles, CA 90035
310-369-1000
Stephanie Gilula

Franchise Pictures
8228 Sunset Blvd. Suite 305
Los Angeles, CA 90046
323-848-3444
Elie Samaha, Mimi Steinbauer

Gold Circle Releasing
9420 Wilshire Blvd, Suite 250
Beverly Hills, CA 90212
310-278-4800
Paul Brooks, David Garber

HBO Films
2049 Century Park East, 41st Floor
Los Angeles, CA 90067
310-201-9300
Colin Callendar, Sheila Nevins,
Jonathan Miller

THE ULTIMATE FILM FESTIVAL SURVIVAL GUIDE

IFC Films
11 Penn Plaza, 15th Floor
New York, NY 10001
646-273-7200
Johnathan Sehring

Jeff Dowd & Associates
3200 Airport Ave., Suite 1
Santa Monica, CA 90405
310-572-1500
Jeff Dowd

Keystone Entertainment
23410 Civic Center Way
Malibu, CA 90265
310-317-4883
Michael Strange

Kino International
333 West 39th Street, #503
New York, NY 10018
212-629-6880
Donald Krim

Koch Entertainment
22 Harbor Park Drive
Port Washington, NY 11050
516-484-1000
Michael Rosenberg

Lakeshore International
5555 Melrose Ave.
Gloria Swanson Building, 4th Floor
Hollywood, CA 90038
323-956-4222
Tom Rosenberg, Bic Tran

Lions Gate Films
2700 Colorado Ave.
Santa Monica, CA 90404
310-449-9200
212-966-4670
Tom Ortenberg, Michael Paseornek

Lot 47 Films
13 Laight Street, 6th Floor
New York, NY 10011
212-925-7800
Gregory Williams

Media 8 Entertainment
1875 Century Park East Suite 2000
Los Angeles, CA 90067
310-226-8300
Mark Damon

Miramax Films
375 Greenwich St.
New York, NY 10013
212-941-3800
Harvey Weinstein

Myriad Pictures
405 S. Beverly Drive, 5th Floor
Beverly Hills, CA 90212
310-279-4000
Kirk D'Amico, J.C. Rappaport

Newmarket Films
597 Fifth Ave. 7th Floor
New York, NY 10017
212-303-1700
Bob Berney

Palm Pictures
601 W. 26th Street, 11th Floor
New York, NY 10001
212 320-3678
Chris Blackwell, David Koh

Paramount Classics
5555 Melrose Ave. Chevalier,
Suite 215
Hollywood, CA 90038
323-956-2000
Ruth Vitale, Joe Matukewicz

Seventh Art Releasing
7551 Sunset Blvd. #104
Los Angeles, CA 90046
323-845-1455
Udy Epstein, Stephanie Kral

Showtime Networks
10880 Wilshire Blvd., Suite 1600
Los Angeles, CA 90024
310-234-5200
Matthew Duda

Sloss Law Office/Cinetic Media
555 W. 25th Street
New York, NY 10001
212-627-9898
John Sloss

Sony Pictures Classics
550 Madison Ave., 8th Floor
Nw York, NY 10022
212-833-8833
Michael Barker, Dylan Leiner

Strand Releasing
1460 Fourth St., #302
Santa Monica, CA 90401
310-395-5002
Marcus Hu, Jon Gerrans

Stratosphere Entertainment
767 Fifth Ave., #4700
New York, NY 10153
212-605-1010
Angela Schapiro

Sundance Channel
1633 Broadway, 8th Floor
New York, NY 10019
212-654-1500
Christian Vesper

ThinkFilm
155 Ave. of the Americas, 7th Floor
New York, NY 10013
2646-214-7908
Jeff Sackman, Randy Manis

Troma
733 Ninth Avenue
New York, NY 10019
212-757-4555
Lloyd Kaufman

Tulchin Entertainment
11377 W. Olympic Blvd., 2nd Fl.
Los Angeles, CA 90064
310-914-7979
Harris Tulchin

Zeitgeist Films Limited
247 Centre Street, 2nd Floor
New York, NY 10013
212-274-1989
Emily Russo, Nancy Gerstman

Zenpix, Inc.
506 Santa Monica Blvd., Suit 210
Santa Monica 90401
310-395-3500
Susan Jackson, Todd Olsson

Literary Agents for Writers and Directors

Above the Line Agency
9200 Sunset Blvd., Suite 804
Los Angeles, CA 90069
310-859-6115

The Agency
11350 Ventura Blvd., Suite 100
Studio City, CA 91604
818-754-2000

APA/Agency for the Performing Arts
9200 Sunset Blvd., #900
Los Angeles, CA 90069
310-888-4200

The Artists Agency
1180 S. Beverly Drive, Suite 400
Los Angeles, CA 90035
310-277-7779

Becsey-Wisdom-Kalajian
9200 Sunset Blvd., #820
Los Angeles, CA 90069
310-550-0535

Broder • Webb • Chervin • Silberman Agency
9242 Beverly Blvd., #200
Beverly Hills, CA 90210
310-281-3400

Don Buchwald & Associates
10 E 44th St.
New York, NY 10017
212-867-1200

Creative Artists Agency
9830 Wilshire Blvd.
Beverly Hills, CA 90212-1825
310-288-4545

Endeavor
9701 Wilshire Blvd., 10th Fl.
Beverly Hills, CA 90212
310-248-2000

The Gage Group
14724 Ventura Blvd., Suite 505
Sherman Oaks, CA 91403
818-905-3800

The Gersh Agency
232 N. Canon Dr.
Beverly Hills, CA 90210
310-274-6611

Innovative Artists
1505 Tenth Street
Santa Monica, CA 90401
310-656-0400

International Creative Mgmt.
8942 Wilshire Blvd.
Beverly Hills, CA 90211
310-550-4000

Metropolitan Talent Agency
4526 Wilshire Blvd.
Los Angeles, CA 90010
323-857-4500

William Morris Agency
151 El Camino Dr.
Beverly Hills, CA 90212
310-859-4000

Paradigm
360 N. Crescent Dr.
North Building
Beverly Hills, CA 90210
310-288-8000

Preferred Artists
16633 Ventura Blvd., #1421
Encino, CA 91436
818-990-0305

Jim Preminger Agency
450 N. Roxbury Dr., PH 1050
Beverly Hills, CA 90210
310-860-1116

Shapiro-Lichtman, Inc.
8827 Beverly Blvd., #C
Los Angeles, CA 90048
310-859-8877

United Talent Agency
9560 Wilshire Blvd., #500
Beverly Hills, CA 90212
213-273-6700

FiLMMAKER RESOURCES

Screening Rooms—
Los Angeles

Academy of Motion Pictures Arts & Sciences
8949 Wilshire Blvd.
Beverly Hills, CA
310-274-3000

Academy of Television Arts & Sciences
5220 Lankershim Blvd.
North Hollywood, CA
818-754-2800
www.emmys.org

Charles Aidikoff Screening Room
150 S. Rodeo Dr.
Beverly Hills, CA
310-274-0866
www.leaderhollywoodformat.com

American Film Institute
2021 N. Western Ave
Los Angeles, CA
323-856-7681
www.afi.com

Artisan Theatre/Lions Gate
2700 Colorado Ave.
Santa Monica, CA
310-255-4000

Bendetti Mobile, Inc.
1549 11th St.
Santa Monica, CA
310-587-3377/888-834-8439
www.benettimobil.com

Big Time Picture Company
12210-1/2 Nebraska Ave.
Los Angeles, CA
310-207-0921
www.bigtimepic.com

Clarity Theatre
100 N. Crescent Dr.
Beverly Hills, CA
310-385-4092

Culver Studios
9336 W. Washington Blvd.
Culver City, CA
310-202-3253
310-840-8589
www.theculverstudios.com

Directors Guild of America
7920 Sunset Blvd.
Los Angeles, CA
310-289-2021
310-289-2023
www.dga.org

The Walt Disney Studios
500 S. Buena Vista St.
Burbank, CA
818-560-5506
www.disney.go.com/studiooperations

Harmony Gold Preview House
7655 Sunset Blvd.
Los Angeles, CA
323-851-4900

ICS Services, Inc.
920 Allen Ave.
Glendale, CA
818-242-3839
www.icsfilm.com

The Lot/Warner Bros.
1041 N. Formosa Ave.
Los Angeles, CA
818-954-2144
www.wbpostproduction.
warnerbros.com

Metro-Goldwyn-Mayer
2500 Broadway St.
Santa Monica, CA
310-449-3000
www.mgm.com

New Deal Studios
4121 Redwood Ave.
Los Angeles, CA
310-578-9929
www.newdealstudios.com

Ocean Screening Room
1401 Ocean Ave.
Santa Monica, CA
310-576-1831

Pacific Design Center
8687 Melrose Ave., 2nd Fl..
Los Angeles, CA
310-360-6415
www.pacificdesigncenter.com

Paramount Pictures
5555 Melrose Ave.
Los Angeles, CA
323-956-5000
www.paramount.com

Raleigh Studios
5300 Melrose Ave.
650 N. Bronson Ave.
Los Angeles, CA
323-871-5649

Sony Pictures Studios
10202 W. Washington Blvd.
Culver City, CA
310-244-5721
www.spe.sony.com

Sunset Screening Room
8730 Sunset Blvd.
Los Angeles, CA
310-652-1933

2212 W. Magnolia Blvd.
Burbank, CA
818-556-5190

Todd-AO Studios West
3000 W. Olympic Blvd.
Santa Monica, CA
310-315-5000

Twentieth Century Fox
10201 W. Pico Blvd.
Los Angeles, CA
310-369-2406
www.fox.com

Universal Studios
100 Universal City Plaza
Universal City, CA
818-777-1000
www.universalstudios.com

Warner Bros. Studio Facilities
4000 Warner Blvd.
Burbank, CA
818-954-2144
www.wbpostproduction.
warnerbros.com

Wilshire Screening Room
8670 Wilshire Blvd.
Los Angeles, CA
310-659-3875
www.studioscreenings.com

Writers Guild Theatre
135 S. Doheny Dr.
Los Angeles, CA
323-782-4525
www.wga.org

Screening Rooms— New York

Alliance Français
22 E. 60th St.
New York, NY
212-355-6100
www.fiaf.org

Anthology Film Archives
32 Second Ave.
New York, NY
212-505-5181
www.anthologyfilmarchives.org

Broadway Screening Room
1619 Broadway, 5th Fl.
New York, NY
212-307-0990
www.mybsr.com

Disney Screening Room
500 Park Ave.
New York, NY
212-593-8900

Fox Screening Room
1211 Avenue of the Americas
New York, NY
212-556-2406

Grand Screen
Tribeca Grand, 2 Sixth Ave.
New York, NY
212-519-6600
www.tribecagrand.com

Magno
729 Seventh Ave.
New York, NY
212-302-2505
www.magnosoundandvideo.com

MGM
1350 Sixth Ave.
New York, NY
212-708-0300

Planet Hollywood Screening Room
1540 Broadway
New York, NY
212-265-2404

Quad Cinemas
34 W. 13th St.
New York, NY
212-255-8800
www.quadcinema.com

Walter Reade Theater
165 W. 65th St.
New York, NY
212-875-5608
www.filmlinc.com

Sony Pictures
550 Madison Ave.
212-833-7654
Graham Smith

Tribeca Screening Room
375 Greenwich St.
New York, NY
212-941-4000
www.tribecafilm.com

Warner Bros.
1271 Sixth Ave.
New York, NY
212-484-8080

Lab Services/Transfers (Film and Tape)

Big Time Dailies
6464 Sunset Blvd., Suite 1090
Hollywood, CA 90028
323-464-0616

Forde Motion Picture Labs
306 Fairview Ave. North
Seattle, WA 98109
206-682-2510

DuArt Film and Video
245 West 55th Street
New York, NY 10019
212-757-4580

Film Score/ Soundtrack Advice

ASCAP
7920 Sunset Blvd., Suite 300
Los Angeles, CA 90046
323-883-1000
Nancy Knutsen

BMI
8730 Sunset Blvd., 3rd Floor
Los Angeles, CA 90069
310-659-9109
Doreen Ringer-Ross

Production and Screenwriting Software

The Writers Store
2040 Westwood Blvd.
Los Angeles, CA 90025
800-272-8927
310-441-5151

Closed-Captioning, Subtitling, Translations, and Dubbing

TM Systems
12711 Ventura Blvd., #270
Studio City, CA 91604
818-508-3400
www.tm-systems.com
Deeny Kaplan

TM Productions
3348 Overland Ave.
Los Angeles, CA 90034
310-815-9922
david.wiggins@tmproductions.tv
David Wiggins

ODDS OF GETTING INTO TOP TEN FILM FESTIVALS

American Film Institute (AFI) - Los Angeles Intl. Film Festival ....1 in 18
Berlin International Film Festival ....1 in 50
Cannes International Film Festival ....1 in 100
IFP Los Angeles Film Festival ....1 in 12
Seattle International Film Festival ....1 in 20
SXSW: South By Southwest Film Festival ....1 in 20
Sundance Film Festival ....1 in 25
Telluride Film Festival ....1 in 40
Toronto International Film Festival ....1 in 9
Tribeca Film Festival ....1 in 50 (competition), 1 in 13 overall

Overall Odds of Acceptance into a Top Ten Festival............................1 in 25

IFP INDEPENDENT SPIRIT AWARD ELIGIBLE FESTIVALS

Screening at any one of these seven festivals will make one eligible to be nominated for an Independent Spirit Award.

IFP Los Angeles Film Festival
New Directors/New Films Festival
New York Film Festival
Seattle Intl. Film Festival
Sundance Film Festival
Telluride Film Festival
Toronto Intl. Film Festival

ACADEMY AWARDS SHORT FILM FESTIVALS QUALIFICATIONS LIST

To qualify your short film for an Academy Award, the film must have participated in a "recognized" competitive film festival from the list below and must have won the "Best-in-Category Award." Proof of award must be submitted with the film print. Television or Internet exhibition anywhere does not disqualify a film, provided such exhibition occurs after its Los Angeles theatrical release, or after receiving its festival award. The festivals/events listed may change, so get the latest list and more info about how to submit your film for Oscar consideration at www.oscars.org

Ann Arbor (Michigan) Film Festival
Annecy Festival Intl. Du Cinema D'animation
Aspen Shortsfest
Athens (Ohio) Intl. Film Festival
Atlanta Film Festival
Austin Film Festival
Berlin Intl. Film Festival
Bilbao Intl. Festival of Documentary & Short Films
Black Maria Film Festival
British Academy of Film and Television Arts (BAFTA) Awards
Cannes Festival Intl. Du Film
Cartagena Intl. Film Festival
Chicago Intl. Children's Film Festival
Chicago Intl. Film Festival
Cinanima Intl. Animation Film Festival
Cinequest
Clermont-Ferrand Short Film Festival
Cracow Intl. Festival of Short Films
Flickerfest Australian Intl. Outdoor Short Film Festival
Florida Film Festival
Foyle Film Festival
Gijon Intl. Film Festival for Young People
Hamptons Intl. Film Festival
Hiroshima Intl. Animation Festival
Huesca Intl. Short Film Festival
India Intl. Film Festival
Locarno Intl. Film Festival
Los Angeles Intl. Short Film Festival
Melbourne Intl. Film Festival
Montreal Intl. Festival of New Cinema
Montreal World Film Festival
Nashville Independent Film Festival
Oberhausen Intl. Short Film Festival
Ottawa Intl. Animation Festival
Palm Springs Intl. Short Film Festival
Rhode Island Intl. Film Festival
San Francisco Intl. Film Festival
Santa Barbara Intl. Film Festival
Short Shorts Film Festival
Shorts Intl. Film Festival
Siggraph
Slamdance Film Festival
St. Louis Intl. Film Festival
Stuttgart Intl. Animation Festival
Sundance Film Festival
Sydney Film Festival
Tampere Film Festival
Toronto Worldwide Short Film Festival
Turin Intl. Film Festival of Young Cinema
Uppsala Intl. Short Film Festival
USA Film Festival
Venice Intl. Film Festival
World Animation Celebration (Los Angeles)
Zagreb World Festival of Animated Films

Creating a Film Festival Promotion Budget

Percentage-wise, it's hard to say how much of your total film budget should be used for festival promotion, but you need to consider setting aside somewhere between 5 percent for festival travel, marketing, and promotion — which includes postcards, posters, flyers, website, etc. I would recommend allotting no less than $5,000, but a comfortable figure is somewhere around $25,000+. That may sound excessive, but when you include travel and all the other marketing materials necessary, even that figure is low when you begin to break it down. For some filmmakers, $25,000 is the budget of their entire film! You could certainly spend a lot more, but $25,000 is average based on a festival tour that includes between ten and twenty festivals over the course of a year.

You really need to maximize all your resources and I don't mean money — I mean people. Favors are like money, so cash them in with your pals. Find a friend who works in advertising to do the poster, postcard, and website, so you've got a focused campaign that truly represents the film. When it comes to any travel involved, you just have to search for deals on the web and use those airline miles programs. You could also ask family and friends to donate miles and that may cover several flights.

Bottom line, create a budget for festival promotion and break it down the same way you did the budget for your film, ideally, when you are creating your initial production budget. If you get lucky enough to snag distribution at your first festival, then those extra dollars you set aside for travel may not even be necessary. However, if you choose to ignore this very important line item, it *will* cost you in the end. Playing the festival circuit can go on as long as two years, and while most festivals provide some travel expenses (most will provide accommodations, some provide airfare, a very few offer per diem) there will always be limitations, such as the number of people who can attend the festival.

Sample Festival Submission, Travel, and Promotion Budget (assuming ten to twenty festivals)

$1,500	Festival entry fees (about forty festivals)
$1,000	Festival submission costs (tapes/DVDs/shipping)
$2,500	Website
$1,000	Press kit/EPK (writing, xeroxing, labels, tapes)
$1,000	Postcards/posters/flyers/stickers/promo items
$5,000	Publicist (for one month, used for your festival premiere)
$5,000	Airfare
$5,000	Hotel
$1,500	Car rental/taxi/mass transit
$1,500	Meals, tips, incidentals
$25,000	**Total**

Note on travel: Assuming that the average filmmaker goes to a festival with at least one other person — a producer, an actor, and many times, both — travel may cost an average of $1,000 total for each festival. But there are many cost-effective ways to fly on a budget and many festivals will be able to assist with portions of your expenses, so it's difficult to project a totally accurate budget. This just gives you a place to start; use it as a loose guide. If you're a smart traveler, you can get to a festival cheaply by getting deals on flights and living on energy bars and the free meals provided at the fest. You could also, with donated services and other variables, such as the number of people accompanying you, easily get this budget down to less than $5,000. But whether you budget $5,000 or $50,000, do what you have to in order to make it work.

SUBMiT YOUR FiLM FESTiVAL LiSTiNG

Send Us Your Data or Update Your Entry
for the Next Edition of Chris Gore's
Ultimate Film Festival Survival Guide

In order to be included in the next edition of Chris Gore's *Ultimate Film Festival Survival Guide*, drop me a line. Please contact us via e-mail and we will then send you instructions for precisely how to submit information for a new festival as well as how to correct, update, or add any information to your entry. If you are a new festival, please send as much information as possible. In the meantime, send any additional promotional materials, including press kits, and especially photos — promo items like T-shirts, hats, posters and invites to festivals are also appreciated!

And for your own files, here's our contact info:

Mail: Chris Gore
           c/o Lone Eagle Film Festival Book Listing
           5055 Wilshire Blvd.
           Los Angeles, CA 90036

E-mail: filmfestivals@loneeagle.com